Introduction to Programming with C++ for Engineers

Bogusław Cyganek
AGH-University of Science and Technology
Kraków
Poland

This edition first published 2021
© 2021 John Wiley & Sons Ltd

The right of Bogusław Cyganek to be identified as the author of this work has been asserted in accordance with law.

Registered Offices
John Wiley & Sons, Inc., 111 River Street, Hoboken, NJ 07030, USA
John Wiley & Sons Ltd, The Atrium, Southern Gate, Chichester, West Sussex, PO19 8SQ, UK

Editorial Office
The Atrium, Southern Gate, Chichester, West Sussex, PO19 8SQ, UK

For details of our global editorial offices, customer services, and more information about Wiley products visit us at www.wiley.com.

Wiley also publishes its books in a variety of electronic formats and by print-on-demand. Some content that appears in standard print versions of this book may not be available in other formats.

Library of Congress Cataloging-in-Publication Data
Names: Cyganek, Bogusław, author.
Title: Introduction to programming with C++ for engineers / Bogusław Cyganek.
Description: Chichester, West Sussex, UK ; Hoboken, NJ, USA : Wiley-IEEE Press, 2021. | Includes bibliographical references and index.
Identifiers: LCCN 2020003379 (print) | LCCN 2020003380 (ebook) | ISBN 9781119431107 (softback) | ISBN 9781119431176 (adobe pdf) | ISBN 9781119431138 (epub)
Subjects: LCSH: C++ (Computer program language) | Engineering—Data processing.
Classification: LCC QA76.73.C153 C94 2020 (print) | LCC QA76.73.C153 (ebook) | DDC 005.13/3—dc23
LC record available at https://lccn.loc.gov/2020003379
LC ebook record available at https://lccn.loc.gov/2020003380

Cover Design: Wiley
Cover Images: © SEAN GLADWELL /Getty Images,
Courtesy of Bogusław Cyganek

Set in 9.5/12.5pt STIXTwoText by SPi Global, Chennai, India

10 9 8 7 6 5 4 3 2 1

In memory of my father,
Marian Cyganek

Contents

Preface

For the last half-century, the development of modern and effective programming languages has greatly influenced technology and our society in general. The technological revolution we are observing – artificial intelligence; everything being smart, from cities, cars, and homes, to phones; modern telecommunication; 5/6G; the Internet of Things; autonomous cars and drones; aerospace; etc. – is the outcome of this advancement. To an important degree, these enormous scientific and technological developments were possible due to the C++ programming language; with its object-oriented features, it paved the way for the fast construction of advanced computer systems and is the heart of the technology we observe today.

The latest revisions of C++ offer dozens of powerful new features, the huge Standard Library, and hundreds of software packages supported by thousands of enthusiasts, as well as years of experience and legacy code. C++ remains one of the most popular and widely used programming languages in the world. And when it comes to performance, it is number one.

But a language such as C++ is only a transmission line between humans and computers. What really counts is what we want computers to do and how we tell them to do it. This is the knowledge expressed by programming. Therefore, the primary purpose of his book is to teach the basics of programming, which goes alongside teaching modern C++.

Learning programming relies to a great degree on matching previously seen example patterns and then adapting them intelligently to our current needs. Thus this book lays special stress on properly chosen, nontrivial software examples. The majority of the topics are explained based on real programming problems: we show how to solve them, what techniques should be employed, and how they operate. And with content also comes form: the material is organized with dozens of diagrams, schemes, and tables, which help with understanding, memorizing, and referencing what we need when learning and what we will be looking for when working on exciting projects. Have fun!

Bogusław Cyganek
Kraków, Poland

Acknowledgments

Writing a book is an immense task. It would not be possible without the help of friends, colleagues, collaborators, and many other people, to whom I would like to express my deepest gratitude.

Particularly, I would like to thank numerous colleagues from the AGH University of Science and Technology in Kraków, Poland. In this respect I would like to express special thanks to Professor Artur Rydosz for his meticulous verification of the manuscript, as well as to PhD students Mateusz Knapik and Jakub Grabek for their help in preparing the book.

Special thanks also go to Professor Kazimierz Wiatr, Director of the Academic Computer Centre Cyfronet, for his continuous support and good wishes.

Furthermore, I'm very grateful to the Wiley team who greatly helped in making this book happen. They did brilliant work to make this book as good as possible.

I'm also very grateful to my many colleagues around the world, and especially to my students and readers of this and my previous books, for their e-mails, questions, suggestions, and bug reports, and all the discussions we have had. All of these helped me to develop better text and software. I also ask for your support now and in the future!

Finally, I would like to thank my family: my wife Magda, my children Nadia and Kamil, and my mother, for their patience, support, and encouragement while I was working on this book.

Abbreviations

ALU	arithmetic-logic unit
API	application programming interface
ASCII	American Standard Code for Information Interchange
BCD	binary coded decimal
BIN	BINary
C	carry flag
C1	one's complement
C2	two's complement
CPU	central processing unit
CRTP	curiously recurring template pattern
DEC	DECimal
DSP	digital signal processing
DP	design pattern
ECMA	European Computer Manufacturer's Association
ELF	executable and linkable format
FB	fraction binary
FIFO	first in first out
FP	floating-point
FPGA	field programmable gate array
FX	FiXed-point
GPU	graphics processing unit
GUI	graphical user interface
HEX	HEXadecimal
HTTP	Hypertext Transfer Protocol
IB	integer binary
IDE	integrated development environment
IEEE	Institute of Electrical and Electronics Engineers
ISO	International Organization for Standardization
IoT	Internet of things
LIFO	last in first out

LSB	least significant bit
MSB	most significant bit
NaN	not a number
NL	new line
OCT	OCTal
OO	object-oriented
OOD	object-oriented design
OOP	object-oriented programming
OS	operating system
PC	program counter
PE	portable executable
Q	quotient
R	remainder
RAII	resource acquisition is initialization
RPN	reverse Polish notation
RVO	return value optimization
RTTI	run-time type identification
SDK	software development kit
SM	sign-magnitude
STL	Standard Template Library
SL	Standard Library
SP	stack pointer
TDD	test driven development
UB	undefined behavior
ULP	units in the last place
UML	Unified Modeling Language
V	oVerflow flag
VFT	virtual function table
XML	Extensible Markup Language
Z	zero flag

About the Companion Website

This book is accompanied by a companion website:

http://home.agh.edu.pl/~cyganek/BookCpp.htm

The website includes:

- Example code
- Useful links that further improve the reader's coding ability

Scan this QR code to visit the companion website.

1

Introduction

Success is not final, failure is not fatal: it is the courage to continue that counts.

Winston Churchill

This book arose as a result of my fascination with computers and programming with the C++ language. It is also a result of my over 20 years of teaching the basics of computer science and particularly the C++ language to the students of the faculties of electrical engineering as well as mechanical engineering and robotics at AGH University of Science and Technology in Krakow, Poland. I have also worked as a programmer and consultant to several companies, becoming a senior software engineer and software designer, and have led groups of programmers and served as a teacher for younger colleagues.

Learning programming with a computer language is and should be fun, but learning it well can be difficult. Teaching C++ is also much more challenging than it was a decade ago. The language has grown up significantly and provided new exciting features, which we would like to understand and use to increase our productivity. As of the time of writing, C++20 will be released soon. In the book, we use many features of C++17, as well as show some of C++20. On the other hand, in many cases, it is also good to know at least some of the old features as well, since these are ubiquitous in many software projects, libraries, frameworks, etc. For example, once I was working on a C++ project for video processing. While adjusting one of the versions of the JPEG IO libraries, I discovered memory leaks. Although the whole project was in modern C++, I had to chase a bug in the old C code. It took me a while, but then I was able to fix the problem quickly.

The next problem is that the code we encounter in our daily work is different than what we learn from our courses. Why? There are many reasons. One is *legacy* code, which is just a different way of saying that the process of writing code usually is long and carries on for years. Moreover, even small projects tend to become large, and they can become huge after years of development. Also, the code is written by different programmers having different levels of understanding, as well as different levels of experience and senses of humor. For example, one of my programmer colleagues started each of his new sources with a poem. As a result, programmers must not only understand, maintain, and debug software as it is, but sometimes also read poems. This is what creates a discrepancy between the nice, polished code snippets presented in classes as compared to "real stuff." What skills are necessary to become a successful programmer, then?

Why did I write this book, when there are so many programming Internet sites, discussion lists, special interest groups, code examples, and online books devoted to software development?

Introduction to Programming with C++ for Engineers, First Edition. Bogusław Cyganek.
© 2021 John Wiley & Sons Ltd. Published 2021 by John Wiley & Sons Ltd.
Companion website: http://home.agh.edu.pl/~cyganek/BookCpp.htm

Although all of these frequently are great and highly useful as instant references, it is sometimes difficult to find places or sources that lead us step-by-step through the learning process. It is even more difficult to find good examples that teach key programming techniques and at the same time are short, practical, and meaningful. So, I would like to share with you the synergy of theory descriptions underpinned with project examples that I have collected during my years of programming and teaching.

Let us now look at a short overview of the main subject of this book. The C++ programming language is one of the most influential, commonly used, and fascinating languages, initially developed by Bjarne Stroustrup in the 1980s. In the last decade, it has undergone vast and fundamental changes. The roots of C++ are in the C and Simula programming languages (Stroustrup B., Evolving a language 2007) (Stroustrup B., The C++ Programming Language 2013). As we will see, basic constructions such as expressions and statements, for instance, are almost the same for the two. Also, for years, all C++ compilers have been able to swiftly compile C code. C is the language that greatly influenced our technological revolution, proving to be a key tool in the development of the highly influential Unix operating system, followed by all the other OSs, including Windows, Linux, and Android. Due to its multiplatform compatibility and light footprint, C is still used in embedded systems, field-programmable gate array (FPGA) devices, and graphics cards (graphics processing units GPUs), as well as in code acceleration on parallel platforms. There are also tons of libraries written with C and still in use, such as those with efficient numerical algorithms or for image processing, to name a few. Simula, on the other hand, was one of the first languages equipped with classes, and it fostered the methodology of object-oriented software development. This became a cornerstone of the majority of technological endeavors. Hence, paraphrasing, C++ inherited from these two: from C in public, and from Simula in private.

Although there are many programming languages, learning C++ is worth the effort, especially for people planning to work or already involved in any kind of computer programming, especially for systems and performance. To grasp the main features of C++, it is sufficient to read this book; we will explore them in depth. However, as an introduction here, let us briefly list the most characteristic ones, as follows.

- *Programmer freedom and wealth of features* – Both low-level and highly abstract constructions can be used in many contexts. As with a Swiss army knife, there is a danger of misuse, but freedom and a wealth of features lead to the highest productivity level in various contexts and broad applications. But most of all – freedom is what we love
- *High performance* – This has always been a primary goal of the language. The key point in this respect is to be able to adjust many programming features to a particular need without much overhead. C++ was designed to meet this requirement – it can be paraphrased as "Don't pay for what you don't use." As always, there is a price to pay, though, such as uninitialized variables and un-released resources. However, the new features of modern C++ make these less severe, still placing C++ code in the top-performing league
- *System low-level and high-level object-oriented programming (OOP) on the same platform* – C++ has been used to implement systems requiring low-level access. Many times, C++ is used to construct bridges between other languages: for example, in a numerical domain, to Fortran; and in systems programming, to C and Assembly. On the other hand, the same language has been used to implement high-level applications, such as word processors, CAD platforms, databases, and games. C++ is a strongly object-oriented (OO) language, fulfilling all the OO paradigms such as abstraction, encapsulation, inheritance, polymorphism, operator overloading, etc.

These features, augmented with templates and design patterns, constitute strong support in software development, especially for large systems

- *Strongly typed language* – Each object is characterized by its type. This strong type requirement leads to code that is verified by a compiler, not by a user at runtime, as is the case with some languages that do not possess this feature. Nevertheless, objects can be converted from a type to another type due to built-in or user-provided conversion operators. Also, the relatively new type-deduction mechanism with the `auto` keyword has greatly simplified the use of types and simply lets us save on typing

- *Exception handling* – How to handle computational problems at runtime has always been a question. For example, what should be done in code if a file with crucial settings cannot be opened, or a division by zero is encountered? The solid exception handling system, with a built-in stack unwinding mechanism, greatly facilitates management in such situations

- *Input-output (IO)* – C++ was the first language that beat its competition in providing a clear, extensible, and highly efficient hierarchy of IO objects, as well as getting control over dozens of formatting styles and flags. This feature, although not without some limitations and criticism, can be used to add IO abilities to user-defined types in a fast and elegant way, with the help of overloaded operators

- *Move semantics* – One of the primary goals of C++ has always been performance. A large number of processed objects negatively affects this, especially if the objects are large and extensively copied. However, in many cases, object copying is not necessary, since data can be simply and efficiently swapped. This is the data-swapping mechanism behind the highly efficient move semantics available in modern C++, which have also increased the quality of the generated code

- *Lambda expressions* – This relatively new way of writing expression-like functions greatly improved the process of passing specialized actions or traits to algorithms. Together with `auto`, lambdas lead to more elegant code and increased productivity

- *Smart pointers* – Although smart pointers are among dozens of programming constructions from the Standard Library (SL), they changed the way C++ operates with system resources. For years, possible memory leaks that could easily happen in carelessly written C or C++ code were claimed as the main reasons against approving C++ code in high-security systems, as well as in network and web programming. Smart pointers impressively changed this picture – if consistently used, they can prevent memory leaks with no need for mechanisms such as memory garbage collectors, which negatively influence system performance

- *Templates and generic programming* – When writing massive code, it has been observed that many structures and functions repeat themselves, with almost the same arrangement and only a few types changed. Templates alleviate the problem of repeating code by allowing us to write functions and classes for which concrete types and parameters can differ and be provided just before such a construct needs to be instantiated. Because of this, code has become more generic, since it is possible to code components that can operate with various types – even those not known when the components are implemented. A good example is the `std.::vector` class from the SL, representing a dynamically growing array of objects; it is able to store almost any object that can be automatically initialized

- *Libraries* – The SL has dozens of data containers, algorithms, and sub-libraries for regular expression search, parallel programming, filesystems, and clock and time measurements. There are also other high-performance libraries for computations, graphics, game programming, image processing and computer vision, machine learning and artificial intelligence, sound processing, and other utilities. This resource frequently comes with an open-access policy

- *Automatic code generation by a compiler* – This also touches on *metaprogramming* and is due to the recent constant-expression mechanism, which allows us to compile, and execute parts of code in order to enter the results of these operations into the destination code
- *Rich programming toolchain* – This includes compilers, linkers, profilers, project generators, versioning tools, repositories, editors, integrated development environment (IDE) platforms, code analysis tools, software design CADs, and many more

This is just a brief overview of the characteristics of the C++ language. In many discussions, it is said that the price we pay for all these features is language complexity, which also makes the learning curve relatively steep. That can be true, but let us remember that we do not need to learn everything at the same time. That is, paraphrasing Oprah Winfrey, when you learn C++ features, "You can have it all. Just not all at once."

You may have also heard of the 80/20 rule, also called the *Pareto principle*. It says that 80% of the CPU time will be spent on 20% of the code, or that 80% of errors are caused by 20% of the code, and so on. The point is to recognize that the majority of things in life are not distributed evenly, and usually 20% of the effort will be responsible for 80% of the effect. With respect to learning C++, my impression is that, to some extent, we can apply the Pareto principle. The goal of the first two chapters of this book is just to provide the necessary basics. How many programs can be written with this knowledge? Hopefully, many. However, this does not mean the rest of the book is not important. On the contrary, the introductory parts give us a solid foundation, but the more advanced features provide the top gears we need to take full advantage of C++ and to become professional software designers and programmers. How do we achieve these goals? As in many other disciplines, the answer is practice, practice, and practice! I hope the book will help with this process.

Here are some key features of the book.

- The goal is to present the basics of computer science, such as elementary algorithms and data structures, together with the basics of the modern C++ language. For instance, various search algorithms, matrix multiplication, finding the numerical roots of functions, and efficient compensated summation algorithms are presented with C++ code. Also, the basic vector and string data structures, as well as stacks, lists, and trees are described with C++ code examples
- Special stress is laid on learning by examples. Good examples are the key to understanding programming and C++. However, the most interesting real cases usually happen in complicated production code that frequently contains thousands of lines and was written by different people during years of work. It is barely possible to discuss such code in a book of limited size, aimed at students. So, the key is the nontrivial, practical code examples, which sometimes come from real projects and are always written to exemplify the subjects being taught
- Regarding the editorial style, the goal was to use figures, summaries, and tables, rather than pages of pure text, although text is also provided to explain the code in sufficient detail. The tables with summaries of key programming topics, such as C++ statements, operators, the filesystem library, SL algorithms, etc. should serve as useful references in daily programming work
- Basic containers and algorithms of the C++ SL are emphasized and described, together with their recent parallel implementations
- Special stress is laid on understanding the proper stages of software construction, starting with problem analysis and followed by implementation and testing. It is also important to understand software in its execution context on a modern computer. Although the top-down approach is always presented, topics such as the organization of code and data in computer memory, as well as the influence of multi-core processor architectures with layered cache memories, are also discussed

■ Software construction with object-oriented design and programming (OOD, OOP) methodologies is emphasized

■ The methodology and key diagrams of the Unified Modeling Language (UML) are explained and used

■ Some of the most common and practical design patterns, such as the handle-body and adapter, are presented in real applications

■ We do not shy away from presenting older techniques and libraries that may still be encountered in university courses on operating systems or embedded electronics, as well as in legacy code. For this purpose, a self-contained section in the Appendix provides a brief introduction to the C programming language, as well as to the preprocessor, as always with examples

■ A separate chapter is provided with an introduction to the various number representations and computer arithmetic, with a basic introduction to the domain of floating-point computations and numerical algorithms. This information will be useful at different levels of learning computer science

■ The software development ecosystem, with special attention devoted to software testing and practical usage of tools in software development, is presented with examples

■ The chapters are organized to be self-contained and can be read separately. However, they are also in order, so the whole book can be read chapter by chapter

The book is intended for undergraduate and graduate students taking their first steps in computer science with the C++ programming language, as well as those who already have some programming experience but want to advance their skills. It is best suited for programming classes for students of electrical engineering and computer science, as well as similar subjects such as mechanical engineering, mechatronics, robotics, physics, mathematics, etc. However, the book can also be used by students of other subjects, as well as by programmers who want to advance their skills in modern C++. The prerequisites to use the book are modest, as follows:

■ A basic introduction to programming would be beneficial
■ Mathematics at the high school level

The book can be used in a number of scenarios. As a whole, it best fits three or four semesters of linked courses providing an introduction to programming, OOP, and the C++ programming language in particular, as well as classes on advanced programming methods and techniques. The book can also be used in courses on operating systems and embedded systems programming, and it can serve as supplementary reading for courses on computer vision and image processing. This is how we use it at the AGH University of Science and Technology.

On the other hand, each chapter can be approached and read separately. And after being used as a tutorial, thanks to its ample summaries, tables, figures, and index, the book can be used as a reference manual for practitioners and students.

1.1 Structure of the Book

The diagram in Figure 1.1 shows the organization of the book and possible paths for reading it. The following list describes the contents of the chapters:

■ Chapter 2: "Introduction to Programming" – A basic introduction to programming. We start by presenting the hardware model, which is useful to understand what computer programs do. Then, the goal is to present the C++ development ecosystem, available online compilers, and

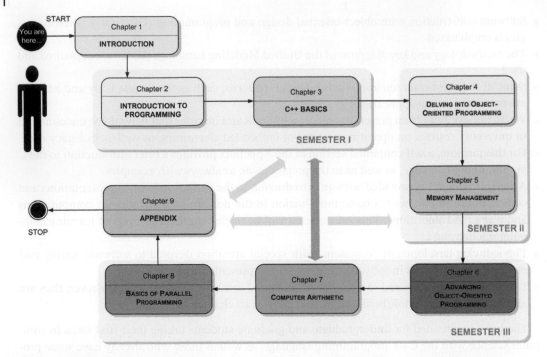

Figure 1.1 The structure of the book, shown as a state diagram in Unified Modeling Language (UML). Chapters 2 and 3 introduce the subject. The advanced level is built from Chapters 4, 5, and 6. These are followed by Chapter 7, on computer arithmetic, and Chapter 8, dealing with parallel programming. The Appendix can be referred to from each of the previous chapters.

integrated development environment (IDE) platforms, followed by three example projects, mostly focused on computations in a single `main` function with a very limited set of statements and operators. The ubiquitous `std::cout` and `std::cin` objects from the SL, representing output to the screen and input from the keyboard, respectively, are presented. In the last example, `std.::vector` and `std.::string` are introduced, for a dynamic array and a text string representation, respectively. Although limited, the set of C++ mechanisms introduced in this section allows us to write a fairly large group of simple programs

- Chapter 3: "C++ Basics" – Provides a solid introduction to the basic but very important features of programming with C++. First, the built-in data types and their initialization methods are discussed. Then, `std::vector` and `std::string` are approached again, with a greater degree of detail. The following sections present the `auto` keyword, an introduction to some SL algorithms, structures and classes, fixed-size arrays with `std::array`, references, pointers, statements, functions (including lambda functions), tuples with `std::tuple`, and structured binding, as well as operators. Along with many small examples, three relatively simple but complete projects are presented: representation of matrices, a class to represent quadratic equations, and a project containing two custom classes for the representation and exchange of various currencies. The aim of the examples and this chapter is to teach how to properly create and use a single class with its data and function members

- Chapter 4: "Delving into Object-Oriented Programming" – Leads to mastering intermediate and advanced techniques of C++ with special stress on OOD and OOP. After discussing the main paradigms of OOD and OOP, the anatomy of a class with access rules is presented. Then, operator overloading is introduced and immediately trained on an example class for representing complex numbers. After that, special class members are discussed, with such topics as shallow vs. deep copying, as well as the benefits of move semantics. An introduction to templates and generic programming follows, as always deeply underpinned with examples. After that, class relations are analyzed, followed by the presentation of class hierarchies and dynamic, as well as static, virtual mechanisms. The "has-a" vs. "is-a" relation is then analyzed, including some hints about when to use each one

- Chapter 5: "Memory Management" – Devoted to various aspects of object lifetime and scope, as well as to object creation, access, and disposal. The vast majority of this chapter is dedicated to smart pointers. Code examples are provided for constructing a list with shared smart pointers, as well as the factory design pattern

- Chapter 6: "Advanced Object-Oriented Programming" – Presents a few additional, highly practical programming techniques and methods. The aim is to practice the methods presented in the previous chapters, as well as to become acquainted with functional objects, pattern matching with regular expressions, implementation of the state machine and the handle-body design pattern, filesystem, system clock and time measurement, ranges, and the user interface. Also, such programming techniques as expression parsing, tree building, and traversing with the visitor design pattern are presented, as well as interpreting expressions with the interpreter design pattern

- Chapter 7: "Computer Arithmetic" – This chapter is divided into two subsections devoted to fixed-point and floating-point numbers, respectively. It starts with very basic information about computer arithmetic, such as byte interpretation, systems conversions, etc. So, it can also be used as an introductory lesson after Chapter 2. However, it includes much more than simple computations. We delve into important topics such as roundoff errors, catastrophic cancelation, and the IEEE 754 floating-point standard. We also investigate some advanced programming techniques, e.g. when a compiler can generate code during compilation, as well as how to compute function approximations and how to properly sum up buffers with big data

- Chapter 8: "Basics of Parallel Programming" – Enters the realm of parallel computations. First, new phenomena are explained associated with the concurrent operation of many cores at once and accessing shared objects. Then, we present and test three software components for parallel computations. The simplest calls a parallel version of the algorithms from the SL. However, C++ contains a separate library that allows parallel computing – in this respect, asynchronous tasks are presented. The last is the OpenMP library. With it, we test how to write parallel sections, how to parallelize `for` loops, and how to measure execution time with examples of matrix multiplication

- Appendix – Presents different programming topics. We start with a short presentation of the preprocessor, followed by a brief introduction to the C language. Although learning C++ does not require prior knowledge of C, the latter helps with understanding some features of the former. For example, the parameters of the `main` function, simple arrays, unions, and C-like string representations are encountered in daily programming life. Other topics, such as linking and binary organization of C/C++ programs, graphical user interfaces (GUIs) available to C++ programs, software testing, and a programming toolchain composed of CMake, Git, and GitHub, as well as the Profiler, are also presented

As already mentioned, the book does not need to be read linearly. The chapters are organized in such a way as to facilitate their separate use. The book's Appendix and many summaries and references can also be used independently when working on the code projects.

In addition, it is important to realize that presenting highly detailed programming topics in a linear fashion is basically impossible. Therefore, some constructions, although used in a given context, may not be well understood on first reading but are explained in later sections.

1.2 Format Conventions

For easier navigation, a few different formats are used in this book, as follows:

- Bullets are used at the beginning and end of some sections to present key programming constructs and/or techniques that will be introduced in that section
- C++ code is written using color to emphasize different language categories. It is then presented on a light blue background and with numbered lines, as in the following example

Listing 1.1 An example of C++ code formatting used in the book (from *main.cpp*).

```
1   #include <iostream>
2
3   int main()
4   {
5       // Display a message in the terminal window
6       // Prefix std:: tells to use objects from the standard library (SL).
7       std::cout << "Good day to you!" << std::endl;
8   }
```

The output in the *terminal window* (also known as the *console* or *command line*) is then presented, also on a color background, as follows:

```
Good day to you!
```

Code on a white background is either older legacy code in C, such as that presented in Appendix A.2, or code that for some reason is not recommended to be used in C++ but is shown as part of the explanation of some phenomenon. This way, we can easily distinguish between the two types of code.

At the beginning of each code snippet is a caption, such as Listing 1.1 in the previous example. It describes the intention of the code and – if the code comes from one of the project files – includes the name of the file containing this code, in parentheses and written in italics, such as *main.cpp*. For better readability, long sections of code are frequently split into a number of shorter code snippets. In such cases, a caption is included only once, above the first snippet, and the line numbering continues until the end of the entire code component.

- The lines are numbered in most of the code listings. These numbers are then referred to using square braces []. For example, in Listing 1.1, the standard *iostream* header is included in line [1], the main function is defined in lines [3–8], and lines [5, 6] contain comments, which in C++ start with double slashes //. To emphasize the importance of the latter, comments are in red
- Code such as the std::cout object, which represents a screen, is written with a special monospaced font. On the other hand, file names – such as *iostream* and *main.cpp* – are in an italic font
- Many functions and objects are presented that belong to the Standard Library. These can be easily distinguished by the std:: prefix, as we have already seen. However, the prefix can be

omitted as for example `endl` if the `using std::endl` (meaning "end-of-line") directive is placed at the top of the code. Hence, two versions are used in the presented code, depending mostly on the context, but also on the available space
- There are two types of sections:
  - Sections presenting new material
  - Example project sections, built around self-contained projects with the goal of practicing specific programming techniques
- Sections that contain additional or advanced material, but do not necessarily need to be read immediately in the current presentation context, are marked with ✗
- The ends of sections with important material frequently have a "Things to Remember" list, as follows

Things to Remember

- Prefer easy-to-read names for functions and objects
- In the code, add meaningful comments to emphasize the main ideas

- To represent algorithms in *pseudo-code*, the following format is used

Algorithm 1.1 Example algorithm in Pseudo-code

Input:	A value x
Output:	A square of x
1	Set threshold: t ← 1e-10
2	...

- There are two types of references:
  - Hard references to books, conference and journal papers, and Internet websites, such as (Stroustrup B., The C++ Programming Language 2013; Cppreference.com 2018)
  - Soft references (usually web links), placed in footnotes
- Chapters end with "Question & Exercise" sections (Q&E), which usually contain extensions to the presented techniques
- If special keys are mentioned, they are indicated, such as `Ctrl+Alt+T` (which opens a terminal window in Linux)

1.3 About the Code and Projects

As alluded to previously, the book contains dozens of code examples. The learning process relies on making the code run and understanding why and what it does. So, here are some hints on how to use the code:

- All of the code is available online from the GitHub repository (*https://github.com/BogCyg/ BookCpp*). A short intro to GitHub is in Section A.6.2
- Although the code can be easily copied, compiled, and executed, the best way to learn programming skills is to write the code yourself. This can involve simple retyping or, better,

after understanding the idea, attempting to write your own version. Once you have done so, try to make it run; and if you are not sure about something, refer to an example from the book. Then update your solution and try again

- The fastest way to compile the code and see what it does is to copy the code (only the code, not the formatting characters or line numbers) to one of the online compilation systems – more on this in Section 2.4.2. This works well, but only for relatively small projects. Also, online platforms have some limitations with regard to input and output actions, such as writing to a file, for example

- For larger projects, a recommended approach is to build the project yourself on your computer with your programming tools. To do this, two things are necessary: a relatively new C++ building environment, such as an IDE, as presented in Sections 2.4 and 2.5; as well as the CMake tool, described in Appendix A.6.1. Although the projects can be built locally with only an IDE, CMake greatly facilitates this process, considering many operating systems, programming platforms, tools, source versions, etc. It is also a de facto industry standard that is good to know. In addition, some IDEs include CMake

- Since software constantly evolves, there may be differences between the code in the book and the code in the repository. Therefore, for an explanation of programming techniques and C++ features, the code from the book should be referenced. However, to build an up-to-date version of a project, the code from the repository should be used

Modern C++ compilers are masterpieces. For instance, prior to the construction of the complete executable, a modern compiler can even precompile parts of the code; these can be then immediately executed by the compiler to compute any results obtainable at this stage, which can be then directly put into the final code to avoid computations at runtime. We will also discuss how to benefit from these features. However, if something is incorrect and the code does not compile, sometimes it is not easy to figure out the cause and, more important, how to solve it. A compiler tries to tell us precisely what is wrong. But because errors can happen everywhere and at different levels, an error message can be a real mystery. Compilers are still far from being able to tell us exactly how to get out of trouble. Maybe AI will bring new possibilities in this area. At the moment, such language features as *concepts* in C++20 are available. As always, some experience and contact with worldwide programming colleagues are the best resources to help.

So, what do we do if code does not compile? – Here are some hints for beginners:

- First of all, do not write long sections of code without checking whether it compiles. A much better approach is to organize your code, if possible, even in a slightly nonlinear way: e.g. write an empty function with only parameters provided, and then compile. Then write a few lines, also nonlinearly (e.g. an empty loop), and see if it compiles. Add more lines, compile, and so on. At each stage, check for errors; if they appear, modify the code to make it compile

- When you encounter compilation (or linker) errors, always scroll the error pane to the top and check only the first error. Frequently, the rest of the errors are just the result of the compiler stumbling on the first one

- Carefully read each error message. If necessary, copy it to an editor and split it into parts so you can understand it better. Error messages include codes, so you can always look them up on the Internet by citing such a code: for example, "`error C2628: 'MonthDays' followed by 'void' is illegal (did you forget a ';'?)`." Yes, indeed, I forgot the semicolon `;` just after a definition of the `MonthDays` structure. Adding the missing `;` fixes the problem in this case. But that was easy

- Sometimes the cause of an error is a letter, line, function, etc. just a few lines before the erroneous line indicated by the compiler. If you stumble due to an error, try to verify a few lines before the indicated place
- Search for clues on the Internet. Pages such as *http://stackoverflow.com*, *http://codeguru.com*, etc. offer a lot of practical advice from skillful programmers. However, always check the date of a given post – there is a lot of outdated information on the Web as well!
- If a section of code persistently does not compile and you have no idea what's going on, disable it temporarily. This can be done either by commenting it out, i.e. placing `//` in front of a line, or by enclosing the code with `#if 0` *`temporarily_disabled_code`* `#endif` directives. If the rest compiles, then narrow the disabled area, and check again
- Code can be written in many ways. For example, there are many types of loops; the `switch-case` statement can be written with `if-else`, etc. However, do not abandon non-compiling code before you find out and understand why it does not compile. It can take some time, but this way, you learn and avoid losing time in the future when you encounter a similar problem. Only after you *understand* what you did wrong should you consider using another or better language construction
- Last but not least, consult your colleagues at college or working at the next desk, or ask your teacher – send them an e-mail, ask for advice, etc. It is always good to communicate

2

Introduction to Programming

To create a computer program to solve a given task, we need to specify the operations a computer must perform for us. This knowledge comes from the problem analysis, and sometimes it is the most difficult stage of the software creation process. Once we know these operations, they need to be written in a form a computer – that is, its processor – can understand. Although each processor speaks its own language, called *assembly* or *machine languages*, these are too primitive to be used efficiently for coding by humans. Instead, many high-level computer languages have been developed for this purpose. C++ is one of them: it is well known; it has the best possible tools and libraries; and it has significant support from the C++ community, which has years of experience using it.

C++ has hundreds of features that can be used in various ways to translate our expectations into an optimal representation that a computer can understand. Learning about C++'s features is an interesting endeavor, but it can take time. However, knowing selected parts of C++ will enable us to write a large number of programs. In this chapter, we will present an introduction to programming with C++. To begin, we will discuss the hardware-software ecosystems. More precisely, we will present the computational models that constitute a foundation for understanding how the software operates and what its development process is.

2.1 Hardware Model

Computers are highly integrated but also complicated systems, composed of dozens of chips, each composed of thousands of transistors, etc. Modeling – that is, the creation of models – is the process of *simplifying reality to expose some of the most important features* that are necessary to explain part of that reality. Figure 2.1 depicts a computational model of a computer system equipped with a multi-core processor, main memory, a system support chipset, as well as a number of connected external devices, such as a keyboard, a screen, disks, and network devices.

The central part constitutes a processor with a number of cores, which themselves are independent computational units. The most important external module is the main memory, which contains both code and data. This type of organization follows the well-established von Neumann computer architecture.

In addition to the main processor, computations can be done by cores on the graphics processing unit (GPU), which is also equipped with its own on-board memory. Although we will not directly address this platform in the programming exercises, it is good to know that its native programming languages are C and C++.

Introduction to Programming with C++ for Engineers, First Edition. Bogusław Cyganek.
© 2021 John Wiley & Sons Ltd. Published 2021 by John Wiley & Sons Ltd.
Companion website: http://home.agh.edu.pl/~cyganek/BookCpp.htm

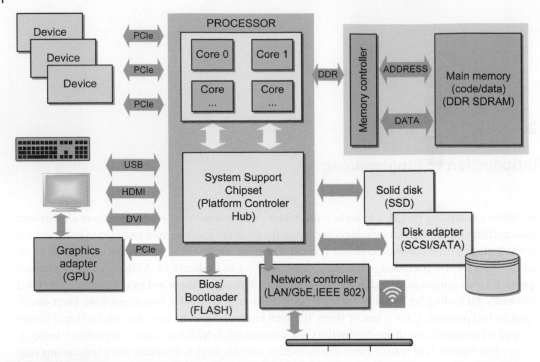

Figure 2.1 Model of a computer system. The central part consists of a processor with a number of cores that are independent computational units. A processor is usually augmented by a system support chipset, which is responsible for interfacing with various modules external to the processor. The most important is the main memory that contains code and data. In addition to the main processor with its cores, computations can be performed by cores in the graphics processing unit (GPU).

Figure 2.2 depicts a model of a multi-core processor with various types of memory. The multi-core processor has a series of onboard memory caches and has an external main memory module attached. We will now explain the functions of these hardware components from the computational point of view.

The arithmetic logic unit (ALU) is the heart of every core and performs basic low-level operations. These are in the form of binary-encoded commands stored in memory, which, after decoding, tell the ALU what to do: for example, with values stored in other memory regions. These commands are in an encoded form called *machine language* and are not human-readable. They can be represented in an equivalent *assembly language* that can be understood and even, in rare cases, used to write software; however, each processor has its own machine language, so writing in assembly is tedious, error-prone, and decidedly hardware dependent. Fortunately, these days we can avoid such inconvenience with the help of *high-level languages* such as C++. These are much easier for humans to understand and are independent of processors and operating systems. In addition, code written with their help can be easily translated into almost any known machine representation with the help of a compiler.

As shown in Figure 2.2, the ALU usually has relatively limited access to a particular block of the core's registers. Depending on the processor, these are a few memory locations that are able to store only a very limited number of computer words, mostly for ALU operations. In addition to the universal registers, there are two special ones: PC, the program counter, which indicates the current position of the executed code; and SP, the stack pointer, which points at an external memory region

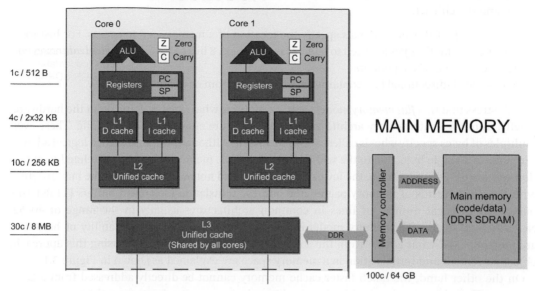

PROCESSOR

Figure 2.2 A model of a multi-core processor with various types of memory. The arithmetic logic unit (ALU) performs low-level machine operations. The closest memory storage consists of registers. In addition to the universal registers, there are two special ones: PC (the program counter that indicates the current position of the executed code) and SP (the stack pointer, which points at the memory region called the stack, containing return addresses to the procedures and some parameters). L1, L2, and L3 are memory caches with different sizes and access times (1c denotes a single processor cycle). The cores can operate independently, sharing only part of the upper-level memory. The processor is connected with external main memory that stores both code and data (von Neumann architecture).

called the *stack* that contains return addresses to procedures and sometimes call parameters (see Section 3.14.3). Figure 2.2 also shows two specific flags: zero (Z) and carry (C). In practice, these are two of many flags, usually encoded as specific bits in one of the control registers. The reason we have highlighted them is that they help to understand some numerical operations discussed in Chapter 7 of this book.

L1, L2, and L3 are memory blocks called memory *caches* and have different sizes and access times. Their characteristic feature is that the further from the ALU such a memory cache is, the larger its capacity – but its access time is also longer. At the very end of this specific capacity-speed triangle is the main memory: its capacity is a few orders of magnitude greater than that of the memory caches, but it also has the longest access times. This is due to the hardware technologies used to manufacture it. Registers and caches are internal processor memory (cores). But this is the external *main memory*, which, in the von Neumann architecture,[1] contains the entire body of compiled executable code for a program as well as most of its data. More specifically, this is *operational memory*, which, unlike disk storage, can be directly addressed by a processor in order to execute a program. From the *programming* point of view, it is important to realize that to access any cell in

---

1 The second distinct type is the Harvard architecture, in which memory is strictly divided into code memory and data memory. Such architectures are sometimes used in digital signal processors (DSP) to implement the single instruction, multiple data (SIMD) strategy at the cost of additional signal buses. See *https://en.wikipedia.org/wiki/Von_Neumann_architecture*.

the operational memory, the following two specialized signal buses need to be handled by the processor and the chipset:

- *Address* – All of this bus's signals specify the location of a memory cell to access. For historical reasons, the smallest possible cell to address is a byte, i.e. 8 bits of data. The *logical addresses* correspond to the C/C++ pointers
- *Data* – This bidirectional bus contains data to be read from or written to memory

Let's stress that this *flat memory model* greatly simplifies what is really going on in the hardware. Briefly, in many contemporary architectures, data buses are either 32 or 64 bits long. These even multiples of bytes specify what is called a *computer word*. Although, as mentioned, a logical address can refer to a single byte, due to the width of the data bus, memory accesses are related to operations on words. For this reason, the lower address bits need not be directly set on the bus. Together with the mechanisms of memory paging and address translation lookahead buffers (TLBs), this makes the physical number of lines in common architectures usually in the range of 40–52. Nevertheless, such a flat memory model is a fair trade-off between the variability of hardware architectures and what is seen from the software perspective. For example, using this approach, object placement and initialization in a memory space are explained as shown in Figure 3.1.

On the other hand, the much faster cache memory cannot be directly addressed from a C++ program. There is no need to do this, since caches only store copies of data from the main memory to allow for faster access. Nevertheless, they can be efficiently employed in the execution of C++ programs by proper data placement in the operational memory. We will address these issues in Chapter 8 when discussing memory access and concurrent operations of the cores.

After this brief introduction to modern computer architectures, notice that older and simpler processor architectures were usually based on an unsophisticated ALU, few registers, no cores, and no memory caches. All of these features allow us to run C++ programs even in a multithreading fashion. Hence, simple processors connected with external memory constitute an even simpler, but still highly usable, computational model. Such approaches are still in use on some embedded platforms, due to their lower cost and frequently lower energy consumption. The latter is also an issue when it comes to software design.

In this introduction, we have only touched on the domains of computer architectures and the computational programming model. Nevertheless, this discussion will be useful for understanding the programming techniques discussed in the following chapters of this book. For further reading, we recommend Patterson and Hannessy (2018) and Bryant and O'Hallaron (2015).

2.2 Software Development Ecosystem

Software makes computers run. On the other hand, computers are used in software development. This dichotomy can be observed in Figure 2.3: it presents the software development ecosystem, elements of which will be the topics of later chapters of this book. Let's briefly characterize each of them.

The first steps shown in Figure 2.3 are software design and coding. Although these are the first steps in this diagram, we will soon discover that they are the end of a very important – perhaps the most important – conceptual phase of software development. After part of the code is completed, it needs to be translated into a representation that the processor can understand, as discussed in

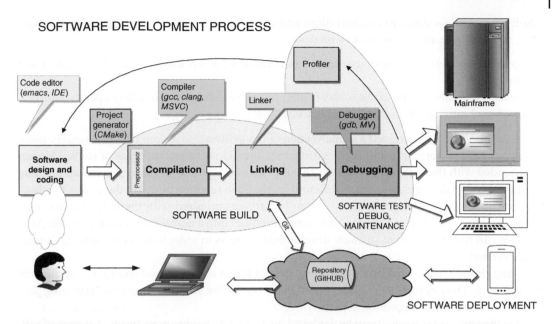

Figure 2.3 Software development ecosystem. To execute software written in C++, it needs to be translated by the compiler into a machine representation. Since software can be created in parts and can use previously created libraries, all of them need to be joined into one executable. This is done by the linker. These are the software build stages. Next, the executable needs to be properly tested and debugged to remove malfunctions. Then, the operation of the current version can be further optimized by launching the profiler. Its role is to measure the performance of software components to discover hot spots – code fragments that consume the most execution time. After that, the entire software development process can be repeated to build the next, better version. During this process, we cannot forget to protect and control the versions of our software. This can be accomplished by using a source control and versioning platform. After the software is ready, it can be deployed on a concrete hardware platform.

the previous section. This process of translating from the C++ language is done by a program commonly known as a *compiler*. Shoulder to shoulder with operating systems, compilers are very complex and sophisticated programs, as we will have many occasions to observe. In the C++ environment, software components can be created independently; and to build a final program, these pieces need to be joined together. This task is performed by a *linker*. After its successful operation, we have a code component that can be executed by a computer.

However, we are still a few steps ahead of saying that we have finished our job. In fact, new development stages commence: code testing and debugging. Since even short programs can implement complicated concepts, we should have no illusion that we will write the correct version from the very beginning. Therefore, we should also write software that controls what other software is doing. This can be, for instance, in the form of *unit tests*, which we will also discuss. When problems are spotted in software, it can be run step by step with a *debugger*. This is yet a third program in our toolchain; in addition to the line-by-line code execution, it lets us add breakpoints, examine the values of variables, look into memory regions and call stacks, and even examine the registers of a processor, if necessary. Debugging is the best way to learn what code is doing. Therefore, we use debuggers extensively when working on the code examples presented in this book.

Software can have different configurations and versions. Although many configurations are possible, usually there are two distinctive modes:

- *Debug* – A software version that usually is not optimized and is used for "in house" testing and debugging
- *Release* – A stable version of the software after intensive testing, which is fully operational, optimized, and intended to be distributed to users

Let's assume we have attained a stable version of our software, so we can run real computations. In many cases, performance still is not satisfactory due to long execution times or stalls. This can be amended with the help of a *profiler*. Its role is to measure the performance of software-building components and discover *hot spots* at different levels. Such reported places in the code – i.e. those that consume the most execution time – can be further optimized with the help of other algorithms or *refactoring* (i.e. redesigned and reimplemented) into a *parallel* version, if possible. After that, we can repeat the entire software development process in order to build the software's next, better version.

During the software development cycle, we cannot forget to protect and control the versions of our software. This, in turn, can be accomplished by one of the source control and versioning platforms discussed in the Appendix, Section A.6.2.

After the software is ready, it can be deployed on a concrete hardware platform. A degree of software-hardware (S/H) dependence is a function of software features. That is, some programs can easily run on almost any hardware platform, whereas others may require significant computational power or can be tuned for specific displays, for instance. Hence, if appropriate, such features need to be taken into account during the software development steps.

Thus the software development process resembles a spiral: the same tasks are repeated over and over until a satisfactory solution is obtained. In other words, we operate in cycles with larger and larger diameters. Indeed, we enter a *spiral development model*, which is a recognized software development strategy used by many companies. If properly organized, such an approach can be highly efficient in practice. In the next section, we will look in more detail at the software development steps.

Last but not least, note that the programming ecosystem in Figure 2.3 shows only one person – but software development and construction usually requires teamwork. The human factor, which frequently is overlooked in books on programming, can have a significant impact on the success or failure of any project. Although this serious issue is out of the scope of this book, smooth operation entails project organization and cooperation (McConnell 2004). To some extent, these are supported by the modular structure of C++ projects, as well as by tools that perform source versioning and maintaining, such as Git and GitHub in Figure 2.3.

2.3 Software Development Steps

Just as there is more than one way to design a house, a bridge, or a car, there is also more than one way to design software. However, in all of these cases, the ultimate criterion indicating success or failure is the performance of the final product. As in other engineering fields, based on years of experience and thousands of projects, some common rules can be recognized that help us avoid common pitfalls in future designs. Such software development steps are depicted in Figure 2.4, and we will take a closer look at each of them.

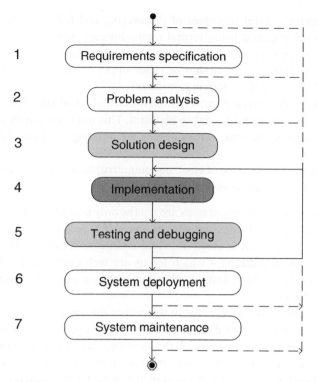

Figure 2.4 UML activity diagram presenting the steps of the software development process.

In this book, we focus mostly on correct implementations in C++. However, there can be no good implementation of a flawed design. Also, even good design and implementation do not guarantee a successful solution if software does not undergo extensive testing. Therefore, although C++ is our main subject, we will also pay attention to other software development steps. Let's describe each of them briefly in the order shown in Figure 2.4:

1. *Requirements specification* – A process of defining the main tasks to be solved, as well as functionality and applications of the product. Involves cooperation between many parties, such as end users, system architects, managers, etc. A proper statement of the allowable costs and foreseen deadlines is also essential at this stage (Dick et al. 2017).
2. *Problem analysis* – Based on the previous step: the process of establishing the main relations in the system, recognizing the governing rules of the critical system processes, identifying the most difficult components, and sketching the main stages of the critical algorithms with special focus on the most problematic ones. In some cases, this can be one of the most expensive and tedious steps, involving experts from other domains.
3. *Solution design* – Based on the previous steps: the process of specifying the architecture of the whole system, considering all of its components and their interfaces. Includes specification of tools and implementation strategies. Frequently, this process involves the preparation of *Gantt charts* that capture interdependencies between system implementation stages, human resources, deadlines, and milestones.
4. *Implementation* – The process of software creation based on the previous steps. The main product of this stage is the source code. The executable can be built, as shown in Figure 2.3.

5. *Testing and debugging* – Joint processes of discovering and fixing malfunctioning software. Tests should be well designed using formal methodologies such as test-driven development (TDD) and unit testing (Appendix A.7). However, problems arise when a malfunctioning implementation is due to flaws in the design or other upper levels of the development process. Therefore, the role of the design steps is paramount.

6. *System deployment* – The process of system integration and installation to ensure proper operation on a specifically configured hardware platform. This usually requires adjustments to specific hardware components that, for example, are missing or have different parameters (Sommerville 2016).

7. *System maintenance* – The practice of ensuring uninterruptable system operation and allowing for system evolution and seamless system changes.

Certainly, these software development steps are not the only possible path to follow in this highly demanding engineering domain; they are simply one of the possible models. Design strategies developed in other domains, such as electronics and architecture, can also be of help in software design. Interestingly, design patterns – which for us are well-established software components with specific characteristics – were first postulated as common patterns encountered in building construction (Alexander 1977).

The previous steps should also be reflected in the project documentation, the structure of which could be the topic of a much longer discussion. Needless to say, such documentation should as precisely and concisely as possible describe all the steps necessary to solve a given problem. In our projects, we will deal mostly with code documentation. In this respect, the principle of *self-documenting code* has proven useful in many practical realizations. This is based on the assumption that proper comments are added during software implementation. These should succinctly convey the most important concepts and, most importantly, be up-to-date. We will return to this issue in future sections.

Finally, let's stress that the development process shown in Figure 2.4 is just one of the possible processes and does not reflect all of the important aspects of software development, such as the human factor. A design that follows all of these steps is still not guaranteed to be successful. However, as a heuristic finding, not following any design strategy, especially when developing complex systems, is a good recipe for disaster. There are many more comprehensive strategies for IT project development, such as PRINCE2, Scrum, and Agile, to name a few. Further investigation of these subjects is definitely worth the effort; see, for example, Hinde 2018, Cohn 2019, and Sommerville 2016.

2.4 Representing and Running Algorithms

At last, in this section, we will implement a C++ program. It will ask a user to enter a number and, after checking whether it is a positive value, display the number's square root. That is, if 16 is entered, 4 will be displayed, and so on. However, before we go to the C++ code, which is one of the forms of representing algorithms, let's first reflect on what an algorithm is and the ways to express it.

In this section, we will learn the following:

- What an algorithm is, and how to represent it
- What the Unified Modeling Language (UML) is, and what can be represented with UML activity diagrams

- How to write a simple C++ program that computes the square root of a value entered by a user
- How to compile and execute simple C++ code using online platforms
- How to write a C++ source file, compile it, and run its executable in a Linux environment

2.4.1 Representing Algorithms

An algorithm describes steps for execution. Algorithms are frequently encountered not only in computer science but also in daily life. For example, fire alarm instructions in every office provide the steps to be followed in the event of a fire; selecting a given program on a dishwasher specifies the steps to be performed by the machine to clean our precious glass; etc.

Much depends on the *abstraction level* at which we are operating. The concept of *abstraction* in computer science is frequently encountered: when representing algorithms, it simply tells what level of details is necessary. In some cases, especially if we wish to view the entire form of an algorithm, a more general *coarse level* is preferred, and an image can be used: more specifically, a diagram that uses commonly agreed-on symbols. Such diagrams are used in many domains, such as electric engineering and architecture. In computer science, we are lucky to have a common system of diagrams under the umbrella of UML (see *http://uml.org* and *www.visual-paradigm.com*). UML is much more than a simple collection of common symbols – this framework facilitates the entire software development process shown in Figure 2.4. We will return to it many times. However, let's now present the UML activity diagram that represents the steps required by our program, shown in Figure 2.5.

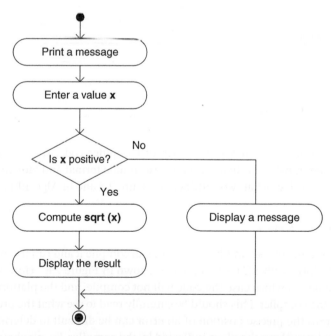

Figure 2.5 UML activity diagram presenting an algorithm for computing the square root of a value x entered from the keyboard. All actions can be expressed by two symbols: activities (procedures) and decision blocks.

Basically, there are two types of symbols in Figure 2.5. Actions are in rounded rectangles, and decision blocks are in diamonds. Lines ending in arrows show the control flow. Therefore, such diagrams are sometimes called *flow charts*. Usually, in simple diagrams, the main flow proceeds from top to bottom. But observe that the flow can be easily redirected, forming loops in execution. There are also black circular symbols denoting the beginning and end of an action, respectively. Although simple and straightforward, the ending symbol reminds us about a very important problem in algorithm design: the *stop problem*. Put simply, this means a well-designed algorithm should have well-defined stop conditions, i.e. it should not hang up forever in an undefined state. Some software, such as operating systems, operates in an indefinite loop; however, it should never find itself in an undefined state or behavior.

Note that in Figure 2.5, the whole program can be seen in one glance. But at the same time, the steps express certain general actions, such as "Compute sqrt(x)," without in-depth details. This is what we call the coarse level or, more generally, a *top-down* approach. On the other hand, going into detail means entering finer and finer levels: that is, "going down" the design. Usually, this involves more symbols; to avoid clutter, these are usually presented in separate diagrams. Nevertheless, in some tasks, it is possible to start from the details. Such a *bottom-up* approach is much less useful in our domain and usually results in designs in which upper-level components do not interface well.

Yet another way to present algorithms is in the form of the pseudo-code. This is a mixture of simple computer commands interspersed with more general statements, usually written in the form of human-readable commands or short sentences. Algorithm 2.1 presents this approach.

Algorithm 2.1 An algorithm for computing the square root of a real value expressed in pseudo-code (a mixture of programming commands and human-readable commands).

Input:	A real value x
Output:	Square root of x
1	**if** $x \geq 0$
2	Print sqrt (x)
3	**else**
4	Print an error message

The ultimate representation comes in the form of computer code, such as that presented in Listing 2.1. This can be translated into a computer-executable format and launched.

The code in Listing 2.1 does what was outlined in Figure 2.5 and in Algorithm 2.1.

2.4.2 Using Online Compilers

Before we explain each line of code in Listing 2.1, we can compile it and run its executable with the help of an online platform with a C++ compiler, as shown in Figure 2.6.[2] However, when typing, we may make a mistake, in which case the code will not compile, and the platform will display an error message from the compiler. This should be carefully read to see what the problem is, in order to fix it. But sometimes the precise position of an error can be difficult to determine, and the real culprit may be a few lines above the place indicated by the compiler. So, we should also check the preceding lines.

---

2 For example, to quickly evaluate short programs, we can use one of the following platforms: *http://ideone.com*, *https://wandbox.org*, *http://coliru.stacked-crookd.com*, *https://repl.it*, *www.onlinegdb.com*, or *http://cpp.sh*.

Listing 2.1 `main` function for computing the square root of an entered value (from *main.cpp*).

```cpp
1   // This is a C++ comment in the program to compute the square root of a value
2
3   #include <cmath>         // A header for std::sqrt
4   #include <iostream>      // A header for std::cout, std::cin, std::endl
5
6   int main()               // A program in C++ consists of a function main()
7   {
8     double x { 0.0 };      // Define and initialize a variable x
9
10    std::cout << "Enter x="; // Print a message
11    std::cin >> x;           // Enter value of x from the keyboard
12
13    if( x >= 0.0 )           // Check if x is positive
14      std::cout << "\nSqrt(" << x << ") = " << std::sqrt( x ) << std::endl;
15    else
16      std::cout << "\nWrong value - cannot compute Sqrt\n";
17  }
```

(a)   (b)

Figure 2.6 The *http://ideone.com* online C++ compiler environment running in the Mozilla Firefox viewer with the code from Listing 2.1 (a). The source code has been copied into the editor pane. Under it is the input pane, simulating `std::cin`. After we click Run, the source is compiled and executed. Results are shown in (b).

Online compilers are very useful when it comes to testing short code snippets, as frequently shown in this book. However, for larger, multi-file projects, we will frequently use an IDE to build executables.

2.4.3 Structure of a C++ Program

To understand the roles of the various code components, a simplified version of the C++ program has been extracted from Listing 2.1 and is shown and explained in Figure 2.7. A detailed description of the code from Listing 2.1 will be presented in the next section.

A program consists of a series of statements, separated by semicolons ;. Forgetting this ending symbol is one of the most frequent errors in early programming. However, notice that there is no semicolon at the end of the block of the `main` function, which continues inside a region enclosed by braces { }.

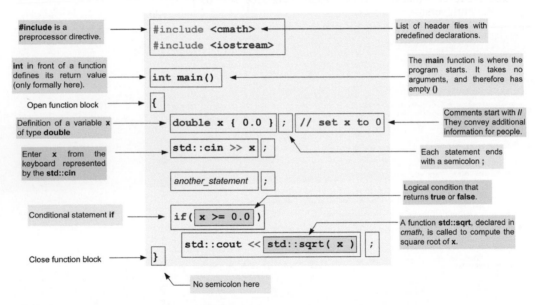

Figure 2.7 Structure of a simplified C++ program that consists of a `main` function. Header files containing definitions of other components are brought in by the #include directive. Each statement, such as the `double x {0.0}` definition, ends with a semicolon ;. However, there is no semicolon at the end of the function block, delineated with { } braces. The `std::cin` object represents a keyboard, whereas `std::cout` represents the screen for output. Inside `main`, other functions can be called to produce results, such as `std::sqrt( x )`, which computes the square root of a value x.

2.4.4 Code Analysis

Let's return to the code presented in Listing 2.1. The first line [1] contains a simple comment: that is, text that is intended only as additional information for the programmers. In C++, comments start with two slash symbols // and end at the end of the current line. We will see more such symbols that are composed of multiple single characters – these are necessary due to the limited set of special symbols on the computer keyboard. Lines [3, 4] contain two #include statements, each followed by a file name in <> brackets. These are preprocessor directives, discussed in Appendix A.1, that effectively copy and paste the contents of the indicated file into the current position. This is done to introduce programming components already written by other programmers, which we can easily reuse rather than bothering with self-implementation. Examples are the `std::cout` object and the `std::sqrt` function, which we will use in upcoming lines. Fortunately, the whole copy-and-paste is done invisibly when compilation starts, so we do not see any clutter in our code.

In our example, the `main` function is defined on line [6], and its body – a set of code lines – is contained between the curly braces on lines [7–17]. `int` in front of `main` means it is supposed to return a value, but this is irrelevant in this case.

The first object, a variable named x, is defined and initialized on line [8]. We see that it is of the `double` type. It is used to represent *floating-point* numbers, which approximate real numbers, as presented in Section 7.4. The curly braces `{ 0.0 }` mean x is initialized with the value 0, which in the floating-point domain is precisely expressed as the 0.0 constant.

Line [10] instructs the computer to display the text `"Enter x="` on the screen, i.e. in a window. This is accomplished with the help of the `std::cout` object, representing the output stream (a screen), and the `<<` operator (again, two characters that together have a new meaning). The latter, in its default version, means a left-shift of bits in an integer; but we will see that in C++, operators can be assigned different meanings, depending on the context they operate in. This is quite a useful feature.

The opposite action is encoded on line [11]: the computer will wait for the user to enter a value of x. This is accomplished with the help of the `std::cin` object and `>>` operator, respectively. In effect, just after the user hits the `Enter` button, x will change its contents to whatever value was typed in.

However, not all values of x can be used to compute a square root. Therefore, on line [13], the condition `x >= 0.0` (that is, whether x is greater than or equal to 0.0) is checked with the `if-else` statement (Section 3.13.2.1). Then there are two options: either the condition is fulfilled, in which case the code from line [14] is executed; or it is false, and the alternative line [16], just after the `else` part on line [15], is executed.

Line [14] deserves a short explanation. It is a bit more complicated than line [10], since, in addition to text, it displays a series of objects. All of them are separated by the `<<` operator. `std::sqrt( x )` is a call to a function named `sqrt`, contained in the Standard Library[3] – hence the `std::` prefix and the `#include <cmath>` – with x as its parameter. That is, once we know that x is positive, we call an already-written function that computes the square root for us. The question arises, what would happen if x was negative? It depends, but definitely nothing good. Such a situation is known as *undefined behavior* (UB), which we must avoid.

The last object sent to the screen on line [14] is `std::endl`. It instructs the computer (i) to put the caret on a new line and (ii) to flush the output, with the result that all of the symbols will be transferred to the screen. The first action, passing to the new line, can also be achieved by inserting `\n` to the text constant, as shown on lines [14, 16].

Finally, let's explain the ubiquitous *scope resolution operator* `::` (two colons). It is used to access members of namespaces, such as data and functions, classes, as well as structures, as will be discussed later in the book. Its syntax is shown in Figure 2.8.

For instance, `std::cout` in the previous code means the `cout` object from the `std` namespace. The latter denotes the namespace of the Standard Library.

---

3 For more on the Standard Library, see *https://en.wikipedia.org/wiki/C%2B%2B_Standard_Library* and *https://en.cppreference.com/w/cpp/header*.

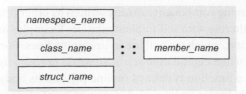

Figure 2.8 Syntax of the scope-resolution operator ∷ to access members of namespaces, structures, and classes.

2.4.5 (✂) Building a Linux Executable

In this section, we will show how to build an application by typing a few commands in the Linux OS.[4] Not surprisingly, actions to perform are also summarized in the form of an algorithm, as follows.

- Open a terminal window (in Linux, use the `Ctrl+Alt+T` shortcut)
- Run the `ls -l` command to list files and directories. The following is some example output:

```
boxy@PARSEC:~$ ls -l
total 0
drwxrwxrwx 1 boxy boxy 512 Aug 16 18:32 Desktop
drwxr-xr-x 1 boxy boxy 512 Aug 16 18:32 Videos
```

- With the `mkdir` command, create a new directory, such as *Projects*, and list its contents:

```
boxy@PARSEC:~$ mkdir Projects
boxy@PARSEC:~$ ls -l
total 0
drwxrwxrwx 1 boxy boxy 512 Aug 16 18:32 Desktop
drwxrwxrwx 1 boxy boxy 512 Aug 30 19:51 Projects
drwxr-xr-x 1 boxy boxy 512 Aug 16 18:32 Videos
```

- Go into *Projects* by calling `cd Pro*` (to save typing, the special *grep* character * is used, which substitutes for zero or more characters):

```
boxy@PARSEC:~$ cd Pro*
boxy@PARSEC:~/Projects$ ls -l
total 0
```

- Now type, or copy-paste, the code from Listing 2.1. To do so, we can call one of the installed text editors, such as GNU *nano* or *emacs*. However, to create a *sq.cpp* file, a simple `cat` command can be used. Just after typing `cat > sq.cpp`, paste the code from the clipboard (or type it), as follows

```
boxy@PARSEC:~/Projects$ cat > sq.cpp
// This is a C++ comment in the program to compute the square root of a
value
```

---

4 In this example, we use Ubuntu 18.04 installed as a Linux bash in Windows 10. However, it can be any distribution of Linux with *gcc* installed (see, for instance, *https://linuxize.com/post/how-to-install-gcc-compiler-on-ubuntu-18-04*).

```
#include <cmath>          // A header for std::sqrt
#include <iostream>       // A header for std::cout, std::cin, std::endl

int main()                // A program in C++ consists of a function main()
{
    double x { 0.0 };     // Define and initialize a variable x

    std::cout << "Enter x=";     // Print a message
    std::cin >> x;        // Enter value of x from the keyboard

    if( x >= 0.0 )        // Check if x is positive
      std::cout << "\nSqrt(" << x << ") = " << std::sqrt( x ) << std::endl;
    else
      std::cout << "\nWrong value - cannot compute Sqrt\n";
}
^Z
[1]+  Stopped                      cat > sq.cpp
```

To indicate that we wish to stop redirecting what we type or paste to *sq.cpp*, press `Ctrl+Z` to terminate the redirection pipe.

- Now we are ready to compile our program by calling the GNU *gcc* compiler, as follows:

```
boxy@PARSEC:~/Projects$ g++ sq.cpp -o sq
```

To make *gcc* use the C++ compiler, rather than C, the `g++` command is invoked, as shown. Its second argument is the source file *sq.cpp*, after which the –o option and the name of the executable (*sq*) are provided. However, before doing that, make sure *gcc* is already installed.

- We list our files with `ls  -l`:

```
boxy@PARSEC:~/Projects$ ls -l
total 20
-rwxrwxrwx 1 boxy boxy 13248 Sep  3 18:14 sq
-rw-rw-rw- 1 boxy boxy   611 Sep  3 18:10 sq.cpp
```

We see that, in addition to our source file *sq.cpp*, a new *sq* file appears with an executable x attribute turned on. Congratulations! This means we have successfully created the executable.

- Run the program and see its actions, as follows:

```
boxy@PARSEC:~/Projects$ ./sq
Enter x=123.45

Sqrt(123.45) = 11.1108
boxy@PARSEC:~/Projects$
```

- If we made an error when typing or simply wish to work further to modify the source, a text editor is a convenient solution. Open it, for instance, by typing this:

```
boxy@PARSEC:~/Projects$ nano sq.cpp
```

After making any changes and saving *sq.cpp*, repeat the previous compilation process.

Certainly, some practice in managing the Linux environment is necessary. There are ample online resources (such as *www.linux.org*, or *https://askubuntu.com* for Ubuntu users), as well as many books (Dalheimer and Welsh 2006). However, even more fascinating is Linux programming. This has gained further attention in recent years, mostly due to embedded systems powered by Linux. There are also plenty of online resources for this subject, including the outstanding book *Linux Programming Interface* by Michael Kerrisk (Kerrisk 2010). Since the Linux OS is written in C, examples of Linux programming are also provided with C. To understand them, reading Appendix A.2 will be beneficial. Linux is also a perfect environment for modern C++, as will be shown in this book.

Although Linux is a great operating system with hundreds of useful features and applications, sometimes it is good to have Linux and Windows coexist on a single computer. Windows 10 comes with excellent facilities for Linux programming. First, the Ubuntu and Debian Linux distributions can be downloaded and installed from the Windows Store' and allow us to run the Windows Subsystem for Linux (WSL) like any other Windows application, providing full Linux services at the same time. Second, a Linux development plug-in is available in Microsoft Visual 2019[5] (MV'19).

The MV'19 environment is also our main development platform. Therefore, unless stated otherwise, the majority of the projects – that is, the whole platform, with all files and settings to create a complete program – presented in this book were first developed and tested with MV'19 in Windows 10. However, the projects were generated automatically with the help of the *CMake* program. This greatly facilitates maintaining up-to-date projects in environments with multiple operating systems and various compiling platforms, as described in Appendix A.6.1. Organization of C++ projects and the roles of various files are discussed in Section 3.15.

Summarizing, in this section, we have learned the following:

- What an algorithm is, and how to represent it with a UML activity diagram, as pseudo-code, or as C++ code
- How to implement the `main` function that constitutes the entry to any C++ program
- Defining and initializing a variable of the `double` type to represent real numbers
- Using the `std::cin` object for input and the `std::cout` object for output
- Using the conditional `if-else` statement to check the value of a variable and, depending on the result, execute a code path
- Editing a C++ source file, compiling it, and running it online, as well as in the Linux environment

---

5 For more information, see *https://devblogs.microsoft.com/cppblog/linux-development-with-c-in-visual-studio* and *https://devblogs.microsoft.com/cppblog/c-with-visual-studio-2019-and-windows-subsystem-for-linux-wsl*.

2.5 Example Project – Compound Interest Calculator

In this example, we will make a simple program that can facilitate financial investments. Let's assume we have $1000 (the original principal amount), and we want to safely invest it in a bank at an interest rate of 3% per year. It is easy to determine that after a year, we will gain $1000 · 3% = $30, so our final principal amount will be $1030. What happens if we repeat the same thing? Now our initial principal amount is $1030, so after a year, we will have a gain of $1030 · 3% = $30.90. This time we earn slightly more than in the first year, since we started with a slightly higher principal amount. Let's write a C++ program that does these computations for us. As discussed in Section 2.3, these are our requirements. However, before writing a single line of code, we should spend some time on the problem analysis, as shown in Figure 2.4. In this case, we will begin by writing some simple equations that will guide our implementation.

2.5.1 Compound Interest Analysis

Given initial capital denoted as C_0, interest rate r, and a number of periods t, the interest is computed as follows:

$$I_1 = C_0 \cdot r \cdot t \tag{2.1}$$

Hence, the new capital after t is C_1, which is the sum of C_0 and I_1. Then C_1 can be invested again, and so on. The entire process can be written as follows

$$
\begin{aligned}
C_1 &= C_0 + I_1 = C_0 + C_0 \cdot r \cdot t = C_0 \cdot \left(1 + r \cdot t\right) \\
C_2 &= C_1 \cdot \left(1 + r \cdot t\right) = C_0 \cdot \left(1 + r \cdot t\right)^2 \\
C_3 &= C_0 \cdot \left(1 + r \cdot t\right)^3 \\
&\ldots \\
C_i &= C_0 \cdot \left(1 + r \cdot t\right)^i
\end{aligned}
\tag{2.2}
$$

where r denotes an income rate in the compounding period t. However, banks usually provide the value of r with respect to a yearly period, i.e. 12 months, whereas there can be many compounding periods per year. Hence, we need to be more granular and set as our basic unit the compounding period. In other words, our index i will count the number of fully finished compounding periods in the total investment time. Say we invest for 24 months, and the compounding period is 4 months; in this time, we will have 6 periods. How did we compute this? 24/4 = 6. In general, the periods are $i = m/t$, where m denotes the total investment time expressed in months. On the other hand, in each period, the investment rate is $r/12 \cdot t$. For example, if r is 3% and t again is 4 months, then the interest in this period is 0.03/12 · 4 = 0.01. Thus, we obtain the following equation that will serve as the basis for our implementation:

$$C_i = C_0 \cdot \left(1 + \frac{r}{12} \cdot t\right)^{\frac{m}{t}} \tag{2.3}$$

where

C_0 is the initial capital.

C_i is the final capital after m months of investment (i.e. $i = m/t$ compounding periods).

r is the annual investment rate (expressed as a fraction, so if provided as a percentage, we need to divide by 100).

t denotes the compounding period in months (e.g. for quarterly compounding, t is three months).

m is the total investment time in months.

Let's see how this works in practice. Assume we have \$2500 to invest, the annual rate is 3.4%, and the investment and compounding periods both are six months. What will our income be? If we put all the data into Eq. (2.3), we obtain $C_1 = 2500\$ \cdot (1 + 0.034/12 \cdot 6)^{(6/6)} \approx 2542.50$. Thus, the gain is $C_1 - C_0 = \$42.50$. Unfortunately, in some countries, this gain is taxed, so our investment will be slightly less lucrative.

2.5.2 Implementation of the Interest Calculator

We are almost ready to start our implementation. The only thing we need to know is how to write an equation like (2.3) in C++. Writing *expressions* is similar, more or less, to writing equations in mathematics. However, we have to keep two obstacles in mind. First, for clarity and to address various terminals, expressions have to fit in a line or lines of plain text. In other words, subscripts and superscripts are not allowed. The second limitation is the number of symbols available to represent operators. Hence, to form some operators in C++, terminal symbols are glued together: +=, &&, ::, etc. A complete table of C++ operators is presented in Section 3.19.

This is how we write Eq. (2.3) as a C++ expression:

```
C_i = C_0 * std::pow( 1.0 + r / 12.0 * t, m / t );
```

First, all the symbols, such as C_i, r, t, etc. need to be defined – that is, they must have an associated type. In our case, the built-in `float` or `double` type should be chosen to best represent fractions. Also, variables need to be initialized. Second, there is no power operator in C++. Therefore, we need to call the function `std::pow` from the C++ mathematical library. It accepts two arguments and then returns as a result its first argument raised to the power of its second argument. This function comes in a ready-to-use library, but we need to let the compiler know that we are going to use it. Finally, note that for the constant values, instead of 1 we wrote 1.0, and instead of 12 we wrote 12.0. We did so to use the floating-point format and avoid converting from an integer representation.

Now we are ready to start our implementation. The result looks like the following code, which is split into parts for easier reading.

Listing 2.2 `main` function from the *CompInterest* application (from *main.cpp*).

```
1   #include <cmath>        // To use the pow function
2   #include <iostream>     // To use the std::cout and std::cin
3
4   // Introduce names of the I/O objects from the std namespace
```

```
 5    using std::cout, std::cin, std::endl;
 6
 7
 8    // This program computes the compound interest rate
 9    int main()
10    {
11        // --------------------------------------------------------
12        cout << "Enter the initial amount to invest: " << endl;
13        double C_0 {};    // Initial amount
14        cin >> C_0;
15
16        if (C_0 <= 0.0 )
17        {
18           cout << "Wrong value, exiting..." << endl;
19           return -1;
20        }
```

On lines [1] and [2], two header files from C++ libraries are included. Thanks to this, we can use the already mentioned `std::pow` function, as well as the `std::cout` and `std::cin` objects representing the output screen and the input keyboard, respectively. To avoid repeating the `std::` prefix over and over again, on line [5], the names of the input-output objects from the `std` namespace are introduced with the help of the `using` directive (see Section 3.5).

Line [9] begins defining the `main` function. C++ applications are required to contain exactly one definition of `main`. Further details of various forms of `main` are presented in Appendix A.2.2.

On line [12], we output text on the screen using the `cout` object, the `<<` operator, as well as a text constant in quotation marks. (We will see that the action of an operator such as `<<` can differ, depending on the types of objects it is used to act on.) `endl` means to move the cursor to the next line and update the screen.

On line [13], a variable named `C_0` is created to hold an initial amount. The names of variables are very important for conveying useful information. So, this variable could be named something like `initial_amount`. However, when implementing equations, such as Eq. (2.3), it is usually better to keep the names of the equation's elements; and mathematical equations are usually written with single letters and subscripts. The variable (object) `C_0` can hold any positive value, including fractions. Because of this, `double` was chosen for its type. `C_0` is created and, on the same line immediately initialized to 0 by typing { }.

Next, on line [14], we wait for the user to enter the real value of the initial capital. After that, we check this value on line [16]. If it is not correct, the program writes out a message and, on line [19], the error code −1 is returned. Checking for incorrect values is one of the very important, but frequently forgotten, actions that need to be performed in real code – always try to stay on the safe side. In C++, there are more advanced mechanisms to deal with errors than returning an error code; these are discussed in Section 3.13.2.5.

This process of printing, defining variables, waiting, and then checking the correctness of the user input data is repeated a few times. This is shown in the following code and should be clear by now:

```
21
22      // -------------------------------------------
23      cout << "Enter the annual rate [% per 12 months]: " << endl;
24      double r {};
25      cin >> r;
26      if ( r <= 0.0 || r >= 100.0 )
27      {
28         cout << "Wrong value, exiting..." << endl;
29         return -1;
30      }
31
32      // -------------------------------------------
33      cout << "Compound frequency is a period in months between computing interest" << endl;
34      cout << "(e.g. if 2 times a year, enter 6)" << endl;
35      cout << "If you don't know, enter 12 for a yearly compound frequency." << endl;
36      cout << "Enter the compound frequency [months 1-72]: " << endl;
37      double t {};
38      cin >> t;
39      if ( t <= 0.0 || t > 72.0 )
40      {
41         cout << "Wrong value, exiting..." << endl;
42         return -1;
43      }
44
45      // ---------------------------------------------------
46      cout << "Enter the investment time [months 1-100]: " << endl;
47      double m {};
48      cin >> m;
49      if ( m <= 0.0 || m >= 100 )
50      {
51         cout << "Wrong value, exiting..." << endl;
52         return -1;
53      }
54
```

Having read all the data, we start our computations and define two constants on lines [58] and [59], respectively. Their names convey information about their role. As we already know, adding the keyword const ahead of double makes an object read-only. Omitting const here would not change the computations, but it would harm the code's resistance to unwanted errors. So, if a value should remain constant, we should declare it const.

```
55      // -----------------------------
56      // Do computations
57
58      const double kMontsPerYear    = 12.0;
59      const double kPercentageDiv   = 100.0;
60
61      double i = m / t;    // compounding periods
62
63      double C_i =C_0 * std::pow( (1.0 + ( r/kPercentageDiv ) / kMontsPerYear*t ), i);
64
65      cout << "Your balance before tax, after " << m;
66      cout << " months of investment is: " << C_i << endl;
67
68      // Compute the net income
69      double income = C_i - C_0;
```

```
70    cout << "Your income is " << income << endl;
71    const double kIncomeTax = 19.0;                    // 19%
72    cout << "After " << kIncomeTax << "% tax deduction you get: ";
73    cout << ( 1.0 - kIncomeTax / kPercentageDiv ) * income << endl;
74
75    return 0;
76  }
```

Given a total number of investment months *m* and a compounding period *t*, also in months, line [61] computes a number *i* of compounding periods. Then, on line [63], the final sum is computed, exactly as in Eq. (2.3). On lines [65–66], the computed values are displayed on the screen. Finally, on lines [69–73], our income and also income after tax deductions are computed and displayed.

2.5.3 Building and Running the Software

We can easily launch the previous code in one of the online C++ compiler platforms, as mentioned in Section 2.4.2. However, building an application that can be launched like any other program in our system is a more convenient option in this case. To build the *CompInterest* application for Linux, we can follow the steps presented in Section 2.4.5. But because the code in Listing 2.2 uses only standard C++ mechanisms, this software component is rather general. Hence, it could work on any platform if we had the tools to create and maintain multi-platform projects. For each software development environment, we can manually create a suitable project and build the application. However, considering the number of such platforms and operating systems, doing so would be tedious. Instead, we can use the *CMake* project generator. With its support, not only this but all future projects can be automatically generated to fit different development platforms and various operating systems. All we need to do is install this free tool and write the *CMakeList.txt* file, which contains commands that tell *CMake* what to do. (These are described in Appendix A.6.1.) Fortunately, a suitable *CMakeList.txt* file is attached to the example projects and can be downloaded with the other sources from GitHub (*https://github.com/BogCyg/BookCpp*). Also fortunately, all of our projects use an almost-identical *CMakeList.txt* file.

Having built the *CompInterest* application, to test it, let's assume we have $1000, the annual investment rate is 2.7%, and we wish to invest our capital for four months. After launching *CompInterest,* our interest can be easily computed as follows:

```
Enter the initial amount to invest:
1000
Enter the annual rate [% per 12 months]:
2.7
Compound frequency is a period in months between computing interest
(e.g. if 2 times a year, enter 6)
If you don't know, enter 12 for a yearly compound frequency.
Enter the compound frequency [months 1-72]:
4
Enter the investment time [months 1-100]:
4
Your balance before tax, after 4 months of investment is: 1009
Your income is 9
After 19% tax deduction you get: 7.29
```

The previous `main` function can act as a simple template for similar programs that read data, do some simple computations, and output the result. Also, this project can be used as a startup to build an application with a graphical user interface (GUI) for a mobile platform or as a web component. We will discuss some of these ideas later.

In this section, we learned:

- How to define and initialize integers with int, values with fractions with double, and constant strings with " "
- The common arithmetical operators +, −, *, /, and how to write simple expressions
- How to print text and variables on the screen with the built-in cout object and << operator, and how to enter their values with the cin object and >> operator

2.6 Example Project – Counting Occurrences of Characters in Text

We have already seen how to represent a simple algorithm and how to build it and run it in an online platform, as well as how to create an executable. We have also learned about a few useful features of C++, such as the main function, creating and initializing variables, the input and output objects, as well as the conditional if-else statement. Here, we will extend this list of C++ features by adding the for statement to implement software loops, as well as containers to store objects of the same type. In this section's example, we will show how to compute a histogram of occurrences of the letters *a–z* in a sentence.

2.6.1 Problem Analysis and Implementation

Assume that we wish to compute a histogram of occurrences of the letters *a–z* in a given sentence. How do we set about this problem? Let's start with a simple example and analyze the process of building such a histogram from the word *Alcatraz*, as shown in Figure 2.9.

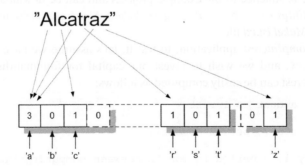

Figure 2.9 Building a histogram of characters: a use case analysis. Each bin contains the number of occurrences of a given letter.

A *histogram* is a data structure composed of *N* bins, each containing a number of occurrences of an event associated with its bin. Each bin corresponds to a particular letter in our example or other *event* in general. Thus, histograms are commonly used to measure the frequency with which events occur. They can also be used to measure probability – the higher the frequency, the higher the probability. Initially, all numbers in the histogram are set to 0. Then, when traversing the text to be measured, an occurrence of a given letter increases the corresponding bin by 1. Hence, in our example, the bin that corresponds to the letter *a* gets the number 3, since there are 3 occurrences of *a* in *Alcatraz*, and so on (upper- and lowercase letters are treated the same). The following C++ code performs these actions.

Listing 2.3 `main` function of *CharHistogram* (in *CppBookCode, letter_histogram.cpp*).

```cpp
1   #include <iostream>
2   #include <string>
3   #include <vector>
4
5   // Listing them here allows omitting std::
6   using std::cout, std::cin, std::endl;
7   using std::string, std::vector;
8
9
10  int main()
11  {
12      // Make a slot for each letter, from 'a' to 'z'
13      // Initial count set to 0 for each.
14      vector histogram( 'z' - 'a' + 1, 0 );
15
16      string in_str;
17
18      cin >> in_str;
19      in_str = "AGH University of Science and Technology";
20
21      for( auto c : in_str )        // c takes on successive letters from in_str
22        if( std::isalpha( c ) )   // isalpha( c ) returns true if c is alphanumeric
23          ++ histogram[ std::tolower( c ) - 'a' ];// ++ adds 1 to the letter position
24
25      cout << endl;
26
27      for( auto c { 'a' }; c <= 'z'; ++ c )  // c takes on codes from 'a' to 'z'
28          cout << c << " ";                  // Print all characters 'a' to 'z'
29
30      cout << endl;
31
32      for( auto h : histogram )    // h takes on successive values of the histogram
33          cout << h << " ";        // Print histogram values
34  }
```

2.6.2 Running the C++ Code with the Online Compiler

Before we explain how this code operates, let's see what it does. How do we run the code? The simplest way is to open one of the web pages with an online C++ compiler, such as *Coliru*, copy and paste the code, and click the "*Compile, link and run…*" button. See the screenshot in Figure 2.10. Given the examples from the previous sections, building a standalone application also should not be a problem.

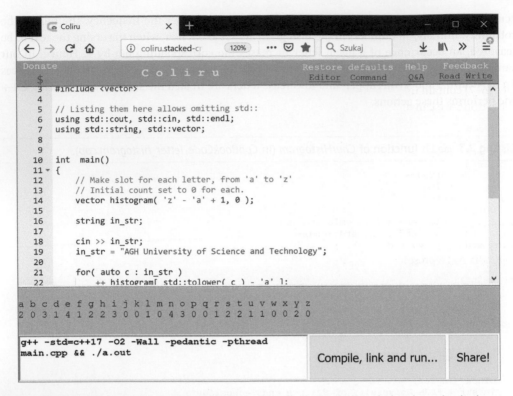

Figure 2.10 The Coliru online compiler environment (*http://coliru.stacked-crooked.com*) running in the Mozilla Firefox viewer with the code from Listing 2.3 copied and pasted into the editor pane. Under it is the output pane. The lower-left pane contains the command line to build and run the program. At lower right are the action buttons.

We obtain the following output:

```
a  b  c  d  e  f  g  h  i  j  k  l  m  n  o  p  q  r  s  t  u  v  w  x  y  z

2  0  3  1  4  1  2  2  3  0  0  1  0  4  3  0  0  1  2  2  1  1  0  0  2  0
```

That is, each letter is associated with the frequency of its occurrence in the input sentence.

2.6.3 Histogram Code, Explained

Let's now split up the code from Listing 2.3 and explain what it does, line by line. On lines [1–3], #include <*file_name*> is called, where *file_name* corresponds to a header file. As alluded to earlier, headers contain already-written code that we can use to simplify our lives as programmers. Figuring out what header to choose for a given language component is sometimes difficult – the easiest way is to look it up on the Internet. Here we include *iostream* for the std::cout and std::cin objects, which represent the screen and the keyboard, respectively. Then the *string* file is introduced, to use the std::string class to store plain text. Finally, a *vector* that contains the definition of the std::vector class that allows us to store the histogram is included, as shown in Figure 2.9.

```
1   #include <iostream>
2   #include <string>
3   #include <vector>
4
```

Lines [6–7] contain using directives. These are optional but let us save on typing, since instead of std::cout we can omit the prefix std:: and succinctly write cout:

```
5   // Listing them here allows omitting std::
6   using std::cout, std::cin, std::endl;
7   using std::string, std::vector;
```

The actual program starts on line [10]. A program in C++ is composed of the main function and all the functions it calls from inside. A function is outlined with braces, such as { on line [11] and } on line [34]. main on line [10] returns an object of type int, but we are not using this option here (Appendix A.2.2 presents more about main).

```
8
9
10  int main()
11  {
```

Now we are inside main. On line [14], the object histogram of the vector type is defined and initialized with two parameters (both forms, std::vector and vector, are OK in this context). The first one reads 'z' - 'a' + 1. Since 'z' and 'a' are numeric code values of the last and first letters in the English alphabet, subtracting the two and adding 1 gives a total number of 26 letters. Later, we will see how to treat upper- and lowercase letters the same way. Thanks to this, a structure of 26 counters is created, as shown in Figure 2.9. The second initialization parameter for the histogram is 0, which sets the initial counters to 0. vector is a very useful data structure that can contain a number of other objects of the same type.

On line [16], a string object named in_str is created (we can skip the std:: prefix again). This is also a kind of vector, but it is specialized to store and process vectors of characters (text):

```
12      // Make a slot for each letter, from 'a' to 'z'
13      // Initial count set to 0 for each.
14      vector histogram( 'z' - 'a' + 1, 0 );
15
16      string in_str;
17
```

The object in_str is empty at first, but not for long. On line [18], it waits until the user types a sentence in the terminal window and presses the Enter key. This would be sufficient; but since we are running the program in an online compiler that does not easily accept user input, on line [19] we hard-coded some example text to in_str:

```
18      cin >> in_str;
19      in_str = "AGH University of Science and Technology";
```

Now it is time for some action. We need to access all the letters in the in_str object and increment the histogram at the bin positions that correspond to each letter. So, if the letter is 'a', then the index should be 0, if 'b', then the index is 1, if 'z' then 25, and so on. Note that for *N* elements, the indices go from 0 to *N* − 1. To access each letter, on line [21], a for loop is created. In it, auto c means c will take consecutive letters of in_str, which is on the other side of the colon :. Thanks to auto, we do not need to bother with the type of c – it will be inferred automatically by the compiler from the type of letters stored in in_str.

Line [23] operates under the supervision of the closest for loop. Hence, for each letter c, we find the corresponding index in the histogram vector by subtracting the code 'a'. Then that entry is increased by 1 by calling the ++ operator. To treat upper- and lowercase letters the same way, each letter c is converted to lowercase by calling the std::tolower function (here we have to explicitly write the prefix std:: since std::tolower has not been listed with using). To reset the prompt position in the output window to the beginning of the next line, on line [25], the endl object is sent to the screen object cout.

```
20
21      for( auto c : in_str )        // c takes on successive letters from in_str
22         if(std::isalpha( c ) )     // isalpha( c ) returns true if c is alphanumeric
23            ++ histogram[ std::tolower( c ) - 'a' ];// ++ adds 1 to the letter position
24
25      cout << endl;
26
```

Lines [27–28] show the next for loop. Its purpose is to print all the letters on the screen. However, this time for is composed of three fields, separated with a semicolon ;. Its first part, auto k { 'a' }, is executed only once – it creates an object k with the initial value 'a'. The second part, the condition k <= 'z', is checked during each iteration; if it is fulfilled, line [28] is executed, which simply prints a letter represented by k, followed by a space. Just after that, the third part of the for loop is executed. In our example, this is the ++ k expression, which advances k by 1: that is, to the next letter code. Then, the loop repeats from the point of condition checking. However, if at any iteration the condition is not fulfilled, i.e. it evaluates to false, the loop breaks, and the next line of code just after the loop is executed. If more than one statement needs to be executed at each iteration of the loop, the statements can be grouped into a block with braces { }.

```
27      for( auto k { 'a' }; k <= 'z'; ++ k )    // c takes on codes from 'a' to 'z'
28         cout << k << " ";                     // Print all characters 'a' to 'z'
29
```

Finally, the loop on lines [32–33] displays computed values of the histogram. Again, the first form of the for loop is used, so at each iteration, h gets the value of a consecutive element stored in the histogram object.

```
30      cout << endl;
31
32      for( auto h : histogram )     // h takes on successive values of the histogram
33         cout << h << " ";          // Print histogram values
34   }
```

That's it. How can we use this code further? Just copy it, change something, and play. And keep reading, since all the constructs used here will be explained in the following chapters.

In this section, we learned the following elements of C++ programming:

- How to implement a simple C++ program
- What the int main() function is used for
- What header files to #include, and why
- What using directives need to be placed at the beginning of a program
- How to define a simple array of elements with std::vector
- How to input text from the keyboard, and how to store it in the std::string object
- How to automate object type deduction with the auto keyword
- How to implement a loop with the for statement
- How to check logical conditions with the if statement
- How to call predefined functions for text manipulation, such as std::isalpha and std::tolower

In the following chapters, we will polish these techniques in further examples.

2.7 Summary

Things to Remember

- Analyze the problem before beginning a design
- Make a proper design before implementation. Prefer the top-down approach
- Understand your hardware, and remember its limitations. Also know your software development tools
- You can use the projects from this chapter as blueprints for simple C++ applications
- Wherever possible, use the objects from the Standard Library
- Keep objects in a meaningful state
- Document your code with terse, meaningful comments
- Understand your code
- Continuously improve your programming skills. Read books and blogs. Learn about your programming environment

Questions and Exercises

1. The *greatest common divisor* (GCD) of two positive integers a and b is the largest integer that divides each of them without any remainder. The solution to this provides the Euclidean algorithm (*https://en.wikipedia.org/wiki/Euclidean_algorithm*):

Algorithm 2.2 The Euclidean algorithm for finding the greatest common divisor of two numbers.

Input:	Two positive integers: a, b	
Output:	GCD(a, b)	
1	**while** b != 0	(iterate as long as b is not 0)
2	tmp ← b	(copy b to a temporary variable tmp)

(Continued)

3	$b \leftarrow a \% b$	(copy the remainder of a divided by b to b)
4	$a \leftarrow tmp$	(copy the value of `tmp` to a)
5	Return: a	(return a containing the greatest common divisor)

    a. On a sheet of paper, work out an example: for instance, setting $a = 255$ and $b = 221$.

    b. Implement Algorithm 2.2. Hint: To implement the loop use the statement **while** $(b \ != 0)$, or **for** `( ; b != 0 ; ) { loop_statements 2-4 }`.

    c. Verify the operation of your program by setting different values of a and b.

2. Analyze the following bisection algorithm for computing an approximation of the square root from an integer value.

    a. Write an implementation of Algorithm 2.3.

    b. Compare the returned values with those produces by the code in Listing 2.1.

Algorithm 2.3 A bisection algorithm for integer square root approximation.

Input:	An integer value x
Output:	Approximation of the square root of x
1	`lower_bnd` $\leftarrow$ 1 `upper_bnd` $\leftarrow$ x / 2 (for x > 4 sqrt cannot be larger)
2	**while** `upper_bnd >= lower_bnd` (iterate as long as fulfilled)
3	`mid_val` $\leftarrow$ `(lower_bnd + upper_bnd ) / 2` (compute a middle value)
4	**if** `mid_val * mid_val > x` (check which half)
5	`upper_bnd` $\leftarrow$ `mid_val - 1` (lower the upper bound)
6	**else**
7	`lower_bnd` $\leftarrow$ `mid_val + 1` (advance the lower bound)
8	Return: `(lower_bnd + upper_bnd ) / 2` (return a middle value)

---

3. The bisection algorithm has other applications. It is helpful in search tasks over monotonic values (*https://en.wikipedia.org/wiki/Bisection_method*). Use the bisection algorithm to find the root of a function (i.e. its zero-crossing point).

4. There can be problems when entering values using the `std::cin` object. For example, on line [14] of Listing 2.2, a numeric value is expected, but the user can enter `abc`. To prevent such errors, the status of the reading operation can be checked as in the following code snippet:

```
if( ! ( cin >> C_0 ) )
{
  cout << "Error entering a value\n" << endl;
  return -1;
}
```

This works because the `cin >> C_0` expression converts to a `bool` value of `true` or `false`, depending on whether the operation succeeded or not, respectively. Then, the `!` operator negates this result, so if `false` was returned, the code inside `if` is executed, and the program terminates.

Using this method, update the value-reading lines of code in Listings 2.2 and 2.3.

5. Refactor the *CharHistogram* source code in Listing 2.3 to print the histogram as vertical bars composed of the `*` symbol, rather than numbers of occurrences.

6. A second-order polynomial can be expressed as follows

$$a x^2 + b x + c = 0 \tag{2.4}$$

where a, b, and c denote real coefficients. The question is whether there are values of x that fulfill this equation. If they exist, they are called *roots* of the second-order polynomial. Recall that to answer this question, it is sufficient to compute the delta coefficient d as follows:

$$d = b^2 - 4ac \tag{2.5}$$

If $d \geq 0$, we can compute the solution to Eq. (2.4) (its roots) as follows:

$$x_1 = \frac{-b - \sqrt{d}}{2a}, \ x_2 = \frac{-b + \sqrt{d}}{2a} \tag{2.6}$$

Otherwise, there are no roots. Write a C++ program that asks the user for the three coefficients a, b, and c; resolves whether there are roots; and, if possible, computes them. First rewrite the previous equations into equivalent C++ expressions, and then adapt them.

7. Implement the *Secret Chamber* game – its 10×10 grid board looks as follows.

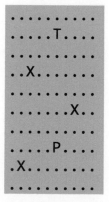

You can move a player 'P' up, down, left, or right but only one position at a time (e.g. by pressing the buttons 'U', 'D', 'L' and 'R'). You win if you step 'P' onto the treasure 'T'. However, you lose if you step onto one of the traps 'X'. Moreover, at each turn 'X' can randomly change its position by one spot. Pay attention not to step outside of the game board range.

8. Compute a sum of two positive integer values. However, the sum to compute is given as a string, e.g. "123 + 37", "78+ 99", etc. Write a program that performs the following steps:
   a. Prompt a user to enter a string;
   b. Eliminate extra spaces from the string;
   c. Extract the two substrings representing the two arguments, such as "123" and "37";
   d. Compute integer values of these two substrings, so "123" is transformed to the value 123, etc.
   e. Print the sum of the two values;
   f. Extend your solution to handle potential errors.

9. There are many ways to compare texts. A simple one is to compare the two histograms of their letter occurrences. Two histograms of the same length can be compared by summing up squares of differences of the corresponding bin values.
   a. Extend the program from Listing 2.3 to compute and compare histograms of two texts.
   b. Test your procedure comparing few paragraphs.
   c. Better results will be obtained if the histograms are normalized before the comparison. After normalization, the sum of all bins in a histogram is 1.0. To normalize the histogram, divide each its bin value by the total sum of all bins in that histogram. Hint: make the histogram vector to store floating-point values, e.g. in line [14] of Listing 2.3 change the initialization value from 0 to 0.0.

3

C++ Basics

This chapter presents the basics of the C++ programming language. The top-level programming topics we will learn about are as follows:

- Constants, variables, `auto`, and built-in data types
- Common containers and algorithms from the Standard Library
- Basics of data structures and their initialization
- Introduction to classes
- Indirect object access with references
- Indirect object access with pointers
- C++ statements
- Functions, passing objects from and to functions, and lambda functions
- C++ operators

We will analyze and present detailed implementations of several projects that we hope will be interesting. Our goal is to show some programming techniques and, in particular, C++ features in action.

3.1 Constants and Variables – Built-In Data Types, Their Range, and Initialization

To perform computations, we need to represent data and define operations on it. Data is stored in the dedicated computer's memory regions as what we will call *objects*, although we will extend this concept soon. All computer languages have ways to reserve sufficient memory, initialize such objects, and read from and/or write to them. However, all of them require a means of access. This can be

- *Direct*, by providing a direct *name* for an object, or
- *Indirect*, by providing a *link* to an object (a reference or a pointer)

Objects can be further divided into the following two groups:

- *Mutable* – After creation and initialization, the objects can be further changed. These are also all variables
- *Immutable* – Such objects can be created and initialized, but they cannot be changed. These are called *constants*

Introduction to Programming with C++ for Engineers, First Edition. Bogusław Cyganek.
© 2021 John Wiley & Sons Ltd. Published 2021 by John Wiley & Sons Ltd.
Companion website: http://home.agh.edu.pl/~cyganek/BookCpp.htm

Soon we will see that objects can contain operations, which is one of the paradigms of the object-oriented programming. However, in this section we will focus on aspects related to representing data.

Figure 3.1 depicts three stages of variable creation and initialization and their imprint in the computer's memory. In raw memory, each byte has an undefined value. Defining a variable by instructing the computer to perform `char c` reserves a byte of memory in the computer's address space, as shown in Figure 3.1b. As a result, instead of writing a numeric address, we use the identifier of an object, such as c in this example. However, c still contains a garbage value, so it has to be initialized. Initializing writes a known value (state) to a variable. In our case, this is `'Z'` – that is, code for the letter Z.

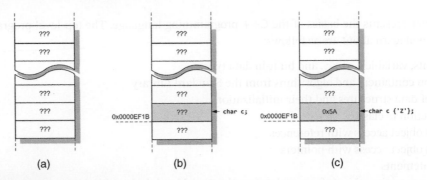

Figure 3.1 Stages of variable (object) creation and initialization and their imprint in the computer's memory. In raw memory, each byte has an undefined value (a). Defining a variable by instructing the computer to perform `char c` reserves a byte of memory in the computer's address space. Instead of writing addresses, we use its identifier, c. (b). However, c is not initialized, so it can contain any value. Initializing sets a known value to the variable. In our case this is code of the letter 'Z' i.e. 0x5A in the hexadecimal representation (c).

We stress here that although it is possible to write and compile an uninitialized variable, such as

```
char c;    // Avoid uninitialized objects!
```

the object can then have *any value* that happened to be in memory! This can lead to serious errors that are difficult to spot. Therefore, *always initialize all the objects you create*! In C++, it is sufficient to add { }, as follows:

```
char c {};   // Ok :)
```

When creating an object, consider the following aspects:

- Choose a name for the object[1] that reflects important information about the object's role in the code. In C++, a name for an object, such as a variable, constant, function, structure, or class,

---

1 The notion of an object is a broad concept in computer science. It is a construct placed in a memory, such as a variable or a constant of a given type. In object-oriented programming, a structure or a class denotes a type, which is an abstract concept, whereas instantiations of these types that reside in memory are objects. However, in some interpretations, a function is also considered an object. Objects in the object-oriented context will be discussed further in Section 3.9.

comes in the form of an *identifier*. An identifier is a series of characters and digits, starting with a character. The underscore symbol _ counts as a character and is frequently used to separate parts of names, as we will see in many examples

- If an object is not intended to change its state, define it constant with the `const` keyword
- Do not operate on raw numbers – give them names by defining constant objects
- Choose the proper types for objects
- Properly *initialize* each object
- Do not mix variables of different types

Mixing types can lead to nasty errors. Let's consider the simple conversion from degrees Fahrenheit to Celsius, which is given by the following formula

$$T_C = \left(T_F - 32\right) \cdot \frac{5}{9} \tag{3.1}$$

To convert $T_F = 100$ to T_C, we can translate the previous formula into the following code:

```
1   double TF { 100.0 };
2   double TC {};
3
4   TC = ( TF - 32 ) * ( 5 / 9 );   // Compiles but does not compute what is expected...
5   cout << TF << " Fahrenheit = " << TC << " Celsius" << endl;
```

However, after compiling and running, the following message appears in the terminal window

```
100 Fahrenheit = 0 Celsius
```

which obviously is not correct. So, what happened? The problem is in the wrong data type on line [4]. Division of the integer constant 5 by another integer constant 9 results in 0. On the other hand, the variables `TF` and `TC` are correctly declared with the `double` type. So the subtraction `TF - 32` on line [4] is not a problem since the integer constant 32 will be promoted to `double`, and the result will also be `double`. But this result multiplied by 0 promoted to `double` will produce 0, as shown. The correct version is as follows:

```
4   TC = ( TF - 32.0 ) * ( 5.0 / 9.0 );
```

Here we do not mix data types, and we do not count on behind-the-scenes promotions. On line [4], all variables and constants are of the same `double` type. Now the division is correct, and the correct answer is displayed:

```
100 Fahrenheit = 37.7778 Celsius
```

Table 3.1 presents some of the basic built-in types along with their properties, such as length in bytes and value representation. This knowledge is necessary when deciding what type to choose to represent quantities in a program. The value representation specifies whether we can store positive or negatives values, as well as whether they can be fractions. A variable's length affects the precision of the stored representation. These issues are further discussed in Chapter 7. The length (in bytes) occupied by a given type can be determined using the `sizeof` operator (see the description of the *GROUP 3* operators in Table 3.15). As shown in Table 3.1, only `char` has a length equal to exactly 1 byte.[2] The other types require more than 1 byte. Their exact lengths are system dependent and can change from system to system. However, the following is guaranteed to hold:

```
sizeof( char ) == 1    <= sizeof( short )
                       <= sizeof( int )
                       <= sizeof( long )
                       <= sizeof( long long )
```

In C++, when an object is created, two things happen:

- A sufficient amount of memory is allocated to store the object
- The object is initialized (if a proper initialization function, called *a constructor*, is available)

As alluded to previously, all objects need to be initialized during the creation process. It is very important for a variable to have a predictable value at all times. Usually, this is easily achieved in more complex objects, since they usually have special initialization functions called *constructors* (see Table 3.2, as well as Section 3.15). However, for performance reasons, the basic types – such as those in Table 3.1 – do not initialize automatically. Their initialization can be performed with *literals*, i.e. a fixed value or another object that has already been created. Table 3.1 contains examples showing the creation of variables and their initialization with literals. There are many versions of them, though (Stroustrup 2013). Interestingly, there is no problem with constant objects – the compiler always enforces their initialization.

For historical reasons, there are many ways to initialize objects (i.e. variables and constants). Table 3.2 shows three such mechanisms. Currently, the most popular and versatile approach is initialization with the *initializer list*, as shown in the first row of Table 3.2. The second row of Table 3.2 shows initialization by a constructor call.

On the other hand, assigning a value with the assignment operator (=) looks natural, especially when coding mathematical formulas. However, in this case, we have to be aware that such assignment means first creating an object with a default or undefined value, and then assigning to it a value on the right side of the =. This doesn't seem like an issue when assigning to, for example, `int` or `double`, but assigning large objects like matrices this way may incur excessive operation time.

As already mentioned, for a given type T, the operator `sizeof` (T) returns the number of bytes necessary to store an object of type T (see also Table 3.15). This works fine with basic types, but calling `sizeof` on more complex objects usually does not return what we expect, since data can be spread throughout many memory locations. In such cases, we should call a specific member function, such as `size`, which is usually provided by the object.

---

2 The primary role of `char` is to store characters in the one-byte ASCII code representation (*www.ascii.com*). However, for international symbols, multiple-byte Unicode is used.

Table 3.1 Built-in basic data types and their properties and literals.

Type	Bytes	Description	Examples

char	1	Stores signed integer values that fit in 1 byte, i.e. in the range −128...+127. Used to store the ASCII codes for characters.	```cpp
			// Create and init c
			char c { 'Y' };
			
			std::cout << "Press N to exit" << endl;
			std::cin >> c;
			
			// Operator == to compare, || is logical OR
			bool exit_flag = c == 'N' || c == 'n';
			if(exit_flag)
			    return; // Exit now
			``

short	≥2	Signed integer values (an optional signed keyword can be put in front).	```cpp
			int x { 100 }; // Create x and set 100
			
			x = 0x64; // in hex (leading 0x)
			x = 0144; // in octal (leading 0)
			x = 0b01100100; // as binary (0b, C++14)
			``

int	≥2		
long	≥4		
long long	≥8		

unsigned [char, short, int, long]	As for signed types	Unsigned integer values.	```cpp
			// Set to 1111111...111
			// Operator ~ negates all bits
			// 0UL is an unsigned long version of 0
			unsigned long light_register { ~ 0UL };
			``

bool	≥1	Boolean value: true or false.	Various formats for literals (constants) are possible (dec, hex, oct, bin). The type of a literal should comply with the type of a variable, as in the last line: 0 is of type int, 0L is long, and 0UL is unsigned long.

float	≥4	Single-precision floating-point (IEEE-754).	```cpp
			std::cout << "Enter value \n";
			// Create double and init with 0.0 (0 int)
			double val { 0.0 };
			
			std::cin >> val;
			if(val >= 0.0)
			    cout << "sqrt(" << val << ") = "
			         << sqrt(val) << endl;
			else
			    cout << "Negative value" << endl;
			``

double	≥8	Double-precision floating-point (IEEE-754).	
long double	≥8	Extended-precision floating-point.	A literal to initialize float and double should have a dot, such as 0.0, .3, −13, etc. Pure 0 is of int type. The sqrt function (from *cmath*) computes a square root. Constant text is provided in quotation marks " ".

wchar_t	≥2; 4 for Unicode	Wide character representation.	```cpp
			// Unicode letter
			wchar_t w_letter { L'A' };
			
			// Its memory size in bytes
			size_t w_letter_bytes = sizeof(w_letter);
			
			// wcout is necessary to display Unicode
			std::wcout << w_letter << L" bytes = "
			           << w_letter_bytes << std::endl;
			``

size_t	≥4	Unsigned integer type; the result of the sizeof operator (*GROUP 4*, Table 3.15).	To enter constant wide letters, use L'A'. Constant wide text is provided as L"": in quotation marks with the prefix L.

Table 3.2 Syntax for defining and initializing variables and constants (objects) in C++.

Operation	Syntax	Examples

Definition of a variable or constant (object) named by *identifier* and with features set by *type*.
 	
 The initial *value* is set with the initializer list { }.
 	
 If const is added, then the object cannot be changed (no new values are allowed).
 	
 This is the *preferable* way to initialize objects in C++.
 	
 { } is called zero-initialization since an object is guaranteed to have its default constructor called, which for built-in types sets its value to 0.
	const type identifier { value } ;	```// Vars and const initialized with {}```
		 ```int x {}; // Create x and set to 0```
		 ```x += 1; // Can increase by 1```
		
		 ```// Create const y and set to 100 - cannot change```
		 ```const int y { 100 };```
		 ```//y += 1; // Error, cannot change constant```
		
		 ```// Create c and set to ASCII code of 'A'```
		 ```char c { 'A' };```
		 ```// Can display on the screen```
		 ```std::cout << "c = " << c << std::endl;```
		
		 ```// A variable of floating arithmetic```
		 ```double radius { 2.54 };```
		
		 ```// Create const kPi of floating type```
		 ```const double kPi { 3.14159263589 };```
		 ```// Compute and display area```
		 ```std::cout << "Area = " << kPi * radius * radius;```
		
		 ```bool flag { true }; // A logical var init to true```

Operation	Syntax	Examples
| | | ```
// Vars and const initialized with ()
//int x(); // x is int and set to 0?? No !!
int x ( 0 );        // Create x and set to 0
x += 1;             // Can increase by 1

int y( 100 );       // Ok, var x with 100
y += 1;

// A variable of floating-point arithmetic
double radius ( 2.54 );

// Create const kPi of floating type
const double kPi ( 3.14159265589 );
// Compute and display area
std::cout << "Area = " << kPi * radius * radius;

bool flag ( true );    // A logical var init to true
``` |
| As in the previous item, but initialization is in the form of a call to a constructor (i.e. an initialization function defined for *type*). | const [*type*] [*identifier*] ([*value*]) ; | Using () for initialization looks like calling a function, and indeed it is. This function is called a *constructor*, which performs an action defined by the object's type. If no arguments are provided, then the *default constructor* is called. With parameters, this is the *parametric constructor*. These are discussed in Section (3.15).

Writing int x(); can be confusing. It does not create a variable x with a call to its default constructor. Instead, the compiler treats it as a declaration of a function named x that takes no arguments and returns int. |

(Continued)
```

Table 3.2 (continued)

Operation	Syntax	Examples
| As in the previous item, but initialization is in the form of a copy.<br><br>A value can also be provided in the initializer list { }. (This is how initialization is done in C.) | const `type` `identifier` = `value` ; | ```cpp
// Vars and const initialized with assignment =
int x = 0;        // Create x and set to 0
x += 1;           // Can increase by 1

// A variable of floating arithmetic initialized
// from an initialization list
double radius = { 2.54 };

// Create const kPi of floating type
const double kPi = 3.14159265389;
// Compute and display area
std::cout << "Area = " << kPi * radius * radius;

bool flag = true;   // A logical var set to true
```<br><br>Initialization by assignment works fine but may not be efficient in some cases. This is the case because two steps are executed: first an object is created with its default value, and then it is initialized with a value on the right side of the assignment operator `=`. |
```

Other parameters of basic types, such as values of `lowest`, `min`, `max`, etc. can be determined using the `numeric_limits< T >` class (from the *limits*), as shown in Listing 3.1.

Listing 3.1 Displaying values and measuring the size in bytes of basic C++ built-in data types (from *CppBookCode, Variables.cpp*).

```
1   #include <limits>      // for basic types' limits
2
3   using std::cout, std::endl, std::numeric_limit;
4
5   // Print basic facts about char
6   cout << "bytes of char = " << sizeof( char )    << endl;
7   cout << "char lowest = "  << +numeric_limits< char >::lowest() << endl;
8   cout << "char min = "     << +numeric_limits< char >::min()    << endl;
9   cout << "char max = "     << +numeric_limits< char >::max()    << endl;
10
11  // Print basic facts about int
12  cout << "bytes of int = " << sizeof( int )       << endl;
13  cout << "int lowest = "   << numeric_limits< int >::lowest()  << endl;
14  cout << "int min = "      << numeric_limits< int >::min()     << endl;
15  cout << "int max = "      << numeric_limits< int >::max()     << endl;
```

To use `numeric_limits`, we need to include the `limits` header, as shown on line [1]. On lines [7–9], we print the `lowest`, `min`, and `max` value of the type `char`. However, to properly display values, we use a small trick here: adding a + sign in front of the `numeric_limits` objects. This causes the values to be treated as integers and displayed properly.

To store a value, we need to check whether the chosen representation has a sufficient number of bits. In the following example, we simply ask if type `long` is sufficient to store the number containing up to 11 digits. The computations are simple, but they require calling the `log` function to return a value of the natural logarithm, as shown on line [18] of Listing 3.2. The answer to the question of whether `long` is long enough is found using the comparison (<) on lines [18–19]. This `true` or `false` result goes to the `bool` variable `longFitFlag`.

Listing 3.2 Computing the number of bits for a value representation (from *CppBookCode, Variables.cpp*).

```
16  // Check whether long is long enough to store 11-digit values
17  const int bits_in_byte = 8;
18  bool longFitFlag = ( std::log( 99999999999.0 ) / std::log( 2.0 ) + 1 )
19              < sizeof( long ) * bits_in_byte - 1;
20
21  cout   << "We " << ( longFitFlag ? "can" : "cannot" )
22      << " store 11 digits in long in this system" << endl;
```

On line [21], a message is displayed depending on the value of the flag `longFitFlag`. To check it, the conditional ? : operator is used, the details of which are presented in *GROUP 15* (Table 3.15). Finally, the following is shown in the terminal window:

```
bytes of char = 1
char lowest = -128
char min = -128
char max = 127
bytes of int = 4
int lowest = -2147483648
int min = -2147483648
int max = 2147483647
We cannot store 11 digits in long in this system
```

We see that in this system, `long` is not long enough to store a value composed of 11 digits. Also, we need to be very careful here, since `long` denotes a signed type. That is, it can store both positive and negative values. This means one bit needs to be used for sign representation. Hence, 1 is subtracted on line [19]. Further differences between signed and unsigned types are discussed in Section 7.1.4. As a rule of thumb, if no specific requirements are set, signed integers should be chosen, and types should not be mixed.

`wchar_t` can be used to store all kinds of international characters. The following code snippet shows how to create and initialize a wide character, as well as how to assign text composed of wide characters using the `std::wstring` object.

```
23    wchar_t pl_letter = L'Ą';
24    wcout << pl_letter << L" needs " << sizeof( pl_letter ) << L" bytes." << endl;
25
26    std::wstring holiday_pl( L"święto" );
27
28    // We cannot use sizeof here - we need to call size()
29    size_t holiday_pl_len = holiday_pl.size();
30
31    std::wcout << holiday_pl << L" has " << holiday_pl_len << L" letters\n";
```

Also note that to display wide characters properly, we need to use `std::wcout` rather than `std::cout`. In addition, on some platforms, we need to call a platform-specific function to display the national letters properly. The results of running the previous code are as follows:

```
Ą needs 2 bytes.
święto has 6 letters
```

Finally, note that the wide text literals begin with the prefix `L`. To conclude, if we write applications that can be used in international markets, using `wchar_t`, `wstring`, `wcout`, etc. from the start is a good option. We will see examples in later chapters of this book.

Things to Remember

- Choose meaningful and readable names (identifiers) for objects (variables, constants, functions, classes, etc.)
- Choose the proper data type for computations
- Prefer signed types
- Always initialize variables. For zero-initialization, it is sufficient to add { }

3.2 Example Project – Collecting Student Grades

So far, we have seen how to define and use single variables and constants of different types. However, quite frequently, we need to store many such objects one after the other. Sometimes we do not know how many will be needed. To do this, we can use a data structure called *a vector* (or an *array*).[3] A vector containing four numerical objects is depicted in Figure 3.2.

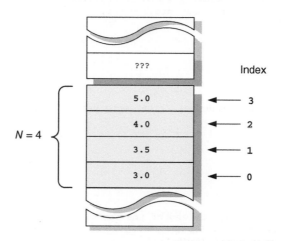

Figure 3.2 A vector is composed of a number of objects occupying contiguous space in memory. Here we have $N = 4$ objects that can store floating-point data. Each cell of a vector can be accessed by providing its index. The first element is at index 0, and the last is at index $N - 1$.

To begin with, a vector is a data structure with the following characteristics:

- It contains objects of the same type
- The objects are densely placed in memory, i.e. one after another (no holes)
- Each object in a vector can be accessed by providing its *index* to the *subscript operator* []. The valid indices are 0 to $N - 1$, where N denotes the number of elements in the vector

In C++, there are many ways of creating vectors. The most flexible is to use the `std::vector` object from the SL library, which

- Can be empty at the start
- Can be attached to new objects once they become available
- Contains many useful functions

Before we go into detail about what `std::vector` can do for us, let's start with a simple example program in Listing 3.3. Its purpose is to collect students' grades and compute their rounded average.

---

3 The term *array* is usually reserved for fixed-sized structures (Section 3.10); *vector* is used for objects with dynamically changing size.

Listing 3.3 A program to collect and compute average student grades (in *StudentGrades*, *main.cpp*).

```cpp
#include <vector>        // A header to use std::vector
#include <iostream>      // Headers for input and output
#include <iomanip>       // and output formatting
#include <cmath>         // For math functions

// Introduce these, to write vector instead of std::vector
using std::cout, std::cin, std::endl, std::vector;


int main()
{

  cout << "Enter your grades" << endl;

  vector< double >    studentGradeVec; // An empty vector of doubles

  // Collect students' grades
  for( ;; )
  {
    double grade {};

    cin >> grade;

    // If ok, push new grade at the end of the vector
    if( grade >= 2.0 && grade <= 5.0 )
      studentGradeVec.push_back( grade );


    cout << "Enter more? [y/n] ";
    char ans {};
    cin >> ans;

    if( ans == 'n' || ans == 'N' )
      break;     // the way to exit the loop
  }
```

To use `std::vector` and to be able to read and write values, a number of standard headers need to be included, as on lines [1–3]. Then, to avoid repeating the `std::` prefix over and over again, on line [7], common names from the `std` namespace are introduced into our scope with the help of the `using` directive. We already know the role of the `main` function, which starts on line [10]: it defines our C++ executable. Then, the central part is the definition of the `vector` object on line [15]. Notice that the type of objects to store needs to be given in `<>` brackets. To be able to store objects, the `vector` class is written in a generic fashion with the help of the template mechanism, which will be discussed in Section 4.7.

Then, on line [18], the `for` loop starts (see Section 3.13.2.2). Its role is to collect all grades entered by the user. However, we do not know how many will be entered. Therefore, there is no condition in `for`: it iterates until the `break` statement is reached on line [34] when the user presses `'n'`, as checked for on line [33].

During each iteration, on line [20], a new 0-valued `grade` is created, which is then overwritten on line [22] with a value entered by the user. If its value is correct, i.e. between 2.0 and 5.0, then on line [26] it is pushed to the end of the vector object `studentGradeVec` by a call of its `push_back` member function. The object and its member function are separated by a dot operator (`.`) – its syntax is presented in Section 3.9, as well as in the description of the *GROUP 2* operators (Table 3.15).

In Polish school systems, we have grades from 2.0 to 5.0, with 3.0 being the first "passing" grade. The valid grades are { 2.0, 3.0, 3.5, 4.0, 4.5, 5.0 }.

The rest of this program is devoted to computing the final grade, which should be the properly rounded average of the grades that have been entered:

```
36    // Ok, if there are any grades compute the average
37    if( studentGradeVec.size() > 0 )
38    {
39      double sum { 0.0 };
40      // Add all the grades
41      for( auto g : studentGradeVec )
42        sum += g;
43
44      double av = sum / studentGradeVec.size();    // Type will be promoted to double
45
46      double finalGrade {};
47
48      // Let it adjust
49      if( av < 3.0 )
50      {
51        finalGrade = 2.0;
52      }
53      else
54      {
55        double near_int  = std::floor( av );    // get integer part
56        double frac      = av - near_int;       // get only the fraction
57
58        double adjust { 0.5 };                  // new adjustment value
59
60        if( frac < 0.25 )
61          adjust = 0.0;
62        else if( frac > 0.75 )
63          adjust = 1.0;
64
65        finalGrade = near_int + adjust;
66      }
67
68      cout << "Final grade: "
69        << std::fixed << std::setw( 3 ) << std::setprecision( 1 )
70        << finalGrade << endl;
71
72    }
73
74
75    return 0;
76  }
```

We start on line [37] by checking whether `studentGradeVec` contains at least one grade. To see this, the `size` data member is called. It returns the number of objects contained by the vector (but not their size in bytes!).

On line [39], a 0-valued object `sum` is created. Then, on lines [41–42], a `for` loop is created, which accesses each element stored in `studentGradeVec`. For this purpose, `for` has a special syntax with the colon operator `:` in the middle, as presented in Section 2.6.3. To the left of the colon, the `auto g` defines a variable `g` that will be copied to successive elements of `studentGradeVec`. Thanks to the `auto` keyword, we do not need to explicitly provide the type of `g` – to make our life easier, it will be automatically deduced by the compiler. Such constructions with `auto` are very common in contemporary C++, as will be discussed later (Section 3.7). After the loop sums up all the elements, on line [44] the average grade is computed by dividing `sum` by the number of elements returned by `size`. We can do this with no stress here since we have already checked that there are elements in the vector, so `size` will return a value greater than 0. Also, since `sum` is of `double` type, due to the type promotion of whatever type of value is returned by `size`, the result will also be `double`. To be explicit, `av` is declared `double`, rather than with `auto`.

We are almost done, but to compute `finalGrade`, defined on line [46], we need to be sure it is one of the values in the set of allowable grades in our system. Thus, on line [49], we check whether the average `av` it is at least 3.0. If not, then 2.0 is assigned. Otherwise, `av` needs to be rounded ± 0.25. In other words, if the entered grades were 3.5, 3.5, and 4.0, their average would be 3.666(6). This would need to be rounded to the 3.5, since $(3.5 - 0.25) \leq 3.666(6) < (3.5 + 0.25)$.

For proper rounding, `av` is split on lines [55] and [56] into its integer `near_int` and fraction `frac` parts. The former is obtained by calling the `std::floor` function, which returns the nearest integer not greater than its argument.[4] On the other hand, `frac` is computed by subtracting `near_int` from `av`. The variable `adjust` on line [58] is used to hold one of the possible adjustments: 0.0, 0.5, or 1.0. Depending on `frac`, the exact value of `adjust` is computed in the conditional statement on lines [60–63]. That is, if `frac` is less than 0.25, then `adjust` is 0, and `near_int` represents the final grade. If `frac` is greater than 0.75, then `adjust` takes on 1, and `near_int` increased by 1 will be the final grade. Otherwise, the final grade is `near_int` + 0.5. The adjustment takes place on line [65].

Finally, the final grade is displayed on lines [68–70]. Since we want the output to have a width of exactly three digits, and only one after the dot, the `std::fixed << std::setw( 3 ) << std::setprecision( 1 )` *stream manipulators* are added to the expression (see Table 3.14).

As with the previous projects, we can run this code in one of the online compiler platforms. However, a better idea is to build the complete project with help of the *CMake* tool, as mentioned in Section 2.5.3. In this case, we will be able to take full advantage of a very important tool – the debugger.

3.3 Our Friend the Debugger

So far, we have written simple code examples and, if they were built successfully, immediately executed them to see their results. However, such a strategy will not work in any serious software development cycle. One of the key steps after the software building process is testing and debugging, as shown in the software development diagram in Figure 2.3. This would not be possible without one of the most important tools – *the debugger*. Running freshly baked software in an uncontrolled way can even be dangerous. A debugger gives us necessary control over the execution of such a software component. For example, it allows us to step through our programs line-by-line and see if the values of objects are correct, or to terminate the entire process if things do not go in the right direction. However, most important, a debugger allows us to really comprehend the operation of our software and make the software behave as intended. In this section, we will trace the basic functionality of debuggers, illustrating with examples.

Before we start debugging, the program has to be built with the debug option turned on. This is either preset in the *CMakeLists.txt* file or set in an IDE. The debug version of a program is fully operational software but without any code optimization, and it includes debugging information. This allows for the exact matching of the current place of execution with concrete lines

---

4 The nearest higher integer is returned by `std::ceil`.

of the source code, as well as complete information about the symbols being used. The release version is built once the software is fully debugged and tested, with all required optimization flags turned on.

Table 3.3 lists the basic operations that can be performed with a program under the control of a debugger. The most common approach is to set breakpoints at the beginning of particular function(s) and then trace software execution by stepping to the next line and observing the state of the involved objects. However, more sophisticated operations, such as setting breakpoints on selected conditions, observing the function call stack, and observing the processor registers and system memory can be useful as well. For example, in Section 3.7, we will show how a debugger can be used to demystify the type of an object declared with the `auto` keyword.

Table 3.3 Basic debugger operations.

Operation	Description (gdb shortcut)	Operation	Description (gdb shortcut)
`run`	Runs a program (process) under control of the debugger (`r`).	`step out`	Steps up one level in the calling stack. This means stepping out of the current function (`fin`).
`breakpoint` `conditional` `breakpoint`	Sets a breakpoint to pause a program at a given line of code (`b`). Optionally, pauses on the occurrence of a given condition (`cond`).	`print object` `state`	Shows the state (value) of an object by providing its name (`p`).
`continue`	Continues execution from the current stop point (`c`).	`set object` `state`	Lets us change the current state (value) of an object. Used to test different settings or to temporarily fix an incorrect value (`set`).
`continue from` `different line`	Continues execution, immediately jumping to the new line (`jump` *newline*).	`show stack`	Shows functions' call stack in the form of data blocks called *stack frames*, each showing the location and arguments of the function call, as well as the local variables of the function being called. A rundown of stack frames, showing how the program got where it is, is called a *backtrace* (`bt` `where`).
`step to next`	Steps to the next line, skipping all lower-level calls (`n`).	`list`	Lists the currently executing portion of the source code (`l`).
`step into`	Steps into lower-level function call (`s`).	`disassemble`	Shows the currently executing portion of the machine code and lets us inspect registers, memory, etc. (`disas`).

Debugging within an IDE is very simple, as shown in Figure 3.3a for the Student Grades project from Section 3.2. However, although various IDE(s) can be installed and used in the Linux OS,[5] we recommend getting acquainted with the gdb debugger, which is frequently used in embedded systems.

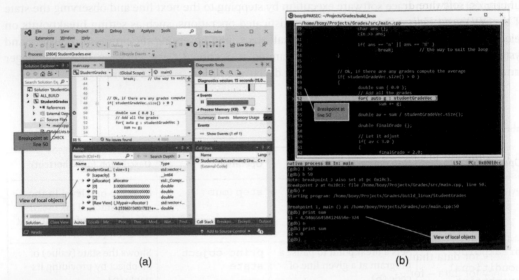

(a)   (b)

Figure 3.3 Example debugging sessions for the Grades project (a) in Visual Studio on Windows; (b) using gdb in the terminal window on Linux. A breakpoint at line 50 lets us inspect the values of the accessible objects. In this context, note the garbage value in the not-yet-uninitialized variable `sum`.

Like coding, software debugging requires practice. Here are some hints:

- Run the software with different data and parameters. Usually it is not possible to test all possible states. However, choosing borderline cases can help to reveal many problems in a much shorter time. Together with serious debugging goes the creation of sufficient code tests. We explore this issue in Section 3.17.2 and Appendix A.7
- Isolate the problem. Sometimes, what manifests as an error is a result of preceding steps
- Read what the tools tell you. In addition to errors, compiler warnings are also valuable
- Understand the problem and your proposed solution – do not guess. Be sure you can state the objectives behind a proposed way out of software misbehavior
- Make sure you fix the problem and not just its symptoms
- If you are still not sure, ask colleagues for help, and look for an answer on the Internet

Not less important is realizing that debugging is a psychological process. It is difficult, since it reveals *our* mistakes, which not only may be due to simple typing errors but, more painfully, also may be related to insufficient knowledge of the subject or misunderstanding of concepts and

---

5 Such as Eclipse or Visual Studio Code.

programming techniques. When learning to program, we may struggle with the new language. Although stressful at first, this should not distract us from using the debugger. So, learn everything you can about debugging, and use it when working on all projects, not only those presented in this book. Soon you will discover that debugging is a fun intellectual adventure. Other helpful programming tools are described in Appendix A.6.

More on software debugging can be found in the following books: *The Art of Debugging with GDB, DDD, and Eclipse* (Matloff and Salzman 2008) and *Inside Windows Debugging. Practical Debugging and Tracing Strategies* (Soulami 2012). Other highly recommended books are *The Pragmatic Programmer* (Thomas and Hunt 2019) and *Code Complete* (McConnell 2004), which provide insightful information on the software development process.

3.4 The Basic Data Structure – `std::vector`

In the program in Listing 3.3, we saw that `std::vector` allowed use to store any number of grades entered by the user. We could add new values by calling its `push_back` function and access the number of elements by calling the `size` function. These and other popular member functions of `std::vector` are summarized in Table 3.4.[6]

Figure 3.4 shows a possible memory location of a `vector` object and its data. There are two different locations: one for the `vector` and the other for its data. Also, a `vector` can reserve more memory for data than is required by its current number of elements. If it does not have enough memory for data – for example, due to many calls to `push_back` – then the `vector` allocates a new, larger buffer, copies its data, and releases the old one. Thus data can be copied back and forth behind the scenes.

To obtain information about the exact amount of data the `vector` holds, its `size` member should be called (not the `sizeof` operator, which returns the number of bytes allocated for the `vector` object alone, and which probably is not what we are interested in). The other options for creating arrays in C++ will be discussed in the following sections.

Things to Remember

- To store many objects of the same type, we can use `std::vector`
- The number of elements in a `vector` is given by calling its `size()` function. In general, this is not the number of bytes occupied by the vector
- The range of elements to process is indicated by providing an iterator (a pointer) to the first element (inclusive) and an iterator to the *one-after-the-last* position (exclusive)
- When using the subscript [*index*], we need to be sure that the `vector` is not empty. If it is not empty, the provided *index* must be located in the range `0 ... size() - 1`

---

6 For clarity in this book's summaries and tables, we use a simplified function call syntax. However, many functions come in variety of versions that can be easily looked up online.

Table 3.4 Basic member functions of `std::vector` (in header `<vector>`).

Member function	Description	Examples

`vector`
 	
`vector( num, init_val )`
	The default class constructor creates an empty vector.
	
	The second constructor creates a vector containing `num` elements, each with `init_val`.
		In this example, an empty vector is first created. Then, a few elements are inserted by calling push_back. The function `size` returns the number of elements in the vector. The function `find` returns the position of the element with the value being sought. This is assigned to an object pos, whose type is automatically determined by the compiler as discussed in Section 3.7. If 0 is not found, then cend is returned. `erase` removes elements in the provided range.
		
		```vector< int > intVec; // Create an empty vector```
		
		```cout << "intVec.size() == " << intVec.size() << endl;```

`push_back`	Pushes (attach) a new element to the end of the vector. Its size is increases by 1.	```intVec.push_back(-13);```
		```intVec.push_back(0);```
		```intVec.push_back(1);```
		```intVec.push_back(13);```
		
		```cout << "intVec.size() == " << intVec.size() << endl;```

`size`	Returns the number of elements stored in the vector (this is not the number of bytes).	```// Find position of the element with value 0```
		```auto pos = find(intVec.cbegin(), intVec.cend(), 0);```
		```if(pos != intVec.cend())```
		``` intVec.insert(pos, -1); // insert -1 before 0```

`[n]` `operator []`	Accesses an element at position `n`. The vector must be large enough to have at least `n` +1 elements. Otherwise, an exception is thrown.	

Member function	Description	Examples
| begin<br>cbegin | Returns an iterator pointing at the first element in the vector.<br><br>Second form – returns a constant iterator. | ```cpp
cout << ":intVec.size() == " << intVec.size() << endl;

for( auto elem : intVec )
    cout << elem << " ";    // Print all elements
cout << endl;
``` |
| end<br>cend | Returns an iterator pointing at the *one-after-last* element of the vector.<br><br>If the container is empty, then begin and end are equal.<br><br>Second form – returns a constant iterator. | ```cpp
// Erase from beginning up to but excluding 0 element
intVec.erase( intVec.begin(),
    find( intVec.cbegin(), intVec.cend(), 0 ) );
``` |
| insert( *pos* ) | Inserts a new element at *pos*. | ```cpp
cout << "intVec.size() == " << intVec.size() << endl;

for( auto elem : intVec )
    cout << elem << " ";    // Print them all
``` |
| resize(*new_
elems, new_init*) | Changes the size of the vector to *new_elems*. Only newly added elements are initialized to *new_init* (old ones are untouched). | |
| erase(*from,
end*) | Removes elements from *from* (including) to *end* (exclusive) | The result is as follows: |
| clear | Removes all elements. After that, the vector is empty. | ```
intVec.size() == 0
intVec.size() == 4
intVec.size() == 5
-13 -1 0 1 13
intVec.size() == 3
0 1 13
``` |

Table 3.4 (continued)

Member function	Description	Examples

		A vector can be constructed from the initializer list of values. Elements can be accessed with the subscript operator [ ]. The function `accumulate` returns the sum of all elements.
		
		``cpp
		vector< char > monthDays { 31, 28, 31, 30, 31, 30,
		                           31, 31, 30, 31, 30, 31 };
		
		// Print them out
		for(size_t i = 0; i < monthDays.size(); ++ i)
		   cout << "Month " << i + 1 << " has "
		        << +monthDays[i] << " days" << endl;
		
		cout << "Total days = "
		      << accumulate(monthDays.cbegin(),
		                     monthDays.cend(), 0) << endl;
		``
		
		This prints the following:
		
		``
		Month 1 has 31 days
		. . .
		Month 12 has 31 days
		Total days = 365
		``

Member function	Description	Examples

		We can construct a vector with a number of elements:
		
		`vector< double > dobVec( 5, 0.0 ); // 5 elems with 0.0 value`
		
		`// Add 5 more and init ONLY the NEW ONES to 1.0`
		`dobVec.resize( 10, 1.0 );`
		
		`// Another way to copy (print) all to the screen`
		`copy( dobVec.cbegin(), dobVec.cend(),`
		`    ostream_iterator< double >( cout, " " ) );`
		
		`dobVec.clear();    // Remove all`
		
		The function `resize` only initializes new elements. The function `copy` copies the range of elements from the vector to the output stream, which is redirected by the `ostream_iterator` to the screen by providing the `cout` object and the separation sign " " (a space). The output is
		
		`0 0 0 0 0 1 1 1 1 1`

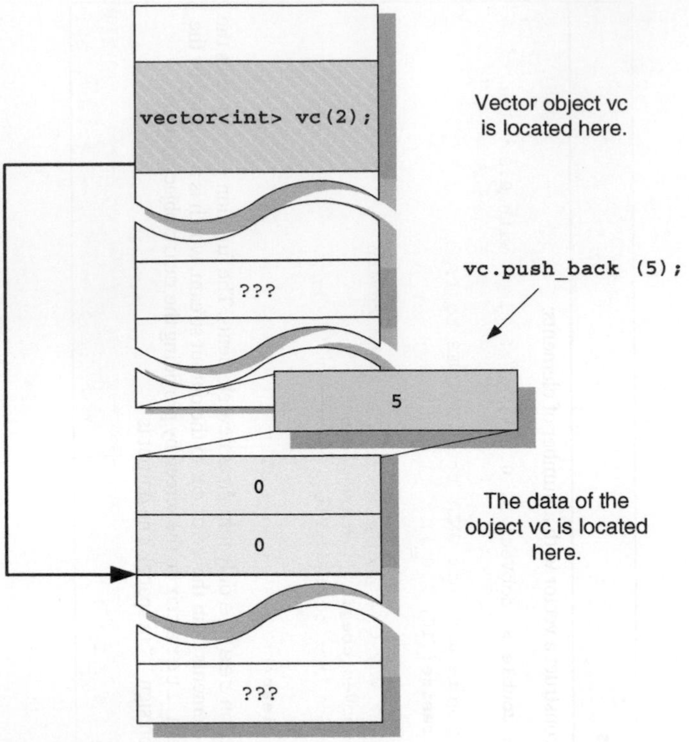

Figure 3.4 Memory placement of vector `vc` storing `int` values. The vector itself is an object that is constructed and placed somewhere in the memory. Then, it creates its own data buffer where its data is stored. Hence, more memory is necessary than would be required for the data alone. To ask for the number of elements, we call `vc.size()`.

3.5 Example Project – Implementing a Matrix as a Vector of Vectors

A *matrix* is a rectangular table containing numerical values, like the following (Korn and Korn 2000):

$$\mathbf{A}_{2\times3} = \begin{bmatrix} 1 & 0 & -5 \\ 7 & 12 & 0 \end{bmatrix} \tag{3.2}$$

The characteristic feature of any matrix is its number of rows and columns. In the previous example, there are two rows and three columns. Matrices have many applications in science. However, they can easily be extended to store not only numbers but also other objects, such as strings, graphics, other matrices, etc. In such representations, matrices are very popular – an Excel sheet is just a matrix of data. How can we represent matrices in C++? In this section, we will try to answer this question and provide some examples.

In this section, you will learn:

- How to implement a matrix using only `std::vector`
- How to declare type aliases with the `using` directive

From the previous section, we know how to create a `std::vector` storing values like `int`s or `double`s. Imagine now that we read a matrix row by row. A matrix is simply a collection of rows, and a row can be represented as a vector. In programming terms, a matrix is a `vector` of `vector`s of `double`s. This idea is brought to life in Listing 3.4.

Listing 3.4 Declarations of basic data types for easy matrix operations based on `std::vector` (in *EasyMatrix, EMatrix.h*).

```
1   #include <vector>
2
3
4   // A type alias declaration for a vector of double values (real approx.)
5   using RealVec = std::vector< double >;
6
7   // A type alias for vector dimensions (size)
8   using Dim     = RealVec::size_type;
9
10  // A type alias for vector type (e.g. double)
11  using DataType = RealVec::value_type;
12
13
14  // A type alias for a vector of vectors with doubles = a real matrix
15  using RealMatrix = std::vector< RealVec >;
```

In this code, we see four declarations of a few types. More precisely, with the `using` directive, we introduce a new name for a longer or more cumbersome declaration. In other words, `using` lets us declare a *type alias* for a known type.

Let's explain each of the previous declarations. `RealVec`, defined on line [5], is the same as writing `std::vector< double >`, but much shorter. Its name better conveys our intentions: we will use it as a vector of real values. `Dim`, on line [8], is the same as a type used in `std::vector< double >` to represent its size, whatever this type really is. Such indirect access to types saves us trouble if something changes in the future in the vector. It also saves us from mixing types. The situation is the same with `DataType` on line [11], which represents a type of data stored in the vector. We know it is `double`, but why repeat `double` in so many places? Also, if we want to change it to anything else, such as a `FixedFor` from Section 7.3.2, we can do this in one line – everything else will adapt automatically. This is a bonus of creating a kind of separation layer for the types we use in our software components, such as a class or a namespace. All containers from the SL define useful `size_type` and `value_type` aliases; we will see them many times.

Finally, on line [15], the `RealMatrix` type is defined as a `std::vector< RealVec >`. That is, it is a `vector` of `vector`s of `double`s, as expected.

This matrix is ready for use, as shown in the `Easy_Matrix_First_Test` function in Listing 3.5.

Listing 3.5 Definition of the `Easy_Matrix_First_Test` function using `RealMatrix` for matrix operations (part of *EMTest.cpp*).

```
16  void Easy_Matrix_First_Test( void )
17  {
18    // Using RealMatrix as it is
19
20    RealMatrix    m = {
21                        { 2, 2, 0, 11 },
22                        { 3, 4, 5, 0 },
23                        { -1, 2, -1, 7 }
24                      };
25
26    // Add next row
27    m.push_back( { 5, 3, 5, -3 } );
28
29    // Accumulate elements except the diagonal
30    double non_diagonal_sum {};
31
32    for( int r = 0; r < m.size(); ++ r )
33      for( int c = 0; c < m[ 0 ].size(); ++ c )
34        if( c != r )
35          non_diagonal_sum += m[ r ][ c ];
36
37    std::cout << "Sum of m except the diagonal " << non_diagonal_sum << std::endl;
38  }
```

A matrix m of type `RealMatrix` is defined and initialized on lines [20–24]. As we already know, `RealMatrix` is a vector of vectors. Therefore, it is initialized exactly the same way. More precisely, the initializer lists, each encompassed in { } brackets, are used to set up values for each row. Then the rows are set in order, one after the other, to constitute a matrix. This matrix's dimensions are three rows by four columns. However, we would like to have a square matrix, so on line [27], another row is pushed back. After that, m represents a 4×4 matrix.

Then, on lines [32–35], the sum of only the diagonal elements of m is computed. To do this, two `for` loops are used (Section 3.13.2.2). The first, from line [32], advances its iterator r from 0 to the number of rows in m. This is read as m.size(), since the size of m is its number of elements: that is, the number of vectors of vectors, each containing data from the consecutive row. The second `for` on line [33] traverses each element in a single row: that is, in a single vector. To do this, its iterator variable c iterates from 0 to m[0].size(). Let's explain this: m[0] is the first element: the first row. This is a std::vector< double >, so it has its own size, which is accessed by calling the `size` function on it (with help of the dot . operator). Then, on line [34], to verify whether a diagonal element is processed, the row number is compared to the column number. Only non-diagonal elements of m are added together and finally displayed on the screen identified by the std::cout object.

As we can see, `RealMatrix` allows for some matrix operations. However, its use is limited, so we will expand this example in Section 3.15.

Things to Remember

- A type alias declaration with a `using` directive introduces a name that can be used as a synonym. This directive can also be used to introduce to the current scope a name that is defined elsewhere
- All SL containers are equipped with the `size_type` and `value_type` aliases to represent an appropriate type for the container size and the type of objects it contains

3.6 Special Vector to Store Text – `std::string`

So far, we have seen `std::vector`, which stores objects of type `int` or `double`. A separate category of vectors stores characters and is a text array, or simply text. However, to make the best use of text, instead of using `std::vector< char >`, a specialized `std::string` class is provided. The difference is significant, since the latter offers a number of additional functions specific to text processing. For example, consider the following simple C++ program:

```
1   #include <iostream>   // to use std::cout
2   #include <string>     // to use std::string
3
4   using std::string, std::cout, std::endl;
5
6
7   int main()
8   {
9     string str( "The quick" );
10    str += " brown fox.";
11    cout << str << "\nContains "
12         << str.size() << " characters." << endl;
13    return 0;
14  }
```

After being compiled, built, and run, this program will produce the following output:

```
The quick brown fox.
Contains 20 characters.
```

On line [9] of the previous code, the `string` object `str` is created from the string literal `"The quick"`. Unlike vectors, strings can be joined, i.e. concatenated, as on line [10]. On line [11], both a string and a string literal are shown in the terminal window. Notice that frequently, a text literal, i.e. characters in quotes `" "`, is used. Is this also a string? Yes, but of a different type: it is C-style text that is even more basic, but less useful than `std::string` (see Appendix A.2.6). We have already seen that there is an easy conversion from text in quotes to `std::string`. But `std::string` can perform more useful operations than those shown in the previous short program. So, staying with `std::string` for text processing helps in many ways. Its commonly used member functions with further examples are summarized in Table 3.5.

Table 3.5 Basic member functions of `std::string` (in header `<string>`).

Member function	Description	Examples
`string`	Class constructor.	In this example, the initial string `filePath` is decomposed to find out the name of a file, as well as its extension. Then, the extension is replaced with a new one. For this purpose, the `if` statement with the initializer is used. It lets us first create and initialize the `pos` object and then check if `pos` is pointing at the end of the string. Conditional statements are discussed in Section 3.13.2.1. In the following code, a number of string objects are created with different constructors:
`string( const char * )`	1. Default (no params.) 2. From C style string.	
| `string( num, init_ch )` | 3. A string with *init_ch* repeated *num* times. | ```cpp
// A full path of a C++ source file
string filePath( "C:\\Projects\\test.cpp" );
``` |
| `string( const string& )` | 4. Create a string and copy its contents from another string object. | ```cpp
// Now find the file name and its extension
// and the name of its header.
string name( filePath );
if( auto pos=filePath.rfind('\\'); pos != string::npos )
    name = filePath.substr( pos + 1 );
``` |
| `push_back` | Attaches a new element at the end of the string. Its size is increased by 1. | ```cpp
cout << "file name is: " << name << endl;

// Find old extension and exchange to a new one
string new_ext( "h" );
if( auto pos= name.rfind('.'); pos != string::npos )
{
``` |
| `size`<br>`length` | Returns the number of characters in the string. | ```cpp
    // Extract the extension
    ++ pos; // Advance from '.' to the first letter
    string ext { name.substr( pos ) }; // Create ext
``` |
| `[n]`<br>`operator []` | Accesses an element at position *n*.<br>There must be at least *n* + 1 characters in the string. Otherwise an exception is thrown. | ```cpp
    // Check if a source file and replace extension
    if( ext == "cpp" || ext == "cp" )
        name.replace( name.begin() + pos, name.end(),
                      new_ext );
``` |
| `find`<br>`rfind` | Finds a character and returns its position.<br>1. Find first from beginning.<br>2. Find first from end. | ```cpp
    // now we have a name of a header file
    cout << "header name is: " << name << endl;
}
``` |
`substr`	Returns a new string extracted from the given one, from the provided position until the end of the string.	
`replace`	Replaces a series of characters in the string.	
`operator +=`	Concatenates strings.	

Member function	Description	Examples

operator ==
operator !=
operator <
operator <=
operator >
operator >=
	Lexicographical comparison of strings.	The function rfind searches for a character, starting from the end of the string. If it is not found, then string::npos is returned. substr extracts a substring, and replace replaces part of a string with a new one. Strings can be compared with the == and < operators. *Lexicographical* order is assumed.
		
		In the following example, text is read from the keyboard until an end-of-line special character is entered. Then, all of the text is are joined together by accumulate:
		
		``cpp
		vector< string > textVec; // An empty vector of string
		
		string str; // An empty string
		while(cin >> str) // Read text until EOL (^Z)
		    textVec.push_back(str + " "); // Add space and push
		
		// Add i.e. concatenate all the strings together
		// and move the result to outMsg
		string outMsg;
		outMsg = accumulate(textVec.begin(),
		                     textVec.end(), outMsg);
		
		cout << outMsg << endl;
		``

(Continued)

Table 3.5 (continued)

Member function	Description	Examples

to_string(*v*)	Converts an object *v* to a string.	In this example, a file is opened and read line by line in the while loop (Section 3.13.2.2) with a call to the getline function. Then, the number of lowercase characters is counted and stored in cnt_lower:
		
		`// Count all lowercase letters in the string`
		`string filePath( "test.cpp" );`
		`ifstream inFile( filePath );`
		
		`int cnt_lower {}; // Set to 0`
		
		`string line; // Empty buffer for a line`
		
		`while( getline( inFile, line ) ) // Read line-by-line`
		`  for( const auto c : line ) // For each char`
		`    if( islower( c ) ) // Increment if lowercase`
		`      ++ cnt_lower; // Increment if lowercase`

stoi(*str*) stod(*str*) stof(*str*)	Converts string *str* to: 1. int 2. double 3. float	
getline(*stream*, *str*)	Reads a line from a *stream* to the string *str*.	

Member function	Description	Examples
		In the following code snippet, a fileName object of std::string type is created, containing a digit number of digit characters:

```cpp
int digit { 3 };   // 333.txt, 4444.txt, ...
// cin >> digit;   // Can enter new digit

// Make a file containing digit digits
assert( digit >= 0 && digit < 9 );
//         repeat    char
string fileName( digit, '0' + digit );// ASCII codes '0'

// Open the output file
ofstream outFile( fileName + ".txt" );

outFile   << filePath << " has " << cnt_lower
          << " lower capital letters" << endl;
```

For this purpose, a string constructor is called with the number of repeated values and the value of the character to be repeated. Adding a value of digit to the literal '0' is a simple way of computing the ASCII code corresponding to digit. The assert function verifies a condition in a debug version of the code.

Color functions are separate from std::string. An analogous set is available in std::wstring for international character sets.

A special version of std::string for international character sets is std::wstring. Examples are presented later, e.g. in Section 3.18. The complete functional specification of std::string is much longer and contains more calls and syntactic variants than are shown in Table 3.5; so, online references will be helpful.

In this book, we will use std::string and std::wstring quite often. But in some applications, manipulating strings back and forth can lead to inefficiencies. Therefore, SL has the std::stringview class that implements a kind of proxy to the string pattern and in some cases leads to a significant speedup.

More information on C-style text arrays and their manipulating functions is provided in Appendix A.2.6.

3.7 Using the auto Keyword and decltype for Automatic Type Deduction

In Section 3.1, we discussed the basic built-in C++ objects such as int, double, etc. as well as how they are initialized. We have seen that when assigning an initial value to a variable, their types should match. For example, we wrote the following:

```
1   int x { 0 };
2
3   double y { 0.0 };
4
5   cout << "x=" << x << endl;
6   cout << "y=" << y << endl;
```

That is, int is initialized with 0, since it is an integer constant; double is initialized with 0.0, since it is a double constant; and so on. On the other hand, from the previous example, we see that by investigating the types of the initializing values, we can automatically deduce the types of the objects x and y. This idea has been incorporated into modern C++ with the help of the auto keyword. By using it, the compiler will automatically determine the type of an object, if possible. For example, the previous code can be rewritten as follows using the auto keyword:

```
7    auto x { 0 };
8
9    auto y { 0.0 };
10
11   cout << "x=" << x << endl;
12   cout << "y=" << y << endl;
```

The code compiles and prints the same output. Internally, variable x on line [7] is assigned the int type by analyzing the type of its initializer 0, and y on line [9] gets the double type because of its 0.0. We did not gain much from using auto in this example, but in more complex constructions the benefits can be significant. There are also other reasons for using `auto`, as we will discuss.

However, let's stop for a moment: Is it dangerous to use `auto` and rely on automatic type deduction? How can we be sure the deduced types are correct and agree with our intentions? There are a few mechanisms that can help to dismiss our doubts. The first comes from the compiler itself – if the code with `auto` compiles, this means the compiler was able to deduce all types. But explicit proof can be obtained from the debugger, which shows all the parameters of processed objects, such as their type and contents. Figure 3.5 shows the MV'19 debugger windows while stepping through the code lines in our example. We see that despite the `auto` keyword in the object definition, the object types are explicitly shown in the *Watch* pane.

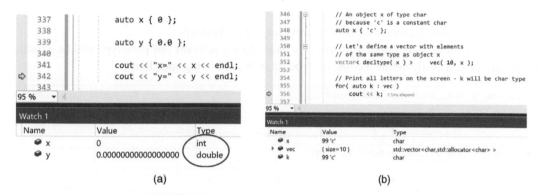

Figure 3.5 Reading object types in the debugger: (a) code from lines [7–9]; (b) code from lines [15–22]. All `auto` defined objects show their inner types and values.

But on lines [7–9], we missed something. If a type is automatically deduced from the type of its initialization object, then x should be `const int`, and y should be `const double`. Right – but `auto` does not operate this way. Implicitly, it strips off `const`, `ref`, and other attributes. A more detailed analysis of type deduction with `auto` can be found in (Meyers 2014). If we really want to have a constant object, we write `const auto`, as shown in the following examples.

A new question arises – is there a way back? That is, if an object is available, is there a way to tell its type in the code? If we wish to have such a type at compilation time, we can use the `decltype` function, as shown in the following example:

```
13    // An object x of type char
14    // because 'c' is a constant char
15    auto x { 'c' };
16
17    // Let us define a vector with elements of the same type as object x
18    vector< decltype( x ) >    vec( 10, x );
19
20    // Print all letters on the screen - k will be char type
21    for( auto k : vec )
22        cout << k;
```

On line [15], a new object x is created with the help of `auto`. As we already know, it will be of `char` type, since `'c'` is `const char` but `auto` will leave only `char`. However, on line [18], we wish to define a vector that stores objects of the same type as x. Let's assume that we do not know explicitly what type it is: how do we write it? For this purpose, we can use `decltype( x )`, which will return the type of object x in this case. This works fine, so `vec` will be created, containing 10 elements, each initialized with a copy of x (Table 3.4). We can easily access each element of a vector in the `for` loop, as on line [21]. Here `auto` again simplifies writing the code, although an explicit type can also be used, as follows:

```
23      // The same with explicit type
24      for( char k : vec )
25          cout << k;
```

But `auto` is more flexible compared to providing an explicit type.

As we have already mentioned, if `auto` is used, then a relevant but pure type will be chosen. However, we can easily define a constant type, as in the following code lines:

```
26      // Now k will be const char type
27      for( const auto k : vec )
28          cout << k;
```

Or we can define a constant reference type:

```
29      // Now k will be const char reference type
30      for( const auto & k : vec )
31          cout << k;
```

This allows for indirect access to the elements of `vec`, to avoid making copies of them. Here we signal such a possibility; a full discussion of references is postponed until Section 3.11. But the results of all the previous `for` loops are to print this:

cccccccccc

Using `auto` can be tricky in some cases. For example, what type do we expect in the following example?

```
32      auto text { "The quick brown fox" };
33
34      // What type is text? Do we need to know?
35      cout << text << endl;
```

The type of text is not `std::string`, neither `char*` - it is `const char*` . However, if we used the following initialization

```
32      auto text = { "The quick brown fox" };
```

the code would not compile, and the problem would be on line [35]. This happens because the deduced type for `text` would be `std::initializer_list`. Fortunately, such nuances are scarce; in the majority of cases, `auto` is easy to use.

As alluded to previously, `auto` provides many benefits. Not only do we save on typing, but we also gain code flexibility since we can set proper type dependencies, as in the following code snippet:

```
37      // By using auto we avoid searching for an exact type
38      // and unwanted type conversions.
39      auto vec_size { vec.size() };
40
41      cout << "vec_size=" << vec_size << endl;
```

Thanks to `auto` on line [39], we do not need to look up or, even worse, guess the exact type of whatever is returned from the `size` function. Its type will be automatically and correctly deduced by the compiler, based on the type of the returned value in the definition of the `vector::size`. On the other hand, if we explicitly wrote `int vec_size{ vec.size() }`, there would be a conversion from `size_t` to `int`. Maybe not harmful, but why go to the trouble?

Last but not least, there are also lambda expressions (functions), which we discuss in Section 3.14.6. It is not possible to explicitly provide their type, though. In this case, `auto` is the only option. So, let's use `auto`!

3.8 Common Standard Algorithms

Table 3.6 shows SL functions that implement some common algorithms. Unlike member functions, these do not belong to any object. The benefit is that they can operate on any SL container, such as `std::vector` (Section 3.2), `std::string` (Section 3.6), `std::map` (Section 3.18.4), and a few more.

Note that the functions in Table 3.6 are presented with simplified syntax. Almost all of them have *many variants* that can be looked up in the references, such as (cppreference 2019; Josuttis 2012). On the other hand, the previous algorithms have many similarities to the calling rules. We will use the `std::transform` as an example. Its operation is shown in Figure 3.6. Recall that to define the `src` range, the position of the first element in the range (inclusive) and one-after (exclusive) need to be provided. On the other hand, for `dst`, only the position of the first element is required, since the number of elements is already known. However, we must ensure there is enough room in `dst`. If there is not, a special inserting object can be used, such as `std::back_inserter`.

At each iteration, the function `fun` is used to transform a source element into the corresponding destination element. Lambda functions are the best fit for this role; they are discussed in Section 3.14.6.

Table 3.6 Common SL algorithm functions (in header *<algorithm>*). They can operate on any SL collections, such as vector, string, map, etc.

SL algorithm function	Description	Examples
| find( *start, to, what* ) | Searches for a value *what* in a collection (vector, string, map, etc.), from the position *start* up to but not including *to*. | ```cpp
vector< int > vec;
for( int i = -5; i <= 5; ++ i )
    vec.push_back( i );

vector< int > neg_vec;
``` |
| copy( *src_start, src_to, dst_start* ) | Copies elements from the range [*src_start, src_to*) in one container to the other, starting at *dst_start*. The destination must have enough space, or back_inserter must be used. | ```cpp
// Copy all values up to 0
copy(vec.begin(),
    find( vec.begin(), vec.end(), 0 ),
    back_inserter( neg_vec ) );

// Copy (print) vec to cout
cout << "vec : ";
copy( vec.begin(), vec.end(),
    ostream_iterator<int>( cout, " " ) );

cout << endl << "Sum( vec ) = "
    << accumulate( vec.begin(), vec.end(), 0 )
    << endl;
``` |
| back_inserter( *container* ) | Instructs a process to push incoming elements to the end of the *container* (vector, string, map, etc.). | ```cpp
// Copy (print) neg_vec to cout
cout << "neg_vec : ";
copy( neg_vec.begin(), neg_vec.end(),
    ostream_iterator<int>( cout, " " ) );
``` |
| accumulate(*src_start, src_to, init_val*) | Returns a sum of *init_val* and all elements from the range [*src_start, src_to*) of a container. | The output is as follows:

```
vec : -5 -4 -3 -2 -1 0 1 2 3 4 5
Sum( vec ) = 0
neg_vec : -5 -4 -3 -2 -1
``` |
```

SL algorithm function	Description	Examples
| generate( start, to, fun ) | Fills a container in the range [start,to) with a value returned by fun. fun is a function pointer or a functional object. | ```cpp
vector< unsigned int >randVec( 10 );

// Put some random values with Mersenne twister
generate( randVec.begin(), randVec.end(),
          std::mt19937( std::random_device {}() ) );

// Sort the values
``` |
| sort(start, to) | Arranges in ascending order all elements of a container in the range [start,to). | ```cpp
sort(randVec.beg-n(), randVec.end());

// Copy to the screen
copy(randVec.begin(), randVec.end(),
      ostream_iterator< unsigned int >(cout, " "));
```

For each element of randVec, generate assigns a random value, as returned by the std::mt19937 object, initialized with std::random_device (Section 3.17.3). sort sorts all elements of randVec, whereas copy copies them to cout. |

(Continued)

Table 3.6 (continued)

SL algorithm function	Description	Examples
transform (*src_start*, *src_to*, *dst_start*, *fun*)	Transforms elements from the range [*src_start*, *src_to*), applying *fun* to each and copying the result starting at *dst_start*. The destination must have enough space, or back_inserter has to be used.	```// Convert texts into absolute values and displays` `vector< string > str_vec{ "10", "12", "-13.13" };` `vector< double > dbl_vec;` `` `            // src_start src_end` `transform( str_vec.begin(), str_vec.end(),` `           back_inserter( dbl_vec ),  // dst_start` `           [] ( auto & s )  // the lambda function` `           { return fabs( stod( s ) ); } );` `` `copy( dbl_vec.begin(), dbl_vec.end(),` `      ostream_iterator< double >( cout, "\n" ) );` `` `transform operates as follows: Each string from str_vec is first converted to double by stod, then its absolute value is taken with fabs, and finally this is back-inserted into dbl_vec. The last argument of transform is the lambda function, discussed in (Section 3.14.6).```

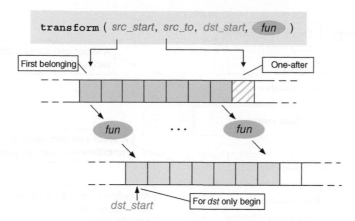

Figure 3.6 Operation of `std::transform` transforming elements from the `src` collection into elements of the `dst` collection by applying the function `fun`. To define the `src` range, we provide the position of the first element (inclusive) and one-after (exclusive). For `dst`, only the first position is necessary. However, we must ensure that there is enough room in `dst`.

3.9 Structures: Collecting Objects of Various Types

We have already discussed basic C++ constructions such as built-in objects (Section 3.1) and `std::vector` to store collections of objects (Section 3.2), as well as `std::string` for storing and processing text (Section 3.6). `std::vector` can store elements of the same type, such as students' grades, as in the example in Listing 3.3. Similarly, `std::string` can efficiently store a series of letters. However, what if we wish to collect objects of different types, such as `std::string` and `int`? For this purpose, C++ offers the *structure*, which can be visualized as shown in Figure 3.7.

Before we set about analyzing a structure or a class – in this context, they are the same – let's explain what a structure/class is and what an *object* of that class is. The relation is exactly as we have already seen between, for example, a type `int` and a variable of that type. We can write this:

```
int x {};
```

Here, `int` is the name of a type (class), whereas `x` is the name of a variable (object) of that type. In the object-oriented domain, a structure (or a class) definition introduces *a new type*, whereas an object of that class is simply placed somewhere in memory and behaves as defined by that type. In this sense, a type superimposes a kind of *abstraction* on raw memory. In other words, the same fixed piece of memory can be interpreted differently, depending on an assumed type. One of the simplest examples is the following:

```
class MyClass
{};

MyClass myObject;
```

In this code snippet, `MyClass` is the name of an empty class. The class definition is placed in curly braces { }, always followed by a semicolon (forgetting the ; is a frequent coding error). On the other hand, `myObject` is an instantiation of the `MyClass` type and, if any data is defined, has a memory imprint. Also notice that both data and functions belonging to a structure/class are frequently called its *members*.

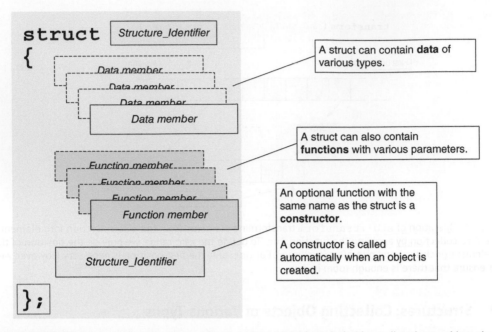

Figure 3.7 Visualization of a C++ structure, using bold for terminal symbols (those directly typed into the terminal window, such as commands, code, etc.). The structure can contain data of various types, as well as functions. If a function is named exactly the same as the structure, it is a structure constructor: a function that is automatically called when the structure is created. The same is true for C++ classes, except that by default all members of a class are private.

Let's now analyze a structure that is able to convey information about a month's name and the number of days in that month. Listing 3.6 shows the definition of the struct MonthDays. It follows the general scheme shown in Figure 3.7. The structure is contained within the opening { brace on line [3] and closing } brace on line [6], and ends with a semicolon ;. There are two data member definitions: fName on line [4], which is of the std::string type; and fDays on line [5], of type int. Also note that each data item ends with {}. As we already know, because of this, the data is properly initialized; fName is set to an empty string,[7] while fDays is set to 0, as presented in Section 3.1.

Listing 3.6 Definition of the struct MonthDays (in *CppBookCode, Calendar_struct.cpp*). Using {}, the members are initialized to their specific zero state: an empty string for fName and 0 for fDays.

```
1    // Joins two different objects under one roof
2    struct MonthDays
3    {
4        std::string    fName {};    // Use {} to initialize data members.
5        int            fDays {};    // Empty braces {} to initialize to 0.
6    };
```

---

7 Even without {}, the std::string would be properly initialized, since it has its own default constructor (Section 3.15). However, int without {} would be left with some garbage values (Section 3.1).

Comparing the diagram in Figure 3.7 and the structure in Listing 3.6, we can easily observe that the latter does not contain a function. There is not even a constructor. To hold a simple pair of objects, such as fName and fDays, this is perfectly OK, assuming the two have an initialization mechanism. As alluded to previously, initialization is performed for each data item with the initialization list { }. Hence, we do not need to implement a constructor – this is called *the rule of zero*. Further rules for special member functions, such as constructors, are discussed in Chapter 4.

On the other hand, the following SimpleCalendar function, whose definition starts on line [8], shows the application of the vector that contains MonthDays objects. The calendar object of type std::vector, which stores MonthDays objects, is defined on line [10]. Its initialization follows on lines [10–23]. Note that for each MonthDays object, a pair of values – one string and one integer value – need to be provided in the initializer list { }: for example, { "May", 31 }. In addition, the string constant "May" is sufficient to initialize the std::string object.

```cpp
7    // Creates and displays a simple calendar
8    void SimpleCalendar( void )
9    {
10       const std::vector< MonthDays > calendar {
11                                       { "January",    31 },
12                                       { "February",   28 },
13                                       { "March",      31 },
14                                       { "April",      30 },
15                                       { "May",        31 },
16                                       { "June",       30 },
17                                       { "July",       31 },
18                                       { "August",     31 },
19                                       { "September",  30 },
20                                       { "October",    31 },
21                                       { "November",   30 },
22                                       { "December",   31 }
23                                   };
24
25       // Print them on the screen
26       auto sum_days { 0 };
27       for( auto month : calendar )
28       {
29          sum_days += month.fDays;
30          std::cout << month.fName << " has " << month.fDays << " days\n";
31       }
32
33       std::cout << "\nTotal days: " << sum_days << std::endl;
34    }
```

Objects stored in the calendar vector are accessed one by one in the loop. This is done on lines [27–31] using the range for. More precisely, each successive object from the calendar is copied to the month object, which despite being declared with auto, is also of the MonthDays type. From this, on line [29], the fDays field is accessed with the help of the dot . operator and added to the variable sum_days. On line [30], both fName and fDays are accessed from the month object and streamed to the screen. After all the months from calendar are displayed, and the total number of days has been accumulated in sum_days, the latter is also displayed on line [33].

After launching the previous code (e.g. in one of the online compilers, after adding the proper #include), the following output is obtained:

```
January has 31 days
February has 28 days
March has 31 days
```

```
April has 30 days
May has 31 days
June has 30 days
July has 31 days
August has 31 days
September has 30 days
October has 31 days
November has 30 days
December has 31 days


Total days: 365
```

So far, we have only seen data members inside a structure. Soon we will start to add member functions. Then, we will learn how to superimpose restrictions on access to member data and functions (Section 4.3). However, all not restricted data and members function of a struct or class can be accessed from the object level with member access operators. Their syntax is shown in Figure 3.8.

Figure 3.8a shows the familiar scheme of calling a member from an object using the dot operator. This method of calling is also used when instead of directly providing an object, a reference to it is provided (Section 3.11). For completeness, calling via a pointer to an object is also shown in Figure 3.8b. In this case, the - > operator is used. Both belong to the *GROUP 2* operators (Table 3.15).

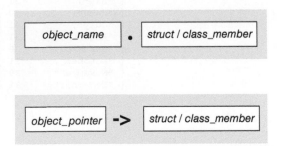

Figure 3.8 Syntax of member access (a) from an object or a reference to an object; (b) by a pointer to an object.

A discussion of pointers is postponed until Section 3.12.

Data members can also be initialized by placing the initialization in the constructor, as will be discussed in the next section. If no constructor is explicitly written, then the compiler will automatically embed data members with default behavior for us. The default behavior in this context is to initialize and copy objects by calling their proper constructors, such as for the std::string. However, the simple built-in types are left uninitialized; if copied, they are copied byte by byte. Therefore, it is important to implement proper initialization in this case.

As we have already seen, C++ defines classes, which are semantically very similar to structs. The main difference is that in a class, all of its members are hidden from direct access by default, whereas a struct does the opposite: that is, all members of a struct can be freely read and written by external components. The difference, although subtle at first glance, has an impact on programming, and we will return to this issue in the next sections. But the two share many similarities, especially when it comes to initializing data members.

Things to Remember

- Structures (classes) are used to gather data and functions intended for a specific functionality or role. This should be clearly expressed by the structure (class) name
- The definition of a structure (class) introduces a new type to the scope
- Objects are instantiations of structures (classes)
- Data members can be initialized using an initializer list { } containing initialization parameters
- Data members can also be initialized by placing the initialization code in a constructor. However, if no special initialization is necessary, it is recommended to skip writing constructors – this is "the rule of zero"
- If constructors are not explicitly written by the programmer, the C++ compiler will automatically generate the default (and copy) constructors with the default semantics (calling default/copy constructors on the data members). But this does not initialize the simple built-in types, such as int and double

3.10 (✄) Fixed-Size Arrays

As we have already seen, in C++, arrays can be easily created and manipulated with the std::vector, as discussed in Section 3.2. However, std::vector consumes slightly more memory than absolutely necessary, as shown in Figure 3.4. Moreover, memory for data is allocated on the heap, which in some constructions is not the option we wish (Section 5.1). A more frugal array can be created with the std::array class. The main differences between std::vector and std:array are as follows:

- std::array has a fixed size, given in its template parameters (std::vector can grow if necessary)
- std:array is an *aggregate class* and does not automatically initialize its elements (except the fundamental types; their default constructors are called, as we will explain later). However, the elements can be set by providing a suitable initializer list

Let's start with simple examples that show the most basic functionality of the std::array (we need to #include <array>); see Listing 3.7.

Listing 3.7 Examples of using the std::array class for fixed-size arrays (in *CppBookCode, VectorsStringsArrays.cpp*).

```
1    // Create a fixed-size array - its first two
2    // elements will get 1, 2,
3    // the rest will be set to 0.
4    array< int, 10 > arr = { 1, 2 };
5
6    assert( sizeof( arr ) == arr.size() * sizeof( arr[ 0 ] ) );
7
8    // Traverse and print all elements of array
9    for( size_t i = 0; i < arr.size(); ++ i )
10      cout << arr[ i ] << " ";
```

The first `std::array`, named `arr`, is created on line [4]. It has exactly 10 elements, each of type `int`. These two parameters are provided in the template part of the type, i.e. inside the `<>` brackets (Section 4.8.5). The `arr` object is initialized by the initialization list. However, it contains only two values: 1 and 2. What will happen to the rest? They will automatically be set to 0. So, if the ending values are 0, we can omit them – very helpful.

Comparing `std::array` with `std::vector`, notice that the size of `std::vector` can vary. That is, it can grow, or some of its elements can be removed. This is not possible with `std::array` – it is of a fixed size. Another difference is that `std::array` will not initialize its elements unless an initializer list is provided, as in the previous example, or its values are using separate code.

`std::array` is very memory efficient – it will occupy a contiguous block of memory that is the exact size of the sum of all of its elements. Nothing more. This feature is checked by the `assert` on line [6]. As pointed out in Table 3.5, `assert` is a special function that verifies logical conditions – but only in the debug version of the code. It helps to put *invariants* in the code for easier debugging, as we will see many times.

We know that `std::vector` is not that frugal, as shown in Figure 3.4. Moreover, if we define `std::array` as on line [4], it will be treated like all other local objects and will be allocated on the local stack, as discussed in Section 5.1. But if we allocate it on the heap by using `std::unique_ptr`, as discussed in (Section 5.2), then the `std::array` object will be entirely on the heap, as requested.[8]

Elements of the `std::array` can be accessed with the subscript operator, as shown on line [10]. Also, its size can be read by calling its `size` member function, as on line [9]. These are exactly the same semantics as for `std::vector`.

On line [12], a new `std::array` named `theArray` is defined. It contains exactly 13 elements, but they are not initialized; so, on line [16], the `std::generate` function is launched, as presented in Table 3.6. Again, the `std::mt19937` object, representing the Mersenne twister, is used. It is initialized with `std::random_device`, as discussed in Section 3.17.3. Thus, we see that similar to `std::vector`, `std::array` offers the pair of iterators `begin` and `end`. They are used again on line [19], where the `std::sort` function is called on `theArray`, so its elements are set in order. Finally, the elements are shown using the range `for` loop, as shown on lines [21–22].

```
11      const int kArrSize { 13 };
12      array< unsigned int, kArrSize > theArray;
13
14
15      // Put some random values
16      generate( theArray.begin(),    theArray.end(),
17                                 std::mt19937( std::random_device{}() ) );
18
19      sort( theArray.begin(), theArray.end() );
20
21      for( const auto e : theArray )
22         cout << e << " ";
```

---

[8] An example can be found in the *VectorsStringsArrays.cpp* source file of the attached project.

theDbArray, which is the same size as theArray, is created on line [24]. This time, it holds elements of double type. We already know that it will not be initialized automatically. Therefore, on line [27], elements of theArray are copied to the theDbArray object with the std::copy function. Note that the elements are converted from unsigned int to double on the fly.

```
23    // Make the same size as theArray
24    array< double, theArray.size() > theDbArray;
25
26    // Copy and convert int to double
27    copy( theArray.begin(), theArray.end(), theDbArray.begin() );
28
29    copy(    theDbArray.begin(),theDbArray.end(),
30             ostream_iterator< double >( cout, " " ) );
```

Finally, std::copy is used again on lines [29–30] to display all the elements of the theDbArray array. More precisely, the output is performed by the ostream_iterator for double, attached to the std::cout stream.

It is worth noting that std::array is a wrapper class around the built-in fixed-size arrays, discussed in Appendix A.2.1. A wrapper class will be presented in Section 3.15.

3.10.1 Multidimensional Fixed-Size Arrays

In a straightforward way, we can create arrays that contain other arrays and thus obtain multidimensional fixed-size arrays. Let's consider Listing 3.8, which shows how to create a simple 2D structure with two rows and three columns (i.e. a matrix), holding floating-point objects.

Listing 3.8 Examples of using std::array to define multidimensional fixed-size arrays (in *CppBookCode, VectorsStringsArrays.cpp*).

```
1     enum ArrayDims { kCols = 3, kRows = 2 };    // Define two constants
2
3     using ArrayElem = double;
4
5     // Declare a single array of kCols elems
6     using _1D_Array = std::array< ArrayElem, ArrayDims::kCols >;
7
8     // Declare a matrix with kRows
9     using _2D_Array = std::array< _1D_Array, ArrayDims::kRows >;
10
11
12    _2D_Array matrix { 0.0 };  // Create a matrix and init with zeros
```

The dimensions of a fixed-size array need to be known at compile time. For this purpose, we can define a const int object; but in this example, we use the other option, which is the enumerated type ArrayDims and its constant values kCols and kRows, as defined on line [1]. This is an *unscoped enumerated* type, which is sufficient in this context. The newer *scoped enumerated* type is presented in Section 3.14.6.

Now we can define a `std::array` with the chosen dimensions. However, when dealing with long names composed of namespaces, classes, etc., it is useful to declare name aliases with the `using` directive, as shown on lines [3, 6, 9]. As we will see in a moment, creating proper alias names with `using` makes code shorter, clearer, and more flexible. For instance, if we want to change the type of the elements, then only line [3] needs to be changed – all subsequent elements will adjust automatically during compilation. Armed with these aliases, on line [12], the matrix object is defined. Its elements are immediately initialized to 0.0 by providing the initializer list { 0.0 }.

```
13    double val { 0.0 };    // Initial value
14
15    // Initialize matrix with increasing values
16    for( auto & r : matrix )
17       for( auto & c : r )
18          c = val ++;       // Each element gets 1 higher value
```

Our 2D structure can be accessed to write new values, as on lines [13–18]. On line [16], rows of `matrix` are accessed by reference `r`. Then, on line [17], each element of the row is accessed thanks to reference `c`, which is then assigned the current `val`. Using references, which are discussed in the next section, offers two benefits:

- We avoid making copies of rows and elements
- We change the real elements of `matrix`, not their local copies

After running the previous code, the memory layout of our 2D structure looks as shown in Figure 3.9. We see that `kCols` defines the dimensions of the innermost array, while `kRows` is the number of such arrays: i.e. the number of rows in the matrix.

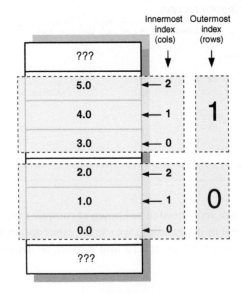

Figure 3.9 Memory layout and indexing of a multidimensional array with two rows and three columns.

Alternatively, the elements of `matrix` can be accessed using the subscript operators `[]`, as shown on lines [20–22].

```
19    // Make the same initialization with subscripts
20    for( _2D_Array::size_type r = 0; r < matrix.size(); ++ r )
21      for( _2D_Array::size_type c = 0; c < matrix[ 0 ].size(); ++ c )
22        matrix[ r ][ c ] = val ++;
```

In this case, the outer `for` traverses the rows (there are as many rows as the size of `matrix`). The inner `for` traverses each element in the row, so we need the size of a row. We get this by calling `matrix[ 0 ].size()`. Unlike with `std::vector`, in this case we can be sure that both dimensions are greater than 0.[9]

3.11 References

References in C++ provide indirect access to objects. Pointers can also be used for this purpose (Section 3.12). However, the two techniques differ significantly, with greater emphasis in C++ on using references. In this section, we discuss the basic properties of left references. Right references and forward (universal) references are discussed in Section 4.5. Table 3.7 summarizes the syntax of the references with some examples.

A reference denotes a kind of alias to an object. However, let's not confuse this with name aliases obtained with the `using` directive. A *reference type* is defined by joining a type with the `&` symbol. Following are some examples of defining and using references:

```
1    int x { 10 };
2
3    int & x_ref = x;
4
5    x     = 12;        // Directly set x,    x == 12
6    x_ref = 12;        // Indirectly set x,  x == 12
```

On line [1], an object `x` is created and initialized with the value 10. On line [3], a reference `x_ref` to the `int` is defined and joined with the `x` object. From this moment on, `x_ref` will always refer to `x`. Such a liaison requires that object `x` live at least as long as its reference does. Now, all operations that can be done directly using `x` can also be performed using `x_ref`. To show this, on line [5], the value 12 is assigned to `x`. Functionally, the same effect can be achieved by assigning 12 to `x` through the reference `x_ref`, as on line [6]. Hence, by looking at a single line, it is not possible to tell a direct operation from an indirect one done by a reference.

---

9 For some of the reasoning behind zero-length arrays, see *https://herbsutter.com/2009/09/02/when-is-a-zero-length-array-okay/*.

Table 3.7 Summary of reference syntax. Reading from and writing to an object directly, and reading from and writing to the object indirectly through a reference to that object, produce the same result.

Operation	Syntax	Examples

Defining and initializing a reference	`const` `object_type` `&` `ref_identifier` `=` `object` `;`	```double sum = 0.0; // object```
		 ```double & sum_ref = sum; // ref to sum```
		
		 ```// const ref to constant```
		 ```const double & kPi { 3.141592653 };```
		
		 ```sum = kPi; // set kPi to sum```
		 ```sum_ref = kPi; // the same via ref```

	`const` `object_type` `&` `ref_identifier` `{` `object` `}` `;`	

It is important to note that *a reference must be initialized* on the line where it is created, as shown in the previous examples. A non-const reference must be initialized with a mutable object, i.e. one that can be read from and written to. Thus, lines [7] and [9] in the following code snippet are incorrect and will not compile. On the other hand, a constant object, i.e. the one that can be only read, can be assigned only to a const reference, such as the constant 10 on line [11].

```
7    int & x_ref;                    // Wrong - a reference must be initialized !
8
9    int & x_ref = 12;               // Wrong - a non-const reference to const !
10
11   const int & kBase_10 = 10; // Ok, kBase_10 refers to value 10 and cannot be changed
```

If we foresee only read operations to an object, a good design practice is to create a const reference to it, as on line [12] in the following code example:

```
12   const int & x_const_ref = x;
13
14   cout << x_const_ref << endl;    // Ok - read through reference
15
16   x_const_ref = 12;                // Wrong - const ref only to read
```

The const reference can be used to read from the object, as on line [14], but it cannot be used to write to it. Hence, line [16] will not compile. In other words, const protects us from unintentional writes to an object if only read operations are expected.

Once attached to an object, a reference cannot be reattached to another object. So, in the following code, after executing line [19], x_ref still refers to object x; it will be assigned the value of object y, and thus x will hold 13.

```
17   int y = 13;
18
19   x_ref = y;      // x == 13
20   // x_ref is not connected to the new object "y".
21   // Instead, object "x" was assigned a new value of "y", i.e. 13.
```

Finally, a reference can only be made to a valid, accessible object. A reference cannot be made to another reference, so the following code line will not compile:

```
22   int & & x_ref_ref = x_ref;      // Wrong - reference to reference not allowed !
```

However, a reference to a reference can happen with the using alias, as follows:

```
23   // a reference to reference by aliasing
24   using int_ref = int &;
25   using int_ref_ref = int_ref &;
26
27   int_ref_ref    xx_ref { x };  // the same as int &
28
29   xx_ref = 12;                // change object x to 12
30
31   * ( & xx_ref ) = 13;        // we can take an address / dereference via reference
32                               // and change object x to 13
```

With the double `using` directives on lines [24–25], a kind of reference-reference-`int` is defined. However, C++ will treat all such chains as a single reference: `int &` in this case. On line [27], `xx_ref` is defined and immediately bound to `x`. If we take a look at the previous code snippet, on line [3], we notice that this is the second reference to the object `x`. Thus, many references to an object can exist. On line [29], the value of `x` is changed to 12. Finally, on line [31], `x` is again changed, and now holds 13. But this is done with help of pointers (discussed in the next section) operating on a reference exactly as if they were operating on the original object `x`. That is, first the address of `x` is obtained with the `&` operator. Then, 13 is written under this address: i.e. to the object `x`, with help of the dereferencing operator `*` (see the description of *GROUP 4* in Table 3.15). Here we see why references are sometimes called *aliases*, since the effect of their use is exactly the same as direct access to objects.

Things to Remember

- References allow for indirect access to an object without creating copies
- A reference must be initialized with an object that lives as long as that reference
- A constant reference can be initialized with a constant object
- After initialization, a reference cannot be detached from its object

3.12 (⚒) Pointers

Pointers and references are language mechanisms that allow us to access objects (variables, constants) in an indirect way. But despite this similarity, there are major differences between them as well. Pointers are available in C and C++, whereas references are used only in C++. References play the primary role in C++, although pointers are useful in some cases. Since C++ 11, there are also *smart pointers*: fully fledged small objects that safely perform the functionality of ordinary pointers for heap allocations and deallocations, as discussed in Section 5.3. However, it is also advisable to know how ordinary pointers work, and we will discuss them in this section.

3.12.1 Object Access with Pointers

For the majority of object types, we can define a corresponding pointer type by adding an asterisk after the type name: for `double`, the corresponding pointer type is `double *`; for `char`, the pointer type is `char *`, and so on. The two parts are considered a unit, defining a *pointer-to-type* type. For those of us who are more machine-oriented, pointers might seem like objects containing memory addresses (Figure 2.2). However, since each type has a corresponding pointer type, pointers in C/C++ are different than bare signals on the address bus. Namely, a pointer not only represents a memory location, but also conveys information about the size of the memory occupied by the object it points to. This has repercussions when advancing pointers or adding an offset to a pointer, as we will discuss later. But creating a pointer that points at an object also means creating a separate object that must reside in memory, be initialized, etc. Thus, since a pointer is also an object, it is possible to create a pointer to a pointer, and so on. We will also discuss these issues.

Let's consider the following code example.

```
1    char c = 0;          // a variable initialized to 0
2
3    char * ptr = & c;    // a pointer initialized to point at c
```

On line [1], an object (a variable) c of type char is defined, and its value is set to 0. This means if program execution reaches this point, a 1-byte object will be allocated in operational memory, and its value will be set to 0. On the other hand, on line [3], an object of type pointer-to-char is created and set to point at c using the *object address operator* & (*GROUP 4*, Table 3.15). Example locations of the two objects, as well as their initial values and relations, are shown in Figure 3.10.

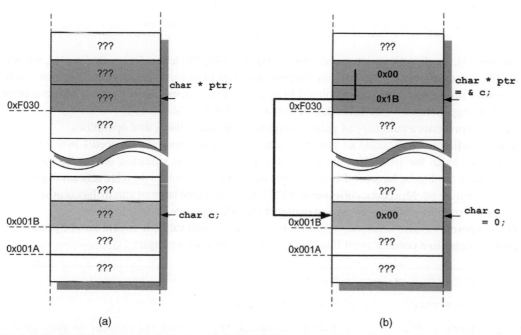

(a)   (b)

Figure 3.10 Example memory location in a simplified address space for an object (variable) of type char and a pointer of type char *. The two objects occupy different memory regions: for c, this is one byte; but for ptr, enough bytes are needed to convey the system's address. In our case, we assume two bytes are sufficient, although in newer systems multiple bytes are needed. (a) Be aware of uninitialized data objects – they can contain undefined garbage values. (b) After initialization, c holds a 0 value, whereas ptr is set to point at c, which in practice means holding its address.

Object c occupies only 1 byte of operational memory space, since in C++ char is defined this way. But the number of bytes for a pointer depends on the system, since it must be large enough to hold the address of another object in that system. For 64-bit systems, a pointer can occupy up to 8 bytes. However, in C++, a pointer is not a simple system address: it also "knows" the size of the object it points to. Thanks to this property, pointers can be advanced forward or backward – they have *scalable arithmetic*, as we will discuss.

Note that it is important to initialize objects where they are created – if this is not done properly, data can contain harmful garbage values, as shown in Figure 3.10a. After proper initialization, c is set to 0, while `ptr` points at c, as shown in Figure 3.10b. As we have seen, C++ objects facilitate this by providing many ways to initialize objects.

Looking at the previous code snippet, and considering all this information, why do we need all these pointers? The answer is that we can manipulate the value of object c two ways (Section 3.1):

- *Directly*, by setting/reading values of c
- *Indirectly*, by performing the same action but via a pointer (or a reference) to c

The following code example shows these two possibilities:

```
4    c = 'A';           // DIRECTLY assign code value of 'A' to c
5
6    * ptr = 'A';       // INDIRECTLY assign 'A' to c via the pointer ptr
```

On line [4], we directly assign a code value[10] representing the letter *A* to c. On line [6], we perform the same action via `ptr`. For this purpose, we need to instruct the compiler not to assign to the pointer but rather to an object pointed to by `ptr` – to do so, we precede `ptr` with the pointer dereferencing operator * (see Table 3.8, as well as *GROUP 4* in Table 3.15).

Table 3.8 presents a summary of pointer definitions, initializations, and operations.

Why is indirect object access so attractive, since in the previous code we need 1 byte for c and many more bytes for `ptr`? The answer is that in practice, the situation is usually the opposite – objects tend to be large, and to avoid copying them back-and-forth, relatively small pointers can be used instead. Moreover, collections of uniformly arranged large or small objects of the same type (arrays) can be easily accessed and operated on with only one pointer to them.

Since a pointer is also an object with a memory location and value, it should also be possible to create a pointer to a pointer, as on line [7] in the following code example:

```
7    char * * ptr_2_ptr = nullptr; // a pointer to a pointer init to nullptr (0)
8
9    ptr_2_ptr = & ptr;             // now ptr_2_ptr points at ptr
10
11   * * ptr_2_ptr = 'B';           // INDIRECTLY assign 'B' to c via the pointer to pointer
```

A pointer to a pointer is indicated by a second *, which can be read as a pointer to `char` *: a pointer to a pointer to `char`. On line [7], we create a pointer, and we want to initialize it to a neutral, or zero, value. For this purpose, there is the special C++ keyword `nullptr`,[11] as used on line [7].

---

10 This is an ASCII (American Standard Code for Information Interchange) code. For international symbols, Unicode values are used – but they are longer than 1 byte.

11 In C and early C++, a simple 0 integer value was used for this purpose, sometimes in the guise of the NULL preprocessor-defined constant.

Table 3.8 Summary of pointer syntax and operators.

Operation	Syntax	Examples

Defining a pointer	const `object_type` * `pointer_identifier` = `nullptr` / & `object` ;
	
	 const `object_type` * `pointer_identifier` { `nullptr` / & `object` };
		`int x = 100;`
		 `int * ptr = & x; // create`
		 `// pointer ptr and set it to x`
		
		 `std::string s { "Fox" };`
		 `const string * s_ptr { & s };`
		
		 `double d {}; // C++ init`
		 `double * d_ptr { nullptr };// C++`
		
		 `d_ptr = & d;`

Address operator	& `object`	

Dereferencing operator	* `pointer_identifier`	`* ptr = 112;`
		 `// assign 112 to x via ptr`
		
		 `cout << * s_ptr + * s_ptr;`
		 `// print "FoxFox"`

On line [9], a `ptr_2_ptr` is assigned with the address operator & to the `ptr` object, which in turn points at object c. Then, on line [11], the code value `'B'` is assigned to c via twofold pointer dereferencing. To disentangle the syntax, reading from right to left, we get the following:

- `ptr_2_ptr` is a pointer.
- `* ptr_2_ptr` is an object pointed to by `ptr_2_ptr` (that is, `ptr`)
- `* * ptr_2_ptr` means the same thing as `* ptr`: this is the object c

To help us understand this, the relations of these pointers in an example memory map are depicted in Figure 3.11.

Pointers to pointers are used e.g. when operating with arrays of arrays, such as arrays of strings passed to the `main` function (for more information, see Appendix 9.2.2).

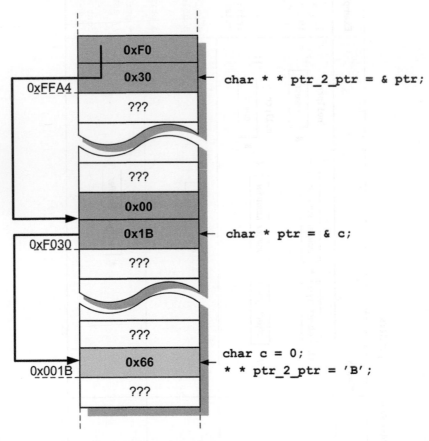

Figure 3.11 Example pointer-to-pointer operations in a simplified memory space. An object c of type `char` is pointed to by pointer `ptr`, which in turn is pointed to by `ptr_2_ptr`. A value of the constant `'B'` can be indirectly written to the object c by a twofold dereferencing of `ptr_2_ptr`.

Things to Remember

- Pointers are objects that allow for indirect access to other objects
- Pointer types are defined in relation to the type of object they point to. Syntactically, a pointer type is obtained by joining an object type with the * symbol
- Pointers are more than bare object addresses in memory space since they "know" the object type they point to. As a result, pointers can be incremented or decremented to point at the next object, not at the next memory location
- There is a special type void * that is not associated with a particular type and that can be used to express a system address to any object
- Like all objects, pointers should be initialized during creation. To express an empty pointer, a special nullptr value is assigned to a pointer
- For indirect access in C++, references should be considered rather than bare pointers (Section 3.11)

3.13 Statements

Statements are language constructions that let us control code execution. The first statements to learn and understand are the conditional statement if and the loop statement for. In Section 2.5.2, we created expressions. An expression that ends with a semicolon becomes a statement. But unlike expressions, statements do not have a value. In addition, declarations are statements; blocks (groupings) of statements are also statements. To begin, we will investigate the role of braces in C++.

3.13.1 Blocks of Statements and Access to Variables – The Role of Braces

In C and C++, pairs of braces { } play an important role. Their two contexts are as follows:

- Grouping type definitions of a class, struct, enum, or namespace (in the first three cases, the closing } should be followed by a semicolon ;). For example, let's analyze the following C++ code:

```
1   namespace CppBook
2   {
3       // Defines an RGB pixel with three byte values
4       class RGB_Pixel
5       {
6           public:
7
8               enum EColor
9               {
10                  kRed, kGreen, kBlue
11              }; // Semicolon after enum definition
12
13              unsigned char GetRed( void ) const { return fData[ kRed ]; }
14              // ...
15
16          private:
17              // An array with 3 byte values
18              std::array< unsigned char, kBlue + 1 > fData;
19      }; // Semicolon to close class definition
20
21  } // No ; when closing a namespace (namespace can be split in many places)
```

There are three pairs of braces in this code. The first pair, between lines [2–21], serves to encompass the CppBook namespace. There is no semicolon after } on line [21] since namespaces can be split into separate parts. The second pair of braces, lines [5–19], defines a simplistic version of the RGB_Pixel class for RGB pixel representation. There is a semicolon after the closing brace on line [19]. Finally, on lines [9–11], we see the definition of the enum EColor type, belonging to the RGB_Pixel class, which is also closed with a semicolon. On the other hand, the braces on line [13] outline the body of a function – this is the second category, discussed in the next bullet.

EColor in the previous code is an example of the *unscoped enumerated type* (the newer scoped enums are discussed in Section 3.14.6). This old-style enum can be directly used to serve as an array bound or array index (IBM: "C++0x, scoped enums" *https://www.ibm.com/developerworks/ rational/library/scoped-enums/scoped-enums-pdf.pdf* Accessed 2020). If not directly specified, the first constant, kRed in this case, is assigned the value 0, the second is assigned 1, and so on. Thus on line [18], the size of the fData array is set to kBlue + 1, whereas on line [13] a value of a red color is read simply as fData[kRed].

■ Grouping statements of a *function* or a *statement* and defining a *local variable context*. To see this in action, let's analyze the following function, which is used to compute Fibonacci numbers (also discussed in Section 3.14.4):

```
1   // Returns a vector with Fibonacci numbers up to max_val
2   vector< int > FibonacciNumbers( const int max_val )
3   {   // LOCAL STACK no. 0 CREATED for local objects (variables)
4
5       vector< int > fibo_num_vec;   // local object, scope in the function
6
7       int a = 0, b = 1; // two variables a and b created - scope only in the function
8
9       while( a < max_val )
10      {   // LOCAL STACK no. 1 CREATED for local objects (variables)
11
12          fibo_num_vec.push_back( a );
13
14          int tmp = a; // a temporary to exchange a and b - scope only in the while
15
16          a = b;        // a becomes "old" b
17          b = tmp + b; // b becomes a sum of "old" a and b
18
19      } // LOCAL STACK no. 1 DELETED - tmp is destroyed
20
21      return fibo_num_vec;     // returned local object
22
23  } // LOCAL STACK no. 0 DELETED - a, b, max_val, fibo_num_vec dead after this line
```

The braces between lines [3–23] define the body of the FibonacciNumbers function. They group all the statements and expressions of this function and also define the scope for local variables. This means each variable (object) defined within the block delimited by the current level of braces is alive, visible, and accessible only in this block (unless it is declared static). After execution exits the block defined by the braces, *all local variables are destroyed and cannot be used in any form!* This is sometimes forgotten, which leads to nasty bugs (e.g. returning the address of a local variable that is destroyed, etc.). To accomplish such functionality, the framework (the compiler) defines special data structures called *local stacks*, which serve to store local variables (see Section 5.1).

In the scope of the `FibonacciNumbers` function, one object `fibo_num_vec` of type `vector< int >` is defined on line [5]. This is a local object that will be available inside the function. Hence, its *scope* is the body of the function, i.e. between lines [3–23]. It is also visible in this scope. The scope and visibility are the same for objects a and b defined on line [7].

The second pair of braces, between lines [10–19], defines a block of the `while` loop, presented in Section 3.13.2.2. On line [14], a `tmp` object (variable) of type `int` is defined, which is placed on the second local stack associated with the `while` context. However, unlike a, b, and `fibo_num_vec`, the scope of `tmp` is limited exclusively to the body of the `while` loop. In other words, `tmp` cannot be accessed before or after the `while` and its block. The `tmp` is used as an auxiliary variable to change the values of a and b on lines [16–17]. The latter, as well as `fibo_num_vec`, are also visible in the `while` block since it is embedded in the broader scope of the function body. Regarding *visibility*, the name `tmp` is visible only in the `while` scope, and it would hide all other `tmp` names if they were defined outside of the `while` loop.[12]

After the `while` terminates on line [19], the second local stack is destroyed, which entails the destruction of the local `tmp` object. This behavior is desirable since it frees us from having to worry about explicitly deleting objects. Hence, such local objects are *automatic variables*. Other types of objects are discussed in Section 5.1. Last but not least, local stacks usually have limited capacity, so they should not be used to store very large objects (say, hundreds of megabytes or more).[13] Instead, the heap and dynamic allocations should be used for large objects, as discussed in Section 5.2.

The two language constructions just discussed should not be confused. In this section, dealing with statements, we will primarily use the second context.

3.13.2   C++ Statements

In this section, we summarize all the statements in C++.[14] Versions available in the C++11 standards are marked with color. Understanding the details of statement operations is a key factor in learning the language, as well as in writing correct code.

3.13.2.1   Conditional Statements

Conditional statements let us follow a path of execution based on the value of a given Boolean condition. In this group, we have the `if-else` and the `switch` statements, explained in Table 3.9. Starting from C++11, we have new versions of these with inherent initialization blocks, which are also highlighted.

---

12 As an interesting experiment, we can substitute `tmp` for `fibo_num_vec`. Then two variables named `fibo_num_vec` – one of type `vector< int >` and the second of type `int` – would coexist in the `while` scope. However, such code is obfuscated and by no means recommended.
13 Stack and heap sizes can be set in the linker settings.
14 With only a few exceptions, the same statements can be used in C. Details are provided in Appendix 9.2.

Table 3.9 C++ statements.

Flowchart	Description	Syntax	C++ examples
| | Conditional statement that executes only one branch of its instruction(s), depending on the value of its Boolean condition. If it evaluates to true, then *statement_t* is executed. If it evaluates to false, then *statement_n* in the else part is executed. The else part is optional and can be omitted.<br><br>If more than one instruction is necessary, they can be grouped within a block { }.<br><br>If many if-else statements are chained together, the last else pertains to the last if. | | ```cpp
double val {};     // read val from keyboard
cin >> val;
if( val > 0.0 ) // if val larger than 0.0
    cout << std::log( val ); // out a natural logarithm
else
    cout << "Error - Negative argument" << endl;
```<br><br>The if statement is used here to guard against calling the std::log function with a negative argument. |

if – conditional statement
```

Flowchart	Description	Syntax	C++ examples

		`if (  condition  )`
		`{`
		`    statement_t ;`
		`}`
		`else`
		`{`
		`    statement_n ;`
		`}`
			```bool flag = false; // define a flag```
			```char c = 'Y'; // define a variable```
			```cout << "Proceed with computations? (Y/N)" << endl;```
			```cin >> c; // get answer```
			
			```if(c == 'Y')```
			```{```
			``` cout << "Continue" << endl; // "Yes"```
			``` flag = true;```
			```}```
			```else```
			```{```
			``` cout << "Stop" << endl; // "No"```
			``` flag = false;```
			```}```
			
			```// continue computations if flag == true ..```

		`if ( initializer ; condition )`
		`{`
		`    instruction_t ;`
		`}`
		`else`
		`{`
		`    instruction_n ;`
		`}`
		
		`(C++17+)`
			```// is open returns bool (true if ok)```
			```if(ofstream outFile("Log.txt"); outFile.is_open())```
			```{```
			``` outFile << "Operation successful" << endl;```
			```}```
			
			In the initializer part, an output (write) file object named `outFile` of the `ofstream` class is created. A file named *Log.txt* is provided in its constructor, so there will be an attempt to create or open that file. This operation may not need to succeed, so in the condition the `is_open` function is called from the `outFile` object.

(Continued)

Table 3.9 (continued)

Flowchart	Description	Syntax	C++ examples

switch – conditional statement

Flowchart:

Description:

A switch statement checks the runtime value of the expression and transfers control to one of the branches depending on its associated values. These need to be known at compile-time (if not, an if statement is the only option).

The branches are labeled by the case keyword, followed by a value and a colon :. Statements for a particular case are grouped and usually closed by the break statement to jump out of the switch. Otherwise, the next group of statements is executed. For all values not listed in the case branches, there is a default branch that usually is also closed with the break statement.

Syntax:

```
switch ( expression )
{
    case val_0 :
        statement_0
        break ;
    case ...
    case val_n :
        statement_n
        break ;
    default :
        statement_d
        break ;
}
```

C++ examples:

```cpp
// A function reads a video and converts into a
tensor
string TensorFromVideo( const string & videoPath,
                        const string & outFileName = string(""),
                        const string & outFileExt = string("") );

// argc - num of arguments; argv - text arguments
int main( int argc, char ** argv )
{
    string outMsg;
    switch( argc )
    {
    case 2:
        outMsg = TensorFromVideo( argv[1] );
        break;
    case 3:
        outMsg = TensorFromVideo( argv[1], argv[2] );
        break;
    case 4:
        outMsg = TensorFromVideo( argv[1],
                argv[2],argv[3]);
        break;
    case 1:
    default:
        outMsg = "Exiting - wrong number of
                params.\n";
        break;
    }
    cout << outMsg; // write out output message
    return 1;
}
```

Flowchart	Description	Syntax	C++ examples
			In this main function, the `switch` statement is used to decide on an action depending on the number of parameters provided in a command line (Section 9.2.2). `argc` conveys the number of parameters, separated by white space, and `argv` is a pointer to these parameters (i.e. text, in other words – this is a table of `char *`). The function `TensorFromVideo` requires at least one parameter of type `string` and, optionally, two additional parameters. These are resolved in the `case` 2, `case` 3, and `case` 4 branches. The old-style `char *` text will be converted to `string` objects using one of the constructors (Table 3.5). Note that after each action, the `break` statement is called to jump out of the `switch` statement. Otherwise, the action would pass to the lower branches. Also note that `case` 1 and all other possible calls represented by `default` are processed in one place. Thus, there is no break after `case` 1.
			The following code shows a newer version of the `switch` statement, which can be used in C++17 and newer. It is used to locally collect the user's answer and switch between different selections.

```cpp
bool answer_expected { true };
cout << "Do you want to play a game? [Y/N]" << endl;
do
{
    cin.clear(); // clear the input buffer
    switch( char c {}; std::cin >> c, c )
    {
        case 'Y':
        case 'y':
            answer_expected = false;
            cout << "Let us play our game" << endl;
            //PlayGame(); // Call a function to play
            break;
``` |

(Continued)

Table 3.9 (continued)

Flowchart	Description	Syntax	C++ examples
			``
    case 'N':
    case 'n':
        answer_expected = false;
        cout << "Let us stop our game" << endl;
        break;

    default:
        answer_expected = true;
        cout << "Press only \'Y\' for yes
                or \'N\' for no" << endl;
        break;
    }
} while(answer_expected == true);
```

The entire switch is embedded in the *do-while* loop to allow only yes/no selections. In switch( char c {}; std::cin >> c, c ), the first part char c {} defines and initializes to 0 a variable c of type char in the scope of the switch statement. The second part is more interesting here, since it should return a value that is then compared to the series of case statements. However, in this case, the comma , operator lets us tweak two statements into one place. Namely, first std::cin >> c is executed that reads c from the keyboard. Then a second part of comma is executed that is simply c. Since result of the comma operator is the rightmost expression, then a value of c is returned (Table 3.15, *GROUP 16*). |

Since a block of statements is also a statement, the first version of syntax would suffice. The second version, with explicit { and }, is shown for convenience.
```

3.13.2.2 Loop Statements

Loop statements constitute a second and very important group of language constructions. In C++, the most important and frequently used is the for loop.[15]

Starting from C++11, a new and very useful range version of for is available.

Flowchart	Description	Syntax	Examples

	The for statement first (and only once) executes its *initializer*. Then it iterates, executing its statement(s) as long as its *condition* is true. After executing its last statement, the *iterator* part is executed.
	
	If more than one statement needs to be processed, the statements should be grouped between { }.
	
	Each of the *initializer*, *condition*, and *iterator* parts can be empty: e.g. for (; ;) is a valid loop that iterates indefinitely.
			`const size_t kSize { 16 }; // size_t for dimensions`
			`std::vector< int > tab( kSize ); // Reserve kSize ints`
			
			`// Set consecutive kSize odds`
			`for( auto i { 0 }; i < tab.size(); ++ i )`
			`    tab[ i ] = 2 * i + 1;`
			
			This loop sets all elements of the vector tab to consecutive odd values: 1, 3, and so on. The scope of the i variable is limited exclusively to the for loop and its statement[16] (i.e. it is not accessible outside the for loop).
			
			The following code opens two text files inFl and outFl for reading and writing. If successfully opened, then the for loop inFl is read line by line to the str of the std::string type. To read a line, the getline function is used, which returns true if a line was successfully read.
			
			Then, std::transform is called to *in situ* convert the characters in str from lowercase to uppercase. This is done by providing the std::toupper function as an argument to std::transform. Finally, outFl << str << endl is called, which writes str to outFl, followed by the end-of-line symbol.
			
			`ifstream inFl( "InFile.txt" );`
			`ofstream outFl( "OutFile.txt" );`
			
			`if( inFl.is_open() && outFl.is_open() )`
			`    for( string str; getline(inFl,str); outFl<<str<<endl )`
			`        transform( str.begin(), str.end(),`
			`                   str.begin(), toupper );`

for – loop statement

---

15 for is the only loop that can be parallelized, using the OpenMP framework (8.3).

16 This functionality was changed; in the earliest version of C++, the scope of i was beyond the for loop, as if int i was defined outside the for loop.

(Continued)

Flowchart	Description	Syntax	Examples

	In a third version – called *range-for-statement* and available only in C++11 and above – for iterates for each element in a collection. It is a common practice to include the auto keyword for automatic type deduction for the *iterator*.	`for ( auto iter : container )`
		`{`
		   statement `;`
		`}`
		C++11+
		
		`for ( initializer ; auto iter : cont )`
		`{`
		   statement `;`
		`}`
		C++20
			``// This function changes endianness

// i.e. it reverts the order of bytes in the input arg.
// Example: 0x78ABCDEF will be changed to 0xEFCDAB78
auto RevertEndianness(unsigned long in)
{
unsigned long out { 0 };
for(auto i {0}; i < sizeof(in); ++i) // rotate bytes
{
out <<= 8;
out |= in & 0xFF;
in >>= 8;
}
return out;
}``` The function reverts the order of bytes (the *endianness*, as discussed in Section 4.15.2) of its input parameter in. The for loop iterates for the number of bytes occupied by unsigned long provided by the sizeof operator. The loop contains three statements: it left-shifts the out variable by a byte (eight bits), and then in & 0xFF extracts a single byte from in, which is OR-ed to out (see *GROUP 15*, Table 3.15). After that, in is shifted right by eight bits to expose its next byte for processing. In this case, we exploit in being passed by value, so no other data copies are necessary.

Flowchart	Description	Syntax	Examples
			``
vector< int >   vec;

// fill vec with even values
for(auto i : { 0, 1, 2, 3, 4, 5 })
    vec.push_back(2 * i);
```

The *range* for iterates for each element of the container specified by the { } list. It contains six values, so in each iteration the iterator i successively takes these values. After the loop finishes, vec contains successive even values.

This version of the for loop can be further simplified when using the range class (Section 6.5), as in the following example:

```
// Introduce the range class to facilitate range for
#include "range.h"   // "" are for user-created headers

// Display values from -10 up to -64 (excl.) with step -2
for(auto i : range(-10, -64, -2))
    std::cout << i;
``` |

(Continued)
```

Flowchart	Description	Syntax	Examples
| 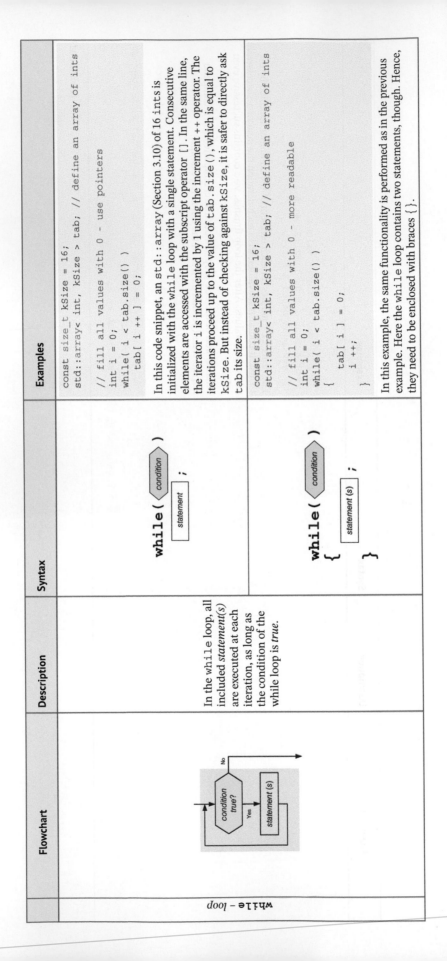 | In the `while` loop, all included *statement(s)* are executed at each iteration, as long as the condition of the while loop is *true*. | `while (` *condition* `)`  *statement*  `;` | ```
const size_t kSize = 16;
std::array< int, kSize > tab; // define an array of ints

// fill all values with 0 - use pointers
int i = 0;
while( i < tab.size() )
    tab[ i ++ ] = 0;
```  In this code snippet, an `std::array` (Section 3.10) of 16 ints is initialized with the while loop with a single statement. Consecutive elements are accessed with the subscript operator `[]`. In the same line, the iterator `i` is incremented by 1 using the increment `++` operator. The iterations proceed up to the value of `tab.size()`, which is equal to `kSize`. But instead of checking against `kSize`, it is safer to directly ask `tab` its size. |
| | | `while (` *condition* `)`  `{`  *statement (s)*  `;`  `}` | ```
const size_t kSize = 16;
std::array< int, kSize > tab; // define an array of ints

// fill all values with 0 - more readable
int i = 0;
while( i < tab.size() )
{
    tab[ i ] = 0;
    i ++;
}
```  In this example, the same functionality is performed as in the previous example. Here the while loop contains two statements, though. Hence, they need to be enclosed with braces {}. |

while – loop

Flowchart	Description	Syntax	Examples

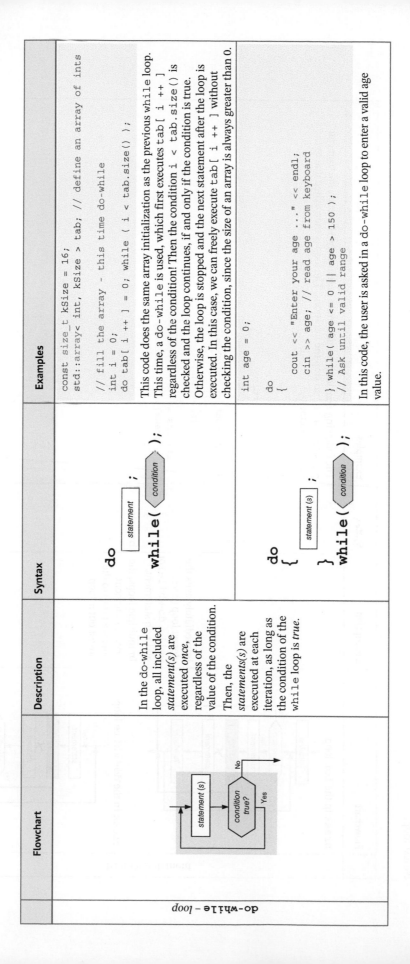	In the do-while loop, all included *statement(s)* are executed *once*, regardless of the value of the condition. Then, the *statements(s)* are executed at each iteration, as long as the condition of the while loop is *true*.	do
		
		`statement`
		
		while(`condition` **);**
			```const size_t kSize = 16;```
			 ```std::array< int, kSize > tab; // define an array of ints```
			
			 ```// fill the array - this time do-while```
			 ```int i = 0;```
			 ```do tab[i ++] = 0; while (i < tab.size());```
			
			 This code does the same array initialization as the previous while loop. This time, a do-while is used, which first executes `tab[ i ++ ]` regardless of the condition! Then the condition `i < tab.size()` is checked and the loop continues, if and only if the condition is true. Otherwise, the loop is stopped and the next statement after the loop is executed. In this case, we can freely execute `tab[ i ++ ]` without checking the condition, since the size of an array is always greater than 0.

		do
		`{`
		
		`statement (s)`
		
		`}`
		while(`condition` **);**
			```int age = 0;```
			
			 ```do```
			 ```{```
			
			 ``` cout << "Enter your age ..." << endl;```
			 ``` cin >> age; // read age from keyboard```
			
			 ```} while(age <= 0 || age > 150);```
			 ```// Ask until valid range```
			
			 In this code, the user is asked in a do-while loop to enter a valid age value.

3.13.2.3 Auxiliary Statements – continue and break

Loop operations can be facilitated with the break and continue statements. The former is also used in the switch statement. It is important to understand their functionality, as well as their differences. When dealing with nested loops it is also important to remember that they act on the *closest* loop.

Flowchart	Description	Syntax	Examples

break in the for loop
 	
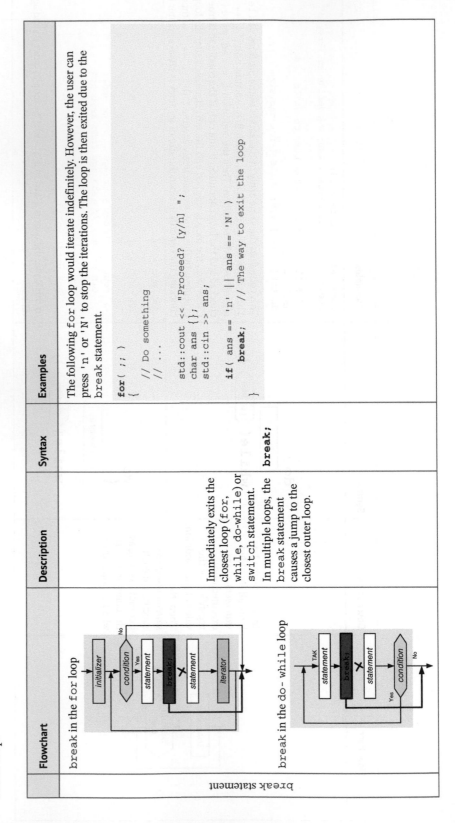
 	
break in the do-while loop
			The following for loop would iterate indefinitely. However, the user can press 'n' or 'N' to stop the iterations. The loop is then exited due to the break statement.
			
			``cpp
			for(;;)
			{
			    // Do something
			    // ...
			
			    std::cout << "Proceed? [y/n] ";
			    char ans {};
			    std::cin >> ans;
			
			    if(ans == 'n' || ans == 'N')
			        break; // The way to exit the loop
			}
			``

	Immediately exits the closest loop (for, while, do-while) or switch statement. In multiple loops, the break statement causes a jump to the closest outer loop.	break;	

break statement

Flowchart	Description	Syntax	Examples

Examples

The following code snippet first creates a _2D_array object that is an array of arrays of int objects. Then, after reading in its content, the sum of all elements except those on the diagonal is computed.

```cpp
const auto kRows { 12 };
const auto kCols { 12 };

std::array< std::array< int, kCols >, kRows > _2D_array;

// ... read array from a file

// Add all components of the array
// except for the diagonal
double sum = 0.0;
for( int r = 0; r < kRows; ++ r )
{
    for( int c = 0; c < kCols; ++ c )
    {
        if( r == c )
            continue;        // if diagonal, skip

        sum += _2D_array[ r ][ c ];
    }
}
```

When using continue in multiple loops, as in the previous code, remember that it refers to its *closest* loop.

Syntax

```cpp
continue;
```

Description

The continue statement is used exclusively in loops (for, while, do-while). When encountered, it causes the omission of all following statements in the loop and immediately jumps to the *iterator* part of the closest loop. Then, if the condition is still true, iteration of the loop continues.

Flowchart

continue in the for loop

continue in the do-while loop

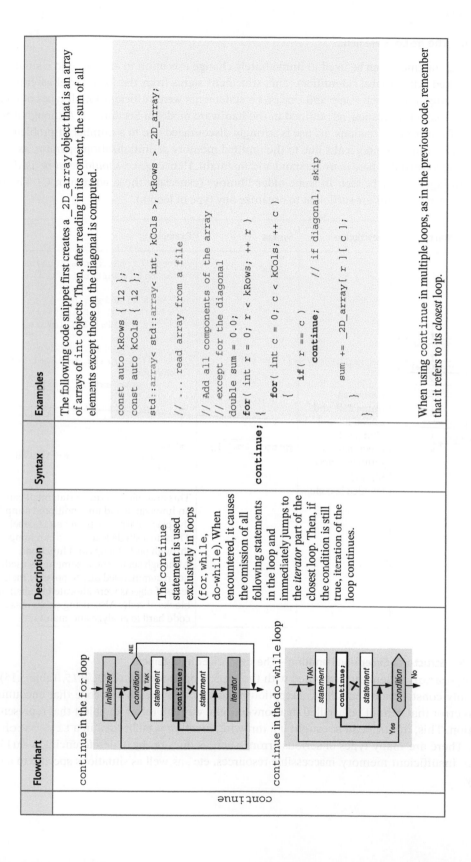

continue

3.13.2.4 The `goto` Statement

The `goto` statement can be used to immediately change execution to any place in a single function, marked with a label (identifier). This statement stems from the lower-level assembly language paradigm in which `jump` and `compare` statements were sufficient for all types of control, including loop organization, as outlined in the hardware model in Section 2.1. Although it might seem useful in some situations, its use is strongly discouraged due to a number of problems. The most frequent are memory leaks due to the omitted memory de-initialization operator, as well as obfuscated code that is hard to understand and maintain. Hence, `goto` *should never be used in new code*, although it may be seen in some older libraries (especially those written in C). The other language constructions are sufficient to organize any type of loop(s).

	Flowchart	Description	Syntax	Examples

goto statement		Causes an immediate and unconditional change of execution – a jump to a *label*. Should be avoided in code.	**goto** `label` **;**	```const int kBufLen = 1024;```
				```char buf[kBufLen];```
				
				```// Read line-by-line```
				```for(ifstream inFile("File```
				```.txt"); inFile && ! inFile```
				```.eof();)```
				```{```
				``` if(! inFile.getline(buf,```
				```kBufLen))```
				``` goto exit; // exit the loop```
				
				``` // process buffer ...```
				```}```
				
				```exit:```
				``` cout << "Loop terminated" <<```
				```endl;```
				
				This example of a `goto` statement causes an immediate and unconditional jump to the place marked with the `exit` label. Thus, in a single leap, `goto` can jump through nested loops and functions. Although such code is sometimes used, it is not recommended due to possible memory leaks if objects were allocated in abandoned blocks of code. Also, using `goto` makes code hard to analyze and maintain.

3.13.2.5 Structural Exception Handling – The `try-catch` Statement

The `try-catch` statement, combined with the `throw` operator (see *GROUP 15*, Table 3.15), is a C++-only construction that allows exception handling. This means any code that encounters a serious error that cannot be handled in a conventional way can throw an object that represents an exception. This, in turn, can be caught if a throwing function is embedded in a `try-catch` construct. There are many types of serious errors, such as division by 0, dereferencing a `nullptr` pointer, insufficient memory, inaccessible resources, etc., as well as situations specific to a given library.

Flowchart	Description	Syntax	Examples
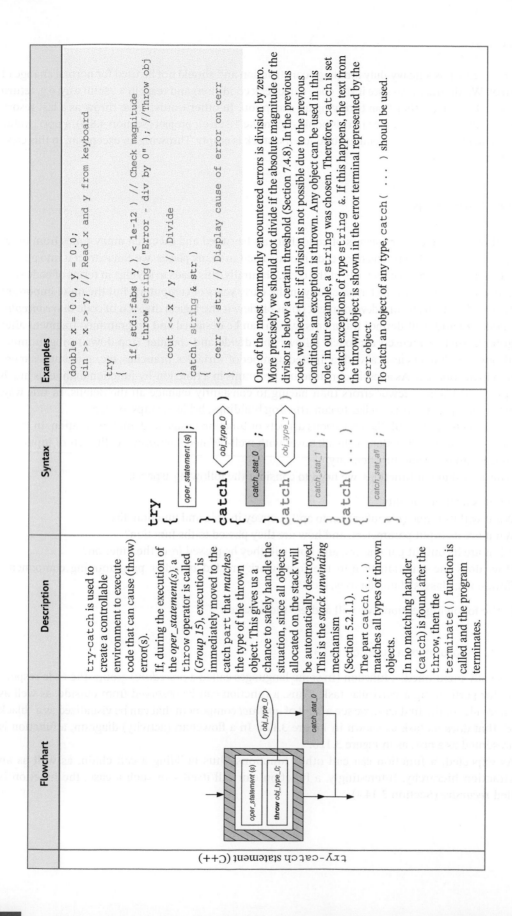	try-catch is used to create a controllable environment to execute code that can cause (throw) error(s).

If, during the execution of the *oper_statement(s)*, a throw operator is called (*Group 15*), execution is immediately moved to the catch part that *matches* the type of the thrown object. This gives us a chance to safely handle the situation, since all objects allocated on the stack will be automatically destroyed. This is the *stack unwinding* mechanism (Section 5.2.1.1).

The part catch(...) matches all types of thrown objects.

In no matching handler (catch) is found after the throw, then the terminate() function is called and the program terminates. | **try**
{
  oper_statement(s) ;
}
catch(*obj_type_0*)
{
  catch_stat_0 ;
}
catch(*obj_type_1*)
{
  catch_stat_1 ;
}
catch(...)
{
  catch_stat_all ;
} | ```
double x = 0.0, y = 0.0;
cin >> x >> y; // Read x and y from keyboard
try
{
   if(std::fabs(y) < 1e-12) // Check magnitude
      throw string("Error - div by 0"); //Throw obj

   cout << x / y ; // Divide
}
catch(string & str)
{
   cerr << str; // Display cause of error on cerr
}
```
One of the most commonly encountered errors is division by zero. More precisely, we should not divide if the absolute magnitude of the divisor is below a certain threshold (Section 7.4.8). In the previous code, we check this: if division is not possible due to the previous conditions, an exception is thrown. Any object can be used in this role; in our example, a string was chosen. Therefore, catch is set to catch exceptions of type string &. If this happens, the text from the thrown object is shown in the error terminal represented by the cerr object.

To catch an object of any type, catch( ... ) should be used. |

**try-catch statement (C++)**
```

`try-catch` is a heavy-duty language construction and should not be used for normal change of control. We should always see if the code can check conditions and react in a useful way, e.g. return a `bool` flag, etc., rather than throwing an exception. In other words, leave throw as a last resort. Many examples are presented in this book: e.g. in the `TStack` project (Section 4.8.4), a `bool` value is returned from the `Pop` member function if a stack is empty. Throwing an exception, in this case, would be overkill.

3.14 Functions

Functions are selected fragments of code that can be called and executed many times from other fragments of code. If a fragment of code repeats itself in many places, we can extract it into a function that is called from other parts of the code. Naturally, this leads to savings in terms of code size, which was an important factor especially in the early years of computers. But the more important feature of functions from a development point of view is the logical division of code into *conceptually coherent* and well-defined fragments, which can be designed and programmed fragment after fragment. Such a focused approach follows the divide-and-conquer (top-down) programming methodology that lets us deal with a limited number of variables, branches, etc. at a time, as mentioned in Section 2.3. As a result, constructing programs in a function-by-function manner is much simpler and leads to fewer errors than having to constantly manage all the details. In this way, constructing programs is similar to constructing buildings, bridges, ships, or cars.

In this section, we will discuss various aspects of function design and implementation. In many places, we will treat functions as black boxes with well-defined *interfaces*, i.e. the sets of input and output parameters and functionality.

When thinking of functions, we need to consider the following aspects:

- What is its functionality?
- What will its name (identifier) be, to aptly convey its role and functionality?
- What are its input parameters, and how are they passed to the function?
- What are its output parameters, and how will they be passed from the function?
- How does the function fit into the framework created by other programming components (functions, classes, data, libraries, etc.)?

In the following sections, we will address these issues.

3.14.1 Anatomy of a Function in C++

As already mentioned, a function (in some languages called a *procedure*) groups the code responsible for performing a particular task. Thus, a function can be observed from outside, as well as from inside. In the first case, we see a kind of *abstract* component that can be visualized as a "black box" that does its task as shown in Figure 3.12a. In a flowchart (activity) diagram, a function is represented as a box, as in Figure 3.12b.

As expected, a function can call other functions, thus building a call chain, as well as an abstraction hierarchy. Interestingly, a function can call itself – in such a case, the function is called *recursive* (Section 3.14.4).

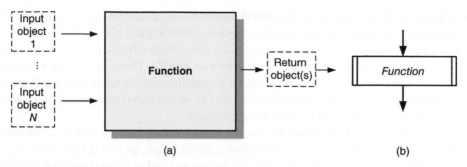

Figure 3.12 (a) A function as a black box that optionally takes the number of input objects and also optionally returns an object. The input/output objects can be passed in various ways, and they can be of different types and sizes. Thus, functions can operate on various data. (b) A function as a subprocedure in the flowchart diagram.

To perform its tasks, a function needs data on input, as well as a way to return its results. Thus, a function can optionally accept a number of parameters, given in its parameter list, as well as output an object. Although the parameter list can be long and a function can output only one object, we can freely model the function's ability to convey information, as will be discussed. Also important is the way objects are passed to a function: whether objects are *copied* and then passed to a function for its exclusive use, or *links* are passed for *indirect access* to the objects, while the objects themselves are not copied due to their size or other issues. In the latter case, link to objects are provided by references or pointers, as discussed in Sections 3.11 and 3.12.

Let's take a look inside a function by analyzing the short C++ program in Listing 3.9. It prompts the user to enter two numeric values and then returns the sum of their squares. In this section, we are mostly interested in two functions – SumOfSquares and main – and what objects they accept as inputs and return as output.

Listing 3.9 Declaration and call of the SumOfSquares function (in *CppBookCode, Functions.cpp*).

```cpp
1   #include <iostream>
2
3   using std::cout, std::cin, std::endl;
4
5
6   // Function declaration - we introduce a function.
7   // Its full definition is elsewhere.
8   double SumOfSquares( double a, double b );
9
10
11  void main( void )
12  {
13      double x { 0.0 }, y { 0.0 };      // two floating-point variables
14
15      cout << "Enter two values" << endl;
16      cout << "x = ";
17      cin >> x;
18      cout << "y = ";
19      cin >> y;
20
21      // Sum will contain the value returned by SumOfSquares
22      double sum = SumOfSquares( x, y );
23
24      cout << "x*x + y*y = " << sum << endl;
25  }
```

As already pointed out, to successfully compile this code, we need to let the compiler know what other functions and libraries we will be using. Since we wish to print text on the screen and read from the keyboard, on line [1] we include the iostream header file with the relevant declarations, followed by type aliases with using directives on line [3]. Then, on line [8], we introduce our SumOfSquares function, providing only its declaration, i.e. its name and a full list of the types of its input and output parameters. The former go in the parameter list in parentheses (), whereas the latter go on the left side of the function name.

On lines [11–25] is the full definition, i.e. the complete code, of the main function, which is the primary function in every C++ program. Its action is simple. First, on line [13], two floating-point variables (objects) x and y, identified by double, are created and initialized with 0.0. As we mentioned earlier, it is very important to always initialize variables as soon as possible, in their definitions. Then, on lines [15–19], text is output to the terminal, asking the user to enter values for x and y. After this, control goes to line [22], where two things happen. First, a new variable sum, also of type double, is created. Then, it is initialized with whatever value is returned by the SumOfSquares function, called with the x and y objects as its input parameters. In the last line [24] of main, a message with the computed value is output to the terminal, and main (as well as the entire program) ends; it also automatically cleans out all allocated objects. But we have not yet seen the full definition of the SumOfSquares function.

Let's move on to function declarations. Figure 3.13 shows an organizational diagram of a function declaration in C++. As alluded to previously, function declaration is basically composed of three parts: the function name, a list of its arguments, and the type of any returned object. A function can have no arguments – in this case, instead of the list, we use void. Similarly, if a function does not return a value, void is used as a placeholder.

A relatively new feature of C++ is automatic deduction of the return type, using the auto keyword as a return object (Section 3.7). We will see these semantics in further examples in this book. Using auto makes sense if complicated long types (e.g. templates) are returned. In other cases, it is usually OK to explicitly write return types if doing so helps increase code readability (this is a manifest type declaration). Also, with the auto keyword alone, it is not possible to split the locations of the declaration and definition, since the compiler will not be able to deduce the returned type exclusively from a declaration and auto.

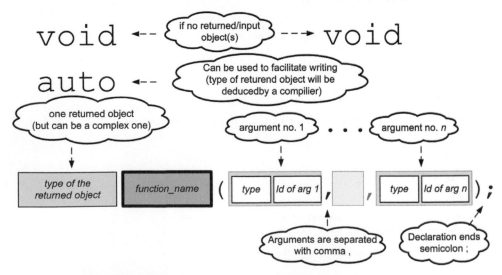

Figure 3.13 Function declaration in C++.

Returning to our practical example, notice that providing only a function declaration is sufficient to compile the previous code but not to build the entire program. Why is that? Because for full operation, we need the complete code for `SumOfSquares`. Otherwise, despite successful compilation, our program will not link properly (there will be a linker error complaining about a missing definition). Thus, to satisfy the compiler and the linker, and to be able to build a complete program, we put a complete version of the `SumOfSquares` function in the same file after `main`, as shown in Listing 3.10.

Listing 3.10 Definition of the `SumOfSquares` function (in *CppBookCode, Functions.cpp*).

```
26   ////////////////////////////////////////////////////////////
27   // Computes and returns sum of squares of its arguments
28   ////////////////////////////////////////////////////////////
29   //
30   // INPUT:
31   //     a, b - floating-point input values
32   // OUTPUT:
33   //     Sum of squares of a and b, i.e.:
34   //     a * a + b * b
35   //
36   // REMARKS:
37   //     Parameters passed by value (copies)
38   //
39   double SumOfSquares( double a, double b )
40   {
41      return a * a + b * b;
42   }
```

On line [39], we see a copy of the declaration from line [8]. However, instead of a semicolon (;) at the end, on lines [40–42], the full body of the function is contained within braces { }. The function is fairly simple: it computes the squared values of each of its arguments, sums them up, and returns this computed value – all in a single line [41].

An important exercise is to compare the function, treated as an entity defined on lines [39–42], with the place where it is called on line [22]. Let's count how many objects are involved and how they are connected; see Figure 3.14.

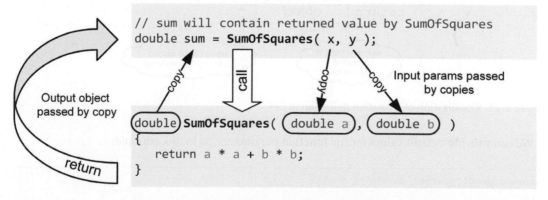

Figure 3.14 Matching a function call to its definition. In the place of a function call with x and y objects, their copies are created and named a and b. Upon return from a function, a temporary object with no explicit name is created and returned. It is used to initialize the variable sum.

When SumOfSquares is called with the x and y objects as its input parameters, code execution is moved to the actual code of SumOfSquares; the objects a and b are local copies of x and y. Upon returning from the function, a temporary object with no explicit name is created, and control returns to the next instruction after the function call. In this case, the returned object is used to initialize the variable sum. It is important to point out that SumOfSquares contains its own copies of the passed objects. Objects a and b will be only used to compute the returned result. These copies are local and available exclusively in the scope of SumOfSquares. In other words, whatever happens with these objects will not affect the originally supplied objects x and y. However, sometimes it is beneficial to be able to change external objects, such as x and y, using instructions inside a function. Such functionality requires us to pass the objects indirectly using references or pointers to the real objects, instead of making copies. We will discuss this later.

To conclude with the happy finish of our simple program, Figure 3.15 shows a general diagram of a function definition. It is easy to spot that it consists of a function declaration followed by the function body delimited by the braces { }. Inside are lines of code that define the function's behavior.

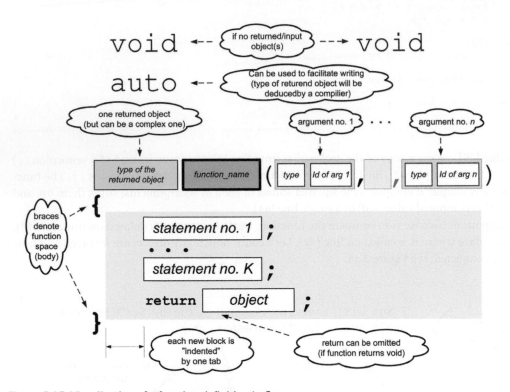

Figure 3.15 Visualization of a function definition in C++.

We can provide default values for the function parameters, as in this example:

```
double SumOfSquares( double a, double b = 0.0 )
{
    return a * a + b * b;
}
```

Then, if the value of a parameter is not provided during a call, its default will be used. In our example, we can provide values for a and b or only for a. In the latter case, b will be set to its default 0.0, as in the following call:

```
cout << SumOfSquares( 10.0 ) << endl;     // returns 100.0
```

Default parameters can be provided for one, two, or all function parameters. However, they must be set consecutively starting from the rightmost parameter.

When developing a function, giving proper names (identifiers) to the function and its types and parameters is important, to convey sufficient, clear information about their role and purpose. As a rule of thumb (McConnell 2004),

- Names should be short and distinctive
- If a name is composed of multiple words, the words should be separated by capital letters or underscore symbols (_)

Not less important is the comment placed before the function, which briefly conveys its role and the roles of its parameters. Other important lines of code should also be commented.

Things to Remember

- Functions are a very important software design concept that let us group conceptually coherent code for multiple use
- Functions can take zero or more input objects of various types, and can return zero or one object of various types
- The input parameters can be passed
  - By making a copy (by value)
  - By providing a reference to an outside object
  - By providing a pointer to an outside object
- Functions can have default values for their parameters
- Two functions can have the same name, provided their sets of input parameters differ. These are called *overloaded* functions

3.14.2 Passing Arguments to and from a Function

After deciding on a function's role and name, the most important thing is to determine the number and type of its input and output parameters, as well as the mechanism of passing them to the function (copy or indirect). Formal parameters can contain default values. If the value of such a parameter is not explicitly provided, a default value is used. Default values can be added in a continuous fashion starting from the rightmost parameter. Although they may be convenient in a given context, be careful about using too many default parameters, since they can obscure the necessity of providing a runtime computed value, for instance. We will see examples of default parameters in many examples provided in this book.

To show the various ways of passing parameters to and from functions, we will examine variants of the Deg_2_Rad function, which simply converts the value of an angle passed in degrees into the equivalent radians: 60 degrees is approximately 1.047 radians, and so on.

3.14.2.1 Argument Passing by Copy (Value Semantics)

Figure 3.16 illustrates passing an object to a function by making a copy that is processed by the function. Such a scheme of passing objects by copying them was presented earlier in Figure 3.14.

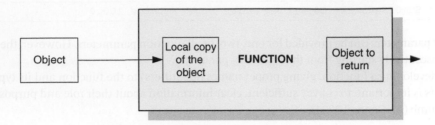

Figure 3.16 Visualization of passing an object to a function by copying.

The same thing happens to every object declared to be passed this way: it is copied. Also, if a function declares a return object, a temporary object of the declared type is created and returned. With this information, let's look at an example. First, in Listing 3.11, we define a constant `kPi` representing the value of π.

Listing 3.11 Context of passing copies of objects to and from a function (in *CppBookCode*, *Functions.cpp*)

```
1   // Let's define an external constant pi
2   const double kPi { 3.14159265 };
```

Our first version of `Deg_2_Rad` accepts an input object (variable) `deg`, which lets us pass floating-point values because it is defined as a `double`. Additionally, the `const` keyword means we do not allow any changes to `deg` inside the function: we want this variable to be *read-only*. We also protect ourselves from errors that could arise from inadvertent changes when using `deg`. This is important especially when writing larger and more complicated functions.

```
3    // Converts degs to radians.
4    // Pass "deg" by a copy
5    double Deg_2_Rad( const double deg )
6    {
7      // Whatever happens to deg here
8      // has an effect only here
9      return kPi * deg / 180.0;
10   }
```

The only computation is performed in a single line [9]. To obtain radians, the value of `deg` is multiplied by `kPi` and divided by 180.0. The result, in the form of a temporary object of type `double`, is then passed outside the function via the `return` statement. Thus to fully understand what happens when we call a function and pass objects to and from it, it is necessary to analyze its calling context, as shown in the following code snippet:

```
11    double d { 0.0 };      // holds degrees
12
13    cout << "Enter degs: ";
14    cin >> d;
15
16    double r { 0.0 };      // here we'll store radians
17
18    r = Deg_2_Rad( d );      // call Deg_2_Rad, d won't be affected
19
20    cout << d << " degs = " << r << " rad" << endl;
```

On lines [11–14], we create and initialize a variable d, print a message, and wait for the user to enter a value for d. Then, on line [16], a variable r, also of type double, is created and initialized. On line [18], Deg_2_Rad is called with d as its parameter. The value returned by Deg_2_Rad is then copied to r. Finally, degrees and radians are shown on line [20]. We introduce the variable r here to aid in understanding the example; but in practice, if r is not used afterward, the code can be simplified by calling Deg_2_Rad in the expression and displaying its returned temporary object with the computed value of radians, as follows:

```
21    cout << d << " degs = " << Deg_2_Rad( d ) << " rad" << endl;
```

Passing objects by copying is sometimes referred to as *value semantics*, as opposed to *reference and pointer semantics*, which assume indirect access to objects, as discussed in the following sections.

3.14.2.2   Indirect Argument Passing by Reference

References were discussed in Section 3.11 as a general technique of providing indirect access to objects. Passing an object to a function with a *left reference* means the object is not copied and only a reference to it is provided, as shown in Figure 3.17. On the other hand, *right references* allow for the application of move semantics to objects, which means an exchange (swap) of data between objects takes place. Interestingly, there is also a hybrid approach: the *forward reference* (also known as a *universal reference*). In this section, we will focus mostly on object passing using left references. The other types of references are discussed in Section 4.6.4.

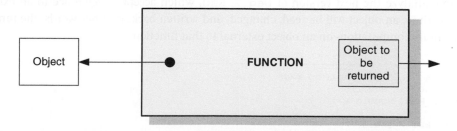

Figure 3.17 Visualization of passing an object to a function by a reference (C++ only).

Since objects are frequently quite large, avoiding copies can save significant time and memory. Even more important, indirect access allows a function *to make changes to an external object* through the references to it. Thus the results of a function operation do not vanish after we return from that function.

The code in Listing 3.12 shows a version of the `Deg_2_Rad` function with a reference parameter `deg` that provides access to an object somewhere outside this function.

Listing 3.12 Context of indirect object passing by reference (in *CppBookCode, Functions.cpp*).

```
22   // The same action but indirect access
23   // by a const reference.
24   // In C++ we can use the same function names
25   // provided that their params are different (overloading)
26   double Deg_2_Rad( const double & deg )
27   {
28       // deg is a reference to an object
29       // defined outside Deg_2_Rad;
30       // deg can only be read since it is const reference
31       return kPi * deg / 180.0;    // the same formula as before
32   }
```

It is important to notice that `deg` on line [26] is a constant reference to an object of type `double`. This means such an object can only be read and cannot be changed via this reference. (A version with a reference that allows both reading and writing is discussed later.) Interestingly, the rest of `Deg_2_Rad` is exactly the same as the version that passes a copy of the input object, discussed in the previous section. Thus its calling context is also exactly the same as the one we saw on lines [11–20], so it is not repeated here.

Also notice that the returned object is still passed as a copy, since it must be alive and accessible after the function finishes, destroying all its local objects. This explains why we cannot pass a reference to a local object as a return object – such an object will be destroyed after the function exits, so a reference would point at a dangling object and lead to destructive behavior if used in subsequent lines of code.

Finally, note that we have two functions with exactly the same name – `Deg_2_Rad` – operating in the same scope. In C++, this is fine and is called *function overloading*. The only requirement is that the functions' lists of formal parameters are different, to allow the compiler to make an unambiguous choice in a given context. We will return to this important issue in Section 3.14.5.

Let's now analyze the next version of `Deg_2_Rad`, which accepts a reference to an external object. This time, an object will be read, changed, and written back. In other words, the function will perform its computations on an object external to that function.

```
33   // Converts "val" from degs to rads in place
34   // Works but can surprise ...
35   void Deg_2_Rad( double & val )
36   {
37       val *= kPi / 180.0;
38   }
```

Note that on line [35], a non-`const` reference `val` to a `double` object is passed. Also, this function does not return a value, so the `void` keyword is used at the front of its declarator. In this version, the code is different as well – `val` only needs to be multiplied by a constant `kPi` / `180.0`. For better readability, we left it as a division of two values – no need to worry, because the compiler will cope with them for us.

With this new version of `Deg_2_Rad`, we also need a different calling context, as presented in the following code:

```
39   double d { 0.0 };      // holds degrees
40
41   cout << "Enter degs: ";
42   cin >> d;
43
44   double d_storage = d;      // here we'll store degrees for later
45
46   Deg_2_Rad( d ); // call Deg_2_Rad, d will be changed (!)
47
48   cout << d_storage << " degs = " << d << " rad" << endl;
```

Since `Deg_2_Rad` will change the value of its supplied object d, to store an original value of degrees we have to use an auxiliary variable `d_storage`, which is defined and initialized with d on line [44]. Then, on line [46], the function `Deg_2_Rad` is invoked, which converts the value of d from degrees to radians. Finally, on line [48], values in degrees and radians are shown.

Note that such a call, which changes the value of its passed object, can be surprising if not well documented. Having a passed value be stealthily changed by a function can lead to programming errors. Although in many cases this technique is justified, in this case, a version with an object passed with a constant reference as on line [26] would be preferable.

3.14.2.3 (✗) Passing by Pointer

To complete the picture of indirect object access, let's present a version of `Deg_2_Rad` that takes a pointer to an external `double` object containing a value of degrees to be converted to radians. See Listing 3.13.

Listing 3.13 Context of indirect object passing with a pointer (in *CppBookCode, Functions.cpp*).

```
49   // An indirect version with a pointer. (The only way in old C)
50   // deg must be a valid pointer.
51   void Deg_2_Rad( double * deg )
52   {
53      // should we check whether deg is not nullptr?
54      assert( deg != nullptr );
55
56      * deg = kPi * * deg / 180.0;
57
58      deg = nullptr;      // deg is a local pointer - we can zero it here
59                          // but nothing happens to the outside object
60   }
```

On line [51], an object deg of type pointer to double (`double *`) is declared. It is supposed to point at an external object of type `double`. However, an immediate difference between a pointer and references is that a pointer can be empty, i.e. its value can be `nullptr` (or simply 0 if converted to an integer). If this is the case, the pointer cannot be dereferenced, since doing so would mean an inevitable program crash. On the other hand, constantly checking for a valid pointer will negatively affect performance; so in this case, we specify that the function can be called only with a valid pointer, and we guard this assumption with the assert function on line [54] (which is active only in the project's debug mode). All of the computations are performed on line [56]. Compared with the previous versions, the main difference is the syntax necessary to access an object through its pointer: * deg. Because of this, the first * denotes multiplication, whereas the second * simply means pointer dereferencing (Section 3.19.1).

An interesting observation is that a pointer by itself, i.e. the object deg on line [51], is passed by a copy of another pointer used in a call of Deg_2_Rad. Thus, deg is a local pointer to the Deg_2_Rad function. To show this, on line [58], we set it to nullptr with no effect, since after the function returns it is destroyed. But these have no effect on an object pointed to by deg. Figure 3.18 illustrates indirect access via pointers.

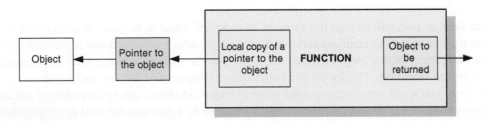

Figure 3.18 Visualization of passing an object to a function by a copy of a pointer to that object.

Finally, the context for calling a pointer-based version of Deg_2_Rad is presented next. It is exactly the same code as in the case of deg passed by a non-const reference defined on line [35]. The only difference is on line [68], where the address of d is taken with the "address of" & operator (see *GROUP 4*, Table 3.15).

```
61    double d { 0.0 };     // holds degrees
62
63    cout << "Enter degs: ";
64    cin >> d;
65
66    double d_storage = d;     // here we'll store radians for later
67
68    Deg_2_Rad( & d );          // call Deg_2_Rad; d will be changed
69
70    cout << d_storage << " degs = " << d << " rad" << endl;
```

We can achieve read-only semantics with a pointer to a const object. Such constructions are common when processing "old" style text, identified via the const char * type (see Appendix A.2.6).

Passing an object by a pointer is the only way to indirectly access objects in C. In C++, passing objects by pointers is avoided, if possible. To some extent, this role has been taken over by references as well as smart pointers (see Section 5.3). The one case where they are still used is when a passed object may not exist. In that case, `nullptr` conveys the information about a missing object. For example, if a parameter is optional to a function, it can be passed this way. Nevertheless, in modern C++, such cases are well managed with `std::optional` objects.

With a simple function, we have seen various ways to pass parameters, with their benefits and drawbacks. These can be easily extended to real cases of functions with many more parameters. However, always consider the context and correctness of the software.

Things to Remember

- Passing by a copy is safe since the function operates on its own copy of an object. However, if the object is "heavy," this might require significant time and memory resources. Also, this approach cannot be used on objects that are forbidden to be copied (Section 4.15.5.1)
- If an object is "heavy" (uses a large amount of memory, or is not allowed to be copied), it should be accessed indirectly:
  - Indirect access to *read* only should be made with a constant reference to an object
  - Indirect access to *read and write* should be made via a non-`const` reference
- Indirect access with pointers should be avoided if possible or used with care
- In addition to objects indirectly accessed via read-and-write access, an object of arbitrary size can be returned by a function as its "return value." However, take care not to return a pointer or reference to an object that does not exist or was just deleted

3.14.3 Function Call Mechanism and Inline Functions

Figure 3.19 depicts various aspects of function calls. Repeated identical code fragments, as shown in Figure 3.19a, can be replaced by calls to a single function located elsewhere in the code space, as shown in Figure 3.19b. In such a case, when the execution unit calls (jumps) to another code fragment, it has to know to what part of the code to return to when it has finished. This is accomplished by saving the return address on the data structure (memory) called the *stack*. When chained function calls take place, the corresponding return addresses are also stored on the stack, as shown in Figure 3.19c. When the innermost function returns, its return address is taken from the top of the stack, and so on. Thus, the stack operates in a *last-in-first-out* (LIFO) fashion. This type of data organization is beneficial for some computations, such as expression parsing. Implementation of the stack data structure is discussed in Section 4.8.4.

When calling functions, input and output objects need to be passed, in addition to the return address. This is commonly accomplished by pushing and then popping data to and from the stack. However, the stack usually occupies a relatively small area of memory, so the number of nested calls, the number of passed objects, and the objects' size need to be limited.

In some cases, instead of calling a function whose code is elsewhere, we may wish to repeat and embed the function code everywhere it is called, as shown in Figure 3.19a. This is known as *function inlining*, and it reduces execution time, especially when there are many calls to a relatively small function. The performance improvement is due to saving on extra call and return instructions, as well as avoiding additional resources such as registers and the stack. Also, contemporary microprocessor architectures provide significant benefits if code and/or data are located in a relatively compact space rather than in interspersed and distant memory spaces (Section 2.1). The way to benefit from fast memory access is to maintain the microprocessor's cache coherency (Patterson and Hennessy 2018).

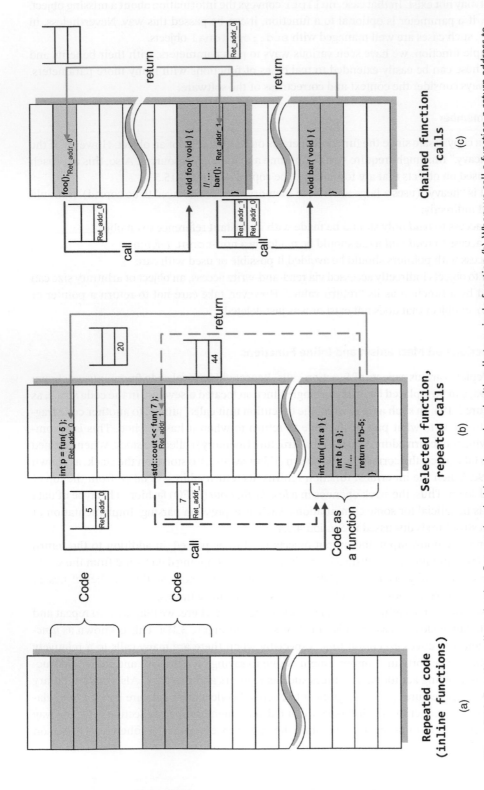

Figure 3.19 Function call mechanism. Repeated code (a) can be replaced with calls to a single function (b). When we call a function, a return address to the place just after the function call has to be stored on the stack. When we return from a call to a function, the return address is popped off the stack. The call parameters, as well as the return objects, can also be passed through the stack (or, on some architectures, via the processor's registers). When chained calls to functions take place (c), the successive return addresses are placed on top of the stack. These are then taken in last-in-first-out (LIFO) order when returning back.

Function inlining can be performed by placing the `inline` keyword just before the function declaration. Also, all functions defined in a class definition are by default the inline type (Section 4.2).

3.14.4 Recursive Functions and the Call Stack

The Fibonacci series follows a simple pattern: the next element is the sum of the two previous elements. So, starting with a pair of values 0, 1, in the first step we obtain 1, then 2, followed by 3, 5, 8, 13, and so on. Following this pattern, in Section 3.13.1 we saw a function that computed consecutive values of the Fibonacci series. But the computations can be performed in a simpler way by using a function that repeatedly calls itself. Such functions are called *recursive*. The most important point when using them is to ensure that after meeting a certain condition, they stop calling. Otherwise, we will quickly run into trouble, including *stack overflow*.

Going into a little mathematics, the Fibonacci series is defined as follows:

$$a_0 = 0$$
$$a_1 = 1$$
$$\ldots \tag{3.3}$$
$$a_n = a_{n-1} + a_{n-2}$$

Such a recursive definition gives rise to an easy recursive implementation, shown in Listing 3.14.

Listing 3.14 Definition of a recursive function (in *CppBookCode, Functions.cpp*).

```
1   // Returns nth element of the Fibonacci series.
2   // Recursive function
3   const int FiboRecursive( const int n )
4   {
5       assert( n < 100 ); // a "fuse" not to overrun the stack
6
7       if( n == 0 || n == 1 )
8           return n;
9       else
10          return FiboRecursive( n - 1 ) + FiboRecursive( n - 2 );
11  }
```

The definition of the `FiboRecursive` function starts on line [3]. The function does not change anything, so its input and output parameters are `const int`. In accordance with formula (3.3), the first two elements of the series need to be treated specially. In the code, this is accomplished by checking the condition on line [7]; if it is fulfilled, we return n. Interestingly, these are our stop conditions for the recursive calls. For values of n larger than 1, on line [10], the recursive part of formula (3.3) is called. As discussed in the previous section, each call to a function is accomplished by placing its parameters on the processor stack alongside the return address. However, such a mechanism, as well as a limited stack size, mean the depth of such chained function calls cannot be indefinite. In practice, they need to be quite small, which in many cases limits applications of recursive functions. Nevertheless, we always have the option to rewrite a recursive function into a non-recursive, but functionally equivalent, version. In our code, to be on the safe side, on line [5] we include a kind of "fuse" in the form of the `assert` function.

The following code to test `FiboRecursive` is straightforward:

```
12   void FiboRecursive_Test( void )
13   {
14       cout << "Enter Fibonacci level: ";
15
16       int fibo {}; // define and init to 0
17       cin >> fibo; // read from the keyboard
18
19       // display it out
20       cout << "Fibonacci at level " << fibo << " is "
21                               << FiboRecursive( fibo ) << endl;
22   }
```

Problems that can be written in the form of a recursive formula, such as factorials, binary search, and the graphical flood fill algorithm, are usually easy to implement this way. But due to the afore-mentioned limitations, in practice, recursive functions are rarely used. The other interesting mechanism is recursive templates (Section 4.8).

3.14.5 Function Overloading – Resolving Visibility with Namespaces

Unlike C, where functions are resolved only by name, in C++ what counts is the function name along with *all* of its parameters from the function's formal parameter list. As a result, in C++, *functions can have the same name*, providing their parameters differ in at least one type so they can be uniquely distinguished. However, even if the function types differ, there can be ambiguity between functions. The compiler choosing a function unexpected by the programmer is a source of stealthy errors. This is one of the reasons C++ has *namespaces*. In this section, we will see how they can be used to uniquely resolve function names.

Let's look back at the two versions of the function `Deg_2_Rad`, as defined in Sections 3.14.2.1 and 3.14.2.2:

```
double Deg_2_Rad( const double deg );
```

```
double Deg_2_Rad( const double & deg );
```

These are overloaded versions that can be put together in one file. However, a problem arises if we try to call one of them, as in the following line:

```
r = Deg_2_Rad( d );     // call Deg_2_Rad, d won't be affected
```

(The full context can be seen around line [18] in Section 3.14.2.1.) Such a call will result in a compiler error complaining about the ambiguous choice of `Deg_2_Rad`. This happens since, to the compiler, the choices of calling with a value, as in the first version, and calling with a constant reference are equally good in this context. To our rescue come namespaces, as outlined in Listing 3.15.

Listing 3.15 Resolving function name clashes with namespaces (in *CppBookCode, Functions.cpp*).

```
1   namespace Deg_2_Rad_Val
2   {
3
4       // Converts degs to radians.
5       // Pass "deg" by a copy
6       double Deg_2_Rad( const double deg )
7       {
8           // Whatever happens to deg here
9           // has an effect only here
10          return kPi * deg / 180.0;
11      }
12
13  }
```

The first version of Deg_2_Rad is enclosed in the Deg_2_Rad_Val namespace (notice that there is no semicolon at the end of the namespace).

```
14  namespace Deg_2_Rad_Ref
15  {
16
17      // The same action but indirect access
18      // by a const reference.
19      // In C++ we can use the same function names
20      // provided that their params are different (overloading)
21      double Deg_2_Rad( const double & deg )
22      {
23          // deg is a reference to an object
24          // defined outside Deg_2_Rad;
25          // deg can be only read since it is const reference
26          return kPi * deg / 180.0;    // the same formula as before
27      }
28
29  }
```

The second version of Deg_2_Rad, i.e. the one that accepts const double &, is in the Deg_2_Rad_Ref namespace. Finally, calling the two functions looks like this:

```
30  // Function call examples
31  void FunctionCallTest( void )
32  {
33      {
34          double d = 0;    // holds degrees
35
36          cout << "Enter degs: ";
37          cin >> d;
38
39          double r = 0;    // here we'll store radians
40
41          r = Deg_2_Rad_Val::Deg_2_Rad( d );    // call Deg_2_Rad, d won't be affected
42
43          cout << d << " degs = " << r << " rad" << endl;
44      }
45
46      // ----------------
47
48      {
49          double d = 0;    // holds degrees
```

```
50
51          cout << "Enter degs: ";
52          cin >> d;
53

54          double r = 0;      // here we'll store radians
55
56          r = Deg_2_Rad_Ref::Deg_2_Rad( d );      // call Deg_2_Rad, d won't be affected
57
58          cout << d << " degs = " << r << " rad" << endl;
59      }
60  }
```

This time, each call to the `Deg_2_Rad` function is preceded with a namespace and the scope resolution operator `::`, as shown on lines [41] and [56] and as presented in Section 2.4.3. The `::` operator belongs to *GROUP 1* of the C++ operators (Table 3.15). Also note that thanks to the new scopes introduced by blocks [33–44] and [48–59], enclosed between braces { }, we can have objects with the same names that are local within their scope.

The technique of guarding functions inside namespace(s) is very powerful and useful. It is used in libraries, such as SL and Boost. In some cases, it can be considered as an alternative to classes, especially those that contain only functions but no, or a limited number, of data members (no state). This methodology is used in many projects presented in this book: for example, see Section 3.18.

3.14.6 Lambda Functions

Lambda expressions, also called *lambda functions*, let us write function code in the form of an expression, rather than a function definition, as discussed previously. Let's start with a simple example enclosed in `SimpleLambda_TestFun`; see Listing 3.16.

Listing 3.16 Definition and call of a simple lambda function (in *CppBookCode*, *Functions_Lambdas.cpp*).

```
1   #include <iostream>
2
3   using namespace std;   // Open the whole std since we use many objects in this source
4
5   void SimpleLambda_TestFun( void )
6   {
7
8       // This is the lambda closure
9       auto cm_2_in =
10          // This is the lambda expression
11          [] ( const double cm ) { return 2.54 * cm; };
12
13
14      cout << "Enter cm: ";
15
16      double val {};
17      cin >> val;
18
19      // Call lambda expression
20      cout << " = " << cm_2_in( val ) << " in" << endl;
21
22  }
```

Before we get down to the code analysis, notice on line [3] the `using namespace std` construction. It opens the entire standard namespace of all standard headers that have been included in the currently compiled software, i.e. the *translation unit*. As a result, the `std::` prefix can be omitted from the standard functions and classes. A downside is that a name clash can occur if there is already a function or a class with the same name as one in the opened namespace. So, the previous construction *should be avoided,* especially in header files. This means the `std::` prefix should be explicitly used, especially if doing so does not diminish code readability. An alternative, also used in the majority of our examples, is to literally introduce each construction that we wish to use without the `std::` prefix, such as `using std::cout`, `using std::string`, etc. Nevertheless, it is sometimes justified to open the entire `std` or other namespace in a source file (*.cpp*) that uses dozens of functions and classes from that namespace, if potential name clashes are well controlled (as in *Functions_Lambdas.cpp*, only a small fragment of which is shown in Listing 3.16). Our primary goal should be *software correctness,* and this and other rules should be chosen with care and applied only if they support this primary objective.

Our first lambda expression (a lambda function) is written entirely on line [11] in Listing 3.16. Compared with a "classical" function definition, instead of a name, it has a pair of square brackets: `[]`. Then, in parentheses, we see the definition of a formal parameter cm, followed by the function body in braces `{}`. Its role is simple – take the parameter cm, expressing centimeters, and convert it to inches by multiplying by 2.54. We mentioned that the lambda expression has no name; in many cases, there is no need to give a lambda a name. However, when necessary, the entire lambda expression can be assigned to an object, such as in our example on line [9]. This is a *lambda closure object,* which lets us make further references to that expression, such as the call on line [20]. Note, however, that there is no way to declare a type for this lambda closure object except using the `auto` keyword. At the end of this section, we will look further at this feature.

As shown in Figure 3.20, lambda expressions are composed of the following parts:

- *Caption* – Introduces external objects into the scope of the lambda
- *Formal arguments list* – A list of types and names defining formal arguments, as in any other function
- *Optional return type* – The `->` operator followed by the type of the returned object
- *Lambda body* – A set of statements and expressions, including `return`, contained within braces `{}`

Each lambda includes a runtime object, called *a lambda closure.* If a lambda expression is attached to an identifier, it can be used to pass a function, like any other object, or to store it in an

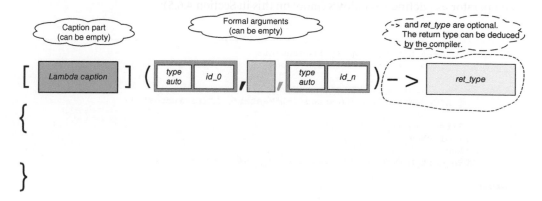

Figure 3.20 Lambda expressions are composed of three parts: caption, formal arguments list, and optional return type. The lambda body is contained within braces `{}`.

Listing 3.17 Implementation of a database to store participants in SCUBA classes (in *CppBookCode, Functions_Lambdas.cpp*).

```
1    // SCUBA class student information
2    struct StudentInfo
3    {
4        wstring    fFirstName;  // will be automatically initialized to
5        wstring    fFamilyName; // empty wide strings
6
7        int        fAge {};        // {} denotes a default initialization to 0
8
9        enum class SCUBA_Cert { kOpenWater, kAdvanced, kMaster, kInstructor };
10
11       SCUBA_Cert fCert { SCUBA_Cert::kOpenWater }; // init to kOpenWater
12   };
```

array, for instance. But lambdas are especially useful for specifying unnamed code to be passed to other functions.

Let's consider the example shown in Listing 3.17, in which we will build a simple database of people attending SCUBA classes. First, we define a simple `struct` containing four data members.

`StudentInfo` is similar to the structures presented in Section 3.9. The new construction, however, is the enumerated `SCUBA_Cert` type, defined on line [9]. We already presented enumerated types in Section (13.3.1). However, `SCUBA_Cert` is a *scoped enumerated* type. This means that to use numerated constants, such as `kOpenWater`, we have to use the fully qualified name `SCUBA_Cert::kOpenWater`, and so on. The benefits of the scoped enumerated types include the following:

- Safety, because we are less likely to confuse strongly scoped names
- Safety, because scoped enums are strongly typed. This means that to convert them to other types, such as `int`, we have to use the `static_cast` operator (Table 3.15, *Group 2*)
- More safety and flexibility, because we can explicitly specify the underlying type for the `enum`. So, for example, if we wish to use `unsigned char` for this purpose, we write `enum class SCUBA_Cert : unsigned char { };`

We also need a function to print out the data members of the `StudentInfo` structure. Instead of writing a `PrintAll` function, in C++ there is a common framework in the form of the overloaded operator `<<`, defined as follows (more on this in Section 4.6.5):

```
13   // We need to tell how to display StudentInfo
14   wostream & operator << ( wostream & o, const StudentInfo & s )
15   {
16       const vector< wstring > SCUBA_Cert_Names
                 { L"OpenWater", L"Advanced", L"Master", L"Instructor" };
17
18       o << s.fFirstName << L" ";
19       o << s.fFamilyName << L", ";
20       o << s.fAge << L" ";
21       o << SCUBA_Cert_Names[ static_cast< size_t >( s.fCert ) ] << L" ";
22
23       return o;
24   }
```

Lines [18–20] should be straightforward, considering that the parameter `o` can represent any stream, such as `std::cout`, as well as an open file or a network port. To print out human-readable information, on line [21], text defined in the vector from line [16] is output.

Now we create a simple database with information about a few people taking a SCUBA diving course. This is represented by a vector named `SCUBA_Class`, containing `StudentInfo` objects:

```
25    // Let us create a SCUBA class
26    vector< StudentInfo >    SCUBA_Class {
27
28        { L"Phil", L"Curtis",      18,    StudentInfo::SCUBA_Cert::kAdvanced },
29        { L"Kamil", L"Cyganek",     15,    StudentInfo::SCUBA_Cert::kOpenWater },
30        { L"John", L"Kowalski",     23,    StudentInfo::SCUBA_Cert::kOpenWater },
31        { L"Michal", L"Brajta",     61,    StudentInfo ::SCUBA_Cert ::kInstructor },
32        { L"Anna", L"McLaghlan",    18,    StudentInfo::SCUBA_Cert ::kAdvanced },
33        { L"Bog", L"Cyganek",       49,    StudentInfo::SCUBA_Cert ::kInstructor },
34        { L"Megan", L"Plant",       26,    StudentInfo::SCUBA_Cert::kMaster }
35
36    };
```

Finally, in the following `SCUBA_Course` function, we display information about SCUBA students who fulfill certain conditions. First, the `SCUBA_Class` vector is sorted with the `std::sort` function, invoked on lines [43–44]. Since each `StudentInfo` object contains many data fields, we need to tell `sort` which one should be used for sorting. This is accomplished by providing `sort` with the lambda function defined on line [44]. It takes two constant references to `StudentInfo` objects and returns the Boolean value of a lexicographical comparison of `fFamilyName` strings. This does not require any further intervention since the compiler already "knows" how to compare strings. Then, on lines [47–48], the sorted vector is copied to the screen with the `std::copy` function (see Table 3.6).

Similar sorting and printing is done in the next few lines [54–59] of the function. However, this time we sort by `fAge`. Also, the `auto` keyword is used to automatically deduce the object types.

Finally, on line [65], `std::copy_if` is called: it outputs only those objects for which the `fCert` field is identical to the externally supplied `cert` object. This checking is done by another lambda function, defined on line [67]. However, unlike the two previous lambdas, this one uses a `copy` caption to bring `cert` into its scope:

```
37    void SCUBA_Course( void )
38    {
39        wcout << endl << L"Sorted by family name:" << endl;
40
41        // --------------------
42        // Sort by family name
43        sort( SCUBA_Class.begin(), SCUBA_Class.end(),
44            [] ( const StudentInfo & a, const StudentInfo & b )
            { return a.fFamilyName < b.fFamilyName; } );
45
46        // Print them on the screen
47        copy( SCUBA_Class.begin(), SCUBA_Class.end(),
48            ostream_iterator< StudentInfo, wchar_t >( wcout, L"\n" ) );
49
50        wcout << endl << L"Sorted by age:" << endl;
51
52        // -----------
53        // Sort by age
```

```
54    sort( SCUBA_Class.begin(), SCUBA_Class.end(),
55        [] ( const auto & a, const auto & b )
      { return a.fAge < b.fAge; } );
56
57    // Print them on the screen
58    copy( SCUBA_Class.begin(), SCUBA_Class.end(),
59        ostream_iterator< StudentInfo, wchar_t >( wcout, L"\n" ) );
60
61    wcout << endl << L"Instructors in the group:" << endl;
62
63    // Find all with a given certificate
64    const auto cert = StudentInfo::SCUBA_Cert::kInstructor;
65    copy_if( SCUBA_Class.begin(), SCUBA_Class.end(),
66        // [ cert ] caption to access a copy of cert
67        ostream_iterator< StudentInfo, wchar_t >( wcout, L"\n" ),
          [ cert ] ( const auto & a ) { return a.fCert == cert; } );
68
69    wcout << endl << endl;
70  }
```

When run, the program prints the following information about the SCUBA class:

```
Sorted by family name:
Michal Brajta,    61       Instructor
Phil Curtis,      18       Advanced
Kamil Cyganek,    15       OpenWater
Bog Cyganek,      49       Instructor
John Kowalski,    23       OpenWater
Anna McLaghlan,   18       Advanced
Megan Plant,      26       Master

Sorted by age:
Kamil Cyganek,    15       OpenWater
Phil Curtis,      18       Advanced
Anna McLaghlan,   18       Advanced
John Kowalski,    23       OpenWater
Megan Plant,      26       Master
Bog Cyganek,      49       Instructor
Michal Brajta,    61       Instructor

Instructors in the group:
Bog Cyganek,      49       Instructor
Michal Brajta,    61       Instructor
```

What have we learned in this example?

- Lambda functions can be captioned by copy and by reference
- A simple `StudentInfo` structure holds personal information with the scoped, enumerated type `SCUBA_Cert`
- An overloaded stream insertion `operator <<` for `StudentInfo`
- The functions `std::sort` and `std::copy_if` from SL with supplied lambda functions and different captions

3.14.7 (✂) More on Lambda Functions

When using a lambda, it is very important is to properly specify the type of its caption. Examples of lambdas with different captions and various call conditions are shown in Table 3.10.

Table 3.10 Lambda captions with examples.

Caption	Meaning	Examples
[]	No object is captured.	```
vector< int > vec;

// Insert 10 random values into vec
generate_n(back_inserter(vec), 10, rand);

// Print only if element is less than 100
copy_if(vec.begin(), vec.end(), ostream_iterator< int >(cout, " "),
        [] (auto x) { return x < 100; });
```

The previous code creates a vector with a few random values. Then, values less than 100 are output to the screen by using the `std::copy_if` function, which allows for an extra lambda to check a user-supplied condition. The lambda does not capture anything from the surrounding scope. |
| [=]<br>[a]<br>**[cpy=a]** | Capture by value:<br>1. Capture all objects by copy (by value). This opens access to all local objects from the lambda's outer scope.<br>2. A better way is to explicitly specify what local objects we wish to access, as in the second version.<br><br>Capture object a by copy:<br>3. Init capture. The third version creates a local copy cpy of an object a, exclusively for the lambda (generalized lambda capture, C++14).<br><br>Objects passed by value are immutable: i.e. they can only be read, not written to. | A common task for system administrators is to add new users and send them initial passwords. The following code performs this task: it generates passwords composed of eight randomly chosen characters from three groups of symbols. The generated passwords are not guaranteed to be unique; our intention is only to show a simple example of a few lambda functions.<br><br>```
 1   // Generate random identifiers
 2
 3   // Chars used to generate passwords
 4   const vector< string > rand_strings =
 5   { "ABCDEFGHIJKLMNOPQRSTUVWXYZ",
 6     "abcdefghijklmnopqrstuvwxyz",
 7     "0123456789_@&#"
 8   };
 9
10
11   std::srand( time( 0 ) );     // seed random generator
``` |

(Continued)

Table 3.10 (continued)

Caption	Meaning	Examples
| | | ```
12    // Generated value can be from 0 .. max_val-1
13    // We could use default caption [=] to access RAND_MAX;
14    // However, a better way is to create a local copy rm
15    // via the "init capture" (generalized captures).
16    // -> int to explicitly convert return value from double to int
17    auto rand_index = [ rm = RAND_MAX ] ( const int max_val ) -> int
18    {
19
20        return  static_cast< double >(std::rand()*max_val)// static_cast to make
21                / static_cast< double >( rm + 1 );         // division on double
22    };
23
``` |
| | Capture by reference: | ```
24    // Let's generate a few example passwords ...
25    const int kPswdToGenerate { 10 };
26    for( int cnt = kPswdToGenerate; cnt > 0; cnt -- )
27    {
``` |
| [&] | 1. Capture all local objects by reference. This opens access to all local objects in the lambda. Capture by reference is potentially risky since a lambda expression can outlive its parameters. In such a case, the lambda may attempt to access a dangling pointer or reference. Thus, a safer way is to create copies of passed objects. | ```
28
29        string pwd;
30
31        // Insert kPasswordLen random chars via lambda function
32        const int kPasswordLen = 8;
33        generate_n ( back_inserter( pwd ), kPasswordLen,
34
35        //  -------------------------------------------------
36        // Use lambda which calls another lambda passed by reference
37
``` |
| [&a] | 2. Explicitly specify exactly what local objects needs to be accessed (safer). Capture object a by reference. | |
```

Caption	Meaning	Examples

```
38        // However, avoid default [&]
39        [ & rand_strings, & rand_index ] ()
40        {
41            const auto & s = rand_strings[ rand_index( rand_strings.size() ) ];
42            return s[ rand_index( s.size() ) ];
43        }
44        // ----------------------------------------
45        );
46
47        cout << "Proposed password: " << pwd << endl;
48    }
```

Lines [4–8] define a vector rand_strings containing three strings with character sets. This is to promote passwords that contain a mixture of uppercase and lowercase letters, as well as digits and symbols such as # and @. These will be used to generate a password. Since we wish to be terse, the rand and seed functions are used to initiate and generate random numbers. However, a better choice is to use one of the new random number generators, such as the one presented in Section 3.17.3.

Our first lambda expression is defined on lines [18–22] and assigned to the rand_index identifier (a closure). It utilizes the init capture, copying a global constant RAND_MAX to the variable rm, which is local exclusively to that lambda. The formal parameter max_val defines the maximum value that can be generated by this lambda. Finally, a return value is explicitly defined by the -> int part of the definition. This ensures that the floating-point value is explicitly cast to the integer type, since this lambda is used to generate random integer indices. Due to the applied float to integer type conversion, the function can generate values in the range 0 ... max_val-1, inclusive. Then a loop is formed that generates a few example random passwords, each with eight characters.

The main password generation is performed by the generate_n function from the SL library. Its first argument back_inserter(pwd) tells the function to insert new elements at the end of the pwd string of length kPasswordLen, which is the second argument of this function. The most interesting parameter of generate_n is the third, which is a second lambda function defined on lines [39–43]; it performs two random draws.

(Continued)

Table 3.10 (continued)

Caption	Meaning	Examples
		This time we use a caption [& rand_strings , & rand_index], explicitly providing the named objects rand_strings and rand_index. Interestingly, rand_index is the previously defined lambda closure object, since it will be used by this lambda. Also interesting is that this lambda does not take any arguments in its argument list, so it is left empty. As mentioned earlier, there are two random actions. The first, on line [41], selects one of the three strings in the rand_strings container. From the selected string, on line [42], a random character is selected that is returned to the generate_n algorithm. As a result, a series of randomly generated eight-character strings is obtained. The output of the previous code looks like the following (it will vary for each run):
		``` Proposed password: eb#V#V4k Proposed password: ZzCxV_K8 Proposed password: 12Js6@3A ```

[...]	Capture with a variadic template.	This example is a little advanced, but it can be used in practice (templates are discussed in Section 4.8). Here we will create a template function multi_print_helper that accepts any number of parameters, which will be output to the output stream. It can be used as a diagnostic tool, for example, as will be shown.
		
		``
		61 // First function in the series
		62 template < typename T >
		63 auto & multi_print_helper(ostream & o, const string sep, const T & val)
		64 {
		65 o << val << sep;
		66 return o;
		67 }
		68
		69 // A template function accepting an arbitrary number of parameters
		70 template < typename T, typename ... Args >
		71 auto & multi_print_helper(ostream & o, const string sep, const T & val,
		     Args... args)
		72 {
		73 o << val << sep;
		74
		75 // Recursively call
		76 return multi_print_helper(o, sep, args...);
		77 }
		``

Caption	Meaning	Examples
		To define a variadic template function, we need two versions of that function: the startup version defined on lines [62–67], and the version with the template parameter pack Args, defined on lines [70–77]. This structure follows the recursive call type that happens on line [76]. Hence, at the end of the recursion, the startup version ends the call chain.

```
78   void multi_print_helper_test( void )
79   {
80       // Make a log file
81       ofstream log_file( "log_file.txt" );
82
83       // A helper variadic lambda that joins multi_print_helper with the log file
84       auto diagnostic_print = [ & log = log_file ] ( auto... params ) -> ostream &
85       {   // Each output separate with " ", then add end-of-line
86           return multi_print_helper( log, " ", params ... ) << endl;
87       };
88
89
90       int x { 1 }; double y { 2.0 }; string z { "three" };
91
92       // Output objects of arbitrary type to the log file
93       diagnostic_print( x, y, z );
94
95       diagnostic_print( x, y, z, "Text", x == y, 5.0 );
96   }
```

The multi_print_helper_test function shows a use context for the variadic template multi_print_helper function. However, since we wish to redirect output to the diagnostic file created on line [81], a helper lambda with variadic parameters is introduced on lines [84–87]. The only action it performs, on line [86], is to call multi_print_helper with properly organized parameters. Finally, the previous lambda is called on lines [93] and [95], each time with a different number of input parameters of arbitrary types. Finally, the content of the *log_file.txt* looks like the following:

```
1 2 three
1 2 three Text 0 5
```

Lambdas can mix object access types in their captions. Some examples are included in the following table:

Lambda caption variants			
`[a,&b]`	Capture object `a` by copy (value), `b` by reference	`[&,a]`	Capture all by reference except `a`, which is captured by copy
`[=,&a]`	Capture all by copy, but object `a` by reference	`[&,this]`	Capture all objects by reference but `this` by copy (`this` can only be accessed by copy)
`[a, this]`	Capture `a` and the `this` pointer (see Section 4.4).	`[this, ...]`	Capture the `this` pointer and variadic template

As alluded to previously, an interesting thing about lambda expressions is that the only way to declare their type is to use the `auto` keyword. This is because each lambda expression has a unique and unnamed type (the type of its associated closure object). However, the lambda expression can be converted (cast) to a pointer to a function (discussed in the next section) that has the same formal parameters and the same return type. In this case, rather than using a raw function pointer, a better idea is to use `std::function` (see Section 3.14.9).

Lambda functions are constant objects. This means they cannot change the values of the objects passed in their captions. However, declaring them `mutable` will allow for such changes; see Section 7.4.7.

3.14.8 (✂) Function Pointers

Sometimes we need to pass a function as an argument to another function, or include it as a member in a structure. Sometimes a function provider wants a function to be called when an event occurs – this is called *a callback mechanism*. There are many options to deal with such situations. The lowest-level one, available in C/C++, is a simple function pointer. Its syntax is shown in Figure 3.21: it follows the function declaration pattern, except that the function name is replaced by `(*` *function_ptr_name*`)`, where *function_ptr_name* is simply an identifier of a function pointer.

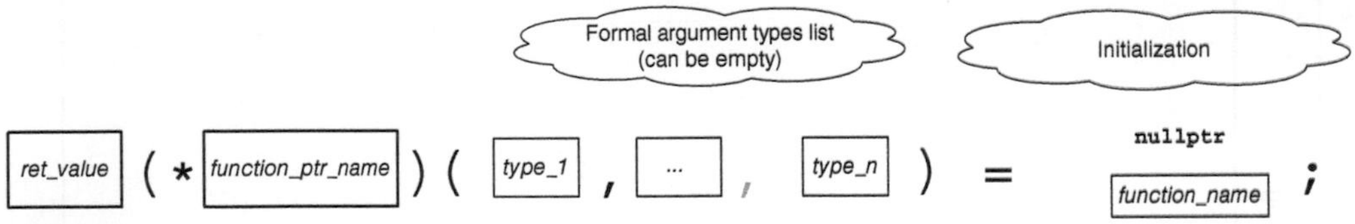

Figure 3.21 Syntax of a function pointer.

In the following example, we wish to write a short program to compute a function derivative at a single point. Before we start, let's recall some mathematics. For a given continuous function f, its derivative f' is defined as follows (Korn and Korn 2000)

$$f'(x) = \lim_{\delta \to 0} \frac{f(x+\delta) - f(x)}{\delta} \tag{3.4}$$

where δ is a parameter. For sufficiently low values of δ, the previous equation can be approximated as follows (Press et al. 2007):

$$f'(x) \approx \frac{f(x+\varepsilon) - f(x)}{\varepsilon} \qquad (3.5)$$

The previous formula gives us a practical method for computing f', given f and x and choosing ε. In practice, the latter is set as a small value, but large enough compared to the computer's precision to avoid excessive rounding errors (Section 7.4).

The `deriv` function follows Eq. (3.5):

```
1    double deriv( double ( * f ) ( double ), double x, double eps = 1e-5 )
2    {
3        // Let us use the definition of a derivative
4        return ( f( x + eps ) - f( x ) ) / eps;
5    }
```

To allow computations for any function, a function pointer of type `double (*) ( double )` is supplied on line [1] as the first argument of `deriv`. The next two arguments are a point x, at which we compute the derivative, and (obviously) the parameter `eps`. All of the computations take place on line [4], where a function, supplied by a pointer `f`, is called as if it were an ordinary function name.

Now we are able to compute real values. Let's choose an interesting function $f(x)=x^x$, which can be easily coded as the following `pow_x_2_x`:

```
6    double pow_x_2_x( double x )
7    {
8        return pow( x, x );
9    }
```

We can compute the derivative of the previous function at a given point value. The necessary computations are performed in the following `deriv_test_fun` function:

```
10   void deriv_test_fun( void )
11   {
12       double x = 1.3;
13       cout << "x2x'(x=1.3)" << deriv( pow_x_2_x, x ) << endl;
14   }
```

An interesting thing happens on line [13]: the `deriv` function takes as its first argument a function pointer that is simply the name of a function – `pow_x_2_x`, in this case. This works only under the condition that the formal and return parameters of the function and the function pointer agree. Hence it is important to remember that:

- The function name *itself* is a pointer to that function (i.e. its code)

This sometimes leads to unexpected errors. For example, the following code

```
deriv_test_fun;
```

will compile, but it does nothing, while we expected a function call. Instead, we should write[17]

```
deriv_test_fun();
```

In the previous section, we said that one of the main differences between C and C++ structures is that we cannot include functions in C structures (Section 9.1). True? Not exactly, since function pointers can be used in a `struct`, providing a way of calling a function. However, these functions need to be defined elsewhere in the global space, which is something we avoid doing.

3.14.9 (⚒) Functions in an Object-Oriented Framework

In an object-oriented framework, more often than not, functions are members of classes. Moreover, some of them can be overridden in derived classes to adjust their behavior (see Section 4.11).

There are also classes especially devoted to representing a function – these are called *functors* or *functional objects*, i.e. classes with an overloaded function call `operator ()`. Details of functional objects will be presented in Section 6.1. However, we have already seen them, since lambdas, discussed in Section 3.14.6, are examples of function objects (although they are special).

C++ also offers much more than bare function pointers. In SL, there is the `std::function` template classes, which lets us wrap almost any callable object, such as those already mentioned. Listing 3.18 shows how `std::function` can be used instead of the simple function pointer discussed in the previous section.

Listing 3.18 Function and function derivatives represented with `std::function`. Examples of computing function values and their derivatives (in *CppBookCode, Pointers.cpp*).

```
1   using Real_Fun = std::function< double( double ) >;
2
3   // Derivative is also a 1D real function
4   auto deriv( const Real_Fun & fun, double x0, double eps = 1e-5 )
5   {
6       // Let us use the definition of a derivative
7       return ( fun( x0 + eps ) - fun( x0 ) ) / eps;
8   }
```

On line [1], a type alias `Real_Fun` is declared as a `std::function`, which accepts all forms of functions that accept one argument of type `double` and return a result, also of type `double`. `deriv` is the first function we define on line [4] of this code fragment. On line [7], it computes a derivative of any function passed as its first argument `fun` of type `Real_Fun` (a type alias).

There are two more functions. The first, defined on line [10], simply computes the square root of its argument x. Actually, it is defined as a lambda expression, as discussed in Section 3.14.6. The second function, defined in the usual way on line [13], computes a compound call on line [15] to two other mathematical functions `pow` and `tanh` (declared in the `cmath` header).

```
9   // Define a square function (lambda expression)
10  Real_Fun x2_fun = [] ( double x ) { return pow( x, 2.0 ); };
11
12  // Define a compound function ("normal" function definition)
```

17 The compiler will warn us, saying something like *function call missing argument list*. So, it is always a good idea to check all compiler warnings and eliminate them.

```
13    double fun_tan( double x )
14    {
15       return tanh( pow( x, 3.0 ) );
16    }
```

On line [21], a few vector< double > objects are created, which are empty at first. These are filled in the for loop, starting on line [22]. It traverses the range of −3.0 to +3.0 values, using the range object. Its operation is intuitive. However, to better understand its structure, more information on object-oriented programming (OOP) is required, as provided in the following chapters of this book. Specifically, the range class is presented in Section 6.5. The older version of for would work here as well, but writing this is left as an exercise.

```
17    void deriv_test_fun( void )
18    {
19
20       // Fill vectors with arguments, value of x2_fun, derivatives of the two functions
21       vector< double > x, fx, dfx_1, dfx_2, d2fx;
22       for( auto arg : range( -3.0, +3.0, 0.1 ) )
23       {
24          x.      push_back( arg );
25          fx.     push_back( x2_fun( arg ) );
26          dfx_1. push_back( deriv( x2_fun, arg ) );
27          dfx_2. push_back( deriv( fun_tan, arg ) );
28       }
```

On lines [24–27] of the deriv_test_fun function, the vector objects are filled with the arguments, values of x2_fun, and the results of two calls to the deriv function. In this case, it is interesting to observe that the first arguments of deriv in the calls on line [26] and [27] are functions defined in different ways, as alluded to previously. However, a uniform call interface is possible thanks to the application of std::function.

```
29       // Store results in one file
30       ofstream outFile( "x_fun_plot.txt" );
31
32       // Copy each vector to the outFile
33       copy( x.begin(), x.end(), ostream_iterator< double >( outFile, " " ) );
34       outFile << endl;
35       copy( fx.begin(), fx.end(), ostream_iterator< double >( outFile, " " ) );
36       outFile << endl;
37       copy( dfx_1.begin(), dfx_1.end(), ostream_iterator< double >(outFile, " " ) );
38       outFile << endl;
39       copy( dfx_2.begin(), dfx_2.end(), ostream_iterator< double >(outFile, " " ) );
40       outFile << endl;
41    }
```

On line [30], an output file object is created. Starting from line [33], this file is used to stream out all vectors with computed function values. Writing to a stream is accomplished with the std::copy function (Section 3.8). Two iterators to the beginning and end of the input sequence are provided as its arguments, as well as to the beginning of the output sequence. However, the latter is provided by the `ostream_iterator` attached to the `outFile` object. As a result, each vector's data goes to that file, rather than to a data collection in memory.

Figure 3.22 shows a plot of the values stored in the *x_fun_plot.txt* file generated by the code from Listing 3.18.[18]

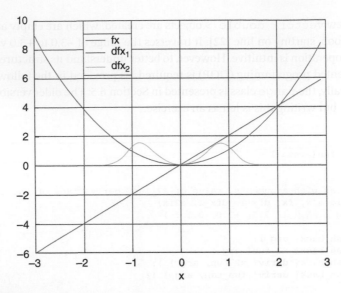

Figure 3.22 Plot of the functions generated with the code fragment from Listing 3.18. For the x^2 function (blue) we easily identify its $2x$ derivative (red). We also see that a point at the minimum of x^2 coincides with its derivative $2x$ crossing 0. The derivative of $tanh(x^3)$ is shown in yellow.

As we will soon see, `std::function` can also be used to store functional objects. Indeed, lambda functions are a kind of functional object.

3.15 Example Project – Wrapping Objects in a Structure with a Constructor

In Section 3.5, we showed how to define a matrix with the help of the `std::vector` class. We used classes and their instantiations, which we call objects. For example, in

```
RealMatrix   m;
```

`RealMatrix` denotes a type, whereas m is an object of this type. We have also seen the ways in which `RealMatrix` can be used in computations. But in some cases, the `RealMatrix` interface may not be satisfactory. For example, a drawback is the lack of a flexible method of initialization to a predefined size. Also, it is possible to have rows of different sizes, which would lead to weird matrices.

In this section, you will learn:

- How to put a matrix in a structure and add a constructor function for its initialization
- How to write basic algorithms on matrices, such as matrix addition and multiplication

---

18 There are many libraries for graphics and plots, such as GnuPlot (*www.gnuplot.info*) . See also Appendix A.4.

We will show how to make a *class* with data and functions in order to facilitate the use of `RealMatrix`. But first, we will make something slightly simpler – *a structure with a constructor* and a few helper *member functions*. In C++, both classes and structures can contain data and functions.[19] As alluded to previously, a structure behaves exactly like a class but with all of its members publicly accessible. This means whatever is in a structure can be read and written at will. This is not a desirable feature in OOP in general, but we will remedy this later. At this point, we wish to have something simple, useful, and ready for basic computations.

The definition of our structure `EMatrix` (which stands for "easy matrix") extends through lines [3–25] in Listing 3.19. It contains only one data member: the object `fData` on line [6] of the familiar type `RealMatrix`.

Listing 3.19 Definition of the `EMatrix` structure that wraps a `RealMatrix` object and adds a constructor (in green) for easy initialization; and two member functions (in *EasyMatrix, EMatrix.h*).

```
1    // EMatrix is a wrapper to RealMatrix.
2    // A role of a wrapper is to facilitate some actions.
3    struct EMatrix
4    {
5
6        RealMatrix fData; // data structure
7
8
9        // A parametric constructor
10       // rows, cols - number of rows and columns of a matrix (should be > 0)
11       // initVal - an initial value of elements of a matrix
12       EMatrix( Dim rows, Dim cols, DataType initVal = 0.0 )
13           : fData( rows, RealVec( cols, initVal ) )
14       {
15           // matrix == a vector of vectors of double
16           assert( cols > 0 );
17           assert( rows > 0 );
18       }
19
20
21       // Helpers
22       auto GetCols( void ) const { return fData[ 0 ].size(); }
23       auto GetRows( void ) const { return fData.size(); }
24
25   };
```

In addition to the data member, `EMatrix` contains member functions. The most specific is the first one, `EMatrix`, which accepts up to three parameters. Its name is the same as that of the entire structure; this is a characteristic feature of functions called *constructors*. These are *special functions*, which are called automatically when an object is created. This is the first feature from the realm of OOP. In other words, when an `EMatrix` object is created, its constructor function `EMatrix` is called. As shown on line [12], it expects three arguments, one of which has assigned a default value. These are easily identified as the number of rows and columns. The last provides an initial value to be set for all elements of the matrix.

An interesting construction follows on line [13]: after the semicolon `:` in *the constructor initialization list*, the member object `fData` is called with two parameters. You may think, how is it

---

19 In C, `struct` can contain only data and function pointers, but no function definitions (see Appendix A.2.3).

possible to "call" an object? The answer is that this is a function. What is called is a constructor of fData. Since it is of class std::vector, this constructor expects as its first argument the number of elements, and the second parameter is an initial value for these elements (see Table 3.4). In this case, the number of elements is the number of rows. However, the initial value is an example row – therefore, the object RealVec(cols, initVal) is provided as an initial value as a kind of a prototype. After that, on lines [14–18], the body of the EMatrix constructor-function follows. It is almost empty, though. The only two lines [16–17] are occupied by calls to assert functions. As we already know, these are special fuse-like functions that are usually active only in the *debug* version of software. Their role is to check the correctness of constructions or, as in this case, of passed parameters. In our EMatrix constructor, we require both dimensions to be larger than 0. This is to verify whether the passed dimensions of a matrix are greater than 0, since, although possible, a matrix of size 0 is not well-defined. However, if someone mistakenly tries to create EMatrix by providing 0 as its dimension, the program is stopped, a message is shown, and we can check the reason in the debugger window. This is a good way to control the behavior of our code in the testing stage.

Certainly, the requirement that the dimensions of a matrix be greater than 0 can be relaxed. As already mentioned, this is a mathematical, rather than a programming, constraint. For example, by adding default parameters to the EMatrix constructor, as follows

```
12    EMatrix( Dim rows = 0, Dim cols = 0, DataType initVal = 0.0 )
```

a constructor is obtained that can be called without providing any arguments – this is *a default constructor*. And as mentioned in Section 3.9, if data can be initialized with only { }, a constructor can be omitted. We will see many examples in future sections.

Moreover, the requirement to always pass dimensions during object construction has a consequence – an object does not have a default means of construction (i.e. without any additional parameters). In other words, explicitly defining the parametric constructor suppresses the automatic generation of a default constructor by the compiler. The lack of a default constructor imposes limitations on an object, as we will discuss.

Another design question is whether to allow or disallow changes to a matrix's dimensions after it has been created. We have to make such design decisions quite often. They should be thoroughly analyzed, taking the consequences into consideration; and, even more important, they should be well commented in the code.

Returning to the definition of EMatrix, notice that there are two more member functions – GetCols on line [22] and GetRows on line [23] – that return the number of columns and rows in EMatrix. The operation of these functions should be clear by now, since in previous sections we discussed how to access the dimensions of a RealMatrix. However, two things that deserve explanation. First is the return type, which here is defined with auto. We could use Dim, but using auto is more versatile, as we will show many times. Second is the keyword const. Declaring functions const means the function has no intention of changing any member data (state).

Since EMatrix contains fData and extends its functionality, this construction is an object *wrapper* or an *adapter* design pattern (Gamma et al. 1994). We will see this ubiquitous and useful construction in many examples in this book (Section 4.8.4).

Things to Remember

- Data member initialization in a struct (class) can be performed with a constructor that belongs to the group of *special member functions*

- A constructor that can be called without any argument is called a *default* constructor
- A constructor that takes arguments is called a *parametric* constructor
- Initialization of the data members in a constructor should be performed in *the constructor initialization list*, i.e. after the colon : and before the constructor body
- Data members are always initialized in the order in which they are declared in the class definition, so they also should be written in that order in the constructor initialization list
- Adding a parametric constructor to a struct (class) will suppress the automatic generation of the default constructor by the compiler (and other special members)

3.15.1 *EMatrix* in an Object-Oriented Environment

`EMatrix` was defined with the help of `struct`, which implies that all of its data and member functions are widely accessible and can be freely called from any `EMatrix` object.

```
1  struct EMatrix
2  {
3
4      RealMatrix fData; // data structure
```

The equivalent with the `class` keyword is as follows:

```
1  class EMatrix
2  {
3    public:
4      RealMatrix fData; // data structure
```

Since `class` assumes all members to be private, adding the `public` keyword makes all data members and function members wide open, as is the case with `struct`. But obtaining the same functionality, just with different keywords, is not interesting. What *is* interesting is using OOP paradigms in our designs. The current version of `EMatrix` is close to being in the OO domain. To enter that domain, though, we at least need to make data private and add member functions. In Section 4.7, we will practice re-making `EMatrix` in the OO domain. Such changes to enhance the code's features and quality are called *code refactoring* (Fowler 1999).

3.15.2 Basic Operations with *EMatrix*

Having defined `EMatrix`, let's do some matrix computations, as shown in Listing 3.20. On lines [12–19], we print instructions to the user. On line [22], an object `matrix_1` with dimensions 3×4 is created. This invokes the `EMatrix` constructor, which we discussed in the previous section. As a result, we can be sure that all matrix elements are set to zero.

Instead of writing all the computation steps in one big function, it is almost always better to organize the code into a number of specialized functions. Therefore, to enter and print matrix data, we use the `AskUserForMatrixData` and `ShowMatrix` functions. Similarly, `MultMatrix` performs matrix multiplication. To call them, we only need to provide their declarations, such as the ones on lines [4–6]. This way, we can use them now and postpone their full definitions until later in the code.

Listing 3.20 Definition of the `Easy_Matrix_Second_Test` function with examples of using `EMatrix` to define, initialize, and multiply matrices (in *EasyMatrix, EMTest.cpp*).

```cpp
1    // To use a function we only need to provide its declaration.
2    // However, to make a full program, function definitions must
3    // be added in some of the source files.
4    void       AskUserForMatrixData( EMatrix & m );
5    void       ShowMatrix( const EMatrix & m );
6    EMatrix    MultMatrix( const EMatrix & a, const EMatrix & b );
7
8
9    // Here we show how to use EMatrix
10   void Easy_Matrix_Second_Test( void )
11   {
12       std::cout << "-----------------------------------------------" << std::endl;
13       std::cout << "In this example we will:" << std::endl;
14       std::cout << "* Create a 3x4 matrix M1 (you will enter its data)" << std::endl;
15       std::cout << "* Print M1" << std::endl;
16       std::cout << "* Create a 4x2 matrix M2 (you will enter its data)" << std::endl;
17       std::cout << "* Print M2" << std::endl;
18       std::cout << "* Compute and print a product M1 * M2" << std::endl;
19       std::cout << "-----------------------------------------------" << std::endl;
20
21
22       EMatrix    matrix_1( 3, 4 );
23       AskUserForMatrixData( matrix_1 );
24
25       std::cout << "You've just entered M1 - is it correct?" << std::endl;
26       ShowMatrix( matrix_1 );
27
28
29       EMatrix    matrix_2( 4, 2 );
30       AskUserForMatrixData( matrix_2 );
31
32       std::cout << "You've just entered M2 - is it correct?" << std::endl;
33       ShowMatrix( matrix_2 );
34
35
36       std::cout << "The matrix product of M1 * M2 is:" << std::endl;
37       ShowMatrix( MultMatrix( matrix_1, matrix_2 ) );
38   }
```

On line [23], the `AskUserForMatrixData` function is called to let the user enter values for the elements of `matrix_1` from the keyboard . To verify its contents, `matrix_1` is printed out on the screen by the `ShowMatrix` function, invoked on line [26].

Similarly, on lines [29–33], the `matrix_2`, this time with dimensions 4×2, is acquired and shown. Finally, the product of the two matrices is computed and immediately shown on line [37] by successive calls to the `MultMatrix` and `ShowMatrix` functions. More precisely, `MultMatrix` returns a temporary `EMatrix` object that is taken by `ShowMatrix` as its argument, which is then shown. As we know from matrix algebra, their product is a 3×2 matrix. We will return to the details of these computations shortly.

Note that of these functions, only `AskUserForMatrixData` changes the matrix passed to it. For this purpose, its argument is declared as a reference to an `EMatrix` object: that is, as `EMatrix &`. The other two functions only read values from their passed `EMatrix` arguments. Therefore, these are declared as constant references: `const EMatrix &`. This way, the passed objects are safe (immutable), since no changes to them are allowed. Passing by reference has been chosen for two reasons. In the case of `AskUserForMatrixData`, it is necessary since we want the passed matrix object's original values to be overwritten. Hence, passing by value is not an option, since the original values would stay intact. For the two other functions, passing by reference saves time. Object copies that were passed by value would also work well. However, creating copies of relatively large objects is an obvious waste of resources. The ways to pass objects to and from functions are discussed in Section 3.14.2.

3.15.3 Input and Output Operations on *EMatrix*

As alluded to previously, we postponed the definitions of functions that perform specific actions on `EMatrix` objects. In this section, we will analyze the two functions, `AskUserForMatrixData` and `ShowMatrix`, to read in and display matrix values.

The `AskUserForMatrixData` function is defined on lines [3-18] of Listing 3.21. It is always a good idea to include information explaining the function's action, as well as the roles of its parameters; a few comment lines are sufficient in this case.

Listing 3.21 Definition of the `AskUserForMatrixData` function to read values for a matrix m from the keyboard (in *EasyMatrix*, *EMUtility.cpp*).

```
1    // Ask the user to enter values for matrix m
2    // from the keyboard.
3    void AskUserForMatrixData( EMatrix & m )
4    {
5       const Dim kCols = m.GetCols();
6       const Dim kRows = m.GetRows();
7
8       for( Dim r = 0; r < kRows; ++ r )
9       {
10         std::cout << "Enter data for row no. " << r << " of " << kRows << std::endl;
11         for( Dim c = 0; c < kCols; ++ c )
12         {
13            std::cout << c << ": ";
14            std::cin >> m.fData[ r ][ c ];  // read a value from the keyboard
15         }
16      }
17      std::cout << std::endl; // new line again
18   }
```

Lines [5–6] read the number of columns and rows of the input object m. These are stored in two constant values `kCols` and `kRows`, which will be used as delimiters when accessing elements of m. `Dim` is a type designated to index elements of vectors and matrices, as declared in Listing 3.4.

Since a matrix is two dimensional, to access its elements we need two program loops that iterate over its rows and columns. For this purpose, the first `for` loop that traverses the matrix rows commences on line [8]. All the statements on lines [9–16] are repeated with a variable (iterator) r that takes values from 0 to kRows − 1. After each iteration, r is incremented by 1 by ++ r. On line [10], we display a message to the user, indicating the row number we are about to enter.

The second, nested `for` loop starts on line [11]. It performs two operations between the braces on lines [12–15]. First, on line [13], it prints text indicating the column number. Then, line [14], expects a read from the keyboard. The value entered by the user is assigned to the matrix element at position r, c. This is accomplished by a number of calls. First, `m.fData` finds the `fData` member of object m. This can be done with no problem, since fData is a publicly available member of EMatrix in Listing 3.19, as we know. Then, m.fData[r] accesses the rth row. Finally, m.fData[r][c] accesses the cth element in the rth row. Simple. However, it would be much easier if we could directly write m[r][c]: that is, with no explicit access to the fData member. Why isn't it possible? Because EMatrix does not have the subscript [] operator defined. Later, in Section 4.7, we will see how we can achieve this functionality as well.

The following ShowMatrix function has a simpler task: displaying the matrix data on the screen.

```
19   // Prints contents of a matrix m on the screen
20   void ShowMatrix( const EMatrix & m )
21   {
22       for( const auto & row : m.fData )        // go row-by-row
23       {
24           for( const auto & data : row )       // go through the data in a single row
25               std::cout << data << "\t";       // separate data with tab
26
27           std::cout << std::endl;              // print new line
28       }
29       std::cout << std::endl;                  // new line again
30   }
```

This function also has two for loops to traverse and display the elements of the matrix passed to it as a constant reference m. However, this time we show newer versions of the loops. The first one, on line [22], traverses each row of m.fData. This is done with const auto &, which defines a constant reference row. In successive iterations, row will refer to consecutive rows of m.fData. As discussed in Section 3.7, auto is a special keyword that lets the compiler automatically deduce the type of an object, if possible; auto by itself would assume that row was a copy of a row from m.fData. As we know, copies are expensive, so we decided to use a reference by using auto &. Since we only wish to read data, we finally used const auto &.

The second for on line [24] accesses the elements of a single row passed from the first for. The access is done by a constant reference data, again defined with const auto &. This way, retrieved elements of m are shown one by one on line [25]. At the end, note the symbols \t. This is the *escape sequence* that adds one horizontal tab to the output stream. Recall the \n sequence, which add a new line (NL) code.

Why do we use two different versions of the for statement in these two functions? AskUserForMatrixData uses the classical version with an iterator, because we also want to print each row and column number for the user. On the other hand, in ShowMatrix, we do not need to count the matrix indices, so the auto versions are faster to type and use. Thus the version of for depends on the context. Nevertheless, it is easy to write both functions with the opposite versions of for (this is left as an exercise).

Soon we will see more general input/output functions for matrices, which can operate in a more uniform fashion with any data stream, not only to the screen or keyboard. These are overloaded streaming operators, which are presented in Section 4.7.

3.15.4 Basic Mathematical Operations on *EMatrix*

In this section, we will analyze two functions: one to add and the second to multiply matrices represented with the EMatrix type. In Listing 3.22, the AddMatrix function on line [4] accepts two constant references a and b to access external EMatrix objects to be added together. As we know, to add two matrices, their dimensions must be the same; this condition is verified with `assert`. If the dimensions agree, then on line [9], an output matrix c is created and immediately initialized with data from the first matrix a. This is possible since the compiler will assume that only data member c.fData needs to be copied from the a.fData member. Moreover, this operation will be performed automatically, since – as we remember – these are `std::vector` objects that know how to copy from each other. This explains what is happening inside the code, although a detailed explanation of the copy and move constructors is left until Section 4.4.

Listing 3.22 Definition of functions for basic matrix operations (in *EasyMatrix*, *EMUtility.cpp*).

```
1    // Add two matrices, return the result:
2    // c = a + b
3    // Dimensions of a and b must be the same.
4    EMatrix    AddMatrix( const EMatrix & a, const EMatrix & b )
5    {
6        assert( a.GetRows() == b.GetRows() );     // dim must be the same
7        assert( a.GetCols() == b.GetCols() );
8
9        EMatrix c { a };     // Make c the same as a
10
11       for( Dim row = 0; row < b.GetRows(); ++ row )
12           for( Dim col = 0; col < b.GetCols(); ++ col )
13               c.fData[ row ][ col ] += b.fData[ row ][ col ];
14
15       return c;
16   }
```

Adding matrices requires two `for` loops, as shown on lines [11, 12]. These traverse the rows and columns of fData exactly as in the `AskUserForMatrixData` function. On line [13], the elements of the b matrix are added to the corresponding elements of c using the += operator. Writing x += y is the same as x = x + y, as explained for the *GROUP 15* operators (Table 3.15). Object c is finally returned on line [15].

Let's have a brief refresher on matrix multiplication. As an example, consider the following two matrices **A** and **B**:

$$\mathbf{A}_{2\times3} = \begin{bmatrix} 1 & 0 & -5 \\ 7 & 12 & 0 \end{bmatrix}, \mathbf{B}_{3\times3} = \begin{bmatrix} 0 & -1 & 4.5 \\ 2.2 & 0 & 3 \\ 3 & 5 & 0 \end{bmatrix}, \tag{3.6}$$

These matrices can be multiplied as follows:

$$\mathbf{A}_{2\times3} \rightarrow \begin{bmatrix} 1 & 0 & -5 \\ 7 & 12 & 0 \end{bmatrix} \quad \begin{bmatrix} 0 & -1 & 4.5 \\ 2.2 & 0 & 3 \\ 3 & 5 & 0 \end{bmatrix} \leftarrow \mathbf{B}_{3\times3} \\ \begin{bmatrix} -15 & -26 & 4.5 \\ 26.4 & -7 & 67.5 \end{bmatrix} \leftarrow \mathbf{A}_{2\times3} \cdot \mathbf{B}_{3\times3} \tag{3.7}$$

We arranged the matrices to show that matrix multiplication relies on multiplying each row of the first matrix by each column of the second matrix – therefore these dimensions must be the same. The corresponding elements are multiplied together, and these products are added to yield the final result, which goes in the output matrix at the row-column position. For instance, multiplying the first row by the first column goes like this: $1 \cdot 0 + 0 \cdot 2.2 + (-5) \cdot 3 = -15$.

Armed with this knowledge, we are ready to write the code in Listing 3.23. The function MultMatrix for matrix multiplication is defined on line [20]. Again, it expects two EMatrix objects representing real matrices, passed by constant references a and b. But unlike matrix addition, matrix multiplication requires the number of columns of a be the same as the number of rows of b. After reading the numbers of rows and columns on lines [22–26], this condition is checked with assert. Then, on line [30], the return matrix c is created with values explicitly initialized to 0.0 (if not provided, 0 is used anyway).

Listing 3.23 Definition of the matrix multiplication function (part of *EMUtility.cpp*).

```
17    // Multiply two matrices, return the result:
18    // c = a * b
19    // Dimensions of a and b must comply for multiplication
20    EMatrix    MultMatrix( const EMatrix & a, const EMatrix & b )
21    {
22        const auto a_cols = a.GetCols();
23        const auto a_rows = a.GetRows();
24
25        const auto b_cols = b.GetCols();
26        const auto b_rows = b.GetRows();
27
28        assert( a_cols == b_rows );             // Dimensions must be the same
29
30        EMatrix c( a_rows, b_cols, 0.0 );      // Output matrix has such dimensions
31
32        for( Dim ar = 0; ar < a_rows; ++ ar )          // Traverse rows of a
33            for( Dim bc = 0; bc < b_cols; ++ bc )      // Traverse cols of b
34                for( Dim ac = 0; ac < a_cols; ++ ac    // Traverse cols of a == rows of b
35                    c.fData[ ar ][ bc ] += a.fData[ ar ][ ac ] * b.fData[ ac ][ bc ];
36
37        return c;
38    }
```

From the previous example, we discover that matrix multiplication requires three loops: the first iterates through the rows of a, the second through the columns of b, and the third through the columns of a (which must number the same as the rows of b). These three loops are realized on lines [32–34] with for statements. Consecutive sums of products of corresponding elements of a and b are added on line [35] to the corresponding position of matrix c.

Finally, the resulting matrix c is returned on line [37]. Note at this point that c is returned by value,[20] which can involve expensive object copying. This should not be a major problem thanks to the optimization mechanisms discussed in Section 4.6.4.

3.15.5 Organizing the Project Files and Running the Application

The previous code fragments come from the *EasyMatrix* project available from the book's project web page (Cyganek 2018). The definition of the EMatrix structure is placed in the *EMatrix.h* header. Matrix operations are located in the *EMUtility.h* and *EMUtility.cpp* files, and test functions are in

---

20 Returning by reference would be a significant error in this case, as explained in Section 4.5.3.

EMTest.cpp. Finally, *main.cpp* contains calls to the test functions. To visualize the organization of the *EasyMatrix* project, Figure 3.23 shows the UML *artifact diagram* showing the structure of the files.

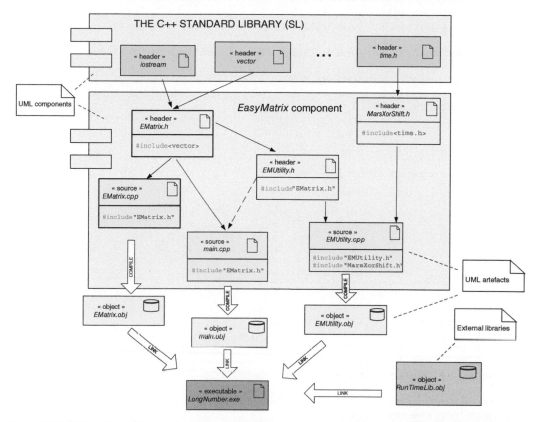

Figure 3.23 UML artifact diagram showing the relations and roles of the files in the *EasyMatrix* project. Code is placed in two types of files: headers and sources. Headers usually contain only declarations and definitions, whereas source files contain full definitions. Sometimes the code is contained in headers (e.g. templates). The source files need to be compiled to generate object files. These contain computer-executable code but usually are not complete. Each separate compilation is performed in a translation unit, i.e. a source with all its #includes. To build a final executable or a library, all object files, as well as external object files and libraries, need to be joined together by the linker. A group of files that constitutes a separate project or library is called a software component (symbols with two rectangles). Comments in UML are in rectangles with a bent upper-right corner.

   Project code is placed in two types of files: headers and sources. Headers usually contain only declarations and definitions. Larger parts of the code, including full function bodies, usually are placed in the source files. Exceptions are template functions and classes, whose code is contained in the headers (Section 4.8.5). The source files need to be compiled to generate the object files. These contain computer-executable code, but it usually is not yet complete (Section 2.1). Each separate compilation is done in a *translation unit*, which contains the source code with all relevant headers included. To build a final executable or a library, all object files, as well as external object files and libraries, need to be joined together. This process is performed by the linker. One of its roles is to find and join objects defined in various translation units. The groups of files that constitute a separate project or a library are called software *components*. In UML, these are represented with the characteristic two rectangles. Comments in UML are placed in rectangles with a bent upper-right corner.

After building and running *EasyMatrix.exe*, the following output appears on the screen:

```
----------------------------------------------------------------
In this example we will:
* Create a 3x4 matrix M1 (you will be asked to enter its data)
* Print M1
* Create a 4x2 matrix M2 (you will be asked to enter its data)
* Print M2
* Compute and print a product M1 * M2
----------------------------------------------------------------
Enter data for row no. 0 of 3
0: 0.00
1: 1.11
2: 2.22
3: 3.33
Enter data for row no. 1 of 3
0: 4.44
1: 5.55
2: 6.66
3: 7.77
Enter data for row no. 2 of 3
0: 8.88
1: 9.99
2: 10.10
3: 11.11

You've just entered M1 - is it correct?
0          1.11      2.22      3.33
4.44       5.55      6.66      7.77
8.88       9.99      10.1      11.11
Enter data for row no. 0 of 4
0: 0.00
1: 1.11
Enter data for row no. 1 of 4
0: 2.22
1: 3.33
Enter data for row no. 2 of 4
0: 4.44
1: 5.55
Enter data for row no. 3 of 4
0: 6.66
1: 7.77
You've just entered M2 - is it correct?
0          1.11
2.22       3.33
4.44       5.55
6.66       7.77
The matrix product of M1 * M2 is:
34.4988 41.8914
93.6396 120.746
141.014 185.503
```

Naturally, the previous results depend on the matrix values entered by the user. Also, you may wonder about the format of the values. In C++, this can be set as well. If you are interested, see Table 3.14.

3.15.6 Extending Matrix Initialization with a Simple Random Number Generator

In this section, we will further explore the idea of joining data using functions under the umbrella of a `struct`. At the same time, we will learn about the following:

- How to implement a simple function to generate random numbers with good random properties
- Object initialization with an initializer list inside `struct/class`
- Bit shifts, XOR, and AND operations with hexadecimal masks

Listing 3.24 shows our `MarsXorShift` structure, which begins on line [9]. On line [12], it contains one data member `r_a_n_d` of `unsigned long` type. On line [16], the `GetNext` function is defined, which on each call will return a random number computed by the *XorShift* algorithm.

Listing 3.24 Definition of the `MarsXorShift` structure implementing a random number generator based on the Marsaglia algorithm (in *EasyMatrix, MarsXorShift.h*).

```
1   // System headers in < >
2   #include <ctime>
3
4
5   // -----------------------------------
6   // A helper simple random number generator
7
8   // Marsaglia's Xorshift random numbers
9   struct MarsXorShift
10  {
11      // Start value - must be different from 0
12      unsigned long r_a_n_d { (unsigned long) time( nullptr ) & 0xFF };
13
14      // These values were found by G. Marsaglia
15      // to generate quite good random values
16      unsigned long GetNext( void )
17      {
18          r_a_n_d ^= r_a_n_d << 13;    // << is bit left shift
19          r_a_n_d ^= r_a_n_d >> 17;    // ^= is XOR-and-assign
20          r_a_n_d ^= r_a_n_d << 5;
21
22          return r_a_n_d;
23      }
24  };
```

The method presented here is based on the *XorShift* algorithm proposed by the American mathematician George Marsaglia (*https://en.wikipedia.org/wiki/Xorshift*). It is a very efficient method that operates by consecutive bit shifts obtained with the << and >> operators, followed by the XOR operator ^, as implemented on lines [18–20]. These operators are further explained in the operator tables for *GROUP 8* and *GROUP 12* (Table 3.15).

`MarsXorShift` does not contain a constructor – see "the rule of zero" in Section 3.9. However, initialization of the `r_a_n_d` member takes place on line [12] with the help of the initializer list in { }. To start with a random value, `time( 0 )` is called, which returns the number of seconds since January 1, 1970 (we talk more about time functions in Section 6.3). This value is cropped to one byte by the bit AND operation & 0xFF. To access this library function, the *ctime* header is included on line [2].

Such a random number generator can be used to assign random values to `EMatrix` objects. This is done by the `RandInit` function, defined on lines [26–32] of Listing 3.25.

Listing 3.25 Definition of the `RandInit` function for matrix initialization with the Marsaglia random number generator object (*MarsXorShift.h*).

```
25    // Does random initialization of a matrix m
26    void RandInit( EMatrix & m )
27    {
28        MarsXorShift randMachine;
29        for( auto & row : m.fData )      // go row-by-row
30            for( auto & data : row )      // go through the data in a single row
31                data = randMachine.GetNext() & 0xFFFF; // cast, type promotion
32    }
```

Again, the input object is passed as a reference m to `EMatrix`. Then, on line [28], the `MarsXorShift` object is created. Thanks to the aforementioned time-based initialization, each call to `RandInit` will generate a different initialization – a desirable feature. Then, two `for` loops are organized on lines [29, 30] to traverse each row, and each element `data` in each row. Since `data` is defined as a reference, assigning a random value to it on line [31] automatically assigns the same value to the `fData` member of the object m. More precisely, to avoid values that are too large, the value is cropped to two bytes by ANDing with the `0xFFFF` mask, and implicitly converted to a `double`.

C++ offers a library to generate random numbers in various distributions (Stroustrup 2013). An example is the `CreateRandomVector` function, presented and discussed in Section 3.17.3, as well as `MathFun_RandTest`, discussed in Section 6.4. However, `MarsXorShift` is probably the fastest; it is also a convenient solution for hardware implementations.

3.16   Example Project – Representing Quadratic Equations

We have already seen how to write functions and structures. In this section, we will design and implement our first class to *represent* quadratic equations of the form

$$a x^2 + b x + c = 0 \tag{3.8}$$

where *a*, *b*, and *c* denote real coefficients. This polynomial, as well as its solution, i.e. finding its roots, were presented in question 4 in Section 2.8. However, in this section, we are primarily interested in the *object-oriented representation* of the equation; its solution is a secondary problem. In Section 3.15, we created the `EMatrix` structure that implements a simple matrix. We noticed that in C++ structures, `EMatrix` can contain both data and functions that manipulate it. However, `EMatrix` grants open access to all of its data and function resources. Such behavior, although justified in some cases, is not desirable in general. First, unrestricted access to data makes it vulnerable to manipulation by external objects. Second, a structure can contain functions that, once implemented, should be called only inside that structure. To meet these requirements, *object-oriented technology* was devised for software design and implementation. One of its main paradigms is *member encapsulation*, as will be further presented in Section 4.1. This means all data and some member functions should be protected from uncontrolled external access. To achieve this goal, in C++ the `private` keyword can be added before a data or function member. To allow external access, i.e. from the object level, the `public` keyword should be used. Such publicly accessible members are called *class interfaces*. If neither of these keywords is used, `struct` treats all of its members as public by default, whereas `class` does the opposite – all of its members are private by default. This is the only difference between them.

Member encapsulation also has a positive effect on design. As mentioned in Section 2.3, in the top-down approach, we are first interested in understanding a system on a coarse scale. Then we focus on the details of each particular system component. Properly designed and implemented classes with well-encapsulated members relieve us from unnecessary bother about details, leaving time to properly connect their interfaces. Nevertheless, member encapsulation demands proper design to hide sensitive data and allow for proper functionality. In this section, we will show how to achieve these goals. We will return to this issue many times: for example, in Section 4.7, when converting the `EMatrix` structure into a fully fledged class.

In this section, we will follow the rules of OOP. To represent quadratic equations, we will design the `TQuadEq` class. Its data and some internally used functions will be declared private. A few functions will be declared public to allow for class functionality such as initializing data members and computing the roots of the equation.

The project's organization will be analogous to that in Figure 3.23. However, we will focus on the OO aspects of writing C++ classes, as follows:

- Class members access rules:
  - Private members declared with the `private` keyword
  - Publicly accessible members declared with the `public` keyword
- Why and how to encapsulate data in a class
- What functions to add to the class to allow easy access to private data
- Proper formation of class constructors
- Design and implementation of the class interface
- Methods and levels of error handling
- Definitions of the overloaded stream insertion `operator <<` and stream extraction `operator >>` for a class

3.16.1 Definition of a Class to Represent Quadratic Polynomials

There is no one best way to design and implement a class. The first step is to identify the principal role of the class, as well as to select its data and member functions. But in programming, many approaches are possible, as well as styles, patterns, naming conventions, and other nuances that come with years of experience. Nevertheless, in many cases it is possible to distinguish characteristic parts of a class, such as those of the `TQuadEq` class shown in Table 3.11.

A more detailed treatment of the arrangement of a class and the roles of its components is left to Section 4.2. However, although `TQuadEq` is simple, it and the following classes can serve as patterns to write your own. The complete code can be obtained after gluing together all of the code fragments from Table 3.11, and the entire project can be downloaded from the book's web page (Cyganek 2018).

Table 3.11 Organization of the TQuadEq class (in *QuadEq, QuadEq.h*).

Class member	Description	Example
| | Data members are objects aggregated in the class. These can be any of the previously introduced types. Data members can be mutable or immutable (constant) objects. | ```
1  #include <iostream>
2  #include <cassert>
3
4  ////////////////////////////////////////////////////
5  // This class implements the quadratic equation of the form:
6  //
7  // a*x*x + b*x + c = 0
8  //
9  ////////////////////////////////////////////////////
``` |
| Class data members | Class data members are usually *hidden from uncontrolled access* by placing them in the `private` area. | ```
10  class TQuadEq
11  {
12      private:
13
14          double fa {}, fb {}, fc {}; // the coefficients of the equation
``` |

On lines [1–2], two SL headers are included: *iostream* for the input/output hierarchy, and *cassert* for the assert macro. The class definition begins on line [11]. On line [13], the `private` area of the class is opened, after which three data members `fa`, `fb`, and `fc`, corresponding to the coefficients of the quadratic equation, are defined and initialized with { } as their zero values.

Class member	Description	Example

Default constructor	A function with the same name as the class and no input parameters:
	
	X::X(void)
	
	Called once during creation of an object. Its role is to initialize *this* object.
	
	The characteristic part just after the colon : and before the constructor's body is the *member data initializer list*. Here the constructors of the data member objects are invoked.
		```17 public:18192021222324252627``` *(see text)*
		
		```17 public:18192021 // class default constructor20 TQuadEq(void) : fa(0.0), fb(0.0), fc(0.0)21 {}22```
		
		On line [17], the public region is opened to enter the class *default constructor* on line [20]. It is the function TQuadEq, which has the same name as the class. Being a default constructor, it does not take any arguments, as indicated with the void keyword. Also, like any constructor, it does not return an object or void.
		
		This constructor is very important and allows e.g. initialization of objects in an array. Just after the closing parenthesis of its argument list, a colon : introduces the *member data initializers*. Since a TQuadEq object is composed of three other objects, fa, fb, and fc, these are initialized by calling their respective constructors: fa (0.0), and so on. This type of initialization is preferred over initialization in the constructor body. Finally, the empty body of the constructor is located on line [21].
		
		If not explicitly written, the default constructor is automatically generated by the compiler. We had to explicitly write it here, since having a parametric constructor suppresses the automatic generation mechanism.

Parametric constructor	A function with the same name as the class and with input parameters: X::X(*type_ list*) Called once during creation of an object. Its role is to initialize *this* object using the objects from *type_list*.	```23 // class parametric constructor24 TQuadEq(double a, double b, double c)25 : fa(a), fb(b), fc(c)26 {}27``` The second constructor of TQuadEq is defined on lines [24–26]. This is a parametric constructor, since it accepts three arguments a, b, and c. These are used to initialize the class data members fa, fb, and fc. Initialization is performed in the constructor initializer list on line [25]. Since data is already initialized, the constructor body on line [26] is empty.

(Continued)

Table 3.11 (continued)

Class member	Description	Example
| | | ```
28
29    public:
30        // Getters & setters
31        double Get_a( void ) const { return fa; }
32        double Get_b( void ) const { return fb; }
33        double Get_c( void ) const { return fc; }
34
35
36        void Set_a( double a ) { fa = a; }
37        void Set_b( double b ) { fb = b; }
38        void Set_c( double c ) { fc = c; }
39
``` |
| Getters / setters | A group of functions to read and write the (usually private) data members of a class. | Getters are commonly called member functions of a class that let us read all or selected data members. In the TQuadEq class, three such functions are defined on lines [31–33] to read the fa, fb, and fc members. Additionally, the functions have the const specifier, which indicates that they will not change the state of the object (i.e. they are read-only). Such a declaration helps ensure safe access to objects and their data. Also, a function whose body is defined in the class definition space is assumed to be an *inline* function (Section 3.14.3). This means the function code is located where it is called. This accelerates performance by minimizing call latency.

Similarly, three setters functions are defined on lines [36–38]. They let us set the respective values of the three data members of TQuadEq. Thus, the setters change the state of the TQuadEq object. |
| Class public interface | Member functions located in the public section of a class are called the class public interface. They provide functionality for calling objects. | ```
40
41    public:
42        // Helper functions to compute the discriminant of the quadratic equation;
43        // This is an inline function (definition of a function in the class)
44        double ComputeDelta( void ) const { return fb * fb - 4.0 * fa * fc; }
45
46        // Define some constants for the class - using the scoped enum type
47        enum class EEqType { kNone, kOne, kTwo, kLinOne, kLinContra };
``` |

Class member	Description	Example
		48
		49 ///
		50 // This function checks type of the equation
		51 ///
		52 //
		53 // INPUT:
		54 // delta
		55 //
		56 // OUTPUT:
		57 // The exact type of the equation
		58 // represented by the parameters f_a, f_b, f_c
		59 //
		60 // REMARKS:
		61 // Separation of problem analysis from
		62 // problem solution
		63 //
		64 EEqType GetNumOfRoots(const double delta) const;
		65
		66 ///
		67 // This function computes the roots of the equation,
		68 // if possible.
		69 ///
		70 //
		71 // INPUT:
		72 // theRoot_1 - a reference to an object that
		73 // contains root 1 if returned kLinOne, kOne, or kTwo
		74 // theRoot_2 - a reference to an object that

(Continued)

Table 3.11 (continued)

Class member	Description	Example
		``
75   //   contains root 2 if returned kOne or kTwo
76   //   (in the first case root_1 == root_2)
77   //
78   // OUTPUT:
79   //   status of the equation (number of roots)
80   //
81   // REMARKS:
82   //   The values referenced by theRoot_1 and theRoot_2
83   //   are undefined in all other cases than stated above.
84   //
85   //
86   EEqType GetRoots(double & theRoot_1, double & theRoot_2) const;
87
88 };
```

Lines [40–88] of the class definition contain public member functions specific to the TQuadEq class.

The inline function ComputeDelta, defined on line [44], returns the discriminant delta of the quadratic equation. On line [47], the EEqType *scoped enumerated* type is defined. It contains definitions of constant values that identify specific types of quadratic equations, which depend on the values of fa, fb, and fc.

The function GetNumOfRoots, declared on line [64], returns a type of equation. On line [86], GetRoots is declared, which computes the roots of the quadratic equation. Both are defined outside of the class definition. |
```

Class member	Description	Example
| Input / output overloaded operators | Most C++ operators can be overloaded (Section 4.4). This boils down to writing an operator-function that defines a specific behavior of an operator for the given class.<br><br>An overloaded operator-function can be a member of a class or a function external to that class. | ```
89
90     ////////////////////////////////////////////////
91     // Input/Output operations (external functions)
92     std::ostream & operator << ( std::ostream & o, const TQuadEq & equation );
93     std::istream & operator >> ( std::istream & i, TQuadEq & equation );
```<br><br>On lines [91–92], outside of the class definition, the overloaded streaming in and out operators are declared. They let us write TQuadEq objects to and from any stream object from the iostream hierarchy, such as the keyboard, the screen, or a file. Their full definitions are in the source file. |
```

3.16.2 *TQuadEq* Member Implementation

As we saw in the previous section, the header file contains a full definition of the TQuadEq class. However, this does not that this class is fully implemented and finished. For longer member functions, to save space, it is a common practice to put only function declarations in the class definition; their implementations are placed in a source file, as shown in Figure 3.23. In such a case, since the definitions are outside of the class scope, the names of the class components need to be preceded with the class name and scope resolution operator `::` (*GROUP 1*, Table 3.15), whose syntax is shown in Figure 2.8.

Listing 3.26 contains the definitions of the TQuadEq members, as well as related streaming functions, excerpted from the *QuadEq.cpp* file, as shown in Figure 3.23.

Listing 3.26 Definitions of some TQuadEq member functions and streaming operators (in *QuadEq, QuadEq.cpp*).

```
1   #include "QuadEq.h"
2   #include <cmath>
3
4
5   //////////////////////////////////////////////////////////
6   // This function checks the type of the equation
7   //////////////////////////////////////////////////////////
8   //
9   // INPUT:
10  //      delta
11  //
12  // OUTPUT:
13  //      An exact type of the equation
14  //          represented by the parameters f_a, f_b, f_c
15  //
16  // REMARKS:
17  //      Separation of the problem analysis from
18  //      the problem solution
19  //
20  TQuadEq::EEqType TQuadEq::GetNumOfRoots( const double delta ) const
21  {
22      if( fa == 0.0 )
23      {
24        return fb == 0.0 ? EEqType::kLinContra : EEqType::kLinOne;
25      }
26      else
27      {
28         if( delta < 0.0 )
29             return EEqType::kNone;
30         else
31             return delta == 0.0 ? EEqType::kOne : EEqType::kTwo;
32      }
33  }
34
35
```

First, on line [1], the *QuadEq.h* header is included to create a complete translation unit containing all necessary definitions. Note that because *QuadEq.h* is a user-created header file, it needs to be provided in quotation marks `""` rather than `<>`, since the latter are used for system headers (Appendix A.1). This is followed by the inclusion of *cmath*, from which the `std::sqrt` function is used. The operations of the functions are explained in comment lines in the code. When developing a project, always maintain self-explaining source files.

The function `GetNumOfRoots` returns a constant of type `EEqType` indicating the type of the quadratic equation, including the number of roots if applicable. Notice that both identifiers are preceded by the class name and the scope operator, i.e. `TQuadEq::`.

```
36    /////////////////////////////////////////////////////////
37    // This function computes the roots of the equation,
38    // if possible.
39    /////////////////////////////////////////////////////////
40    //
41    // INPUT:
42    //      theRoot_1 - a reference to an object which
43    //         contains root 1 if returned kLinOne, kOne, or kTwo
44    //      theRoot_2 - a reference to an object which
45    //         contains root 2 if returned kOne or kTwo
46    //         (in the first case root_1 == root_2)
47    //
48    // OUTPUT:
49    //      status of the equation (number of roots)
50    //
51    // REMARKS:
52    //      The values referenced by theRoot_1 and theRoot_2
53    //      are undefined in all other cases than stated above.
54    //
55    //
56    TQuadEq::EEqType TQuadEq::GetRoots( double & root_1, double & root_2 ) const
57    {
58       auto delta( ComputeDelta() );     // call a constructor for the built-in type
59
60       EEquationType equationTypeFlag = GetNumOfRoots( delta );
61
62       const double kDivThresh { 1e-36 };     // Used in assert to verify divisions
63
64       // It is a good idea to explicitly place ALL the cases here (to be sure)
65       switch( equationTypeFlag )
66       {
67          case EEqType::kLinContra:
68          case EEqType::kNone:
69
70             break;          // if none, then do nothing
71
72          case EEqType::kLinOne:
73
74             assert( fa == 0.0 );
75             assert( std::fabs( fb ) > kDivThresh );
76
77             if( std::fabs( fb ) < kDivThresh )
78                throw std::overflow_error( "Too low fb" );
79
80             root_1 = root_2 = - fc / fb;
81
82             break;          // return with one root
83
84          case EEqType::kOne:
85                           // no break here - for these two cases, one solution
86          case EEqType::kTwo:
87
88             { // We need a block {} here for local variables
89
90                assert( delta >= 0.0 ); // just in case, who knows?
```

```
91
92              double delta_root = std::sqrt( delta );
93
94              double denominator = 2.0 * fa;
95              assert(std::fabs( denominator ) > kDivThresh);
96
97              if( std::fabs( denominator ) < kDivThresh )
98                  throw std::overflow_error( "Too low fa" );
99
100             root_1 = ( - fb - delta_root ) / denominator;
101             root_2 = ( - fb + delta_root ) / denominator;
102          }
103
104          break;
105
106      default :
107
108          assert( false );     // this should not happen - an error in programming?
109          break;
110      }
111
112      return equationTypeFlag;
113  }
114
115
```

GetRoots, defined on line [56], returns the type of the equation, as well as its root or roots, depending on the value of its discriminant, computed on line [58]. Based on its value, on line [60], the number of roots is returned by the GetNumOfRoots function. On line [62], a threshold value is defined that will be used to verify the feasibility of divisions. The switch statement on line [65] determines the processing method. For example, if the equation is not a quadratic equation, as checked on lines [67–68], the function simply exits. Note that the two cases are processed in the same way, since there is no break between them. Similarly, the two cases checked on lines [84, 86], are also processed the same way. The two roots are computed in accordance with formulas (2.6). Note that on line [97], the denominator is checked before the division takes place. If it is smaller than a predefined threshold, an exception is thrown on line [98]. If this happens, the thrown std::overflow_error object should be caught, as described in Section 3.13.2.5. However, if the divisor is large enough, the two roots are computed. Finally, although other options in the switch are not expected, it is a coding practice to include the default branch, as on line [106]. In our implementation, it contains only the assert fuse, followed by the break on line [109]. On line [112], the function returns the type of the equation.

Let's briefly summarize the various methods and levels of error handling and software verification:

1. The assert function is active only in the debug version of the project (Section 3.15). When writing software, we make mistakes; assert, operating as a kind of fuse, greatly facilitates bug removal and software updates during the early stages of software development (see Figure 2.4). In other words, the responsibility of assert is to check conditions that the programmer assumes should be true in all software runs. In a production (release) version, assert is inactive. Until that point, asserts should never fail.

2. If we expect that some conditions cannot be fulfilled in a program flow, a simple if construction should be used, with a proper condition and action. This will be active in all versions of the software.

3. As a last resort, to cope with unexpected errors, we can use the throw operator and the `try-catch` statement.

In the `GetRoots` function, we have all three methods of error handling.

The streaming operators are external to the `TQuadEq` class. The *stream insertion operator* – that is, the overloaded `operator <<`, defined on line [118] – is straightforward: it simply outputs all data members of the `eq` object. The *stream extraction operator* – i.e. the overloaded `operator >>` – is slightly more complicated. Its definition starts on line [124]. At the start, a separate variable `tmp` needs to be created, as on line [126]. It is then used to capture consecutive values coming from the input stream. They are used to initialize the output `eq` object. Note that the two operators *need to be compatible*: they must follow same format for writing and reading.

```
116   /////////////////////////////////////////////////////////////
117   // Input/Output operations (usually as external functions)
118   std::ostream & operator << ( std::ostream & o, const TQuadEq & eq )
119   {
120       o << eq.Get_a() << " " << eq.Get_b() << " " << eq.Get_c() << std::endl;
121       return o;
122   }
123
124   std::istream & operator >> ( std::istream & i, TQuadEq & eq )
125   {
126       double tmp { 0.0 };
127       i >> tmp; eq.Set_a( tmp );
128       i >> tmp; eq.Set_b( tmp );
129       i >> tmp; eq.Set_c( tmp );
130       return i;
131   }
```

As already mentioned, the streaming `operator <<` and `operator >>` are always placed outside the class definition. This is because they join two class hierarchies: `iostream` and the given class (`TQuadEq` in our example). In this case, due to the getter and setter functions of `TQuadEq`, the streaming operators can easily access all of the class's data members for reading and also for writing. If this is not the case, and the operators need to access a class's private data, the streaming operators should be declared as `friend` in the class. We will see examples of this method in Section 3.18.4.

The two streaming operations need to be compatible. That is, the same writing and reading format must be implemented so an object that is streamed out can be fully retrieved by calling the streaming-in operator. Also note that both operators return their stream object (the first argument), to allow operator chaining.

3.16.3 *TQuadEq* in Action

The *main.cpp* source file contains the `main` function. It implements a simple application that reads the coefficients of the quadratic equation from the keyboard, checks its type, and computes the roots of the equation, if possible. Finally, the results are displayed on the screen. All computations are performed using the TQuadEq object, presented in Listing 3.27. The *iostream* header is included on line [1], followed by *QuadEq.h*. This brings TQuadEq into the scope of main.

Listing 3.27 Definition of the main function (in *QuadEq*, *main.cpp*).

```
1   #include <iostream>
2   #include "QuadEq.h"
3
4   using std::cout, std::cerr, std::cin, std::endl; // write cout and not std::cout
5
6   // In C++ there are overloaded main functions
7   int main( void )
8   {
9       // Text corresponding to TQuadEq::EEquationType
10      const string eq_types_text[] = { "No real roots",
11                                       "One real root",
12                                       "Two real roots",
13                                       "Linear equation, one root",
14                                       "A contradictory equation"
15                                     };
16
17      cout << "Enter coeffs of the quadratic equation: a*x*x + b*x + c" << endl;
18      double a = 0.0, b = 0.0, c = 0.0;
19      cin >> a >> b >> c;
20
21      TQuadEq    eq( a, b, c );      // Create an initialized object
22
23      // For the roots
24      double x1 {}, x2 {};          // {} to initialize x1 and x2 to zero
25      TQuadEq::EEqType eq_type {};
26
27      try
28      {
29          eq_type = eq.GetRoots( x1, x2 ); // This can throw
30      }
31      catch( const std::exception & e )
32      {
33          cerr << e.what() << endl; // If here, then error, so print the reason
34          return -1;                // Exit with a failure code
35      }
36
37      // Everything ok, so print results
38      cout << eq_types_text[ eq_type ];
39
40      // In addition, if there are roots, then print them out
41      switch( eq_type )
42      {
43          case TQuadEq::kOne:
44          case TQuadEq::kLinOne:
45              cout << ": " << x1;
46              break;
47
48          case TQuadEq::kTwo:
49              cout << ": " << x1 << ", " << x2;
50              break;
51
52          default :
53              break;
54      }
55
56      return 0; // Exit with ok code
57  }
```

On line [4], the `using` directives introduce common IO objects into the scope. Because of this, instead of writing `std::cout`, we simply write `cout`, and so on. The definition of the `main` function starts on line [7]. Note that in C++ we have a choice of overloaded versions of `main` – in this example, we choose the one that does not take any arguments but returns an integer, which can convey an error code. A more detailed discussion of the various versions of `main` is contained in Section A.2.2.

On lines [10–15], an auxiliary text array is created, which reflects the order of the `EEquationType` constants defined in `TQuadEq`. It will be used as a very simple user interface for the application. On lines [18–19], the three coefficients are read from the keyboard, represented by the `cin` object from the standard library. These are used on line [21] to initialize the `TQuadEq` object `qe`. On line [29], the public member function `GetRoots` is called from the `qe` object, which evaluates the type of the equation and computes the roots, if any.

Since an exception can be thrown on line [29], as described earlier, lines [27, 31] use a `try-catch` statement. If an exception is caught, an error message is printed on line [33] and, on line [34], the function safely exits with an error code.

On line [38], the user's text is printed out. Additional information is output after checking the type of the equation in the `switch` statement on lines [41–54].

After building and launching the *QuadEq* application, the following output is observed:

```
Enter coefficients of the quadratic equation: a*x*x + b*x + c
1.0 5.0 4.0
Two real roots: -4, -1
```

Notice that the three example coefficients were entered on one line, separated by spaces.

3.17 Example Project – Tuples and Structured Bindings for Converting Roman Numerals

In this example, we will develop a C++ program to convert from decimal numbers to Roman numerals. In addition to counting in the Roman system, we will learn about the following C++ techniques:

- `std::tuple` for auxiliary collections of objects of various types
- The `vector` container with `std::tuple< int, string >`, as well how it is initialized with an initializer list
- The structured binding mechanism to access the fields of a tuple
- Using the random number library

Roman numerals are part of a system invented in ancient Roma (Wiki:Roman_numerals 2020). Although they are not very popular these days, in some countries Roman numerals are still used e.g. to express the month in a date. The following 10 numerals form the basis of the Roman system:

1	2	3	4	5	6	7	8	9	10
I	II	III	IV	V	VI	VII	VIII	IX	X

The upper row are the Arabic symbols used in our decimal system. In the lower row are the corresponding Roman numerals. There are additive numerals, such as III, which is composed of I+I+I; and VII, made up of V+I+I. Other digits are represented in a subtractive form: for instance, IV means V − I, which corresponds to $5 - 1 = 4$. This is to avoid such confusing constructions as IIII and VIIII. As a result, in any Roman numeral, a given symbol does not appear more than three times. Summing up, we have three distinct symbols and five distinct settings for symbols. The remaining five settings are obtained by adding multiples of I.

In this example, we will develop a procedure for converting decimal values into Roman numerals. For this purpose, let's supplement the previous table with all the Roman numerals, as follows:

XL	L	XC	C	CD	D	CM	M
40	50	90	100	400	500	900	1000

In addition to the new symbols L, C, D, M, we again see subtractive numbers: XL for 40, XC for 90, CD for 400, and CM for 900. In this basic setup, we do not have additive combinations. Hence, we have 13 different combinations. The converting algorithm is simple: analogous to converting a number such as 1993 into decimal components, all we need to do is find out how many 1000s are in the number, followed by how many 100s are in the remainder, then how may 10s, and finally how many 1s. For Roman numerals the process is similar, but using the values shown in the previous tables. Thus, we check how many 1000s are in the number, and then we check the remainder to see if it contains 900, then 500, then 400, and so on down to 1s. The `ConvertDecimal_2_Roman` function in Listing 3.28 implements this idea using helpful mechanisms in modern C++.

On line [9], the function `ConvertDecimal_2_Roman` is defined. It accepts an integer decimal value, which will be converted into a corresponding `string` representation of the Roman value. The return type of the function, declared using `auto`, is deduced by the type of the returned value on line [29]. On line [12], `vector` is defined, which contains pairs consisting of a value and a string with its corresponding Roman numeral. These pairs are defined as `tuple< int, string >`. A tuple is a relatively new C++ construct, which allows for simple grouping of objects of various types. It is similar to a struct, as discussed in Section 3.9. However, tuples are very flexible and useful in many programming contexts.[21] Also note that the tuples in our example need to be stored in descending order of the `value` parameter. Thus, `vector` is the best-fitting data structure in this case.

An interesting programming construction can be observed on line [25]: a loop whose operation is shown in Figure 3.24. It is a `for` loop (see Section 3.13.2.2) that traverses all of the value-string pairs, represented as `[ val, str ]`, stored in the `RomanValueTranslator` object. Accessing two or more fields of a tuple simultaneously is called *structured binding* (Filipek 2018).

Note that to access a `[ val, str ]` pair, instead of a simple `auto`, we use `const auto &`. As a result, more efficient access with a constant reference is utilized, avoiding the creation of unnecessary copies.

Finally, on lines [26–27], if the remaining value of `in_dec_num` is still larger than the value of the currently processed Roman numeral `val`, it is successively subtracted from `in_dec_num`.

---

21 Its predecessor was `std::pair`, which can join two objects together.

During the same iteration, the corresponding Roman digit, represented by the `str` string, is added to the final `outStr` object.

Listing 3.28 Function to convert decimal numbers to Roman numerals (in *CppBookCode, Dec2Roman.cpp*).

```cpp
#include <iostream>
#include <vector>
#include <string>

using std::cout, std::cin, std::endl;
using std::vector, std::string, std::tuple;

// Converts decimal number in_dec_num into a Roman numeral string
auto ConvertDecimal_2_Roman( int in_dec_num )
{
    // The values need to be sorted from the largest one
    const vector< tuple< int, string > > RomanValueTranslator =
    {
        { 1000, "M" },    { 900, "CM" },
        { 500,  "D" },    { 400, "CD" },
        { 100,  "C" },    { 90,  "XC" },
        { 50,   "L" },    { 40,  "XL" },
        { 10,   "X" },    { 9,   "IX" },
        { 5,    "V" },    { 4,   "IV" },
        { 1,    "I" }
    };

    string outStr { "" };
    // Traverse all tuples [ val, str ], starting from the largest val
    for( const auto & [ val, str ] : RomanValueTranslator ) // structured binding
        while( in_dec_num >= val )                  // iterate subtracting
            outStr += str, in_dec_num -= val; // the largest possible value

    return outStr;
}
```

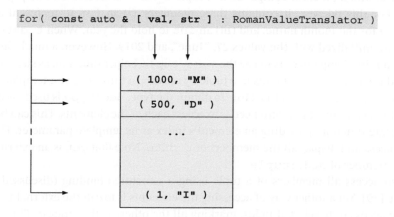

Figure 3.24 Accessing elements of vector< tuple< int, string > > with a structured binding.

For testing, the following `Dec_2_Roman_Test` function calls the conversion function for some decimal values:

```
void Dec_2_Roman_Test( void )
{
  cout << "1593 <=> " << ConvertDecimal_2_Roman( 1593 ) << endl;
  cout << "1968 <=> " << ConvertDecimal_2_Roman( 1968 ) << endl;
  cout << "1999 <=> " << ConvertDecimal_2_Roman( 1999 ) << endl;
  cout << "2008 <=> " << ConvertDecimal_2_Roman( 2008 ) << endl;
}
```

After we launch `Dec_2_Roman_Test`, the following output is displayed on the screen:

```
1593 <=> MDXCIII
1968 <=> MCMLXVIII
1999 <=> MCMXCIX
2008 <=> MMVIII
```

3.17.1 More on `std::tuple` and the Structured Binding

At this point, let's take a closer look at what *tuples* are and how they can be useful in programming. Tuples are ordered collections of data objects that can be of the same or different types. In this respect, their functionality is similar to `struct` (and `class`), discussed in Section 3.9. Tuples, being recently added to the language, are simpler and have specific applications. On the other hand, `struct` and `class` have much more functionality in the context of OOP. Adding the following lines facilitates the use of `std::tuple` in code:

```
#include <tuple>
using std::tuple, std::get, std::tie, std::tuple_size;
using std::cout, std::endl;
// ...
```

Because `struct` is a built-in language construction, it does not need any headers.

Listing 3.29 shows a practical comparison. A tuple `t_date` is created on line [3]: its role is to store a date. For this purpose, it contains three members: (i) an `int` to represent a day, (ii) a `std::string` for the month name, and (iii) an `int` to hold the year. When `t_date` is created, its members are initialized with the values 27, "June", and 2019. However, a much faster method of creating and initializing tuples is to use the `make_tuple` helper function, as shown on line [6].

We can read the number of elements in a tuple by creating a `tuple_size` template, initialized with the tuple's type, as shown on line [10]. To obtain the type, `decltype` is used, as discussed in Section 3.7. However, a more frequent need is to access each of the elements. This can be done with the `get` template function, providing an element's index as its template parameter. Thus on lines [13–15], we access and display all the members of `t_date`. Note that `get` is an external function, rather than a member of `std::tuple`.

We can also access all members of a tuple using a structured binding (discussed earlier), as shown on line [19]. Yet another way of accessing the elements is to call the external `tie` function. This time, we access only selected fields, marking all the others with `ignore`. This way, on line [29], only the day and month are read.

Listing 3.29 Comparison of `std::tuple` and `struct` for date definition (in *CppBookCode, tuple_vs_struct.cpp*).

`std::tuple`	`struct`
`std::tuple` is an ordered collection of unnamed objects of the same or different types. Each can be accessed with the `std::get< N >` function, for read as well as for write, where *N* denotes a zero-based index to the objects in a tuple.	`struct` (as well as `class`) is an ordered collection of named members, which can be data objects of various types, as well as functions. It can also be inherited from. Hence, the application spectrum of `struct` is broad.

```
1   // Let us store a date in a tuple
2   //    day   month   year
3   tuple< int, string, int > t_date( 27, "June", 2019 );
4
5   // It can be easier with make_tuple
6   auto t_date_2 = make_tuple( 27, "June", 2019 );
7
8   // tuple_size<>::value returns the number of elements
9   cout << "t_date has " <<
10  tuple_size< decltype(t_date) >::value << " elems" <<
11  endl;
```

```
1   // The same with struct with no name
2   struct
3   {
4       // Each field has its name
5       int     fDay    { 27 };
6       string  fMonth  { "June" };
7       int     fYear   { 2019 };
8   } s_date;
9
10  // We cannot enumerate a struct,
11  // just provide its field names.
12
```

(Continued)

Listing 3.29 (continued)

std::tuple

```
12    // Print the elements - do not confuse the order
13    cout << "D/M/Y:" << get< 0 >( t_date ) << "/" <<
14                        get< 1 >( t_date ) << "/" <<
15                        get< 2 >( t_date ) << endl;
16
17    // Retrieve the elements to separate objects
18    // with the structured binding
19    const auto [ d, m, y ] = t_date;
20
21    // Print the elements
22    cout << "D/M/Y:" << d << "/" << m << "/" << y << endl;
23
24    // Use tie with ignore to retrieve a few elements
25    int dd {};
26    string mm {};
27
28    // Retrieve only day and month, ignore the year
29    tie( dd, mm, ignore ) = t_date;
30
31    // Print the elements
32    cout << "D/M:" << dd << "/" << mm << endl;
```

struct

```
13    // Print the elements
14    cout << "D/M/Y:" << s_date.fDay << "/" <<
15                        s_date.fMonth << "/" << s_date.fYear << endl;
16
17    // Retrieve the elements to separate objects
18    // with the structured binding
19    const auto [ d, m, y ] = s_date;
20
21    // Print the elements
22    cout << "D/M/Y:" << d << "/" << m << "/" << y << endl;
```

If a tuple has more objects, then accessing them by index can lead to confusion. In our case, the first and last elements are of the same type: `int`. So, writing `t_date( 2019, "June", 27)` on line [3] could confuse the day with the year, since field semantics are assumed.

A similar data structure, this time obtained with `struct`, is shown in the right pane of Listing 3.29. The definition of the unnamed `struct` starts at line [2]. Then, on lines [5–7], the structure's data members, `fDay`, `fMonth`, and `fYear` are defined. Unlike in the tuple, these can be accessed only[22] by providing the name of the object followed by a dot operator (*GROUP 2*, Table 3.15), followed by the member name. Then, on line [8], the `s_date` object is created. Its members are already initialized with the default values provided in their definitions. The data members of `s_date` are accessed and printed to the screen, as shown on lines [14–15]. Interestingly, structural binding also works with `struct`, as shown on lines [19–22].

So, when should we use `std::tuple`, and when should we use `struct`? Here are some hints. Use `std::tuple` when:

- A collection of a few data objects of potentially different types is necessary. Storing too many objects can lead to confusion, since their meaning (semantics) is based on their position in a series
- No stress is laid on naming the data members
- It is fine that all elements are equally accessible to all objects that have access to the tuple
- We want to return multiple objects from a function (see Section 7.4.8)

Use `struct` (`class`) when:

- A collection of data objects with potentially different types is necessary
- Data member objects need to be easily identified by their names (strong semantics)
- Access rights need to be assigned to the members (i.e. `private`, `public`; see Section 4.3)
- Member functions are expected
- Inheritance is expected

But as always, there are cases when the two are equally good choices. And if the objects are of the same type, then `std::vector` or `std::array` can also be considered.

3.17.2 How to Write a Software Unit Test

Even more important than writing code is ensuring that the code executes the way we expect. This can be a tedious task even for short functions, not to mention huge software systems composed of dozens of libraries written over many years, etc. How can we get closer to certainty that our software is working properly? One way is to use *unit tests* – test functions that are embedded in a software testing framework and that run and verify the correctness of the corresponding software components. Some teams even start writing their code from unit tests, before they write any operational code. More information on software testing is provided in Appendix A.7. In this section, we will write a simple test function for our Roman numeral converter; see Listing 3.30.

`ConvertDecimal_2_Roman_UnitTest` checks the number of decimal values and, using `assert`, compares the output of the `ConvertDecimal_2_Roman` function with the corresponding Roman numerals. All must pass to return true. Otherwise, `assert` fires and stops execution. In practice, a more subtle behavior can be more useful, such as an entry to the log file, etc.

---

22 This is a normal, natural, and recommended path, although there are some other tricky techniques with pointers.

Listing 3.30 Unit test function for the decimal to Roman converter (in *CppBookCode*, *Dec2Roman.cpp*).

```
// Unit test for ConvertDecimal_2_Roman
bool ConvertDecimal_2_Roman_UnitTest( void )
{
    assert( ConvertDecimal_2_Roman( 2000 ) == "MM" );
    assert( ConvertDecimal_2_Roman( 137 ) == "CXXXVII" );
    assert( ConvertDecimal_2_Roman( 1999 ) == "MCMXCIX" );
    assert( ConvertDecimal_2_Roman( 2018 ) == "MMVIII" ); // a mistake to catch
    return true;
}
```

3.17.3 Automating Unit Tests – Using the Standard Random Number Library

In the previous section, we showed a simple unit test. The question remains, how many tests are enough? More often than not, we are not able to check all possible settings. In practice, randomly selected values or border conditions can be an option. In this section, we will learn:

- How to generate a vector of uniformly distributed random integers in a given range
- How to run automated tests on Roman-to-decimal and decimal-to-Roman conversions

For years, the function pair rand and seed was used to generate random integers. This was fine in simple applications, but in many cases the generated values were not truly "random" as expected. Since C++11, an advanced library is available to generate random numbers in various distributions (Stroustrup 2013). With the help of this facility, Listing 3.31 shows how to create a vector of uniformly distributed random integers.

To create a series of random numbers, three things are necessary: an initialization object, a random generation engine, and a random distribution, as shown in Figure 3.25.

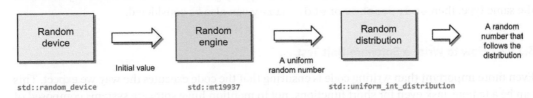

Figure 3.25 C++ chain for generating random numbers in a given distribution.

This example uses the Mersenne twister random engine mt19937. To do its job, it needs to be properly initialized. For this purpose, on line [17], a random_device object is created, which is then called in the constructor of mtRandomEngine.

On line [21], a uniform_int_distribution object is created. It will be responsible for generating a series of uniformly (but not yet randomly) distributed numbers in the range from kFrom to kTo. This series will be driven by the random engine created on line [19]. To generate random numbers of a given distribution and range, the following scheme has to be followed.

On line [23], an empty vector of ints is created. This is filled with random values on line [27] using the generate_n function from the SL library. Since random_decimals was created

Listing 3.31 Function to create a vector containing random values (in *CppBookCode, Dec2Roman.cpp*).

```
1   #include <random>
2
3   /////////////////////////////////////////////////////////////
4   // Creates a vector with random integers
5   /////////////////////////////////////////////////////////////
6   //
7   // INPUT:
8   //      kFrom, kTo - range of values
9   //      kNumOfTrials - the number of values
10  // OUTPUT:
11  //      vector< int > with random values in the range
12  //
13  auto CreateRandomVector( const int kFrom, const int kTo, const int kNumOfTrials )
14  {
15      // To generate random values we need:
16      // (1) a random initialization object
17      std::random_device rd;
18      // (2) a random engine
19      std::mt19937 mtRandomEngine( rd() ); // Mersenne twister MT19937? Why not?
20      // (3) a distribution
21      std::uniform_int_distribution uni_distr( kFrom, kTo ); // vals from_val-to_val
22
23      std::vector< int > random_decimals; // will hold random integers
24
25      // Generate kNumOfTrials random values through the lambda function joining
26      // uni_distr with mtRandomEngine. We use back_inserter since vector is empty.
27      std::generate_n( back_inserter( random_decimals ), kNumOfTrials,
28                  [&](){ return uni_distr( mtRandomEngine ); } );
29
30      return random_decimals;
31  }
```

empty, the `back_inserter` function is used to make new random values to be properly inserted into this container. However, `generate_n` by itself does not know how to generate random values. Therefore, on line [28], a lambda function is provided, which calls `uni_distr` with `mtRandomEngine`.

This simple function can be easily modified to create other random distributions. But remember that the subject of random number generation is much more involved, and our example only scratches the surface. More can be found e.g. in (Stroustrup 2013).

Now that we have random numbers, let's investigate how to automate the testing process for the decimal-to-Roman numeral converter function. The simplest way is to convert each random number to Roman and back, and check whether the result matches the original value. To do so, we need a second conversion function, this time working from Roman to decimal. The first version can be sketched out as follows (its full implementation is left as an exercise):

```
auto ConvertRoman_2_DecimalNumber( const string & Roman_str )
{
    int out_dec_num {};
    // Write the conversion algorithm ...
    return out_dec_num;
}
```

This is harnessed to the automated `Decimal_2_Roman_Chain_UnitTest`. It takes each randomly generated decimal value, converts it into a Roman numeral and then back into a decimal value, and compares the results:

```
/////////////////////////////////////////////////////////
// Unit test to randomly test both conversions
/////////////////////////////////////////////////////////
//
// INPUT:
//      kFrom, kTo - range of values to test
//      kNumOfTrials - a number of random test values
// OUTPUT:
//      true if all tests passed ok, false otherwise
//
// REMARKS:
//      Calls assert()
//
bool Decimal_2_Roman_Chain_UnitTest( const int kFrom = 1, const int kTo = 3999,
                                     const int kNumOfTrials = 1000 )
{
   // Check each random decimal if it converts ok
   for( const auto & val : CreateRandomVector( kFrom, kTo, kNumOfTrials ) )
    if( ConvertRoman_2_DecimalNumber( ConvertDecimal_2_RomanNumber(val) ) != val )
        return false; // test failed, exiting ...
   return true; // if here, then we passed all tests ;)
}
```

All of the programming techniques used in `Decimal_2_Roman_Chain_UnitTest` should be clear at this point. Note that in the `for` loop, `CreateRandomVector` function is called and returns a temporary object containing random values that are immediately used in the loop. This is a common technique and, thanks to the move semantics, it does not cause large computational overhead due to unnecessary copying of temporary objects. This is further discussed in Section 4.6.4.

So far, we have written test functions to test two concrete functions. In practical software projects, we will face dozens of functions, classes, components, libraries, etc. Therefore a more versatile unit test framework can be very helpful. The most popular are Google Test (Google 2019); Boost.Test (Rozental and Enficiaud 2019), Catch2 (Catch Org 2019); and the latest Microsoft Visual Studio, which comes with unit testing features (Augustin 2019). For more, see Section 9.7.

3.18 Example Project – Building a Currency Calculator Component

Exchanging currencies is a common financial operation in international trading. In this example, we will develop a simple program to perform currency exchanges. As shown in the software development diagram in Figure 2.4, let's start by specifying our requirements. Actually, there is only one, and it is very simple:

- The program will let us exchange a value in one currency for a corresponding value of another currency, based on an exchange rate acquired from a currency exchange authority

As also shown in Figure 2.4, before we begin our favorite activity (which is coding), we need to analyze the problem and prepare for the steps toward solving it. Most of all, we need to explain the details of the currency exchange mechanisms that will affect the implementation and outcome of our work.

3.18.1 Currency Exchange Problem Analysis

How do we set about the problem analysis and design? UML is helpful once again, not only because of its diagrams, but because of the methodology behind those diagrams. In Section 2.3, we discussed UML activity diagrams, which help to visualize the steps of actions or algorithms during the late stages of the design process. But at the beginning, it is better to focus on *use cases*. To facilitate this design stage, UML has *use case diagrams*. They capture major *patterns of behavior* in the system by entities such as people and objects, called *actors*. Hence, UML use case diagrams show the relationships between actors and use cases in a system.

Figure 3.26 shows a UML use case diagram for our currency exchange system. Since it is very simple, there are not many actors and use cases. In more advanced projects, the more details we can include, the better.

As expected, in Figure 3.26 we see an actor named User who can buy or sell a certain amount of currency. We expect two potentially different exchange ratios for the two cases. The Admin actor can make changes to the system, such as choosing the currency exchange authority and listing allowable currencies for exchange. This UML use case diagram will guide the later design stages. But first, let's take a look at how currencies are named and exchanged.

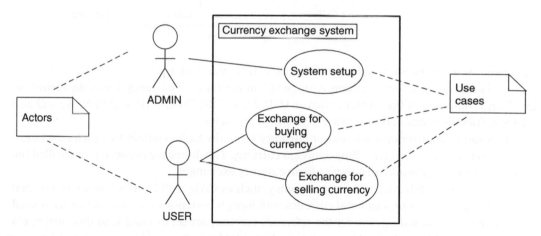

Figure 3.26 UML use case diagram for the *CurrencyCalc* system. Two actors are envisioned: users and administrators. Users can buy or sell currency. An administrator can specify system settings such as the reference bank that provides the exchange ratios.

For the purpose of currency exchange, national banks and other financial organization keep a list of currencies and their exchange ratios. Examples are presented in Tables 3.12 and 3.13.

First is the currency name, which frequently includes the country this currency is used in. Currency names are usually expressed in different languages, and because of this they are specific to a given country. Thus, for each currency, it would better to have a *unique identifier* called *a key*.

Table 3.12 A spreadsheet with currency names, acronyms, and buying and selling exchange ratios from the Bank of Canada.

Country	Name of currency	The bank buys	The bank sells
United States	DOLLAR	1.2520	1.3220
European Union	EURO	1.4250	1.5380
England	POUND	1.6165	1.7275
China	YUAN	0.1685	0.2065
Japan	YEN	0.01093	0.01161
Australia	DOLLAR	0.8760	0.9495
Switzerland	FRANC	1.2525	1.3465

Source: *https://www.nbc.ca* .

Table 3.13 A spreadsheet with currency names, acronyms, and buying and selling exchange ratios from the National Bank of Poland.

Currency name	Currency code	Buy ratio	Sell ratio
dolar amerykanski	1 USD	3.6987	3.7735
dolar australijski	1 AUD	2.6211	2.6741
dolar kanadyjski	1 CAD	2.8742	2.9322
euro	1 EUR	4.2602	4.3462

Source: *https://www.nbp.pl*.

This need was envisioned years ago; the ISO 4217 standard (*https://en.wikipedia.org/wiki/ISO_4217*) was created, which assigns a unique identifier for each currency. Currency identifiers are always composed of three letters, such as USD, EUR, GBP, CHN, CAD, and PLN. We will also use these friendly codes in our software to identify currencies.

In addition to a currency name and/or currency code, the tables contain two exchange ratios: one for buying and second for selling a foreign currency. The difference between them, called the *spread*, is the way the banks earn money from currency exchanges.

Also note that each bank has its own currency, such as CAD or PLN, which is set as a special reference. This is the bank's national currency, and foreign currencies exchange ratios are related to it. The buying and selling rates for the reference currency are set to 1 and 1, so this currency is frequently omitted from the bank's currency exchange tables.

Summarizing, a currency exchange table is a kind of simple *database*. Each line in such a database is called *a record*. To uniquely identify a record, it has to contain a *unique key*.

To design our software components, we need to identify the basic functionality as well as the data structures. Based on the previous problem analysis, we make the following assumptions:

- The program will be able to represent each currency with four attributes: the currency code, the currency name, the currency buying ratio, and the currency selling ratio, as shown in each row of Table 3.13
- The exchange ratios are referred to a chosen single reference currency
- The currencies will be stored in the local database

- The currency code attribute will be used as a key to uniquely identify a currency record in the currency database
- The currency database can be stored for further program initialization
- It will be possible to add new currencies, as well as to find and access the existing ones
- The amount to exchange will be computed with reference to the reference currency. There will be two options:
  - To buy currency
  - To sell currency

3.18.2   *CurrencyCalc* Software Design

Let's move on and develop the basic building blocks of our currency exchange system (see Figure 2.4). Currency records will be represented with a class named `TCurrency`, which will contain the four data attributes and functions to facilitate data access. The currency records will be held in the currency database. Each record will be uniquely identified by a currency code, as mentioned earlier. Such a *dictionary*-like data structure can be efficiently created using the `std::map` container class from the SL, as shown in Figure 3.27.

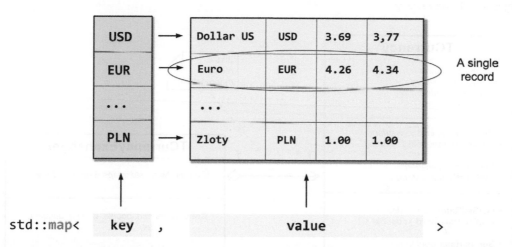

Figure 3.27 A dictionary data structure with key and values. To uniquely identify a value, each key must be different. In our project, the three-letter currency code is chosen as a key. All other attributes are represented as record values. A dictionary data structure can be implemented with the `std::map` container from the Standard Library.

In the previous sections, we used classes from the SL, such as `std::vector` and `std::string` (Section 2.6), or `std::tuple` (Section 3.17). Their functionality was provided in the form of a text description, as in Table 3.4. However, in a top-down design, after the main actors and use cases are identified, but before the implementation, the general *view* of the system is more descriptive. Therefore, during design, instead of a text description, we create a visualization of the classes and their relations using UML *class diagram*, which show the most important content and the primary relations between classes.

A class in a UML class diagram is represented by a rectangle, usually split into the following parts:

- *Class name* – Should clearly convey the purpose and primary functionality of the class
- *Data members* (called *attributes* in UML) – Represented by identifiers that are separated from their type with a colon :
- *Member functions* (called *operations* in UML) – Represented by identifiers with an attribute list in parentheses, separated from the return type with a colon :

Due to the limited space in a drawing, usually only the most important data and function members, and their most important parts, are shown. Each is preceded with a +, -, or # descriptor, which stands for public, private, or protected access rights, respectively. These are further discussed in Section 4.3, and more details about class relations and UML will be presented in Section 4.9.

The UML class diagram in Figure 3.28 shows the relation between two classes: TCurrency and TCurrencyExchanger. TCurrency represents a single record with a currency name, a code, and exchange ratios. TCurrencyExchanger aggregates the currency records and computes the conversions. Because TCurrencyExchanger will aggregate objects of the TCurrency class, in Figure 3.28 the relation between them is drawn with an arrow that ends in a diamond, showing that one object of the TCurrencyExchanger class can contain zero or more (encoded as a star *) objects of TCurrency.

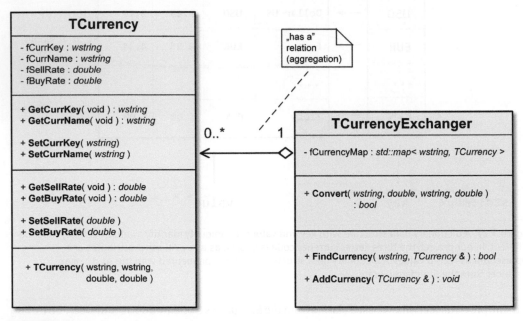

Figure 3.28 Relation between the TCurrency and TCurrencyExchanger classes. TCurrency represents a single record with the currency name, code, and exchange ratios. TCurrencyExchanger aggregates the currency records and computes the conversions.

We are ready to move to the implementation details of these components.

3.18.3 *TCurrency* Class Representing Currency Records

To represent a given currency, we need to identify what types of objects will best convey information about the currency name, code, and exchange ratios. Since we will need to work with international names, we decided to use the `std::wstring` type, rather than `std::string`. Unlike the ASCII character encodings used in `std::string`, `std::wstring` lets us use Unicode to represent international letters, such as ł and à (Unicode Consortium 2019). Exchange ratios will be expressed using the numeric value `double`.

Listing 3.32 presents the complete *Currency.h* header file with the definition of the `TCurrency` class representing each currency in our currency exchange calculator. The preprocessor directive `#pragma once` on line [1] instructs the compiler to include this header only once in the translation unit (Appendix A.1). This is important since a header file can be implicitly included many times, causing errors due to multiple definitions. Lines [3–5] include the necessary SL headers, which contain the definitions of objects used in `TCurrency`. Then, on line [10], the `using` directive introduces `wstring` to the context, so the namespace prefix `std::` can be omitted when using `wstring`. We discussed ways to introduce classes from other namespaces in Section 3.14.6.

Listing 3.32 Definition of the `TCurrency` class in the `CppBook` namespace (in *CurrencyCalc_Lib, Currency.h*).

```
1   #pragma once      // include this header in the translation unit only once
2
3   #include <iostream>
4   #include <string>
5   #include <cassert>
6
7   namespace CppBook
8   {
9
10  using std::wstring;
11
12  class TCurrency
13  {
14      private:
15
16          wstring     fCurrKey;     // a 3-letter code, such as USD, EUR, PLN
17          wstring     fCurrName;    // a unique name of a currency to be displayed
18
19          double      fSellRate {}; // selling rate - always add {} to stand. types
20          double      fBuyRate {};  // buying rate
21
22      public:
23
24          // Two constructors in one (default and parametric)
25          TCurrency( const wstring & currCode = L"", const wstring & currName = L"",
26              const double sellRate = 0.0, const double buyRate = 0.0 )
27          : fCurrKey( currCode ), fCurrName( currName ),
28              fSellRate( sellRate ), fBuyRate( buyRate )
28          {}
29
30      public:
31
32          // Functions to read data
33          wstring     GetCurrKey( void ) const { return fCurrKey; }
34          wstring     GetCurrName( void ) const { return fCurrName; }
```

(Continued)

Listing 3.32 (continued)

```
35
36          double    GetSellRate( void ) const { return fSellRate; }
37          double    GetBuyRate( void ) const { return fBuyRate; }
38
39
40          // Functions to write data
41          void      SetCurrCode( const wstring & s ) { fCurrKey = s; }
42          void      SetCurrName( const wstring & s ) { fCurrName = s; }
43
44          void      SetSellRate( double r ) { fSellRate = r; }

45          void      SetBuyRate( double r ) { fBuyRate = r; }
46     };
47
48    // "w" for wide-character streams
49    std::wostream & operator << ( std::wostream & o, const TCurrency & c );
50
51    std::wistream & operator >> ( std::wistream & i, TCurrency & c );
52
53
54     }    // CppBook
```

All of the classes in our example are additionally embedded in the CppBook namespace, which in *Currency.h* opens on line [7]. The definition of the TCurrency class commences on line [12] inside this namespace. Note that unlike class definitions, namespaces can be opened and closed many times to encompass consecutive components. The class constructor, defined on lines [25–28], performs two tasks. On the one hand, it has parameters, which are used to initialize the member variables defined in the private portion of the class. On the other hand, it provides all the default values, so it also becomes the default constructor of that class. The rest of the class contains getter and setter member definitions on lines [33–45].

Outside the class definition, on lines [49, 51], are two declarations of the streaming operators for the TCurrency class. Notice that to deal with Unicode wstring objects, we need to use the wide versions of the input and output streams: the wistream and wostream types. These streaming operators are fully defined in the *Currency.cpp* source file in Listing 3.33.

Listing 3.33 Definitions of the streaming operators for TCurrency objects (in *CurrencyCalc_Lib*, *Currency.cpp*).

```
1     #include "Currency.h"
2
3     namespace CppBook
4     {
5
6     // "w" for wide-character streams
7     std::wostream & operator << ( std::wostream & o, const TCurrency & c )
8     {
9         const int kOutWidth { 10 };      // total width of numeric output
10        const int kOutPrec { 4 };        // precision for the rates
11
12        o << c.GetCurrKey() << "\t";
13        o << c.GetCurrName() << "\t";
14
15        o << std::fixed
16           << std::setw( kOutWidth )
```

```
17          << std::setprecision( kOutPrec )
18          << c.GetSellRate() << "\t";
19
20       o << std::fixed
21          << std::setw( kOutWidth )
22          << std::setprecision( kOutPrec )
23          << c.GetBuyRate()  << "\t";
24
25       return o;
26    }
27
28    std::wistream & operator >> ( std::wistream & i, TCurrency & c )
29    {
30       wstring s {};      // empty temporary string
31       i >> s; c.SetCurrCode( s );
32       i >> s; c.SetCurrName( s );
33
34       double tmp {};     // temporary double
35       i >> tmp; c.SetSellRate( tmp );
36       i >> tmp; c.SetBuyRate( tmp );
37
38       return i;
39    }
40
41    } // CppBook
```

On line [3], the CppBook namespace is opened again to include the definitions of the streaming operators. The stream insertion operator << on lines [7–26] is straightforward – all class data objects are streamed out in order, separated by tab characters. Lines [15, 16, 17] set the std::fixed, std::setw, and std::setprecision manipulators. These specify that the output has a fixed length of 10 characters, including 4 characters for precision, i.e. for the number of digits after the dot (Table 3.14).

The extraction operator defined on lines [28–39], must be compatible with the insertion operator. First, a temporary wstring object is created on line [30], which is then used to collect consecutive characters for the wstring objects. These are then set by calling SetCurrCode and SetCurrName. A similar action is performed for the numerical values.

Table 3.14 presents the most frequently used C++ input/output manipulators. When using them, it is important to precede each one with the std namespace (the older prefix ios may result in different behavior).

3.18.3.1   C++ Input/Output Manipulators

The input and output (IO) operations belong to the most common ones in data-processing components. C++ pioneered a revolution by providing efficient IO class hierarchies (for comparison with IO in C, refer to Section 9.2.4). As we have already seen many times in this book, each custom struct or class can easily be attached to this IO hierarchy by overloading the stream insertion << and extraction >> operators. The more we use them, the more special formatting is necessary. Table 3.14 summarizes most of the C++ IO manipulators (*https://en.cppreference.com/w/cpp/io/manip*). Using these objects, the input and output streams process data in the prescribed way. Even more exciting in C++ is the possibility of adding our own manipulators (Stroustrup 2013). An example is the custom endl, defined in Section 7.3.4, that lets us insert multiple end-of-line symbols at once.

Table 3.14 C++ input/output manipulators (in header *<iomanip>*).

Input/output manipulator	Description	Example

setw	Sets the width of the output (the total number of shown chars, including a dot).	`#include <iomanip>`
		
		`double e = exp( 1.0 );     // e value, default precision is 6`
		`cout << " [defaultfloat]              e = " << e << endl;`
		`cout << " [sc]                        e = " << std::scientific << e << endl;`
		`cout << " [fx]                        e = " << std::fixed << e << endl;`
		`cout << " [p=4]                       e = " << std::setprecision( 4 ) << e << endl;`
		`cout << " [w=10]                      e = " << std::setw( 10 ) << e << endl;`
		`cout << " [fx] [w=14] [p=12]          e = " << std::fixed << std::setw( 14 )`
		`                                        << std::setprecision( 12 ) << e << endl;`
		`cout << " [fil_] [fx] [w=10] [p=4] e = " << std::setfill( '_' ) << std::fixed`
		`                                        << std::setw( 10 ) << std::setprecision( 4 )`
		`     << e << endl;`

precision	Sets the precision: ■ In fixed or scientific mode, this is the number of digits after the dot. ■ In defaultfloat, this is the total number of digits before *and* after the dot.	

fixed	Enforces the floating-point values to be written with no exponent term and with the number of digits in the fractional part set by precision.	Output:
		
		`[defaultfloat]          e = 2.71828`
		`[sc]                    e = 2.718282e+00`
		`[fx]                    e = 2.718282`
		`[p=4]                   e = 2.7183`
		`[w=10]                  e =     2.7183`
		`[fx] [w=14] [p=12]      e = 2.718281828459`
		`[fil_] [fx] [w=10] [p=4] e = ____2.7183`

scientific	Sets the scientific format of the output (e.g. −12e-36).	
defaultfloat (C++11)	Sets the floating-point numbers in the default notation: i.e. the precision field means the total number of digits before and after the dot.	
setfill	Lets us set the fill character that is used if necessary to make the output the chosen width. Use left, etc. to set the symbol position.	
left		
internal		
right		

Input/output manipulator	Description	Example
setbase	Sets the base of the output (allowed values are 8, 10, and 16, or 0 to reset to decimal).	```cout << "100d = " << 100 << " dec" << endl;
cout << "100d = " << std::hex << 100 << " hex" << endl;
cout << "100d = " << std::setbase(8) << 100 << " oct" << endl;
cout << "100d = " << std::dec << 100 << " dec" << endl;```
dec oct hex	Sets the base of the output to 10, 8, or 16.	Output: ```100d = 100 dec
100d = 64 hex
100d = 144 oct
100d = 100 dec```

3.18.4 *TCurrencyExchanger* Class for Exchanging Currency

The role of the `TCurrencyExchanger` class defined in Listing 3.34 is to define a kind of database containing all the currency records represented by objects of the `TCurrency` class defined in the previous section. Once again, the entire definition is placed in the `CppBook` namespace.

Listing 3.34 Definition of the `TCurrencyExchanger` class embedded in the `CppBook` namespace (in *CurrencyCalc_Lib*, *CurrencyExchanger.h*).

```
1    #pragma once
2
3    #include "Currency.h"
4    #include <map>
5
6
7    namespace CppBook
8    {
9
10
11   class TCurrencyExchanger
12   {
13       public:
14
15           // a key-value data structure
16           using CurrencyMap = std::map< wstring, TCurrency >;
17
18       private:
19
20           CurrencyMap          fCurrencyMap; // a map will store TCurrency objects
21
22       public:
23
24            // Let the compiler generate these
25           TCurrencyExchanger( void ) = default;
26           virtual ~TCurrencyExchanger() = default; // virtual destr. for inheritance
27
28       public:
29
30           ///////////////////////////////////////////////////////////
31           // This function converts a value of one currency into
32           // the other currency
33           ///////////////////////////////////////////////////////////
34           //
35           // INPUT:
36           //      from_key - a 3-letter code of a currency (USD, PLN, etc.)
37           //      from_val - value to convert
38           //      to_key - a code of a destination currency
39           //      to_val - output value
40           //
41           // OUTPUT:
42           //      true if ok, false otherwise
43           //
44           // REMARKS:
45           //      If from_key or to_key is not included in the map
46           //      the function will throw an exception; a given currency
47           //      code can be checked by calling FindCurrency member
48           //
49           bool Convert( const wstring & from_key, const double from_val,
                           const wstring & to_key, double & to_val ) const;
```

```
50
51
52        ///////////////////////////////////////////////////////
53        // A helper to access fCurrencyMap for read only
54        ///////////////////////////////////////////////////////
55        //
56        // INPUT:
57        //      none
58        // OUTPUT:
59        //      the internal map data structure (for read only)
60        //
61        // REMARKS:
62        //
63        //
64        const CurrencyMap & GetCurrencyMap( void ) const { return fCurrencyMap; }
65
66
67        ///////////////////////////////////////////////////////
68        // Find and return currency by its code;
69        // Returns true if ok, false if cannot find.
70        ///////////////////////////////////////////////////////
71        //
72        // INPUT:
73        //      currency_code - the 3-letters currency code, such
74        //          as "USD", "EUR", etc.
75        //      outCurrency - contains found currency if returned true
76        // OUTPUT:
77        //      true if ok, false if cannot find
78        //
79        // REMARKS:
80        //
81        //
82        bool FindCurrency( const wstring & currency_code, TCurrency & outCurrency ) const;
83
84
85        ///////////////////////////////////////////////////////
86        // Adds new currency record to the database
87        ///////////////////////////////////////////////////////
88        //
89        // INPUT:
90        //      new_currency - new currency record. If it
91        //          already exists, it is obliterated by this one
92        // OUTPUT:
93        //      none
94        //
95        // REMARKS:
96        //
97        //
98        void AddCurrency( const TCurrency & new_currency );
99
100  private:
101
102        // Friends to read and write to fCurrencyMap
103        friend std::wostream & operator << ( std::wostream & o,
104                                        const TCurrencyExchanger & c );
          friend std::wistream & operator >> ( std::wistream & i,
                                        TCurrencyExchanger & c );
105  };
106
107
108  }     // End of the CppBook namespace
```

The key data structure of the `TCurrencyExchanger` class is `std::map< wstring, TCurrency >`, abbreviated to `CurrencyMap` with the `using` directive on line [16]. The `fCurrencyMap` object is defined on line [20]. As shown in Figure 3.27, the `std::map` container is useful in the construction of dictionary-like structures that contain < *key, value* > pairs and ensure unique keys for their elements. This is a very useful feature, which in our example ensures that there will be at most one currency definition in the `map` object. In our implementation, we decided to use the currency code, such as USD or EUR, as the unique key. Thus, `CurrencyMap` resembles the currency tables discussed at the beginning of Section 3.18.

An interesting new construction is the application of the `default` keyword at the end of the constructor on line [25], as well as the declaration of the `virtual` destructor on line [26]. `default` tells the C++ compiler to automatically generate a default constructor and a default destructor for this class. (This would also happen if their declarations were omitted. And it would work fine, since the compiler knows how to initialize, copy, and delete the only data member, `std::map`.) The `virtual` keyword in front of the destructor allows future inheritance from the `TCurrencyExchanger` class. That is all for now; we will return to this issue in Section 4.10.

Probably the most practical member function of `TCurrencyExchanger` is `Convert`. It takes one currency code `from_key` and an amount `from_val` in that currency, and converts them to the output `to_val` of the currency identified by the `to_key` parameter. If the operation is successful, `Convert` returns `true`.

The other member functions of `TCurrencyExchanger` are self-explanatory. However, this time the streaming operators need to be declared as `friends` of the class. This is because they must be able to stream in and out the internal `fCurrencyMap` object, which, being external functions, they otherwise would not be able to access. An access exception is possible if we declare the operators `friends` of the `TCurrencyExchanger` class. The streaming operators are defined in the *CurrencyExchanger.cpp* source file, shown in Listing 3.35.

Listing 3.35 Implementation of the streaming operators for `TCurrencyExchanger` (in *CurrencyCalc_Lib*, *CurrencyExchanger.cpp*).

```
1   #include "CurrencyExchanger.h"
2
3   namespace CppBook
4   {
5
6   using std::wostream, std::wistream; // Introduce these std objects to the scope
7
8
9   wostream & operator << ( wostream & o, const TCurrencyExchanger & c )
10  {
11      for( const auto & currency : c.fCurrencyMap )
12          o << currency.second << L"\n";
13      return o;
14  }
15
16  wistream & operator >> ( wistream & i, TCurrencyExchanger & c )
17  {
18      TCurrency currency;    // temporary currency (one line from file)
19
20      // Read record-by-record and insert to the map;
21      // The fCurrKey becomes the map key.
```

```
22        while( i >> currency )
23            c.AddCurrency( currency );
24
25        return i;
26    }
```

In the `for` loop on line [11], each element of the `fCurrencyMap` object is accessed with the currency reference. Then, `currency.second` is used to access only the *<value>* part: that is, the `TCurrency` object. Finally, `TCurrency` is output to the stream on line [12]. The *<key>* part of each element is not used at this time.

```
27    // This function converts a value of one currency into the other currency
28    bool TCurrencyExchanger::Convert( const wstring & from_key, const double from_val,
      const wstring & to_key, double & to_val ) const
29    {
30        try
31        {
32            // Get the exchange ratios
33            double fromCurr_ExchRatio    = fCurrencyMap.at( from_key ).GetSellRate();
34            double toCurr_ExchRatio      = fCurrencyMap.at( to_key ).GetBuyRate();
35
36            // First we buy to the reference
37            double val = from_val * fromCurr_ExchRatio;
38
39            // The we sell
40            assert( toCurr_ExchRatio > 1e-6 );   // check that we don't divide by 0
41            to_val = val / toCurr_ExchRatio;
42        }
43        catch( ... )
44        {
45            return false;    // problems, sorry
46        }
47
48        return true;       // operation ok
49    }
```

The `TCurrencyExchanger::Convert` function is defined on lines [28–49]. The buy and sell exchange ratios for the two exchanged currencies are accessed on lines [33–34]. Then, the conversion takes place on lines [37–41]. The requested currencies may not exist in the `fCurrencyMap` map object, or their exchange ratios may be close to zero; in such an unusual situation, the conversion code can throw an exception. Thus, it is enclosed in a `try-catch` statement (Section 3.13.2.5). If an exception is thrown, `false` is returned. Otherwise, the function returns `true`. The additional `assert` on line [40] catches incorrect exchange values in the debug version of the code.

The `FindCurrency` function returns the `TCurrency` object, if it exists in `fCurrencyMap`. On line [55], the new version of the `if` statement is used (Section 3.13.2.1). If `currency_code` cannot be found in `fCurrencyMap` by its `find` member, then the iterator `pos` indicates the end of the map, conveyed by `fCurrencyMap.end()`. Otherwise, if the currency is found, it is copied to the `outCurrency` object [57].

```
50    // Find and return currency by its code;
51    // Returns true if ok, false if cannot find.
52    bool TCurrencyExchanger::FindCurrency( const wstring & currency_code, TCurrency &
      outCurrency ) const
53    {
54        // This is a new C++17 feature
55        if( auto pos = fCurrencyMap.find( currency_code ); pos != fCurrencyMap.end() )
56        {
57            outCurrency = ( * pos ).second;
58            return true;
59        }
60
61        return false;
62    }
63
64
65    void TCurrencyExchanger::AddCurrency( const TCurrency & new_currency )
66    {
67        fCurrencyMap[ new_currency.GetCurrKey() ] = new_currency;
68    }
69
70
71    }  // End of the CppBook namespace
```

Finally, AddCurrency adds a new_currency object of TCurrency type to fCurrency
Map. It is inserted on line [67] by the map's subscript operator, providing the currency's key. Note
that if a given key is inserted many times, only the last one will be held in the fCurrencyMap
object.

3.18.5 Putting It All Together – The Complete Currency Exchange Program

So far, we have created the parts that we will now glue together to make the complete
CurrencyExchanger program component, as shown in the UML component diagram shown in
Figure 3.29. It will expose a publicly accessible interface composed of several functions that load
information for the currencies that will then be used for currency exchange.

A *software component* usually consists of a set of classes, functions, variables, etc. that provide a
conceptually coherent platform to perform well-defined actions. This can be a library, module, or
application, such as *CurrencyExchanger*, offering everything needed for exchanging currency. The
key roles are played by the two classes TCurrency and TCurrencyExchanger, developed as
described in the previous sections. But we need additional code to glue together the parts that are
necessary for the user to create and then use TCurrencyExchanger. For such "glue code," it
would be natural to create another class – this has been the "natural" way of thinking for years.
However, modern C++ offers other options, such as *namespaces*. Since we already know how to
compose classes, in this section we will take a closer look at how similar functionality can be
achieved using namespaces. We applied this technique in Section 3.14.5 to resolve function names.
Let's take a closer look at the possible solution to this task in Listing 3.36: the CurrExchanger
namespace and the functions it contains.

On lines [1–10], common headers, as well as our custom *CurrencyExchanger.h*, are included.
Then, names from the CppBook and std namespaces are brought into the scope.

Our `CurrExchanger` namespace opens on line [19]. As we already know, a namespace can be split into separate chunks. The first object in the `CurrExchanger` namespace is `initDefault-FileName`, defined on line [22]. It contains a string with the default name of the initialization file for the `TCurrencyExchange` object.

An interesting new object is introduced on line [25]: `std::optional< TCurrency Exchanger >`, which will be used to convey the `TCurrencyExchanger` object. `std::optional` can be empty; in other words, it lets us convey information about a nonexistent object. This will be useful if for some reason `TCurrencyExchanger` cannot be created; hence its name, `optional`. As usual in C++, there are many ways to express the fact that we may or may not have an object (Section 4.5.2). However, `std::optional` is a viable new option in this respect, and it complies with the OO rules.

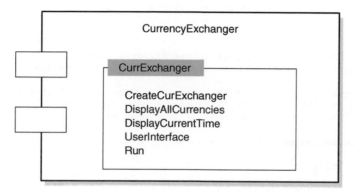

Figure 3.29 UML component diagram of the *CurrencyExchanger* component.

Listing 3.36 Definition of the `CurrExchanger` namespace containing the `CreateCurExchanger` function (in *CurrencyCalc_Lib*, *CurrencyCalcPlayGround.cpp*).[23]

```
1   #include <iostream>
2   #include <fstream>
3   #include <string>
4   #include <ctime>
5   #include <cassert>
6   #include <optional>
7   #include <filesystem>
8
9   #include "CurrencyExchanger.h"
10
11
12
13
14
```

(Continued)

---

23 The software presented here is a slightly modified version of the `CurrencyCalc_Lib` library project discussed in Section 6.2. The `main` function has been added so it can run as a standalone application. Also, due to limited space, only the most important parts of the software are presented and discussed. The entire project can be accessed from the book's web page.

Listing 3.36 (continued)

```
15   using std::wstring, std::wcout, std::wcin, std::endl;
16   using std::string, std::wifstream, std::wofstream;
17   using std::ostream_iterator;
18
19   namespace CurrExchanger
20   {
21
22       wstring initDefaultFileName { L"Currency.txt" };
23
24
25       using CurrExch_Optional = std::optional< TCurrencyExchanger >;
26
27       /////////////////////////////////////////////////////////////
28       // Creates and initializes the TCurrencyExchanger object
29       /////////////////////////////////////////////////////////////
30       //
31       // INPUT:
32       //     initFileFullPath - full path to the ini file containing
33       //         formatted information for currencies and exchange ratios
34       // OUTPUT:
35       //     There are two options for the return CurrExch_Optional object:
36       //         - It is either TCurrencyExchanger if properly built
37       //         - or empty CurrExch_Optional if it cannot be created
38       //
39       auto CreateCurExchanger( const wstring & initFileFullPath )
40       {
41           wifstream inFile( initFileFullPath );
42
43           if( inFile.is_open() == false )
44               return CurrExch_Optional(); // no init file, no object, what to return?
45
46           TCurrencyExchanger currencyExchangerObj;
47
48           // Read data from the file
49           inFile >> currencyExchangerObj;
50
51           return CurrExch_Optional( currencyExchangerObj );
52       }
```

On line [39], the definition of the CreateCurExchanger function begins. Its main role is to create the TCurrencyExchanger object. However, its proper creation requires the existence of an initialization file containing properly formatted data with currencies and exchange ratios. Various things can happen to files, so there is no guarantee that our initialization file even exists. Hence, if the initialization file cannot be opened, TCurrencyExchanger cannot be properly created. To indicate this, an empty CurrExch_Optional object is returned on line [44]. If we proceed further in this function than line [44], then we have a good chance on line [46] to create and on line [49] to initialize the TCurrencyExchanger object. In that case, CurrExch_Optional is returned on line [51], this time holding a valid TCurrencyExchanger object.

Most of the following functions take the TCurrencyExchanger object as their argument. For example, DisplayAllCurrencies, defined on line [53], displays all the currencies contained in the TCurrencyExchanger object supplied as its argument:

```
53   void DisplayAllCurrencies( const TCurrencyExchanger & currencyExchangerObj )
54   {
55       // Display available currencies
```

```
56        const TCurrencyExchanger::CurrencyMap & cur_map
                                    = currencyExchangerObj.GetCurrencyMap();
57
58        wcout << L"Available currencies:" << endl;
59
60        // Use structured binding
61        for( const auto & [ key, val ] : cur_map )
62            wcout << val.GetCurrKey() << L" : " << val.GetCurrName() << endl;
63
64        wccout << endl;
65    }
```

An interesting construction on line [61] is the structured binding used to simultaneously access the `cur_map` object obtained on line [56]. We discussed structured binding in Section 3.17.

The role of `DisplayCurrentTime`, defined on line [66], is simple: to display the current date and time. It uses timer functions, as described in Table 6.4:

```
66    void DisplayCurrentTime( void )
67    {
68        using timer = std::chrono::system_clock;
69        std::time_t time_point = timer::to_time_t( timer::now() );
70        string time_str( std::ctime( & time_point ) );
71        wcout << wstring( time_str.begin(), time_str.end() ); // string --> wstring
72    }
```

On line [68], the alias `timer` is created for `std::chrono::system_clock`. On line [69], `timer::now` is called to get the current time, which is then converted using the `timer::to_time_t` function. This, in turn, is converted to the `time_str` string object on line [70]. Finally, on line [71], this `string` is converted to `wstring` by calling the `wstring` constructor with `time_str.begin()` and `time_str.end()` as its parameters. This is a simple workaround that works in limited contexts; therefore it cannot be treated as a universal character converter between the character locales. These are discussed e.g. in (Josuttis 2012).

The role of the `UserInterface` function, defined on line [74], is to interact with the user and let them exchange currency by typing currency codes and values on the terminal screen:

```
73    // Perform currency exchange based on user's commands.
74    void UserInterface( const TCurrencyExchanger & currencyExchangerObj )
75    {
76
77        // Work with the user
78        wstring answer;
79        do
80        {
81            try
82            {
83                wstring from_curr, to_curr;
84                wstring from_val {}; // double would work but what user enters ...
```

```
85              double to_val {};
86
87              wcout << L"Enter from currency code:"; wcin >> from_curr; wcout << endl;
88              wcout << L"Enter value to exchange:";  wcin >> from_val; wcout << endl;
89              wcout << L"Enter to currency code  :"; wcin >> to_curr; wcout << endl;
90
91              if( currencyExchangerObj.Convert( from_curr, stod( from_val ),
                                   to_curr, to_val ) == true )
92                  wcout  << from_val << L" " + from_curr + L" ==> " << to_val
                                << L" " + to_curr << endl;
93              else
94                  wcout << L"Cannot convert these currencies" << endl;
95          }
96          catch( ... )
97          {
98              wcout << L"Error - wrong input." << endl;
99          }
100
101         // Ask the user what to do next
102         wcout << endl << L"New conversion [y/n]?";
103         wcin >> answer;
104         wcout << endl;
105
106
107     } while( answer.find( L"y" ) != wstring::npos );
108
109
110     }
```

UserInterface operates in a do-while loop, starting on line [79]. On lines [81–96], inside the loop, a try-catch statement is set to intercept a potential exception object thrown from the called functions. One of them is stod, called on line [91] to convert string to a double value.

On line [112], the Run function is defined, taking the TCurrencyExchanger object. It simply calls three functions we have already seen: DisplayCurrentTime [115], DisplayAllCurrencies [118], and UserInterface [120]:

```
111     // Run if we already have the currency exchanger object
112     void Run( const TCurrencyExchanger & currExchObj )
113     {
114         wcout << "*** Welcome to the currency exchanger ***" << endl;
115         DisplayCurrentTime();
116         wcout << endl;
117
118         DisplayAllCurrencies( currExchObj );
119
120         UserInterface( currExchObj );
121     }
```

The other overloaded function, Run, is defined on line [123]. This time, it internally creates the TCurrencyExchanger object by calling CreateCurExchanger. As we already pointed out, to create it, an initialization file is necessary. This is accessed on line [125] with std::filesystem[24] and by creating iniPath on line [127]. (Further details about the C++ filesystem are presented

---

24 In some compilers, the filesystem is still in the std::experimental::filesystem namespace.

in Section 6.2.7.) `CreateCurExchanger` is then called on line [130]. If a valid object is returned, `Run` is called on line [132]. Otherwise, an error message is displayed on line [136], and the program terminates.

```
122    // All actions
123    void Run( void )
124    {
125       namespace fs = std::filesystem;
126
127       wstring iniPath( fs::current_path() / fs::path( initDefaultFileName ) );
128
129       // At first try to get the currency object
130       if( CurrExch_Optional all_my_options { CreateCurExchanger( iniPath ) };
                                  all_my_options )
131       {
132          Run( * all_my_options );
133       }
134       else
135       {
136          wcout << L"Error, check Currency.txt file." << endl
137               << L"Exiting ..." << endl;
138       }
139    }
140
141
142 }    // End of CurrExchanger namespace
```

Finally, the `main` function looks like the following. On line [156], the `setmode` function is called to set up the display mode for the terminal. This is done to properly process Unicode characters. Then, on line [157], `CurrExchanger::Run` is called. Finally, a success code is returned on line [158].

```
143 #include <io.h>
144 #include <fcntl.h>
145
146
147 namespace CurrExchanger
148 {
149    void Run( void );
150 }
151
152
153 // Keep main() simple
154 int main( void )
155 {
156    setmode( _fileno( stdout ), _O_U16TEXT );
157    CurrExchanger::Run();
158    return 0;  // Although not absolutely required, return a value also from main
159 }
```

The question of when to use class(es) and when to use namespace(s) or both is open, and software designers' opinions differ. As usual, there is no single answer or universal recipe, and the chosen approach depends on the particular problem. In such situations, it is helpful to try to foresee future use cases and call contexts for a given component and choose the most natural, simple, and versatile solution. Usually, this is obtained in an iterative way, after the first version is refined. The beauty of programming comes from the fact that the same thing can be achieved many different ways, frequently with different consequences. This was also the story behind the *CurrencyExchanger* presented in this section. An alternative approach is left as an exercise.

We have learned about the following while working on the *CurrencyCalc* project:

- Creating simple classes with a constructor to initialize data
- Creating classes with default special members and `virtual` destructors for future inheritance
- Using a `std::map` container to store *<key,value>* pairs
- Using structured bindings when accessing elements of a `std::map`
- Input/output:
  - Overloaded `operator <<` and `operator >>` for data output and input
  - Stream manipulators
  - Using wide characters (Unicode) with the `std::wstring, std::wcout, std::wifstream,` and `std::wofstream` objects
  - Writing to and reading from a file using elements of the filesystem in the `std::filesystem`
- Converting `std::wstring` to `double` with the `stod` function
- Using `std::optional` to express an optionally available object
- Working with `try-catch` statements
- Creating software components with defined namespaces
- Accessing the system time with objects from `std::chrono::system_clock`

In Section 6.2 we will further extend the *CurrencyCalc* project.

3.19 Operators

In the tables in this section, we list all of the C++ operators, ordered by their precedence, with short explanations and brief examples. Remember that not all operators are equally important when writing C++ programs. Also, some of them are rarely used or obsolete. For some, a full description appears in future chapters. For completeness, differences between C- and C++-specific operators are indicated (Appendix A.2). Let's introduce an *lvalue* and an *rvalue*:

- *lvalue* – Informally, an object that has a name and can be taken address of, so it can be used on the left side of the assignment operator (=), e.g. x in const int x = 10; if const is omitted, then x becomes a modifiable *lvalue*; an *lvalue* can be converted to an *rvalue*, e.g. if placed on the right side of =
- *rvalue* – Not an *lvalue*, such as no-name, temporary, literal constant, with no specific memory location objects; cannot be on the left side of the assignment, e.g. 10 in const int x = 10; cannot be converted to an *lvalue* (*https://en.cppreference.com/w/cpp/language/value_category*)

The next important concepts are operator precedence and associativity:

- *Precedence* – When evaluating an expression, a rule indicating which operation should be performed before the others
- *Associativity* – A rule for selecting the first operator to execute when there is a choice between operators of the same precedence. Most of the C++ operators are left-associative except for the unary and assignment operators, which are right-associative. An associative rule must be

checked if an operand is between operators of the same precedence, such as in a + b − c; see Figure 3.30. In this case, b is between + and −, which are in the same precedence group. Both are left-associative, so first b "will be taken" by +; thus a + b will be executed, and c will be subtracted from this result. Thus the original equation will be evaluated as (a + b) − c. On the other hand, an example of the right-associative operator is shown in Figure 3.31

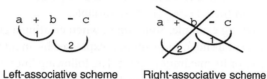

Left-associative scheme   Right-associative scheme

Figure 3.30 Example of the order of expression evaluation for left-associative (left) and right-associative cases (right). In C++, the addition + and subtraction − operators have the same precedence and are left-associative. Therefore, the order of evaluation on the left is used: operand b is first used by its left operator +, and a + b is computed; then the result of this operation is used for the subtraction − c. This second result is the value of the expression.

Left-associative scheme   Right-associative scheme

Figure 3.31 Example of the right-associative assignment operator. For proper, intuitive results, first c has to be assigned to b, and then b to a.

Let's consider the following example:

```
char * ptr = "The book";
char first_letter = * ptr ++;
```

In the first line, * is not an operator, since in this context it has a type name on its left; together, they mean "a pointer to char," which we name ptr. The pointer ptr is an l-value since it is located on the left side of the assignment operator =. To its right is the string literal "The book", which must be an *r*-value since it cannot be changed. More precisely, the text is placed somewhere in the program's constant memory, while a pointer to its beginning is used as the r-value, which is then assigned to ptr.

In the second line of the example are two objects indicated by the first_letter and ptr identifiers. Here, first_letter serves as the l-value, since it is assigned to. We have three operators here: =, *, and ++. Their order of evaluation is strictly defined by their level in the hierarchy of all operators, as shown in the tables in the next section. To find their proper precedence, first let's identify exactly what operators we are dealing with, since many symbols, such as *, mean totally different things when used in different contexts. For example, * is used in the first line with the char keyword, but * can also mean the binary multiplication operator or unary pointer dereferencing. In this example, * is not in between two operands. Instead, * is in front of a pointer ptr, so it means pointer dereferencing. Investigating the tables in the following sections, we easily find that it belongs to *GROUP 3* (Table 3.15).

Now, let's consider the increment-by-one ++ operator. It has two versions – *prefix* and *postfix* – that return different values. Here, ++ is behind the variable ptr, so it is the postfix version, which belongs to *GROUP 2*. So, how does it work? The postfix ++ increases a pointer value to indicate the next object, which is char in this case. Thus, from this moment on, ptr points at the second letter in "The book". However, a value of ptr ++ returned to the rest of the expressions is still the "old" value of ptr. This is how postfix ++ behaves. Then, * is performed on this old value of ptr, which still points at the letter *T*, whereas the new value of ptr points at *h*. Finally, the assignment is performed, which places *T* in the first_letter variable.

Now let's analyze the following example. Sometimes, when creating a graphical user interface, we need to set the initial value of a slider. Its position is expressed by an integer, and we would like to set it to something like 75% of its maximum extent. The following lines of example code accomplish this task. Let's consider what they do, especially in the context of operator precedence and associativity, but also considering the domain of integer arithmetic:

```
1   long slider_position = 256;

2   long initial_slider_pos {};      // let us set this to 75% of the slider_position

3   initial_slider_pos = 75 / 100 * slider_position;      // oops, 0 ?
4   initial_slider_pos *= 75 / 100;                       // 0 again
5   initial_slider_pos = 75 * slider_position / 100;      // 192, ok but ...
6   initial_slider_pos = ( 75 * slider_position ) / 100;  // this is more pronounced

7   initial_slider_pos = 0.75 * slider_position; // ok, but implicit type conversions
```

As we notice on line [3], there are three operators: an assignment, which as we already know is low in the hierarchy, so it will execute last; and two arithmetic operators / and * that happen to belong to the same precedence group (*GROUP 5*, Table 3.15). So, how will the right side of line [3] be interpreted? In this case we need to take into account the left associativity of the two operators. The value 100 between / and * will be first taken to the left operation: i.e. at first 75 / 100 will be evaluated, which equals 0 in integer arithmetic. Therefore, the result of line [3] is probably not the one we want. Simple exchanging the order of the operands, as shown on line [5], results in the multiplication 75 * slider_position, followed by division by 100. In this case, the result is 192. It is always better to explicitly express our intentions, such as on line [6]. This example shows how important it is to understand the consequences of changing the order of operands, as well as that manipulating fractions in integer arithmetic can be error-prone. For such computations, floating-point types should be considered, such as on line [7]. Here we also obtain expected 192, but at the cost of two type implicit conversions (from long to double and from double to long).

Let's analyze yet another code fragment, which may look surprising, especially to those who program in other languages, like Python. What will be the result of the following two lines?

```
int a { -1 }, b { -2 };
a, b = 3, 4;
```

To answer this question, the first thing to do is to look up is the precedence of the operators in the second line. The comma operator , belongs to the lowest group, *GROUP 16* (Table 3.15).

The assignment operator = from *GROUP 15* has higher precedence. Therefore the latter will be executed first: the variable b will be assigned 3. Then the comma expressions will be evaluated from left to right, which will have no effect in this case. If the last line was as follows

```
int c = ( a, b = 3, 4 );
```

then the expression in parentheses would be evaluated first: b would be assigned 3, as before, whereas the result of the two comma operators, executed in order from left to right, would be the rightmost value 4. Thus c would be assigned 4.

3.19.1 Summary of the C++ Operators

The operators in a given group have the same precedence (the same hierarchy level). Groups marked ® contain right-associative operators. All others are left-associative.

Operator legend	C++	Exclusively C++ operators (if in a table caption, then all operators in this group are C++-only; otherwise they are C/C++)
	C++11	Exclusively in C++ from revision 11 onward
	®	Right-associative operators
	Colors	Arithmetic / Comparisons / Bitwise / Logical

Category	**Description**	**Category**	**Description**
expr	An expression	*capture_list*	Possibly empty list denoting context dependencies of lambda expressions
expr_list	A list of expressions, separated by commas; It can be empty	*type_list*	Possibly empty list of types (comma separated)
pointer	An expression yielding a pointer to an object	*statement_list*	Possibly empty list of statements
object	An expression yielding an object	*type*	A name of a valid built-in or user-defined type
member	Denotes a member of a class (a function or data)	*rvalue*	A value can be used on the right side of the assignment operator
ptr_to_member	A pointer to a class member function	*lvalue*	An object that can be assigned to (located on the left side of the assignment operator)

A couple of additional remarks on C++ operators:

- Most C++ operators can be *overloaded*, i.e. a class can contain its own version of an operator with its own behavior (Section 4.4). Exceptions are the member access operators . and .*, sizeof, typeid, scope resolution ::, and the ternary conditional ?:
- Since C++ 11, there are counterparts to some of the comparison, logical, and bitwise operators: != ⇔ not_eq, ! ⇔ not, && ⇔ and, || ⇔ or, ~ ⇔ compl, & ⇔ bit_and, | ⇔ bit_or, ^ ⇔ bit_xor, &= ⇔ and_eq, |= ⇔ or_eq, ^= ⇔ xor_eq

Table 3.15 C++ operators.

GROUP 0

Operator	Description	Examples

Expression in parentheses
 	
(*expr*)
	Parentheses let us group subexpressions. Used to change the order of expression evaluation.	```double x = 1.3, sigma = 0.5;```
		```double gauss_val = exp(- x * x / (2.0 * sigma * sigma));```
		
		To compute the formula $g(x) = \exp\left(-\dfrac{x^2}{2\sigma^2}\right)$, we need to use parentheses in the denominator. Otherwise the numerator will be multiplied twice by sigma. In C/C++, there is no power operator. Thus we must either multiply or use the standard ```pow(x,c)``` function (c is the exponent).

Lambda expression (C++11, lambda function)
 	
[*capture_list*]
(*type_list*)
{ *statement_list* }
	Defines a lambda expression (lambda function).	```const double kPi = 3.14159;```
		```// [=] caption denotes accessing external objects by value```
		```auto area_fun = [=] (const double & r) { return kPi * r * r ; };```
		```cout << area_fun(13.7); // area of a circle with r=13.7```
		
		Lambda functions are used to define local functions. The caption [=] allows the previous lambda to access external objects by value. The other options are described in Section 3.14.6.

GROUP 1

Operator (C++)	Description	Examples
class_name :: member	Scope resolution – To access class members	SafeSqrt is a class in the User namespace whose role is to define the square root function sqrt, which can safely take any value, positive or negative. User::SafeSqrt accesses the User namespace and its SafeSqrt class. SafeSqrt::sqrt accesses the sqrt function, which is a static member of the SafeSqrt class (only static member functions can be accessed this way). Finally, ::sqrt accesses the sqrt function from the *global namespace*.
namespace_name :: name	Scope resolution – To access namespace members	
:: name	Global access – To access identifiers from the global scope (out of namespaces)	<pre>namespace User
{
    class SafeSqrt
    {
      public: // in   out
        static bool sqrt(const double & val, double & result)
        {
            if(val >= 0.0) // call global scope sqrt, then return true
                return result = ::sqrt(val), true;   // comma operator
            return false;
        }
    };
}

double x {}, res {};
cin >> x; // user enters a value
if(User::SafeSqrt::sqrt(x, res) == true)
    cout << "sqrt(" << x << ")=" << res << endl;
else
    cout << "A value must be positive." << endl;</pre> |

(Continued)

Table 3.15 (continued)

GROUP 2

Operator	Description	Examples

object . *member*	Member selection (access) through an object.	```cpp
		// The class (struct) to hold partial accuracies of a classifier
		struct Accuracy
		{
		    double fTP {}, fFP {}, fTN {}, fFN {}; // true-positive, false-positive, etc.
		} a; // let us define the class "Accuracy" and the object "a"
		``

pointer -> *member*	Member selection (access) through a pointer.	```cpp
		a.fTP ++; // let us access and increase fTP
		// ...
		Accuracy * ptr = & a; // create a pointer ptr and make it point at a
		ptr->fTP ++; // access and increase fTP through a pointer
		(&a)->fTP ++; // can do this way
		``

pointer [*expr*]	Subscript operator; allows access to objects in an array.	```cpp
		// Create a 2D array
		const int kRows = 3, kCols = 4;
		int table[kRows][kCols] = { { 1, 2, 3, 4 },
		                                { 5, 6, 7, 8 },
		                                { int {} } }; // fill last row with "default" int (=0)
		``

expr (*expr_list*)	Function call.	
type (*expr_list*)	Type conversion (function-like cast).	

type{ *expr_list* }
(C++11)
	Value construction.	```cpp
		double sum {}; // default "double", the same effect as sum = 0.0
		``

Operator	Description	Examples
| | | ```
// let us compute a sum of square roots (sqrt) of all elements in "table"
for( int r = 0; r < kRows; ++r )
    for( int c = 0; c < kCols; ++c )
        sum += sqrt( double ( table[ r ][ c ] ) ); // type convert and call sqrt()
```<br><br>The last line can be alternatively written with pointer dereferencing and the old-style cast:<br><br>```
sum -= sqrt( (double) * ( ( table + r ) + c ) ); // alternatively use this
```<br><br>In C, a variable can be only initialized with the assignment operator =. In C++, we can also use the list expression { }. In C++, int { } denotes an integer object with a default value of 0. The expression double ( expr ) denotes constructor-like type conversion. C/C++ also has another conversion in the form (double) *expr* (old C style). |
| lvalue ++ | Postfix increment (by 1).<br><br>*lvalue* is saved and then incremented by 1, and the saved (original) value is returned. | ```
// Copy length bytes from src to dst memory area
void MemCopy( unsigned char * src, unsigned char * dst, int length )
{
    while( length -- > 0 ) // copy length bytes. At each iteration decrement length by 1
        * dst ++ = * src ++;    // copy bytes, then advance pointers
}
``` |
| lvalue -- | Postfix decrement (by 1). *lvalue* is saved and then decremented by 1, and the saved (original) value is returned. | The loop is executed exactly length times. The counter length is first affected by the postfix decrement operator --, which saves the unchanged value of length, decreases it by 1, and returns the saved original value. The loop iterates until the value of length is greater than 0. At each iteration, both pointers dst and src are incremented by the postfix increment operator ++. However, before this happens, their original values are saved (in temporary objects), and these are returned to the pointer dereferencing operator * since it has lower precedence than the postfix ++ operator. In the last step, a right value is read from the location pointed to by src, which is then copied to the memory location pointed to by dst, and the loop proceeds. |

(Continued)
```

Table 3.15 (continued)

Operator	Description	Examples
typeid (*expr*) (C++)	The runtime type identification (RTTI) mechanism; see also Section 6.6.9.2.	``` void workerFun(void); // function declaration try { workerFun(); // call some action; can throw an exception } catch(std::exception & e) // catch exception { cerr << "Caught: " << e.what() << endl; // find what it is cerr << "Type: " << typeid(e).name() << endl; // print to error stream } catch(...) { cerr << "Unknown error" << endl; } ```
typeid (*type*) (C++)	Type identification.	
		Here, workerFun is a function that does something, and it may throw an exception with the throw operator (*GROUP 15*). An exception can be handled by the try-catch statement (Section 3.13.2.5). Any object can be used to represent an exception; here, we assume that workerFun can throw an object, referenced by e, of the std::exception class hierarchy from the SL. The first branch of catch is used for this purpose. Once execution jumps into this branch, it is useful to print the reason for the exception, to see what happened during execution of workerFun. But the point is that the exception hierarchy can be very large – it can contain many classes, whereas we have a reference e to the base, which can be a reference to any object in that hierarchy (this is how inheritance works). Hence, to print the right information about the cause of the problem, the what member is called. In the same fashion, to get the exact type of the throwing object, we call typeid(e), which is a kind of information-passing object. From this, we invoke the function name to print its type name on the error stream (commonly identified by the cerr object). Finally, if any other type of exception occurs, the thrown object is caught by the final branch of catch(...). Here we cannot do much except print a message. In practice, however, we should avoid such situations and design our code in such a way that exceptions, if they happen, can be uniquely identified and properly handled.

Operator	Description	Examples
| **dynamic_cast** < *type* > ( *expr* ) (C++) | *Runtime* checked conversion. dynamic_cast can be used to perform runtime checked conversions of pointers and references within a class hierarchy. Conversion is performed during program execution (runtime); if this is not possible, then nullptr is returned when casting a pointer, or an std::bad_cast exception is thrown if casting a reference. | ```cpp
class Fl_Widget;

// The class to create GUI (FLTK framework)
class SCUBA_Log_GUI_Creator
{ // ...
  public:
    // Callback function for GUI button click;
    // Upon call "obj" points to "this" of this class
    static void theButtonCallback( Fl_Widget * widgetPtr, void * obj )
    {
      // Now convert void * to SCUBA_Log_GUI_Creator *
      SCUBA_Log_GUI_Creator * theObj =
            reinterpret_cast< SCUBA_Log_GUI_Creator * >( obj );
      theObj -> Action_On_Button(); // call local function for action on button
    }
  protected:
    virtual bool Action_On_Button( void ) // local virtual function
    {
      // Do something here...
      return true;
    }
  public:
``` |
| **static_cast** < *type* > (*expr*) (C++) | *Compile-time* checked conversion. static_cast can be used for conversions between related types such as pointers in the same hierarchy, or arithmetic types, as well as conversions by constructors and conversion operators. Conversion is performed during compilation; if it is not possible, a compiler error is issued. | |

(Continued)
```

Table 3.15 (continued)

Operator	Description	Examples
| **const_cast** <br> < *type* > <br> ( *expr* ) <br> (C++) | const type conversion. <br><br> Converts between types using *const* (or *volatile*). | ```cpp
    // Create the main window with the FLTK library
    virtual int CreateGUI( void )
    {

        Fl_Window main_win( 100, 200, "SCUBA diving log" );

        // Add some widgets such as buttons, combos, ...
``` |
| **reinterpret_ cast** <br> < *type* > <br> ( *expr* ) <br> (C++) | Unchecked conversion. <br><br> reinterpret_cast is used in all type conversions other than the three previous. For example, it can be used to convert an integer to a pointer or vice versa. It is equivalent to the old cast style. | ```cpp
        // Add a button as a local object
        Fl_Return_Button theButton( 20, 20, 80, 20, "Action button" );

        // Link action on button via the callback function
        theButton.callback( theButtonCallback, this );

        // Finalize adding new widgets ...

        return Fl::run();    // Show the main window and widgets
    }
};
```<br><br>The previous excerpts from the SCUBA_Log_GUI_Creator class show an example of a *callback function* mechanism, embedded with class member functions in order to implement a simple GUI that uses the FLTK framework (FLTK 2019). A static function theButtonCallback is defined, which is supplied to the theButton.callback function alongside the this pointer of that class. As a result, FLTK calls theButtonCallback when the button widget is clicked. Then, theButtonCallback needs to cast *obj* to the TClassRegistry_GUI_Creator class, since it is the this pointer supplied during callback registration. This is performed by the reinterpret_cast operator, after which the Action_On_Button function is called, which eventually handles the button click. |

Operator ®	Description	Examples

sizeof *expr*	Returns std::size_t with the size of the object in bytes. In C++, the operand *expr is not evaluated,* and only its type is used to determine its size.	`int x = 5;`
		`std::size_t dummy = sizeof x;`
		
		After the last line, dummy contains the *size* of x in *bytes* (e.g. four bytes in a test system), and the value of x is not changed (even if we set x++ to sizeof, the value of x would *not* be changed since sizeof does not evaluate its operand expression – so beware of such errors!).
		
		With arrays, a common practice to count the elements is to divide the total number of bytes by the number of bytes occupied by the first element, as in the following code:
		
		`long arr[ 16 ]; // array of 16 long integers`
		`// a way to compute the number of elems of an array`
		`assert( sizeof( arr ) / sizeof( arr[0] ) == 16 );`
		
		`long * arr_ptr = arr;  // make a pointer to the first elem of arr`
		
		`// sizeof( arr_ptr ) returns size of the pointer by itself (not an array!)`
		`assert( sizeof( arr_ptr ) != sizeof( arr ) );`
		
		`long ( & ref_arr )[ 16 ] = arr;   // make a reference to long [16]`
		`// reference returns size of the array`
		`assert( sizeof( ref_arr ) / sizeof( ref_arr[0] ) == 16 );`
		
		A common mistake is to use a single pointer for that purpose, since in this case, sizeof will return the size of that pointer in bytes, as shown in the second assert. Assigning a reference to an array works perfectly – see the third assert.

(Continued)

Table 3.15 (continued)

Operator ®	Description	Examples

`sizeof`
`( type )`
	Returns the size of the provided type in bytes.	Each object occupies a number of bytes that can be looked up by the `sizeof` operator. However, to meet hardware requirements, objects of various sizes need to be placed on memory addresses that are properly aligned – this can be looked up with the `alignof` operator. We have to take this into consideration when placing objects together in structures, such as in the following example: due to data alignment, the size of the whole can be greater than the sum of sizes of its parts.
		
		`// Not well spaced in memory`
		`struct NotTooGood`
		`{`
		`    char c {}; double d {}; int i {};`
		`};`
		
		`// The same information but fewer bytes`
		`struct BetterPacked`
		`{`
		`    double d {}; int i {}; char c {};`
		`};`
		
		`cout << "NotTooGood :\t" <<    sizeof( NotTooGood ) << " - " <<`
		`                            alignof( NotTooGood ) << endl;`
		`cout << "BetterPacked :\t" << sizeof( BetterPacked ) << " - " <<`
		`                            alignof( BetterPacked ) << endl;`
		
		On a test computer, the results are 24-8 for NotTooGood, and 16 – 8 for BetterPacked. That is, for NotTooGood 24 bytes are required for storage, and for BetterPacked only 16 bytes are required. But both are 8-byte aligned (i.e. their addresses are multiples of 8).

`alignof`
`( type )`
`(C++11)`
	Returns the alignment of the provided type in bytes.
	
	For instance, an alignment of 4 means an object has to be stored starting at an address that is a multiple of 4 (i.e. the last two bits of the address will be always 00).	

Operator ®	Description	Examples
| `"expr"_expr` (C++11) | User-defined literals. | ```cpp
// constexpr for the compile-time constant
constexpr const long double kPi = 3.141592653589793238463;

// User-defined literal - to convert xx deg into radians
constexpr long double operator"" _deg ( long double deg )
{
    return deg * kPi / 180.0;
}

void UserTypeConstant_Test( void )
{
    //                  cos() expects radians
    cout << "cos( 30_deg )=" << cos( 30.0_deg ) << endl;
}
``` |
| | | User-defined literals let us define a custom suffix for selected type literals. Using proper conversions or scaling, a function can be defined. For example, we can write `112_km + 80_m` with mixed dimensions and still obtain the correct result. In the previous example, using the custom `_deg` suffix, it is possible to provide angle values in degrees, instead of radians as expected by trigonometric functions.

In addition, using constexpr in front of the constant and function lets the compiler evaluate them during compilation, rather than at program execution time (Section 7.3). |
| `- expr` | Unary minus. | ```cpp
double a {}, b {};
// ....
double p = - b / (+ 2.0 * a); // unary + before the binary *
``` |
| `+ expr` | Unary plus. | |

(Continued)

Table 3.15 (continued)

Operator ®	Description	Examples

`++ lvalue`	Prefix increment (by 1). `lvalue` is incremented by 1, and this is the value of the expression. The same as
	
	`lvalue =`
	`lvalue + 1`
		``// Copy memory starting from the higher addresses down

void BackwardMemCopy(unsigned char * dst, unsigned char * src, int num_of_bytes)
{
    src += num_of_bytes;   // src is one address after the source buffer
    dst += num_of_bytes;   // dst is one address after the destination buffer

    while(num_of_bytes -- > 0) // return original value, then decrement
        * -- dst = * -- src;   // first decrement, then copy bytes
}``` |
| `-- lvalue` | Prefix decrement (by 1). `lvalue` is decremented by 1, and this is the value of the expression. The same as

`lvalue =`
`lvalue - 1` | ```// ...
const int kBytes = 256;
unsigned char source[kBytes];
unsigned char destination[kBytes];
// ...
BackwardMemCopy(& destination[0], & source[0], kBytes);``` |
| `& lvalue` | Address of an object. | BackwardMemCopy can be used to copy overlapping memory blocks, if src < dst. To do so, copying starts with the uppermost addresses and proceeds downward. Bytes are copied by a while loop that performs exactly num_of_bytes iterations. The dst and src pointers are affected by the * and -- operators, which belong to the same precedence group; since they are right-associative, -- takes place first. As a result, each pointer is decremented by 1, and the new value of the pointer is returned to the * operator. In the next step, the source byte is read and is copied to the memory location pointed to by the current value of the dst pointer.

When calling BackwardMemCopy, the address to the first element (& destination[0]) is used to get a pointer to the destination memory block. The same value is obtained by writing destination, since the name of an array is a constant pointer to its first element. |
| `* expr` | Dereferences a pointer. | |

Operator ®	Description	Examples
`~ expr`	Bit complement (each bit is changed: 0→1 and 1→0).	```typedef short DATA_TYPE;
// For a given type kSignMask has 1 only on its MSB
const int kSignMask = 1 << 8 * sizeof(DATA_TYPE) - 1;
// ~kSignMask holds all 1s except MSB
// works with the sign/mag format
DATA_TYPE DataValueAbs(DATA_TYPE value) { return value & ~kSignMask; }```
`! expr`	Logical NOT.	```ifstream inputFile("image.raw", ios::binary | ios::in);
if(! inputFile.is_open())
return;   // cannot open, exiting ...```
`new` *type* `( )` (C++)	Creates an object – Allocates memory on the free store (heap), and calls the default constructor.	The MiniMatrix class, which is responsible for handling 2D matrices, uses the new [] and delete [] operators in its constructor and destructor. The allocated data buffer is always 1D, so the access functions SetElem and GetElem need to compute the corresponding index from the two coordinates. However, in modern C++, *smart pointers are recommended as a safe replacement* for new and delete. These and other details of memory allocation are discussed in Section 5.3.
`new` *type* `( expr-list )` `new` *type* `{ expr-list }` (C++11)	Creates an object – Allocates memory on the free store (heap), and initializes with *expr-list*.	```class MiniMatrix
{
    double * fData;   // data buffer
    int fCol, fRow;   // dimensions

public:

    MiniMatrix(int col, int row) : fCol(col), fRow(row)
    {``` |
| `new` `( expr-list ) type` (C++) | Creates an object – Allocates memory in the supplied memory area (*expr-list*), and calls the default constructor. | |

(Continued)

Table 3.15 (continued)

Operator ®	Description	Examples
| **new** ( *expr-list* ) *type* (C++) | Every new operator has a first argument of *size_t*, conveying the size in bytes of the allocated object. | ```cpp
fData = new double [ col * row ]; // alloc buffer

  ~MiniMatrix() { delete [] fData; }      // free memory

  void SetElem( int c, int r, double v ) { * ( fData + r * fCol + c ) = v; }
  double GetElem( int c, int r ) { return * ( fData + r * fCol + c ); } }
};
``` |
| **new** ( *expr-list* ) *type* ( *expr-list* )<br><br>**new** ( *expr-list* ) *type* { *expr-list* } (C++11) | Creates an object – Allocates memory in the supplied memory area (*expr-list*), and initializes with the second *expr-list*. | CommExcept_Handler is a struct that contain the machine code to process a communication exception on an embedded microprocessor platform. This code needs to be allocated at a specific and fixed address region in the microprocessor's memory map given by CommExcept_Addr. The new operator with the location address does its job and copies the code in the specified memory area.<br><br>```cpp
struct CommExcept_Handler
{
  enum { kExcSize = 256 }; // exception vector size
  // Assembly code for this handler goes here (just an example ...)
  const unsigned char asm_code[ kExcSize ] = { 0x01, 0x02, 0x03, 0x04 };
                                             // the rest fill with 0
};
``` |
| **delete** *pointer* (C++) | Destroys an object pointed to by *pointer* – Calls the object's destructor and deallocates its memory. | ```cpp
size_t CommExcept_Addr = 0x00000200;      // Comm Exception vector address
                                          // (in uP space)
// Allocate the CommExcept_Handler containing assembly code in the exception handler
void * CommExceptPtr =
  new( reinterpret_cast< void * >( CommExcept_Addr ) ) CommExcept_Handler;
``` |
| **delete** [] *pointer* (C++) | Destroys an array of objects pointed to by *pointer* – Calls the objects' destructors and deallocates their memory. | |
```

Operator ®	Description	Examples
`(type) expr`	Type conversion. Used to force a type change using a value-conversion procedure, which sometimes leads to data loss (e.g. converting `double` to `char`).	```char * text = "The quick brown fox";std::cout << text << " @ 0x".std::cout.setf(std::ios::hex, std::ios::basefield);std::cout << (size_t) text << " address." << endl;```To print the address of `text`, and not `text` itself, we need to cast `text` into the `size_t` type. Here the old C-style cast is used, which is equivalent to the C++ `reinterpret_cast`. We also use the function `cout.setf` to set the `std::ios::hex` flag in order to have a hexadecimal display (Table 3.14).

GROUP 4

Operator (C++)	Description	Examples
`object . *` `ptr_to_member`	Class member selection from an object.	```// A matrix with row or column -major data organizationtemplate < typename T >class OrdMatrixFor{ T * fData; // data buffer int fCol, fRow; // dimensions T * (OrdMatrixFor::*data_offset)(int c, int r); // ptr to a member fun // Two alternative member functions for data access in memory T * col_major_ind(int c, int r) { return fData + c * fRow + r; } T * row_major_ind(int c, int r) { return fData + r * fCol + c; } // default```
`pointer->*` `ptr_to_member`	Class member selection from a pointer to an object.	

(Continued)

Table 3.15 (continued)

Operator (C++)	Description	Examples
		``
public:
    // If row_major is true (default), data is set row-major
    OrdMatrixFor(int col, int row, bool row_major = true)
    : fCol(col), fRow(row), // init the pointer member function
      data_offset(row_major == true ? & OrdMatrixFor::row_major_ind :
                                       & OrdMatrixFor::col_major_ind)
    {
        fData = new T [col * row];   // alloc buffer
    }
    ~OrdMatrixFor() { delete [] fData; }   // free memory

    // Access an element using right data offset (two equivalent alternatives)
    void SetElem(int c, int r, double v) { * (this->*data_offset)(c, r) = v; }
    double GetElem(int c, int r) { return * ((*this).*data_offset)(c, r); }
};

const int kCols = 13, kRows = 20;
OrdMatrixFor< double > matrix_r(kCols,kRows,true), matrix_c(kCols,kRows,false);

matrix_r.SetElem(1, 2, 3.0);
matrix_c.SetElem(1, 2, 3.0);
```

A pointer to a function member of a class can be used to select a proper internal function at the runtime. In OrdMatrixFor, this role is played by data_offset. It is initialized by the constructor depending on the way matrix elements are stored: row-major or column-major. When a matrix element is accessed in the SetElem and GetElem members, the proper function is called via data_offset. |
```

GROUP 5

Operator	Description	Examples
| *expr* * *expr* | Arithmetic multiplication. | ```
double T_Cels {}, T_Fahr { 100.0 };      // init in C++ 0x11 - or use T_Cels = 0.0
T_Cels = 5 / 9 * ( T_Fahr - 32 );        // oops, a bug, always 0, why?
T_Cels = 5.0 / 9.0 * ( T_Fahr - 32.0 );  // correct with floating-point data
``` |
| *expr* / *expr* | Arithmetic division. | |
| *expr* % *expr* | The remainder of *integer* division.<br><br>For two integers *x*, *y*, such that y != 0, the remainder (and its sign) are computed to fulfill the following:<br><br>x%y == x - (x/y) *y<br><br>Otherwise, it is undefined. On some older platforms, % is also undefined for negative operand(s). | ```
int year = 2020;  // Check whether it is a leap year
// Divides by 4 and not by 100, or divides by 400
bool is_leap_year = ( year % 4 == 0 ) && ( year % 100 != 0 ) || ( year % 400 == 0 );
``` |

GROUP 6

Operator	Description	Examples
| *expr* + *expr* | Arithmetic addition. | ```
int x = 7;
int y = -8;
int z = 0;
``` |
| *expr* - *expr* | Arithmetic subtraction. | ```
z = x + y;   // "z" becomes -1
z = x - y;   // 15
``` |

(Continued)

Table 3.15 (continued)

GROUP 7

Operator	Description	Examples

`expr_a <<`
`expr_b`
	Bitwise left shift.
	
	Shifts *expr_a* left the number of bits specified by *expr_b*.
		```unsigned int x = 13;```
		```// << as binary and overloaded operator```
		```cout << x << 1 << endl; // print 13, then 1 ==> 131 in result```
		```cout << (x << 1) << endl; // mult by 2 ==> print 26```
		```cout << (x >> 1) << endl; // div by 2 ==> print 6```

`expr_a >>` `expr_b`	Bitwise right shift. Shifts *expr_a* right the number of bits specified by *expr_b*.	Shifting an expression by one bit to the left multiplies it by 2, and shifting to the right divides by 2. However, avoid using << and >> for signed integers since their behavior is not defined by the standard and can be either arithmetical or logical, depending on the computer platform (see Section 7.2).

GROUP 8

Operator	Description	Examples

`expr < expr`	*Less than* comparison.	```float a = 2.0f, b = 10.0f, c = 4.0f; // add suffix f to define float constants```
		```float delta = b * b - 4.0f * a * c;```
		```float x1 = 0.0, x2 = 0.0; // always initialize the variables```

`expr <= expr`	*Less than or equal to* comparison.	

`expr > expr`	*Greater than* comparison.	```if (fabs(a) > 1e-12f && delta >= 0.0f) // better than: a != 0.0```
		```{```
		``` float sq_delta = sqrt(delta);```
		``` x1 = (- b - sq_delta) / (2.0f * a);```
		``` x2 = (- b + sq_delta) / (2.0f * a);```
		```}```

`expr >= expr`	*Greater than or equal to* comparison.	The first comparison ensures that subsequent division by (2.0f * a) is feasible. Usually this is the proper way to check for division by zero in order to avoid numerical instabilities, rather than a != 0.0f. The second comparison, delta >= 0.0f, ensures that delta is non-negative so that we can compute its square root by calling the sqrt function from the standard mathematical library (*cmath*). The second condition is evaluated *only if* the result of the first condition is true. The suffix f explicitly defines a float constant (otherwise double is assumed).

GROUP 9

Operator	Description	Examples
`expr == expr`	*Equal* comparison.	```char c = getchar();\nif(c == 'Y' || c == 'y') // operator == has higher precedence than ||\n{\n // Proceed if user pressed 'Y' or 'y'...\n}```
`expr != expr`	*Not equal* comparison.	

GROUP 10

Operator	Description	Examples
`expr & expr`	Bitwise AND $1 \& 1 \rightarrow 1$ $0 \& 1 \rightarrow 0$ $1 \& 0 \rightarrow 0$ $0 \& 0 \rightarrow 0$	```unsigned char bulb_control_register = 0xAB; // '1' means 'on', '0' is 'off'\nunsigned char bulb_index = 3; // counting from the right\n\n// turn off bulb at bulb_index\nbulb_control_register = bulb_control_register & ~(1 << bulb_index); // can use &=``` To turn off a bulb, we need to set its corresponding bit to 0. For this purpose, we shift 1 a number of bits left, after which we negate all the bits. The resulting flag contains exactly one 0 at the corresponding position. After the bitwise AND, the bit that is the value in `bulb_control_register` will be 0.

GROUP 11

Operator	Description	Examples
`expr ^ expr`	Bitwise XOR $1 \wedge 1 \rightarrow 0$ $0 \wedge 1 \rightarrow 1$ $1 \wedge 0 \rightarrow 1$ $0 \wedge 0 \rightarrow 0$	```unsigned char bulb_control_register = 0xAB; // '1' means 'on', '0' is 'off'\nunsigned char bulb_index = 3; // counting from the right\n\n// toggle bulb at bulb_index: if on, then off, and vice versa\nbulb_control_register = bulb_control_register ^ (1 << bulb_index); // can use ^=\n// ^ is not the power operator```

(Continued)

Table 3.15 (continued)

GROUP 12

Operator	Description	Examples

expr | expr	Bitwise OR
	
	1 | 1 → 1
	0 | 1 → 1
	1 | 0 → 1
	0 | 0 → 0
		``cpp
		unsigned char bulb_control_register = 0xAB; // '1' means 'on', '0' is 'off'
		unsigned char bulb_index = 3; // counting from the right
		
		// turn on bulb at bulb index
		bulb_control_register = bulb_control_register | (1 << bulb_index); // can use |=
		``

GROUP 13

Operator	Description	Examples

expr_1 &&
expr_2
	Logical AND.
	
	Operands are treated as Boolean true or false (true / false keywords in C++; integer in C).
	
	In && joined expressions, *expr_1* is always evaluated first; if it is false, then *expr_2* is not evaluated at all! However, this holds only for the built-in types – the user-defined overloaded versions always evaluate both operands.
		``cpp
		double x {};
		cin >> x;
		
		const double kValMin = -1.0, kValMax = +2.0; // define the range
		
		if(x >= kValMin && x <= kValMax) // check whether "x" is in the range
		{ // when "x >= kValMin" is false, then the rest is not evaluated at all
		    // proceed ...
		}
		``

Operator	Description	Examples
expr_1 || expr_2	Logical OR. Operands are treated as Boolean true or false (true / false keywords in C++; integer in C). In || joined expressions, expr_1 is always evaluated first; if it is true, then expr_2 is not evaluated at all! However, this holds only for the built-in types – the user-defined overloaded versions always evaluate both operands.	```// see previous definitions ...
if(x < kValMin || x > kValMax)   // check whether "x" is out of the range
{ // when "x < kValMin" is true, then the rest is not evaluated at all
// proceed ...
}```

Operator ®	Description	Examples
expr_c ? expr_t : expr_n	Ternary conditional expression. expr_c is computed first. If it is true, then expr_t is evaluated; otherwise, expr_n is evaluated. The value of the evaluated expression is returned.	```double x {};
// ...
// sign_of_x contains -1 or 1 depending on sign of "x"
int sign_of_x = x < 0.0 ? -1 : +1;``` On the last line, we have an assignment operator and a conditional operator. Since the latter has higher precedence, it is executed first and checks whether x < 0.0. If so, -1 is returned and then assigned to the sign_of_x variable. Otherwise, sign_of_x gets the value +1.

(Continued)

Table 3.15 (continued)

GROUP 15

Operator ®	Description	Examples

`lvalue = expr`	Assignment.	`short s = -31000;    // pay attention to the maximum range of a variable`
		`const long double kPi = 3.14159265358979;`
		`vector< long > v = { 1, 2, 3, 4 };  // assign with an initializer list`
		`const double kPi = 3.14159;    // first in degs`

`lvalue *= expr`	Multiply and assign (the same as `lvalue = lvalue * expr`).	`double angle { 60.0 };    // first in degs`
		
		`angle *= kPi;       // the same as angle = angle * kPi`
		`angle /= 180.0;     // the same as angle = angle / 180.0 - now angle is in rad`
		
		`angle *= kPi` has the same effect as `angle = angle * kPi` but is shorter to write.

`lvalue /= expr`	Divide and assign.	This holds for all operators of this type. The symbol of the operator and the assignment = must be kept together. Written this way, they form a new type of operator.
`lvalue %= expr`	Modulo divide and assign.	
`lvalue += expr`	Add and assign.	

`lvalue -= expr`	Subtract and assign.	`// The number of bits reserved for the "short" type`
		`unsigned int bits_in_type = sizeof( short );`
		`bits_in_type <<= 3;    // mult by 8`

`lvalue <<= expr`	Bitwise left shift and assign.	
`lvalue >>= expr`	Bitwise right shift and assign.	Notice that the binary shift operations `<<=` and `>>=` are not defined by the language standard for signed arithmetic values and therefore should be avoided.

`lvalue &= expr`	Bitwise AND assign. Don't overuse it with other types, such as `bool`.	The following code shows how to exchange two integers using only XOR and assign:
		
		`unsigned int a = 0xAB, b = 0xCD;`
		
		`a ^= b;    // Exchanging two ints without an auxiliary variable`
		`b ^= a;`
		`a ^= b;`

`lvalue |= expr`	Bitwise OR and assign. Don't overuse it with other types, such as `bool`.	
`lvalue ^= expr`	Bitwise XOR and assign.	`assert( a == 0xCD && b == 0xAB );    // Now values are exchanged`
`{ expr_list }` (C++11)	An initializer list.	`vector< string > words { "The", "quick", "brown", "fox" };`

GROUP 15

Operator ° (C++)	Description	Examples
| **throw** *expr* | Throws an exception object to react to atypical runtime conditions. | ```cpp
double x {}, y {}, z {};
const double kEpsilon = 1e-32;

if( fabs( y ) > kEpsilon )
    z = x / y;
else
    throw std::overflow_error( "Div by 0" ) ;
``` |

GROUP 16

Operator	Description	Examples
| *expr_1* , *expr_2* | Comma sequencing operator that separates expressions.<br><br>Introduces a *sequence point*, i.e. it is guaranteed to execute in order from left to right (*expr_1*, then *expr_2*).<br><br>The value of the *rightmost* expression (i.e. *expr_2*) is returned.<br><br>(This is not a comma in a list of function parameters.) | ```cpp
// Convert Cartesian (x, y) into polar (mag, angle) coordinates
bool Cart_2_Polar( const double & x, const double & y, double & mag, double & angle )
{
    // write everything in 1 line
    return fabs( x ) > 1e-32 ? mag = sqrt(x*x+y*y), angle = arctan(y/x), true : false;
}
```<br><br>The comma operator can be used to write expressions in a succinct way, which is not necessarily the most readable. Cart_2_Polar converts (xy) Cartesian coordinates into polar coordinates (*magnitude*, *angle*). In the return statement, the conditional ? : operator is used. If the absolute value of the input variable x is sufficiently large, the first expression, i.e. the one between ? and :, is chosen and evaluated. It contains two comma operators, which partition this entire expression into three sub-expressions. These, in turn, are guaranteed to be evaluated in *left-to-right order*. The result of *the rightmost* one is returned, which is true in our case. Otherwise, false is returned, and the values of mag and angle remain undefined. |

3.19.2 Further Notes on Operators

Be careful not to assume any special *evaluation order* for subexpressions. For example, the following dependencies should be avoided:

```
int f( int & x )
{
    return x += 2;
}

int g( int & x )
{
    return x *= 3;
}

void h( void )
{
    int x = 10;
    int p = f( x ) + g( x ); // can be 48 or 42
    // ...
}
```

The result of p can be different depending on whether f is called before g or g before f, which is not defined in the C++ standard. On the other hand, the logical operators && (*and*) and || (*or*), as well as , (comma), guarantee that the left-hand operation is performed *before* the right-hand operation. For example,

```
f( x ) && g( x )
```

is guaranteed to call function f before g. But for built-in types, the && operator's second operand is *not* evaluated if the first operand has been evaluated to `false` (since the result is obviously `false` in such a case). Similarly, the || operator's second operand is evaluated only if the first one returned *false* (this is known as *short-circuit evaluation*). This is especially useful to check for null pointers before accessing objects, as in the following function:

```
bool check_if_not_empty_string( char * p )
{
    // the second cond is evaluated only if first is true
    if( p != nullptr && * p != 0 )
        return true;
    else
        return false;
}
```

In this `if` statement, the pointer p is first checked to see if it is a null pointer (denoted by 0 in C/C++ or `nullptr` in C++11). If it is `nullptr`, then we cannot evaluate its dereferencing expression * p, since it would throw a software exception. However, if p is a valid pointer, we check the first letter of the text pointed to by p; if it is not zero, we return `true` to indicate that the text is not empty. Otherwise, we return `false`.

Since this short-circuit evaluation feature is guaranteed *only* for the built-in types, we cannot rely on it if we call a class's overloaded && and || operators. Therefore, if we really need to overload these operators, we should do so carefully (Section 4.4).

Operators can be grouped based on the expected types, as follows:

- *Arithmetic* – Operators that perform arithmetic operations. If we use objects of different types, we must performs type conversions (this process is are automatic for built-in types, although in many cases it can lead to value and precision loss and therefore should be avoided)
- *Comparisons* – Operators that compare objects for which the comparison operators are defined. The result is `true` or `false`, both of type `bool`
- *Logical* – Operations on objects of type `bool`. The result is `true` or `false`, both of type `bool`
- *Bitwise* – Operations on integer types, such as (unsigned) `char`, `int`, `short`, and `long`. These operations are performed in a bit-by-bit fashion

In C++, operators can be overloaded: we can change their meaning to serve specific purposes for objects (Section 4.4). In this fashion, the bitwise left-shift `<<` operator has been overloaded and is commonly used with output streams, such as the `std::cout` object representing a screen. However, operator precedence and associativity rules cannot be changed.

Note that, unlike the address and pointer dereferencing operators, a reference is not an operator. It is always preceded by a type, and together they mean "reference-to-a-type."

In C++20, the "spaceship operator" `<=>` has been added. Its official name is the *three-way comparison operator*, since basically it compares two objects, say `x` and `y`, and gives the answer: `x<y`, or `x>y`, or `x==y`. However, `<=>` does much more than return information about the strength of the relation between objects, and whether it allows only equality or ordering as well. For more on comparisons, see *https://en.cppreference.com/w/cpp/language/operator_comparison*.

3.20 Summary

Things to Remember

- Learn all aspects of the operators. Check their precedence and associativity
- Try not to mix types in expressions – do not count on implicit type conversion
- Only the `&&` (*and*), `||` (*or*), and `,` (comma) operators have a strict left-to-right evaluation order. Do not assume any specific order for other operators
- For built-in types, the second operand of `&&` is *not* evaluated if the first one evaluates to `false`. Similarly, the second operand of `||` is *not* evaluated if the first one evaluates to `true`
- If possible, split expressions instead of using complicated ones. Use parentheses to enhance readability
- For indirect access to objects, prefer references versus pointers
- Split code into relatively small fragments – functions – each of which has a well-defined purpose, a meaningful name, and a short list of parameters. If more parameters are necessary, compose them into a class or a structure
- Embed data and its related functions in a class. Designate a compact set of functions as the class's public interface. Put everything else in the private sections of the class. Be sure to initialize all data members (with initializer lists { } and/or constructors)
- Prefer using containers (e.g. `vector`, `string`, `array`) and algorithms (e.g. `find`, `copy`, `accumulate`, `transform`) from the Standard Library rather than writing your own
- Well analyze the problem before design. Make a design before implementation

Questions and Exercises

1. Write a simple program to convert temperatures expressed in Fahrenheit to Celsius using formula (3.1). First convert the formula, and then use variables with the proper types and names. After writing and compiling your program, verify its operation with the help of the debugger.

2. Refactor the code in Listing 3.3, replacing the summation `for` loop on lines [41–42] with the `std::accumulate` function presented in Tables 3.4 and 3.6.

3. Refactor the function `AskUserForMatrixData` in Listing 3.21 to use `auto` instead of `Dim`.

4. Convert the following `for` loop

```
std::vector< double > vec( 123 );
for( auto k { 0 }; k < vec.size(); ++ k )
{
    vec[ k ] = 2 * k + 1;
}
```

    a. To the equivalent `while`
    b. To the equivalent `do-while`

5. In the `FibonacciNumbers` function defined in Section 3.13.1, refactor the `while` loop to the equivalent `for`.

6. Write a function to convert the values of a vector containing length measurements expressed in centimeters into equivalent values in inches. Hint: use `transform`, presented in Table 3.6, with `fun` set to the `cm_2_in` the lambda from Listing 3.16.

7. A prime number is an integer greater than 1 that divides with no remainder only by 1 and by itself. So, the first prime is 2, the second is 3, and next are 5, 7, 11, 13, and so on. One of the methods of finding all prime numbers in a certain range is the *Sieve of Eratosthenes* (*https://en.wikipedia.org/wiki/Sieve_of_Eratosthenes*). First a vector of consecutive values is created, starting with 2 and with all values initially marked as "prime." Then, beginning with the first marked value, which is 2, all of its multiples are marked "not prime" in the vector. Then all multiples of the next value marked "prime" are found and marked "not prime," and so on. The algorithm stops if all of the values have been accessed. Implement this algorithm. Hint: think of data structures to store values and mark information, e.g. two `std::vector< int >` of the same length, or a `std::vector< std::tuple< int, bool > >`. Do we need to store the even values? Verify your solution's correctness, and measure its performance.

6. Write a test function for the `RevertEndianness` function in Section 3.13.2.2.

7. A cyclic redundancy code (CRC) can be used to compute a special signature for a series of data (*https://en.wikipedia.org/wiki/Cyclic_redundancy_check*). It can be used for error correction in a transmission line or to verify the authenticity of data, for instance. The following function computes a simple CRC sum based on the $x^8 + x^2 + x + 1$ CRC polynomial:

```
///////////////////////////////////////////////////////////////
// Returns a remainder of the CRC sum.
///////////////////////////////////////////////////////////////
//
// INPUT: crc - previously computed crc value
//        byte - new value to be reflected by the new crc
//
// OUTPUT: new crc value
//
//
```

```
// REMARKS:  At the beginning the crc parameter should be set to 0.
//           The function counts 8-bit CRC for transmission of bytes
//
unsigned char CalcCRC( unsigned char crc, unsigned char byte )
{
  // A representation of the polynomial
  const unsigned short kPoly = 0x107;

  unsigned short x { crc };
  x ^= byte;

  // Check each bit of x
  const auto kBitsInByte { 8 };
  for( auto count { 0 }; count < kBitsInByte; ++ count )
  {
     bool carry = ( x & 1 ) != 0;
     x = ( x >> 1 ) & 0x7fff; // Shift right and mask
     if( carry )
         x ^= kPoly;             // XOR with the polynomial
  }

  return x & 0xFF;              // Return CRC as a single byte
}
```

a. Write a function to test computation of the CRC value over a buffer with randomly generated bytes.

b. After attaching the computed CRC value to the end of the buffer and computing the CRC again, what will be the result?

c. Repeat the computation of the CRC in the buffer after changing a single bit in one data item. Compare the results.

8. Expand the SCUBA_Course function in Section 3.14.6 into a fully operational program with a user interface.

9. In Listing 3.24, exchange struct MarsXorShift for class MarsXorShift. Refer to Section 3.15.1.

10. Modify the RandInit function from Listing 3.25 to set random values in a provided range, such as exclusively from 10 to 35, etc.

11. Analyze the performance of the recursive function FiboRecursive, discussed in Section 3.14.4. How efficient is it? Since computations of some values are repeated, consider adding a data structure – a cache – to store intermediate results that can be reused (e.g. vector< int > would serve this purpose).

12. Write a full implementation of the ConvertRoman_2_DecimalNumber function in Section 3.17.3 to convert Roman numerals into decimal numbers.

13. In the Linux OS, the environmental variable PATH stores paths to registered programs, separated by colons :. Write a program to print each path in a separate line on the screen. Use getenv("PATH"), returning char * to PATH.

14. Devise and implement a sorting method for a vector of integers. (Hint: a simple insertion and a bubble sort [https://en.wikipedia.org/wiki/Bubble_sort] are the first candidates.) Test it with a vector filled with random values.

15. Design and implement a simple database to store information about films and music in your library. What is the record structure and how should it be implemented? What container should be chosen to store the records? Add basic functionality to add/remove a record, save/load from a file, etc.

a. Write a function to test computation of the CRC value over a buffer with randomly generated bytes.

c. After attaching the computed CRC value to the end of the buffer and computing the CRC again, what will be the result?

e. Repeat the computation of the CRC in the buffer after changing a single bit in one data item. Compare the results.

18. Expand the scuba_Courses function in Section 3.14.6 into a fully operational program with a user interface.

19. In Listing 3.24, exchange `MatrixGetInt8()` for `MatrixGetInt32()`. Refer to Section 3.15.1.

20. Modify the ReadInt16 function from Listing 3.25 to set random values in a provided range, such as exclusively from 10 to 35, etc.

21. Analyze the performance of the recursive function FiboSequence(), discussed in Section 3.14.4. How efficient is it? Since computations of some values are repeated, consider adding a data structure – a cache – to store intermediate results that can be reused (e.g. `vector<int>` – would serve this purpose).

22. Write a full implementation of the ConvertRoman2DecimalNumber function in Section 3.17.3 to convert Roman numerals into decimal numbers.

23. In the Linux OS, the environmental variable PATH stores paths to registered programs separated by colons. Write a program to print each path in a separate line on the screen. Use `getenv("PATH");` returning `char *` to PATH.

24. Devise and implement a sorting method for a vector of integers. (Hint: a simple insertion and a bubble sort [Programiz pgBubbleSort, Wiki_Sort] are the best candidates.) Test it with a vector filled with random values.

25. Design and implement a simple database to store information about films and music in your library. What is the record structure and how should it be implemented? What container should be chosen to store the records? Add basic functionality to add/remove a record, save/load from a file, etc.

4

Delving into Object-Oriented Programming

Most of the difficulty of software design and programming arises from the requirements that have to be met, domain complexity, and the implications of software behavior and use that have to be expected. We can use *modeling* to make this process easier by focusing on the most important aspects of the system. By partitioning the system into smaller, conceptually easier modules, we can work out the details one module at a time.

In this chapter, we will delve into the domain of the object-oriented (OO) approach to software design and object-oriented programming (OOP), which helps with software system modeling. The central concept is the *class* and its instantiations – *objects*. Objects, in turn, can represent real things or actions. OO paradigms are formed based on this concept, as we will discuss; they are the result of decades of experience by the worldwide programming community.

OOP has been proven in many successful projects. On the other hand, we could probably find projects that used OO methods but failed. So, the OO approach is not a Holy Grail that unconditionally guarantees success. OOP is simply a set of principles, programming techniques, patterns, and recommendations. Therefore, it is important to understand the basic concepts of OOP and to use its best features to improve our software designs and implementations. Improving our software means it will be better when we apply OOP than if we did not use it. However, this is not an ideological issue – what counts is a successful result: reliable, well-behaved software that is clear, understandable, straightforward to use, and easy to maintain and extend. Isn't it amazing that similar concepts like module encapsulation in silicon chips started the electronics revolutions of integrated circuits? The synergy of these two domains – hardware and software – brought us to today's artificial intelligence (AI) and Internet of Things (IoT) breakthroughs.

The principles of OOP are rooted back in the 1960s and 1970s with the development of such programming languages as Simula and Smalltalk. Most modern programming languages draw from this legacy. The C++ programming language, derived from the principles of Simula and C, is one of the first players in the OOP league. In this chapter, we will delve into the OOP properties of C++, starting with OOP concepts and then examining code examples.

4.1 Basic Rules and Philosophy of Object-Oriented Design and Programming

One of the successful software engineering paradigms from the 1970s was the famous equation *Algorithms + Data structures = Programs*, coined by professor Niklaus Wirth as the title of his renowned book on programming (Wirth 1976). For years, algorithms were treated separately from

Introduction to Programming with C++ for Engineers, First Edition. Bogusław Cyganek.
© 2021 John Wiley & Sons Ltd. Published 2021 by John Wiley & Sons Ltd.
Companion website: http://home.agh.edu.pl/~cyganek/BookCpp.htm

data structures. Such an approach led to loose cooperation of functions and data structures, each existing separately, as can be observed in code written in C, for example. This can work, but problems arise over the years as projects grow. It became problematic to ensure synergy between the two domains. For example, how could we obtain smooth interfacing or guarantee proper initialization of structures? Also, the maintainability of such huge projects became an issue – for example, how could we write a new or slightly updated version of an operating function or structure? The advent of high-level OO languages like C++ helped to overcome or, at least, mitigate some of these problems.

Classes encompass data *and* the functions that operate on it, at the same time providing a publicly accessible interface and hiding unimportant details. The C++ principle of *resource acquisition is initialization* (RAII) – which means resource acquisition is performed in the constructor of an object, followed by the safe deallocation of resources in the object's destructor when the object is destroyed – helped to overcome the initialization and de-initialization issues (Section 5.2.1.1). Together with the *exception handling* mechanism (Section 3.13.2.5), RAII allows for relatively predictable software behavior in error situations encountered during code execution. In addition, polymorphism and class inheritance improved the process of growing and updating software, leading to a much higher degree of software *reusability*. All of these things greatly influenced the technological advances observed today. For example, in many cases, releasing new versions of complex software products has become a matter of months, rather than years or decades. Plus software is better able to accommodate dynamic hardware changes, so we can concentrate on new features rather than on new families of chips and the intricacies of their interfacing.

OOP is based on the following four principles. We will define them here and present examples in later sections:

- *Encapsulation* – Relates to protecting data by hiding it from direct and uncontrolled access. It also concerns hiding local member functions that are not directly involved in a class *interface* (a set of publicly available functions). Encapsulation means not only hiding data and functions but, more importantly, hiding unimportant details. This frees us from thinking about too many issues at once and makes us focus on the principal ones. Once well implemented, data and functions operate as expected, saving us from having to pay attention to hidden details. This has a tremendous impact on design and implementation, since it lets us concentrate on higher-level abstractions. As a rule of thumb, all data in classes should be hidden by declaring it `private`
- *Inheritance* – A process that lets new classes reuse the functionality and data of previously created classes. A class derived from another class, called the *base class* or *superclass*, inherits all of its data and functions. Hence, the derived class only needs to add specializations or change parts of the existing functionality. This is possible due to virtual functions and overriding, as we will discuss
- *Polymorphism* – Means "many forms," and in OOP relates to the possibility of expressing actions and relations in terms of the base class's functionality. This will still operate even if the class is greatly extended by inheritance in the future. For example, a menu command mechanism can have a fully operational action-call mechanism and still be open to the addition of new objects that add menus and their associated actions
- *Abstraction* – A way of showing models while hiding the details. This usually boils down to separating ideas from implementation details. In other words, abstraction lets us focus on what the class does, rather than on how it does it

In C++, the OOP domain gets further strong support from the template functions and classes (Section 4.8.5). This led to the development by Alex Stepanov of the Standard Template Library (STL), which was a forerunner of the Standard Library (SL) we use today. It also gave rise to what is called *generic programming* or *metaprogramming*: both let us write general software constructions in an abstraction of the concrete types that can be chosen just before instantiation. Also, more and more programming actions are being performed by the compiler, which can generate and execute code and insert only the results of its operations. This is a significant step toward computers writing software.

After OOP became established in the coding community and demonstrated its productivity, people observed further relations between classes and objects that repeated from project to project with the same principal structure and behavior and only the details changed. This is how *design patterns* (DPs) were recognized and incorporated into modern software design. In OOP, they significantly increase code readability, maintainability, reusability, and productivity. We will see and apply a few examples of the most popular DPs in our example projects.

Further heuristic findings about OOP and software development in general have been discovered, including the appropriately named SOLID methodology. It is based on five principles that were first proposed by Robert C. Martin (Martin 2009); the SOLID acronym was then coined by Michael Feathers. Since these principles also can help us develop better software, we cite them here with short explanations:

1. *Single responsibility principle* – A class should be responsible for only one, well-defined piece of functionality. Robert C. Martin defined responsibility as a "reason to change." This principle means a class should have one, and only one, reason to be changed. It is difficult to give general rules for how to achieve this goal, but it begins at the class design stage when a class's functionality and name are specified. If we have problems with one or the other (e.g. the class name seems too long or clumsy), we should think again and perhaps split the class into a few smaller ones.
   For instance, in Section 3.15, the EMatrix structure was introduced for the simple representation of matrices. It could also be used to represent a monochrome image, since it is a rectangular matrix of numerical values representing pixel intensities. But to save space, images are usually written in a specific encoding, such as JPEG or TIFF. Introducing this option to EMatrix would violate the single responsibility rule, since any change to the JPEG format, such as a new version, would require the recoding of EMatrix. Most matrix applications have nothing in common with JPEG format; therefore, these two should be decoupled.
   The single responsibility principle can also be extended to the rule regarding data member independence. From this perspective, only independent data members should be part of a class. Otherwise, changing one would require recomputing and updating the others. For example, the TQuadEq class, presented in Section 3.16, has three data members – fa, fb, and fc – each representing a separate coefficient of the polynomial. We might be tempted to include a delta parameter as a member. But what would happen if, for example, fa changed? Such a change would need to immediately launch a function to recompute and update the delta member, since its value would depend on all three parameters. That would be overkill for this class.
   Single responsibility is strongly connected to the "Don't repeat yourself" (DRY) rule. In short, it says that "Every piece of knowledge should have a single, unambiguous, authoritative representation within a system" (Thomas and Hunt 2019). If this is the case, then having two logically unconnected components means a change to one of them does not entail a change to the other.
2. *Open-closed principle* – According to Bertrand Meyer, this means "Software components (classes, functions) should be open for extension, but closed for modification" (Meyer 1997). In other words, classes and functions should be designed and implemented in such a way that they need not ever be changed. When a change or update is necessary, they can be extended by adding new code rather than by changing the old code that has already been tested and is called

from many places. How do we achieve such a goal in C++? By using abstraction, inheritance, polymorphism, and encapsulation.

For example, the TQuadEq class finds the roots of quadratic equations, but only in the domain of real numbers (Section 3.16). How can we extend its functionality to operate in the complex domain? We could change the code of TQuadEq, but doing so could break other components' dependencies on it. Plus any new code should be tested from the start. In addition, we do not always have access to the original code, e.g. code that is part of a library. But in C++, we can easily extend the functionality of TQuadEq by deriving TComplexQuadEq from it, as we will demonstrate in Section 4.10. The new class extends the functionality to the complex domain without changing anything in the existing class. The two can be used independently.

3. *Liskov substitution principle* – This says that wherever the base object was used, a derived can be substituted for it without altering the correctness of the program (Liskov 1988). Returning to our example, in code that uses of TQuadEq objects, objects from the derived TComplexQuadEq class can be inserted instead and will give the same effect. Examples of the Liskov substitution principle will be shown in Section 4.11 when we discuss virtual functions. In Section 6.1, we will present the TEventHandlers class, which invokes overloaded functional operators from its registered action handler objects without even knowing what concrete type they will have. What they have in common is their derivation from the same abstract class THandler, which defines an "abstract" action, whatever it may be.

4. *Interface segregation principle* – A *class interface* is a set of all of the class's public member functions. Sometimes, however, classes are called interfaces, especially if their primary responsibility is to provide a particular interface or adapt to a particular interface. The interface segregation principle is about keeping class interfaces cohesive and not polluting them or making them "fat" by overusing inheritance. More specifically, this principle says that client classes should not be forced to depend on interfaces that they do not use. We will see various interfaces in many projects presented in this book. For example, in the extended version of the *CurrencyCalculator* presented in Section 6.2, a currency-converting interface is decoupled from the user interfaces. As a result, the former can be used in both a simple terminal window and the graphical user interface.

5. *Dependency inversion principle* – High-level components should not depend on low-level ones, and both should depend on abstractions (Martin 2009). For example, let us again consider the TQuadEq class (Section 3.16). It has three data members (fa, fb, and fc) that need to be initialized. This is done by a default constructor, as shown on line [20] in Table 3.11. But to make things faster, we might consider doing data initialization in the constructor by reading the data from a keyboard, such as std::cin >> fa;. Would it work? Is it a good design? Well, it would mean whenever a TQuadEq object was created while the application was operating in a terminal window, the program would freeze, waiting for the user to type values; TQuadEq would be glued to std::cin. What if we wanted to use TQuadEq in a window-based system rather than a terminal window? What if the input came from a file? This is not a good design, because the upper-level class depends on the lower-level mechanism. The way out is to move reading from the keyboard (if we want this functionality) to a function external to TQuadEq. Such decoupling would allow TQuadEq to be used in other constructions not involving std::cin.

Another way to express the dependency inversion principle is that abstractions should not depend on details, but details should depend on abstractions. For example, in Section 6.2.4, we will investigate a component for HTTP file downloads, which can operate in different operating systems. This flexibility is achieved using the handle-body (bridge) design pattern, which, using a built-in action delegation mechanism, facilitates the decoupling of an abstract interface from its implementation on a concrete system. Hence, by using design patterns, we can avoid overly tight dependencies.

As we alluded to previously, these OO rules are not a panacea for all the problems we encounter in software development. Good designs come from years of learning and experience. Sometimes, checking if a class fits the existing components reveals a better design. In addition, explaining and discussing a design with colleagues forces us to answer important questions or admit that we should change this or that (this works especially well if the colleagues are from a competing team). One way or the other, the rules can help us develop a good design. We will return to them many times.

4.2 Anatomy of a Class

Now let's take a closer look at the internal structure of a class. Figure 4.1 shows the schematic organization of a class into specific areas. The bold names relate to *terminal symbols*, i.e. what we explicitly write in our software. The box-like regions indicate proper identifiers, names, etc.,

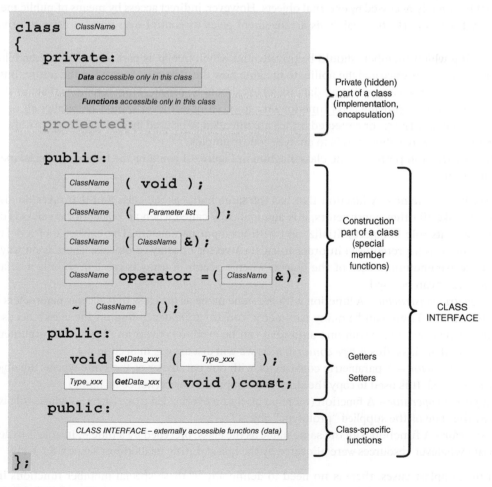

Figure 4.1 C++ class diagram.

depending on the context. The first is a class name, which, similar to the name of a function or a variable, should tersely convey the role of that class. Devising the name of a class sometimes is not easy, so this is the first test of whether we know what the class is intended to do. (More on the subject of function and class naming can be found in McConnell 2004.) It is also a good idea to use naming conventions to distinguish the type of the class and other objects. If systematically used, naming conventions add readability to the code. We follow this idea in this book, as discussed in the next section. The diagram in Figure 4.1 does not cover all possible classes and their organization but gives a coarse view of the possible structure of many of them. In this section, we will take a closer look at characteristic fields within a class. In subsequent sections, we will analyze their roles in a number of example projects.

In Figure 4.1, notice that a class can be split into a number of interspersed parts in the `private` and `public` sections as well as the `protected` section, which comes into play in class inheritance and will be discussed in Section 4.3. As mentioned earlier, data is usually located in the `private` section of a class, in addition to member functions that are only used internally by that class. This does not mean they are less important or more important than public member functions. This key idea behind hiding data and member functions is that doing so lets us control their access. In other words, private members can be easily accessed by all other members of that class, but they cannot be directly accessed by external objects. However, indirect access by means of public member functions is perfectly legal. This arrangement gives us control over what is done to private members.

Deciding which members should be private, and which public, is part of the OO methodology and requires experience and the ability to imagine how the class may be used in the future. But in most cases, we can assume that all data members should be private. Only functions that are absolutely necessary to provide class functionality from an object level should be public; all others should be either private, or protected if they are intended to be used by derived classes. As always, the best way to learn about this is to analyze code examples.

The construction portion of the class diagram in Figure 4.1 contains the following special member functions:

- *Default constructor* – A function that has the same name as the class and that takes no arguments. Like all other constructors, it is automatically called when an object of that class is created, and its role is object initialization with no input parameters. The existence of a default constructor is a prerequisite in order to create a vector or array of objects. There is no way to provide parameters to each of the objects when a vector or array is created, so only a default constructor can be used
- *Parametric constructor* – A function with the same name as the class that accepts parameters for initialization. There can be many parametric constructors, depending on the class's needs. A parametric constructor with one argument can be used to convert an object of its argument's type into that class; this is *type conversion*, as we will discuss e.g. in Section 4.4
- *Copy constructor* – A parametric constructor with one parameter of the same type as the object being created. It is used to copy the state of the supplied object (hence its name)
- *Assignment operator* – A function (more precisely, an overloaded `operator =`) whose role is to copy the state of the supplied "prototype" object
- *Destructor* – A function with the same name as the class, preceded by a tilde ~. Its role is to deallocate whatever resources were allocated by the object during its lifetime (Section 5.2.1.1)

In the simplest cases, there is no need to define any of these special member functions in a class; we saw the "rule of zero" principle in Section 3.9. However, there are cases when explicit definitions of some or all of these functions are necessary. We will return to these issues in Sections 4.4.1 and 4.5. A class can also contain the move constructor and the move assignment operator (Section 4.6.4).

The next items in Figure 4.1 are *getters* and *setters*. These are simple public member functions whose role is to read and write all, or a selected number, of the private data members. In upcoming sections, we will encounter many examples of these.

Last but not least is the *class interface*. This consists of all member functions that can be called on behalf of the class objects, as designed and implemented by a programmer.

4.2.1 Naming Conventions and Self-Documenting Code

We discussed the issue of properly naming objects such as constants, variables, and functions in Section 3.14.1. An object's name, i.e. its *identifier*, should convey the primary role of that object in a meaningful way. But in order to pass additional information, we can also augment names with prefixes and other styles in the form of additional naming conventions. Table 4.1 contains one of the possible conventions, which is OOP-oriented and based on the Taligent proposals (Taligent 1994); these rules are applied in the examples presented in this book.

Table 4.1 Naming conventions for classes and class members.

Prefix	Example	Language category
T	`TMatrix`	Base classes
f	`fData`	Class data members
E	`EException`	Enumerated type names
k	`kPi`	Constants; also those of enumerated types
fg	`fgCommonPath`	Non-constant static data members
g	`gCounter`	Global variables
M	`MFontTrait`	Mixin classes – see Section 4.13
V	`VKernel`	Virtual base classes – see Section 4.12

4.3 Rules for Accessing Class Members

As we have already seen, a class's data and member functions can be assigned to the private or public groups. If not explicitly assigned, then by default, members of a class are private. Although derived classes will be presented in Section 4.9, the complete set of access rules is illustrated in Figure 4.2. They can be summarized as follow:

- `private` – Members of this group can be accessed only by members of the class and friends of the class. They cannot be accessed by members of derived classes or from the object context
- `protected` – Like private members, these can be accessed by members of derived classes and their friends. They cannot be accessed from objects
- `public` – These members can be accessed by all members of a class and its derivatives and their friends, as well as from the object level

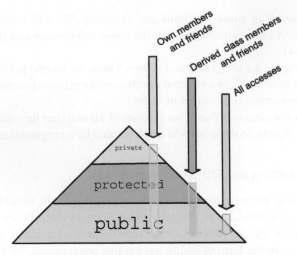

Figure 4.2 Access control rules in C++. A class's own members and class friends can access all members (private, protected, and public). Derived class members and derived class friends can access protected and public members of the given class. All other accesses can be to public members only.

As mentioned earlier, access rules also apply to class inheritance, as we will discuss. In such a context, they act as cut-off filters to the members of the base class. That is, class D can be derived from B, where B is:

- *A public base class* – (The most frequent choice.) All public and protected members of B can be accessed from D, keeping their public or protected status. Private members of B are not accessible in D
- *A protected base class* – All public and protected members of B become protected in D. Private members of B are not accessible in D
- *A private base class* – All pubic and protected members of B become private in D. Private members of B are not accessible in D

Inheritance is most frequently public, since it lets us extend the base class, which is in concordance with the main principle of inheritance. Naturally, this is called *extending inheritance*. The other types of inheritance, protected and private, are limited since members of the base class are no longer accessible from derived classes. This will be discussed in later sections.

Regarding the previous access rules, we can also distinguish the following member access types:

- Access from an object of a class with the member selection operator
- Access to static members and friends of a class
- Access within a hierarchy of classes, i.e. members called from derived classes

We have already seen examples of the first two access types in the code presented in previous chapters. Access to a member from an object, or a pointer to an object, can be obtained using one of the member selection operators (*GROUP 2*, Table 3.15). Their syntax is shown in Figure 4.3a and b.

An important aspect of member access from an object is that only public members of a class can be accessed this way. But members of a class declared `static` can be accessed by providing the name of the class followed by the scope resolution operator `::` and the name of the member (see *GROUP 1* in Table 3.15, and Figure 2.8). No class objects are involved in these calls, but again, only public members can be accessed.

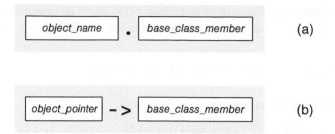

Figure 4.3 Syntax for selecting class members from an object or a reference to an object (a) and with a pointer to an object (b).

A characteristic feature of static members is that there is exactly one of each of them, even if no objects of this class have been created. Hence, no objects are necessary, and static members can be accessed by providing only the name of the class. This also means each static member is shared among all objects of that class. This rarely is a problem when using static member functions. However, non-constant static member data can cause problems in a multithreading environment, since it has to be protected from unsynchronized thread accesses (see Chapter 8.) Therefore, using non-constant static members is discouraged. When there is no data and only static member functions, a better approach is to put the functions in a namespace rather than a class (Section 3.14.5).

We will discuss class inheritance and access to members within class hierarchies in Section 4.10.

4.4   Example Project – *TComplex* Class for Operator Overloading

In this section we will learn how to make another class, this time to represent complex numbers: two-valued entities with their own arithmetic rules, which are used e.g. in electronics and physics (Korn and Korn 2000). Our purpose is to learn about several new programming techniques, as follows:

- Representing *complex numbers*. We will show how to write the construction group, where to put the data members, and how to implement getters/setters and overloaded streaming operators
- *Operator overloading*. In C++, it is possible to write our own versions of most operators so they behave in accordance with class requirements. This way, we can multiply complex numbers using a simple asterisk *, or stream out a complex number with the << operator, as we have seen for other classes. Overloaded operators are defined in almost the same way as other class member functions; the only difference is the `operator` keyword in their name, followed by an operator symbol (or multi-symbol)
- *Special member functions*: constructors, a destructor, and assignments
- The class pointer-to-self: `this`

Recall that basically, a complex number is nothing more than a pair of real values

$$z \equiv (a,b) \tag{4.1}$$

where a and b are real: that is, $a, b \in \mathfrak{R}$.

However, there are additional assumptions that change the game, as follows:

$$z = a + ib, \text{ and } i^2 = -1 \tag{4.2}$$

This equation is interesting. Because of it, all four basic algebraic operations are possible. For example, assuming that $u = c + id$ is also a complex number, the difference $z - u$ can be expressed as follows:

$$z - u = (a + ib) - (c + id) = (a - c) + i(b - d) = (a - c, b - d) \tag{4.3}$$

Division, on the other hand, can be expanded as follows:

$$\frac{z}{u} = \frac{a + ib}{c + id} = \frac{(a + ib)(c - id)}{(c + id)(c - id)} = \frac{(ac + bd) + i(bc - bd)}{c^2 + d^2} = \frac{ac + bd}{c^2 + d^2} + i\frac{bc - bd}{c^2 + d^2} \tag{4.4}$$

Addition is the same as Eq. (4.3), but with all plus signs; and multiplication is used in Eq. (4.4). Due to the properties we have briefly sketched here, complex numbers have found many applications: for example, in physics, circuit theory, and, with extensions, in the representation of colors. And this is all the background we need to implement a computer model of a complex number.

4.4.1 Definition of the *TComplex* Class

As usual, a class is written in two files: the header and the source file (see Listing 4.1). In the *Complex.h* header, the CppBook namespace starts on line [5]. Then, the definition of the TComplex class follows on line [12]. Also as usual, data is located in the private section of the class, which begins on line [14]. The real part of the number fRe is defined on line [18], while the imaginary part fIm is defined on line [19].

Listing 4.1 Definition of the TComplex class in the CppBook namespace (in *Complex, Complex.h*).

```
1   //////////////////////////////////////////
2   // Our own namespace to uniquely identify
3   // contained classes
4   //////////////////////////////////////////
5   namespace CppBook
6   {
7
8
9   //////////////////////////////////////////
10  // A class to represent complex numbers
11  //////////////////////////////////////////
12  class TComplex
13  {
14      private:
15
16          // Data members should be in the private section of the class
17
18          double fRe {};          // real part
19          double fIm {};          // imaginary part
20
```

Interestingly enough, we do not need to store an object to represent the imaginary value i, as used in Eq. (4.2). All we need to do is remember that fRe is meant to store the real part and fIm the imaginary part of a complex number. In other words, the pair in Eq. (4.1) is ordered, and the values cannot be mixed. This can be understood through closer scrutiny of Eq. (4.3).

In the next section of the `TComplex` definition, we see the group of *special member functions*. This group can contain the following items:

- A default constructor to create and initialize an object with no external parameters
- Parametric constructor(s) to create and initialize an object with parameters
- A copy constructor to create and initialize an object based on another object of the same type
- An assignment operator to copy the state from another object of the same type
- A destructor to deallocate whatever was allocated during an object's lifetime
- A move assignment, which is usually more efficient than a copy assignment because we can use data from the supplied object (Section 4.6.4)
- A move constructor to create and initialize an object, which can be more efficient than a copy constructor because we can use data from the supplied object (Section 4.6.4)
- Type-converting constructor(s) that create and initialize an object based on a passed parameter of a different type than its class (similar to the copy constructor)

As we have already seen, in most classes, few of these are needed. Some are for special occasions, as we will explain later. Also, some of them can be automatically deduced and implemented by the compiler, as we have seen. Returning to `TComplex`, its default constructor is on line [26], in the `public` section of the class beginning on line [21]. The characteristic part is the constructor's initializer list, on line [27]. Its role is to call the constructors of its member data objects. If it is omitted, then the default constructors of the members are called. In that case initialization is possible but less efficient, since an object is first created with its default constructor, and then initialized as on line [29].

The definition of the parametric constructor begins on line [36]. It takes two arguments, which are immediately used in the constructor's initializer list in the same line. Not surprisingly, in this case, the parametric constructors of the member objects are invoked, providing the appropriate parameters.

When designing a class, sometimes we have the option of not providing any constructors, since the data will be initialized using initialization lists. This is the rule of zero, explained in Section 3.9. But a decision to explicitly provide a parametric constructor has implications. More concretely, when we declare (write) a special member function other than the default constructor, the compiler will suppress the generation of other special functions. Therefore, if we decide to add a declaration of the parametric constructor or a destructor, *we should explicitly add all six other special functions*. This is called the *rule of six* (or five, depending on what we count). And this is exactly what we do here: the copy constructor is declared on line [43], the assignment operator on line [49], and the destructor on line [54]. In all of these functions, we use `= default`, since the default functionality is all we need – that is, data members are copied if necessary. Also, we skipped the special move functions, since we only have two small data members and so there is nothing to gain from move semantics. We will explain the construction and operations of these special members in upcoming sections.

```
21    public:
22
23        //////////////////////////////////////////////////////////
24        // Default constructor
25        //////////////////////////////////////////////////////////
26        TComplex( void )
27            : fRe( 0.0 ), fIm( 0.0 )      // special data initialization
```

```
28      {
29          //fRe = 0;        // such initialization is possible but the above is better
30      }
31
32
33      ////////////////////////////////////////////////////////////
34      // A parametric constructor
35      ////////////////////////////////////////////////////////////
36      TComplex( double re, double im ) : fRe( re ), fIm( im ) {}
37
38      ////////////////////////////////////////////////////////////
39      // Copy constructor - make this object and make its state
40      // the same as the supplied one (i.e. "c").
41      // default means to copy fRe and fIm from "c".
42      ////////////////////////////////////////////////////////////
43      TComplex( const TComplex & c ) = default;
44
45      ////////////////////////////////////////////////////////////
46      // Overloaded assignment operator - default means to
47      // copy fRe and fIm.
48      ////////////////////////////////////////////////////////////
49      TComplex & operator = ( const TComplex & c ) = default;
50
51      ////////////////////////////////////////////////////////////
52      // Destructor does nothing, but stated explicitly
53      ////////////////////////////////////////////////////////////
54      ~TComplex() = default;
55
```

The last item in this group is the constructor defined on line [63]. It takes only one real argument, declared with `double`, and initializes only the real part of the complex number, leaving the imaginary part set to 0.0. But it is more than a constructor – this is the *type-converting constructor*. Its role is to take an object of a different type, in this case `double`, and convert it into the type of its class: `TComplex` in our example. As a result, we can, for example, add a real number to the complex one, which – because real numbers are special cases of complex numbers with an imaginary part of zero – is a perfectly acceptable operation from a mathematical point of view. However, there is no corresponding reverse operation: we cannot convert `TComplex` to `double`. We can write such a conversion function, but we cannot be sure what its action would be (returning only the real part, or a module?). We will return to this `double` form of type conversion in Section 7.3.

```
56      public:
57
58          ////////////////////////////////////////////////////////////
59          // Converting constructor - allows the creation of TComplex
60          // from a double type object (i.e. it is a conversion
61          // from double to TComplex).
62          ////////////////////////////////////////////////////////////
63          TComplex( double re ) : fRe( re ), fIm( 0.0 ) {}
64
```

After the group of special functions, the familiar getter and setter member functions are located on lines [68–72]. Note that it is a common practice in OOP to hide data but provide public access to it, or to a selected set of it. As a result, access is controlled, and we can refuse to assign values, for instance. But these functions are inline, since their full definitions are in the definition of a class, so indirect access does not add any time penalty. Also note that `GetRe` and `GetIm` are declared `const` to indicate that they do not change the state of the class. All member functions that are not intended to change member data should be declared `const`: this practice makes code safer since any inconsistencies will be caught by the compiler.

```
65   public:
66
67       // Getters & Setters to access data members of the class
68       double GetRe( void ) const { return fRe; }     // "const" since we only read
69       double GetIm( void ) const { return fIm; }     // data, not changing the state
70
71       void SetRe( double re ) { fRe = re; }          // here we change the state
72       void SetIm( double im ) { fIm = im; }          // so it is not "const"
73
```

Finally, we came to the *overloaded operators*. The first one, defined on line [79], is the comparison `operator ==` (do not confuse it with assignment =). On line [81], it simply returns the result of the comparison of both data members. But let's stop for a moment – to compare, we need two objects, whereas only c is provided as an argument in the definition of `operator ==`. Where is the other object? To answer this, note that, as for any other non-static member, the `operator ==` code is executed on behalf of an object. We can easily see that this is the first object necessary for the comparison, while c is the second one. On the other hand, note that there is no definition of how to implement the ordering `operator <`.

```
74   public:
75
76       ////////////////////////////////////////////////////////////
77       // Overloaded "equal" compare operator
78       ////////////////////////////////////////////////////////////
79       bool operator == ( const TComplex & c ) const
80       {
81           return fRe == c.fRe && fIm == c.fIm;
82       }
83
```

At this point, we will provide a few facts about the overloaded operators in C++:

- Overloaded operators are overloaded functions that define special behavior for the operators
- Overloaded operators can be members of a class, or they can be standalone functions
- An overloaded operator is defined exactly like any other function, except that its name follows the pattern shown in (Figure 4.4)

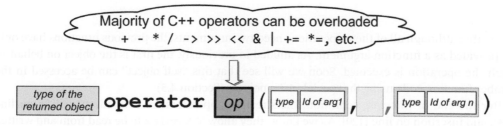

Figure 4.4 Syntax of the overloaded operators in C++.

- The association rules and precedence of the overloaded operators cannot be changed and remain as defined in Table 3.15
- The vast majority of C++ operators can be overloaded (there are only a few exceptions, e.g. member access . and scope resolution : :)

As alluded to previously, all four basic arithmetic operations are defined for the complex numbers. Therefore, it is a good idea to define the overloaded operators of the corresponding arithmetic operations in the TComplex class. As a result, we will be able to write z + u, instead of calling a function like Add(z, u) to perform the operation. Actually, since the implementations will be slightly different, we define a pair of functions for each arithmetic operation: one for an operator, and the second for its operator-update version. For example, on lines [91, 93], respectively, operator + and operator += are defined. This is done for all four operations, and thus we have eight member operators.

```
84      public:
85
86          ///////////////////////////////////////////////////////////
87          // Overloaded arithmetic operators
88          ///////////////////////////////////////////////////////////
89
90          // +
91          TComplex operator + ( const TComplex & second_op ) const;
92
93          TComplex & operator += ( const TComplex & second_op );
94
95
96          // -
97          TComplex operator - ( const TComplex & second_op ) const;
98
99          TComplex & operator -= ( const TComplex & second_op );
100
101
102         // *
103         TComplex operator * ( const TComplex & second_op ) const;
104
105         TComplex & operator *= ( const TComplex & second_op );
106
107
108         // div - can throw and exception of division by zero
109         TComplex operator / ( const TComplex & second_op ) const;
110
111         TComplex & operator /= ( const TComplex & second_op );
112
113      };
114
```

Note that although all of these operations need two arguments, the previous functions have only one provided as a function argument. As alluded to previously, the first is the object on behalf of which the operation is executed. Soon we will see that this "self object" can be accessed in the member function code using the special this pointer (Section 4.5).

After the end of the class definition, the streaming operators are defined: extraction on line [118], and insertion on line [120]. As we know, they allow TComplex to be read from and written to any streamable object, such as std::cin for the keyboard and std::cout for the screen.

Finally, the `abs` function is declared, also external to the class definition but in the namespace. It returns a module of a complex number.

```
115    /////////////////////////////////////////////////////////////////
116    // Overloaded streaming operators - always outside the class
117
118    std::istream & operator >> ( std::istream & i, TComplex & complex );
119
120    std::ostream & operator << ( std::ostream & o, const TComplex & complex );
121
122    /////////////////////////////////////////////////////////////////
123
124    // Returns module of a TComplex
125    double abs( const TComplex & c );
126
127    }          // end of the CppBook
```

As we mentioned, the two streaming operators are defined outside the `TComplex` class. This is necessary since they need to operate with the streaming classes as well. But we have a choice for the arithmetic operators: they can be either class members or external operators. This possibility will be further evaluated in Section 4.7.

4.4.2 Definition of the *TComplex* Class Members

As we have seen, the class's definition is usually contained in its header file, while the implementation is postponed to the source file. This structure allows for the independent processing of different translation units, while information can be exchanged through the headers, as shown in Figure 2.3 and Figure 3.23. Such an arrangement, in which only headers and object files are distributed, also lets us prevent expensive sources from being revealed or tampered with. But it is possible to provide full definitions of member functions in the header. In this case, the member function has the `inline` attribute. This means instead of being called indirectly, the code is inserted at the call location, as discussed in Section 3.14.3. In addition, `inline` defines the static type of linking – that is, the same definition can be included many times in different translation units without the linker complaining about the symbols being defined multiple times, as we will discuss in Section 5.1. As alluded to previously, longer implementations are left to the source file(s).

As we mentioned, the header with the class definition needs to be included before the definitions, as on line [2] in Listing 4.2. Then, on line [6], the namespace is reopened. An auxiliary constant `kDivThresh` is defined on line [11]: it will guard against division by values that are too low, which could lead to numerically incorrect results (Section 7.4).

`TComplex::operator +` is defined on line [19]. Note that since we are outside the class definition, all externally provided class types need to be prefixed with the class name and the scope-resolution operator: `TComplex::` in our case (Figure 2.8). `operator +` adds two `TComplex` objects: the one for which the function is executed, and `second_op` passed as the constant reference (Section 3.11). Finally, the result is returned on line [22] as a third object. It is locally created on line [21] using the parametric constructor with the passed sums of the corresponding components, as expected. Such a return by value might look like a waste of time for object copying, especially if we are returning a larger object, such as a matrix or a video object. However, the return value optimization (RVO) mechanism, as well as move semantics, mitigate this greatly, as we will discuss in Section 4.5.

Listing 4.2 Definition of members of the `TComplex` class (in *Complex, Complex.cpp*).

```
1    // Let us include the definition of the TComplex class
2    #include "Complex.h"
3
4
5
6    namespace CppBook
7    {
8
9        // Used to check against division by 0
10
11       const double kDivThresh { 1e-36 };
12
13
14       //////////////////////////////////////////////////////////
15       // Overloaded arithmetic operators for the TComplex class
16       //////////////////////////////////////////////////////////
17
18       // +
19       TComplex TComplex::operator + ( const TComplex & second_op ) const
20       {
21           TComplex retComplex( fRe + second_op.fRe, fIm + second_op.fIm );
22           return retComplex;      // Return object by value
23       }
24
25       TComplex & TComplex::operator += ( const TComplex & second_op )
26       {
27           fRe += second_op.fRe, fIm += second_op.fIm;
28           return * this;               // Return object by reference
29       }
30
```

Quite similar, but usually more efficient, is the implementation of the add-and-update `operator +=` beginning on line [25]. In this case, the members of the current object are updated on line [27], and then the current object is returned on line [28] via dereferencing of the pointer-to-self: `* this`.

We skip the definitions of the subtraction and multiplication operators since they operate in a similar fashion. But the division operators deserve a little attention. Looking at Eq. (4.4), we can see that if the value of the denominator $c^2 + d^2$ is 0 or close to 0, the result will be incorrect computations. What should we do in such a situation, and what result, if any, should be returned? There is no good result in this case, so the solution is to break execution by throwing an exception, as discussed in Section 3.13.2.5. If properly caught, it will let us safely abandon the difficult spot and begin the action from a well-defined state. The situation is detected and remedied, if necessary, on lines [35–36]. We could throw any object, even a simple text constant; however, a better idea is to throw a more meaningful object. Again the Standard Library offers ready solutions – `std::overflow_error`, for instance, or allows for a custom exception class derived from the `std::exception` base – see Section 4.10.

```
31       // div - can throw an exception on division by zero
32       TComplex TComplex::operator / ( const TComplex & second_op ) const
33       {
34           auto div = second_op.fRe * second_op.fRe + second_op.fIm * second_op.fIm;
35           if( fabs( div ) < kDivThresh )      // don't divide by small number or 0
36               throw std::overflow_error( "div by 0 error" );// better than: div==0.0
```

```
37
38          auto re = fRe * second_op.fRe + fIm * second_op.fIm;
39          re /= div;
40
41          auto im = fIm * second_op.fRe - fRe * second_op.fIm;
42          im /= div;
43
44          return TComplex( re, im );           // Return object by value
45      }
```

Finally, let's look at the overloaded streaming operators for the TComplex class, defined on lines [50, 60]. Since we have discussed the streaming operators many times, the code should be clear. We will only observe that, because easy access to all data members is provided by the class getters and setters, the streaming operators need not be declared friend, as was the case for the CurrencyExchanger object presented in Section 3.18.4.

```
46      //////////////////////////////////////////////////////////
47      // Streaming operators - they do not need to be declared
48      // as friends
49
50      istream & operator >> ( istream & i, TComplex & complex )
51      {
52          double re {}, im {};
53          i >> re;
54          i >> im;
55          complex.SetRe( re );
56          complex.SetIm( im );
57          return i;
58      }
59
60      ostream & operator << ( ostream & o, const TComplex & complex )
61      {
62          o << complex.GetRe() << " " << complex.GetIm();
63          return o;
64      }
65
66      //////////////////////////////////////////////////////////
67
68      double abs( const TComplex & c )
69      {
70          return std::sqrt( c.GetIm() * c.GetIm() + c.GetRe() * c.GetRe() );
71      }
72
73  }       // end of the CppBook namespace
```

Finally, the abs function is defined. Since the sum of squared values is always positive, then call to the square root function std::sqrt is safe here.

4.4.3   Test Functions for the *TComplex* Class

The TComplex class is coded, but it is not finished yet – we need to test its functionality and, if necessary, trim the code. For this purpose, two functions are proposed, as shown in Listing 4.3.

Listing 4.3 Test functions for the `TComplex` class (in *Complex, ComplexTest.cpp*).

```
1   #include <fstream>
2
3   #include "Complex.h"
4
5
6   using std::cout, std::cin, std::endl;
7   using std::ofstream, std::ifstream;
8
9   using CppBook::TComplex;
10
11
12
13  // Simple operations with complex numbers
14  // using the keyboard and the screen
15  void Complex_Test_Screen( void )
16  {
17      /////////////////////////////////////////
18      // Let us create few TComplex objects:
19      CppBook::TComplex        a, b,       // a and b by default constructor
20                          c( 10, 20 ); // c by the parametric constructor
21
22      TComplex d( c );        // Yet another one, this time d contains a copy of c
23
24      // Let us test how to stream out object d to the screen
25      cout << d << endl;
26      operator << ( cout, d );        // We can also write like this
27      cout << endl;                   // then move to the new line
28
29      cout << "Write re, press Enter, then im, press Enter" << endl;
30      cin >> a;       // From the keyboard read new values to the object a
31
32      c = b = a;      // Copy a to b, then b to c (= is right-associative)
33
34      // Let us add two complex numbers b and d and display the result
35      cout << "( " << a << " ) + ( " << b << " ) = ( " << a + b << " ) " << endl;
36
37      // To assign 5.0 to b, 5.0 needs to be converted to TComplex, then assigned.
38      b = 5.0;
39      cout << "( " << a << " ) +.( " << b << " ) = ( " << a + b << " ) " << endl;
40  }
```

In `Complex_Test_Screen`, first three `TComplex` objects a, b, and c are created on lines [19–20]: the first two with a call to the default constructor, and the third with a call to the parametric constructor. On line [22], object d is created with a call to the copy constructor with the object c as its parameter; as a result, the state of d will be a copy of the state of c.

These objects are then involved in IO operations, as shown on lines [25–30]. They are straightforward, although on line [26], an explicit call to `operator >>` has been used. Here we see that an overloaded operator can be used like any other member function – by providing its name and passing it parameters in the list enclosed by parentheses (). Such a call syntax is useful in some situations.

Line [32] is interesting: it has three assignments in a row. As we know from Section 3.19, the assignment `operator =` belongs to the rare group of right-associative operators. This is for a reason: the right assignment b = c is performed first, by calling the overloaded `operator =` from within object b. The result of this operation is a temporary object that will be passed to the first `operator =`, this time called on behalf of the a object. The result is that all three objects will possess a state identical to that of object c. Finally, on line [35], the results of the arithmetic operations on a and b are printed.

On line [38], the real value 5.0 is assigned to the complex object b. But this is a twofold operation: first, the converting constructor (line [63] in Listing 4.1) is called to convert a `double` object into a `TComplex` object, which is then assigned to b with the assignment operator, defined on line [49] in Listing 4.1. The result of a + b is displayed on line [39].

The second test function `Complex_Test_File`, defined on line [43], creates two default `TComplex` objects on line [46]. These are then initialized on lines [50, 53] from the keyboard.

The results of the arithmetic operations are output to a text file *ComplexTest.txt*, which is opened in appending mode so its existing contents are preserved (Section 6.2.7). Since division can throw an exception – we do not know what the user will enter – it needs to be enclosed by a `try-catch` statement, starting on line [71]. If an exception is thrown, the first chance to catch it is the `catch` on line [76]. The exception to be caught must be of the `std::exception` (or derived) type. Otherwise, if the type of the thrown exception object is incompatible with the former type, the second "last chance" branch on line [81] will catch it. In both cases, an error message is output to the error stream, represented by the `std::cerr` object. In the first case, `std::exception` has a chance to print a message using a call to its `what` member.

```cpp
41    // Simple operations with complex numbers
42    // using the keyboard, the screen, and a file
43    void Complex_Test_File( void )
44    {
45        // Create two complex objects
46        TComplex     a, b;
47
48        // Enter two from the keyboard
49        cout << "Enter 1st complex" << endl;
50        cin >> a;
51
52        cout << "Enter 2nd complex" << endl;
53        cin >> b;
54
55        // Let us try to copy results to a file opened in appending mode
56        ofstream theFile( "ComplexTest.txt", std::ios::app );
57
58
59
60
61        // Always check if the file opened correctly
62        if( theFile.is_open() == true )
63        {
64            // Perform operations and print the results to the file
65            theFile << "a = " << a << ", b = " << b << endl;
66            theFile << "a + b = " << a + b << endl;
67            theFile << "a - b = " << a - b << endl;
68            theFile << "a * b = " << a * b << endl;
69
70            // However, division is different - it can throw an exception
71            try
72            {
73                // Keep it in the try-catch clamp
74                theFile << "a / b = " << a / b << endl << endl;
75            }
76            catch( std::exception & e )            // catch exceptions
77            {
78                // Standard exceptions will be processed here
79                std::cerr << "Exception caught: "    << e.what() << endl; // print the cause
80            }
81            catch( ... )
82            {
```

```
83          // Any other exception will be caught here
84          std::cerr << "Unknown error" << endl;
85      }
86
87  }
88
89 }
```

Finally, the two test functions are launched in the main function in the *Complex* application, as shown in Listing 4.4.

Listing 4.4 Definition of the `main` function with calls to the test functions (in *Complex, main.cpp*). Function declarations are sufficient; no header files are necessary.

```
1   // Declarations are sufficient to call functions
2   void Complex_Test_Screen( void );
3   void Complex_Test_File( void );
4
5
6   // In C++ there are few versions of the main function
7   int main( void )
8   {
9       Complex_Test_Screen();
10      Complex_Test_File();
11
12      return 0;
13  }
```

4.5 More on References

In this section, we discuss some more advanced, but important and practical, issues associated with references and indirect access to objects. Here we focus on *right-references*, which let us use *move semantics* to avoid expensive, unnecessary copying of objects. For indirect object accesses, the problem of object lifetime is also important, so we will touch on it as well.

In this section, we will learn about the following:

- Right references and the move semantics
- Relations between references and pointers
- Object lifetime issues when returning objects from functions

4.5.1 Right and Forward References

C++11 introduced the very important concept of *move semantics* (Stroustrup 2013). This is simply a smart way of avoiding unnecessary object copying in some contexts. Instead of performing a full copy of an object and its data, usually pointed to by the object's internal pointer, it suffices to exchange the internal pointers to data, thus avoiding time-consuming memory operations. The two actions are shown in Figure 4.5.

When performing a copy[1] operation (Figure 4.5a), both the object and data are copied to form a new object with its own copy of the data. As a result, two identical objects are available. On the

---

1 Actually, this is a type of deep copy, as opposed to a shallow copy – see Section 4.6.4.

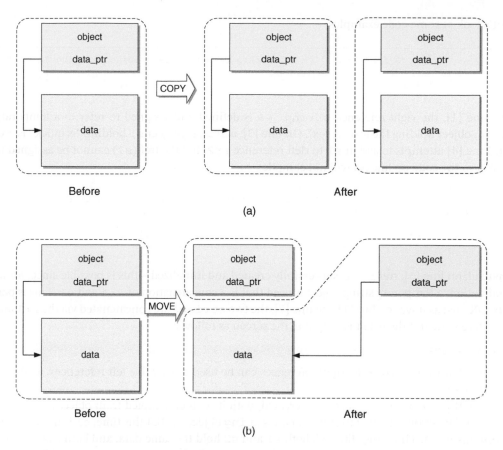

Figure 4.5 The difference between copy and move operations for an object containing external data. When copying (a) an entirely new object, a new version of the data is created. On the other hand, a move (b) creates an object and steals data from the original object. After the move operation, the original object is changed; it has no data and should not be used.

other hand, a move operation (Figure 4.5b) creates a new object but takes the data from the original object. Thus, after the move, the original object is left with no data and should not be used. Modern C++ compilers know when copy and move should be performed. But how to copy an object, and how to steal data, must be implemented by the programmer. In other words, for objects to have copy and move available, the two operations need to be implemented as separate member functions, as we will discuss in Section 4.6.4.

To distinguish copy from move, the concept of *right-value references* (*rvalue reference, rref* for short) was introduced.[2] These are denoted with the && symbol to distinguish them from left-value references (*lvalue reference; lref* for short) denoted with a single &, as explained in Section (3.11). In other words, the main concept behind the rvalue reference is that it refers to a temporary object, which the owner of that reference can freely exploit (e.g. drain data from); we assume this temporary object will never be used again. Thus, object access via rvalue references is sometimes called a *destructive read* (Stroustrup 2013).

---

2 For a discussion of left values (lvals) vs. right values (rvals), see Section 3.19.

Let's look at some code examples:

```
1    string &&   rr1( "A fox" );        // rr1 refers to a temporary object holding "A fox"
2
3    string   s1( "is quick" );
```

On line [1], the right reference string && is defined and assigned to refer to a temporary string object holding the text "A fox". On line [3], a string object s1 holding "is quick" is created. Line [4] attempts to assign s1 to rleft reference rr2; but the lref (s1) cannot be assigned to the rref, so the code on line [4] will not compile:

```
4    string && rr2( s1 );              // error, cannot directly assign lref to rref
5    string && rr2( " " + s1 );        // OK, bound to a temporary object
6
7    cout << rr1 + rr2 << endl;        // output concatenation of strings
```

Instead, on line [5], rref rr2 is successfully created and initialized – this is possible since, for its initialization, a temporary string object is used that is a concatenation of " " and s1. This is perfectly OK, just as it was on line [1]. On line [7], the two strings are concatenated via the rr1 and rr2 references, and the result is output to the screen as follows:

```
A fox is quick
```

We see that to access objects, right references can be used exactly like left references, as shown in Section 3.11.

On line [8], a new string object s2 is created, with its contents copied from object s1. On line [10], a similar action is started to create a new string object s3. But this time, s1 is used to *move* its contents to s3. Thus, after line [8], both s1 and s2 hold the same data, and both can be freely used. However, after line [10], only s3 contains "is quick" and can be used: s1 now has no data and should not be used. On line [12], yet another rref rr3 is created and initialized with a temporary string object returned by the Conv2Upper function. Finally, on line [14], a temporary object is displayed, holding a concatenation of the uppercase versions of both pieces of text:

```
8    string s2( s1 );                  // copy s1 to s2, both strings can be used
9
10   string s3( std::move( s1 ) );     // move s1 to s3 - no longer use of s1
11
12   string && rr3( Conv2Upper( s3 ) ); // take over an uppercase temporary
13
14   cout << Conv2Upper( rr1 ) + " " + rr3 << endl; // uppercase version
```

After execution of this fragment of code, the following string will appear on the terminal :

```
A FOX IS QUICK
```

What is new here is the std::move function, which simply casts s1 to the corresponding rref. Thus, its call is equivalent to the following:

```
string s3( static_cast< string && >( s1 ) );
```

Because of this cast, a proper initialization member function from the `string` class can be invoked by overloading the `string` function (Section 3.14.5). Not surprisingly, this will be a move initializer, if available (in `string` it is; in other classes we do not know, or we have to write them ourselves). If such a move initializer is not available (e.g. the class is old), a copy constructor will be called instead. Thus the operation is safe. In other words, `move` indicates to the compiler that an object will no longer be used, and its contents can be moved out of it.

In light of the move semantics, it is interesting to analyze the function `Conv2Upper` called on lines [12, 14] of the previous code snippet. In both calling contexts, it returns a temporary `string` object holding an uppercase copy of a `string` passed to it as an input parameter through a `const` lref [16]. The function is defined as follows:

```
15   // Returns an uppercase copy of str
16   string      Conv2Upper( const string & str )
17   {
18      string ret_str;      // transform will copy-and-convert to uppercase
19      transform( str.begin(), str.end(), back_inserter( ret_str ), toupper );
20      return ret_str;   // return ret_str via a temp object
                          // - use move semantics thanks to string implementation
21   }
```

On line [19], the `std::transform` function copies the input `str` from beginning to its end, converting each character to its uppercase version and inserting each character into the `ret_str` object using `std::back_inserter`. The conversion is performed using the `std::toupper` function. Finally, on line [20], the function returns a temporary `string` object that will be moved since move operations are implemented in the `string` class. If `string` did not support move semantics, the object would be copied (although the compiler could still apply the copy elision strategy – see Section 4.5).

Similar to left references, right references also have to be initialized in their definition. As mentioned earlier, they can be initialized with other right reference like objects, such as temporary objects. But they cannot be initialized with left references. However, a left-referenced object can be moved to an object referred to with a right reference via typecast. The syntax and examples of right references to access `vector< int >` are shown in Table 4.2;

As shown in Table 4.2, there is no use of `const` rvalue references, since most of the benefits from their use involve modifying objects they refer to. But these references have another interesting feature: for some contexts that require *type deduction*, such as

- Function template parameters (Section 4.8)
- `auto` declarations

the meaning of `T&&`, where `T` denotes a type, is more general and can be either

- An rvalue reference or
- An lvalue reference

In other words, depending on the context, `T&&` can bind either to an rvalue, as expected, or to an lvalue. Such references are called *forward* or *universal references* (Meyers 2014). Since, for each reference, a forward reference also needs to be initialized, the way it is initialized determines

Table 4.2 Syntax and examples of right references.

Operation	Syntax	Examples

Right reference definition and initialization	`object_type` `&&` `ref_identifier` `=` `object` `;`
	
	`object_type` `&&` `ref_identifier` `{` `object` `}` `;`
		``// rvalue can be assigned to rref

int && ir2 = 25 + 7;   // OK, ir2 ==> 32
ir2 = 55;   // OK, ir2 ==> 55

using int_vec = vector< int >;

// rref to a temporary object
int_vec && rv1 { 1, 5, 7, 13 };

// create iv1 and init based on rv1
int_vec iv1(rv1);

// create iv2 and (move) take over data from iv1
int_vec iv2(move(iv1));
// iv1 is empty and should not be used``` |

what it binds to. That is, if it is initialized with an rvalue, then it is an rvalue reference. Otherwise, if it is initialized with an lvalue, it is an lvalue reference. Consider, for instance, the following code snippet:

```
22  string str( "is quick" );
23
24  auto && rref = "Fox";   // a forward reference + type deduction ==> rref
25
26  auto && lref = str;     // a forward reference + type deduction ==> lref
27
28  lref = " " + lref;      // append space in front of str
29
30  cout << rref + lref << endl;    // "Fox is quick"
```

To be a forward reference, the reference's form in the function template must be exactly `T&&`. Right references are also used for *perfect forwarding* of function arguments using `std::forward`, as shown in the time measurement example in Section 6.4. For details, see (Stroustrup 2013; Meyers 2014).

Things to Remember

- For some objects, a move operation, which basically means data swapping with another object, is faster and consumes less memory than a copy. To distinguish the two, right-value references were introduced
- Right-value references identify objects that can be moved. Similar to copy operations, move operations (construction, assignment) must be implemented in the object
- Right-value references must be initialized with temporary objects or other right references
- A left-value object can set to be moved by its cast to an rvalue with the `std::move` function

4.5.2   References vs. Pointers

References and pointers are two alternative ways to access objects indirectly. This is their similarity. However, the two concepts differ significantly, as follows:

- A reference is always attached to its object – there are no empty or unattached references. But there is a special empty pointer (`nullptr`; previously 0 or represented with the NULL macro)
- Unlike with references, there can be a pointer to another pointer, and so on
- Accessing an object via its reference does not require any special operators – the syntax is the same as in the case of direct object access. Pointers, on the other hand, require the use of the `*` and `&` operators

In many cases, indirect access to objects can be coded with pointers or references. Probably the most important semantic difference between references and pointers is the concept of an empty pointer. For instance, a pointer argument of a function can express the state of not having an object, such as an optional value, etc. But in contemporary C++, references play a primary role; to express an optional argument, C++ offers the `std::optional` mechanism (see Section 3.18.5).

4.5.3 Pitfalls with References

When dealing with indirect access, we operate with two objects: the proper object and a link object to it in the form of a reference or a pointer to the former. But in some situations, there can be a link (a reference) that refers to a nonexistent object. Consider the following code:

```
1    // Very nasty error - a function returns a reference
2    // to an object which was destroyed.
3    // "returning address of local variable or temporary: char_counter_vec"
4    vector< int > &    CountCharsIn( const string & fileName )
5    {
6
7        vector< int >    char_counter_vec;
8
9        // open the file, read line by line
10       // count chars and push them back to char_counter_vec
11       // ...
12
13       // finally, return the counted results
14
15       assert( false );          // do NOT use this code
16
17       return char_counter_vec;  // WRONG!! char_counter_vec will be destroyed
18                                 // since it is local to this function
19   }
```

The problem arises in the last line – a reference to the `char_counter_vec` object is returned. However, since `char_counter_vec` is a local object, it is automatically destroyed after leaving the function on line [19]. The rref will not help in this respect, either. Thus, anyone who wants to use that object will be in trouble:

```
20   void CountCharsIn_Test( void )
21   {
22       const string fileName( "Test.txt" );
23
24       vector< int >    v = CountCharsIn( fileName );    // serious error lurks here ...
25
26       // display results ...
27
28   }
```

There are a few solutions to this situation, of which the following is also the simplest. Return a copy of the `char_counter_vec` vector.

```
29   // Return a copy (or move)
30   vector< int >    CountCharsIn_copy_( const string & fileName )
31   {
32
33       vector< int >    char_counter_vec;
34
35       // open the file, read line by line
36       // count chars and push them back to char_counter_vec
37       // ...
38
39       // finally, return the counted results
40
41       return char_counter_vec;    // OK, char_counter_vec can be copied (in effect it
42                                   // will be moved since std::vector is smart enough)
43   }
```

In this version, we simply return a copy of the `char_counter_vec` local object. That is, a temporary local object is created from `char_counter_vec` using the copy constructor, to be returned as a return value at line [41].[3] But in modern C++, if an object has a move constructor, the compiler will be smart enough to figure out the situation and call it instead of making heavy and usually unnecessary local copies of an object. In short, move semantics allow the simple exchange of pointers to data instead of moving the entire data pool, as we will discuss (see Section 4.6.4).

Obviously, the problem of referring to live objects is also important when dealing with pointers. In this case, we have another potential pitfall associated with object ownership passing from pointer to pointer.

Every rose has its thorns; and because of their value syntax but pointer semantics, some programmers consider references confusing (see *https://google.github.io/styleguide/cppguide.html*). We can be surprised when calling a function with an object as its parameter since this object's state can be stealthy changed in the function when passing an object with a reference (see Section 3.14.2.2).

4.6 Example Project – Mastering Class Members with the *TheCube* Class

There are many different types of classes, since they represent a variety of real objects. Nevertheless, common construction patterns can be identified for a broad group of them. In this section, we will investigate the details of a class for modeling cubes of data like the one shown in Figure 4.6a. In this section, we will learn about the following:

- How to define a container class to store data organized as a 3D cube (a tensor)
- Class special member functions
- Deep vs. shallow copying
- Implementation of move semantics

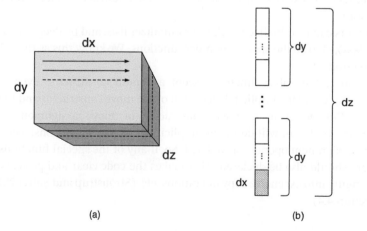

(a)   (b)

Figure 4.6 Illustration of TheCube and memory allocation in its internal data buffer.

---

3 There is no need to perform a cast on a return value with `std::move` – a modern C++ compiler will know what to do.

- Dynamic memory allocations on the heap: resource management and access with the smart pointer `std::unique_ptr`
- Transforming a 3D element's position to the 1D memory layout
- Streaming operators in a binary format
- Copy elision and the RVO mechanism

Such multidimensional collections of data arise in many scientific and technical applications, such as processing video sequences: even a single color frame can be seen as a 3D cube of pixel values (Cyganek 2013). The class to represent cubes of data, named `TheCube`, serves us as a class definition with nontrivial special member functions. Table 4.3 presents a systematic overview of the most important parts of this class. However, there is no unique way to express a given concept in the C++ language. A construction usually reflects the expected usage scenarios but also depends on the programmer's style and experience.

Figure 4.6b shows the possible alignment of the data in a linear memory model, as presented in Section 2.1. In this case, *dx* is the innermost index, followed by *dy* and then *dz*.

4.6.1   Automatic vs. Explicit Definition of the Constructors

Do we need to write all of the special member functions for each class we define? The short answer is no; the slightly longer answers is, it depends. Undoubtedly, we need to know the rules to pick the right solution. As we have already seen, we have written constructors, assignments, and so on for the classes used previously in this book.

If we do not provide a constructor or an assignment operator, it will be automatically generated by the compiler using code that performs simple member-after-member copies. In many cases, this is OK; but as we see in `TheCube`, for some classes, a simple copy of a pointer to the data buffer is wrong (this is called a *shallow copy*). Nevertheless, if the default constructor were to initialize class members to their defaults, it could be omitted. To summarize:

- If a default definition is desired, use `=default`
- To disable a special function, use `=delete`[4]
- If a class is intended to be derived from, define an explicit destructor that is declared `virtual`, even if it is empty
- If all data members can be initialized with their initializer lists, and no deep copy is expected (no pointers in a class), skip all the special member functions. We know this as the rule of zero, first presented in Section 3.9
- Declaring any special member function except a default constructor, even as `=default` or `=delete`, will prevent the implicit declaration of the move constructor and the move assignment operator. But declaring a move constructor or move assignment operator, even as `=default` or `=delete`, will define an implicitly generated copy constructor or implicitly generated copy assignment operator as deleted. So, if any of the special functions are declared, all of the others should also be declared. This makes the code clear and protects against move operations changing into expensive copy operations, etc. (Stroustrup and Sutter 2019). This is the rule of six (Section 4.4)

---

4 A similar effect can be obtained by placing a special member in the class's `private` section. For example, making a destructor = `delete`, or private, prevents the direct creation of such an object.

Table 4.3 Characteristic structures of a class (in *TheCube, TheCube.h*).

Class members	Description	Examples
Class data members	Objects embedded into *this* one. Can be any of the previously introduced types. Can be variable or constant objects.	1 #include <iostream> 2 #include <fstream> 3 #include <array> 4 #include <cassert> 5 6 7 using std::cout, std::cin, std::endl; // Name aliases

Static class members	Static data and member functions connected with a particular class instead of an object.
	
	There is only one instance of each static data member for a class, regardless of the number of objects for that class.
	
	Static data members can be accessed with the prefix X::.
		8
		9
		10 class TheCube
		11 {
		12 public:
		13
		14 using value_type = double;
		15 using size_type = std::size_t;
		16
		17 static const size_type kDims { 3 }; // the same for all objects of class
		18
		19 enum EDims { kx, ky, kz }; // shortcuts for 3 dimensions
		20
		21 private:
		22
		23 // A 'smart' pointer to the 1D buffer with all data
		24 std::unique_ptr< value_type [] > fDataBuf;
		25
		26 // An array of 3 dimensions
		27 std::array< size_type, kDims > fDim;

(Continued)

Table 4.3 (continued)

Class members	Description	Examples
		On lines [1–4] we include four header files: *iostream* for the input/output classes, *fstream* for the file input/ output operations, *array* for the fixed-size array to store cube dimensions (Section 3.10), and *cassert* for the assert macro, used for code verification (see Section 3.17.2). To avoid repeating the `std::` prefix, some of the common `std` objects are introduced by the `using` directive on line [7]. The definition of the `TheCube` class starts on line [10]. Lines [14, 15] introduce two type aliases: `value_type` to represent the type of the stored data (`double`), and `size_type` to represent the dimensions of the cube. Such aliases are very convenient – imagine, for example, that we wish to change `double` to `float`. Then we only need to modify line [14].Then we define two constant data object of this class. The first, on line [17], is the `static const size_type` object kDims, which conveys the common dimension of all objects of the `TheCube` class: 3. This is the domain of static members. Their characteristic feature is that they are related to the class, not to the objects of that class: `TheCube::kDims`. Only one copy of a static object of a class exists at a time, regardless of the number of objects of that class. But the static members are shared by all objects. Therefore, static non-const objects should be avoided if we think of using the code for parallel processing (Chapter 8). Another way to define static values for a class is to use the enum type, such as enum `EDims` on line [19]. An unscoped enum is a trade-off here for easy indexing (Section 3.14.6). Both of these constants will be available for all objects, since they are public.

TheCube contains private data members that are local to each object of this class. The first, defined on line [24], is the `fDataBuf` *smart pointer* to the data buffer containing all the data of TheCube. It has two functions: (i) it serves as a pointer to the memory buffer allocated on the heap, and (ii) it ensures *the automatic deallocation of this memory buffer* (explained in Section 5.2).TheCube has three dimensions. These are stored in the `std::array` defined on line [27], using `static kDims`. Each object of the TheCube class, always contains kDims==3 but could have different integer values. Their product is equal to the total number of elements in each TheCube object.

```
28    public:
29
30        // Default constructor
31        TheCube( void )    // empty buffer
32            : fDataBuf( nullptr ), fDim { 0, 0, 0 }
33        {
34        }
35
``` |
| Default constructor | A function with the same name as the class and no input parameters X::X (void). Called once during the creation of an object.Its role is to initialize *this* object. | |

In *each constructor*, after the colon `:`, the *member data initializer* list can be used to invoke constructors of the member data objects. This is the preferred way to initialize data members.	The class default constructor is defined starting on line [32]. This special function is named exactly like the class TheCube, takes no arguments (default), and never returns an object. The specific part of each constructor of a class is the member data initializer list - a list of member objects of this class with initial parameters, starting after the colon `:` and before the body `{ }` of the constructor function (Section 3.16.1). In other words, for each of the class members, its default or parametric constructor is called. On line [33], we initialize the entire array at once, using the list initializer `{ }` (*GROUP 15*, Table 3.15). Also note that no data is allocated in the default constructor since all dimensions of TheCube are set to 0, and fDataBuf is set to nullptr.

Notice that for all member functions of a class, we have two options for where to put its body. It can be put directly in the class definition, as previously. In such a case, non-virtual and non-static functions also have *implicit inline* properties (Section 5.1). But a function can only be declared in the class definition, whereas the function itself is defined outside the class definition. In this case, we need to use its fully qualified name. For instance, if the constructor is defined outside, we should write TheCube::TheCube (void). Finally, if a member is used inside the class definition, then we can skip the prefix TheCube:: and write TheCube (void). This is how the member functions are defined in this example. |
| **Parametric constructor**

A function with the same name as the class and with input parameters:

X::X (*type_list*). Called once during the creation of an object.

Its role is to initialize *this* object using the objects from the *type list*. | ```
35   // Parametric constructor
37   TheCube(const size_type dx, const size_type dy, const size_type dz)
38   : fDim{ dx, dy, dz }
39   {
40   // Allocate a 1D array of value_type elements and assign to fDataBuf
41   fDataBuf = std::make_unique< value_type [] >
42   (fDim[kx] * fDim[ky] * fDim[kz]);
43   }
```

The definition of the parametric constructor of TheCube starts on line [37]. It takes three parameters, which are the dimensions of the cube. They are used to initialize the fDim array in the member data initializer list on line [38], using the list `{ }` operator. We assume that each of the dimensions, dx, dy, and dz, is greater than 0. On lines [41–42], a data buffer whose size is the product of all the cube dimensions is allocated on the computer heap and assigned to the fDataBuf object. Data allocation is performed by the helper function std::make_unique. The most important advantage of std::unique_ptr is that it automatically takes care of the buffer deallocation (which is not the case if the new operator is used, as explained in Section 5.2). |

*(Continued)*
```

Table 4.3 (continued)

Class members	Description	Examples

Copy constructor	A function with the same name as the class and with one input parameter – a (const) reference to an object of the same class:
	
	X::X(X &)
	
	X::X(const X &)
	
	Called once during creation of an object. Its role is to copy the state of *this* object from the input object.
		``cpp
		44 // Copy constructor
		45 TheCube(const TheCube & cube)
		46 {
		47 fDim = cube.fDim; // First copy the dimensions
		48
		49 const auto elems = fDim[kx] * fDim[ky] * fDim[kz];
		50
		51 // Whatever was held by fDataBuf will be first deleted.
		52 // Then, a new buffer will be allocated and attached to fDataBuf
		53 fDataBuf = std::make_unique< value_type [] >(elems);
		54
		55 // Finally, "deep" copy data to the "this" buffer
		56 // dest source bytes
		57 std::memcpy(fDataBuf.get(), cube.fDataBuf.get(),
		58 elems * sizeof(value_type));
		59 }
		``

The role of the copy constructor, as shown on line [45], is to create an object as a copy of an existing object (hence its name). It copies all data members from the supplied object. First, on line [47], the array with cube dimensions fDim is copied element by element.

However, it is a different story with fDataBuf since if we only copied a value of the held pointer, we would be left with two objects and one data buffer. Obviously, such a *shallow copy* is not what we want. Our wish is to perform a *deep copy*; that is, to copy the entire buffer.

To do this, on line [53] a new memory buffer is allocated, containing elems data of value_type, and assigned to fDataBuf. Just before that, whatever was held in fDataBuf is released. But since this is a copy constructor, fDataBuf held a nullptr, which deallocates nothing.

Finally, data from the cube object's buffer needs to be copied to the newly allocated buffer. This is accomplished on lines [57–58] with the std::memcpy function (Section A.2.6). It copies bytes between two memory buffers, with the destination – which pointer is obtained by the call fDataBuf.get(), and the source – pointed to by cube.fDataBuf.get(). To get the correct number of bytes, we need to multiply the amount of data expressed by the elems variable from line [49] by the number of bytes allocated for each data item, i.e. sizeof(value_type).

Assignment operator	An overloaded assignment operator, with one input parameter const X & and returning X &:
	
	 X & X::operator = (X &)
	
	 X & X::operator = (const X &)
	
	 Its role is to copy the state of an existing object to the previously created *this* object, and then return *this* object.
		60 // Assignment operator
		 61 TheCube & operator = (const TheCube & cube)
		 62 {
		 63 // We cannot copy if the same object
		 64 if(this != & cube)
		 65 {
		 66 fDim = cube.fDim; // First copy the dimensions
		 67
		 68 const auto elems = fDim[kx] * fDim[ky] * fDim[kz];
		 69
		 70 // Whatever was held by fDataBuf will be first deleted
		 71 // The new block will be allocated and assigned to fDataBuf
		 72 fDataBuf = std::make_unique< value_type [] >(elems);
		 73
		 74 // Finally, deep copy data to the "this" buffer
		 75 // dest source bytes
		 76 memcpy(fDataBuf.get(), cube.fDataBuf.get(),
		 77 elems * sizeof(value_type));
		 78 }
		 79 return * this;
		 80 }

this	Each object of a class can access a specific pointer named this, which simply points at *this* particular object. It is passed as an implicit argument to each member function of a class; sometimes it is used in specific constructions, such as to return this object from the assignment operator.	

(Continued)

Table 4.3 (continued)

Class members	Description	Examples
		The assignment operator copies data from the supplied object. In this regard, it is similar to the copy constructor. The difference is that both objects already exist. Because of this, in the assignment operator, we check for a special case of copying from the same object to itself, as in the expression a=a. This does not happen often in explicitly written code, but storage functionality can invoke such actions. Copying from itself to itself is checked on line [64] of the `TheCube` overloaded assignment, whose definition starts on line [61]. It is done by simply checking whether "my" address – i.e. the address of an object on behalf of which all of these actions happen, identified by a `this` pointer – is the same as the address of an object supplied as the parameter cube. But why do we want such *self-assignment protection?* For most simple objects, there is nothing wrong that forbids such copy actions. But problems can arise if the buffers need to be cleared before the data is copied, as is the case of `TheCube`, which in line [72] clears old buffers when assigning a new buffer to `fDataBuf`. If this happened for the self-copy, then we end up first deleting a buffer, from which we will try to copy the next lines of code, which obviously is wrong. For `TheCube`, we have two arrays to copy: one small `fDim`, can be copied by simply calling its assignment operator on line [66]. But the second array, `fDataBuf`, can be large, and therefore the optimized library function `std::memcpy` is called on line [76], which efficiently copies all the data (Appendix A.2.6). The one thing to remember is that its third parameter is expressed in bytes: hence, on line [77], the multiplication by `sizeof`. Finally, `operator =` returns "this object," which is expressed on line [79] as a dereferencing `* this`. This is necessary since in C++, the result of the assignment operator is the leftmost object. In other words, we want to allow expressions like a=b=c.
		``` 81 // Destructor - if planning to derive, make it virtual 82 ~TheCube() {} ``` The class destructor is responsible for the deallocation of all remaining resources that were allocated during the object's lifetime. In `TheCube`, there are two such resources: `fDim` and `fDataBuf` and its held data buffer. Both are automatic data (Section 5.1); therefore, when an object is deallocated, the destructors of these two will be automatically called. `fDataBuf`, in turn, will automatically destroy its held and guarded memory resources. Therefore, `~TheCube` does not have much to do. In the case of derived classes (Section 4.11), a destructor should be declared `virtual` to allow proper disposal of derived objects via a pointer to the base class. Since we do not assume that `TheCube` is the start of a class hierarchy, its destructor is not virtual.
Destructor	A function whose name is the concatenation of the tilde symbol ~ and the name of the class: `X::~X()`. Takes no input parameters (not even `void`) and returns no output. Called once upon object destruction. Its role is to free all the resources allocated by an object during its lifetime. If we plan for a class to be derived from, then its destructor should be declared `virtual` (Section 4.11).	

Move constructor (C++11)	A constructor is similar to the copy constructor. However, it steals data (state) from the supplied object. As a result, data is in effect "moved," which in many cases is more efficient than a copy.
	
	Format X::X(X &&).
	The double && means an rvalue reference (Section 4.5.1).
		```83 // Move constructor (C++11)```
		```84 TheCube(TheCube && cube) noexcept```
		```85 : fDataBuf(nullptr), fDim { 0, 0, 0 }```
		```86 {```
		```87 // Swap (exchange) dimensions```
		```88 std::swap(fDim, cube.fDim);```
		```89```
		```90 // Swap held pointers```
		```91 fDataBuf.swap(cube.fDataBuf);```
		```92 }```

The idea of the move constructor, as opposed to the standard copy constructor, is simply to take over data from the supplied object, leaving it empty in effect. Such a strategy is very efficient when exchanging with a temporary object, for example.

The definition of the move constructor for the TheCube class begins on line [84]. In line [85], in the data member initializer, both fDataBuf and fDim are initialized to a zero state. But the idea of the move constructor is to steal whatever the supplied cube object has. This is done on line [88] and [91], with a simple swapping of data between this and the cube objects. After that, the this object holds whatever cube held, whereas cube is left with fDataBuf(nullptr) and fDim { 0, 0, 0 }, as set on line [85]. This is fine if cube will no longer be used – for example, if it is a temporary object, etc. Data exchange is performed with the std::swap helper function, whereas fDataBuf has swap on board.

Also notice that to be useful, the move constructor should not throw an exception, as explicitly declared here with the noexcept keyword.

Move assignment operator (C++11)	An operator of the form X & X::operator = (X &&) used to take (swap) data from the supplied object.	```93 // Move assignment operator (C++11)```
		```94 TheCube & operator = (TheCube && cube) noexcept```
		```95 {```
		```96 // Swap all data members between this and cube```
		```97 std::swap(fDim, cube.fDim);```
		```98```
		```99 // Only exchange the pointers - do not copy the buffers!```
		```100 fDataBuf.swap(cube.fDataBuf);```
		```101```
		```102 return * this;```
		```103 }```

The move assignment operator defined on line [94] steals data from the supplied cube object. The main idea is that only data members are swapped, whereas data buffers are left untouched. All these operations must ensure that both objects exchange data, rather than copying it, and that their state is valid after these operations so, for example, their destructors will perform correctly. The exchanges take place on lines [97, 100]. Finally, the object pointed to by this is returned or line [102]. As with the move constructor, the noexcept keyword is used to indicate that the move assignment will not throw exceptions.

(Continued)

Table 4.3 (continued)

Class members	Description	Examples
Getters/ setters	A group of functions to read and write data members of a class (which are usually private).	(see code below)

```
104   public:
105
106     // Getters/setters
107
108     // Because of EDims as a parameter we cannot ask for nonexistent dimension
109     auto   GetDim( EDims which_one ) const { return fDim[ which_one ]; }
110
111     // Access elements by reference - bi-directional
112     auto & Element( const int x, const int y, const int z ) const
113     {
114       const auto offset = ( z * fDim[ ky ] + y ) * fDim[ kx ] + x;
115       return * ( fDataBuf.get() + offset );
116     }
117
118     auto  Size( void ) const { return fDim[ kx ] * fDim[ ky ] * fDim[ kz ]; }
119
120     // It is a const function, but it allows for data change
121     auto  GetDataBuf( void ) const  { return fDataBuf.get(); }
```

A common practice in OOP is to restrict direct access to data by placing it in the private section, while providing *controlled access* to the data via a group of member functions commonly called *getters* and *setters* (because they usually have "get" or "set" in their names). The key point is the controlled access: for instance, a function can check whether a value we set has the correct range or sign, such as a circle radius that must not be negative, etc. Getters usually only read data; the const keyword is used after the parameter list to express this fact. But setters never are const since their role is to change an object's state by changing its data. GetDim on line [109] simply returns the value of a given dimension of TheCube. Because we use enum EDims as its parameter, we do not need to check whether the dimension is correct.

A slightly different approach is undertaken in the case of the Element function on line [112], since it returns a data member of TheCube at a given position (computed on line [114]) *by reference*. Therefore it can both read and write to a given data location in the TheCube object. However, Element never changes any data members of the class, so it is also declared as const. Note the expression to compute an offset of a particular data position: this is done as shown in Figure 4.6. Finally, the getters Size on line [118] and GetDataBuf on line [121] return a number of data elements (not bytes) and a const pointer to the data buffer.

| `friend` functions and classes | External functions and external classes that can access *all* members (including private and protected) of *this* class. | |

```
122    public:
123
124        // Streaming operators are functions external to this class
125        friend std::ostream & operator << ( std::ostream &o, const TheCube &cube );
126        friend std::istream & operator >> ( std::istream & i, TheCube & cube );
127
128    };
```

Friend functions and classes do not belong to the class (i.e. are not members of the class) but can still access private and protected members of that class (Section 3.18.4). This obvious breach in security/access rules is sometimes justified by simplified implementations, but we suggest using friends *only* if access to private members cannot be accomplished by the class's getters and setters. In TheCube, we overload the streaming operators << and >>, which require access to two different hierarchies of classes: these are representatives of the iostream hierarchy, but we are streaming a given object (TheCube in our example). The two friend functions are declared on lines [125] and [126], but their definitions are outside the class. Similar to the assignment operator, they are examples of overloaded operators as discussed in Section 4.4.

| Overloaded operators | For most operators, C++ allows for their overloading in the classes; This means writing an operator-function defining specific behavior of an operator for a given class; An overloaded operator-function can be a member of a class or a function external to that class (Section 4.4); | |

4.6.2 *TheCube* Object Layout and Semantics

Figure 4.7 shows a possible memory mapping for an object of TheCube class. The object is composed of other objects, which are data members defined in TheCube. But the objects also govern an external block of memory, which contains all of the cube's data. This is organized as shown on the right side of Figure 4.7. Such a structure is superimposed by the access algorithms of the Element member function and depends solely on our implementation. Therefore it is called *data abstraction* since it cannot be inferred looking only at memory, which is organized linearly in the computer's address space. In other words, other objects can superimpose other types of data organization, even for the same block of memory.

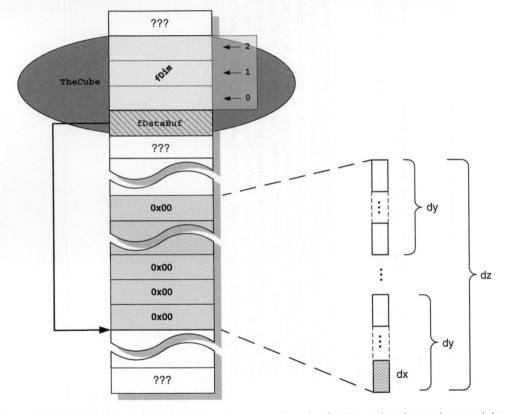

Figure 4.7 Illustration of a TheCube object and memory allocation for its member data and external data buffer. Objects are composed of other smaller objects. Frequently, they also have and control external objects and/or data buffers. Member functions define an abstract organization and interpretation of an inherent data structure.

We will point out that the location of TheCube is distributed in memory. Moreover, its parts are sometimes located in different types of memory. For example, a TheCube object can be declared as an automatic variable and placed on a stack associated with a function, whereas its data buffer is allocated on the heap. Sometimes this can be problematic: for example, when we wish to stream such an object to and out of a file. std::vector behaves in a similar way (Section 3.2).

Also interesting is to measure the size of an object of the class TheCube. Static and constant data members are outside an object since they are unique and can be shared among objects of the same class. Similarly, the code for class functions is shared and placed in a separate memory region.

Thus, the size of a `TheClass` object is the sum of the `fDim` and `fData` data members. But the size of an object depends on the data alignment. This example gives us at least two clues:

- The size of an object is equal to or greater than the sum of its members
- Always measure and verify your programming assumptions

We will see that the size of an object is always larger than the sum of its members if a class contains virtual function(s), as will be presented in Section 4.11. This happens since additional memory is required for the virtual function table associated with the object (Section 4.12).

Notice that the size of the `TheClass` object, computed with the `sizeof` operator (*GROUP 4*, Table 3.15), accounts only for data members and does not include the size of the data buffer. Thus, to determine the number of data elements, we need to call the `TheCube::Size` member function.

4.6.3 Shallow vs. Deep Copy Semantics

Figure 4.8 shows the semantics of shallow and deep data member copies when creating or copying an object b out of a. If only a value of the `fDataBuf` pointer is copied, which we call a shallow copy, then two objects share the same data buffer, which probably is not desirable in this case.[5] But a deep copy allows us to create two separate objects with their own data sets.

But deep copying, although desirable in many cases, can involve more time-consuming operations. Thus, in practice, the choice depends on the context and object functionality. However, notice that if we do not explicitly write our versions of the constructors and the assignment operator, then

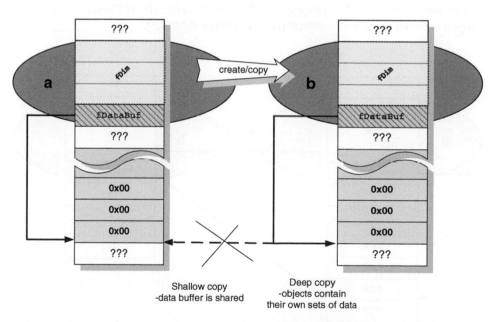

Figure 4.8 Semantics of shallow and deep copying of data members when creating or copying an object b from a. If only a pointer is copied – a shallow copy – then two objects would share the same data buffer, which is not desirable in this case. A deep copy lets us create two separate objects with their own data collections.

---

5 In such a case `std::shared_ptr` would be appropriate, as presented in Section 5.3.

these functions will be generated automatically by the compiler. In such a case, data members are copied byte-by-byte, which results in shallow copy semantics. Be aware of this mechanism, especially if a class contains pointers referencing external objects, since leaving the work to be done automatically can lead to errors.

4.6.4 Move Constructor and Move Assignment Semantics

The move constructor and move assignment operator are relatively new features available in C++ 11 and above. Both operations could be managed by the copy constructor and copy assignment – but the idea is to speed up the operation by exchanging pointers, rather than copying the buffers, between the objects. This is justified when working with temporary objects, i.e. those that go out of scope and will be deleted.

Figure 4.9 shows operation of the move constructor of two TheCube objects: b (a) ; . The primary assumption is that object a will not be used anymore (e.g. it is a temporary object returned from a function), so its allocated data buffers need not be copied (as in the case of the copy constructor) and can be stolen by object b.

This "taking over" operation is performed by swapping pointers held by a . fDataBuf to the b . fDataBuf objects, which immediately disconnects a from its data buffer. This also makes a empty, so this mechanism is useful if we know that a will no longer be used. How do we know that? Such situations happen, for example, if a temporary object is returned from a function and will be disposed of – see, for example, the returned object c from the MultMatrix function in Listing 3.23. Such situations can easily be deduced by modern C++ compilers, so the proper code will be generated automatically. Our role is to supply the move constructor for classes that can benefit from move semantics. What happens to the other data members? These, such as fDim, are also swapped between the a and b objects (see line [88] in Table 4.3).

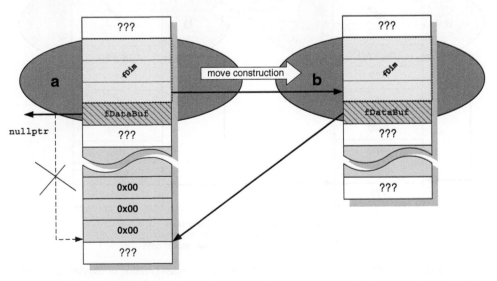

Figure 4.9 Semantics of the move constructor b (a). Data members of object a are taken over by the newly created object b. The data buffer is not copied.

The move assignment operator b = a, illustrated in Figure 4.10, is similar in concept to the move constructor: i.e. we wish to avoid copying of large buffers of data. The only difference is that both objects can have their data buffers and other data members previously allocated, since the two objects already exist.

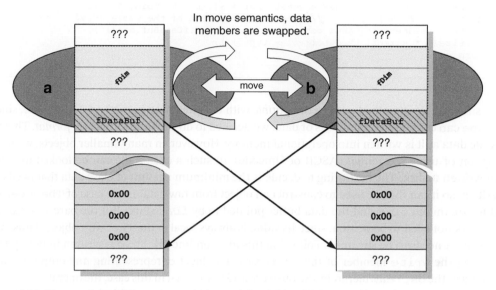

Figure 4.10 Move assignment a = b semantics explained. Objects' data members are simply swapped (moved). Data buffers are not copied.

In the move assignment b = a, data members of both are also swapped, as shown in Figure 4.10: the state of a.fDataBuf becomes that of b.fDataBuf, and the state of b.fDataBuf becomes that of a.fDataBuf. The same thing happens with other data members: in our example, a.fDim is swapped with b.fDim. By doing this, in effect, the objects exchange all of their data rather than making expensive copies. As we have mentioned, this type of operation is useful if we wish to pass the content of an object a that will soon go out of scope, etc. Note that this operation is also different from the copy assignment operator in the sense that after a move assignment, the data buffers can be different, whereas after a copy assignment, both buffers contain *the same* amount of *the same* data. Code examples of the move construction and assignment are presented in Section 4.6.6.

4.6.5   Implementation of the *TheCube* Streaming Operators

What remains to be done is to write implementations of the overloaded streaming operators, as well as to see TheCube in an application (see Listing 4.5). Streaming out is usually simpler to implement, so we start there. This time, the code – see lines [1–7] – is located outside the definition of the class; usually it is located in the source file (with a *.cpp* extension, such as *TheCube.cpp*), whereas the definition goes in the header file (*.h* extension, *TheCube.h*). The first thing to decide when streaming objects is the output format. The streaming-out operator << (insertion operator) has the same format for all objects – that is, when writing our own class, the only thing to do on line [1] is to substitute the name of the class of the streamed object for TheCube.

Listing 4.5 Definitions of the overloaded `operator <<` and `operator >>` for TheCube (in *TheCube, TheCube.cpp*).

```
1   std::ostream & operator << ( std::ostream & o, const TheCube & cube )
2   {
3       // Out data as binary streams
4       o.write(      reinterpret_cast< const char * >(  & cube.fDim[ 0 ] ),
5       sizeof( cube.fDim ) );        // sizeof returns size of the whole array
6       o.write(  reinterpret_cast< const char * >(  cube.fDataBuf.get() ),
7       cube.Size() * sizeof( TheCube::value_type ) );
8       return o;
9   }
```

The streaming-out method *must be compatible* with the streaming-in method. In this case, since TheCube can contain large amounts of data, we decided to do streaming in *binary format*. That is, we write data as it is written into operational memory. However, in many smaller objects, we have the option of using *text format* (ASCII or Unicode). In such a case, a file can be looked up after being written to disk. The next thing to decide is the minimum amount of class data that needs to be written, so it can then be used to construct an object from raw data. In the case of TheCube, we need to stream out fDim and the data buffer pointed to by fDataBuf. But the bare fDataBuf object does not need to be written, since its value is always local to the TheCube object. Thus, not all class data needs to be streamed. Following this idea, on line [4], fDim is written in binary format, using the write member of the ostream class object o, representing *any* output stream belonging to the ostream hierarchy (Stroustrup 2013). Note that in this case, the operator sizeof returns the total number of bytes of this array, as required by write. With the same function, on line [6], the entire data buffer from TheCube is saved. In this case, to find out its size *in bytes*, first the Size member is called, returning a number of data items from the streamed cube object, which is multiplied by the size of each element, obtained with the sizeof operator. How is such free access to private buffers possible for a function that is not a member of the class? Recall that this is a result of letting the class treat the function as a friend (line [125] in TheCube definition). Friend functions and classes should be used sparingly, since they break normal member-access rules. But in some cases, such as object streaming, they can be useful. As we will see in subsequent examples, they can be avoided in many cases through proper class design and getters/setters. Finally, on line [8], the ostream object o is returned, which lets us use << operators in a series.

Streaming-in an object is usually more challenging than streaming-out, as described earlier. But in this case, the streamed object already exists – it is the second argument of operator >>, as shown on line [10]. The streaming-in operator needs to obey the format of the data saved by the streaming-out method. Therefore, on line [13], the fDim array is read in. But when streaming-in, we are more vulnerable, since we have to assume that the opened stream of data contains the right data, set in the right order, etc. In practice, this is not always the case, so the streaming operator needs a number of conditions that check the state of the input stream, such as the one on line [14]. Putting a bare stream object in the conditional statement might look strange, but it is normal practice. It works since the stream object contains an overloaded bool operator, which allows its "conversion" to the bool type, as required by if. However, this conversion does not convert anything – instead, a true or false flag is returned, depending on whether the stream can be further read.

On line [16], the current `cube` buffer is deleted and a new one is allocated and assigned to it. The size can be determined by calling the `Size` member. Then, the buffer data is read by calling the `read` member of stream `i` on line [20]. Finally, on line [22], for debugging purposes, we check the state of the input stream after this operation by calling `assert`.

```
10   std::istream & operator >> ( std::istream & i, TheCube & cube )
11   {
12       // First read dimensions
13       i.read( reinterpret_cast< char * >( & cube.fDim[ 0 ] ), sizeof( cube.fDim ) );
14       if( i )     // Check if the stream OK
15       {
16           cube.fDataBuf = std::make_unique< TheCube::value_type [] >( cube.Size() );
17
18           const auto cube_bytes = cube.Size() * sizeof( TheCube::value_type );
19           // read() accepts a number of bytes
20           i.read( (char*)cube.fDataBuf.get(), cube_bytes );     // Read the rest of the data
21
22           assert( i );
23       }
24       return i;
25   }
```

Then, the input stream object `i` is returned on line [24] to allow stream chaining.

4.6.6   Validation of *TheCube*

After a class is defined and its members are implemented, the functionality and performance of the class should be tested. In some software development strategies, writing tests precedes class implementation. Also, in larger systems, tests are usually included in the test-driven library for automatic software testing. More on various approaches to testing software can be found in Appendix A.7.

To test the functionality of the `TheCube` class (Listing 4.6), we define the `TheCube_Test` function starting on line [11]. First, on line [15], a cube object of dimensions $15 \times 13 \times 11$ is created using the parametric constructor. But remember that although the large data buffer has already been allocated, the data it contains is not yet initialized. Therefore, on line [18], the Mersenne twister random generator is created, which is then used by the `std::generate` function, called on line [21], to initialize the cube with random values (Section 3.17.3).

In this fragment of code, we see that for bulk data operations, instead of the `Element` function, which allows random access to each piece of data of `TheCube`, we can use a much simpler and faster construction that treats the buffer as a linear stream of data. The starting address of the `inCube` data buffer is accessed by `GetDataBuf`, whereas the number of elements is determined by the `Size` member.

On line [25], a `mirror_cube` object is created, which is a copy of `cube`. Here, the copy constructor is used rather than move, since `cube` needs to be used later and therefore cannot be deprived of its data by a potential move. The `Element` function is tested on lines [28–29].

Listing 4.6 Test functions for `TheCube` (in *TheCube, TheCubeTest.cpp*).

```
1    #include <algorithm>
2    #include <random>
3
4    #include "TheCube.h"
5
6
7    TheCube RetAbsCube( const TheCube & inCube );
8
9
10   // Test function for TheCube class
11   void TheCube_Test( void )
12   {
13       const int dx { 15 }, dy { 13 }, dz { 11 };
14
15       TheCube    cube( dx, dy, dz );
16
17       // Random Mersenne twister
18       std::mt19937   rand_gen{ std::random_device{}() };
19
20       // Fill the cube with random values; ref is a reference wrapper
21       std::generate(    cube.GetDataBuf(), cube.GetDataBuf() + cube.Size(),
22                         std::ref( rand_gen ) );
23
24       // Cannot move - only copy from cube since it is used later
25       TheCube    mirror_cube( cube );
26
27
28       cube.Element( 5, 7, 9 ) = -100.0;              // Set an element,
29       assert( cube.Element( 5, 7, 9 ) == -100.0 );   // read and check if the same
30
31       std::ofstream outFile( "TheCube.bin", std::ios::binary );
32       outFile << cube;
33       outFile.close();       // so we can open it in the next line
34
35       std::ifstream inFile( "TheCube.bin", std::ios::binary );
36       TheCube    testCube;
37       inFile >> testCube;
38
39
40       // Check if data the same byte after byte
41       assert( std::memcmp( cube.GetDataBuf(), testCube.GetDataBuf(),
42               cube.Size() * sizeof( TheCube::value_type ) ) == 0 );
43
44       // Call the move constructor
45       TheCube abs_cube( RetAbsCube( cube ) );
46
47       // Explicitly call the move assignment operator
48       cube = static_cast< TheCube && >( abs_cube );
49
50
51       std::ofstream outAbsFile( "TheAbsCube.bin", std::ios::binary );
52       outAbsFile << cube;
53
54   }
```

Next, the `TheCube` streaming operations are tested. On line [31], the output file *TheCube.bin* is opened in binary format. Then, on line [32], the `cube` object is streamed out to this file by calling the overloaded `operator <<`. Just after that, the file is explicitly closed on line [33]. As a result, we can be sure it is flushed to disk and can be immediately reopened, as on line [35]. In line [36], a new `TheCube` object `testCube` is created, this time using the default constructor. It is then streamed in from the file by calling `operator >>` on line [37]. However, we need to be sure that both objects contain the same data. This is checked on lines [41–42] by calling the `assert` function, which calls `std::memcmp`. This is a low-level function that compares two memory buffers (Appendix A.2.6).

The move semantics of the constructor and the assignment operator are tested in the rest of the `TheCube_Test` function. The idea of the move operations is to avoid excessive and usually unnecessary copying of temporary objects. To see this in action, let's analyze what happens on line [45]. The `RetAbsCube` function, defined in the line [55], is called, providing the `cube` object as its constant argument. We will return to `RetAbsCube` soon.

On line [48], the object `abs_cube` is moved to the object `cube`, explicitly calling the move assignment operator. This is enforced in the same line by the cast to the right reference `TheCube &&`. In the move operation, the objects simply exchange data members as well as, in effect, data buffers, without making copies of the buffers. Because of this, move operations usually let us save significantly on data allocation, copying, and deallocation. This can be measured with the profiler, as presented in Appendix A.6.3.

```cpp
55   TheCube        RetAbsCube( const TheCube & inCube )
56   {
57       // Create an empty return cube of the same dimensions
58       TheCube outCube(   inCube.GetDim( TheCube::kx ),
59           inCube.GetDim( TheCube::ky ),
60           inCube.GetDim( TheCube::kz ) );
61
62       // Transform all elements to their absolute values
63       std::transform( inCube.GetDataBuf(), inCube.GetDataBuf() + inCube.Size(),
64       outCube.GetDataBuf(), [] ( TheCube::value_type v ) { return std::fabs( v ); } );
65
66       return outCube;        // Invokes the move semantics
67   }
```

The role of the `RetAbsCube` function is to create a temporary `TheCube` object on lines [58–60], which is then, on line [63–64], filled by the `std::transform` function with the absolute values of the elements of the input `inCube` object. Finally, the temporary object `outCube` is passed outside on line [66]; it is immediately copied to the `abs_cube` object on line [45], as already mentioned. Thus, in an unoptimized environment, we would have one local object `outCube` copied in a deep fashion to the `abs_cube` object, after which `outCube` would be destroyed with its data buffer. But with the move semantics, the `abs_cube` object can simply steal the previously allocated data buffer from `outCube`. This is performed by the move constructor operating on behalf of the `abs_cube` object. This also conforms to *the copy elision* strategy, which is a compiler optimization technique that eliminates unnecessary copying or moving of objects: when returning a named or unnamed object from a function by value, the compiler is allowed to omit the copy and move operations and not call the associated constructor. This *return value optim*ization (ROV) technique is implemented and applied by most C++ compilers.

Things to Remember

- When designing a class, be careful to recognize shallow vs. deep copies of its objects
- Large buffers of data should be allocated on the heap with the `std::make_unique` helper and then kept in `std::unique_ptr` (or another smart pointer)
- If a class can benefit from move semantics, implement the move constructor and move assignment. Then, also implement the copy constructor and copy assignment
- If a class is intended to be derived from, declare its destructor `virtual`
- Use `=default` for the default implementation of a special member function, and use `=delete` to disallow a function

4.7 Example Project – Moving *EMatrix* to the Class

In Section (3.15), we defined a simple `EMatrix` structure containing a constructor and some member functions. In this section, we will learn how to refactor `EMatrix` to an OO framework. We will learn about the following:

- How to refactor `struct` to `class`
- How to write the efficient overloaded streaming functions `operator <<` and `operator >>`, and how to create a stream from `std::string`
- How to write overloaded `operator +` and `operator *` to let us write `m1 * m2` instead of `MultMatrix( m1, m2 )`
- What functions to add to have a range-based `for` loop in a class
- Pre- and post-conditions, and programming by contract

As mentioned earlier, the only issue with going from a struct (with all of its data and member functions publicly open to external access) to a class (with some members hidden and some publicly open) is ensuring better control and security on the hidden members. As we know, this is encapsulation, which can involve both data and member functions. Data is usually hidden to disallow uncontrolled access. For instance, when defining a circle object, we might want to ensure that the radius value is always positive, etc. At the same time, access to hidden data is frequently granted by public getters and setters. Such a mechanism ensures *control and protection of the data*. Hence, we want to move `EMatrix` from a struct to the `EMatrix` class. Let's start with its definition, which will extend the definition of `struct EMatrix` from Listing 3.19.

4.7.1 Definition of the *EMatrix* Class

The definition of the `EMatrix` class starts on line [1] of Listing 4.7 with its first and only data member `fData`, defined on line [5]. Because of the `private` keyword on line [3], `fData` cannot be accessed directly from `EMatrix` objects, unlike the `EMatrix` functions, which can all be freely accessed. Since, as already pointed out, `private` is a default behavior, placing it on line [3] was optional in this case.

Then we open the section for publicly available members by placing `public` on line [7]. The only class parametric constructor begins on line [10]; it is an exact copy of the constructor from Listing 3.19. Also the same are the `GetCols` and `GetRows` functions, defined on lines [19, 20]. However, this time they offer the only possible way to determine the number of columns and rows, since `fData`, being private, cannot be directly accessed.

Listing 4.7 Object-oriented version of `EMatrix` (in *EasyMatrix, EMatrix.h*). Data member `fData` moved to the `private` section to obtain data encapsulation; new `operator []`; `operator <<` and `operator >>` declared as `friend` (new features in bold).

```
1    class EMatrix
2    {
3    private:
4
5        RealMatrix fData;        // private data structure (encapsulation)
6
7    public:
8
9        // A parametric constructor
10       EMatrix( Dim rows, Dim cols, DataType initVal = 0.0 )
11          : fData( rows, RealVec( cols, initVal ) )
12       { // matrix == a vector of vectors of double
13          assert( cols > 0 );
14          assert( rows > 0 );
15       }
16
17
18       // Helpers
19       auto GetCols( void ) const { return fData[ 0 ].size(); }
20       auto GetRows( void ) const { return fData.size(); }
21
22       // As a result of overloaded subscript operators
23       // instead of m.fData[2][3] we can write directly m[2][3]
24       auto &       operator[] ( Dim idx ) { return fData[ idx ]; }
25       const auto & operator[] ( Dim idx ) const { return fData[ idx ]; }
26
27       // We need only these two pairs of functions to have a range-based for loop
28       auto       begin() { return fData.begin(); }
29       auto       end()   { return fData.end(); }
30
31       auto       begin() const { return fData.begin(); }
32       auto       end()   const { return fData.end(); }
33
34       // Let us add some overloaded arithmetical operators
35       EMatrix &       operator += ( const EMatrix & b );       // this can change this object
36       EMatrix         operator + ( const EMatrix & b ) const;
37       // We can add other operators here ...
38
39
40       // friends are functions that can freely access fData
41       friend std::ostream & operator << ( std::ostream & o, const EMatrix & matrix );
42       friend std::istream & operator >> ( std::istream & i, EMatrix & matrix );
43
44   };
```

Also, to allow access to matrix elements, two versions of the overloaded `operator []` are defined on lines [24, 25]. This the subscript operator, which we have used previously to access vector elements. But this is the first time we have written our own versions of the operators, which can then be used to call mathematical operations efficiently. As already discussed, an overloaded operator is defined exactly like any other function, except its name must start with the `operator` keyword followed by the operator symbol (Section 4.4).

We need to write our own version of `operator []` because `fData` is private, so it cannot be directly accessed. Actually, there are two versions of the subscripts: on line [24], for write operations;

and on line [25] – declared as const member – exclusively for read operations. Interestingly, both return fData[idx]. Recall that fData was defined as a vector< vector< double >>. This means if m[2][3] is called, where m is an object of type EMatrix, then m[2] returns the second vector, which is the second row of the matrix. However, if m[2][3] is called, then the second call (the one with [3]) will invoke the operator [] but from the std::vector, rather than one of our subscripts from line [24] or [25]. In effect, a third element of the second row is accessed.

Two pairs of begin and end functions are defined on lines [28–29] and [31–32]. They have exactly the same role as std::vector::begin and std::vector::end, described in Table 3.4. That is, they return an iterator object pointing at the first or one-after-the-last element of their vector. But why do we need them, and why do we need two versions of each one? The answer is simple – to be able to use the novel *range-based* version of the for loop with the auto-declared iterator (see Table 3.9). Note that these four functions do not do anything special; they just *delegate the action* to the fData member. Once again, the const-declared versions are for read-only operations.

Now we are at the point of presenting overloaded mathematical operators like the increment and assign operator += on line [35] and the summation operator + on line [36]. Their role is to allow us to write cool expressions like c = a+b or c += b, where a, b, and c are of type EMatrix. We will discuss their implementations shortly.

Finally, on lines [41–42], we see the two last overloaded operators: the left and right bits shifts. As we know, for the EMatrix objects, these will transfer data to and from data streams, such as the screen or keyboard. For example, instead of writing ShowMatrix(m), we can use the more intuitive cout << m.

As we discussed when presenting the TCube class in Section 4.6.5, although the streaming operators are declared inside the definition of the EMatrix class, they are not its members. This is because they need to take an EMatrix object as their input argument. So, they are external overloaded operators; we will see their full implementations soon, but for now they are declared in EMatrix as its friends. As presented in Section 3.18, the reason is that their syntax disallows being members of a class. But for their operation, they need to access the fData private object. Therefore, we need to break the private restrictions with the friend keyword, although doing so is not pretty. Fortunately, this is the only situation where we use friend in our projects.

Accomplishing OO paradigms and enforcing data privacy may require us to write a few more lines of code than expected, but soon we will see that this effort pays off. For example, because we formatted the streaming operators, we will be able to use them for all streams – not only the keyboard and the screen, but also files or telecom. The bare minimum for EMatrix would be to have operator [] and the streaming operators.

4.7.2 Implementation of the Class Streaming Operators

Not all of the EMatrix class's member functions have been defined. We will now present their full implementations. We start with the streaming operators, as presented in Listing 4.8. In all such cases, we have to develop the following mechanism:

- We need to decide on the format of the output data: how data is saved to the output stream, whether data items are separated with commas or newlines, etc
- The output and input format should be compatible. If we write an object to a file, we should be able to read it back and have the same internal state
- We are not saving the entire EMatrix object, just its data – in this case, the full contents of the fData member. That's all

The definition of the overloaded `operator <<` starts on line [2]. Remember that this is a separate function, declared in `EMatrix` as a friend. It always takes two parameters; the first is the `out` reference to `std::ostream`, which in C++ represents a broad group of output streaming objects, such as the familiar `std::cout`; the second parameter is always an object to be streamed out, `matrix` in our case, passed by a constant reference. Since we have a matrix to be streamed out, two loops are started on lines [4, 6]. The first one traverses rows of the input matrix parameter using the `const auto &` construction (Section 3.7). Such a convenient version of the `for` loop is possible thanks to the `begin` and `end` functions defined in `EMatrix`. Otherwise, we'd be left with the older version of `for`, operating with an iterator and calling the `EMatrix::GetRow` function. The second internal loop on line [6] traverses the data in each row, which is then output on line [7] to the `out` stream, separated by a tabulator (`\t`). After writing the entire row, a newline symbol is output on line [9], and so on, until all the rows are saved. Finally, on line [12], the stream object `out` is returned, so the `<<` operations can be chained in one line, as we have done before.

Listing 4.8 Definitions of the overloaded `operator <<` and `operator >>` for `EMatrix` object streaming (in *EasyMatrix, EMatrix.cpp*).

```
1    // Stream out a matrix to the stream out. Assume text mode.
2    std::ostream & operator << ( std::ostream & out, const EMatrix & matrix )
3    {
4        for( const auto & row : matrix )        // go row-by-row
5        {
6            for( const auto & data : row )        // data in a single row
7                out << data << "\t";
8
9            out << std::endl;
10       }
11
12       return out;        // return the stream, so they can be chained
13   }
```

The implementation of `operator >>`, starting on line [15], is a little bit more complicated, mostly because we need to interpret what is read in. First, let's analyze the two parameters of this function: `in`, which is a reference to the `std::istream`-derived object; and a matrix, which is a reference to an `EMatrix` object. That is, the `EMatrix` object must already have been created, so it can then be passed for input. But it can be empty, since on line [22], its current contents are cleared.

```
14   // Stream in a matrix from the stream in. Assume text mode.
15   std::istream & operator >> ( std::istream & in, EMatrix & matrix )
16   {
17       // Dimensions have to be determined from the data layout.
18       // Each new line constitutes a new row of a matrix.
19       // So, we have to read strings line by line, and
20       // from each string read data by data.
21
22       matrix.fData.clear();        // get rid of whatever was there
23
24       std::string str;        // an empty string
25       while( getline( in, str ) )        // read the entire line into the string
26       {
27           // Create a string-stream from a string
```

```
28        std::istringstream istr( str );
29
30        DataType          data {};   // temporary data
31        RealVec           one_row;   // at first, create an empty row
32        while( istr >> data )        // read from the string-stream to data
33          one_row.push_back( data );     // fill one row
34
35        matrix.fData.emplace_back( one_row );      // emplace the row into the matrix
36      }
37
38    return in;              // return the stream, so they can be chained
39 }
```

Since we expect the input data to be formatted the same way it was saved by the insertion opera-tor, in order to know the row ends, the newline (end-of-line, EOL) symbol need to be detected. Therefore entire lines containing entire rows of data are read and processed. This is done by first defining the auxiliary `std::string` object on line [24]. This is then used to store the entire line read in by the `getline` function [25]. The process operates in a loop, which breaks only if there are no new lines to be read from the input stream.

Once we read the entire row of data into a string, we need to split it into data elements. This can be done a number of ways, but the easiest is probably to define an input stream connected to that string and then read one number after another from it, like from any other stream, taking advan-tage of the automatic input formatting, i.e. splitting on white characters, performed by the streams. This is accomplished on line [28] with the `std::istringstream` object `istr` connected to the `str` string. Then, on lines [30–31], two auxiliary objects are created: `data` to store a single num-ber, and `one_row` to store a single row of numbers. These are then filled on lines [32–33] by read-ing from the `istr` stream. Finally, the resulting row vector is transferred at the end of the `fData` object. To avoid a two-step action of creating a temporary object that is then copied to `fData`, on line [35], the `emplace_back` method (a member of the `std::vector`) is used and performs the action in one move. Then, as always, the stream object is returned on line [38] to allow chaining of the `>>` operator.

Since such an input stream processing scheme is ubiquitous, modern C++ is equipped with a special `std::move_iterator` that further simplifies input operations. Obviously, it relies on the move semantics discussed in Section 4.6.4. Using this iterator, the previous code fragment can be efficiently written as follows:

```
40 // Stream in a matrix from the stream in. Assume text mode.
41 std::istream & operator >> ( std::istream & in, EMatrix & matrix )
42 {
43     // Dimensions have to be determined from the data layout.
44     // Each new line constitutes a new row of a matrix.
45     // So, we have to read strings line by line, and
46     // from each string read data item by data item.
47
48     matrix.fData.clear();        // get rid of whatever was there
49
50     std::string str;             // an empty string
51     while( getline( in, str ) )  // read the entire line into the string
52     {
53         // Create a string-stream from a string
54         std::istringstream istr( str );
55
56         using DType_Iter = std::istream_iterator< DataType >;
57
```

```
58         // Here we move
59         matrix.fData.emplace_back( std::make_move_iterator ( DType_Iter{ istr } ),
60                                     std::make_move_iterator( DType_Iter{} ) );
61
62     }
63
64     return in;              // return the stream, so they can be chained
65 }
```

The previous version operates exactly like the function on line [15] of the previous version of `operator >>`, except for lines [59–60], which contain `emplace_back` fed with the move iterator. Its role is to apply the move semantics instead of object copying. In this version, `emplace_back` operates not on a single object as on line [35] of the previous code, but on a range of objects, created as always by providing the beginning and end of a stream or collection. These are created by calling the `std::make_move_iterator` helper function, first providing `std::istream_iterator` to the `istr` stream for the beginning, and second providing `std::istream_iterator` to denote the end. Equipped with these two iterators, `emplace_back` will know how to create a collection of numbers contained in the stream `istr`. To save typing, line [56] creates a `DType_Iter` alias. `make_move_iterator` is a helper template function that constructs a `std::move_iterator` for an iterator passed as its argument.

Regardless of which version of the extraction operator is chosen, let's test the streaming operators with the following code (in the `Easy_Matrix_Zeroth_Test` function):

```
EMatrix     m ( 2, 3 );
std::cin  >> m;     // Call the extraction operator on std::cin and m
std::cout << m;     // Call the insertion operator with std::cout and m
```

This makes the terminal window wait for us to type. Since matrix m is 2×3, we type as follows:

```
1          2          3
-1         0          5
12         10         -10
```

To inform the input stream `std::cin` that this is the end-of-file (EOF), we press `Ctrl+Z`. After that, the following appears:

```
^Z
1          2          3
-1         0          5
12         10         -10
```

This is the effect of `operator <<` working with the `std::cout` object. Finally, note that the line

```
std::cout << m; // Call the insertion operator with std::cout and m
```

can be written equivalently as

```
operator << ( std::cout, m ); // Call the insertion operator with std::cout and m
```

In other words, an overloaded operator can be called like any other function by providing its full name.

4.7.3 Implementation of the Arithmetic Operators

Let's now move analyze different versions of the addition and addition-and-update operators over-loaded for operations on EMatrix objects. The first, defined in Listing 4.9 on line [3], is the stan-dalone operator +, which takes two EMatrix objects as its arguments and returns a third containing their sum. Since the dimensions of the added matrix must agree, there are two asser-tions on lines [4–5]. These constitute a runtime fuse that works only in debugging mode on a call with improper objects. This is for the caller code, to verify that the dimensions are the same. These two lines constitute *preconditions* for this method. Checking methods' *preconditions, postcondi-tions,* and *invariants* belongs to the broader strategy of software verification methodology called *programming by contract* (Meyer 1997). More on this and software testing is provided in Appendix A.7.

On line [8], the output object c is created as a copy of the first argument a. Then, in the two loops operating on lines [10–12], elements of the second matrix b are added to c; and finally, c is returned on line [14].

Listing 4.9 Overloading operator + for EMatrix (in *EasyMatrix, EMUtility.cpp*).

```
1    // Overloaded operators
2
3    EMatrix    operator + ( const EMatrix & a, const EMatrix & b )
4    {
5        assert( a.GetRows() == b.GetRows() );      // dim must be the same
6        assert( a.GetCols() == b.GetCols() );
7
8        EMatrix    c { a };      // Make c the same as a
9
10       for( Dim row = 0; row < b.GetRows(); ++ row )
11           for( Dim col = 0; col < b.GetCols(); ++ col )
12               c[ row ][ col ] += b[ row ][ col ];
13
14       return c;
15   }
16
```

Here we will add a word on returning an object by value, such as c on line [14]. If this is a large object, then the add-and-assign operator += will always be more efficient. But with the advent of move semantics, constructions like the following

```
r = p + q;
```

are also as efficient as possible. This happens because a big data allocation will be performed to create object c on line [8]. When c is returned on line [14], the compiler knows it will be out of scope soon, so its contents are moved directly to object r, which is external to the scope of opera-tor + in this case. Even before move semantics, compilers were performing an optimization called *copy elision*.

Now let's analyze two addition operations that are members of the EMatrix class; see Listing 4.10. The first is the add-and-assign operator +=, defined on line [4]. Again, the precon-ditions are located on lines [6–7]. Then, exactly as previously, the addition takes place on lines [9–11]. But as a return object, on line [13], * this is returned by reference since operator += is a member of the EMatrix class. No matrix copies or move operations are required. This explains why operator += is more efficient than the two-argument operator +.

Listing 4.10 Overloading operators that are members of `EMatrix` (in *EasyMatrix, EMatrix.cpp*).

```
1    // Overloaded operators
2
3    // Let's add some overloaded arithmetical operators
4    EMatrix &    EMatrix::operator += ( const EMatrix & b )
5    {
6        assert( GetRows() == b.GetRows() );      // dim must be the same
7        assert( GetCols() == b.GetCols() );
8
9        for( Dim row = 0; row < b.GetRows(); ++ row )
10           for( Dim col = 0; col < b.GetCols(); ++ col )
11               fData[ row ][ col ] += b[ row ][ col ];
12
13       return * this;
14   }
15
```

But the `EMatrix` class also has `operator +`, whose functionality is exactly the same as the `operator +` presented in Listing 4.9. Its definition starts on line [16]. However, notice that this time only argument b is necessary: this operator *is a member* of the `EMatrix` class, so its first argument is the object on behalf of which it is called. In other words, the first argument can be identified as `* this`. This sheds more light on all member functions – each of them gets `this` as its implicit parameter.

```
16   EMatrix      EMatrix::operator + ( const EMatrix & b ) const
17   {
18       // Where does matrix "a" come from? It is "this".
19       assert( GetRows() == b.GetRows() );      // dim must be the same
20       assert( GetCols() == b.GetCols() );
21
22       EMatrix c { * this };      // Make c the same as a
23
24       c += b;    // call the add and assign operator +=
25
26       return c;
27   }
```

The operation of `operator +` is simple. First, the preconditions are checked [19–20]. Placing preconditions in each function independently, even if they are the same, helps to catch potential precondition violations as soon as possible. Next, the temporary matrix object c is created on line [22] and immediately initialized with the contents of the current object, identified by `* this`. Then, on line [24], the previously implemented `operator +=` is called to add object b to c, and c is finally returned on line [26].

4.7.4 Testing Matrix Operations

Now it is time to use `EMatrix` in some computations; see Listing 4.11. A matrix identified as `matrix_1`, with dimensions 3×3, is created on line [4] of the test function, which starts on line [2]. After the matrix is created, all of its elements are set to 0. But to include more diverse values, on line [6], it is randomly initialized with the `RandInit` function from Listing 3.25.

Listing 4.11 Examples of using overloaded streaming and arithmetic operators on `EMatrix` objects (in *EasyMatrix, EMTest.cpp*).

```
1    // Here we show how to stream EMatrix objects in and out
2    void Easy_Matrix_Third_Test( void )
3    {
4       EMatrix      matrix_1( 3, 3 );
5
6       RandInit( matrix_1 );
7
```

The first set of streaming operations begins in the block [8–14]. First, the contents of `matrix_1` are displayed on the screen. Due to the random initialization, the results will be different each time we run the code. Then, on line [11], the output file object `oma`, of type `std::ofstream`, is created and opened as *ema.txt*. Now, with *the same* streaming `operator <<`, the contents of `matrix_1` are streamed to this output file [13]. This behavior explains the power of streaming operators in C++; once defined, they can operate on any stream belonging to the hierarchy of streaming devices. Closing the block on line [14] destroys its local objects, which entails closing the file as well. This is an example of the resource acquisition is initialization (RAII) principle, which we will discuss in Section 5.2.1.1.

```
8        {
9            std::cout << matrix_1; // stream it to the screen
10
11           std::ofstream oma( "ema.txt" );
12
13           oma << matrix_1; // with the same operator << stream it to the file
14       }
15
```

The next code block [16–24] starts on line [17] with the creation of a new object `matrix_2`, which contains only one element at first. Then, the `ima` input file object, this time of `std::ifstream` type, is created on line [19] and opened from the *ema.txt* file. The `ima` object is used on line [21] as an input stream to initialize `matrix_2`. Finally, on line [23], its contents are displayed on the screen for comparison.

```
16       {
17           EMatrix matrix_2( 1, 1 );        // there must be at least 1 element
18
19           std::ifstream ima( "ema.txt" );
20
21           ima >> matrix_2;                 // stream in from an input file
22
23           std::cout << matrix_2 << std::endl;    // show it on the screen
24       }
25
```

Next are displayed the matrices that result from the calls on line [27–28] to `operator +` and `operator *`. `operator +` is called like an ordinary function, whereas `operator *` is called in the expression.

```
26      // With overloaded operators operations are even easier
27      std::cout << "M1 + M1 = \n" << matrix_1 .operator +( matrix_1 ) << std::endl;
28      std::cout << "M1 * M1 = \n" << matrix_1 * matrix_1 << std::endl;
29
30  }
```

Since we use the random generator, each time we run the previous code, different results will be generated. These may look like the following:

```
52320          36332          24182
1663           60314          20505
51152          21811          22920
```

Then, this appears on the terminal:

```
52320     36332     24182
1663      60314     20505
51152     21811     22920

52320     36332     24182
1663      60314     20505
51152     21811     22920

M1 + M1 =
104640    72664     48364
3326      120628    41010
102304    43622     45840

M1 * M1 =
4.03476e+09     4.61965e+09     2.56444e+09
1.23618e+09     4.14543e+09     1.74693e+09
3.88495e+09     3.67387e+09     2.20952e+09
```

4.8 Introduction to Templates and Generic Programming

We have already seen classes that can operate with different types provided during the definition of concrete objects. The most prominent example is the `std::vector` class, which can be defined for a concrete type of objects to be stored, such as `std::vector< int >` to store `int`, `std::vector< std::string >` to store `std::string`, etc. This is possible since `std::vector` has been defined as a *template class*. In this section, we will explain what this means and how we can define our own template classes and functions. More precisely, in this section, we will learn about the following:

- Template functions and classes
- How to convert an existing function or class to a more general template version
- How to design a template class and organize template code
- Template parameters and how to provide them
- How to restrict allowable template parameters with conditions
- Template specializations
- Template member functions and how to use them
- More on `constexpr`, `static_assert` and code execution at compilation time

4.8.1 Generalizing a Class with Templates

In Section 4.4, we discussed the details of TheCube class. It is a self-contained class that is able to store the value of the double type, organized as a 3D cube of data. But in Section 4.4, we saw a self-contained class TComplex that models complex numbers. It also implements a number of operations specific to the complex domain. Let's now imagine that we wish to make a 3D cube of data, but instead of double, we wish to store data of the TComplex type. What can we do? The simplest solution, and the only one available in languages like C, is to copy the code of TheCube, paste it, name it differently (TComplexCube, for instance), and exchange all occurrences of double for TComplex. Later, if we want a 3D cube of text, we can repeat this procedure, this time substituting double for string, and so on. However, if we proceed this way, we end up with a dozen almost identical classes, differing only in a few places where double appears. What happens if we decide to improve the original code a bit? It is tempting to create a common pattern: a template in which we indicate the places to change. When an object of such a class is instantiated, we can specify a concrete type to use in these places. Such a mechanism exists in C++ and is called *class templates*. It lets us define classes that are universal enough to operate with objects of any type – even types we will create in the future. This programming approach, which fits (almost) any type, is called *generic programming*. In the same fashion, we can create template functions, either standalone or as class members (Section 4.8.5).

Let's summarize what we will learn about in this section:

- Converting a non-template class into a template version
- Template instantiation

To see how to make a generic class with the C++ template mechanism, let's write a template version of TheCube, whose definition is listed in Table 4.3. To make the task easier, let's work with a smaller version called TinyCube, defined in Listing 4.12.

Listing 4.12 Definition of TinyCube with Specific types underlined (in *CppBookCode*, *TinyCube.cpp*).

```
1    class TinyCube
2    {
3        public:
4
5            static const int kDims = 3;   // the same for all objects of this class
6
7            enum EDims { kx, ky, kz };    // shortcuts for 3 dimensions
8
9        private:
10
11            vector< double >      fDataBuf;  // a vector to store data
12
13            array< int, kDims >  fDim;       // stores range of each dimension
14
15        public:
16
17            // Parametric constructor - dx, dy, dz must be > 0
18            TinyCube( const int dx, const int dy, const int dz )
19                : fDim{ dx, dy, dz }, fDataBuf( dx * dy * dz, 0.0 )
20            {
21                assert( dx > 0 && dy > 0 && dz > 0 );
22                assert( fDataBuf.size() == dx * dy * dz );
23            }
24
```

```
25          // Destructor does nothing; data will be deleted by the vector
26          ~TinyCube() {}
27
28      public:
29
30          // Access elements by reference - bi-directional
31          auto & Element( const int x, const int y, const int z )
32          {
33              const auto offset = ( z * fDim[ ky ] + y ) * fDim[ kx ] + x;
34              return fDataBuf[ offset ];   // subscript returns by reference
35          }
36
37      };
```

TinyCube is a simplified version of TheCube from Table 4.3. Instead of a pointer and explicitly allocated buffer on the heap, std::vector from the SL is used for data storage, as shown on line [11]. It performs a job similar to std::unique_ptr from the previous example. However, unlike std::unique_ptr, it also automatically initializes the entire buffer with the default 0 value. Especially for very large buffers, this is not necessarily what we wish to do in the constructor.

In our case, the two assertions on lines [21–22] of the constructor check for a correct number of allocated elements, but not their values. This is a type of *class invariant* superimposed on TinyCube. As alluded to previously, such a code fuse is active only in debug mode and helps to avoid logical errors during development. Proper assertions can prevent a lot of debugging problems, as discussed in Appendix A.7.

This version of TinyCube will work only with elements of double type. We can easily see that it would be more flexible if there were a simple way to exchange a few occurrences of double for another type. We will soon see that this can be done automatically with C++ templates.

Converting a "normal" C++ class into a template version is straightforward. Usually, it can be done in only two steps:

1. Add a template preamble to state that the class is a template class and to provide the name of the template parameter (or parameters), say T.
2. Exchange all occurrences of a type for an identifier of a template parameter: T in our example.

Figure 4.11 shows a simple visualization of a template class. Comparing with the class diagram in Figure 4.1, we can easily see that the main difference is in the first line, which introduces the template class and a list of *formal type-names*, each preceded by the typename keyword. The template list can also contain parameters that come with concrete types, as we will see. There are also more advanced features, such as a variadic template that lets us pass template parameters in a recursive way. We will not go into details about these, but examples of variadic templates are shown in Section 3.14.7 and in Section 6.4.

Let's apply the previous rules to convert TinyCube into a template version. This is the class name:

```
class TinyCube
{
```

We need to add the following preamble to it. Doing so changes the class into a template class and introduces an identifier ElemType to represent the template parameter:

```
template < typename ElemType >
class TinyCube
{
```

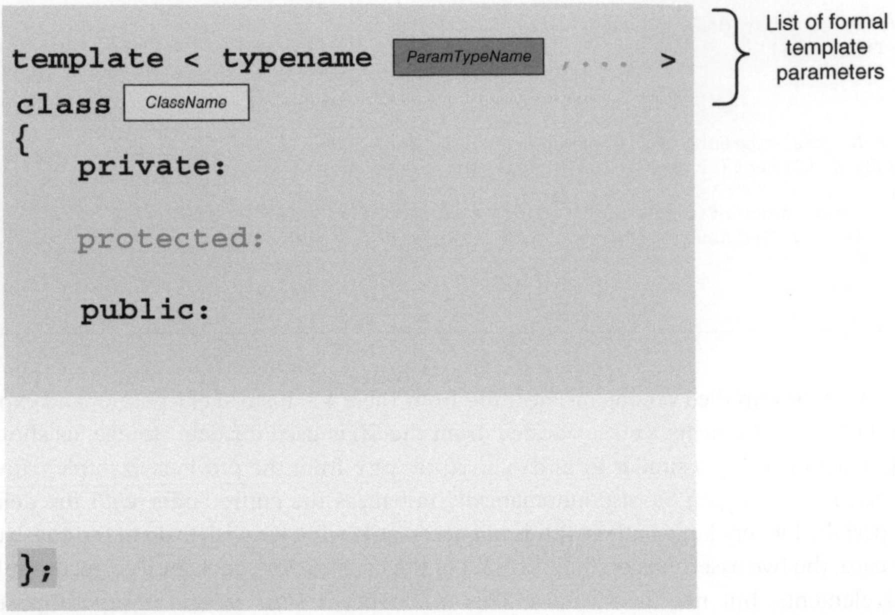

Figure 4.11 A template class diagram. The main difference between this and the class diagram in Figure 4.1 is the first line, which contains a list of template type names and parameters. These formal types can be used like any other types in the definitions of class members.

In the second step, we exchange all specific types – double in TinyCube – for the template name, which we set to ElemType. For example, the following code

```
vector< double >    fDataBuf;    // a vector to store data
```

becomes

```
vector< ElemType >    fDataBuf;    // a vector to store data
```

The complete template version of TinyCube is shown in Listing 4.13.

Listing 4.13 Definition of TinyCube, with the template parameter underlined (in *CppBookCode*, *TinyCube.cpp*).

```
1   template < typename ElemType >    // TEMPLATE preamble - ElemType is a placeholder
2   class TinyCube                     // for a later concrete type
3   {
4      public:
5
6         static const int kDims = 3;    // the same for all objects of this class
7
8         enum EDims { kx, ky, kz };      // shortcuts for 3 dimensions
9
10     private:
11
12        vector< ElemType >    fDataBuf; // a vector to store data
13
14        array< int, kDims >  fDim;      // stores range of each dimension
15
16     public:
17
```

```
18          // Parametric constructor - dx, dy, dz must be > 0
19          TinyCube( const int dx, const int dy, const int dz )
20              : fDim{ dx, dy, dz }, fDataBuf( dx * dy * dz, ElemType() )
21          {
22              assert( dx > 0 && dy > 0 && dz > 0 );
23              assert( fDataBuf.size() == dx * dy * dz );
24          }
25
26          // Destructor does nothing; data will be deleted by the vector
27          ~TinyCube() {}
28
29      public:
30
31          // Access elements by reference - bi-directional
32          ElemType & Element( const int x, const int y, const int z )
33          {
34              const auto offset = ( z * fDim[ ky ] + y ) * fDim[ kx ] + x;
35              return fDataBuf[ offset ];
36          }
37
38      };
```

Finally, let's analyze how to use the TinyCube template. Actually, TinyCube can be used exactly like TheCube. The only difference is the *template instantiation*. This means supplying a concrete type for the formal template parameter ElemType, as in Listing 4.14.

Listing 4.14 Examples of TinyCube instantiations. Each TinyCube with a different template parameter introduces a new type (in *CppBookCode*, *TinyCube.cpp*).

```
1   TinyCube< double > _3D_double_cube_obj( 2, 3, 4 );       // 2x3x4 cube of doubles
2
3   typedef TinyCube< int > TinyCubeForInt;
4   TinyCubeForInt        _3D_int_cube_obj( 1, 1, 1 );       // 1x1x1 cube of ints
5
6   using StringCube = TinyCube< std::string >;             // C++11
7   StringCube   _3D_string_cube_obj( 3, 2, 2 );           // 3x2x2 cube of strings
```

Line [1] instantiates _3D_double_cube_obj of the type TinyCube< double. This is a cube with dimensions $2 \times 3 \times 4$ containing double objects. Since the template definitions tend to be long, a common practice is to define a new shorter name for a template type with the typedef construction, as shown on line [3]. Here, TinyCube is instantiated with ElemType set to int. Thus, it is a cube of integer values. This type is then used on line [4] to define the _3D_int_cube_obj object. However, the using declaration on line [6] is more general than typedef and therefore preferable for use in modern C++ code. Interestingly enough, this time, we have a 3D cube of text strings, as exemplified on line [7]. Thus, template definitions introduce a lot of flexibility. But can we use *any* type for a class template? No: it has to fit into the definition of the class. For instance, TinyCube cannot be instantiated with a type for which the default constructor is not publicly exposed: for example, it cannot be declared with = delete or defined in the private section of the class. In such a case, the code will not compile, since we cannot create an array of elements for which there is no default constructor.

It is worth noting that the types TinyCube< double > and TinyCube< int > are not related. The compiler considers them different types, although they were generated from the same template class.

Looking at the template class `TinyCube` in Listing 4.13, note that the template name `ElemType` plays the role of a parameter: in other words, it is a kind of a variable for class definitions, which is set during code compilation. This type of code development is called *metaprogramming*, since it involves variables that are active during compilation rather than at runtime.

As shown earlier, probably the simplest way of writing a template class is to first write its non-template version, test its behavior, and then convert it to a template version. However, with a little practice, it is straightforward to implement a template class directly.

The example shown is very simple. Soon we will show a few more advanced examples, which will explain template specializations and template members.

4.8.2 (✱) Template Specializations

A template class like `TinyCube` in Listing 4.13, after being instantiated with different template parameters, defines a series of classes with the same structure but different types. Sometimes we can provide a more efficient implementation for a given type that differs not only in type but also in the implementation. C++ lets us define such exceptions to the rule: they are called *template specializations*. Here we will show that we already have a specialization for `TinyCube`. Since the definition in Listing 4.12 is written exclusively for the `double` type, it can be used as an example of specialization for the template definition of `TinyCube` in Listing 4.13. In other words, we exchange the roles of the two definitions in Listing 4.12 and Listing 4.13. However, a simple exchange is not enough: we need to let the compiler know that `TinyCube` in Listing 4.12 is a specialization of the general template `TinyCube` in Listing 4.13. This is accomplished using special syntax. In Listing 4.12, we only need to change the first line

```
class TinyCube
```

to the following two lines:

```
template <>
class TinyCube < double >
```

The rest of the class in Listing 4.12 remains untouched. This way, we obtain a special definition of `TinyCube` if the template parameter is `double`. For all others, the definition in Listing 4.13 will be used.

In this example, we used the same implementations. A more realistic example is a special implementation to store `bool` elements in `TinyCube`; see Listing 4.15. This time we can save on space, since each byte can store eight bits.

Listing 4.15 Definition of the `TinyCube` Specialization for `bool`.

```
template <>
class TinyCube < bool >
{
   // write your implementation as an exercise ...
};
```

Writing its implementation is left as an exercise. Soon we will see more examples that use templates and template specializations.

4.8.3 Template Functions and Type Checking

In Section 3.13.2.2, RevertEndianness was presented as an example of the for loop operation. It reverts the order of bytes in a variable of the unsigned long type only. So, if we wished to revert the byte order in unsigned short or int, we would need to provide almost-exact copies of RevertEndianness with the only changes being the types for its in and out variables. This would work due to the mechanism of the overloaded function, as discussed in Section 3.14.5. However, if we decide to modify details in one copy, then we need to remember to repeat the modification in the remaining copies, too. This is not very convenient, and there must be a better way to define such repeated patterns. Fortunately, C++ provides the template mechanism for functions and classes, which we discuss in this and the following sections. The programming techniques used in this section are as follows:

- Template functions
- Introduction to compile-time computations with constexpr and static_assert
- Verifying the type of the template argument during compilation

Listing 4.16 presents a template version of the RevertEndianness function. It operates exactly like its predecessor, but it allows for different types T due to the template definition on line [8].

Listing 4.16 Definition of a template version of the RevertEndianness function. constexpr allows this function for constexpr-compliant input parameters to be compiled and executed at compile time. is_unsigned_v narrows the group of allowable types T to unsigned integers (in *CppBookCode, RevertEndianness.h*).

```cpp
1   #include <iostream>
2   #include <type_traits>      // for is_unsigned_v
3
4
5   // Template function to change endianness of integer types
6   // i.e. it reverts order of bytes in the input arg.
7   // Example: 0x78ABCDEF will be changed to 0xEFCDAB78
8   template < typename T >
9   constexpr auto RevertEndianness( T in )
10  {
11      static_assert( std::is_unsigned_v< T > );
12
13      T out { 0 };
14      for( auto i { 0 }; i < sizeof( in ); ++ i )      // rotate bytes
15      {
16          out <<= 8;
17          out |= in & 0xFF;
18          in >>= 8;
19      }
20      return out;
21  }
```

What is interesting is that, in addition to being a template function, it is declared on line [9] as constexpr. This means if in is also constexpr, the function can be evaluated at *compile time*. This behavior was recently added to C++ to increase the performance of executable code – what can be precomputed will be precomputed – at the cost of compilation time. We touched on constexpr when discussing the C++ operators in *GROUP 3* (Table 3.15).

Another interesting construction is the compile-time invariant on line [11]. It ensures that the type of the provided argument in is from the group of "unsigned" integers. In other words, we do not allow other types to be byte-reversed. But this condition has to be checked during compilation, rather than at runtime. Therefore, instead of using assert, which is checked at runtime, we need to use static_assert in this case. To check whether the type T provided to a template function is unsigned, we use the std::is_unsigned_v< T > construction. If T is indeed one of the unsigned types, it evaluates to true. Otherwise, the compilation will be aborted with a suitable error message from the compiler. std::is_unsigned_v belongs to the type support libraries, for which a suitable header is included on line [2]. More examples of using constexpr and static_assert are presented in Sections 6.4 and 7.3.2.

The operation of the template version of RevertEndianness is verified in the following RevertEndianness_Test function, whose definition begins on line [22]:

```
22   inline void RevertEndianness_Test( void )
23   {
24       // RevertEndianness can be computed at compilation time
25       // Notice 'u' in 0xABCDu - this makes 0xABCD an unsigned constant
26       std::cout   << std::hex << std::uppercase  << "0xABCD" << "\t <-> "
27                   << RevertEndianness( 0xABCDu ) << std::endl;
28
29       // Compilation time since argument is constexpr
30       constexpr unsigned int ui { 0xABCDu };
31       std::cout   << std::hex << std::uppercase   << ui << "\t <-> "
32                   << RevertEndianness( ui ) << std::endl;
33
34       long l { 0x01234567 };
35       // This will not compile since l is not an 'unsigned' type
36       //std::cout    << std::hex << std::uppercase << l << "\t <-> "
37       //             << RevertEndianness( l ) << std::endl;
38
39       unsigned long ul { 0x01234567ul };
40       std::cout   << std::hex << std::uppercase        << ul << "\t <-> "
41                   << RevertEndianness( ul ) << std::endl;
42
43       unsigned long long ull { 0x0123456789ABCDEFull };
44       std::cout   << std::hex << std::uppercase        << ull << "\t <-> "
45                   << RevertEndianness( ull ) << std::endl;
46   }
```

As already pointed out, if a constexpr type argument is passed to RevertEndianness, as on lines [26–32], the function will be compiled and executed, after which the resulting value will be included in the code. But when mutable objects are provided, RevertEndianness can be called like any other function. However, in the case of the long type argument defined on line [34], RevertEndianness will not compile due to an unfulfilled type-verification condition on line [11].

Also notice the special suffixes such as u, ul, and ull on lines [30, 39, 43], which define integer literal constants (*https://en.cppreference.com/w/cpp/language/integer_literal*).

The output after running RevertEndianness_Test looks as follows:

```
ABCD        <-> CDAB0000
ABCD        <-> CDAB0000
1234567     <-> 67452301
123456789ABCDEF   <-> EFCDAB8967452301
```

The order of bytes is reversed, although the order of bits in the bytes remains the same.

4.8.4 Example Project – Designing Template Classes with *TStack*

In this section, we will learn how to define and implement a very useful data structure called a *stack*. We have already seen this important data structure when we organized nested calls for functions (Section 3.14.3). Recall that for a function call, the return address is automatically pushed to the top of the stack. It is then popped off when the function returns. But the calls can be nested, so a function called from inside another function needs to be served first. Thus, the stack reverses the order of access – what was pushed last will be popped first, and so on. Such an approach is called last in, first out (LIFO), as discussed earlier (Section 3.14.3). However, as we will see, the stack data structure can have much broader applications than storing return addresses (Section 6.6.9). In this section, we will learn about the following:

- A stack and its functionality
- How to define a stack class that can store elements of *any type* by creating a *template* class
- How to add numeric parameters to the template definition
- How to organize files with the template class definition

A stack is a data structure that lets us store objects in a way resembling a pile of books on a desk, as shown in Figure 4.12. A new object N can only be pushed on top of the stack. Similarly, only an object from the top of the stack can be popped off. It is not possible to access objects that are deeper in the structure, such as Z and Q in Figure 4.12a. If there are three objects on a stack, named Q, Z, and N, then to access Z, first we need to pop off N. Also note that if the objects were put onto the stack in the order Q, Z, N, then when taken off, they will be in the reverse order: N, Z, Q. Finally, a stack can be empty or full.

Figure 4.12a illustrates the stack data structure. There must be support for storing data, indicated by fData. There is also the notion of a direct or indirect stack pointer that indicates the first free spot on the stack. This is all we need to know about the stack's underlying data-storage region. But what is really specific to the stack is its functionality (dynamics). Only two operations are possible: *push*, to put a new object on top of the stack; and *pop*, to take an element from the top of the stack.

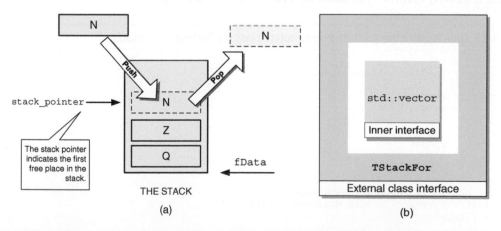

Figure 4.12 (a) Structure and operation of the stack data structure. The stack is accessible only from the top – a new element can be added by pushing it on the top of the stack. Similarly, an element on the top can be popped off. The example stack contains two elements, Q and Z. Element N can be pushed onto the top. It can then be removed from the stack by the pop operation. There is no way to access elements deeper on the stack, such as Q, other than popping off all of the preceding elements. (b) The adapter (wrapper) pattern. The internal object is embedded in the external one. Only the external interface is exposed.

These need to be prepared for two special situations: an empty stack (for *pop*) and a full stack (for *push*), as we will see when implementing our class to represent a stack.

4.8.4.1 Design and Implementation of the *TStackFor* Class

The stack can store objects of the same type. However, we would like to defined the stack for many different types, such as `size_t *` and `double`. We have seen objects that can operate the same way with data of various types – `std::vector` is the best example (Section 3.2). Such functionality is obtained by designing template classes: classes in which a type or types can be specified when a specific object needs to be created, such as `std::vector< double >`.

The SL also contains an implementation of the stack (`std::stack`). But in this section, we will implement our own version (Listing 4.17) for two reasons: (i) to learn how to write template classes, and (ii) because a slightly different interface of the stack will be needed in future applications, as discussed in Section 6.6.6.

To better protect the name of a popular class, first the `CppBook` namespace is reopened. The definition of the template class `TStackFor` occupies lines [13–14]. First, `T` is introduced as a name that represents a parametric type, whereas `MaxElems` is a numeric parameter, which can also be provided in the template definition. The second line of the definition introduces the name `TStackFor`.

As usual, it is convenient to define an alias for the stored type, as done in the `public` section on line [18] and then in the `private` section on line [22]. We can easily guess that our underlying data support will be an object of `std::vector` holding objects of `value_type`, as defined in line [24]. As shown in Figure 4.12b, since `fData` is a private data member, `TStackFor` can be interpreted as *a wrapper* around `std::vector`, greatly narrowing its functionality (Section 3.15). Then, on line [29], the `size_type` alias is created. Interestingly enough, an additional `typename` needs to be located before `DataContainer::size_type` to explicitly tell the compiler that we are specifying the type. This is necessary when operating with type names that are dependent on template parameter(s), as we will discuss in Section 6.6.6.

The main interface of `TStackFor` consists of two functions: `Push`, declared on line [54]; and `Pop`, declared on line [71]. The simple `GetStackSize`, which returns a number of objects on the stack, is entirely defined as an inline member in a single line [34].

Listing 4.17 Definition of the `TStackFor` template class (in *TheStack*, *TheStack.h*).

```
1    #pragma once
2
3
4    #include <cassert>
5    #include <vector>
6
7
8    namespace CppBook
9    {
10
11
12       // Definition of the stack data structure
13       template < typename T, auto MaxElems = 1000 >
14       class TStackFor
15       {
16          public:
17
18             using value_type = T;
```

```
19
20      private:
21
22          using DataContainer = std::vector< value_type >;
23
24          DataContainer              fData;
25
26      public:
27
28          // Here we need an additional typename
29          using size_type = typename DataContainer::size_type;
30
31
32      public:
33
34          auto GetStackSize( void ) const { return fData.size(); }
35
36      public:
37
38
39          /////////////////////////////////////////////////////////
40          // This function puts an element onto the stack
41          /////////////////////////////////////////////////////////
42          //
43          // INPUT:
44          //        new_elem - a reference to the element to
45          //             be put. Actually its copy is put onto
46          //             the stack.
47          //
48          // OUTPUT:
49          //        true - if operation successful,
50          //        false - failure, due to insufficient
51          //           space on the stack (e.g. too many
52          //           elements)
53          //
54          bool Push( const value_type & new_elem );
55
56
57          /////////////////////////////////////////////////////////
58          // This function removes an element from the stack
59          /////////////////////////////////////////////////////////
60          //
61          // INPUT:
62          //      ret_elem - a reference to the object which
63          //         will be copied with  topmost element
64          //         from the stack. Then the topmost element
65          //         is removed from the stack.
66          //
67          // OUTPUT:
68          //        true - if operation successful,
69          //        false - failure, due to empty stack
70          //
71          bool Pop( value_type & ret_elem );
72
73
74  };
```

Push and Pop are short enough that they could also be implemented in the class definition. We take them outside here to show the syntax. In the case of template classes, all definitions are contained in a header file.

Lines [75–76] define the Push function, which is a member of TStackFor< T, MaxElems >. Notice that the full name of a template class is not only its name – it is its name *and* the template parameters. This also indicates that the TStack classes with different types set for T are different, unrelated, classes. In addition, two TStack classes with the same T but different MaxElems are also different types.

Push first checks on line [78] to be sure the stack is not full. For this purpose, the MaxElems parameter is used. If so, false is returned on line [79]. But if there is room in the container, a new object, referred to by the new_elem argument, is pushed back into the fData container. emplace_back is used on line [81], which allows for more efficient move semantics rather than object copying (Section 4.7.2). In this case, true is returned on line [83], as an indicator of success. Hence, TStackFor has built-in error semantics, which lets us use safe push operations on a full stack and safely pop from the empty one. Throwing an exception would be overuse in this case.

```
75   template < typename T, auto MaxElems >
76   bool TStackFor< T, MaxElems >::Push( const value_type & new_elem )
77   {
78     if( GetStackSize() == MaxElems )
79         return false;
80
81     fData.emplace_back( new_elem );
82
83     return true;
84   }
```

Pop, defined on lines [85–86], does the opposite of Push. On line [88], it checks whether there are any elements in storage to be popped off. If the stack is empty, then false is returned on line [89] with no further consequences. However, in the opposite case, the topmost object is first accessed on line [91] and then removed on line [92], and true is returned on line [94].

```
85   template < typename T, auto MaxElems >
86   bool TStackFor< T, MaxElems >::Pop( value_type & ret_elem )
87   {
88     if( GetStackSize() == 0 )
89         return false;
90
91     ret_elem = fData.back();   // Copy the top element
92     fData.pop_back();          // Get rid of the last element
93
94     return true;
95   }
96
97   }       // End of the CppBook namespace
```

As alluded to previously, the entire definition of a template class is usually contained in a single header file. Figure 4.13 shows a Unified Modeling Language (UML) artifact diagram showing the relations of the header containing a template class definition and the source files in a project.[6]

---

6 Some projects prefer the *.hpp* extension to distinguish headers exclusively for C++, such as those with templates.

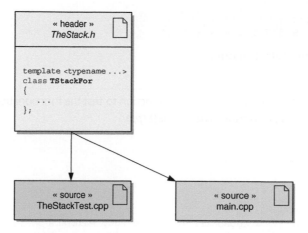

Figure 4.13 UML artifact diagram showing the relations of the header containing a template class definition and source files. Templates are entirely implemented in the header files (there are no source *.cpp* files). These are included in other sources – *TheStackTest.cpp* and *main.cpp* in this example.

4.8.4.2 Testing *TStack*

Listing 4.18 presents a test function that demonstrates the basic operations of the `TStackFor` class. On line [3], the *TheStack.h* header is included, which contains the complete definition of the `TStackFor` class from Listing 4.17. But notice the *template version of the* `using` directive, as shown on lines [7–8]. This partially specialized `using` lets us define an alias with a few template parameters already set to concrete types, and a few left as template parameters. In our case, `StackForInt_VarSize` is a partially specialized alias for all stacks holding `int` objects but with the possibility to specify a different maximum size by providing a value for the `MaxElems` parameter.

Then, on line [11], the `StackForInt` alias is defined, this time with a concrete `int` type and a maximum capacity of 256 objects.

When creating an object based on a template class, first that class has to be created with the specified concrete template types and parameters. This process is called template class *instantiation*. The rules and the entire process of matching template parameters with a compiler can be found in the language specification (Stroustrup 2013; Cppreference.com 2018). The compiler tries to choose the best-fitting parameters from all the possibilities. However, as we have seen, it is also possible to create variants of templates, called template specializations, that address specific types. More information on stack specialization will be presented in Section 6.6.6.

The definition of the `TheStackTest` test function starts on line [18]. In line [20], the `theStackForInt` object of the `StackForInt` class is created. It is an empty stack, so in the loop on lines [25–26], it is filled with consecutive values in the range < 0...16). These values are obtained using the `range` class, contained in the `CppBook` namespace and discussed in Section 6.5. The values are simultaneously written to the screen. Then, in the next loop on lines [31–32], the entire contents of the stack are popped off, one object after another, and printed out on the screen.

After launching the `TheStackTest` function, we obtained the following output:

```
Values pushed to the stack:
0 1 2 3 4 5 6 7 8 9 10 11 12 13 14 15
```

```
Content of the stack:
15 14 13 12 11 10 9 8 7 6 5 4 3 2 1 0
```

We can easily see the LIFO structure.

Listing 4.18 Definition of the `TheStackTest` function to test the functionality of the `TStackFor` class (in *TheStack, TheStackTest.cpp*).

```
1   #include <iostream>
2   #include "range.h"
3   #include "TheStack.h"
4
5
6   // Partially specialized using
7   template < auto MaxElems >
8   using StackForInt_VarSize = CppBook::TStackFor< int, MaxElems >;
9
10  // Full class
11  using StackForInt = StackForInt_VarSize< 256 >;
12
13
14  using std::cout, std::endl;
15
16
17
18  void TheStackTest( void )
19  {
20      StackForInt theStackForInt;
21
22      cout << "\nValues pushed to the stack:\n";
23
24      // Push consecutive values
25      for( auto a : CppBook::range( 16 ) )
26          cout << a << " ", theStackForInt.Push( a );
27
28      cout << "\nContent of the stack:\n";
29
30      // Print taking the top of the stack - for will do all
31      for( StackForInt::value_type v {}; theStackForInt.Pop( v ); cout << v << " " )
32          ;
33  }
```

4.8.5 Template Member Functions

We have already used many functions in which the types of the parameters were specified in the call line, depending on the passed arguments. For instance, see the common SL algorithms listed in Table 3.6, or the `std::make_unique` function used to create a data buffer in Section 4.5. We have also presented some examples of template functions – for instance, `RevertEndianness` in Table 3.9 and `multi_print_helper` presented in Table 3.10. But in this section, let's examine yet another possibility: *a template member function*. It is a definition of a template function inside a template, or non-template, class. We will analyze some example code that shows a template member function.

Let's create a simple class (actually, only the skeleton of a class) to represent 2D points with various types of coordinates. A sketch of a possible definition of the template `TPointFor` class is shown in Listing 4.19.

Listing 4.19 Definition of the `TPointFor` class (in *CppBookCode, PointFor.h*). For full operation, the darker line should be replaced with the code from Listing 4.21

```
1   // Template members within a template class example
2   template < typename T >
3   class TPointFor
4   {
5
6   private:
7
8       T       fx {}, fy {};       // Two coordinates of T type
9
10
11  public:
12
13      void Set_x( T x ) { fx = x; }
14      void Set_y( T y ) { fy = y; }
15
16      auto Get_x( void ) const { return fx; }
17      auto Get_y( void ) const { return fy; }
18
19
20  };
```

The definition of `TPointFor` begins on lines [2–3]. The template parameter `T` defines the type of the two coordinate points `fx` and `fy`, defined and initialized to the zero state on line [8]. To this point, on lines [13–17], we also have the standard getters and setters.

Let's test the basic functionality of the `TPointFor` class; see Listing 4.20. For this purpose, the `PointTest` function is defined, starting on line [21]. On lines [24, 26], two types for the real and integer point coordinates are aliased. Then, two pairs of real and integer point objects are created on lines [29] and [31]. On line [34], the real point `rp2` is copied to `rp1`. Everything is fine so far.

Listing 4.20 Definition of the `PointTest` Function (in *CppBookCode, PointFor.h*).

```
21  inline void PointTest( void )
22  {
23
24      using RealPoint = TPointFor< double >;
25
26      using IntPoint = TPointFor< int >;
27
28
29      RealPoint rp1, rp2;       // Calls default constructor
30
31      IntPoint ip1, ip2;        // Calls default constructor
32
33
34      rp1 = rp2;      // Assignment within the same class
35                      // - no special template assignment needed
36
37      rp1 = ip2;      // Assignment across different classes
38                      // - special template assignment necessary
39
40      RealPoint rp3( ip1 );   // Also copy construction across the different classes
41  }
```

The problem arises on line [37] when we try to copy an integer point `ip2` to the real `rp1`. This should be possible – the integer coordinates can be stored with the real representation. Nevertheless, although the compiler knows how to copy coordinates of the same type – we have not explicitly provided an implementation of the assignment operator, but the assignment on line [34] still works – it fails to copy the objects on line [37] when it encounters the `IntPoint` and `RealPoint` objects of different classes. The same type of issue is encountered on line [40], although this time there is a problem with the copy constructor. To remedy these issues, we need to provide definitions for the copy constructor and the assignment operator for `TPointFor`, but with different instantiation types. Since these can be `TPointFor` objects, instantiated with any other type, we can use the copy constructor and the assignment operator, implemented with *template member functions* as shown in Listing 4.21.

On lines [50–51], the copy constructor template member is defined. That is, an object to be copied from can be another `TPointFor`, but instantiated with any type identified with the `U` template parameter. `T` and `U` may be the same: in such a case, we would operate inside one class definition, so we could also freely access all private data members. But since in general `U` and `T` can be different, then to access the `fx` and `fy` coordinates, we have to use `Get_x` and `Get_y` from the public interface of object `pt`. Initializing `fx` with `pt.Get_x`, and `fy` with `pt.Get_y`, on line [51], entails a type conversion from `U` to `T`. This conversion must be known to the compiler; otherwise an error will be reported. In our case, there is no problem with converting `int` to `double`, so the entire process goes smoothly and quietly.

Listing 4.21 Additional template member copy constructor, and the assignment operator for the `TPointFor` class. Because these special member functions were explicitly added to the class, we are also forced to add the definition of the default constructor since its automatic generation is suppressed (in *CppBookCode, PointFor.h*).

```
42
43    public:
44
45
46        // A template member copy constructor to initialize
47        // from a point with different coordinate types.
48        // To be general must call Get_x and Get_y
49        // Direct access possible only if T == U
50        template < typename U >
51        TPointFor< T >( const TPointFor< U > & pt ) : fx( pt.Get_x() ), fy( pt.Get_y() )
52        {}
53
54        // A template member assignment operator to initialize
55        // from a point with different coordinate types.
56        template < typename U >
57        TPointFor< T > & operator = ( const TPointFor< U > & pt )
58        {
59            //fx = pt.fx;          these two work only
60            //fy = pt.fy;          if T == U
61            fx = pt.Get_x();           // allow conversion
62            fy = pt.Get_y();
63            return * this;
64        }
65
66
67        // A default constructor needs to be explicitly coded
68        // since the copy constructor and the assignment were added
69        // (otherwise could be skipped).
70        TPointFor( void ) = default;
71
```

Similarly, on lines [56–57], the assignment operator's template member is defined. Again, the data access problem is resolved on lines [61–62] by resorting to the public `Get_x` and `Get_y` members, rather than trying to access private data, as shown on lines [59–60]. Such attempts are condemned to fail if `U` and `T` are different, regardless of the existing conversion between `U` and `T`. Naturally, the assignment operator needs to return itself. This is done on line [63].

Notice that since we explicitly added the copy constructor and the assignment operator, we lost the bonus of the automatic generation of the default constructor by the C++ compiler (Section 4.5). If left in this state, the constructions on lines [29] and [31], which previously were fine with the compiler, will now generate a compiler error. Therefore, on line [70], we added the default constructor ourselves.

Finally, note that `PointTest` is declared inline. As we already know, this means two things: (i) a function's code is located directly in the place where it is called, avoiding jumps to other parts of the address space; and (ii) `inline` means local linking: the function is local to the translation unit. This is useful in such cases when the entire implementation of a function is embedded in a header file, which is also the case for `PointTest`. If such a header was included in few different translation units, and if the function were not inline, the linker would report an error associated with a function defined multiple times. Being `inline` mitigates this problem. In modern C++, data can also be declared `inline`, for the same reasons – see Section 4.15.3.

Things to Remember

- Templates let us write code that can operate with different types and parameters, passed when a template function or a class is instantiated
- There can be general template functions and classes, as well as specialized versions that provide implementation optimized for specific template type(s) or parameter(s)
- The stack data structure provides LIFO functionality
- To change the functionality and/or interface of an object of a given type, we can wrap it in an adapter (wrapper) class

4.9 Class Relations – "Know," "Has-A," and "Is-A"

We have seen many examples of classes that contain member data. With only a few exceptions, these data members are objects of other classes. We have used what is probably the most natural relation between classes: the *composition*. For example, the `TQuadEq` class, discussed in Section 3.16.1, is composed of three objects of the `double` type (OK, it is not a "pure" class, but that does not matter in this context – we could also enclose each `double` in a separate class). Also, `TCurrency` from Section 3.18.3 contains `std::wstring` objects at its disposal, etc. But in addition to this natural enclosing relation, in OOP there is a second important relation: inheritance (Section 4.1). It lets us change the behavior of a class by creating a new version of that class that inherits whatever the original possessed, and that can also add new members and change the behavior of old members. As always, there are variants of these two relations, which we will discuss in this section.

In this section, we will learn about the following:

- Class relations: "knows" associations, aggregation and composition, and inheritance
- UML diagrams for class associations
- Simple examples of class relations

Table 4.4 shows and explains the fundamental relations between classes.

Table 4.4 Fundamental relations between classes expressed with UML class diagrams.

Class relation	Description	UML diagram	Examples
The class	The UML class diagram is composed of three compartments: class name, class attributes (data), and class operations (functions). Attributes and operations can have a public (+), protected (#), or private (−) access type. In the case of a template class, the template arguments are shown in a box in the upper-right corner.	*Template arguments* **ClassName** + Public attribute # Protected attribute : *data type = val* − Private attribute : *data type* + Public operation(*arg list*) : *result* # Protected operation(*arg list*) : *result* − Private operation(*arg list*) : *result*	```// Interface to onboard flash memory programming
class Am29_FlashProgrammer
{
public:
    enum EFlashBitMask { k_DQ7_Mask=0x01, k_DQ6_Mask=0x02 };

    using SystemAddress = uint32_t;   // 32-bit address bus
    using DataLen   = uint32_t;   // 32-bit address bus
    using DataWordType = uint16_t;   // 16-bit data bus
private:
    // system flash base address
    const SystemAddress fFlashBaseAddress;
protected:
    // Checks whether a given bit toggles
    bool ToggleBit_PassControl(EFlashBitMask mask,
                    SystemAddress offsetAddress = 0);
public:
    // Class constructor
    Am29_FlashProgrammer(SystemAddress flashBaseAddress);
public:
    // This function ERASES the ENTIRE device
    bool ChipErase(void);
    // This function programs a block of the memory
    bool ProgramBlock(SystemAddress addressInFlash,
                    DataWordType * bufAddr, DataLen dataLen);
};```

The class shows parts of a real class for programming flash memory chips in the embedded system (Am29 family). It contains various private, protected, and public data members and member functions. It has a parametric constructor (no default constructor). However, it does not depend on other classes. |

Association ("Knows")

Class_A "knows" about Class_B, so Class_A can call members of Class_B. This relation is indicated by an arrow from Class_A to Class_B. "Knows" relations can be either one- or bi-directional (bi-directional arrow).

Optionally, the ends of the connections can contain quantities.

Objects of these classes do not depend on each other, but changing the interface of one can affect the other.

```
class PlotServer          // class B
{
  public:
    using DoubleVec = vector< double >;
    virtual void PlotData( const DoubleVec & x,
                           const DoubleVec & y ) const;
};

// common plotting server
static const PlotServer    gPlotServer;

class PartialEquationSolver       // class A
{
  public:
    virtual void operator() ( void )
    {
        vector< double >    a, b;
        // ...
        // action delegation to the server
        gPlotServer.PlotData( a, b );
    }
};
```

The classes have a loose, one-directional relation. PlotServer is a class that facilitates printing services (Class_B). PartialEquationSolver (Class_A) knows and calls for services from PlotServer to print out some of its results. But the two classes are not bound. An object of the Class_B needs to be alive when called by an object of Class_A, which is fulfilled here since gPlotServer is a static object.

(Continued)

Table 4.4 (continued)

Class relation	Description	UML diagram	Examples
| **Aggregation association ("has-a")** | An object of Class_A aggregates an object of Class_B. Aggregation association is also known as a "whole-part" or "has-a" relationship.<br><br>This is a looser version of the whole-part relation in which there is no lifetime dependency between an object of Class_A (whole) and object(s) of Class_B (part). For example, the FacultyRegistry class aggregates objects of the Student class. However, both can exist without the other.<br><br>Class_B can belong to one or more objects – thus its multiplicity can be 1 or more (denoted as 1..*). But a whole, Class_A, can aggregate 0 or more parts (denoted as 0..*). | | ```cpp
class Student            // Class_B (part)
{
    private:
        string      fName, fSurname;
        // ...
    public:
        // Student code here ...
};
class SchoolClassRegistry        // Class_A (whole)
{
    private:
        // registry aggregates students
        vector< Student *>     fStudentGroup;
    public:
        // FacultyRegistry code here
        // A student can be added to a class
        void AddStudent( const Student & );
        // but also removed from a class
        void RemoveStudent( const Student & );
};
```<br><br>One SchoolClassRegistry class (Class_A) can aggregate zero or more Student (Class_B) objects. But the aggregated Student objects can be detached from the SchoolClassRegistry object. That is, if the SchoolClassRegistry object is destroyed, the Student objects are left untouched since they can be aggregated in other "organizations" as well. |
```

Composition is a stronger form of aggregation association since it implies ownership of the Class_B object ("part") by the Class_A object ("whole"). This means a part can belong to at most one composite, and the part object lives as long as the whole composite.

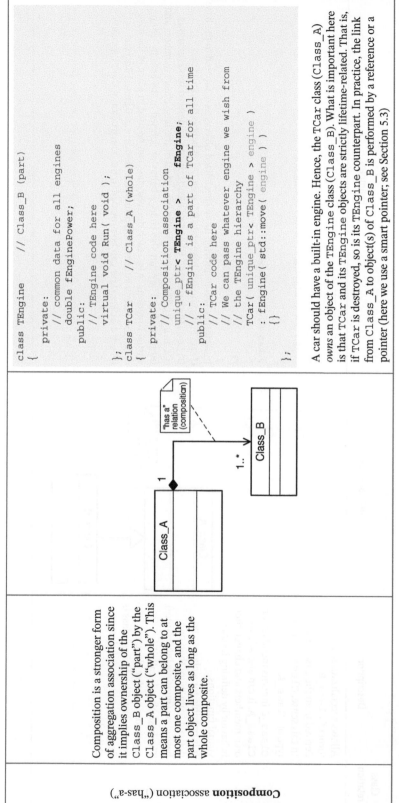

```
class TEngine        // Class_B (part)
{
    private:
        // common data for all engines
        double fEnginePower;
    public:
        // TEngine code here
        virtual void Run( void );
};
class TCar       // Class_A (whole)
{
    private:
        // Composition association
        unique_ptr< TEngine >    fEngine;
        // - fEngine is a part of TCar for all time
    public:
        // TCar code here
        // We can pass whatever engine we wish from
        // the TEngine hierarchy
        TCar( unique_ptr< TEngine > engine )
        : fEngine( std::move( engine ) )
        {}
};
```

A car should have a built-in engine. Hence, the TCar class (Class_A) *owns* an object of the TEngine class (Class_B). What is important here is that TCar and its TEngine objects are strictly lifetime-related. That is, if TCar is destroyed, so is its TEngine counterpart. In practice, the link from Class_A to object(s) of Class_B is performed by a reference or a pointer (here we use a smart pointer; see Section 5.3)

(Continued)

Table 4.4 (continued)

Class relation	Description	UML diagram	Examples
| Inheritance ("is-a") | Allows specialization in the form of Class_B, which is derived from the base Class_A. In this sense, Class_B "is-a" type of Class_A.<br><br>Class_B inherits members of Class_A. It can also add its own members and change their behavior by defining its own virtual functions.<br><br>It is possible for a class to be derived from more than one base class (*multiple inheritance*).<br><br>The base class is called a *superclass*, *mother class*, or *parent class*. The derived class is frequently called a *subclass* or *child class*. | Class_A ◁---- "is a" relation ---- Class_B | ```
class GasEngine : public TEngine
{
};
class DieselEngine : public TEngine
{
};
class ElectricEngine : public TEngine
{
};
```<br><br>Inheritance lets us provide more specialized objects as compared to the base class. TEngine is a base class (Class_A), whereas GasEngine, DieselEngine, and ElectricEngine are all derived specializations (Class_B). The derived classes inherit all of the base class's members and functionality. They can also change behavior defined in the base by using virtual functions. Also, each derived class can be used in place of the base class (the Liskov substitution principle). Hence, e.g. DieselEngine or ElectricEngine can be provided to the constructor of the TCar class. |
```

During derivation, an access filter is provided for the base class, as shown in Figure 4.2. The access filter plus the member access types limit base members to the more restrictive access rule. That is, if a member is declared protected but the derivation is private, then the member becomes private in the derived class, and so on. If no access filter is provided, then private is assumed. In this case, all base members become private in the derived class. Inheritance of this type is called a *dynamic polymorphism*, in contrast to the *static polymorphism* provided by the template mechanism (Section 4.13).

Class diagram legend

Relation multiplicity	Description	Class member visibility	Description	Type of relation	Description
0	No instance	+	Public	→	Association
0..1	No instance or exactly one	-	Private	⇢	Dependency
1	Exactly one instance	#	Protected	▽	Inheritance
0..*	Zero or more instances	/	Derived (inheritance)	◇	Aggregation
1..*	One or more instances	~	Package (libraries)	◆	Composition

In recent decades, more complex relations between classes have been observed, which repeat from project to project regardless of differences in minor details. These are known as *design patterns* (Gamma et al. 1994). In the following sections, we will also present few of the most practical ones.

4.10 Example Project – Extending Functionality Through Class Inheritance with *TComplexQuadEq*

In Section 3.15, we presented the TQuadEq class, which represents quadratic equations in the real domain. Depending on the values of its three parameters, there can be zero, one, or two solutions, or roots. However, two roots always exist in the realm of complex numbers, as we know from Section 4.4. How can we extend TQuadEq to return the TComplex roots? Do we need to write everything from the beginning, or can we somehow *reuse* parts of TquadEq? We can use one of the basic principles of OOP: class inheritance, as shown in Figure 4.14.

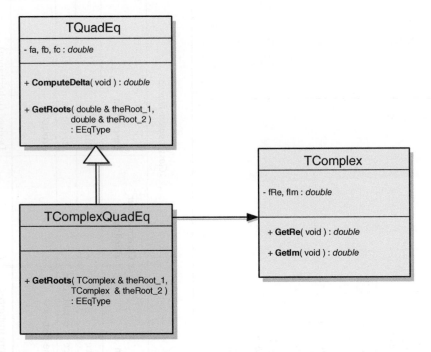

Figure 4.14 UML class diagram showing the inheritance relation between the classes TQuadEq and TComplexQuadEq. TComplexQuadEq inherits data members and the ComputeDelta function from the base class TQuadEq. There is also a relation between the TComplexQuadEq and TComplex classes – TComplexQuadEq knows and uses objects of TComplex.

As already presented in Table 4.4, inheritance allows a derived class, to "possess" all the features of the base class. As a result, the derived class can concentrate on its specific behavior. Also, using the virtual mechanism discussed in the next section, it is possible to adjust the operation of some of the member functions defined in the base class.

Listing 4.22 shows the definition of the TComplexQuadEq class derived from TQuadEq. Inheritance relations are expressed in the class definition, on line [9]. It follows the scheme shown in Figure 4.15.

Figure 4.15 Syntax of class inheritance. The most common form is the public derivation.

As alluded to previously, an access rule specified after the colon : defines access rules for all members of the base class, from the level of the derived class, however. The more restrictive rule is applied here: if a base member is `public` but the derivation was declared as `protected`, then from the derived class, this base member is treated as `protected`; for instance, it will not be accessible from objects of the derived class, for instance.

Before we go further, a note on the project structure. As we see in Figure 4.14, `TComplexQuadEq` is related to two other classes, each from a different project. We could copy the sources to one project; but then we would have two or three versions of *Complex.cpp*, for instance, and if we changed it in one project, we would need to remember to copy it to the other. Therefore, a better option is to have only one version of the source files. For this purpose, assuming that all three projects have the same directory structure, we can use relative paths. Such relative paths are seen on lines [2, 3] in Listing 4.22, where the headers from the associated projects are included. The organization and automatic generation of project files are discussed in Section A.6.1.

On lines [6] and [14], the two `using` directives introduce the respective types into the scope. The difference is that in the second case, the type from the base class is brought only to the scope of the derived class.

Lines [21–33] show the `public` section with special member functions. These follow the definitions from previously presented classes, such as `TComplex` in Section 4.4. But a difference can be seen in the case of the parametric constructor, defined on line [25]. Instead of trying to initialize data members directly, a parametric constructor from the base class is called on line [26], forwarding the arguments.

A good thing about inheritance, both in programming and in life, is that a derived class can reuse whatever has already been prepared. This is also the case for `TComplexQuadEq`. It declares only two member functions: `GetNumOfRoots` on line [47], and `GetRoots` on line [65]. Only these had to be rewritten to adapt to the computations in the complex domain. All the other functions, such as `ComputeDelta` and `Get_a`, and the data members, were inherited from `TQuadEq`. However, notice that since the data was declared `private`, it is not directly accessible even for members of the derived class. Instead, we can use the `TQuadEq` public interface with all the getters, if necessary.

Listing 4.22 Definition of the `TComplexQuadEq` class derived (inherited) from `TQuadEq` (in *ComplexQuadEq, ComplexQuadEq.h*).

```
1  // Paths are relative to the position of the project files
2  #include "../../Complex/include/Complex.h"
3  #include "../../QuadEq/include/QuadEq.h"
4
```

(Continued)

Listing 4.22 (continued)

```
 5
 6    using       CppBook::TComplex;
 7
 8
 9    class TComplexQuadEq : public TQuadEq
10    {
11       public:
12
13          // Introduce the EEqType from the base class
14          using TQuadEq::EEqType;
15
16       public:
17
18          // ====================================================
19
20          // Class default constructor
21          TComplexQuadEq( void )
22          {}
23
24          // Class parametric constructor
25          TComplexQuadEq( double a, double b, double c )
26             : TQuadEq( a, b, c )   // Call the base class constructor
27          {}
28
29          // Class default copy constructor
30          TComplexQuadEq( const TComplexQuadEq & ) = default;
31
32          // Class default destructor
33           ~TComplexQuadEq()= default;
34
35          // ====================================================
36
37       public:
38
39          ///////////////////////////////////////////////////////
40          // This function checks the type of the equation
41          ///////////////////////////////////////////////////////
42          //
43          // INPUT:    delta
44          // OUTPUT:   An exact type of the equation
45          //           represented by the parameters f_a, f_b, f_c
46          //
47          EEqType GetNumOfRoots( const double delta ) const;
48
49
50          ///////////////////////////////////////////////////////
51          // This function computes the roots of the equation, if possible.
52          ///////////////////////////////////////////////////////
53          //
54          // INPUT:  theRoot_1 - a reference to an object that
55          //           contains root 1 if returned kLinOne, kOne or kTwo
56          //         theRoot_2 - a reference to an object that
57          //           contains root 2 if returned kOne or kTwo
58          //           (in the first case root_1 == root_2)
59          //
60          // OUTPUT:  status of the equation (number of roots)
61          //
62          // REMARKS: The values referenced to by theRoot_1 and theRoot_2
63          //          are undefined in all other cases than stated above.
64          //
65          EEqType GetRoots( TComplex & theRoot_1, TComplex & theRoot_2 ) const;
66    };
```

Implementation of the two member functions of the `TComplexQuadEq` class is shown in Listing 4.23. In the complex domain, if this is a proper quadratic equation, then there are always roots. This is expressed on line [11] of the `GetNumOfRoots`, whose definition begins on line [3].

Listing 4.23 Definitions of the `TComplexQuadEq` members (in *ComplexQuadEq, ComplexQuadEq.cpp*).

```
1   #include "ComplexQuadEq.h"
2
3   TComplexQuadEq::EEqType TComplexQuadEq::GetNumOfRoots( const double delta ) const
4   {
5      if( Get_a() == 0.0 )
6      {
7         return Get_b() == 0.0 ? EEqType::kLinContra : EEqType::kLinOne;
8      }
9      else
10     {      // In this class the sign of delta is not important
11        return delta == 0.0 ? EEqType::kOne : EEqType::kTwo;
12     }
13  }
```

`GetRoots`, defined on line [14], also operates in the complex domain. On line [17], the `delta` parameter is computed with a call to the `ComputeDelta` member from the base class. This is possible since `ComputeDelta` was declared public in `TQuadEq`. This parameter is then passed on line [21] to `GetNumOfRoots` from the `TComplexQuadEq` class. Depending on the returned type of the equation, the correct action is undertaken by the `switch` on line [23]. If there are two member functions with the same name, one in the base class and the other in the derived class, then the derived class *hides* definition from the base class, rather than overloading it. But the base function, if accessible, can also be called from the derived class, as we will see soon.

The most interesting two cases, `EEqType::kOne` and `EEqType::kTwo`, are treated together – there is no `break` statement between them. First, the denominator is checked to be sure its value is large enough. If not, then an exception is thrown on line [59]. Then, the two cases related to the sign of the `delta` parameter are resolved on line [62]. In both cases, we need to initialize the two `TComplex` objects. For the complex domain, this is computed on lines [65–69]. However, if there are only real roots, the imaginary parts of both are set to 0.0, as accomplished on lines [75] and [78].

```
14   TQuadEq::EEqType TComplexQuadEq::GetRoots( TComplex & root_1, TComplex & root_2 )
15                                            const
16   {
17      auto delta( ComputeDelta() );        // Call a constructor for the built-in type
18
19      const auto kDivThresh { 1e-36 };     // Used in assert to verify divisions
20
21      EEqType equationTypeFlag = GetNumOfRoots( delta );
22
23      switch( equationTypeFlag )
24      {
25         case EEqType::kNone:
26
27            assert( false );               // should not happen
28            break;
```

```
29
30          case EEqType::kLinContra:
31
32             break;              // do nothing
33
34          case EEqType::kLinOne:
35
36             assert( Get_a() == 0.0 );
37             assert( std::fabs( Get_b() ) > kDivThresh );
38
39             if( std::fabs( Get_b() ) < kDivThresh )
40                throw std::overflow_error( "Too low fb" );
41
42             root_1 = root_2 = - Get_c() / Get_b();
43
44             break;              // return with one root
45
46          case EEqType::kOne:        // no break here - for these two cases, one solution
47          case EEqType::kTwo:
48
49          { // We need a block {} here for local variables
50
51             bool negative_delta = delta < 0.0 ? true : false;
52
53             double delta_root = sqrt( negative_delta ? - delta : delta );
54
55             double denominator = 2.0 * Get_a();
56             assert( std::fabs( denominator ) > kDivThresh );
57
58             if( std::fabs( denominator ) < kDivThresh )
59                throw std::overflow_error( "Too low fa" );
60
61
62             if( negative_delta )
63             {
64                // Negative delta requires a complex domain
65                root_1.SetRe( - Get_b() / denominator );
66                root_1.SetIm( - delta_root / denominator );
67
68                root_2.SetRe( - Get_b() / denominator );
69                root_2.SetIm(   delta_root / denominator );
70             }
71             else
72             {
73                // Positive delta means only real roots
74                root_1.SetRe( ( - Get_b() - delta_root ) / denominator );
75                root_1.SetIm( 0.0 );
76
77                root_2.SetRe( ( - Get_b() + delta_root ) / denominator );
78                root_2.SetIm( 0.0 );
79             }
80
81          }
82
83             break;
84
85          default :
86
87             assert( false );       // This should not happen - an error in programming?
88             break;
89       }
90
91    return equationTypeFlag;
92 }
```

Note that the cases EEqType::kNone, on line [25], and default, on line [85], though unlikely to happen, are included in the code for diagnostics.

As usual, the test function, defined on line [101] of Listing 4.24, contains characteristic functions of TComplexQuadEq. First, the cqe object of the TComplexQuadEq class is created on line [105]. It is initialized with the three parameters a, b, and c, hardcoded on line [103]. The root objects are defined on line [108]. Then, the roots are computed by calling GetRoots from the cqe object, as shown on line [110]. If the roots have been successfully computed, as checked on lines [112–113], two asserts are invoked on line [117–118]. They simply verify whether the computations are correct – that is, whether the roots inserted into the equation lead sufficiently close to 0.

Listing 4.24 Test function for the TComplexQuadEq class (in *ComplexQuadEq, ComplexQuadEqTest.cpp*).

```
93   #include <iostream>
94   #include "ComplexQuadEq.h"
95
96
97   using std::cout, std::endl;
98
99
100
101  void ComplexQuadEq_Test( void )
102  {
103      double a { 5.0 }, b { 2.0 }, c { 1.0 };
104
105      TComplexQuadEq           cqe( a, b, c );
106
107
108      TComplex r1, r2;
109
110      TComplexQuadEq::EEqType eq_type = cqe.GetRoots( r1, r2 );
111
112      if(      eq_type == TComplexQuadEq::EEqType::kOne ||
113               eq_type == TComplexQuadEq::EEqType::kTwo )
114      {
115          // Check if correct - there are many abs functions, but
116          // thanks to the CppBook namespace we do not confuse them
117          assert( CppBook::abs( r1 * ( r1 * a + b ) + c ) < 1e-12 );
118          assert( CppBook::abs( r2 * ( r2 * a + b ) + c ) < 1e-12 );
119
120          // Print out the results:
121          cout << "a=" << a << ", b=" << b << ", c=" << c << endl;
122          cout << "Root_1=" << r1 << ", Root_2=" << r2 << endl;
123      }
124      else
125      {
126          cout << "This is a deficient quadratic equation" << endl;
127      }
128
129  }
```

After calling ComplexQuadEq_Test, the following output is obtained:

```
a=5, b=2, c=1
Root_1=-0.2 -0.4, Root_2=-0.2 0.4
```

We need to point out that the previous implementation has a drawback: in the class hierarchy, the destructor of the base class should be declared `virtual`. This is to ensure that if a derived object is dynamically created and assigned to a pointer to the base class, then when destroying the object through this pointer, a destructor of the derived class is also called. But our base class `TQuadEq`, shown in Table 3.11, does not define a destructor. This section's code example does not use any pointers, so it is safe. We will return to this issue in the next section.

4.11 Virtual Functions and Polymorphism

One of the strengths of OOP is the ability to extend or change the behavior of methods from the base class in a derived class without needing to rewrite everything from scratch. Thus, new, frequently more-specialized versions of previously known objects can easily be created. This falls in the framework of abstraction, represented in a base class, versus specialization or implementation, represented in derived classes.

The key aspect of this functionality – *polymorphism* – is that frequently, a generic algorithm can be described in terms of calls among member functions defined in a base class, and can then be modified by defining custom versions in derived classes. In other words, polymorphism means a call to a member function invokes the execution of a different function, depending on the type of the object being used.

Implementing polymorphism involves *virtual functions*. It is easy to guess that virtual functions are those that can substitute for each other in derived classes. This process is called function *overriding*.[7] To understand what we are talking about, let's analyze an example with two players: the `TCircle` class to represent a circle (see Listing 4.25); and `PrecCircle`, which lets us modify `TCircle`. Their relation is shown in Figure 4.16a in the form of a UML class diagram.

`TCircle` contains one private variable `fRadius` to hold the value of the radius of the circle. There is also a constructor with a default value, so it can serve as a default constructor and a parametric constructor at the same time. In addition, the inline member functions `GetRadius` and `SetRadius` allow access to `fRadius`. Note that such data encapsulation, through data being private with access via public functions, provides additional security for the object because we can control every read and, most important, every write that changes the radius. This way, we can ensure that, for instance, the radius is not negative, not too big, etc. Such control would not be possible if the data was declared public, since every other software component could write whatever it wanted without any control over the values.

`TCircle` also contains a function `ComputeArea` that computes the area of the circle, using the square of `fRadius` multiplied by the `GetPi` function. However, let's assume for a moment that the base version of `GetPi` returns only a roughly approximation *pi*, because we simulate less-precise computations in the base class. We expect that a more precise version of `GetPi` will be defined in a derived class. For this purpose, `GetPi` is defined as *a virtual function*.

Finally, something interesting happens to the destructor of `TCircle`, which on line [24] is also defined virtual. Why that is, we will see soon.

---

7 Do not confuse overriding with overloading. The latter means having a number of functions with the same name but different parameters, as discussed in Section 4.4.

Listing 4.25 Definition of the `TCircle` class (in *CppBookCode, VirtualMechanisms.cpp*).

```cpp
class TCircle
{

private:

    double      fRadius {};          // private data to hold circle radius

public:

    // Declared "const" since it does not change anything
    double GetRadius( void ) const { return fRadius; }

    // Thanks to having fRadius private we can check its initialization
    void SetRadius( double v ) { assert( v >= 0.0 ); fRadius = v; }

public:

    // Default and parametric constructor in one
    TCircle( double r = 0.0 ) : fRadius( r )
    {
        cout << "Constr TCircle called (@" << this << ")" << endl;
    }

    virtual  ~TCircle()
    {
        cout << "Destr TCircle called (@" << this << ")" << endl;
    }

private:

    // Basic version of GetPi (not too precise)
    virtual double GetPi( void ) const
    {
        cout << "TCircle::pi" << endl;
        return 3.14;
    }

public:

    // There is only one version of ComputeArea
    double ComputeArea( void ) const
    {
        return GetPi() * fRadius * fRadius;
    }
};
```

To understand the behavior of virtual functions, it is important to observe that there is only one `ComputeArea` function (not virtual) defined in the public interface on lines [41–44] of the base class `TCircle`. `ComputeArea`, in turn, on line [43] calls a private virtual function `GetPi`. Since `GetPi` is defined on line [32] as virtual, a new and potentially better version can be defined in the derived `PrecCircle` class, as shown in Listing 4.26.

The definition of the `PrecCircle` class begins on line [47]. It is publicly derived from `TCircle`. Thus, `PrecCircle` can access all members except private ones (Section 4.3). That is, `fRadius` is accessible only by calling `GetRadius/SetRadius`. Note the behavior of the `PrecCircle` constructor on line [52]: it calls the constructor of its base `TCircle`, passing it the value `r` for correct member initialization. But the base constructor directly initializes `fRadius`, as shown on line [19].

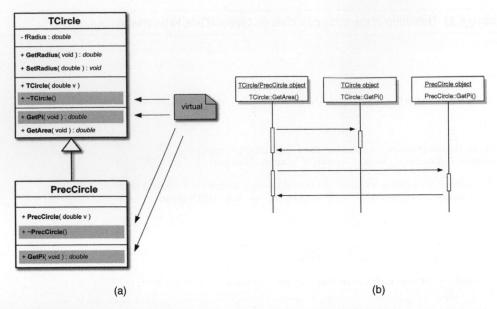

(a) (b)

Figure 4.16 UML class diagram showing the base class `TCircle` and its derived class `PrecCircle`. (a) `TCircle` contains two virtual functions (in gray): the destructor and the private function `GetPi`. `TCircle` also contains one non-virtual function, `GetArea`, which calls `GetPi`. Because it is virtual, `PrecCircle` can define its own version of `GetPi`, which will replace the "old" version in `TCircle`. (b) A UML sequence diagram shows call sequences. For the `TCircle` objects from `TCircle::GetArea`, the `TCircle::GetPi` is called. However, for the `PrecCircle` objects, `TCircle::GetArea` calls `PrecCircle::GetPi`.

Listing 4.26 Definition of the `PrecCircle` class (in *CppBookCode, VirtualMechanisms.cpp*).

```
46   // Slightly more precise for computations
47   class PrecCircle : public TCircle
48   {
49
50   public:
51
52      PrecCircle( double r = 0.0 ) : TCircle( r )
53      {
54         cout << "Constr PrecCircle called (@" << this << ")" << endl;
55      }
56
57      virtual  ~PrecCircle()
58      {
59         cout << "Destr PrecCircle called (@" << this << ")" << endl;
60      }
61
62   private:
63
64      // In this class, we wish to improve GetPi (increase precision)
65      // Place override at the end, skip virtual in front.
66      virtual double GetPi( void ) const override
67      {
68         cout << "PrecCircle::pi" << endl;
69         return 3.14159265358979;
70      }
71
72   };
```

PrecCircle also contains a virtual destructor ~PrecCircle, although having a virtual destructor defined in the base would be sufficient in this case. To express class inheritance, on line [57], we explicitly use virtual~PrecCircle. Nevertheless, PrecCircle does not have much to do. Its only action is defined on lines [66–70] of the new and more precise virtual function GetPi, which overrides its predecessor from the base class. Although not absolutely required, the override is explicitly expressed by adding the override keyword.[8] In long class derivations, it helps to control whether functions really override, since any inconsistency in a function name or parameters would break the overriding. Also, by placing override at the end, we skip virtual in front and avoid clutter (although nothing drastic happens if it is left in).

An important fact about virtual functions is that to be virtual, their declarators *must be exactly the same*. More precisely, their formal arguments must be the same type, and the return type must be the same or at least compatible (e.g. from the same class hierarchy). Thus, when writing virtual functions, a rule of thumb is to *copy-paste* the function declarators (except for the override word, which is added only in derived versions of functions).

Let's imagine now that we have created two objects: one TCircle and one PrecCircle. Let's also recall that there is only one version of the ComputeArea function: it is implemented exclusively in the TCircle class. But GetPi, which is called from within ComputeArea, is implemented in both objects. What happens if we call this function is shown in the UML sequence diagram in Figure 4.16b. When we use the TCircle object, ComputeArea from TCircle is called, which in turn calls GetPi – also from TCircle. But if we do the same thing from PrecCircle, then ComputeArea from the base TCircle is called, which again calls GetPi – but this time the new version, implemented in the PrecCircle class. If GetPi was not virtual, then in both cases, the base GetPi would be called.

Finally, let's test the two objects in action. To do this, we wrote two test functions. The first, PrintInfoFor, is quite simple. Its definition starts on line [75]:

```
73   // This function uses C++ polymorphism to print the radius and area of TCircle object
74   // and ANY other object derived from TCircle.
75   void PrintInfoFor( const TCircle & circ )
76   {
77       double radius     { circ.GetRadius() };
78       double area       { circ.ComputeArea() };
79       cout << "r=" << radius << " ==> A=" << area << endl;
80   }
```

The role of PrintInfoFor is to print the radius and area of a circle object passed to this function with const TCircle &. What is important here is the polymorphism – that is, we explicitly declared the passed parameter to be a constant reference to the *base class* object. The two methods of TCircle that are called here – GetRadius on line [77] and ComputeArea on line [78] – are not virtual. However, ComputeArea calls GetPi, which is virtual and can be implemented differently in each object of the TCircle class hierarchy. In effect, whatever object from this hierarchy will be passed to PrintInfoFor will be displayed in accordance with its defined virtual functions, not the base class. This mechanism works well even with an object whose class will be implemented in the future, assuming it is derived from TCircle. The fact that in the place of a

---

8 Actually it is semi-keyword.

base object, any other derived object can always be substituted, is called the *Liskov substitution principle,* as mentioned in Section 4.1.

Let's now collect and test all the code in the `CircleTest` function:

```
81   void CircleTest( void )
82   {
83
84       // -------------------------------------------------------------
85       cout << "\nExplicitly define two different objects" << endl;
86       cout << "----------------------------------------" << endl;
87
88       {
89           TCircle            c1( 1.23 );
90           PrintInfoFor( c1 );
91
92           PrecCircle      pc1( 1.23 );
93           PrintInfoFor( pc1 );
94
95           // Here, delete all objects
96       }
97
98       // -------------------------------------------------------------
99       cout << "\nLet's access only through a pointer to the base class" << endl;
100      cout << "-----------------------------------------------------" << endl;
101
102      {
103          using TC_UP = unique_ptr< TCircle >;     // TC_UP is a smart pointer
104
105          TC_UP      c1_ptr( make_unique< TCircle >( 1.23 ) ); // create TCircle on heap
106          PrintInfoFor( * c1_ptr );
107
108          TC_UP      pc1_ptr( make_unique< PrecCircle >( 1.23 ) ); // create TCircle on heap
109          PrintInfoFor( * pc1_ptr );
110
111          // Here, delete all objects
112      }
113
114  }
```

To observe object creation and deletion, two code blocks [88–96] and [102–112] are included in `CircleTest`. In the former, the objects are created on the local stack, whereas in the latter they reside on the heap. In C++, the basic functionality to create and then destroy objects on the heap uses the `new` and `delete` operators, as discussed in Section 3.19.1. But in many regards they are too basic; and in the modern programming paradigm, their direct usage is discouraged. Instead, smart pointers are recommended. Our example uses the `unique_ptr` smart pointer object and its associated `make_unique` helper function, both set to the base class `TCircle`. In other regards, smart pointers can be used like ordinary pointers, so this explanation should be sufficient for now; a more in-depth explanation is provided in Section 5.3. As we already observed, all interesting functions display console messages, so by observing these, we can control what functions were called and in what order. To distinguish objects, we also print the `this` pointer, which always contains the system address of the executed object.

On line [89], a base `TCircle` is created; it is passed on line [90] to `PrintInfoFor`. The same thing happens on lines [92] and [93], this time with the `PrecCircle` object. Then, on line [96], the code block ends, the local stack with the two objects is wound: the two objects are destroyed when their destructors are called, and their occupied memory is freed, as discussed in Section 5.1. The output of this code fragment looks like the following:

```
Explicitly define two different objects
----------------------------------------
Constr TCircle called (@000000A16B3FF638)
TCircle::pi
r=1.23 ==> A=4.75051
Constr TCircle called (@000000A16B3FF668)
Constr PrecCircle called (@000000A16B3FF668)
PrecCircle::pi
r=1.23 ==> A=4.75292
Destr PrecCircle called (@000000A16B3FF668)
Destr TCircle called (@000000A16B3FF668)
Destr TCircle called (@000000A16B3FF638)
```

It is not a surprise that calling `ComputeArea` for the two different objects gives different results for the same radius 1.23, and `PrecCircle` gives a slightly more precise value. What is interesting is the order of calling the constructor-destructor pairs, as indicated by the lines. Also interesting, although expected, is the fact that with `PrecCircle`, two constructors and then two destructors are called: their order is `TCircle` → `PrecCircle`, and then `~PrecCircle` → `~TCircle`. Obviously, the values of the `this` pointers will differ from system to system, as well as from run to run. But `this` stays the same for the base class and its derived parts. Let's summarize this. In derived classes, the initialization order is as follows:

1. Base class constructor (if more than one, they are called in their declaration order)
2. Derived class constructor

Destruction operates in the opposite order:

1. Derived class destructor
2. Base class destructor (if more than one, their call order is the reverse of the constructor calls).

The second block on lines [102–112] does almost the same thing, although this time, objects are created on the heap, and access to them is provided with the pointers to the base `TCircle`. These are smart pointers (Section 5.3) that help to safely destroy the objects at the end of the block. On line [103], a `unique_ptr` suitable to point at `TCircle` objects is defined. Then, two objects `TCircle` and `PrecCircle` are created on lines [105, 108] by calling the special function `make_unique`. This way, the objects will be created on the heap but we avoid directly using the `new` and `delete` operators, which can cause memory leaks (*GROUP 4*, Table 3.15). The output after running this code looks like the following:

```
Let us play only through a pointer to the base class
----------------------------------------------------
Constr TCircle called (@000001A7E4A4F3B0)
TCircle::pi
r=1.23 ==> A=4.75051
Constr TCircle called (@000001A7E4A4EA00)
Constr PrecCircle called (@000001A7E4A4EA00)
PrecCircle::pi
r=1.23 ==> A=4.75292
Destr PrecCircle called (@000001A7E4A4EA00)
Destr TCircle called (@000001A7E4A4EA00)
Destr TCircle called (@000001A7E4A4F3B0)
```

Let's take a closer look at the other virtual functions, the destructors of `TCircle` and `PrecCircle`. As we know, after the last line of the code block, the objects `c1_ptr` and `pc1_ptr` will be automatically destroyed since they are located on the block's local stack, launching the destructors of their held `TCircle` and `PrecCircle` objects. However, in both cases, the held pointers are of the `TCircle *` type. This is clear in the case of the first object. But when destroying `PrecCircle` through the `TCircle *` pointer, the virtual call mechanism must be activated. This way, before `~TCircle`, `~PrecCircle` is called, since destructors are declared virtual. Otherwise, only `~TCircle` would be called, leaving part of `PrecCircle` not properly destroyed. Now we see why, when planning class inheritance, it is best to declare the base destructor virtual.[9] Finally notice that the presented setup of the non-virtual public interface (`ComputeArea`) and the hidden private virtual implementation (`GetPi`) constitutes a useful and frequently applied pattern, the Template Method. It provides both: more control to the base class over its functionality (i.e. the same formula for the circle's area) and the class customizable behavior (higher precision).

4.12 (⚒) More on the Virtual Mechanism

The key mechanism behind C++ virtual functions is the *virtual function table* (VFT) associated with each object, which contains at least one virtual function. This table contains function pointers to the object's virtual functions. Thus, calling a virtual function entails reading its slot in the object's VFT to obtain a function pointer and then making an indirect function call through this pointer, as discussed in Section 3.14.8. However, the main point of VFT is that the function pointers can be changed. This happens if a derived object is created. In such a case, the VFT slots of the base object, corresponding to the functions overridden in this derived object, are appropriately updated. As a result, if a virtual function is called by a pointer or reference to the base class, the version suitable for the given object is selected.

Figure 4.17 shows a screenshot from Microsoft Visual Studio 2019 after running the code fragment from the previous section (lines [88–96]). We see that each object containing at least one virtual function, such as `c1` of the `TCircle` type, has a pointer to its VFT, denoted by `_vfptr`. In this example, these are both destructors and both versions of the `GetPi` function. Other non-virtual functions need not be present in each object, and therefore they are not shown by the debugger. Also note that a derived object, such as `pc1`, contains its own members (functions, data) and components of its base class object.

But the C++ mechanism comes at the cost of an indirect function call via function pointers held in the VFT associated with an object. The VFT also consumes memory. Thus, the virtual mechanism adds runtime and memory overhead to the objects.

There are two additional issues related to the virtual mechanism in C++:

- *Pure virtual function* – A virtual function used to define an abstract interface, usually in a class hierarchy. Classes with at least one pure virtual function cannot be instantiated, i.e. no objects of this class can be created. But they can serve as base classes from which concrete classes can be derived. All derived classes must provide an implementation of the pure virtual functions defined in their bases. Details and examples are presented in Sections 6.2.4 and 6.6
- *Virtual base class* – In the case of multiple inheritance, i.e. when a class is derived from more than one class, classes may inherit many times from the same base class. In such a case, shown in Figure 4.18a, in the structure of a derived object `E`, the base sub-object `B` would be repeated multiple times (two times, in this case). If such behavior is not desirable, then *virtual inheritance* can be declared for a given base class, as in the following code example:

9 Although not recommended, it is possible for the base destructor not to be virtual, but only if we avoid destroying the hierarchy objects through pointers to the base class, as discussed in Section 4.10. Such semantics can be enforced by declaring the base destructor protected.

```
330    ⊟void CircleTest( void )
331     {
332
333        // -------------------------------------------
334        cout << "\nExplicitly define two different objects" << endl;
335        cout << "-------------------------------------" << endl;
336
337   ⊟    {
338            TCircle    c1( 1.23 );
339            PrintInfoFor( c1 );
340
341            PrecCircle  pc1( 1.23 );
342            PrintInfoFor( pc1 );  ≤82ms elapsed
343
344            // Here, delete all objects
```

88 % ▾

Locals

Name	Value	Type
▲ ● c1	{fRadius=1.2300000000000000 }	TCircle
▲ ● _vfptr	0x00007ff7af303f68 {CCppBookCode.exe!void(* TCircle::`vftable'[3])()} {0x00007ff7af20a98c {CCppBookCode.exe!'	void * *
◎ [0]	0x00007ff7af20a98c {CCppBookCode.exe!TCircle::`vector deleting destructor'(unsigned int)}	void *
◎ [1]	0x00007ff7af209267 {CCppBookCode.exe!TCircle::GetPi(void)const }	void *
●ₐ fRadius	1.2300000000000000	double
▲ ● pc1	{...}	PrecCircle
▲ ✪ TCircle	{fRadius=1.2300000000000000 }	TCircle
▲ ● _vfptr	0x00007ff7af303fe0 {CCppBookCode.exe!void(* PrecCircle::`vftable'[3])()} {0x00007ff7af20b8b4 {CCppBookCode.∈	void * *
◎ [0]	0x00007ff7af20b8b4 {CCppBookCode.exe!PrecCircle::`vector deleting destructor'(unsigned int)}	void *
◎ [1]	0x00007ff7af2098bb {CCppBookCode.exe!PrecCircle::GetPi(void)const }	void *
●ₐ fRadius	1.2300000000000000	double

Figure 4.17 Debugging C++ objects and virtual functions with the Microsoft MSVC 2019 visual debugger. Each object containing at least one virtual function has a virtual function pointer table, denoted by _vfptr. Other non-virtual functions need not be present in each object, and therefore they are not shown here. A compound object, such as pc1, has its own parts (functions, data) and base component.

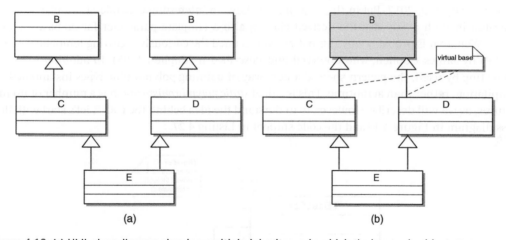

Figure 4.18 (a) UML class diagram showing multiple inheritance in which the base sub-objects B are repeated in the object of class E. (b) To avoid duplication of the base B sub-objects, virtual inheritance can be declared. This results in a diamond-shaped structure.

```
1    class B
2    {};
3
4    class C : public virtual B
5    {};
6
```

```
7   class D : public virtual B
8   {};
9
10  class E : public C, public D // multiple inheritance - diamond structure
11  {};
```

However, multiple inheritance should not be overused, since it adds unnecessary complexity to class relations. As alluded to previously, the Liskov substitution principle says that a derived class can be substituted in place of its base. Therefore, in our case in Figure 4.18, an object of class E can be substituted in different contexts for C or D. But in some contexts, multiple inheritance is helpful: for example, if we are attach our own branch of classes to an existing class. More on class inheritance and order of class initialization can be found in the literature (Stroustrup 2013).

4.13 (�֍) The Curiously Recurring Template Pattern and Static Polymorphism

In Section 4.8, we saw how a class can be templatized to define a kind of class-prototype pattern that, when instantiated with different types for template parameters, creates different classes based on that prototype. When all template parameters are known, a C++ compiler can try to match the provided template arguments to the class prototype and then generate code for that class. Since there can also be template specializations, the compiler will try to find the best match of templates to the class prototype. The rules of template parameter matching are quite detailed and can be found in the following resources: Cppreference.com (2019b); Cppreference (2020a,b,c); and Vandevoorde et al. 2017. But in this section, we show an interesting example of template classes inherited in such a way that the derived class is also a template parameter for its base. Sound weird? Well, that is probably why this pattern was named the curiously recurring template pattern (CRTP) by James Coplien, who observed and described it (Coplien 1995). In addition to being interesting by itself, the pattern showed a new way of defining polymorphic types instantiated at compilation, rather than at runtime. This is called *static polymorphism* and has a number of useful features, as we will describe. However, to understand the idea behind the CRTP, let's start with the class diagram in Figure 4.19 and the code snippet in Listing 4.27.

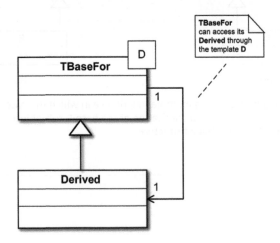

Figure 4.19 UML class diagram of the curiously recurring template pattern (CRTP).

Listing 4.27 A core class relation in the CRTP. TBaseFor is a template class with a template parameter D. Derived is a non-template class derived from TBaseFor< Derived >. TBaseFor has access to parameter D, so it also has access to Derived, which was provided as parameter D.

```
1   template < typename D >
2   class TBaseFor
3   {
4
5   };
6
7
8   class Derived : public TBaseFor< Derived >
9   {
10
11  };
```

The TBaseFor class defined on lines [1–2] is an empty template class with the template parameter D. The Derived class, defined on line [8], is publicly derived from TBaseFor with the template parameter set to Derived. Hence, the CRTP can be read as a sandwich-like Derived-TBaseFor-Derived pattern.

But what is really interesting about the CRTP is that TBaseFor can now access members of Derived, since Derived becomes a template parameter of the former, as shown in Listing 4.28.

The DAction member, defined on line [8], as its first action on line [10] converts the this object to deriv_part, which is a reference to the D parameter. This, in turn, will be one of its derived classes (which one, exactly, we might not know yet). For conversion, the static_cast is sufficient here. Then, the Work method from the derived class can be called, as shown on line [13].

Listing 4.28 Detailed implementation of the CRTP. A Derived class can be accessed in TBaseFor, as shown in DAction. The reference deriv_part is obtained from the static_cast of * this to D &. Through deriv_part, members of Derived can be called, such as Derived::Work (in *CppBookCode, VirtualMechanisms.cpp*).

```
1   template < typename D >
2   class TBaseFor
3   {
4
5   public:
6
7       // No virtual
8       void DAction( void )
9       {
10          D & deriv_part = static_cast< D & >( * this );
11
12          // Do action on a derived class whatever it is ...
13          deriv_part.Work();
14      }
15
16
17  };
18
19
20  class Derived : public TBaseFor< Derived >
21  {
22  public:
23
```

(Continued)

Listing 4.28 (continued)

```
24        // No virtual
25        void Work( void )
26        {
27            // Do something specific to Derived ...
28        }
29
30    };
31
32    // Use Derived in an action
33    void DerivedTest( void )
34    {
35        Derived d;
36        d.DAction();
37    }
```

The `Derived` class [20] has defined only one `Work` method, as shown on line [25]. As we can imagine, the point is to create many versions of `Derived` with different actions performed in their `Work` methods. By doing this, we obtain a kind of polymorphism. However, note that no virtual functions were used here, so the polymorphism we are dealing with is *static*. The lack of virtual functions has the benefit of not adding code to maintain virtual tables, as described in Section 4.12.

Returning to the code analysis, note that an object `d` of the `Derived` class is created on line [35]. Then `d.DAction` is called on line [36]. This invokes the base class `DAction`, which in turn calls `Work` from `Derived`.

Now it is time to compare the static polymorphism, realized with the presented CRTP technique, to the dynamic polymorphism presented in Section 4.11. Recall that in the latter, we had two versions of the class, with two different virtual functions `GetPi` in each one, returning the *pi* constant with different accuracy. The version based on the CRTP is presented in Listing 4.29.

The `TBaseCircle` template class, defined on lines [1–2], contains one data member `fRadius`, the default-parametric constructor defined on line [17], and one function `GetArea` on line [10]. On line [12], `GetArea` accesses `GetPi` from the derived class `D` in the same fashion as in Listing 4.28. There will be two versions of these, as we will soon see.

Listing 4.29 Definition of `TBaseCircle` and its statically derived `SimpleCircle` and `PrecCircle` with the CRTP mechanism (in *CppBookCode, VirtualMechanisms.cpp*).

```
1     template < typename D >
2     class TBaseCircle
3     {
4     private:
5
6         double      fRadius {};
7
8     public:
9
10        double GetArea( void ) const
11        {
12            return fRadius * fRadius * static_cast< D const & >( * this ).GetPi();
13        }
14
15    public:
16
17        TBaseCircle( double r = 0.0 ) : fRadius( r ) {}
18
19    };
```

The definitions of the two derived classes, `SimpleCircle` and the `PrecCircle`, start on lines [20, 38]. Notice that each defines its own version of `GetPi`, different only in the precision of the returned constant *pi*, as shown on lines [26, 44]. Also note the way their base classes are called on lines [31] and [49] to correctly initialize them with the argument `r`.

```
20    class SimpleCircle : public TBaseCircle< SimpleCircle >
21    {
22    public:
23
24        double GetPi( void ) const
25        {
26            return 3.14;
27        }
28
29    public:
30
31      SimpleCircle( double r = 0.0 ) : TBaseCircle< SimpleCircle >( r ) {}
32
33
34    };
35
36    // Don't confuse
37    // class PrecCircle : TBaseCircle< SimpleCircle >
38    class PrecCircle : public TBaseCircle< PrecCircle >
39    {
40    public:
41
42        double GetPi( void ) const
43        {
44            return 3.1415926535;
45        }
46
47    public:
48
49        PrecCircle( double r = 0.0 ) : TBaseCircle< PrecCircle >( r ) {}
50    };
```

The operation of these classes can be observed in the `StaticPolymorphism_Test` function, defined on line [51]. The two derived objects are created on lines [54, 59] with the same radius provided. Then, the same function `GetArea` is called from the two objects, as shown on lines [56, 61]. Note that this function is defined only once in the `TBaseCircle` class. Also, on lines [57, 62], we measure and display the two objects' size in bytes:

```
51    void StaticPolymorphism_Test( void )
52    {
53
54        SimpleCircle sc( 13.13 );
55
56        cout << "A1 = " << sc.GetArea() << endl;
57        cout << "sizeof( SimpleCircle ) = " << sizeof( SimpleCircle ) << endl;
58
59        PrecCircle pc( 13.13 );
60
61        cout << "A2 = " << pc.GetArea() << endl;
62        cout << "sizeof( PrecCircle ) = " << sizeof( PrecCircle ) << endl;
63
64    }
```

The output of the previous code looks like this:

```
A1 = 541.326
sizeof( SimpleCircle ) = 8
A2 = 541.601
sizeof( PrecCircle ) = 8
```

It is interesting to observe that in all cases, the size of each object is just large enough to accommodate the fRadius member from the base. This is one of the main benefits of static polymorphism, as compared to the dynamic version.

4.14 (�) Mixin Classes

An interesting topic related to the CRTP is the *mixin* class pattern (*https://www.fluentcpp.com/2017/12/12/mixin-classes-yang-crtp*). Its general scheme is shown in Listing 4.30.

Listing 4.30 General scheme of a mixin class MMixin. The key idea is to provide the base class as a template parameter to MMixin (in *CppBookCode, VirtualMechanisms.cpp*).

```
1  template < typename Base >
2  class MMixin : public Base
3  {
4      // Can use members of Base ...
5  };
```

Mixin resembles an inverted CRTP pattern. It lets us compose new components from existing simpler ones, as in the example in Listing 4.31.

Listing 4.31 Example of mixin classes to display the date in different formats (in *CppBookCode, VirtualMechanisms.cpp*).

```
1  struct TDate
2  {
3      int             fDay        {};
4      std::string     fMonth      {};
5      int             fYear       {};
6  };
```

The following MPrint_Date_US mixin displays TDate in the US format:

```
7   template < typename B >
8   struct MPrint_Date_US : public B
9   {
10      // US date print format
11      void Print( void )
12      {
13          std::cout << fMonth << "/" << fDay << '/' << fYear << '\n';
14      }
15  };
```

On the other hand, the `MPrint_Date_Eu` mixin knows how to display `TDate` in the European format:

```
16   template < typename B >
17   struct MPrint_Date_Eu : public B
18   {
19      // European date print format
20      void Print( void )
21      {
22         std::cout << fDay << "/" << fMonth << '/' << fYear << '\n';
23      }
24   };
```

Finally, the `MixinTest` function shows the two mixins in action:

```
25   void MixinTest( void )
26   {
27      // Alias is useful with mixins
28      using Date_US = MPrint_Date_US< TDate >;
29      using Date_Eu = MPrint_Date_Eu< TDate >;
30
31      Date_US          dus { 9, "Nov", 2019 };
32      dus.Print();
33
34      Date_Eu          deu { 9, "Nov", 2019 };
35      deu.Print();
36   }
```

The result of running `MixinTest` is as follows:

```
Nov/9/2019
9/Nov/2019
```

4.15 Example Project – The *TLongNumberFor* Class for Efficient Storage of Numbers of Any Length

A *unique key* associated with each record is a requirement when building database systems with classes that represent personal data such as first and last names, address, age, etc. In Poland, each individual has a personal identification number called the PESEL ID (*https://en.wikipedia.org/wiki/PESEL*; similar to a US Social Security number) consisting of exactly 11 digits that are unique to the person and that also convey encoded information about their date of birth and sex. For this example, we decided to include this information in each person's record. Listing 4.32 shows our first attempt to define the `TPerson` class.

Here is our first attempt to set `fID` with an 11-digit PESEL:

```
16        fID = 94120612345;          // try to write the PESEL id
```

This results in a nasty error, which we will see when we try to display `fID`. In systems where `unsigned int` objects are stored in four bytes, the following result appears:

```
fID = 3926299129
```

Listing 4.32 First definition of the `TPerson` class. The type chosen to represent `fID` is inappropriate here since it cannot reliably convey an 11-digit value; it must be replaced.

```
1   class TPerson
2   {
3   private:
4
5       std::wstring          fFirstName;
6       std::wstring          fLastName;
7
8       unsigned char         fAge {};
9
10      unsigned int          fID {};              // PESEL id
11
12      public:
13
14      // ...
15  };
```

We discussed this problem when we introduced various data types in Section 3.1. Listing 3.2 computed the minimum number of bits for a value representation. However, such details are easy to overlook during design and can result in malfunctioning software. To measure if, for example, `unsigned long` would be sufficient, we can modify the code from Listing 3.2 as follows:

```
// Test PESEL ID stored in ID_TYPE
using ID_TYPE = unsigned long;
ID_TYPE           fID {};            // PESEL id

std::cout << "sizeof( ID_TYPE ) = " << sizeof( ID_TYPE ) << std::endl;
std::cout << "Bits for 11 digits = " << (int) ( log(99999999999.0) / log(2.0) ) + 1;
```

We obtained the following output on our system:

```
sizeof( ID_TYPE ) = 4
Bits to store 11 digits = 37
```

Hence, even `unsigned long`, which offers $4 \cdot 8 = 32$ bits, is much too short, since at least 37 bits are necessary to store 11 digits. Since computer memory is byte-addressable, this means using at least five bytes; but an odd number is also not appealing, for performance reasons (Patterson and Hennessy 2018). The 11 digits are nothing to quarrel about – we can put `std::array< unsigned char, 11 >` or another `wstring` in the `TPerson` class, and the problem is solved. However, when we consider storing thousands of such `TPerson` objects in a database, then the extra bytes do not add to software quality. So, in this section, we will show how to design a class to store digits optimally[10] using a *binary-coded decimal* (BCD) representation, which entails only four bits per digit. Then we will scrutinize various ways of designing a special class to represent PESEL IDs. We will consider embedding an 11-digit object, as well as deriving from it. We will also compare their properties and size.

In this example project, we will learn about a number of useful programming techniques:

- BCD data format
- Endianness
- Efficient storage of long numbers

---

10 This is a quasi-optimal representation, being a tradeoff between compression ratio and simplicity.

- Nested classes, i.e. classes defined inside other classes
- Definition and operations with bit fields
- Defining a template class with `auto`
- Type-conversion methods:
  - With a *type-converting constructor*
  - With a *type-converting operator*
- A design issue: aggregation vs. inheritance
- A proxy design pattern to facilitate subscript operators
- Deleted functions
- Conditional compilation

4.15.1   Binary-Coded Decimal Representation

As mentioned earlier, in the BCD representation, a byte is split into two parts called *nibbles*, each occupying four bits. Then, two decimals, such as 13, 56, 00, or 99, can have their digits independently binary-encoded into the corresponding upper or lower nibble, as illustrated in Figure 4.20.

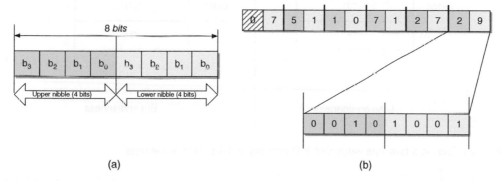

(a)   (b)

Figure 4.20 (a) Binary coded decimals (BCDs) for storing decimal values 0…9 in half a byte (a nibble). (b) An 11-digit number stored in the BCD format. Each byte holds two independently encoded decimal digits.

The following table shows examples of BCD encoding. Encoding and decoding are simple since each digit is placed in its own nibble.

Decimal value	U	L
56	0101	0110
77	0111	0111
89	1000	1001
99	1001	1001
00	0000	0000

As indicated, BCD is used to easily encode two-digit decimal values on a byte. But only 0–99 can be stored this way, whereas there are 256 possible combinations with binary encoding. Hence, in our project, 37 bits mean we will use 6 bytes organized in BCD format.

4.15.2 Endianness

Endianness defines a way to store multibyte words in the computer's memory (Section 2.1). There are two variants:

- *Big endianness* – Most significant byte at the lowest address
- *Little endianness* – Most significant byte at the highest address

Figure 4.21 illustrates two possible types of endianness for the two-byte value 0xABCD.

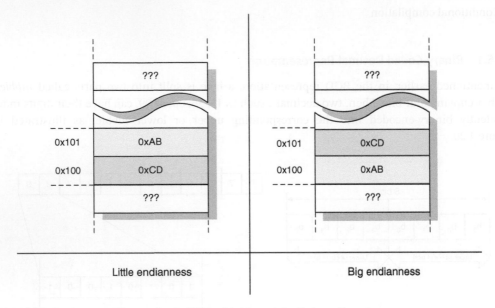

Figure 4.21 Storing a two-byte value 0xABCD with big and the little endianness.

Byte order is defined by the microprocessor architecture standard, and manufacturers usually have their own preferences. For example, little endianness was employed in x86 and new RISC-V architectures (Patterson and Hennessy 2018). But the 68k series of Motorola processors operated in big-endianness mode. There are even some microprocessors for which endianness can be programmatically set (e.g. PowerPC). But big endianness dominates in networking protocols (e.g. TCP/IP). In C++, it is not defined and should not pose a problem on a given platform. However, endianness conversion may be necessary when e.g. sending data structures over different systems. To revert the byte order in a word, the RevertEndianness function from Section 3.13.2.2 can be used.

In our project, endianness needs to be considered when converting strings, such as "12345," into a series of BCD-organized values. For this purpose, big endianness seems to be appropriate, as we will discuss.

4.15.3 Definition of the *TLongNumberFor* Class

Listing 4.33 shows the definition of the TLongNumberFor class that will be used to represent numbers of any length efficiently. As usual, on lines [1–6], the SL headers are included. The last header, i.e. the *exception* header, contains definitions of the `std::exception` class hierarchy, which will be used to represent exceptions that may occur in our code.

Listing 4.33 Annotated definition of the `TLongNumberFor` class (in *LongNumber, LongNumberFor.h*).

```
1    #include <cassert>
2    #include <string>
3    #include <array>
4    #include <iostream>
5    #include <algorithm>
6    #include <exception>
7
8
9    using std::string;
10   using std::istream, std::ostream;
11
12
13
14       // This class efficiently stores a series of numbers, such as 12345678901234567890
15       // of a given length. Each number is stored in a nibble (i.e. 4 bits).
16       //
17       // The auto keyword in a template parameter -
18       // the type is deduced at the point of instantiation.
19       //
20       template < auto MAX_NUMBERS >
21       class TLongNumberFor
22       {
23           public:
24
25               inline static const auto kMaxNumbers { MAX_NUMBERS };
26
27           private:
28
29               // -------------------------------
30               // A class can define another class
31               // This class is just a placeholder
32               struct NibblePair
33               {
34                   unsigned char fFirst     : 4;       // define two bit fields
35                   unsigned char fSecond    : 4;          // of a total size of 1 byte
36
37                   NibblePair() : fFirst( 0 ), fSecond( 0 ) {}
38               };
39               // -------------------------------
```

Then, on lines [9–10], the useful `std` classes are introduced. As a result, the `std::` prefix can be omitted for these explicitly listed classes from `std`, as discussed in Section 3.14.6.

The definition of the `TLongNumberFor` template class starts on line [20] and spans to line [158]. This is an example of a template class with the `auto` keyword in front of the MAX_NUMBERS parameter. The `auto` keyword allows for correct type deduction based on the type of the argument passed during template class instantiation.

On line [25], the template parameter is copied into the local `kMaxNumbers` inline static constant object. As a result, this object is defined only once for the class and does not occupy memory in objects of the `TLongNumberFor` type. If necessary, information about the maximum number of digits can be accessed from a concrete instantiation of `TLongNumberFor`.

A class can contain the definition of another, *nested class*, such as `struct NibblePair` defined on lines [32–38]. It contains two bit fields: `fFirst` on line [34] and `fSecond` on line [35], each occupying four bits. `fSecond` is obtained by providing the `: 4` bit specifier, which defines the number of bits allocated for each member. Hence, each member represents a single digit in the BCD code, as discussed in Section 4.15.1. The two objects together occupy a single byte. Then, on line [37], the `NibblePair` constructor is provided, which sets the two objects to zero.

Line [40] uses an estimation of the number of bytes to represent `kMaxNumbers`. Then, on line [42], a `NibbleArray` alias is created, which on line [43] is used to create the `fData` object. Thanks to the `{ }`, we can be sure it is initialized to zero each time the `TLongNumberFor` object is created.

The `IsFirstNibble` function on line [48] is responsible for returning `true` if the first nibble is accessed. The role of the `ReComputeIndex` function on line [51] is to return the position of the byte that corresponds to the nibble at the `index` position. This is easily achieved by dividing `index` by 2, which is done on line [51] with a simple right shift (Section 7.2).

```
40        static const auto kNumOfBytes = (kMaxNumbers>> 1 ) + ( kMaxNumbers & 0x01 );
41
42        using NibbleArray = std::array< NibblePair, kNumOfBytes >;
43        NibbleArray  fData {};        // Here we efficiently store the nibbles
44                                      // - enforce zero-initialization by adding {}
45
46        // Helper function
47        // Returns true if first nibble
48        bool IsFirstNibble( int index ) const { return ( index & 0x01 ) == 0; }
49
50        // Returns address of a number in the fData structure
51        auto ReComputeIndex( int index ) const { return index >> 1; }
```

The definition of the default constructor of the `TLongNumberFor` class starts on line [55]. It does not perform an action, and `fData` was already initialized with the `{ }`, so it could be omitted. But its role here is to verify preconditions at the moment of object creation. The first, on line [57], checks whether the provided number of numbers to store is greater than 0. On line [58], we verify whether our data structure is correctly aligned (see *GROUP 3*, Table 3.15). Then, on line [60], we check the compactness of `fData`. Finally, in the conditionally compiled code on lines [61–64], the `assert` on line [63] checks whether the size of the entire object is equal to the size of its `fData` member, which is one of our goals in designing this class. But why does this condition hold only if `ALLOW_INHERITANCE` is inactive? Apparently the size of the object will differ if it is designed to be inherited from. We discussed these issues in Section 4.11 and the projects presented in Section 3.18.4. We will return to them here.

```
52    public:
53
54        // Construction part
55        TLongNumberFor( void )
56        {
57            assert( kMaxNumbers > 0 );
58            assert( sizeof( NibblePair ) == sizeof( unsigned char ) );
59            // some bit manipulation, but be careful about the hierarchy
60            assert( sizeof( fData ) == (kMaxNumbers >> 1) + (kMaxNumbers & 0x01) );
61    #if ALLOW_INHERITANCE == 0
62            // that the object does not contain more than the bare data
63            assert( sizeof( * this ) == sizeof( fData ) );
64    #endif
65        }
```

Line [67] defines a virtual destructor. It does nothing special here except that it should be virtual if TLongNumberFor will be derived from. We will investigate two options; the code is encompassed within lines [66–68] by the conditional compilation flag ALLOW_INHERITANCE, which, if set to 1, inserts the destructor into the compiled translation unit.

```
66   #if ALLOW_INHERITANCE == 1
67       virtual ~TLongNumberFor() {}        // A virtual destructor to allow inheritance
68   #endif
```

More on the #if preprocessor directive for conditional compilation can be found in Section A.1.

4.15.3.1 Type-Converting Operations

When we discussed TComplex in Section 4.4, we saw that a real value represented by double can be used to create a TComplex number with the imaginary part set to 0. Hence, we converted from real to complex. But since there is no reverse conversion, we did not implement a conversion from complex to real. In the case of TLongNumberFor, we have two possible approaches: we would like to be able to create a TLongNumberFor object from a string, and to convert it back to the string. The code is as follows

```
TLongNumberFor< 5 > number_1( "1234" ); // Convert number_1 to std::string
```

followed by

```
std::string str { "--" }; // Create a string
str += number_1;          // Convert number_1 to std::string and concatenate with str
std::cout << str;         // Let's see it
```

In C++, we have to implement the following functions to perform the twofold conversion:

- The TLongNumberFor constructor, which accepts std::string as its only parameter
- The overloaded operator string () const member of TLongNumberFor for the opposite conversion, i.e. from TLongNumberFor to std::string

These ways of performing type conversions in C++ are shown in Figure 4.22.

The definition of the TLongNumberFor converting constructor begins on line [72]. Its parameter is const string & s, which is expected to contain a series of digits 0–9. However, its length should not exceed the value of the kMaxNumbers constant. Therefore, on line [74], a suitable precondition is checked. As part of the design, we must decide what to do if the input string is too long or contains non-digit characters. If the object cannot be created, then an exception could be thrown; but exceptions should be a last resort, since if such errors appear in this context, the conversion will be stopped but the TLongNumberFor object will be created. Hence, on line [77], a char_len variable is created and initialized with the minimum value of the string length and kMaxNumber. But since std::min is a template function that expects both its arguments to have exactly the same type, whereas kMaxNumbers depends on the type passed during instantiation of TLongNumberFor, we decided that the value returned by s.length() will be converted to the type of kMaxNumbers. This is achieved using the following construction:

```
static_cast< decltype( kMaxNumbers ) >( s.length() )
```

decltype returns the type of kMaxNumbers (Section 3.7), which is then used by the static_cast operator as its argument (*GROUP 2*, Table 3.15).

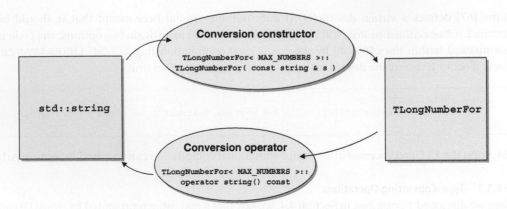

Figure 4.22 Type conversion scheme in C++ for example types. Note that the two conversion procedures are placed in the definition of the type TLongNumberFor< MAX_NUMBERS >.

A condition on line [80] checks whether there are any characters to be processed. If not, then the action is stopped immediately.

The character conversion starts in the for loop on line [83]. Characters are read into the digit object on line [86], starting from the leftmost character (i.e. from the most significant position). Then, if a digit is in the range 0–9, as verified on lines [89–90], this digit is placed in a consecutive position by calling SetNumberAt on line [92]. Notice that for better debugging, on line [88], there is also an assert precondition. Hence, it is assumed that the caller is responsible for checking whether the string for the conversion is the correct length and whether it contains only digit characters.

```
69      // Type-converting constructor - assumes big endianness,
70      // i.e. the rightmost character will be at 0 index,
71      // e.g. "123" will be allocated as: 0 ... 0 1 2 3
72      TLongNumberFor( const string & s )
73      {
74          assert( s.length() <= kMaxNumbers );      // should we throw?
75
76          // template type deduction has to exactly match the passed types
77          auto char_len = std::min(
78          static_cast< decltype( kMaxNumbers )  >( s.length() ), kMaxNumbers );
79
80          if( char_len < 1 )
81              return;              // nothing to do, exit
82
83          for( auto i { 0 }; i < char_len; ++ i )
84          {
85              // Traverse from the leftmost char of the string (endianness)
86              auto digit { s[ char_len - i - 1 ] - '0' };
87
88              assert( digit >= 0 && digit <= 9 );
89              if( ! ( digit >= 0 && digit <= 9 ) )
90                  return;
91
92              SetNumberAt( i, digit );
93          }
94      }
```

The to-string converting operator, defined on line [101], does the opposite conversion. That is, all digits contained in the TLongNumberFor object are read one by one in the for loop on line

[106], converted to the corresponding ASCII code on line [112], and finally added to the return string str. An exception to this rule is leading 0 digits, which we decided to skip; this condition is checked on lines [109–110]. The string str with the converted digits is returned on line [115]. More examples of type conversions will be presented in Section 7.3.

```
95      public:
96
97
98          // Type converter - assumes big endiannes,
99          // i.e. the rightmost character will be at 0 index,
100         // e.g. "123" will be allocated as: 0 ... 0 1 2 3
101         operator string() const
102         {
103             string str;
104
105             // Build the string
106             for( int i { kMaxNumbers - 1 }; i >= 0; -- i )
107             {
108                 auto a_digit { GetNumberAt( i ) };
109                 if( a_digit == 0 && str.length() == 0 )
110                     continue;              // skip leading left 0s
111                 else
112                     str += '0' + a_digit;   // let's use the simple patterns
113             }
114
115             return str;
116         }
```

Sometimes, when writing a one-argument parametric constructor, we wish to forbid such automatic type conversions. In that case, the constructor can be preceded with the explicit keyword. For example, because we have TLongNumberFor(const char * ptr), we do not wish to allow conversions of pointers to char to TLongNumberFor objects. The following declaration would convey our intention:

> **explicit** TLongNumberFor(const char *);

Note that like most of the classes presented in this book, TLongNumberFor does not contain any other constructors, such as a copy or a move, and it does not have an assignment operator. Since their actions are simple – they make a copy of the fData object – these are automatically generated by the compiler.

TLongNumberFor objects can be compared. For this purpose, on lines [117–121], the overloaded operator == is defined. Using std::memcmp, it simply compares, byte by byte, the fData members contained in this object and the object passed by the obj argument (see also Section A.2.6).

```
117         bool operator == ( const TLongNumberFor & obj )
118         {
119             // Treat array as a series of bytes
120             return std::memcmp( & fData[0], & obj.fData[0], sizeof( fData ) ) == 0;
121         }
```

The TLongNumberFor class contains member functions for reading and writing particular digits. GetNumberAt, defined on line [125], returns a digit stored at the position argument. As usual, the precondition on line [127] can greatly facilitate debugging. But if position is out of range at runtime, we have no other choice than to throw an exception, as coded on lines [128–129]. Instead of devising our own exceptions from scratch, it is a good idea to use those provided in the SL. Hence, we use `std::out_of_range`. But if `position` is in the valid range 0..kMaxNumbers, a proper digit is returned on line [131]. The type of a nibble is determined by `IsFirstNibble`. Finally, the `ReComputeIndex` function converts the value of `position` to the index in the `fData` array.

```
122    public:
123
124        // Retuns a digit at position
125        int GetNumberAt( int position ) const
126        {
127            assert( position < kMaxNumbers );
128            if( position >= kMaxNumbers )   // if wrong position then throw
129              throw std::out_of_range( "GetNumberAt position out of range" );
130
131            return IsFirstNibble( position ) ?
132                               fData[ ReComputeIndex( position ) ].fFirst :
133                               fData[ ReComputeIndex( position ) ].fSecond;
134        }
```

`SetNumberAt`, defined on line [135], does the opposite action – it writes the value passed by `val` at the digit position indicated by the `position` parameter. The two preconditions on lines [137–138] verify the correct range of the two parameters. Again, if a position is not correct at runtime on line [139], then a `std::out_of_range exception` is thrown on line [140]. However, such an action is not performed if the wrong `val` is passed. Then, similar to `GetNumberAt`, on lines [141–143], a digit value is written at the correct index in the `fData` array.

```
135        void SetNumberAt( int position, int val )
136        {
137            assert( val >= 0 && val <= 9 );    // check that we don't abuse it
138            assert( position < kMaxNumbers );
139            if( position >= kMaxNumbers )      // if wrong position then throw
140                throw std::out_of_range( "SetNumberAt position out of range" );
141            IsFirstNibble( position ) ?
142                          ( fData[ ReComputeIndex( position ) ].fFirst = val ) :
143                          ( fData[ ReComputeIndex( position ) ].fSecond = val );
144        }
```

A simple `ClearAll` function, defined on line [146], fills all the digits with the value 0. This is accomplished on line [148] by calling the `fill` member function on the `fData` object. As its argument, the default value of `NibbleArray` is passed.

```
145        // Resets all numbers to 0
146        void ClearAll( void )
147        {
148            fData.fill( NibbleArray::value_type() );      // set all to 0
149        }
```

In array-like structures, it is always convenient to have the subscript operator. A version of `operator []`, which lets us read only digit values, is presented on line [152]. It simply delegates the action on line [155] to the `GetNumberAt` function.

```
150        // Overloaded subscript operator but ONLY to READ.
151        // To write, we will need a proxy pattern (see below).
152        const int operator [] ( int position ) const
153        {
154            assert( position < kMaxNumbers );
155            return GetNumberAt( position );            // can throw
156        }
157
158 };
```

Making operator [] able to also write digits at the correct position requires a special *proxy pattern*, as we will discuss in Section 4.15.5.

As usual, external overloaded extraction and insertion operators are defined for TLongNumberFor objects. The first one simply accesses consecutive digits by calling GetNumberAt; the digits are then output to the output stream. A simpler version would be possible by directly accessing the private fData member. However, this entails declaring operator << friend to the TLongNumberFor, which we have avoided in this case.

```
159 ///////////////////////////////////////////////////////////////////////////////
160 // Insertion operator
161 template < typename auto MAX_NUMBERS >
162 ostream & operator << ( ostream & o, const TLongNumberFor< MAX_NUMBERS > & longNumb )
163 {
164     for( auto i { TLongNumberFor< MAX_NUMBERS >::kMaxNumbers - 1 }; i >= 0; -- i )
165         o << longNumb.GetNumberAt( i );
166     return o;
167 }
```

A different strategy is used in the overloaded extraction operator, defined on lines [170–171]. In this case, a simple std::string, created on line [173], is read on line [174]. It is immediately converted and copied on line [175] to TLongNumberFor.

```
168 ///////////////////////////////////////////////////////////////////////////////
169 // Extraction operator
170 template < typename auto MAX_NUMBERS >
171 istream & operator >> ( istream & i, TLongNumberFor< MAX_NUMBERS > & longNumb )
172 {
173     string str;
174     i >> str;                // read as a string
175     longNumb = str;          // call conversion
176     return i;
177 }
```

As always, the stream object is returned, as coded on line [176].

4.15.3.2 *TLongNumberFor* Test Function

Although strict test-driven development (TDD) requires us to write tests first, in a relaxed version we should always write proper tests when finalizing a class or other component. These tests can be in the form of functions or other classes that can be connected to the larger testing environment, as discussed in Section A.7. LongNumbers_Test in Listing 4.34 performs this role for the TLongNumberFor class.

Listing 4.34 Definition of the `LongNumbers_Test` function to test the functionality of `TLongNumbersFor` objects (in *LongNumber_LongNumber_Test.cpp*).

```
1    #include <fstream>
2    #include "LongNumberFor.h"
3
4    using std::cout, std::endl;
5    using std::ofstream, std::ifstream;
6
7
8
9    // A function that checks the main functionality
10   // of the TLongNumberFor class
11   void LongNumbers_Test( void )
12   {
13       try
14       {
15           TLongNumberFor< 11 > pesel;
16
17           pesel.SetNumberAt( 7, 7 );
18           pesel.SetNumberAt( 8, 8 );
19
20           assert( pesel.GetNumberAt( 7 ) == 7 );
21           assert( pesel.GetNumberAt( 8 ) == 8 );
22
23           // Try conversions
24           TLongNumberFor< 5 > number_1( "1234" );
25
26           std::string str { "--" };  // Create std::string from number_1
27           str += number_1;  // Convert number_1 to std::string and concatenate with str
28           std::cout << str << endl;     // Let's see it
29
30           {
31               ofstream testFile( "TLongNumberFor.txt" );
32               testFile << number_1;
33               testFile.close();
34           }
35
36           TLongNumberFor< 5 > number_2;
37
38           {
39               ifstream testFile( "TLongNumberFor.txt" );
40               testFile >> number_2;
41               testFile.close();
42           }
43
44           assert( number_1 == number_2 );
45
46           // Now let's try to access at the wrong position
47           cout << number_1[ 33 ];
48       }
49       catch( const std::exception & e )
50       {
51           std::cerr << "Out of Range error: " << e.what() << '\n';
52       }
53       catch( ... )
54       {
55           std::cerr << "Unknown exception\n";
56       }
57   }
```

First, the system *fstream* header and our *LongNumberFor.h* headers are included, followed by the common `using` aliases. The definition of the test function starts on line [11]. Since exceptions can be thrown, the code is embedded in a `try-catch` statement (Section 3.13.2.5) that starts on line [13].

A TLongNumberFor< 11 > object named pesel is created on line [15]. Then, on lines [17–18], some of its fields are set; they are verified on lines [20–21].

Another object, number_1, is created on line [24]. This time, the conversions to and from std::string are tested on lines [26–27].

The consecutive blocks of statements on lines [30–34] and [38–42] test the correctness of the streaming operators.

Finally, on line [47], access to a nonexistent position is attempted. This fires an exception that should be caught by the first catch branch on lines [49–52] since it is tuned to the std::exception types. If other exceptions occur, the second catch branch on lines [53–56] takes over.

4.15.4 Designing Classes for PESEL IDs

The TLongNumberFor class is a useful container for storing a series of digits, since two digits occupy a single byte. We can now build a special class named PESEL to identify the PESEL ID stored for each person in our example database. Designing a special class for this purpose is useful since the PESEL number conveys additional information that can be efficiently accessed with the methods of the class, as will be shown.

Our basic building block will be a long number class containing exactly 11 digits as required by the PESEL standard; hence we have the TLongNumberFor< 11 > type. However, a question now arises – what relation should it have with respect to the new PESEL class? As we explained in Section 4.9, we have two options:

- The "has-a" relation, which leads to object aggregation (embedding)
- The "is-a" relation, which leads to inheritance

Both versions are shown in Figure 4.23.

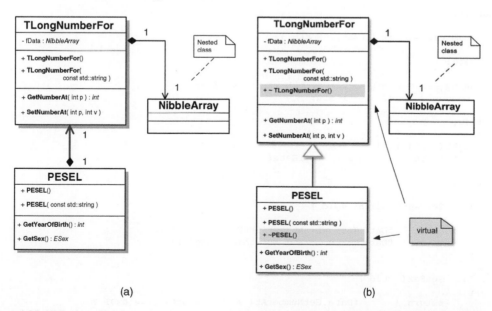

(a)   (b)

Figure 4.23 UML class diagrams showing two versions of the PESEL class: (a) a version that aggregates TLongNumberFor; (b) a version derived from TLongNumberFor. In the latter case, the classes should contain virtual destructors. Such classes contain virtual tables, which make objects larger. NibbleArray is a nested class aggregated by TLongNumberFor.

Note that in addition to the previous two classes, TLongNumberFor defines its own internal NibbleArray. These two are joined by the aggregation relation since the latter's existence is strictly related to the lifetime of the former.

We will now consider the two possible implementations, considering their benefits and drawbacks.

4.15.4.1 Aggregating *PESEL*

Listing 4.35 shows the definition of the PESEL class, which simply embeds the TLongNumberFor< 11 > object, as shown in Figure 4.23a. Hence, PESEL "has" the object of the TLongNumberFor type. In this case, a simpler version of TLongNumberFor is sufficient, so the ALLOW_INHERITANCE flag is set to 0 on line [1]. Then, the *LongNumberFor.h* header is included on line [2].

The alias and the TLongNumberFor object are created on lines [20–21]. Then, two constructors are used on line [25–26]. Finally, since the PESEL ID number contains encoded information about

---

Listing 4.35 Definition of the aggregating PESEL class (in *LongNumber, Embedded_PESEL.h*).

```
1   #define ALLOW_INHERITANCE 0
2   #include "LongNumberFor.h"
3
4
5   /////////////////////////////////////////////////////////////////////////////
6   // The "has-a" version
7   class PESEL
8   {
9       private:
10
11          // Some constants specific to the Polish PESEL number
12          enum { kBirthYear_Dec = 10, kBirthYear_Sngl = 9, kSex = 1 };
13
14      public:
15
16          enum class ESex { kMan, kWoman };
17
18      private:
19
20          using LongNumberObject = TLongNumberFor< 11 >;
21          LongNumberObject      fData;
22
23      public:
24
25          PESEL( void ) {}
26          PESEL( const string & s ) : fData( s ) {}
27
28      public:
29
30          auto GetYearOfBirth( void )
31          {
32              return    fData.GetNumberAt( kBirthYear_Dec ) * 10
33                      + fData.GetNumberAt( kBirthYear_Sngl );
34          }
35
36          ESex GetSex( void )
37          {
38              return (      fData.GetNumberAt( kSex ) & 0x01 ) == 0x01 ?
39                          ESex::kMan : ESex::kWoman;
40          }
41
42      };
```

a person, this data can be read by the functions defined on lines [30, 36]. These are accessed by calling the internal `fData` member.

We have come a long way from trying to use a simple `int` or `long` to store the PESEL ID, all the way to the efficient `PESEL` class that correctly represents the ID in any system, offers additional functionality, and hides the implementation details at the same time. We are interested in measuring the total size of the `PESEL` object, which is done by the following code:

```
#include "Embedded_PESEL.h"
void Embedded_PESEL_Test( void )
{
    std::cout << "Size with wrapped object: " << sizeof( PESEL ) << std::endl;
}
```

The output is

```
Size with wrapped object: 6
```

4.15.4.2 Inherited *PESEL*

In this section, we consider the properties of the second solution, shown in Figure 4.23b. In this case, the `PESEL` class is derived from `TLongNumberFor< 11 >`, so we can say that `PESEL` "is" a kind of `TLongNumberFor`. To allow inheritance, the `ALLOW_INHERITANCE` flag needs to be set to 1, as is done on line [1]. Then, as previously, on line [2], the *LongNumber.h* header is included.

The definition of the `PESEL` class, derived from `TLongNumberFor< 11 >`, starts on line [7] of Listing 4.36. The rest is almost identical to in the definition shown in Listing 4.35, except for the additional virtual destructor defined on line [28]. This is usually necessary for the correct deletion of inherited classes, as discussed in Section 4.11. Also, there is no `fData` member, since all data is stored in the base class. Therefore, the `GetYearOfBirth` (line [32]) and `GetSex` (line [38]) members can directly call the `GetNumberAt` member from the base class. For this purpose, on line [12], `GetNumberAt` is inserted into the scope of the `PESEL` class with the `using` directive.

Listing 4.36 Definition of the `PESEL` class derived from `TLongNumberFor< 11 >` (in *LongNumber, Derived_PESEL.h*).

```
1   #define ALLOW_INHERITANCE 1
2   #include "LongNumberFor.h"
3
4
5   //////////////////////////////////////////////////////////////////////////////////////
6   // The "is-a" version
7   class PESEL : public TLongNumberFor< 11 >
8   {
9       public:
10
11          using BaseClass = TLongNumberFor< 11 >;
12          using BaseClasss::GetNumberAt;
13
14      private:
15
16          // Some constants specific to the Polish PESEL number
17          enum { kBirthYear_Dec = 10, kBirthYear_Sngl = 9, kSex = 1 };
```

(Continued)

Listing 4.36 (continued)

```
18
19    public:
20
21        enum class ESex { kMan, kWoman };
22
23    public:
24
25        PESEL( void ) {}
26        PESEL( const string & s ) : BaseClass( s ) {}      // base class from the string
27
28        virtual  ~PESEL() {}              // this must be virtual, why?
29        // also TLongNumberFor<> should have a virtual destructor
30    public:
31
32        auto GetYearOfBirth( void )
33        {
34            return    GetNumberAt( kBirthYear_Dec ) * 10
35                    + GetNumberAt( kBirthYear_Sngl );
36        }
37
38        ESex GetSex( void )
39        {
40            return ( GetNumberAt( kSex ) & 0x01 ) == 0x01 ?
41                    ESex::kMan : ESex::kWoman;
42        }
43    };
```

With the following code, we can measure the size of this version of the PESEL class and its base:

```
#include "Derived_PESEL.h"
void Derived_PESEL_Test( void )
{
    std::cout << "Size with inherited object: " << sizeof( PESEL ) << std::endl;
    std::cout << "Size of PESEL::BaseClass: " <<
                sizeof( PESEL::BaseClass ) << std::endl;
}
```

Unfortunately, in this case, the output is much larger than it is for the aggregated version:

```
Size with inherited object: 16
Size of PESEL::BaseClass: 16
```

The inherited version is larger by 10 bytes, which is necessary to maintain the VFT due to the presence of the virtual destructors.

Hence, in our example, the aggregated version, which wraps the TLongNumberFor object, is preferred.

4.15.4.3 *LongNumber* Project Organization

Since we have one definition of the TLongNumberFor class with preprocessor-defined symbols that guide compilation, we need to properly organize the project into separate translation units.

The source files that set the compilation flags include the headers and define their function, and are separately compiled into objects. The relations among the project files are shown in the UML artifact diagram shown in Figure 4.24.

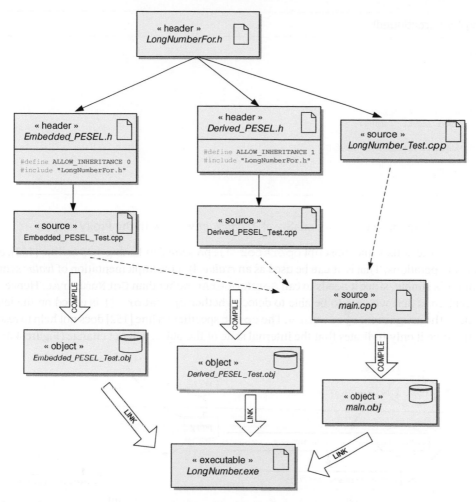

Figure 4.24 UML artifact diagram showing file relations in the *LongNumber* project. Three separate translation units are created.

To maintain the *LongNumberFor.h* header file, which is controlled by the ALLOW_INHERITANCE preprocessor flag, two different translation units are separately compiled. A third is created from the *main.cpp* source file shown in Listing 4.37.

Note that there are only function declarations, which are then invoked. No project headers are included, though.

Listing 4.37 Definition of main with calls to the test functions (in *LongNumber, main.cpp*).

```
1   #include <iostream>
2
3   void LongNumbers_Test( void );
4   void LongNumbersWithProxy_Test( void );
5
6   void Derived_PESEL_Test( void );
7   void Embedded_PESEL_Test( void );
8
```

(Continued)

Listing 4.37 (continued)

```
9    int main()
10   {
11
12       LongNumbers_Test();
13
14       Derived_PESEL_Test();
15       Embedded_PESEL_Test();
16
17       LongNumbersWithProxy_Test();
18
19       return 0;
20   }
```

4.15.5 (�) Extending the Functionality of *TLongNumberFor* with the Proxy Pattern

As alluded to previously, the subscript operator [], presented in Listing 4.33 on line [152], only allows read operations. That is, it can be used as an *rvalue*. But the implementation of *lvalue* semantics is not this simple, since it needs to call SetNumberAt rather than GetNumberAt. Hence, the main problem is that we need to be able to detect whether operator [] is called on the left or right side of the assignment operator =. The const specifier on line [152] does not help to resolve this issue since it only indicates that the internal state of the object will not change (Figure 4.25).

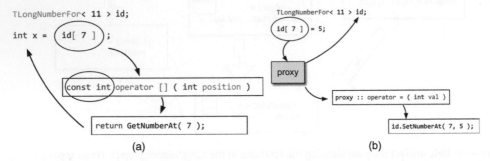

Figure 4.25 Two versions of the subscript operator. (a)The right-side subscript can directly return the value at position 7, which is then assigned to object x. (b) The left-side subscript operator cannot return a reference since a nibble needs to be written. Therefore, a proxy object is returned, which has access to the mother object id. The proxy then calls the assignment operator, which calls id.SetNumber, which finally performs the action.

The situations with the two versions of the subscript operator are shown in Figure 4.25. The right-side subscript operator [] is called with position set to 7. This is almost instantly passed to GetNumberAt, which returns a value that is assigned to the object x, as shown in Figure 4.25a.

The situation with the left-side subscript is a little more complicated. It cannot return just a reference to a location, since a nibble needs to be written rather than the entire byte. However, we cannot address bits or nibbles, so SetNumberAt needs to be called. Hence we need to differentiate between the right- and left-side subscripts. To do this, we can use a trick: operator [] will return another object called a *proxy*. It will have access to TLongNumberFor, which is called the "mother" object, and to the subscript position (Figure 4.25b). Additionally, the proxy object has the assignment operator =, subscript operator [], and conversion to int.

But `TLongNumberFor` needs to be supplemented with another version of `operator []` that returns this proxy object. All of these are added to the definition of the `TLongNumberFor` class, as will be shown.

4.15.5.1 Definition of the Proxy Class

Listing 4.38 contains the definition of the `RetObjProxy` class, which implements the proxy pattern added to the `TLongNumberFor` class to facilitate different versions of data transfer by the overloaded subscript operators.

Listing 4.38 Definition of the `RetObjProxy` nested private class for the proxy pattern to implement full operation of the subscript operator in the `TLongNumberFor` class (in *LongNumber, LongNumberFor.h*).

```
178  #define TURN_ON_PROXY
179  #ifdef TURN_ON_PROXY        // The following code is compiled if TURN_ON_PROXY is defined
180     private:
181
182        // The proxy pattern private area
183
184        // --------------------------------------------------------------
185        // This nested class realized the PROXY pattern
186        class RetObjProxy
187        {
188           public:
189
190           using MotherClass = typename TLongNumberFor< MAX_NUMBERS > ;
191
192           private:
193
194              // A const or reference type data member makes the compiler declare
195              // a copy assignment operator as deleted.
196              // This does not work for us - we need a copy assignment.
197
198              MotherClass * fMyMother {}; // A pointer to the mother class
199
200              int fPosition {}; // Local index storage for the operator []
201
```

The code associated with the proxy pattern is included in the conditional compilation section on lines [179–266]. This is compiled if the flag `TURN_ON_PROXY` is defined, as on line [178]. This is slightly different behavior than the conditional compilation shown on lines [66–68] of Listing 4.33. In that case, a preprocessor flag is not only defined but also assigned a value, so a condition like `ALLOW_INHERITANCE == 1` can be checked. Here, we only check if `#define TURN_ON_PROXY` is present. Preprocessors are discussed further in Section A.1.

The definition of the nested `RetObjProxy` starts on line [186], which is in the `private` section of `TLongNumberFor`. `TLongNumberFor` is aliased on line [190] as `MotherClass`. The `RetObjProxy` class has two private members. The first, defined on line [198], is `fMyMother`, a pointer to the `TLongNumberFor` class for which `RetObjProxy` will work. The second, on line [200], is an auxiliary value to hold the current digit position.

The whole idea of using the proxy pattern for subscript operations is shown in Figure 4.25b. Since we cannot simply code the double-side subscript operation, because we cannot address a nibble, we choose an indirect approach with the proxy: when `operator []` is called, instead of a reference, a `RetObjProxy` object is returned, which holds a pointer to the main

TLongNumberFor object and the current digit position, as shown on line [257]. This is created by the parametric constructor defined on line [207]. At the same time, we wish to disallow the default constructor, since RetObjProxy must always be attached to a TLongNumberFor object. This would be achieved automatically by defining only the parametric constructor. But to explicitly express our intention, we add =delete, as presented in Section 4.6.1. On line [216], the default constructor is marked as deleted, so it cannot be used.

```
202        public:
203
204            // Constructor
205            // myMother - a TLongNumberFor class we connect to
206            // position - index position
207            RetObjProxy( MotherClass * myMother, int position )
208              : fMyMother( myMother ), fPosition( position )
209            {
210              assert( fMyMother != nullptr );
211              assert( fPosition < MotherClass::kMaxNumbers );
212            }
213
214
215            // Forbidden default constructor
216            RetObjProxy( void ) = delete;
217
```

As alluded to previously, the new TLongNumberFor operator [], defined on line [257], returns a RetObjProxy object. But this can happen in two contexts: when a digit is read, or when a digit is written. Naturally, this complies with the right or left value being processed. In both cases, the RetObjProxy members get into the action. Namely, when a RetObjProxy object is on the left side of the assignment and an int object is on the right, then operator = (int), defined on line [230], is called. Line [233] delegates the write operation to the mother object by calling fMyMother->SetNumberAt. Then the proxy is returned on line [234] to allow assignment chaining.

If RetObjProxy object is on the right side of the assignment and an int object is expected, then a simple to-int conversion function is called, as defined on line [223], which returns a digit at a given position. Again, the action to read the digit is delegated on line [226] to the mother object.

Finally, as will be shown in the examples, there may be a RetObjProxy object on both the left and right sides of the assignment. In this case, RetObjProxy & operator = (RetObjProxy & r), defined on line [239], will be invoked. It copies one digit to the other digit, as shown on lines [242–243]. Then the proxy object is returned on line [244] to allow assignment chaining.

```
218        public:
219
220            // Called when: int x = id[ 8 ]
221            // Right side (read) operation
222            // Conversion operator to int - for read operations
223            operator int () const
224            {
225              assert( fMyMother != nullptr );
226              return fMyMother->GetNumberAt( fPosition );
227            }
228
```

```
229        // Called when: id[ 8 ] = 5
230        RetObjProxy & operator = ( int val )
231        {
232            assert( fMyMother != nullptr );
233            fMyMother->SetNumberAt( fPosition, val );
234            return * this;
235        }
236
237        // Another assignment operator
238        // Called when: id[ 8 ] = id[ 7 ]
239        RetObjProxy & operator = ( RetObjProxy & r )
240        {
241            assert( fMyMother != nullptr );
242            fMyMother->SetNumberAt( fPosition,
243                            r.fMyMother->GetNumberAt( fPosition ) );
244            return * this;
245        }
246    };
247    // End of proxy
248    // -------------------------------------------------------------------
249
```

As we mentioned earlier, in addition to adding the definition of the RetObjProxy class, the TLongNumberFor class needs an overloaded version of operator [], as defined on line [257]. It simply returns the RetObjProxy object, created on line [263] and initialized with the parameters this and position.

```
250    public:
251
252
253        // The main idea behind the subscript operator in TLongNumberFor
254        // is to return a proxy object rather than any value.
255        // The returned proxy will behave differently being on the left
256        // or right side of the assignment operator.
257        RetObjProxy operator [] ( int position )
258        {
259            assert( position < kMaxNumbers );
260            // Here we create the proxy object providing "this"
261            // as its "mother" class.
262            // Return by value (copy elision, guaranteed in C++17)
263            return RetObjProxy( this, position );
264        }
265    // -------------------------------------------------------------------
266 #endif
```

Here, RetObjProxy is returned by value, but thanks to the copy elision using the RVO mechanism, as already discussed in Section 4.5, no extra copies are performed.

4.15.5.2 Testing the Functionality of the *TLongNumberFor* Class with the Proxy Pattern

The LongNumbersWithProxy_Test function, defined on line [3] of Listing 4.39, contains example tests that show the operation of TLongNumberFor in various contexts of the subscript operations. The TURN_ON_PROXY preprocessor symbol on line [5] is used to turn on or off the code fragments that require the presence of the RetObjProxy class within TLongNumberFor.

An 11-digit object is created on line [6]. Then it is read from (line [8]) or assigned to (line [10]) at the seventh digit position. The chained assignment takes place on line [12]. After this, all three digit positions should be set to 3, as verified on lines [14–16]. The best way to understand what

Listing 4.39 Test function for the `TLongNumberFor` class using the proxy pattern (in *LongNumber, LongNumber_Test.cpp*).

```
1   // A function that checks the main functionality
2   // of the TLongNumberFor class that has the proxy pattern
3   void LongNumbersWithProxy_Test( void )
4   {
5   #ifdef TURN_ON_PROXY
6       TLongNumberFor< 11 > id;
7
8       int x = id[ 7 ];        // use proxy here
9
10      id[ 7 ] = 7;            // use proxy here
11
12      id[ 6 ] = id[ 8 ] = id[ 7 ] = 3;      // use proxy as well
13
14      assert( id[ 6 ] == 3 );
15      assert( id[ 7 ] == 3 );
16      assert( id[ 8 ] == 3 );
17
18      assert( id[ 10 ] == id[ 0 ] );
19
20  #endif
21
22      // The concordant indexing:        9   ... 0
23      const TLongNumberFor< 11 > cid( "9876543210" );      // cid contains "09876543210"
24      assert( cid[ 10 ] == cid[ 0 ] );          // the leading 11th digit was set to 0
25
26      //cid[ 0 ] = 5;          cannot do that since cid is const
27      // calls const int TLongNumberFor< 11 >::operator [] ( int position ) const
28      int z = cid[ 7 ];
29
30  #ifdef TURN_ON_PROXY
31
32      id[ 7 ] = cid[ 1 ];
33      assert( id[ 7 ] == 1 );
34
35  #endif
36  }
```

function is involved in all of these operations is to set breakpoints in the functions presented in the previous section and watch the function call stack in the debugger.

A constant `TLongNumberFor` object `cid` is created on line [23]. Since it is constant, its digit positions can only be read. Hence, `operator [] const` of the `TLongNumberFor` class is sufficient, as shown on lines [24–28], and the proxy pattern can be avoided. This is not the case on lines [32–33], since again the non-constant object `id` is invoked.

As we have seen, the proxy pattern usually stays invisible and acts in the background. In a similar fashion, it can also be used in other contexts. For example, a proxy can imitate a submatrix embedded in a larger matrix (like a subimage in an image). In this case, such a proxy matrix behaves like any other but does not have its own data, instead relying on data from the larger matrix and recomputing its local coordinates to the corresponding coordinates in the larger matrix. Another application of the proxy is to postpone operations – this is called *lazy evaluation*. In this case, the proxy usually collects references to objects on which to perform operations and does nothing else. An action is performed only if absolutely necessary. For example, an image proxy, when asked for an image from a filesystem, opens the image file but does not load any data into memory. Eventually, an image is loaded into memory only if an operation on the image data is requested (Wiki:Proxy_pattern 2020).

4.16 Strong Types

In the `TPerson` class shown in Listing 4.32, we saw that the `fID` member's type, `unsigned int`, was inappropriate since it could not store an 11-digit value. Therefore, we substituted the `PESEL` class, as discussed in Section 4.15.4. By doing this, we not only can store the correct value but also get functionality such as the date of birth and a correction code that verifies the value's internal integrity.

A similar issue can be observed with the `fAge` data member of `TPerson`. Although its capacity is more than enough (we are not happy about that, either), it is not safe from false initialization. Therefore a stronger type would be more appropriate; an example is presented in Listing 4.40.

Listing 4.40 Definition of the `TAge` class, which is a stronger type than `unsigned char` to represent an age (in *LongNumber, main.cpp*).

```
1  class TAge
2  {
3      unsigned char fAge {};
4
5  public:
6
7      TAge( unsigned char age = 0 ) : fAge( age ) {}
8
9      auto GetAge( void ) const { return fAge; }
10
11     // Verify a precondition on what is written in
12     void SetAge( unsigned char age ) { assert( age < 128 ); fAge = age; }
13
14     // ... more interface
15 };
```

Now `fAge` in `TAge` is private, and `SetAge` has a precondition that will catch all attempts to write unusual values.

Listing 4.41 shows a refactored version of the `TPerson` class from Listing 4.32. Its two data members have been replaced with the stronger types `PESEL` and `TAge`.

Although simple, the technique of using strong types pays off in practice.

For further reading on strong (or named) types, we recommend the blog *Fluent{C++}* (Boccara 2016; Boccara 2018).

Listing 4.41 Refactored `TPerson` class from Listing 4.32 with stronger types (in *LongNumber, main.cpp*).

```
1  class TPerson
2  {
3  private:
4
5      std::wstring    fFirstName;
6      std::wstring    fLastName;
7
8      TAge            fAge {};          // Self-contained class to represent an age
9
10     PESEL           fID {};           // PESEL id - no capacity problem here
11
12 public:
13
14     // ...
15 };
```

4.17 Summary

Things to Remember

- Carefully prepare the contents of a class, and devise a meaningful name that reflects its functions and role in the system. Put all data in the `private` section, and provide a concise interface
- If possible, use self-initialization of class data members and avoid writing special functions such as constructors, assignment and move operators, and destructors
- Function overloading means assigning new functionality to a function or an operator by providing its definition with the same function (operator) name and different parameters
- Most operators can be overloaded. Consider whether an overloaded operator should be a member of a class or if it can be provided outside of a class (analyze the way to access the data)
- Function overriding means writing a function in a derived class that overrides a function with the same parameters but defined in the base class
- In the definition of a base class intended to be inherited from, declare its destructor as virtual
- Declare as virtual all functions that will be substituted for in derived classes
- Virtual functions must have the same set of formal parameters and the same or a compatible return type. For control, use the `override` specifier
- Do not call virtual functions in constructors and destructors since doing so can lead to undefined behavior
- If providing a custom constructor or destructor, also write all the other special functions. If the default action is sufficient, use the `=default` specifier
- Suitably justify whether deep copying is necessary. If so, provide the copy and move special functions
- Use templates to define functions and classes that are intended to operate the same way (the same code) but with different types
- Wherever possible, use strong types
- Always write test functions to test your code
- Provide meaningful comments in your code

Questions and Exercises

1. Measure the performance of the `TCube` copy vs. move operations:
   a. Use the time measurement functions: for example, the one presented in Section 6.4.
   b. Use the profiler, as presented in Appendix A.6.3.
   Hint: base your software on the `TheCube_Test` function, shown in Listing 4.6.

2. In Table 3.6, we presented the `std::sort` function.
   a. Measure its performance with respect to the significantly changed numbers of sorted elements in the vector.
   b. Compare this with the performance of your sorting function from exercise 16 in Section 3.21. What type of relation can you observe?
   c. The amount of time required for execution of an algorithm is determined by its *computational complexity*. This is described in an asymptotic way with big O notation. For example, O(n) means the algorithm executes on average in linear time with respect to the number of elements n, whereas O(n^2) means squared time complexity, etc. Read about computational complexity (*https://en.wikipedia.org/wiki/Time_complexity*) and then, based on the measurements, try to assess the complexity of your tested sorting algorithms.

3. Improve the implementation of `TheCube` class: make it template-like.

4. Make `TQuadEq` template-like.

5. Finish the implementation of the `TinyCube` specialization for `bool`, as started in Listing 4.15. Hint: observe that a byte lets us store eight bits, which can easily be converted to `bool`. Develop a method to translate an address within a cube into an address of a corresponding bit.

6. In the definition of `TStackFor`, replace the template parameter defining the maximum size into the parameters of the `TStackFor` constructor. What is the difference between these two solutions?

7. Read about data sorting with the QuickSort *(https://en.wikibooks.org/wiki/Data_Structures/ Stacks_and_Queues)* approach (Cormen et al. 2009). Implement the method. How can the stack be used in this implementation?

8. Refactor the `ComplexQuadEq_Test` function from Listing 4.24 to properly react to exceptions if thrown by the `TComplexQuadEq::GetRoots` member function.

9. Experiment with the `TCircle` class by removing the `virtual` keyword from the declaration of the `GetPi` member function (Listing 4.25, line [32]). What is the result of running the code?

10. What happens if you remove `virtual` from the destructor of `TCircle` (Listing 4.25, line [24])? Explain.

11. Implement the overloaded comparison `operator <` for the `TLongNumberFor` class defined in Section 4.15.3. Write a test function for sorting objects of this type.

12. To save on memory, the BCD representation was introduced in Section 4.15.1. However, a better compression ratio can be obtained by assigning a special variable-length encoding. An example is the Huffman encoding, which reserves shorter codes for more frequent digits (Wiki:Huffman_coding 2020; Cormen et al. 2009; Cover and Thomas 2006). After reading more about it, try to implement a variable-length encoding to efficiently represent arbitrarily long numbers. Compare it with the BCD.

13. Rethink and extend the implementation of the class `TPointFor` presented in Listing 4.19. How it can be extended to reflect 3D points, 4D points, etc.?

14. Design and implement a class to represent rectangles.
    - What data is necessary?
    - What interface?
    - Add functions to compute an intersection of two rectangles
    - Implement a function that checks whether a 2D point lies inside or outside a rectangle
    - Write test functions to test the class

15. Make the program to play the "21" Blackjack card game.

    a. Read and analyze the rules (e.g. *https://en.wikipedia.org/wiki/Blackjack*).

    b. Make a design – identify the main objects, such as a card, a deck, a player (what kind of players we have?), the rules and the game; recognize and name their attributes and operations; use the UML methodology, apply the use case, sequence, and class diagrams. Split your design into components with well defined interfaces: e.g. the game engine and the user's interface with table display.

    c. Make implementation – use the SL algorithms (e.g. for deck shuffling) and containers (e.g. `vector`, `string`, etc.), put comments where appropriate, make the code self-documenting. Don't wait until everything is written; instead, try to compile and debug whatever parts are ready, write and use test functions.

    d. Create unit tests and verify your application, but most of all enjoy!

5

Memory Management

All objects used in computations must be placed somewhere in computer memory. We touched on memory management when discussing variables, as well as arrays and pointers (Section 3.1). The two most important concepts related to objects and memory are these:

- *Object visibility (scope)* – The rules telling which parts of the code an object can be accessed from. The scope of an object that is not a member of a class starts at a point of its declaration.
- *Object lifetime* – How long an object is "alive" in memory, and which components are responsible for its creation and deletion.

Knowing these is essential for proper code organization. However, although object visibility is an easy concept, understanding object lifetime and responsibility for an object's creation and deletion is much more demanding. Violating these guidelines can result in serious programming errors, such as accessing deleted objects, and in memory leaks. These problems, as well as methods to remedy them, are discussed in this chapter.

5.1 Types of Data Storage

C++ programs use various data structures to store different types of objects (variables and constants); see Appendix A.3 Also, depending on the storage type, there are different rules for object creation and deletion. These are discussed in Table 5.1.

5.2 Dynamic Memory Allocation – How to Avoid Memory Leaks

As alluded to previously, the C++ language has two underground data structures for storing objects: the stack, associated with each block of a function or a statement; and the heap, used for dynamic memory allocation. The stack is created when program execution steps into a function or statement and is automatically destroyed, along with all of its contents, after execution steps out of it. On the other hand, objects allocated on the heap with the `new` operator (*GROUP 4*, Table 3.15) persist until the corresponding `delete` is encountered. If this `delete` is omitted, memory is usually allocated until the end of the process or even until the next computer reboot. This situation is

Introduction to Programming with C++ for Engineers, First Edition. Bogusław Cyganek.
© 2021 John Wiley & Sons Ltd. Published 2021 by John Wiley & Sons Ltd.
Companion website: http://home.agh.edu.pl/~cyganek/BookCpp.htm

Table 5.1 Rules for creating and deleting objects.

Object allocation and/or access type	Lifetime and accessibility	Memory area	Example
| Automatic (local) | Automatic objects (variables) are created within functions. Unless suitable constructors are provided, they are not automatically initialized, so explicit initialization is necessary. They are automatically killed when control leaves the function where a given automatic variable was defined.<br><br>Each new block { } defines a separate scope for its local variables. These exist only when control is in this block or statement. | The stack – a local memory data structure associated with a function or a block { }.<br><br>The stack is automatically created when code execution enters the block, and it is automatically deleted on its exit.<br><br>However, local stacks allow for relatively small objects, so for large allocations (e.g. matrices), the heap should be used. | The following code snippet defines three objects named var. One has global scope, and the other two are automatic variables defined in the function and its inner block, respectively.<br><br>```cpp
1   // A global var - even if not explicitly initialized will be set to 0
2   int var;
3
4   void var_test_fun( void )
5   {   // local stack is created for inner variables
6
7       int var = -1;        // local var that hides the global "var"
8       cout << var << endl; // prints -1
9
10      // {} opens new scope and a local stack
11      {
12          int var = 3;     // hides two prev "var"
13          cout << var << endl; // prints 3
14      }   // here the inner "var" is deleted
15
16      var = ::var;         // set "var" with a global "var"
17      cout << var << endl; // prints 0
18
19  }   // here the first "var" is deleted
``` |
```

Global	Global memory area	The first var, defined on line [2], has global scope. It is placed in a special global memory region created when a program starts (the code is generated by the compiler; see Appendix A.3). It can be accessed in the var_test_fun function and in all other functions of the program.
		The second var, defined on line [7], is a local variable. It is placed on a local stack associated with the var_test_fun function. Then a third var is created on line [12]. It is created within an inner block, which also has a second associated local stack. This third var hides access to the second var because it has the same name. There is no way to access the second var in the inner block. When the block is ended on line [14], the second local stack is destroyed, along with all the local variables from that block.
		On line [16], a first local var is initialized with the global var. To access the global var, we use the global scope operator :: (GROUP 1, Table 3.15).
		The function ends on line [19], which entails deleting the second local stack, containing the second var.
	Global variables are created in the special memory area reserved for the program. They are initialized by special code before the main function is called. They are destroyed automatically after exiting from main. They can be accessed from any place in the translation unit (a compiled file with all of its includes), and in other translation units after being introduced with the extern directive.	
Static	Static memory area	In this example, we show how to use a static variable, defined in a function, to control the number of executions of a block of code in that function:
| | | ```
1   // Example of using static in a function.
2   // No matter how many times we call this function
3   // it will display only N times.
4   void do_action_N_times( const int N, const int to_display )
5   {
6       // This static is alive through the program lifetime.
7       // It can be accessed only from within this function.
8       // This static will be initialized to N only ONCE.
9       static int n_counter = N;
10
``` |
| | Static objects (variables, constants) reside in special memory associated with the C/C++ program. They are automatically initialized to their default (zero) values, after the program starts and before entering the main function, and they are automatically destroyed when the program ends. | |

(Continued)
```

Table 5.1 *(Continued)*

Object allocation and/or access type	Lifetime and accessibility	Memory area	Example
	However, unlike global variables, they can be defined within functions. In this case, a static variable is alive between consecutive calls to that function and is accessible only in the function. Static variables also have a *static linkage* that limits access to an object to the translation unit in which it is defined. Because of this, the static declaration is sometimes used to constrain the visibility of objects (a kind of "private" in C). Since C++17, an object can be declared inline, meaning it has a local linkage in a translation unit and it will hold the same value among translation units, i.e. in the entire program, even though its value can be known not until the run-time (i.e. it does not need to be constant). This feature helps to define objects entirely in the header files with no necessity for source file definitions; see Section 4.15.3.		```\n11 // Allow action at most N times, no matter how many\n12 // times we call this function.\n13 if(n_counter > 0)\n14 {\n15 -- n_counter; // decrement by 1\n16 cout << to_display << endl;\n17 }\n18 }\n19\n20 void do_action_test(void)\n21 {\n22 const int kIterations = 1000;\n23 const int kNumOfActions = 5;\n24\n25\n26 for(int k = 0; k < kIterations; ++ k)\n27 do_action_N_times(kNumOfActions, k);\n28 }\n``` The function do_action:times takes two parameters. The first, N, is used to initialize the inner static variable n_counter, defined on line [9]. The second, to_display, is simply passed to be streamed out to the screen. n_counter has three interesting aspects: (i) it will be initialized at the first (and only the first) execution of the do_action_N_times function; (ii) because n_counter is a static object, it will survive calls to do_action_N_times. N and to_display are automatic and will be destroyed whenever they encounter line [18], whereas n_counter will be untouched; (iii) if do_action_N_times is called from multiple threads, then each call will have different variables N and to_display, since these are private to the function, but only one n_counter throughout all threads, since it is shared (and access should be synchronized in such a case; see Chapter 8).

At each function call, n_counter is decremented on line [15], and a local value goes to the screen on line [16]. On line [27], the function do_action_test calls do_action N_times. This is done kIterations times. However, since n_counter has been set to kNumOfActions, which is 5, only five values are displayed. That is, we will see the following result: 0 1 2 3 4 (with each digit on a new line).

The next two code fragments contain an example of global and static variables and the rules for accessing them in other translation units (e.g. when compiling different source files).

Declaring an object static, as on line [8] of the following code fragment, makes it local to the translation unit (i.e. a currently compiled file named *file_a.cpp* with all of its includes). Such an object can be accessed only in the translation unit where it was declared and is inaccessible in other translation units.

On the other hand, a pure global object like such as x, defined on line [6], can be accessed in this and other translation units using the extern directive.

```
1    // An example of the static linkage
2
3
4    // file_a.cpp
5
6    int x = 5;          // global scope
7
8    static int y = 7;   // static - scope only in this translation unit
9                        // behaves like a global but only in this unit
```

In a separate translation unit, say a file named *file_b.cpp*, using a global object x defined in another translation unit (file) requires the extern directive, as shown on line [3]. On the other hand, the static object y has a *local linkage* and cannot be accessed in other translation units. Even declaring extern on line [5] cannot bring y from the other translation unit: although this code compiles, it generates a linker error since the linker cannot find a global object named y.

(Continued)

Table 5.1 (Continued)

Object allocation and/or access type	Lifetime and accessibility	Memory area	Example
			``
1   // file_b.cpp
2
3   extern int x;
4
5   extern int y;   // this compiles, however trying to use "y" will generate
6   // a linker error (LNK2001: unresolved external symbol "int y")
```

Using static objects in one translation unit makes other translation units free to use their own objects named y. The static specifier can be assigned to the functions and to the class members (see Table 4.3).

There is also a construction extern "C"  {  }  that lets us call C-type functions from within C++ code (see Appendix A.2.7). |
```

Heap-allocated	The heap is a separate and usually large memory region used for object allocations performed with the new operator (*GROUP 4*, Table 3.15), or the malloc function in C (Appendix A.2.6). Such an allocation is not automatically freed and requires an explicit call to the delete operator (or the free function in C). In order to avoid memory leaks, using smart pointers is recommended when working with heap allocations (Section 5.2).	The heap – usually a large memory area reserved by the operating system on behalf of the runring program.	In the following example, a large memory area of 100000 bytes is allocated on the heap. However, to avoid using new and delete explicitly – which can be easily mismatched, leading to memory leaks – we use the make_unique function. It returns the unique_ptr object (a smart pointer), which on line [3] is assigned to large_buffer. For simplicity, we declared the large_buffer declared with the auto keyword.

```
1   #include <memory>
2
3   void HeapAllocExample( void )
4   {
5       // Define a smart pointer large_buffer containing 100000 bytes
6       // allocating on the heap.
7       const auto kSize { 100000 };
8       auto  large_buffer( make_unique< unsigned char [] >( kSize ) );
9
10      // Initialize the buffer to 0
11      std::memset( large_buffer.get(), 0, kSize );
12
13      large_buffer[ 0 ] = 'A';
14      // Do something with large_buffer
15      // ...
16
17
18      // large_buffer is a local object, so it will be automatically
19      // destroyed at the exit of this function - thanks to this
20      // it will also destroy the buffer of 100000 bytes
21  }
```

The memory block can be initialized to 0, as on line [11], and accessed as an ordinary large array, as on line [13]. The interesting action happens when we exit the HeapAllocExample function on line [21]. Since large_buffer is a *local object*, it is *automatically destroyed* on exit from this function. In its destructor, it calls delete [] to free the entire buffer of heap-allocated memory. As a result, the memory-disposal process is automated, which greatly helps avoid memory leaks. Smart pointers are discussed further in upcoming sections.

a serious software error called a *memory leak* that should be always avoided. It is dangerous especially in systems like web servers that repeatedly call a faulty software component. The separation of `new` and `delete` is a feature of the C++ language and allows for deterministic control over memory allocation and deallocation events. Some languages have built-in automatic removal of memory that is allocated for objects that are no longer referenced by other objects; this is called a *garbage collector* mechanism. However, it is also not free from problems and can add significant computational overhead during program execution.

This problem is quite common, so let's take a look at how it can arise in practice:

```cpp
1   // An example of memory leak generation
2   // DO NOT USE THIS CODE !!
3   bool ProcessFile_0( const char * fileName )
4   {
5       const int kBufSize = 256;
6       char * buf = new char[ kBufSize ];      // allocate a buffer on the heap
7
8       ifstream    file( fileName );
9       if( file.is_open() == false )
10      {
11          return false;  // cannot open a file, exiting ...
12      }                  // oops! - buf is not destroyed - a memory leak is generated !
13
14      file.read( buf, kBufSize );  // file open ok, read to the buffer
15      // do something ...
16
17      delete [] buf;  // delete the buffer
18
19      return true;  // everything ok, exit
20  }
```

On line [6], a buffer of 1024 bytes is allocated on the heap. No problem – it can be used as a buffer to read bytes from a successfully opened file. Then, it can be deleted at the end of the function, as indeed happens on line [17]. However, in practice, a file with that name may not exist, so there is another path of execution that terminates the function if the file cannot be opened. Thus, on line [11], the function returns `false` to indicate an error. But we forgot to free memory that is allocated on line [6] and pointed to by `buf`. And because `buf` is a local variable, it will be lost after the function exits. Such situations frequently arise in practice, especially in large functions with many internal calls and alternative execution paths.

So, how can we avoid pitfalls like this? Without changing the function much, we can use a couple of C++ features. The first one is to use an object that is allocated as a local and automatic variable and that will safely allocate and deallocate memory for us. This is the `vector` object (Section 3.2). A version of the file-reading function looks like this:

```cpp
1   // Use std::vector as an underlying data container (data allocated on the heap)
2   bool ProcessFile_1( const string & fileName )
3   {
4       const int kBufSize = 256;
5       std::vector< char >   buf( kBufSize );   // allocate a buffer on the heap
6
7       ifstream    file( fileName );
```

```
8     if( file.is_open() == false )
9     {
10      return false;  // cannot open a file, exiting ...
11    }                 // OK, buf is an automatic object, it will be destroyed
12
13    file.read( & buf[0], kBufSize );  // file open OK, read to the buffer
14    // do something ...
15
16    return true;    // everything ok, exit
17  } // OK, buf is an automatic object, it will be destroyed
```

This time, on line [5], a local automatic object buf of type std::vector< char > is created. In its constructor, it is allocated 256 bytes on the heap. Its destructor deallocates that buffer. But since it is an automatic local variable of the ProcessFile_1 function, no matter what execution path is followed, it will be automatically destroyed: its destructor will be called and the memory deallocated. That's the point – using an automatic local variable and harnessing the automatic object-disposal mechanism! There is also no delete.

To use this version of the function, two minor changes were necessary. First, to use a vector, on line [13], we had to change the access to the memory buffer – we use the address of its first element. Second, we changed the input parameter from const char * to const string &. Unlike calling by a pointer, calling by a constant reference is safe since a reference must point to an object – in this case, a file name.

The second option to avoid the risk of generating memory leaks is to use a smart pointer. Its operation will be explained later, so first, let's take a look at the third version of the function:

```
1   // Use std::unique_ptr smart pointer object
2   bool ProcessFile_2( const string & fileName )
3   {
4       const int kBufSize = 256;
5       auto buf = std::make_unique< char [] >( kBufSize );  // allocate a buffer on
6                               // the heap - but hold it with a unique_ptr C++14
7       ifstream    file( fileName );
8       if( file.is_open() == false )
9       {
10        return false;  // cannot open a file, exiting ...
11      }                 // OK, buf is an automatic object, it will be destroyed
12                        // and it will deallocate memory from the heap
13
14      file.read( buf.get(), kBufSize );  // file open OK, read to the buffer (use get)
15      // do something ...
16
17      return true;    // everything ok, exit
18    } // OK, buf is an automatic object, it will be destroyed
```

This time, on line [5], a buf object is created via a call to the make_unique helper function. Hence, its type is unique_ptr< char [] >, which we avoid writing explicitly thanks to the auto keyword. unique_ptr is an object that behaves like a pointer to an array. But once again, since it is a local automatic object in the ProcessFile_2 function, no matter what the execution path is, `unique_ptr` will be automatically destroyed. This entails a call to the destructor of the `unique_ptr` object and deallocation of the buffer to which it holds a pointer. To access the pointer to the memory buffer, we had to change line [14] and call the `buf.get()` function. In other regards, `unique_ptr` behaves like an ordinary pointer.

Summarizing, when heap memory allocation is required, then the simplest and safest method is to use an SL container, such as the `vector`. But remember that in addition to the memory allocation it is also zero initialized, as well as the vector object itself is created. If this is not desired (e.g. if there are thousands of such objects), then `unique_ptr` is a lighter-weight option.

Allocating blocks of memory through SL containers or smart pointers is the only way to avoid memory leaks, especially if the code *throws an exception*. This is another point advocating for refactoring the old code that calls new directly.

5.2.1 Introduction to Smart Pointers and Resource Management

As we mentioned earlier, the main idea behind the smart pointers is to harness the mechanism of automatic disposal of the automatic objects to the deallocation of the memory blocks from the heap. Let's take a look at what mechanism is actually used in smart pointers. For this purpose a template class a_p of "advanced pointers" may look like follows:

Listing 5.1 Example code of a rudimentary smart pointer class (shown only for explanation; not to be used in the code). The main idea is to use the mechanism of automatic disposal of automatic objects to destroy dynamically allocated objects (in *CppBookCode. SmartPointers.cpp*).

```
1   template < typename T >
2   class a_p      // just an example - use the std::unique_ptr instead
3   {
4   private:
5
6       T * fPtr;  // a pointer to the guarded object
7
8   public:
9
10      a_p( T * p ) : fPtr( p ) {}
11
12      // When a_p is destroyed, then fPtr is also destroyed.
13      ~a_p() { delete fPtr; }
14
15   public:
16
17      // a_p can be used as an ordinary pointer
18      T & operator * ( void ) { return * fPtr; }
19
20      // ...
21   };
```

In the `a_p` constructor on line [10], a pointer to an object of type `T` is passed and stored in local data pointer `fPtr`. When `a_p` is destroyed, its destructor on line [13] is called, which in turn destroys the object pointed to by `fPtr`. To be useful in the role of a pointer, `a_p` must overload the dereferencing operator (line [18]) and define a few more member functions that we omit here. The following function shows a_p guarding an object of type `double`, allocated on the heap:

```
1   void a_p_test( void )
2   {
3       // Create advanced pointer as a local object
4       // - make it hold a pointer to double
5       a_p< double >    apd( new double( 0.0 ) );
6
7       // Do something with apd as with an ordinary pointer to double
8       * apd = 5.0;
9       * apd *= 3.0;
10      cout << "apd=" << * apd << " sizeof(apd) = " << sizeof( apd ) << endl;
11
12      // apd will be destroyed here since it is an automatic object
13      // It will destroy the held object as well
14  }   // <==
```

An object `apd` of type `a_p< double >` is created on line [5] and initialized with a pointer returned by `new double`. Then, `apd` is used on lines [8–10] as if it were an ordinary pointer to `double`. However, since `apd` is a local variable, after reaching the end of the function on line [14] or at any other exit point, it is automatically deleted (the code is generated by the compiler). This, in turn, invokes the `apd` destructor, which simply destroys the `double` object from the heap. This is just a glimpse – in reality, a smart pointer needs to define a few more functions. Fortunately, such classes have been written for us – they are presented in the next section.

An in-depth treatment of smart pointers and contexts for using them can be found in the excellent book by Scott Meyers: Meyers 2014. Also, the following Internet websites provide the newest information with examples: Stack Overflow 2020; Cppreference.com 2019a,b.

5.2.1.1 RAII and Stack Unwinding

The aforementioned mechanism belongs to the principal paradigm of C++: *resource acquisition is initialization* (RAII), discussed at the beginning of Chapter 4. In the previous example, we saw RAII in operation. It is strictly connected to the concept of an automatic call to a constructor when an object is created, and an automatic call to the destructor when that object is deleted. The object's constructor can initialize whatever resources the object needs, and the destructor can release them. Both mechanisms make RAII attractive and functional – thanks to the automation of the constructor/destructor calls, the processes of resource allocation/deallocation are also automated.

Note that in addition to memory, other resources such as opening/closing files, locking/unlocking parallel synchronization objects, etc. need to be managed the same way. Not surprisingly, in these cases the RAII principle is recommended (Stroustrup 2013). For example, in Table 3.9, the `outFile` object of the `std::ofstream` type is created. Implicitly, its constructor tries to open the file *Log.txt*. This requires few calls to system functions, which are handled by the `std::ofstream` class. If they succeed, as verified with the `outFile.is_open()` condition, we can safely write to that file. But what happens next? Do we explicitly close the *Log.txt* file so other components can use it? No: we do not have to do this explicitly, since when `outFile` goes out of the scope, its destructor is called automatically and, in turn, safely closes the file for us. No matter what would happen if, for example, an exception was thrown, if `outFile` is entirely constructed (i.e. its constructor finishes its job), it is guaranteed that the `outFile` destructor will also finish its job (i.e. free the resources). A similar constructor is used in many other examples in this book; For instance, the `CreateCurExchanger` function in Listing 3.36 creates the `inFile` object, which opens an initialization file; when `inFile` is automatically deleted at the end of this function, that file is also closed. The acquisition of a resource (such as a file, in this case) *is achieved by the initialization of the local object embodying that resource*. This also guarantees that a resource does not outlive its embodying object. In addition, the RAII mechanism ensures that resources are released in *the reverse order* of their acquisition, which is a desirable feature.

Closely related to RAII is the *exception-handling* mechanism. An exception object of any type can be thrown with the `throw` operator (*GROUP 15*, Table 3.15). This exception object is then passed from the point where it was thrown *up the stack* to the closest `try-catch` handler that can process the exception (Section 3.13.2.5). When crossing borders of consecutive scopes, the destructors of all *fully constructed* objects are guaranteed to be executed. This means all stack-allocated objects will be properly destroyed and their allocated resources freed. This process is called *stack unwinding*. But what happens to objects that are not fully constructed – for example, if an exception is thrown in the constructor? If members of this class are properly RAII designed, then any members that have been created and allocated resources will also be properly destroyed, and their resources will be released.

Smart pointers, discussed in the next section, realize the RAII principle for managing computer memory resources.

5.3 Smart Pointers – An Overview with Examples

In this section, we will discuss the three smart pointers `unique_ptr`, `shared_ptr`, and `weak_ptr`, as well as the ways they are created and used.

5.3.1 (✗) More on `std::unique_ptr`

5.3.1.1 Context for Using `std::unique_ptr`

Using `unique_ptr` is simple, especially if we remember one rule: a `unique_ptr` cannot be copied, i.e. there should not be two `unique_ptr`s holding a pointer to the same object. However, a `unique_ptr` can be moved: i.e. it can pass its held object to another `unique_ptr`. To force a move rather than a copy, we can use the `std::move` function. This rule also says that we should not initialize `unique_ptr` with a row pointer (see Section 5.3.1.4). Instead, we should use the `std::make_unique` helper, as discussed earlier (Table 5.2).

Table 5.2 Smart pointers explained (in *CppBookCode*, *SmartPointers.cpp*).

Smart pointer	Description	Examples
| unique_ptr | unique_ptr is a template class designed for exclusive ownership of an object or an array of objects, so it automatically deletes its held object(s). A unique_ptr object behaves like a pointer to the held object(s). Its properties are as follows:<br><br>■ Cannot be copied; only the move operation is allowed.<br>■ unique_ptr should be initialized using the make_unique template function.<br>■ Can have a custom delete function to perform an additional action just before object deletion.<br>■ Can be easily copied to the shared_ptr.<br><br>A single unique_ptr< T > takes responsibility for the lifetime of a single object T.<br><br>auto up_0 = std::make_unique< T >();<br><br> | ```cpp
// Heap allocate a single double object, init to 0.0, and create a
// unique_ptr
unique_ptr< double > real_val_0( new double( 0.0 ) );     // good

// Heap allocate a single double object, init to 0.0, and create a
// unique_ptr
// via make_unique. Better, can use "auto".
auto real_val_1( make_unique< double >( 0.0 ) ); // better

assert( real_val_1.get() != nullptr ); // check the allocated memory ptr
* real_val_1 = 3.14; // use like any other pointer

// -----------------------------------------------------------------
// Heap allocate an array of 16 double - access via the unique_ptr
const int kElems = 16;

unique_ptr< double [] > real_array_0( new double[ kElems ] );   // OK
// but elements pointed by real_array_0 are NOT initialized !
``` |

(Continued)
```

Table 5.2 *(Continued)*

Smart pointer	Description
	It cannot be copied, but it can be moved to other unique_ptr< T >.

```
auto up_0 = std::make_unique< T >();
```

std::unique_ptr< T >
| up_0 |
| nullptr |

Object of type T

```
auto up_1 = std::move( up_0 );
```

std::unique_ptr< T >
| up_1 |
| Pointer to the object |

unique_ptr frequently used member functions:

Member	Description
unique_ptr	Class default and parametric constructors
operator *	Pointer dereferencing the held object
operator ->	Pointer access to the held object
operator bool	Checks whether there is an associated object (or empty)
get	Returns a pointer to the object
release	Returns and releases a pointer to the held object (after that, the released object is free and will not be deleted by this smart pointer)
reset	Gets a new object and deletes the old one

Examples

```
auto  real_array_1( make_unique< double [] >( kElems ) );  // better
// Elements of real_array_1 will be value initialized with double(),
// i.e. to 0.0
//-----------------------------------
if( real_array_0 )          // check if memory has been allocated  (calls
// operator bool())
{
    // init elems
    std::fill( & real_array_0[ 0 ], & real_array_0[ kElems ], -1.0 );
    real_array_0[ 0 ] = 2.71;  // use real_array_0 as a simple array
    // ...
}

real_array_0.reset();  // reset the held pointer and delete all elements
```

unique_ptr is used to take over an ordinary pointer returned by calling the new operator (*GROUP 4*, Table 3.15). But in most cases, it is best not to call new at all – instead, the make_unique helper function should be used. It lets us pass value(s) to the constructor of the constructed object, so the objects will be zero-value initialized (i.e. set to their zero state), as for the real_array_1. On the other hand, elements of an array pointed to by real_array_0 are not initialized. In almost the same way, unique_ptr can be used to control the access and lifetime of *arrays* of objects allocated on the heap. The creation of an array is indicated by adding [] to the template type of the unique_ptr.

Smart pointers have overloaded pointer access operators, so they can be used like any other pointers. We can also check to see whether a unique_ptr contains a valid object. It can also be reset to a new object or nullptr. In this case, the previously held object will be immediately deleted, as shown in the last line.

```
class AClass
{
    string fStr;
public:
    AClass( const string & s = "" ) : fStr(s) {}
    ~AClass() { cout << "AClass destructor" << endl; }

    const string GetStr( void ) const { return fStr; }
    void SetStr( const string & s ) { fStr = s; }
}; // ---------------------------------------
// ...
// AClass object on the heap, p_d takes care
unique_ptr< AClass > p_d_1( new AClass( "Good" ) );

// A better way is to use make_unique helper
auto p_d_2( make_unique< AClass >( "Better" ) );

if( p_d_2 )
{
    cout << p_d_2->GetStr() << endl;          // access through the pointer
    cout << ( * p_d_2 ).GetStr() << endl;     // access through the object
}

//unique_ptr< AClass > p_d_3 = p_d_2; // won't work, cannot copy
unique_ptr< AClass > p_d_3 = std::move( p_d_2 );    // OK, can move to
// other smart ptr

// An array of AClass objects on the heap and p_d_4
const int kAClassElems = 4;
auto p_d_4( make_unique< AClass [] >( kAClassElems ) ); // call default
// constr for each
```

make_unique lets us pass any number of parameters necessary to construct an object. Another advantage is the ability to use the auto keyword directly instead of explicitly providing the full type name. Note that unique_ptr cannot be copied, since two smart pointers cannot delete a single object. However, content of one unique_ptr can be easily moved using the std::move function to the other smart pointer – in our example, p_d_2 is moved this way to p_d_3.

(Continued)

Table 5.2 (Continued)

Smart pointer	Description	Examples
| shared_ptr | shared_ptr is used to share access to a single object among multiple parties. Unlike unique_ptr, there can be many shared_ptr objects pointing at a single object. A special *reference counter* is maintained to control how many shared_ptr(s) point at a given object (see the illustrations in this table). If this value falls to 0, the controlled object is destroyed.<br><br>Basic facts about shared_ptr:<br><br>■ Can be copied – many shared_ptr(s) can point at a single object.<br>■ Can be initialized from a unique_ptr.<br>■ weak_ptr counter is attached to the control structure of the shared_ptr.<br>■ In a multithreaded environment, increments and decrements of the reference counter are atomic, which makes shared_ptr operations expensive in terms of time.<br>■ Can have a custom delete. | ```cpp
auto sp_0 = make_shared< AClass >( "Hold by shared" ); // a control block
// is created

assert( sp_0 );   // sp_0 cast to bool to check if it is not empty
assert( sp_0.get() != nullptr ); // the same

auto sp_1 = sp_0;   // copy for shared is ok - now both point at the same
// object, one control block, and the reference counter is 2

cout << sp_0->GetStr() << " = " << (*sp_1).GetStr() << endl; // access
// the same obj
cout << "sp_0 count = " << sp_0.use_count() << ", sp_1 count = "
     << sp_1.use_count() << endl;

sp_0.reset();
cout << "after reset sp_0 count = " << sp_0.use_count() << ", sp_1 count = "
     << sp_1.use_count() << endl;
``` |
```

An example of an object T and its associated shared pointer with the allocated control block:

```
auto sp_0 = std::make_shared< T >();
```

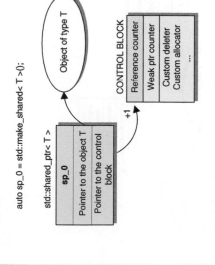

In most cases, it is best to use the make_shared helper function to create a shared_ptr. It lets us use auto to deduce types, and it is thread-safe (exceptions are described e.g. in (Meyers 2014)). It also lets us pass an arbitrary list of parameters to the constructor of the constructed object. If the heap is low on memory, etc., it is good to check whether a shared_ptr holds a valid pointer to the object. This is done in the two assert functions: the first uses an overloaded cast to the bool type, and the second calls the get function to check against the nullptr.

After the shared_ptr is created, the reference counter is incremented. Unlike a unique_ptr, it is perfectly OK to create a copy of a shared_ptr, such as copying sp_1 from sp_0. In such a case, the *common reference* counter is increased to 2. This value can easily be read by calling the use_count member from the board of any of the shared_ptr(s). Analogously to unique_ptr, shared_ptr allows access to the held object like an ordinary pointer. The output of this code snippet is as follows:

```
Hold by shared = Hold by shared
sp_0 count = 2, sp_1 count = 2
after reset sp_0 count = 0, sp_1 count = 1
```

```
// shared_ptr can be made out of the unique_ptr

auto up_0 = make_unique< AClass >( "Created by unique" );

shared_ptr< AClass > sp_2 = move( up_0 );

auto sp_3 = sp_2;

cout << sp_2->GetStr() << " = " << (*sp_3).GetStr() << endl;     // access
// the same obj
cout << "sp_2 count = " << sp_2.use_count() << ", sp_3 count = "
     << sp_3.use_count() << endl;
```

(Continued)

Table 5.2 *(Continued)*

Smart pointer	Description	Examples
	The reference counter is 1; the weak ptr counter is 0. After another shared pointer sp_1 is created and copied from sp_0, the reference counter is increased to 2:	It is also possible to create a shared_ptr from the unique_ptr. However, unlike with the family of shared pointers, we need to use the move function since unique_ptr cannot be copied. In the previous example, an object is taken over by the shared_ptr sp_2, whereas up_0 is left empty. There is no problem with copying sp_3 from sp_2, though. After running the previous code, this is displayed:

```
Created by unique = Created by unique
sp_2 count = 2, sp_3 count = 2
```

```cpp
// shared_ptr to an array

const int kElems = 8;
shared_ptr< AClass [] > sp_4( new AClass[ kElems ] );

cout << "sp_4 count = " << sp_4.use_count() << endl;

for( int i = 0; i < kElems; ++i )
    cout << sp_4[ i ].GetStr() << ", ";

cout << endl;

shared_ptr< AClass [] > sp_5( sp_4 );
cout << "sp_4 count = " << sp_4.use_count() << ", sp_5 count = "
     << sp_5.use_count() << endl;
```

shared_ptr can also take responsibility for the lifetime of an array of objects. It overloads the subscript operator, so it behaves like an ordinary array pointer. Again, there can be more than one shared_ptr attached to such an array of objects – in the previous example, there are two such shared pointers: sp_4 and sp_5. This time the output is as follows:

```
sp_4 count = 1
'','','','','','','','',''
sp_4 count = 2, sp_5 count = 2
AClass destructor
AClass destructor
AClass destructor
AClass destructor
AClass destructor
AClass destructor
AClass destructor
AClass destructor
AClass destructor
AClass destructor
```

Note that at first, sp_4_count is 1. Then all eight empty strings accessed via sp_4 are displayed. After that, sp_4 has been joined with sp_5, which causes the reference counter of each to be increased to 2, as displayed on the next line. Finally, all AClass objects are deleted, as manifested by the messages from the AClass destructor. This happens since all shared_ptr objects went out of scope and have been deleted, which entailed disposal of all their held objects. These are two AClass objects and eight AClass objects from the array.

shared_ptr frequently used function members:

Member	Description
shared_ptr	Class default and parametric constructors
operator *	Pointer dereferencing the held object
operator ->	Pointer access to the held object
operator bool	Checks whether there is an associated object (or empty)
get	Return pointer to the object
reset	Gets a new object; deletes the old one
use_count	Returns the number of shared_ptr(s) attached to the same object

(Continued)

Table 5.2 *(Continued)*

Smart pointer	Description	Examples
| weak_ptr | weak_ptr usually cooperates with a shared_ptr and contains a *non-owning* reference to an object, which is managed by an associated shared_ptr:<br><br>■ Frequently used to accompany a shared_ptr when a double link between objects is required while avoiding circular responsibility for destroying objects (e.g. *cache* of objects, *trees* or *graphs* with mutual dependencies, the *observer design pattern*, etc.).<br><br>■ Unlike unique_ptr and shared_ptr, weak_ptr does not take responsibility for destroying an object it is attached to.<br><br>■ Does not affect the reference counter of the shared_ptr it is created from (see illustration).<br><br>■ To access the held object, weak_ptr has to be converted to another shared_ptr (with the weak_ptr::lock member). | ```
auto sp_0 = make_shared< AClass >( "Goose" );
cout << "sp_0 created" << endl;

cout << "\tsp_0.use_count = " << sp_0.use_count() << endl;

weak_ptr< AClass > wp_0( sp_0 ); // create a weak_ptr assoc with sp_0
cout << "wp_0 created" << endl;

auto sp_1 = sp_0;
cout << "sp_1 created" << endl;

cout << "\tsp_0.use_count = " << sp_0.use_count() << endl; // there is one
cout << "\tsp_1.use_count = " << sp_1.use_count() << endl; // control block

// Check if the object is still alive
if( wp_0.expired() != true )
{
    // We can access the object via lock()
    cout << wp_0.lock()->GetStr() << endl;
}

assert( sp_0 );       // assert that the main object is OK

cout << sp_0->GetStr() << endl; // main object still OK

cout << "sp_0.reset()" << endl;
sp_0.reset();         // detach sp_0

cout << "\tsp_0.use_count = " << sp_0.use_count() << endl; // there is one
``` |
```

```cpp
cout << "\tsp_1.use_count = " << sp_1.use_count() << endl;// control block
cout << ( wp_0.expired() ? "\twp_0 expired" : "\twp_0 not expired" )
<< endl;

ccout << "wp_0.reset()" << endl;

wp_0.reset();    // detach (only) wp_0 from the control block
                 // - does not affect the held object

assert( sp_1 ); // assert that the main object is ok but through sp_1
cout << sp_1->GetStr() << endl; // use the main object via sp_1

cout << "\tsp_0.use_count = " << sp_0.use_count() << endl;
cout << "\tsp_1.use_count = " << sp_1.use_count() << endl;
cout << ( wp_0.expired() ? "\twp_0 expired" : "\twp_0 not expired" )
<< endl;

cout << "sp_1.reset()" << endl;
sp_1.reset(); // detach sp_1

cout << "\tsp_0.use_count = " << sp_0.use_count() << endl;
cout << "\tsp_1.use_count = " << sp_1.use_count() << endl;
cout << ( wp_0.expired() ? "\twp_0 expired" : "\twp_0 not expired" )
<< endl;
```

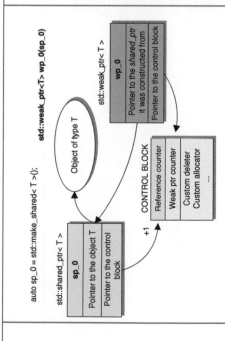

```
auto sp_0 = std::make_shared< T >();        std::weak_ptr<T> wp_0(sp_0)
```

weak_ptr frequently used function members:

Member	Description
weak_ptr	Class default and parametric constructors
expired	Checks whether weak_ptr is pointing at a valid (not destroyed) object
lock	Returns a new shared_ptr to access the attached object
reset	Releases a weak_ptr from the shared_ptr. No effect on the object held by the shared_ptr
use_count	Returns the number of shared_ptr(s) attached to the same object

(Continued)

Table 5.2 (Continued)

Smart pointer	Description	Examples
| | The reference counter is used to count the number of attached shared_ptr(s). If this falls to 0, then the attached object is destroyed. But if this happens, the weak_ptr(s) point to a *dangling* pointer. Such a situation can be detected by calling the weak_ptr::expired function, which checks the reference counter in the control block. This means even if the held object has been destroyed, the control block must exist in memory as long as there are any weak_ptr(s) attached to it. This condition is controlled by the weak pointer counter (see illustration). | ```
sp_0 created
         sp_0.use_count = 1
wp_0 created
sp_1 created
         sp_0.use_count = 2
         sp_1.use_count = 2
Goose
Goose
sp_0.reset()
         sp_0.use_count = 0
         sp_1.use_count = 1
         wp_0 not expired
wp_0.reset()
Goose
         sp_0.use_count = 0
         sp_1.use_count = 1
         wp_0 expired
sp_1.reset()
AClass destructor
         sp_0.use_count = 0
         sp_1.use_count = 0
         wp_0 expired
``` |

In the previous code, first the shared_ptr sp_0 is created and initialized with a pointer to the AClass object. Then, one weak_ptr wp_0 is attached to sp_0. Next, another shared_ptr sp_1 is created and attached to sp_0. Thus there is one control block with a reference counter set to 2 and the weak pointer counter set to 1. The output shown here appears after running the previous code snippet.

The held AClass object can be accessed via each of the shared objects and by wp_0. However, access with wp_0 requires calling the lock function. Resetting sp_0 decrements the reference counter, but the main object and wp_0 remain untouched. Resetting wp_0 does not affect the counter or the shared pointers. Finally, resetting the last shared pointer sp_1 destroys the held AClass object.
```

First, let's create a small `TMatrix` class; see Listing 5.2. With `unique_ptr`, we can easily write a function that creates and returns a `TMatrix` object wrapped up into the smart `unique_ptr`. Some programmers prefix the names of such "creator" functions with *Create_* or *Orphan_* to indicate that the function is creating an object but then giving it away to an "acceptor" function.

Listing 5.2 Ways to access objects from and pass objects to functions with smart pointers (in *CppBookCode. SmartPointers.cpp*).

```
1   class TMatrix
2   {
3   public:
4       TMatrix( int cols, int rows ) {}
5       // ... all the rest
6   };
7
8
9   // ---------
10  // PRODUCER
11  // Returns unique_ptr< TMatrix >
12  auto      OrphanRandomMatrix( const int kCols, const int kRows )
13  {
14      auto retMatrix( make_unique< TMatrix >( kCols, kRows ) );
15
16      // ... do computations
17
18      return retMatrix;   // return a heavy object using the move semantics
19  }
```

An example `OrphanRandomMatrix` is outlined on lines [12–19]. Again, we take advantage of the `auto` keyword to save on typing the full name `unique_ptr< TMatrix >`. After calling the `make_unique` helper on line [14], a smart pointer is created that holds a matrix object of the requested dimensions. Then we are free to do some initializations to the matrix, e.g. with random values. Finally, on line [18], this smart pointer is returned *by value*. As a result, the matrix object is safely passed out of the `OrphanRandomMatrix` function.

The subsequent code fragments show how to pass a matrix object with and without using `unique_ptr`. These can be called *consumers*, and they accept the matrix object in various ways:

- If we wish to perform an action on a `TMatrix` object, then instead of passing `unique_ptr < TMatrix >`, a simpler way is to directly use a reference or constant reference to `TMatrix`, as in the following function:

```
20  // ---------
21  // CONSUMERS
22
23
24  // If always processing an object, then pass an object by a ref
25  // or const ref (read only)
26  double ComputeDeterminant( const TMatrix & matrix )
27  {
28      double retDeterminant {};
29
30      // ... do computations
31
32      return retDeterminant;
33  }
```

- If we need to pass a pointer to a function in the realm of smart pointers, we pass a constant reference to `unique_ptr< TMatrix >`. By doing this, we can access the held object without changing the smart pointer. An example is shown in the second version of the `ComputeDeterminant` function:

```
34  // Ok, unique_ptr is passed by a const reference, however
35  // a pointer to the matrix can be nullptr - we can use this feature
36  // if we wish to have an option to pass an empty object.
37  bool ComputeDeterminant( const unique_ptr<TMatrix> & matrix, double & outRetVal )
38  {
39      if( ! matrix )
40          return false;    // if an empty ptr, then no computations at all
41
42      outRetVal = ComputeDeterminant( * matrix );    // get the object
43
44      return true ;
45  }
```

This method can be used if we wish to express the fact than a passed object is optional or might not exist, which is manifested by passing a `nullptr`. But in that case, `std::optional` provides a viable alternative (Section 6.2.5). As always when working with pointers, before accessing an object, we need to remember to check whether the pointer is a `nullptr`, as shown on line [39].

- If we need to pass an object to a function that will *assume ownership of it,* we do this by passing a non-constant reference to the `unique_ptr`, such as in the following function. By doing this, we can change the passed `unique_ptr` and, for instance, take over its held object:

```
46  // Pass by reference to the unique_ptr - we can take over a held object
47  void TakeOverAndProcessMatrix( unique_ptr< TMatrix > & matrix )
48  {
49      // "it is a deleted function"
50      unique_ptr< TMatrix > myMatrix( move( matrix ) );  // take over the object
51                                          // changes the passed "matrix" to empty
52      // ... do computations
53
54      // when we exit there will be no matrix object at all
55  }
```

On line [50], a new local `unique_ptr< TMatrix >` named `myMatrix` is created, which takes over the `TMatrix` object provided by the `matrix` parameter. This is done with the `std::move` helper. Otherwise, the code will not compile since the `unique_ptr`s cannot be copied to avoid pointing at the same object, as already mentioned. Then, on line [55], the function exits, the local object `myMatrix` is destroyed, the held `TMatrix` object is also destroyed. If not for line [50], the object would not be taken over and would still exist in the code context outside this function.

It is also possible to pass a pointer to a smart pointer, as follows:

```
56  // Such a version is also possible - however, we can have
57  // matrix == nullptr, then it is also possible that matrix.get() == nullptr
58  void TakeOverAndProcessMatrix( unique_ptr< TMatrix > * matrix )
59  {
60      if( matrix == nullptr )
61          return;
62
63      // ...
64  }
```

But in this case, we need to check that the passed pointer is not a `nullptr`, and then check that the held object is not a `nullptr`. So, the usefulness of passing a smart pointer via an ordinary pointer is doubtful.

■ Passing `unique_ptr< TMatrix >` by value forces us to take over the object, as in the following function:

```
65   void AcceptAndProcessMatrix( unique_ptr< TMatrix > matrix )
66   {
67      // if here, then TMatrix object is governed by the
68      // local matrix unique_ptr - it is owned by this function
69
70      assert( matrix );
71
72
73      // ... do computations
74
75      // when we exit there will be no matrix object at all
76   }
```

Since the matrix is a local object of the `AcceptAndProcessMatrix` function, it can hold a `TMatrix` object by itself. However, it can also hold a `nullptr`, so before using the `matrix` object, we have to make sure it is valid. If this is an assumed precondition, it can be verified using `assert`, as on line [70].

Finally, the following function shows some contexts for calling these functions:

```
77    void unique_ptr_OrphanAcceptTest( void )
78    {
79       auto  matrix_1( OrphanRandomMatrix( 20, 20 ) );
80       // matrix_1 is of type unique_ptr< TMatrix >
81
82       assert( matrix_1 );  // make sure the object was created (enough memory, etc.)
83
84       cout << "Det = " << ComputeDeterminant( * matrix_1 ) << endl;
85
86
87       double determinant {};
88       bool detCompStatus = ComputeDeterminant( matrix_1, determinant );
89
90       assert( detCompStatus );
91
92
93       OvertakeAndProcessMatrix( matrix_1 );
         // this will take over the TMatrix object from the passed unique_ptr
94
95       assert( matrix_1 == false );  // no object, only an empty unique_ptr
96
97
98       matrix_1 = make_unique< TMatrix >( 20, 20 );
         // create other fresh object (move semantics)
99
100      assert( matrix_1 );
```

```
101
102        //AcceptAndProcessMatrix( matrix_1 );
           // generates an error - "attempting to reference a deleted function"
103        AcceptAndProcessMatrix( move( matrix_1 ) );       // we need to use move semantics
104


105        assert( matrix_1 == false );             // no object, only an empty unique_ptr
106
107        AcceptAndProcessMatrix( OrphanRandomMatrix( 20, 20 ) );
           // we can also make and pass a temporary object
108
109    }
```

Note that before accessing held objects, we always need to make sure the smart pointer is not empty. This is the same strategy used with ordinary pointers (Section 3.12). Also notice that taking over an object with a called function should be used with care since after its execution, the smart pointer will be empty, as on line [95] of Listing 5.2.

Finally, let's analyze two ways of calling the AcceptAndProcessMatrix function, as shown on lines [103, 107] in Listing 5.2. In the first, we need to use the move helper again to take over an object from matrix_1. But in the second, a temporary unique_ptr< TMatrix > is created, which is then moved to the formal parameter of AcceptAndProcessMatrix by means of the move constructor.

5.3.1.2 Factory Method Design Pattern
Listing 5.3 shows how to create a simple version of the *factory method design pattern,* also known as a *virtual constructor* (Gamma et al. 1994). This is a software component (a class or a function) that, given a class ID, creates and returns a related object. Usually, the factory works for a (larger) hierarchy of related classes, as in the example code.

Listing 5.3 Implementation of the factory method design pattern using smart pointers (in *CppBookCode. SmartPointers.cpp*).

```
1    // Pure virtual base class
2    class B
3    {
4    public:
5       virtual ~B() {}
6
7       virtual void operator() ( void ) = 0;
8    };
9
10   // Derived classes
11   class C : public B
12   {
13   public:
14      virtual ~C()
15      {
16         cout << "C is deleted" << endl;
17      }
18
19      // It is also virtual but override is enough to express this (skip virtual)
20      void operator() ( void ) override
21      {
```

```
22          cout << "C is doing an action..." << endl;
23      }
24  };
25
26  class D : public B
27  {
28  public:
29      virtual ~D()
30      {
31          cout << "D is deleted" << endl;
32      }
33
34      void operator() ( void ) override
35      {
36          cout << "D is doing an action..." << endl;
37      }
38  };
39
40  class E : public B
41  {
42  public:
43      virtual ~E()
44      {
45          cout << "E is deleted" << endl;
46      }
47
48      void operator() ( void ) override
49      {
50          cout << "E is doing an action..." << endl;
51      }
52  };
```

More on this class hierarchy and overloaded functional `operator ()` with the `override` specifier will be presented in Section 6.1. In this section, we concentrate on object management. In this respect, a factory function is designed to operate on a class *ID*, defined with the scoped enumerated type `EClassId` (Section 3.14.6). With this, each object type can be uniquely identified, as in the following code snippet:

```
53  enum class EClassId { kC, kD, kE };
54
55  auto Factory( EClassId id )
56  {
57      switch( id )
58      {
59          case EClassId::kC: return unique_ptr< B >( make_unique< C >() );
60          case EClassId::kD: return unique_ptr< B >( make_unique< D >() );
61          case EClassId::kE: return unique_ptr< B >( make_unique< E >() );
62
63          default: assert( false );   // should not be here
64      }
65
66      return unique_ptr< B >();       // can be empty, should not reach here
67  }
```

Thanks to the `auto` keyword, the compiler automatically infers the type of the return value (the same `unique_ptr< B >`). Here, only lines [59–61] return valid objects. Nevertheless, all function paths need to return a value, so an empty `unique_ptr` is left on line [66]. Finally, we can employ our factory in a short task, as follows:

```
68   void FactoryTest ( void )
69   {
70      vector< unique_ptr< B > > theObjects;      // a vector containing smart pointers!
71
72      theObjects.push_back( Factory( EClassId::kC ) );      // copy or move semantics? move
73
74      theObjects.emplace_back( Factory( EClassId::kD ) );      // this will use move, ok
75
76      theObjects.emplace_back( Factory( EClassId::kE ) );
77
78      theObjects[ theObjects.size() - 1 ] = Factory( EClassId::kD );
         // replace (move) E with D
79
80      for( auto & a : theObjects )
81         ( * a )();            // call actions via the virtual mechanism
82   }
```

A nice thing about `unique_ptr`s is that they can be stored in SL collections, such as the `vector` on line [70]. Since `unique_ptr` cannot be copied, the compiler has to invoke a move version of `push_back` on line [72]. An even better alternative is the direct construction of a `unique_ptr` object "in place," which is accomplished by calling `emplace_back` on lines [74, 76] (Cppreference. com 2018). After exiting, we see the following messages:

```
E is deleted
C is doing an action...
D is doing an action...
D is doing an action...
C is deleted
D is deleted
D is deleted
```

Object E was immediately deleted as a result of the replacement with object D on line [78]. Then actions were invoked on all objects in the collection. Finally, the vector `theObjects`, which is an automatic variable in this context, was destroyed along with its elements. This entailed executing the destructors of the factory objects. An extended version of this project will be presented in Section 6.1.

Because of its behavior, the factory method is sometimes referred to as a *virtual constructor* (Gamma et al. 1994), although in C++, constructors cannot be declared virtual (Section 4.11). Virtual functions also cannot be called from within a constructor.

5.3.1.3 Custom deleter for `unique_ptr`

As mentioned earlier, `unique_ptr` can be endowed with a custom `delete` function. Although we do not often write our own deleter, this is also an occasion to see some interesting constructions, which we will explain.

```
83   // Define a custom delete for AClass - a lambda function
84   auto AClass_delete_fun = [] ( AClass * ac_ptr )
85   {
86      // Print to the log ...
```

```
87      delete ac_ptr;
88   };
89
90   // ...
91   unique_ptr< AClass, decltype( AClass_delete_fun ) >
                 p_d_8( new AClass(), AClass_delete_fun );
```

A custom deleter can be a function or a functor, i.e. a class with an overloaded function operator (Section 6.1). Lines [84–88] of the previous code snippet define the `AClass_delete_fun` lambda function (Section 3.14.6). Note that in this context, we need a semicolon after the lambda function definition. Remember that when adding our own deleter, we take over all actions associated with object disposal. That is, the rest of `unique_ptr` will do nothing. Therefore, `AClass_delete_fun` has to call `delete` on the provided pointer, as it does on line [87]. But before or after doing that task, it can e.g. write to a log file or perform another action, as discussed in the next example. The custom deleter for `unique_ptr` needs to be added to `unique_ptr`'s template parameters, just after the class name of the object to be held. To infer the type of the function on line [91], we use the `decltype` keyword (Section 3.7). Then, in the constructor, since `make_unique` cannot be used with custom deleter, we need to provide a pointer to the object and a custom deleter.

In the second example, rather than deleting a pointer, we use a custom deleter to automatically invoke the `close` function on an opened file. We start with the type definition on lines [1–2]. To provide a function pointer to the second type argument of the `unique_ptr` template, the `std::function` is used (Section 3.14.9).

```
1   template< typename P >
2   using unique_ptr_with_deleter = unique_ptr< P, function< void( P * ) > >;
3
4   // Define a custom delete for FILE - a lambda function
5   auto file_close_fun = [] ( FILE * f) { fclose( f ); };
6
7
8   // ...
9   unique_ptr_with_deleter< FILE > file( fopen( "myFile.txt", "r" ), file_close_fun );
```

The lambda function that closes a `FILE` object[1] through the provided pointer is defined on line [5]. Then, a `unique_ptr` with this custom function is defined on line [9]. It creates and opens a file object from the disk file *myFile.txt* in read mode (`"r"`) and serves as a smart pointer to that object. When the file smart pointer is automatically disposed of, `file_close_fun` is also automatically called, which in turn closes the file object. On the other hand, the default (and also custom) deleter is called only if a held pointer is not `nullptr`. Hence, if a file has not been opened, `fclose` will not be called at all.

Remember that a custom deleter adds to the `unique_ptr` type. Hence, two `unique_ptrs` to the same object type but with different deleters are considered different types.[2]

---

1 FILE is a C-style type that identifies a file stream and contains its control information. We show it here as an example of porting code. In C++, a preferable way of using file streams is with the filesystem library (Section 6.2.7).
2 More on smart pointers with custom deleters and cloning operations can be found in Jonathan Boccara, "Expressive code with C++ smart pointers," Fluent{C++}, *www.fluentcpp.com/2018/12/25/free-ebook-smart-pointers*.

5.3.1.4 Constructions to Avoid When Using `unique_ptr`

Finally, let's discuss a few things to be aware of when using `unique_ptr`. When defining `unique_ptr`, we can use `auto` to automatically infer types and to avoid typing. But this is possible only when using `make_unique`, as shown here:

```
1   // AClass object on the heap, p_d takes care
2   auto p_d_0( new AClass( "No ..." ) );      // oops, an ordinary pointer
3
4   delete p_d_0;                    // get rid of it
```

If we forget about `make_unique` and leave only `auto`, then an ordinary pointer is generated, as on line [2]. It will not be guarded by a `unique_ptr`, so it must be explicitly destroyed, as on line [4]. On the other hand, a `unique_ptr` can be created directly by a return of the `new` operator or as mentioned with `make_unique`:

```
1   // AClass object on the heap, p_d takes care
2   auto p_d_0( make_unique< AClass >( "Yes" ) );
```

We should also be very careful not to create a `unique_ptr` from an ordinary pointer since it is possible to create more than one `unique_ptr` holding a link to a single object. Inevitably this will cause a program error when we try to call `delete` more than once on the same memory location.

```
1   AClass * p_d_5 = new AClass;
2
3   unique_ptr< AClass > p_d_6( p_d_5 );       // do not initialize via ord pointer
4
5   // ...
6   // somewhere else ...
7   unique_ptr< AClass > p_d_7( p_d_5 );       // wrong, two unique_ptr to one object
```

Finally, we must avoid creating a `unique_ptr` on the heap with the `new` operator. For some reason, in the SL, the `new` operator was not forbidden for `unique_ptr`.

5.3.2 (�) More on `shared_ptr` and `weak_ptr`

In this section, we show how to use the `shared_ptr` and `weak_ptr` smart pointers when creating a doubly connected list, as shown in Figure 5.1. `shared_ptr` cannot be used in two directions because such a construction would make the two objects dependent on each other. In effect, both objects cannot be deleted, which will result in a memory leak despite using smart pointers. To overcome such mutual dependencies, the `weak_ptr` comes to play. In our example in Listing 5.4, a backward connection is created by using `weak_ptr`. Let's analyze the code: it consists mainly of the N class, which defines a single node, and a function showing the process of creating and using a list.

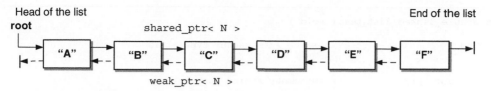

Figure 5.1 A double-linked list needs two different types of pointers to avoid circular responsibility. Forward links are realized with `shared_ptr` and backward links with `weak_ptr`.

Listing 5.4 Implementation of a doubly linked list using the `shared_ptr` and `weak_ptr` smart pointers (in *CppBookCode. SmartPointers.cpp*).

```
1    class N
2    {
3        string fStr; // on-board data
4    public:
5        const string & GetStr( void ) const { return fStr; }
6        void SetStr( const string & s ) { fStr = s; }
7
8    private:
9        shared_ptr< N >    fNext;        // forward reference
10       weak_ptr< N >      fPrev;        // back reference
11
12   public:
13       void SetNext( shared_ptr< N > s ) { fNext = s; }
14       shared_ptr< N > GetNext( void ) const { return fNext; }
15   public:
16       // Default/parametric constructor
17       N( const string & s = "", const shared_ptr< N > & prev = nullptr )
18           : fStr( s ), fPrev( prev ) {}
19       ~N() { cout << "Killing node " << fStr << endl; }
20
21   public:
22       // Adds 3 texts ... <-> [i-1] <-> [i] <-> [i+1] <-> ...
23       string operator() ( void )
24       {
25           string outStr;
26
27           // fPrev is a weak_ptr - first check if a valid pointer
28           if( fPrev.expired() == false ) outStr += fPrev.lock()->GetStr();
29           outStr += fStr;
30           // fNext is a shared ptr - also check if a valid pointer
31           if( fNext ) outStr += fNext->GetStr();
32
33           return outStr;
34       }
35   };
```

The N class implements a node class that stores a `string` and that can make forward and backward connections. The forward connection is realized by the `shared_ptr` fNext, defined on line [9]. This also ensures the proper destruction of the subsequent objects. There is also a backward connection to the preceding object, obtained via the fPrev link, which is a `weak_ptr` [10]. As a result, access in both directions is possible, but object dependency is only in the forward direction, so we avoid a circle. The functional operator defined on lines [23–34] simply returns the concatenation of text from the preceding node, its own text, and text from the successor node. Naturally, a node may not have a predecessor or successor, so each access needs to be carefully checked as on lines [28, 31]. Having defined a node, let's see how to construct and use a list like the one in Figure 5.1.

```
36   void double_linked_list_test( void )
37   {
38      using SP_N = shared_ptr< N >;      // a useful type alias
39
40
41      SP_N root, pr;              // two empty shared ptrs
42
43      // ---------------
44      // Create the list
45      for( const auto & s : { "A", "B", "C", "D", "E", "F" } )
46      {
47         if( pr == false )
48         {
49            root = pr = make_shared< N >( s );      // the first node
50         }
51         else
52         {
53            // Make a new node, and connect to the previous node in the list
54            pr->SetNext( make_shared< N >( s, pr ) );
55            pr = pr->GetNext();   // advance pr on to the end of the list
56         }
57      }
58
59      // ----------------------------------------------------------------
60      // Ok, the list is ready, so traverse the list and call operator()
61      // To check if pointing at a valid object, implicitly use operator bool ()
62      //                  v
63      for( SP_N p = root; p; p = p->GetNext() )
64         cout << ( * p )() << endl;
65   }
```

The list is created based on an initializer list provided in the `for` loop on line [45]. Then we have two possibilities: either we are adding the very first node, in which case line [49] is executed; or we are adding new nodes to an existing list, on lines [54–55]. Going into detail, first a new node is created, which is identified by a shared pointer. This is used to initialize the `fNext` pointer of the current object at the end of the list. Then, we move the end of the list to the just-created object. After the list is ready, the string-composing function is called from each node in the list, as on lines [63–64]. The whole list is traversed, and at each node, the previous, current, and next nodes are accessed to concatenate their strings. A node may be at one end of the list, so each time we access a node, we need to check whether the pointers are pointing at valid objects. The output of our function looks as follows:

```
AB
ABC
BCD
CDE
DEF
EF
Killing node A
Killing node B
Killing node C
Killing node D
Killing node E
Killing node F
```

Notice that the borderline nodes produce shortened output. After the list is processed, the objects are *automatically* deleted thanks to the shared pointers, in the order in which were created, from A to F.

Finally, note that the SL offers the `std::list` class, which implements the list data structure. Therefore, if we need the standard list functionality, we can use a ready and verified solution instead of writing our own code. The `std::list` class will be used and presented in Section 6.1.

5.4 Summary

Things to Remember

- In general, do not use low-level memory management with `new` and `delete`. Instead, use the SL containers (e.g. `vector`, `array`) and/or smart pointers
- If you are not sure which smart pointer to use, think first of using the `unique_ptr`
- Use `make_unique` functions to create `unique_ptrs`
- When changing old code, try to refactor all calls to `new` into smart pointers. In addition, try to refactor all calls to `auto_ptr` into calls to modern smart pointers (`unique_ptr` should be the first candidate)
- Do not make things more complicated than they should be – if all you need is a general-purpose buffer on the heap, then use a `vector` instead of a smart pointer

Questions and Exercises

1. Explain the main idea behind using smart pointers.

2. Explain the main differences between `unique_ptr` and `smart_ptr`.

3. A *ternary tree* is a data structure in which each node can have up to three children (*https://en.wikipedia.org/wiki/Ternary_tree*). Such structures are used, for example, for spell-checking. In such a case, the node also contains a one-letter data member. Implement a ternary tree composed of objects like the N class in Listing 5.4. Each node should have `unique_ptr` members to link to its three children.

4. In the following code snippet, identify the object dependency arising on line [25]:

```
1   #include <iostream>
2   #include <memory>
3
4   // Cyclic dependence problem
5
6   struct Bar;
7
8   struct Foo
9   {
10      std::shared_ptr< Bar > bar;
11      ~Foo() { std::cout << "~Foo()\n"; }
12  };
13
14  struct Bar
```

```
15  {
16      std::shared_ptr< Foo > foo; // ...
17      ~Bar() { std::cout << "~Bar()\n"; }
18  };
19
20  void CyclicPointersProblem_Test( void )
21  {
22      auto foo = make_shared< Foo >();
23      foo->bar = make_shared< Bar >();
24
25      foo->bar->foo = foo;        // oops, a circle ...
26  }
```

Remove the circular dependency between the objects. Hint: change the type of the smart pointer on line [16].

5. Design and implement a simple memory-allocation method for an embedded system. For safety reasons, a single statically allocated memory block can be used from which all partitions resulting from memory requests are created. Hint: read about and then implement the buddy algorithm (*https://en.wikipedia.org/wiki/Buddy_memory_allocation*).

6. Design and implement a class to represent a submatrix (*https://en.wikipedia.org/wiki/Matrix_(mathematics)*) in a matrix object using the proxy pattern, presented in Section 4.15.5. The proxy has no data of its own but operates on the data of its associated matrix. But it defines its own local coordinate system and behaves like any other matrix. Hint: after making some modifications to the EMatrix class in Listing 4.7, derive a proxy class to represent submatrices. Such a proxy should not allocate its own data but should be constructed with a reference to its associated matrix. Accessing an element in the submatrix should result in the data coordinates being transformed to the coordinate system of the associated matrix.

6

Advanced Object-Oriented Programming

You are ready to learn about more methods and techniques of object-oriented programming in C++. Congratulations! In this chapter, we will present programming topics such as processing regular expressions, implementing state machines, building our own libraries, the filesystem, system clock and time measurement, ranges and functional programming, expression parsing, syntax trees, and the composite and interpreter design patterns, all complete with code examples.

6.1 Functional Objects

We have already implemented many classes and created many objects. Usually, these have been related to real objects expressed with nouns, such as TQuadEq or TLongNumber. However, objects can also represent actions expressed with verbs, such as *do_this* or *compare_that*. In such cases, the central part of the object is a function: do_this or compare_that. Sometimes these are accompanied by data. Although not obligatory, if the main goal of a class is *to represent a particular action or a function*, this is usually implemented using the overloaded functional operator (). Objects of such classes are called *functional objects* or *functors*. A call to such an overloaded operator () resembles a call to a simple function, as mentioned in Section 3.14.9. In this section, we will investigate an interrupt-like component to handle various actions that are invoked in response to different external events. Such a component may be a part of an embedded system or, with minor modifications, can serve as a menu-handling module, for instance.

Figure 6.1 shows an event array with attached lists of handlers, performing various actions on an event. The actions are in the form of user-derived classes from the THandler base class with the overloaded virtual operator (). Actions for each event, such as a system interrupt, are arranged as dynamic lists. That is, actions can be added to and also removed from the lists.

Listing 6.1 presents code implementing the event system shown in Figure 6.1. All the definitions are enclosed inside the EventSystem namespace. The THandler class, whose the definition starts on line [6], constitutes the base class for all actions in the system. Not surprisingly, actions are implemented by overloading functional operators in the classes derived from THandler. For this purpose, on line [16], THandler defines the overloaded operator () as a pure virtual function, which is indicated with the = 0 suffix (Section 5.3.1.2). This also means THandler is intended only to be a base class that defines *an abstraction* for the entire hierarchy (here, this is an abstraction of calls). As we already know, the base class's destructors should also be defined virtual. In THandler, this is achieved on line [11]. But interestingly enough, ~THandler is

Introduction to Programming with C++ for Engineers, First Edition. Bogusław Cyganek.
© 2021 John Wiley & Sons Ltd. Published 2021 by John Wiley & Sons Ltd.
Companion website: http://home.agh.edu.pl/~cyganek/BookCpp.htm

not only virtual but a pure virtual function, containing a full body implementation on line [12]. This is sometimes useful – and thanks to this, we will be able to trace calls to the THandler destructor.

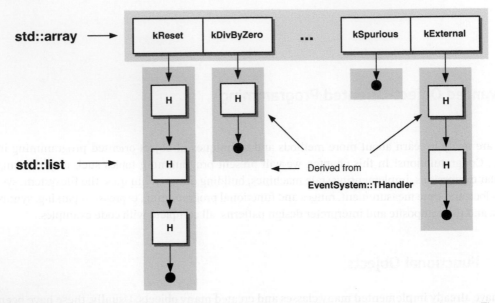

Figure 6.1 An array of lists of handlers with various actions invoked in response to external events. The actions can be user-defined by inheriting from the THandler base class. Such action handlers can then be attached to or detached from the lists of actions associated with each event in the system. There can be empty lists as well.

Listing 6.1 Definition of the EventSystem namespace with classes realizing the system shown in Figure 6.1 (in *CppBookCode, EventSystems.cpp*).

```
1   namespace EventSystem
2   {
3
4       // Base class defining an ACTION
5       // Also can be chained in a list
6       class THandler
7       {
8
9       public:
10
11          virtual ~THandler() = 0              // virtual for proper inheritance
12          { std::cout << "~H()" << std::endl; } // Pure virtual can have a body
13
14          // Main action function ==> functional object
15          // Pure virtual to define INTERFACE for derived classes
16          virtual void operator () ( void ) = 0;
17      };
```

Let's take a closer look at the syntax of the functional operator and its calls. Figure 6.2a shows the syntax of the definition of the functional operator. The syntax of its call is shown in Figure 6.2b, whereas Figure 6.2c shows a call with the explicit operator keyword.

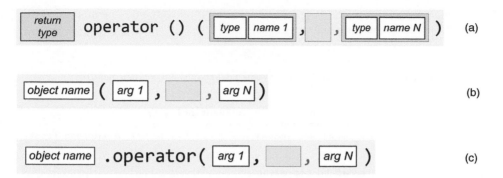

Figure 6.2 (a) Syntax of the definition of an overloaded functional operator. (b) Short syntax for calling a functional operator from an object. (c) A qualified call to the functional operator.

Continuing in the EventSystem namespace, on line [18], the definition of TEventHandlers begins. Using the scoped enum class EEvent, on line [22], example events are defined (these can represent exceptions, main menus, etc.). Note that kSentinel is not an event name but the last value (a sentinel) in this enum. Then, the HandlerList and EventVector data structures are defined with familiar Standard Library (SL) containers [25–29]. HandlerList stores smart pointers to objects to facilitate managing their lifetime.

The fEventVector object, defined on line [32], will store the lists of handlers. This object is used by the AttachHandler_4_Event function, defined on line [36], to attach a new_ handler to the event_to_attach event. Note that new_handler is passed by value since its held object will be moved by a call to the emplace_back member on line [41]. This means after we exit AttachHandler_4_Event, whatever object was passed as new_handler will be empty.

Next is a series of three definitions for the overloaded virtual void operator (). The first, defined on line [45], takes a reference list_of_handlers to HandlerList as its parameter and calls operator () on each of the handler objects that HandlerList contains. That is, on line [48], first an object is dereferenced with the * operator from the smart pointer, and then its operator () is invoked.

operator () on line [51] does the same thing but provides an identifier for an event. Note that the qualified call on line [54] is to operator () from line [45], as illustrated in Figure 6.2c.

Finally, the third operator (), defined on line [58], traverses all of the events on line [60] and, for each list associated with that event, calls all of the registered handlers. Line [61] calls operator () from line [45], but this time using the this pointer.

```
18    class TEventHandlers
19    {
20      public:
21
22        enum class EEvent { kReset, kDivByZero, kExternal, kSpurious, kSentinel };
23
24        using TH_UP         = std::unique_ptr< THandler >;
25        using HandlerList   = std::list< TH_UP >;
26
27        // An array that contains lists of THandler-like objects
28        using EventVector =
29            std::array< HandlerList, static_cast< int >( EEvent::kSentinel ) >;
30      private:
```

```
31
32        EventVector       fEventVector;
33
34    public:
35
36        void AttachHandler_4_Event ( EEvent event_to_attach, TH_UP new_handler )
37        {
38            assert (   static_cast< int >( event_to_attach ) <
39                       static_cast< int >( EEvent::kSentinel ) );
40            fEventVector[ static_cast< int >( event_to_attach ) ].
41                       emplace_back ( std::move ( new_handler ) );  // or emplace_front
42        }
43
44        // Run handlers attached to the event
45        virtual void operator () ( const HandlerList & list_of_handlers )
46        {
47            for ( const auto & handler : list_of_handlers )
48                ( * handler )(); // call a function operator via a pointer to handler
49        }
50
51        virtual void operator () ( EEvent event )
52        {
53            // One way to call a functional operator
54            operator () ( fEventVector[ static_cast< int >( event ) ] );
55        }
56
57        // Run all
58        virtual void operator () ( void )
59        {
60           for ( const auto & list : fEventVector )
61               ( * this ) ( list );   // Call operator () ( EEvent event )
62        }
63
64    };
```

Let's now test this code in the `EventHandlers_Test` function, whose definition begins on line [65]. First, the `theHandlerBoard` object is created on line [68]. Then, two local handler classes `HA` and `HB`, both derived from `THandler`, are defined on lines [74, 90]. Their structure is straightforward: `HA` prints its passed text, while `HB` converts its passed integer from decimal to hex. What is interesting is the way these text and integer objects are passed to `HA` and `HB`. Since virtual functions must have the same list of input parameters, it is not possible to change them from class to class. Therefore, additional parameters, if necessary, must be passed through the constructors to the classes. With this technique, we can overcome the limitations associated with passing parameters to virtual functions.

Also note that in both classes, the overloaded `operator ()` functions have the additional `override` suffix. This relatively new feature of C++ that we saw in Section 4.11 lets us ensure that `operator ()` overrides the `operator ()` from the base `THandler` class. If, for instance, their formats do not match, then the compiler reports an error (which is easy to see after changing `void` to, for instance, `int`). Hence, this optional `override` specifier lets us protect against such inconsistency-related errors.

```
65    void EventHandlers_Test ( void )
66    {
67
68        TEventHandlers      theHandlerBoard;
69
```

```
70
71      // --------------------
72      // Create a few handlers
73
74      class HA : public THandler
75      {
76          std::string fStr;
77
78      public:
79
80          HA( std::string s = "" ) : fStr( s ) {}
81          virtual ~HA() { std::cout << "~HA()" << std::endl; }
82
83          void operator () ( void ) override
84          {
85              std::cout << "I'm HA with text: " << fStr << std::endl;
86          }
87      };
88
89      // --------------------
90      class HB : public THandler
91      {
92          int    fVal;
93
94      public:
95
96          HB( int v = 0 ) : fVal( v ) {}
97          virtual ~HB() { std::cout << "~HB()" << std::endl; }
98
99          void operator () ( void ) override
100         {
101             std::cout    << "I'm HB. " << std::dec << fVal << " = "
102                          << std::hex << fVal << std::endl;
103         }
104     };
105     // --------------------
106
```

On line [107], the ha object is created with a text argument. Then, on line [108], its functional operator is invoked. Note that line [108] looks exactly like any other call to a function with no arguments. Hence, its name – a functional object.

A temporary HB object (no name) is created and immediately invoked on line [110]. Soon we will see the results of this call.

Then, on lines [116–126], two groups of handler lists are created for the kReset and kExternal events. Each handler object is first created by a call to the std::make_unique function, providing suitable construction parameters, and then immediately passed as an argument to the AttachHandler_4_Event function for the chosen event.

Finally, all actions from the handlers are invoked on line [129] by calling operator () with no arguments.

```
107     HA ha( "Standalone HA" );
108     ha();                   // Call the function operator on object ha
109
110     ( HB( 789 ) )();        // Call the function operator on a temporary object HB
111
```

```
112        std::cout << std::endl;
113
114        // Now attach no matter how many handlers to the available event slots
115
116        theHandlerBoard.AttachHandler_4_Event( TEventHandlers::EEvent::kReset,
117                            std::make_unique< HA >( "Reset 0" ) );
118        theHandlerBoard.AttachHandler_4_Event( TEventHandlers::EEvent::kReset,
119                            std::make_unique< HB >( 123 ) );
120        theHandlerBoard.AttachHandler_4_Event( TEventHandlers::EEvent::kReset,
121                            std::make_unique< HA >( "Reset 1" ) );
122
123        theHandlerBoard.AttachHandler_4_Event( TEventHandlers::EEvent::kExternal,
124                            std::make_unique< HB >( 100 ) );
125        theHandlerBoard.AttachHandler_4_Event( TEventHandlers::EEvent::kExternal,
126                            std::make_unique< HB >( 200 ) );
127
128
129        theHandlerBoard();     // Run all
130
131    }
132
133  }
```

Let's now examine the output obtained after building and running the previous code:

```
I'm HA with text: Standalone HA
I'm HB: 789 = 315
~HB()
~H()

I'm HA with text: Reset 0
I'm HB: 123 = 7b
I'm HA with text: Reset 1
I'm HB: 100 = 64
I'm HB: 200 = c8
~HA()
~H()
~HB()
~H()
~HB()
~H()
~HA()
~H()
~HB()
~H()
~HA()
~H()
```

The handlers' actions are as expected. However, it is interesting to observe the order and type of the called destructors. These are automatically invoked due to the operation of the TH_UP smart pointers (Section 5.3). Notice that for each object, first its destructor and then its base class destructor are called, in that order. Hence, for each of the deleted objects, we register two calls to the destructors. The temporary object HB, created on line [110], is destroyed after exiting this line, rather than waiting until the end of the test function.

Finally, notice that THandler realizes what is called a *command design pattern* (an action or transaction pattern). Usually it cooperates with such patterns as the factory pattern (Section 5.3.1.2) and composite pattern (Section 6.6.4).

6.2 Example Project – Extending the Currency Search in XML Files, and Using State Machine and Regular Expressions with the regex Library

In Section 3.18, we saw that the TCurrencyExchanger class can store a number of currencies represented by TCurrency objects. It lets us add new currencies to the repository, as well as drive them in and out to any stream, such as the keyboard and screen or a file. However, entering them by hand would be very tedious. Also, currency exchange ratios tend to change quite often, so we need an automatic mechanism for loading their current values. This can be done by downloading a web page or a file containing all the necessary information. Example content of such a file containing currency data, encoded in the Extensible Markup Language (XML) format (see *www.w3.org/XML* and *https://en.wikipedia.org/wiki/XML*) can look like Figure 6.3 (downloaded from *www.nbp.pl*).

This XML file, although readable, looks quite noisy, partly because most of the words are in Polish. But we can easily spot interesting information placed on consecutive lines in specific XML tags. Because we will be processing general text, rather than std::string, for the correct representation, we need to use std::wstring, which is able to store Unicode characters. However, the main question at this stage is how to find and select interesting information in the XML file. We can do so using the *regular expression search and match (regex)* package, which is now part of the set of C++ libraries.

```
<?xml version="1.0" encoding="ISO-8859-2"?>
<tabela_kursow typ="C" uid="18c190">
    <numer_tabeli>190/C/NBP/2018</numer_tabeli>
    <data_notowania>2018-09-28</data_notowania>
    <data_publikacji>2018-10-01</data_publikacji>
    <pozycja>
        <nazwa_waluty>dolar amerykański</nazwa_waluty>
        <przelicznik>1</przelicznik>
        <kod_waluty>USD</kod_waluty>
        <kurs_kupna>3,6535</kurs_kupna>
        <kurs_sprzedazy>3,7273</kurs_sprzedazy>
    </pozycja>
    <pozycja>
        <nazwa_waluty>dolar australijski</nazwa_waluty>
        <przelicznik>1</przelicznik>
        <kod_waluty>AUD</kod_waluty>
        <kurs_kupna>2,6383</kurs_kupna>
        <kurs_sprzedazy>2,6915</kurs_sprzedazy>
    </pozycja>
</tabela_kursow>
```

Figure 6.3 An example XML file from the National Bank of Poland, containing information about currency buying and selling ratios for various world currencies. All information about a single currency is contained in few consecutive lines, starting and ending with special tags as outlined in the red box. Due to international characters, processing should be done with wide strings.

6.2.1 Pattern Matching with the Regular Expression Library

Regular expressions are used to specify text patterns: for example, to search for a specific phrase or a file name. These are used, for instance, in the `grep` Linux command (Dalheimer and Welsh 2006). C++ contains a rich *regex* library that allows for text pattern matching with regular expressions. To start, we present handy definitions of the most frequently used *regex* symbols and rules, with suitable examples. These operate with the default ECMA script *regex* syntax, although other variants, such as Linux `grep`, are also possible after setting the correct flag.

Returning to our project, let's create regular expressions that match the tag-delimited lines with information about currency. The first line includes a currency name, possibly containing international letters as well as whitespace, enclosed between `<nazwa_waluty>` and `</nazwa_waluty>` tags as follows:

```
<nazwa_waluty>dolar amerykański</nazwa_waluty>
```

To easily find a corresponding regular expression, it is useful to split the pattern into parts:

`<nazwa_waluty>`	`dolar amerykański`	`</nazwa_waluty>`

This is matched by the following regular expression

```
<nazwa_waluty>(.+)</nazwa_waluty>
```

The leftmost part will exactly match the series of letters `<nazwa_waluty>`. Then, the expression `(.+)`, which contains special characters from Tables 6.1 and 6.2, matches any character (denoted with a dot `.`) repeated one or more times (denoted by the `+` symbol). This is enclosed in parentheses `()` to group all matched characters, since after a match, we wish to read them together as a currency name. Finally, `</nazwa_waluty>` literally matches the end tag for this entry. Taken all together, the `<kod_waluty>USD</kod_waluty>` pattern should be matched.

A little bit more demanding is the pattern for the selling rate (i.e. "kurs kupna"):

```
<kurs_kupna>3,6535</kurs_kupna>
```

We would like to see it in the following form

`<kurs_kupna>`	`3`	`,`	`6535`	`</kurs_kupna>`

since in this case, we also want to replace the comma (`,`), used in Poland to separate the integer from the fraction part of a number, with a dot (`.`) for easier conversion from a string to a value. A possible regular expression for this task may look like the following:

```
<kurs_kupna>([[:d:]]+),([[:d:]]+)</kurs_kupna>
```

Here, the `[[:d:]]+` pattern matches any digit repeated one or more times.

Table 6.1 Special characters and groupings of regular expressions (default ECMA standard).

Symbol	Matches	Examples
.	Any character (a wildcard)	`.+`
*	0 or more occurrences of a character	Matches any stream of one or more characters.
+	1 or more occurrences of a character	`0001010102001100`
?	0 or 1 occurrence of a character	`^.*$`
	After any of the repetition notations forces the shortest match (otherwise the longest one is sought)	Matches a whole line: `^` for begin and `$` for end of line. `0001010102001100`
|	Alternative (or)	
^	1) Start of line or 2) negation	`(01)+`
$	End of line	Greedy search – finds the longest match of repeated `01`. `0001010102001100`
\	Next character has special meaning	
[ ]	Defines a character set	`(01)+?`
{ }	Begin-end count { *p* } – *p* times { *p*, } – *p* or more times { *p*, *q* } – *p* to *q* times including	Lazy search – finds the shortest case of `01`. `0001010102001100` `[01]+` Finds the longest string of 0 *or* 1 with at least one char.
( )	Begin-end grouping	`0001010102001100`

\1 \2 \3	Group numbering (starts from 1)	`[^01]+?`
		Finds the shortest substring of *not* 0 and *not* 1. `0001010102001100`
		
		`(123){2}(45){3}`
		With {2}, the pattern 123 will be repeated exactly 2 times, then 45 has to be matched exactly 3 times, etc. `123123123123454545454545`
		
		`<(.+)>(.+)</\1>`
		Matches any XML tag. \1 denotes the first grouping. `<city>New York</city>`

Table 6.2 Frequently used regular expression character sets (ECMA).

Char set	Abbreviation	Matches	Examples
`[:alnum:]`		Any alphanumeric character	`([[:alnum:]._]+)@([[:alnum:]._]+)\.([[:alnum:]]+)` Matches an e-mail address. `\.` matches exactly a dot, not "any" character. `([[:alnum:]._]+)` denotes a grouping which in the e-mail address

(Continued)

Table 6.2 (continued)

Char set	Abbreviation	Matches	Examples
`[:alpha:]`		Any alphabetic character	`jan.koczwara_12@agh.edu.pl` matches as follows: `jan.koczwara_12@agh.edu.pl` `[:alnum:]` is a set of alphanumeric chars. `[[:alnum:]._]` denotes this set extended by a dot and an underscore. `[[:alnum:]._]+` matches any non-empty repetition of chars from this set.
`[:digit:]` `[:d:]`	`\d` `\D not \d`	Any decimal digit	Sometimes it is easier to define a complement, such as "not a digit" `\D`, as opposed to a digit `\d` `\D+(\d+)\D+`. The inner grouping matches digits as follows:
`[:lower:]`	`\l` `\L not \l`	Any lowercase character	`jan.koczwara_12@agh.edu.pl` `[[:alpha:]_][[:alnum:]_]*`
`[:space:]` `[:s:]`	`\s` `\S not \s`	Any whitespace character	Matches any C/C++ identifier. In the function call `normalize_L1( matrix );` it matches a function name: `normalize_L1( matrix );`
`[:upper:]`	`\u` `\U not \u`	Any uppercase character	`[[:w:]]+([[:upper:]]+)[[:w:]]+` Matches as follows: `normalize_L1( matrix );`
`[:cntrl:]`		Any control character	since `[[:w:]]+` matches `normalize_`, `([[:upper:]]+)` matches L (parentheses are not necessary here and are only for selection of this sub-match), and `[[:w:]]+` matches `1` (`(` does not belong to `[:w:]`.
`[:punct:]`		Any punctuation character	
`[:w:]`		Any word character (including underscore)	

6.2.2 State Machine Pattern

Each set of lines shown in the red box in Figure 6.3 presents information about a currency.

These lines are consistent and should be matched in order, one after the other. Thus, we need to write code that first matches a given line, then goes on to match the second line, and so on. This order of actions can be hardcoded with nested `if-else` statements. But a more versatile technique is to use a state machine approach. A *state machine* is a kind of a mathematical model that builds on states and transitions between them. Usually, special start and final states are also selected. Figure 6.4 depicts a *UML state diagram*, sometimes called an *automaton*, for consecutively matching all the lines with information about a currency. Actually, of the five lines in the red box in Figure 6.3, only four convey important information.

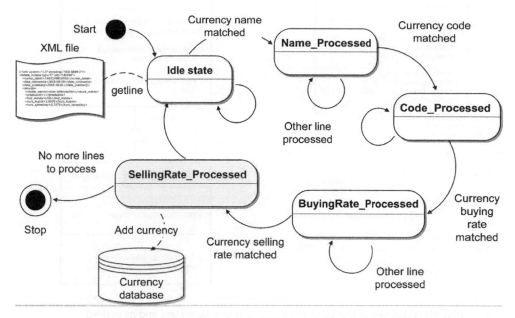

Figure 6.4 UML state diagram for retrieving currency information from an XML file. The system enters an idle state and processes one line after another.

6.2.3 Implementing the Extended Class

The previous ideas have been implemented in the XML_CurrencyExchanger class, which extends the TCurrencyExchanger base class explained in the previous section. Here we clearly see the benefits of object-oriented programming and inheritance. XML_CurrencyExchanger inherits all the functionality of the base class TCurrencyExchanger. All it needs to add is the FillCurrencyTableFrom virtual function, whose role is to fill the currency table from a specified XML file. A UML class diagram with the most important members and relations of these classes is shown in Figure 6.5. Since TCurrencyExchanger and its derived XML_CurrencyExchanger aggregate TCurrency objects, we use an arrow that starts with a diamond (see Table 4.4).

Let's now analyze the code shown in Listing 6.2, from the *XML_CurrencyExchanger.h* header file. Line [1] contains #pragma once to ensure that a given header file is included only once in a given translation unit. The other possibility is to #define a unique preprocessor constant and then check whether it has already been defined, as presented in Appendix A.1. On line [6], the *regex* is included; and on line [8], std::wgrex is introduced into the scope of this header. Then our CppBook namespace is opened between lines [13–65].

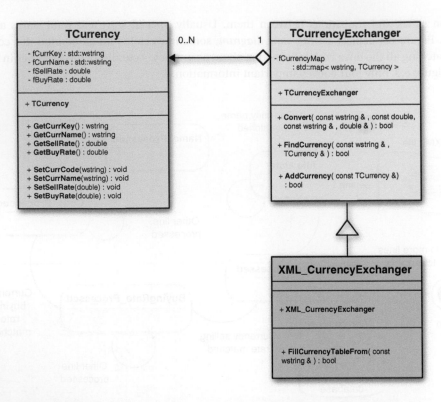

Figure 6.5 UML class diagram of the TCurrencyExchanger base class and its derived XML_CurrencyExchanger. TCurrencyExchanger aggregates objects of the TCurrency class, as indicated by an arrow with a diamond. Only the most important class members are shown.

Listing 6.2 Definition of the XML_CurrencyExchanger class (in *CurrencyCalc_Lib*, *XML_CurrencyExchanger.h*).

```cpp
1   #pragma once
2
3   #include "CurrencyExchanger.h"
4
5   #include <string>
6   #include <regex>
7
8   using std::wregex;
9
10
11
12
13  namespace CppBook
14  {
15
16
17
18  class XML_CurrencyExchanger : public TCurrencyExchanger
19  {
20
21    private:
22
```

```
23
24          // Simple state machine
25          enum class ESearchStates { kIdle, k_Name_Processed, k_Code_Processed,
                                    k_BuyingRate_Processed, k_SellingRate_Processed };
26
27      private:
28
29          // Let's define some patterns
30          // We use raw string formats here R"( )"
31          wregex f_curr_name_pat      { LR"(<nazwa_waluty>(.+)</nazwa_waluty>)" };
32          wregex f_curr_code_pat
33              { LR"(<kod_waluty>([[:upper:]][[:upper:]][[:upper:]])</kod_waluty>)" };
34          wregex f_buy_rate_pat
35              { LR"(<kurs_kupna>([[:d:]]+),([[:d:]]+)</kurs_kupna>)" };
36              // instead of 1.27, in Poland 1,27 is used (with comma)
37          wregex f_sell_rate_pat
38              { LR"(<kurs_sprzedazy>([[:d:]]+),([[:d:]]+)</kurs_sprzedazy>)" };
39
40      public:
41
42          // Allow other patterns
43          void set_curr_name_pat( const wregex & pat ) { f_curr_name_pat = pat; }
44          // ...
45
46      public:
47
48          ////////////////////////////////////////////////////////////
49          // Fills currency table
50          ////////////////////////////////////////////////////////////
51          //
52          // INPUT:
53          //      currencyFile - full path to the XML file
54          //      with currency entries
55          // OUTPUT:
56          //      true if ok, false otherwise
57          //
58          // REMARKS:
59          //
60          virtual bool  FillCurrencyTableFrom( const wstring & currencyFile );
61
62      };
63
64
65  }    // CppBook
```

The definition of the XML_CurrencyExchanger class extends from lines [18–62]. It is publicly inherited from the TCurrencyExchanger class, which was discussed in the previous section. On line [25], the ESearchStates scoped enum (class) is defined. It contains identifiers for states for our state machine, as will be shown.

Lines [31–37] define the four wregex regular expressions. Their operation should be clear at this point. The only thing we need to explain is the construction of the wide raw string literal (constant) using the

```
LR"( )"
```

construction, which can be a little surprising. Wide characters are identified with the L prefix here. Such a construction can contain characters that are not interpreted. Thus, for example, backslashes need not be preceded by backslashes, etc.

Finally, on line [60], the `FillCurrencyTableFrom` member function is introduced. It is declared virtual so that it can be overridden in derived classes, if necessary. The definition of this function is contained in the *XML_CurrencyExchanger.cpp* file, presented in Listing 6.3.

Listing 6.3 Definition of the `XML_CurrencyExchanger` class members (in *CurrencyCalc_Lib*, *XML_CurrencyExchanger.cpp*).

```cpp
1   #include "XML_CurrencyExchanger.h"
2   #include <fstream>
3
4
5
6   namespace CppBook
7   {
8
9
10  bool    XML_CurrencyExchanger::FillCurrencyTableFrom( const wstring & currencyFile )
11  {
12
13          wifstream    inFile( currencyFile );
14
15          if( ! inFile.is_open() )
16            return false;              // cannot open the input file
17
18
19          // Read line by line and look for patterns
20
21
22          ESearchStates    state = ESearchStates::kIdle;
23
24          // Stores currently processed line of the XML
25          wstring line;
26
27          // Stores current match and submatches of the regex
28          wsmatch    match_res;
29
30          // These will gather partial matches of the currency record
31          wstring curr_code, curr_name, buy_rate_str, sell_rate_str;
32
33          // Read params one-by-one
34          while( getline( inFile, line ) )
35          {
36
37            switch( state )
38            {
39               case ESearchStates::kIdle:
40
41                  if(regex_search(line,match_res,f_curr_name_pat)&&match_res.size()>1)
42                  {
43                    // Ok, a currency code was found; let's store it
44                    // require at least one subexpression
45                    curr_name = match_res[ 1 ];          // take the first sub-match
46
47                    // For easier processing, replace white characters
48                    replace( curr_name.begin(), curr_name.end(), L' ', L'-');
49
50                    state = ESearchStates::k_Name_Processed; // change the state
51                  }
52
53                  break;
```

```
54
55      case ESearchStates::k_Name_Processed:
56
57          if( regex_search(line,match_res,f_curr_code_pat) &&    match_res.size()>1)
58          {
59              // Ok, a currency code was found; let's store it
60              // require at least one subexpression
61              curr_code = match_res[ 1 ];    // take the first sub-match
62
63              state = ESearchStates::k_Code_Processed;    // change the state
64          }
65
66          break;
67
68      case ESearchStates::k_Code_Processed:
69
70          // Try to match the buying option
71          if( regex_search(line,match_res,f_buy_rate_pat) && match_res.size()>2)
72          {
73              // Ok, a currency code was found; let's store it
74              // require at least one subexpression
75              buy_rate_str = wstring( match_res[ 1 ] )
76                  + wstring( L"." )
77                  + wstring( match_res[ 2 ] );// assembly the sub-matches
78
79              state = ESearchStates::k_BuyingRate_Processed;    // change the state
80          }
81
82          break;
83
84      case ESearchStates::k_BuyingRate_Processed:
85
86          // Try to match the selling option
87          if( regex_search(line,match_res,f_sell_rate_pat) &&    match_res.size()>2)
88          {
89              // Ok, a currency code was found; let's store it
90              // require at least one subexpression
91              sell_rate_str = wstring( match_res[ 1 ] )
92                  + wstring( L"." )
93                  + wstring( match_res[ 2 ] );        // assembly the sub-matches
94
95              state = ESearchStates::k_SellingRate_Processed;  // change the state
96          }
97
98          break;
99
100     case ESearchStates::k_SellingRate_Processed:
101
102         // Ok, we are ready to insert the new currency record
103         try
104         {
105             // can throw an exception e.g. on an empty string, wrong format, etc.
106             AddCurrency( {   curr_code, curr_name,
107                             stod( buy_rate_str ), stod( sell_rate_str ) } );
108         }
109         catch( ... )
110         {
111             ;
112         }
113
114         state = ESearchStates::kIdle;    // enter the basic state
```

(Coninued)

Listing 6.3 (continued)

```
110
111          break;
112
113       default:
114          assert( false ); // shouldn't be here
115          break;
116     }
117
118
119   }
120
121
122   return true;
123 }
124
125
126 } // CppBook
```

On line [13] of the `FillCurrencyTableFrom` function, an `inFile` file is open with the supplied path. Note that in the domain of wide characters, all streams and containers should be set. This is done using a dual set of objects whose names start with the "w" prefix. For instance, instead of `string`, `wstring` is used on line [25] and `wsmatch` on line [28], etc. On line [31], `wstring` objects are defined, which will be used to store parts of the matched expression.

The main action consists of reading a line of wide characters, checking for potential patterns, and conditionally changing the states based on the matches. This is governed by the `while` loop, starting on line [34]. As long as there are unprocessed lines in `inFile`, the `getline` function copies a consecutive line into the `line` string and returns `true`. Inside the loop, the state machine operates.

One of the methods to implement a state machine of a fixed size, such as the one presented in Figure 6.4, is to use the `switch` statement (Section 3.13.2.1), which will switch between consecutive states until a final state is reached. The initial state, held in the state variable, is set to `ESearchStates::kIdle`. So, line [41] executes first, checking for a potential match of the `f_curr_name_pat` pattern. If this pattern is matched by the `regex_search` function operating on the current line, the state is changed to the next state, as shown in Figure 6.4. The `regex_search` function takes three arguments:

- The input stream of characters (a line object, in our example)
- Output results if a match found (`match_res`)
- Regular expression to be matched, of a `wregex` type

The results of a successful match are stored in the `match_res` object. It contains the entire matched pattern, as well as sub-matches arising from the groups defined in the regular expression. The structure of `match_res` is shown here:

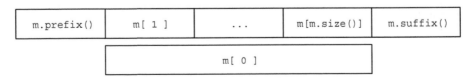

$m[0]$ is the entire matched pattern, $m[1]$ is the first subexpression, and `m.size()` denotes the number of subexpressions; `m.prefix()` and `m.suffix()` denote all characters in the input stream before or after the matched pattern, respectively.

Operation on substrings can be observed on line [75]. In this case, `buy_rate_str` is a concatenation of the first and second matched substrings: the integer and fraction parts of a number, joined with a dot instead of a comma as discussed earlier.

Once we enter the final state, `ESearchStates::k_SellingRate_Processed`, all of the information about the currency has been collected, and the currency object is ready to be added to the database of currencies. The new currency is added on line [102] using the `AddCurrency` function. Wide strings are converted to floating-point numerical values using the `std::stod` function. This is one of the very useful string-conversion functions shown in Table 3.5. Since string conversion can throw an exception, e.g. on an empty string, the wrong format, etc., adding a new currency is encompassed by the `try-catch` statement on line [104]. Finally, if a new currency object is added successfully, the state machine takes on the `ESearchStates::kIdle` state again on line [109], and the entire mechanism is ready to process data, searching for more currency entries in the input XML file.

A sibling function to `regex_search` is `regex_match`. The main difference is that `regex_match` tries to match the entire input to the pattern.

The C++ *regex* library has much more functionality than we have outlined here. More information can be found in the literature (Stroustrup 2013; Josuttis 2012) and on the Internet. For more complex state machine implementations, see the Meta State Machine (MSM; *www.boost.org/doc/libs/1_70_0/libs/msm/doc/HTML/index.html*) from the Boost C++ libraries (Boost.org 2020).

We will summarize what have we learned about in this section:

- Basics of the C++ *regex* library and regular expressions
- `regex_search` functions for regular expression searches and `regex_match` for matches
- Reading and processing XML files
- State machines and UML state diagrams

6.2.4 Project Extension – Loading Currency Information from the Internet

In the previous section, we saw how to find and load information about currencies from an XML file. However, it would be good to have an automatic mechanism for downloading such an XML file from a bank via an Internet connection. Such an operation is certainly possible with a call to a specific HTTP or FTP library. But a subtle problem is that these differ from system to system. So, if we stick to one platform, such as Windows or Linux, that's fine; but what if we wish to write multisystem software that will work equally well on Windows, Linux, Mac, or a mobile? We can imagine a solution that would conditionally compile various versions of the code, depending on the platform type detected at compile-time. A more flexible solution would be to create two software components: one that defines an unchanging interface used by all clients, and a second containing specific implementation suitable on a specific platform. Such a code structure, although it requires slightly more code, gives a very desirable separation of abstraction (i.e. a common calling framework) from implementation (i.e. all the code necessary to perform actions). Figure 6.6 shows a UML class diagram presenting the proposed solution.

Such decoupling of abstraction from implementation is known as the *handle-body* (or *bridge*) design pattern (Gamma et al. 1994).

The external call can be done exclusively to an object of the `HTTP_File_Handle` class through the exposed `Load_HTTP_File` function, whose role is to download a given file from a given web page. But the class does not know how to do this for all the possible OSs. For this purpose, it has an associated hierarchy of body classes that specialize in HTTP file downloads for specific systems. In a concrete system, a body class specialized for this system is created and maintained by

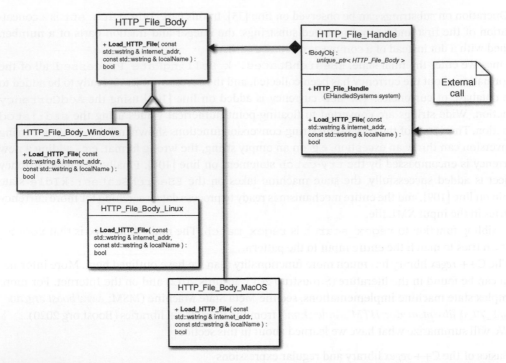

Figure 6.6 UML class diagram of the handle-body (bridge) design pattern used to decouple abstraction, represented by the handle class `HTTP_File_Handle`, from the platform-dependent implementation by the body class hierarchy with the `HTTP_File_Body` base class and its derived classes. An interface for external calls is available only through the handle part.

`HTTP_File_Handle`. Whenever the `HTTP_File_Handle::Load_HTTP_File` function is called, the *action is delegated* to the corresponding `Load_HTTP_File` function in one of the selected body classes, as illustrated in the UML sequence diagram in Figure 6.7. Implementation of the hierarchy of the body classes shown in Figure 6.6 is shown in Listing 6.4.

On line [16], we see a declaration of a pure virtual `Load_HTTP_File` function (see Section 4.11). This means it has to be overridden in the derived classes, as is done for `HTTP_File_Body_Windows` on line [28], `HTTP_File_Body_Linux` on line [37], and `HTTP_File_Body_MacOS` on line [47]. Each class is responsible for implementing `Load_HTTP_File` in a different OS. An overridden function must be an exact copy of its prototype in the base class: a *copy-and-paste*. However, since in practice functions take dozens of parameters of various types, and the hierarchies frequently are deep, it is not unusual to mistakenly break a function override due to inconsistencies in function names or parameters. To remedy this situation, the `override` (contextual) keyword is used. Its use is not compulsory but is recommended, since it forces the compiler to check whether a function decorated with this keyword truly overrides a function in one of the base classes, as discussed in Section 6.1. From the other end, there is the `final` (contextual) keyword, which lets us stop a chain of virtual functions and overriding (Stroustrup 2013).

Since we are designing a hierarchy of classes with virtual functions, which will also allow us to manipulate derived objects via pointers to the base class, it is important to define the destructors of the base classes as virtual, as on line [20]. We can also declare such virtual destructors in derived classes, but this is not necessary when a virtual destructor is defined in the base class. The `=` `default` instructs the compiler to generate a default implementation.

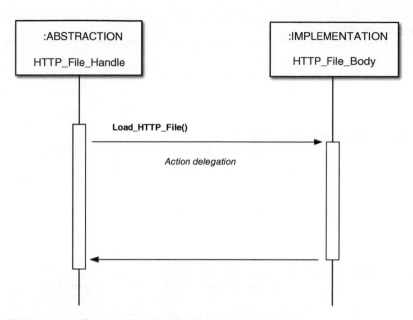

Figure 6.7 UML sequence diagram of the handle-body design pattern.

Listing 6.4 Definition of the `HTTP_File_Body` and its derived classes (in *CurrencyCalc_Lib*, *HTTP_File.h*).

```cpp
1   #pragma once
2
3   #include <cassert>
4   #include <string>
5
6
7   namespace CppBook
8   {
9
10
11  class HTTP_File_Body
12  {
13
14      public:
15
16          virtual bool    Load_HTTP_File(    const std::wstring & internet_addr,
                                                const std::wstring & localName ) = 0;
17
18      public:
19          // a virtual destructor to allow inheritance
20          virtual ~HTTP_File_Body() = default;
21  };
22
23  class HTTP_File_Body_Windows : public HTTP_File_Body
24  {
25
26      public:
27
28          bool    Load_HTTP_File( const std::wstring & internet_addr,
                                    const std::wstring & localName ) override;
29
```

(Continued)

Listing 6.4 (continued)

```
30    };
31
32    class HTTP_File_Body_Linux : public HTTP_File_Body
33    {
34
35        public:
36
37            bool     Load_HTTP_File( const std::wstring & internet_addr,
                                        const std::wstring & localName ) override;
38
39
40    };
41
42    class HTTP_File_Body_MacOS : public HTTP_File_Body
43    {
44
45        public:
46
47            bool     Load_HTTP_File( const std::wstring & internet_addr,
                                        const std::wstring & localName ) override;
48
49    };
```

Neither class in the HTTP_File_Body hierarchy needs to know what will be using it. On the other hand, HTTP_File_Handle needs to know its body hierarchy and properly create and maintain a necessary body object that will be used for further actions. An implementation of the HTTP_File_Handle class is shown in Listing 6.5.

Listing 6.5 Definition of the HTTP_File_Handle class (continued in *CurrencyCalc_Lib, HTTP_File.h*).

```
50    class HTTP_File_Handle
51    {
52        private:
53
54            using BodyPtr = std::unique_ptr< HTTP_File_Body >;
55
56            BodyPtr     fBodyObj;
57
58        public:
59
60            enum class EHandledSystems { kWindows, kLinux, kMac };
61
62            HTTP_File_Handle( EHandledSystems system )
63            {
64                switch( system )
65                {
66                    case EHandledSystems::kWindows:
67                    fBodyObj = std::make_unique< HTTP_File_Body_Windows >();
68                    break;
69
70                    case EHandledSystems::kLinux:
71                    fBodyObj = std::make_unique< HTTP_File_Body_Linux >();
72                    break;
73
74                    case EHandledSystems::kMac:
75                    fBodyObj = std::make_unique< HTTP_File_Body_MacOS >();
```

```
76                  break;
77
78              default:
79                  assert( false ); // not supported
80                  break;
81          }
82
83      }
84
85  public:
86
87      // Interace function to load a file via HTTP (seen by the clients)
88      virtual bool  Load_HTTP_File(   const std::wstring & internet_addr,
                                        const std::wstring & localName )
89      {
90          assert( fBodyObj ); // a pre-condition in programming by contract
91          // delegate an action to the body object
92          return fBodyObj->Load_HTTP_File( internet_addr, localName);
93      }
94
95  public:
96      // a virtual destructor to allow inheritance
97      virtual ~HTTP_File_Handle() = default;
98  };
99
100
101
102  }       // end of namespace CppBook
```

On line [54], the `using` directive is used to define `BodyPtr`, which is a smart `unique_ptr`, discussed in Section 5.3. A pointer `fBodyObj` of this type is defined on line [56] to point at the body object from the `HTTP_File_Body` class hierarchy. However, which one is chosen is decided in the `HTTP_File_Handle` class constructor, defined on lines [62–83]. This is an example of polymorphism. A parameter of the `EHandledSystems` class enumerated type, defined on line [60], tells what system should be chosen. For instance, for the Windows OS, line [67] is executed, which creates the `HTTP_File_Body_Windows` object and assigns it to the `fBodyObj` pointer. The benefit of a smart pointer is that once it is attached to an object, we do not need to bother how to delete the owned object – it will be deleted automatically together with `fBodyObj` when the object itself is deleted. This has an obvious consequence – the lifetime of the `HTTP_File_Body` object is strictly coupled with the lifetime of the `HTTP_File_Handle` handle object. Thus, this relation is called a *composite aggregation*, as shown in Figure 6.6 and discussed in Section 4.9.

On line [88] of the `HTTP_File_Handle` class, the `Load_HTTP_File` function is defined. It simply takes two `wstring` parameters and, on line [92], delegates an action to the analogous `Load_HTTP_File` function – but in the associated body object, held in the `fBodyObj` member. For this to be safe, the latter needs to be properly initialized. For the debug version, this is checked on line [90] in the precondition, as postulated by the "programming by contract" methodology (Section 4.7.3). Take advantage of such debug checks as often as possible since in practice they can save a lot of trouble when it comes to making code running properly. Take our word for it!

Once again, since `HTTP_File_Handle` contains a virtual function and can be derived from in the future, its destructor is defined as virtual on line [97]. Also, `= default` is used.

Finally, let's take a look at the implementation of one of the body objects. More precisely, the only thing to implement is the `HTTP_File_Body_Windows::Load_HTTP_File` function in this case. On the Windows OS, the *urlmon* library and header need to be included – this is done on lines [3–11]: `#include` for the header and `#pragma comment(lib, "urlmon.lib")` for the library. The latter is one of the ways a library can be added to Microsoft Visual C++ projects. However, this happens only if the _WIN32 flag is set, which is true only when compiling for Windows.

```
1    #include "HTTP_File.h"
2
3    #if _WIN32
4
5        #include <urlmon.h>
6
7        #pragma comment(lib, "urlmon.lib")
8
9    #else
10
11   #endif
12
13
14   namespace CppBook
15   {
16
17
18   bool HTTP_File_Body_Windows::Load_HTTP_File( const std::wstring & internet_addr,
                                                  const std::wstring & localName )
19   {
20   #if _WIN32 // Should be 1 on 32-bit and 64-bit Windows
21       return URLDownloadToFile ( NULL, internet_addr.c_str(),
                                    localName.c_str(), 0, NULL ) == S_OK;
22   #else
23       return false;
24   #endif
25   }
26
27
28   }   // CppBook
```

Finally, on line [21], the Windows-specific URLDownloadToFile function is called to download the file. Since this function expects C-style string pointers, c_str needs to be called from each of the supplied wstring objects. This also happens if the _WIN32 flag is set, i.e. exclusively in the Windows OS. In other systems, the code simply boils down to the return false statement. Other systems have their own compile flags set. This is how the entire selection mechanism works in our project.

The downside of this handle-body (bridge) based solution is that in a given OS, only one path is compiled and executed. All of the other $N-1$ classes, where N denotes the total number of supported OSs, are inactive and protected from attempted compilation by the #if - #else - #endif constructions. But the solution is clear and easily extensible without touching the rest of the software components, which communicate only through the handle class.

The previous solution might look like overkill for a simple file-download problem. Indeed, very simple tasks can be done succinctly with only a few lines, and proliferating classes might seem not necessary. But code and interdependencies usually tend to grow, and such a separation of abstraction from implementation almost is always beneficial. Various other techniques are comparably good: for instance, instead of the dynamic object-oriented inheritance used in this example, a static solution employing class templates and compile-time computations offers many benefits.

Nevertheless, our handle-body design pattern (bridge) is one of the most frequently used constructions in many software packages. It is useful to understand its structure and properties in order to spot it in new software designs or software refactoring tasks. Separating an abstraction (handle) from the implementation (body) in general layered architectures increases the number of classes but also adds a lot of flexibility to the solution. A related pattern is the *strategy* pattern, which lets us dynamically choose an algorithm based on external conditions. For example, there are many sorting algorithms that perform differently on small and large databases. So, the correct sorting algorithm is chosen based on the amount of work to do. Also interesting in this context is the *Pimpl* (pointer to implementation) pattern (Meyers 2014). However, its main purpose is to decouple source code compilation dependencies by hiding the implementation.[1]

In this section, we learned about the following:

- The handle-body (bridge) design pattern to decouple abstraction from implementation
- Elements of multiple-platform programming
- Loading HTTP files from the Internet on different platforms

6.2.5 Launching the Extended Version of *CurrencyCalc*

In Section 3.18.5, we discussed the *CurrencyExchanger* component that let us launch our first version of the *CurrencyExchanger* application. It operates in a terminal window and allows a user to do basic currency calculations. In previous sections, we extended this version to allow for automatic downloads of current exchange ratios from the Internet. So, let's make this upgraded *CurrencyExchanger 2.0* version run.

We will further exploit the technique of grouping component elements in namespace(s) rather than classes, as discussed in Section 3.18.5. We have already created the `CurrExchanger` namespace for the basic version of *CurrencyExchanger*. Hence, in Listing 6.6, line [5], we continue in this direction. But since we wish to distinguish the two versions from each other, we separate them by opening a new `OnLine_CurrExchanger` namespace on line [9], nested inside `CurrExchanger`. To some extent, this is an alternative to create a `CurrExchanger` class from which `OnLine_CurrExchanger` would be derived. The two approaches can be seen as alternatives with drawbacks and benefits on both sides. In the former, we simply do not explicitly create the objects.

Listing 6.6 Definition of the project functions in the nested namespaces (in *CurrencyCalc_Lib, CurrencyCalcPlayGround.cpp*).

```
1   #include "XML_CurrencyExchanger.h"
2   #include "HTTP_File.h"
3
4
5   namespace CurrExchanger
6   {
7
8   // A version that can load from a HTTP downloaded XML file
9   namespace OnLine_CurrExchanger
10  {
11      // Internet address of an external XML file
12      wstring nbp_addr { L"http://www.nbp.pl/kursy/xml/LastC.xml" };
13
14      // Name of a temporary local XML file
15      wstring local_xml:file_name { L"LastC.xml" };
16
17      // A flag indicating the current OS
18      HTTP_File_Handle::EHandledSystems kMyOS
                            { HTTP_File_Handle::EHandledSystems::kWindows };
```

---

1 A nice summary of Pimpl can be found on Bartek Filipek's coding blog: *www.bfilipek.com/2018/01/pimpl.html*.

Lines [12, 15] define the `wstring` objects local to the `OnLine_CurrExchanger` namespace. They simply hold the Internet and local default addresses of the XML "from" and "to" files. As already pointed out, the downloaded XML file provides access to current exchange ratios. Moreover, the two addresses can be easily accessed and changed if necessary. On line [18], our local OS is indicated by defining the local variable `kMyOS`.

The `CurExchanger_DownloadCurrencies` function is defined on lines [19–23]. Its role is to create an `HTTP_File_Handle` object named `http_client` and initialize it appropriately on the selected platform. It is then used to download the XML file from the Internet location and save it locally.

```
19      bool CurExchanger_DownloadCurrencies( const wstring & http_addr,
                                              const wstring & local_XML_FullPath )
20      {
21          HTTP_File_Handle    http_client( kMyOS );
22          return http_client.Load_HTTP_File( nbp_addr, local_XML_FullPath );
23      }
```

The downloaded XML file is then used to initialize `XML_CurrencyExchanger`, as we will see. But at this point, it is wise to save the current currency data in a separate initialization file. It can be used in cases when e.g. there is no Internet connection and an XML file cannot be downloaded. This is accomplished by the `CurExchanger_SaveInitFile` function, defined on line [24].

```
24      void CurExchanger_SaveInitFile(    const XML_CurrencyExchanger & obj,
                                           const wstring & initFileFullPath )
25      {
26          // Save to the init file
27          // Use default file to load currencies
28          wofstream  outFile( initFileFullPath );
29          const XML_CurrencyExchanger::CurrencyMap & cur_map = obj.GetCurrencyMap();
30          transform( cur_map.cbegin(), cur_map.cend(),
31                     ostream_iterator< TCurrency, wchar_t >( outFile, L"\n" ),
32                     [] ( const XML_CurrencyExchanger::CurrencyMap::value_type & vt )
                       { return vt.second; } );
33      }
```

In the previous code, the `std::transform` function on lines [30–32] needs some explanation (see also Table 3.6). As we already know, each element of the `std::map` object contains *key* and *value* parts. The role of `std::transform` is to copy only the *value* part of each of the `CurrencyMap` objects to the output file, identified with the `outFile` object. This `CurrencyMap` object is accessed via the local reference `cur_map`. The range to copy from is passed by the first two parameters, i.e. `cur_map.cbegin()` and `cur_map.cend()`. These return constant iterators (which here begin with the letter *c* in front) to the beginning and end of this map collection. The output goes to the `outFile` using the `ostream_iterator`, set on line [31] to process `TCurrency` and wide characters. Each currency is saved using an automatic call to `operator <<` (discussed earlier) on lines [7–26] in Listing 3.33. Each such entry is separated by the wide-new-line symbols `L"\n"`, as provided to the `ostream_iterator`. Last but not least is the lambda function supplied on line [32] as the last parameter to `std::transform`. It is called from inside `std::transform` with the `vt` reference to consecutive elements of `cur_map`. The role of this lambda is simple: skip the *key* and return only the *value* part of the element, identified by `vt.second`.

The definition of the `CreateCurExchanger` function starts on line [40]. It is similar to the function with the same name presented in Section 3.18.5. But the two differ in the type of object they return, which in this case is `XML_CurrencyExchanger` rather than `CurrencyExchanger`. Also, they differ in the way they are initialized, in this case through the XML file downloaded from the Internet. However, as previously, since the object creation process can fail, an `std::optional` object defined on line [34] is returned from `CreateCurExchanger`. It lets us pass a valid object if an object is created successfully, or it is empty if for some reason an object cannot be supplied.

```cpp
34      using XML_CurrExch_Optional = std::optional< XML_CurrencyExchanger >;
35
36
37      // There are two options for the return object:
38      // - It is either TCurrencyExchanger if properly built
39      // - or empty CurrExch_Optional if cannot create
40      auto CreateCurExchanger(  const wstring & http_XML_FileName,
                                    const wstring & initFileFullPath )
41      {
42          XML_CurrencyExchanger   currencyExchangerObj;
43
44          namespace fs = std::filesystem;
45
46          // Create name of a local XML file - its parent is from initFileFullPath
47          wstring local_xml:full_path( fs::path( initFileFullPath ).parent_path()
                                          / local_xml:file_name );
48
49          if( CurExchanger_DownloadCurrencies(http_XML_FileName, local_xml:full_path )
                                                                      == true &&
50              currencyExchangerObj.FillCurrencyTableFrom( local_xml:full_path )
                                                                      == true )
51          {
52              // Success, object initialized from Internet
53
54              // Add the reference currency (PLN) (0xB3 is Polish letter "l-crossed")
55              currencyExchangerObj.AddCurrency( {L"PLN", L"z\xB3oty-polski",1.0,1.0} );
56
57              // Update the ini file with new data
58              CurExchanger_SaveInitFile( currencyExchangerObj, initFileFullPath );
59          }
60          else
61          {
62              // Cannot initialize from the Internet,
63              // so, as a last resort, let's look for a local ini file
64
65              wifstream    inFile( initFileFullPath );
66
67              if( inFile.is_open() == false )
68              return XML_CurrExch_Optional(); // no init file, return empty optional
69
70              // Read data from the file
71              inFile >> currencyExchangerObj;
72          }
73
74          return XML_CurrExch_Optional( currencyExchangerObj );
75      }
```

The two parameters passed to `CreateCurExchanger` are `http_XML_FileName`, which holds the Internet address of the XML file with current data for currency exchange ratios, as well as `initFileFullPath`, holding the full path to the local initialization file. This path is used on line [47] to create the name of another local file – the one that will store the downloaded XML file. These files, i.e. the initialization and local XML files, contain data about currencies, but in different formats. To create a new path, we use the filesystem `path` object and its `parent_path`, as well as the overloaded / (slash) operator, as presented in Table 6.3.

On lines [49, 50], the XML file is downloaded using the `CurExchanger_DownloadCurrencies` function. If and only if this succeeds, the XML file is used to initialize the `currency ExchangerObj` object by calling its `FillCurrencyTableFrom` member. If the file download fails, `FillCurrencyTableFrom` is not called due to the evaluation order of logical expressions (see Section 3.19.2). If these two steps succeed, then on line [55], the reference currency is added (the Polish zloty in this example). Next, on line [58], the new version of the initialization file is saved. This can be used in the future if an Internet download is not possible. Finally, on line [60], this branch returns a valid object: a copy of the local `currencyExchangerObj` object created on line [42].

If the Internet download fails, then on line [67], we try to use a local initialization file to initialize the `currencyExchangerObj` object. If such a file cannot be opened, then we signal the situation by returning an empty `std::optional` object on line [68]. Assuming the initialization file is available, it is used on line [71] to read currency data. This is exactly like the previous version of the `CreateCurExchanger` function (Section 3.18.5). Then, a valid `XML_CurrencyExchanger` object is returned on line [74]: a copy of the local `currencyExchangerObj` object created on line [42].

On line [77], a new version of the Run function is defined. On line [84], the `CreateCurExchanger` function is called, which returns the `XML_CurrencyExchanger` object. However, on line [87], the `CurrExchanger::Run` function is called, which we defined in Section 3.18.5. Interestingly, it is passed the new object of the `XML_CurrencyExchanger` type, whereas this version of Run was defined to accept a constant reference to the `TCurrencyExchanger` object. In an object-oriented framework, this is fine, since an object of the derived class can be used any place an object of its base is used. This is an example of polymorphism and the Liskov substitution rule, discussed in Section 4.1. Also note that this "old" version of Run calls other "old" functions, such as `DisplayAllCurrencies` and `UserInterface`. These also work with this new version of the passed object.

```
76      // All actions
77      void Run( void )
78      {
79          namespace fs = std::filesystem;
80
81          wstring iniPath( fs::current_path() / fs::path( initDefaultFileName ) );
82
83          // First try to get the currency object
84          if( XML_CurrExch_Optional all_my_options
                        { CreateCurExchanger( nbp_addr, iniPath ) }; all_my_options )
85          {
86              // Functions do not overload over namespaces
87              CurrExchanger::Run( * all_my_options ); // so we have to use CurrExchanger::
88          }
89          else
90          {
91              wcout   << L"Error, check Currency.txt file." << endl
92                      << L"Exiting ..." << endl;
93          }
94      }
95
96  } // end of namespace OnLine_CurrExchanger
97
98  } // end of namespace CurrExchanger
```

On the other hand, if `CreateCurExchanger` fails to create the `XML_CurrencyExchanger` object, then an empty `all_my_options` is returned, and an error message is printed on line [91]. In this section, we learned about the following:

- Using the filesystem `path` object
- Composing a namespace inside another namespace (nested namespaces)
- Using `std::transform` to copy elements of `std::map` to a file
- Polymorphism when passing a derived object to a function defined to accept an object of the base class

6.2.6 Building a Static Library and a Terminal Window Application

We could easily add the `main` function to the previous example to create a terminal window version of our application. But since our project is growing and we have further plans to use the *CurrencyCalc* component from Figure 3.29 in various projects, it is a good idea to split it from the `main` function and put into a separate *static library*. The new arrangement of the software components is shown in UML component diagram in Figure 6.8.

To build a static library out of an application project, we need to do the following:

1. Remove the main function (i.e. the entire file containing main). It can then be used in other projects, as we will discuss.
2. Change the *CMakeLists.txt* file to generate *a static library project*,[2] as discussed in Appendix A.6.1.
3. Run *CMake.exe*, build a library project, and then build the library.

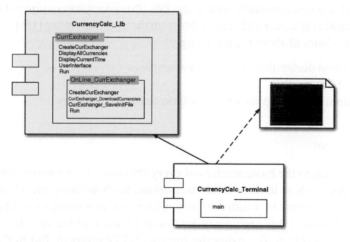

Figure 6.8 UML component diagram of the basic *CurrencyExchanger*.

This way, we can build our first library, named *CurrencyCalc_Lib*. The new *CurrencyCalc_Terminal* component is linked to *CurrencyCalc_Lib*, as shown in Figure 6.8. It contains only the `main` function, as shown in Listing 6.7.

---

2 It is also possible to build a library without using the *CMake* tool. That is, we can create a new project in our programming environment, select its type as a static library, and manually add the files. However, *CMake* gives us flexibility between various platforms and programming tools.

Listing 6.7 Definition of the `main` function (in *CurrencyCalc_Terminal, main.cpp*).

```
99    #include <filesystem>
100   #include <io.h>
101   #include <fcntl.h>
102
103   namespace CurrExchanger
104   {
105     namespace OnLine_CurrExchanger
106     {
107       void Run( void );
108     }
109   }
110
111   // Keep main() simple
112   int main( void )
113   {
114       setmode( _fileno( stdout ), _O_U16TEXT );
115       CurrExchanger::OnLine_CurrExchanger::Run();
116       return 0;  // Although not absolutely required, return the value from main
117   }
```

To enter the previous functions and namespaces into scope of `main`, a `#include` would be appropriate. However, since inside `main` we wish to call the `Run` function, from line [77], it is also OK to provide its declaration, as provided on lines [103–109]. Here we see the structure of the nested namespaces, i.e. `OnLine_CurrExchanger` with `Run`, declared inside `CurrExchanger`. This enables us to call `Run` from line [115] inside `main`, leaving to the linker the task of finding and gluing these functions together. The role of the `setmode` function called on line [114] is to prepare the terminal to output Unicode wide characters, commonly used by the `XML_CurrencyExchanger` object. Last but not least, we must remember to return an integer value from the `main`, as on line [116].

In this section, we learned about the following:

- Introducing function declarations in nested namespaces
- Creating a static library
- Creating a terminal window application that links to the static library

6.2.7 C++ Filesystem

File processing belongs to the basic services of every OS running on a computer equipped with data storage devices, such as hard or solid-state drives, flash memory, etc. However, each system defines these operations in a different way, which makes writing multiplatform software cumbersome. We discussed this problem in Section 6.2.4 when trying to write a universal software component to download files using the Internet HTTP protocol. But in C++17+, a common platform was defined for file and directory processing in the `std::filesystem` namespace. To use it, we need to `#include` the *filesystem* header (Cppreference.com 2018). The most common objects and operations of the C++ filesystem library are summarized in Table 6.3.

Most of the objects and functions presented in Table 6.3 have additional options. Also, there are many subtleties related to parameters of the processed path, file, and directory objects. These can be further explored e.g. in (Cppreference.com 2018).

Table 6.3 Common objects and functions of the C++ filesystem library.

Object	Description	Examples
path	path is a class that represents paths to files, directories, and their links in various systems. It behaves like a container and supports many useful functions for splitting the path and concatenating path parts. Selected members of the path class:	To use the new filesystem features of C++, the filesystem header needs to be included. fs is a short name for the std::filesystem, defined as follows:

Selected members description table:

Member	Description
/=	Path concatenation, which appropriately inserts slash or backslash symbols, depending on the filesystem. Multiple such symbols are compressed to one.
/	
+=	Concatenates paths without adding separators (like string).
filename	Returns a filename (*File.txt*).
stem	Returns a stem (*File*).
extension	Returns an extension (*.txt*).
parent_path	Returns a parent path.[a]
relative_path	Returns a relative path.
root_directory	Returns the root directory.
root_name	Returns the root name.
root_path	Returns the root path.

Examples column continued:

```
1  #include <filesystem>
2
3  namespace fs = std::filesystem;
```

The following function on line [6] converts a wide string std::wstring into a fs::path object. Then, on lines [9–10], each part of the path is printed on the screen.

```
4  void DisplayPathParts( const wstring & inPath_str )
5  {
6      const fs::path inPath( inPath_str );
7
8      // We can iterate through different parts of a path
9      for( const auto & p : inPath )
10         wcout << p << "\n";
11 }
```

For the example input path[b]

```
D:\Research\BC++\Projects\CCppBookCode\ReadMe.txt
```

the following output is obtained:

```
D:
\
Research
BC++
Projects
CCppBookCode
ReadMe.txt
```

(Continued)

Table 6.3 (continued)

Object	Description	Examples
| directory_ iterator<br><br>recursive_ directory_ iterator | Allows for a straightforward iteration through the file tree. The second version does an automatic recursive traversal. Order of iteration is not specified. However, it is guaranteed that each object in the filesystem is accessed only once.<br><br>| Member | Description |<br>|---|---|<br>| * | Accesses an indicated object |<br>| ++ | Advances the iterator to the next object in the tree |<br>| depth | Class default and parametric constructors |<br>| path | Pointer dereferencing to the held object | | The following function performs a recursive traversal of a directory provided as an input wstring object. Its action is to print out a file directory structure, although the output can easily be changed to fulfill other requirements.<br><br>```cpp
1  void RecursivelyTraverseDirectory( const wstring & inDirPath_str )
2  {
3      const fs::path inDirPath( inDirPath_str );
4
5      if( fs::exists( inDirPath ) && fs::is_directory( inDirPath ) )
6      {
7          for( auto iter = fs::recursive_directory_iterator( inDirPath );
8               iter != fs::recursive_directory_iterator(); ++ iter )
9
10             wcout << std::wstring( 3 * iter.depth(), L' ' )
11                  << ( fs::is_directory( * iter ) ? L"[+]" : L"|--" )
12                  << iter->path().filename() << endl;
13     }
14 }
``` |
| exists | Returns true if a file or directory exists or false otherwise. | |
| is_directory | Returns true if a path represents a directory. | |
```

The input directory path name, passed as a wstring object, on line [3] is converted to the inDirPath object of the fs::path class. Line [5] checks to see whether inDirPath exists and whether it represents a directory. If this is true, then on lines [7–8], a loop recursively traverses the directory, advancing the iter object of the fs::recursive_directory_iterator class, and initialized with the inDirPath. Finally, on lines [10–12], the directory structure is printed out. iter.depth returns the depth of the part of the directory tree that is currently being processed. An object of the directory tree is accessed with * iter. If it is a directory, then [+] is printed; otherwise, |-- is printed. The name of a directory tree object is obtained by accessing path and then calling filename functions.

For an example directory with a C++ project, the previous function produces output like the following:

```
|--CMakeLists.txt
[+]include
   |--range.h
|--ReadMe.txt
[+]src
   |--CCppBookCode.cpp
   |--ClassRelations.cpp
   |--Dec2Roman.cpp
```

(Continued)

Table 6.3 (continued)

Object	Description	Examples
`file_size`	Returns the file size in bytes.	The following function prints basic information about the supplied path to a directory or a file:
`is_regular_file`	Returns true if a path represents a regular file (i.e. not a directory and not a link).	
`file_status`	Returns an object with information about a file.	

```
1   void DisplayDirFileInfo( const wstring & inPath_str )
2   {
3       const fs::path inPath( inPath_str );
4
5       wcout << L"exists - \t\t" << fs::exists( inPath ) << endl;
6
7       // Let's call all important members of fs::path
8       wcout << L"filename - \t\t"    << inPath.filename() << endl;
9       wcout << L"stem - \t\t"        << inPath.stem() << endl;
10      wcout << L"extension - \t\t"   << inPath.extension() << endl;
11
12      // If a file, then print its size in bytes
13      if( fs::is_regular_file( inPath ) ) o << val << sep;
14      std::cout << "file size - \t\t"  << fs::file_size( inPath ) << endl;
15
16      wcout << L"parent_path - \t\t"   << inPath.parent_path() << endl;
17      wcout << L"relative_path - \t\t" << inPath.relative_path() << endl;
18
```

```
19    wcout << L"root_directory - \t\t" << inPath.root_directory() << endl;
20    wcout << L"root_name - \t\t"      << inPath.root_name() << endl;
21    wcout << L"root_path - \t\t"      << inPath.root_path() << endl;
22  }
```

To call file_size on line [14], an object is checked on line [13] with is_regular_file to see if it is a valid file. On lines [8–10], as well as [16–21], numerous members of path are called to get parts of the path. For an example C:\Temp\Readme.txt input file in the test system, the following is obtained:

```
exists -            1
filename -          ReadMe.txt
stem -              ReadMe
extension -         .txt
file size -         44
parent_path -       C:\Temp
relative_path -     Temp\ReadMe.txt
root_directory -    \
root_name -         C:
root_path -         C:\
```

(Continued)

Table 6.3 (continued)

Object	Description	Examples
copy	Copies files and/or directories with their contents.	The following function shows how to create two directories [13, 16] and then create a file in one of them [19], copy that file to the second directory [22], move that file back to the first directory [27], and finally remove all files and directories [31]. The last function should be used with great care. To concatenate elements of a path, on line [9], the overloaded /= operator of the path class is used.
remove remove_all	Removes a file or a directory with its contents.	
create_ directory create_ directories	Creates a directory or directories.	
rename	Renames or moves a file.	

```
 1    void CreateDirAndFiles(const wstring& inDirPath_str,
                                const wstring& subDir)
 2    {
 3        try
 4        {
 5            // There are conversions std::(w)string <==> fs::path
 6            fs::path inDirPath( inDirPath_str );

 7            // Use overloaded operator /= to
 8            inDirPath /= subDir;      // add sub directory

 9
10            // Create directories
11            fs::path sub_1_path { inDirPath / L"SubDir_1" };
12            fs::create_directories( sub_1_path );  // create subDir_1

13            fs::path sub_2_path { inDirPath / L"SubDir_2" };
14            fs::create_directories( sub_2_path );  // create subDir_2

15
16            // Create a new file
17
18
```

```
19        wofstream( sub_1_path / L"file_1.txt" ) << L"Fox";
20
21        // Create a second directory & file by fs::copy
22        fs::copy( sub_1_path / L"file_1.txt",    // from
23                  sub_2_path / L"file_2.txt",    // to
24                  fs::copy_options::overwrite_existing );
25
26        // Move file_2.txt to the first directory
27        fs::rename( sub_2_path / L"file_2.txt",  // from
28                    sub_1_path / L"file_2.txt" );// to
29
30        // Remove all dir and files - be careful!
31        fs::remove_all( inDirPath );
32      }
33      catch( fs::filesystem_error & error )
34      {
35        wcout << error.what() << endl;
36      }
37    }
```

Certain fs functions, such as copy, rename, and remove_all, have several different call versions. Some of them can also throw fs::filesystem_error type exceptions related to error situations. Therefore, the try-catch statement should be used, as on line [33].

The previous function can be called to print information about the current file path.

```
38  CreateDirAndFiles( fs::current_path(), L"Playground" );
```

current_ path	Returns a current path (system dependent).

Table 6.3 (continued)

Object	Description	Examples
space_info	A class to convey space information for a directory. Data members are as follows: | Member	Description
---	---
capacity	The total size of the filesystem (bytes)
free	Free space in the filesystem (bytes)

available	Amount of free space available to a non-privileged process (bytes)		The `fs::space_info` object holds information about capacity, free space, and available space of a directory. For a given directory path, the space information can be obtained with the `fs::space` function.
			
			``cpp
			1 void DisplaySpaceInfo(const wstring & inPath_str)
			2 {
			3 fs::space_info dir_space = fs::space(inPath_str);
			4
			5 wcout << L"Space info for: " << inPath_str << endl;
			6
			7 wcout << L"capacity - \t\t" << dir_space.capacity << endl;
			8 wcout << L"free - \t\t" << dir_space.free << endl;
			9 wcout << L"available - \t\t" << dir_space.available << endl;
			10 }
			``
			
			For the `C:\Temp` directory, the following information was output on a test system:
			
			``
			Space info for: C:\Temp
			capacity - 9871509917632
			free - 638753398784
			available - 638753398784
			``

a See the `DisplayDirFileInfo` function.

b To create a wstring object, use wstring (L"D:\\Research\\BC++\\Projects\\CCppBookCode\\ReadMe.txt"). Remember that to enter one backslash symbol \ in the text, you need to type \\ in the string literal.

6.2.8   User Interface

In the previous sections, we saw the evolution of the *CurrencyExchange* project: its two versions, both encompassed in the hierarchical namespaces `CurrExchanger` and its nested `OnLine_CurrExchanger`. `CurrExchanger` defines very basic functionality, whereas `OnLine_CurrExchanger` extends the functionality to automatically load currency information from the Internet. Both were tested as standalone terminal applications. We also saw how to split the project into a static library named *CurrencyCalc_Lib* and another component, *CurrencyCalc_Terminal*, which builds a terminal window application (Section 6.2.6). Now it is time to take the next step and to add a graphical user interface (GUI) to this project. Hence, we will create a third software component to launch *CurrencyExchanger* as a GUI application: `CurrencyCalc_GUI`. The UML component diagram in Figure 6.8 will now change as shown in Figure 6.9.

In this section, we are mostly interested in the `CurrencyCalc_GUI` component, which will be able to draw graphical widgets, as well as process system events, as will be shown. However, the GUI components depend heavily on the type of OS we are working in. This means if we tried to write our `CurrencyCalc_GUI` for two or three different OSs, we would need to write two or three quite different versions of the component. On the other hand, even if our task was much simpler and only one OS was our target, using the raw API would not be the most productive option. A much better solution is to use one of the GUI libraries that create a type of interface between a user application like *CurrencyCalc* and one or many different OSs. Appendix A.4 contains a brief overview of the GUI libraries for C++ projects. Alas, every rose has its thorns, and each has its own peculiarities and limitations. In our example, we choose to test the FLTK library mostly because it is free, it is written entirely in C++, and it runs on many OSs.

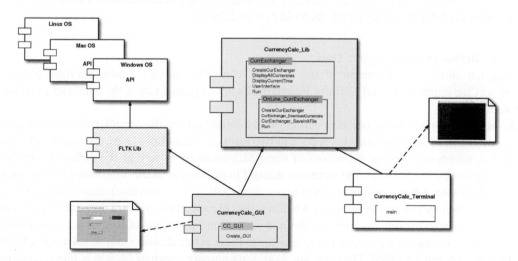

Figure 6.9   UML component diagram of the various software components used in our *CurrencyCalc* project. Because the currency exchange engine is extracted into a separate library, we can easily construct a terminal window or GUI application without interference.

So, let's take a closer look at the UML component diagram shown in Figure 6.9. The most important change is that we have separated all the components strictly related to currency exchange from user-related input-output operations. Now these components are enclosed in a separate library, whereas user actions are moved to different application projects. As a result, we achieve the following important goals:

- *Code readability* – It is now much easier to concentrate on various levels of our system. That is, when working on further mechanisms for currency exchange, we will touch only the *CurrencyCalc_Lib* library. When working on user interfaces, we will not need to change anything in the currency exchange library
- *Code reusability* – It is much easier to reuse our *CurrencyCalc_Lib* library in any other project (with or without a user interface) that requires currency exchange actions. It is also much easier to extend the functionality of the library

Hence, a rule of thumb is not to get involved with the `cout` and `cin` objects in classes. Input/output operations should be implemented using the external overloaded `operator <<` and `operator >>`.

Our code will finally display graphics. To do so, we need to install the FLTK library. Details of this operation are described on the FLTK web page (FLTK 2019) and depend on our OS and installed tools. However, the following short guide can be useful:

1. Download FLTK from its website and unpack it with the *FLTK* and *CurrencyCalc* directories at the same level.
2. Go into the *FLTK* directory, and launch `cmake` . [dot] to build the FLTK project in the current directory.
3. Open the project, and build the library. When finished, the *FLTK/Lib/Debug* directory should contain the *fltkd.lib* library (verify its build date and time).

6.2.8.1 Definition of the `CC_GUI` Class

Listing 6.8 shows the definition of the `CC_GUI` class that defines a user interface for our *CurrencyCalc* application, and Listing 6.9 contains its full implementation. We will briefly explain what these do.

As usual, at the beginning of a new definition, we should inform the compiler about the classes we wish to use. In this example, this is done in two forms. First, on lines [1–5], the header files are included, which contain the definitions of some SL containers as well as the definitions of the `XML_CurrencyExchanger` and functions defined in the *CurrencyCalcPlayGround* header. As a result, all classes defined in this unit will know about `XML_CurrencyExchanger` but not vice versa, as shown by the arrows in Figure 6.9. Lines [8–12] contain the forward declarations. This is the second way to introduce externally defined classes into the scope of the current translation unit. But in this case only pointers and references to these external classes can be used, since their definitions are not provided. Then, on line [14], a namespace shortcut `OL_CE` is introduced, to increase readability and save on typing.

The definition of the `CC_GUI` class starts on line [18]. Thanks to the aforementioned forward declarations, on lines [23–26] we can define pointers to components (widgets) of the GUI. After initialization, these will point at the real widget objects. Although using pointers is not the preferable indirect access technique in modern C++, it is the only option in legacy code like the FLTK library. In many real situations, we face the problem of connecting the two worlds; what is important is to do so safely.

Unlike indirect access by pointers, a connection to the `XML_CurrencyExchanger` component is achieved by the `fXML_CurrencyExchanger` reference defined on line [33] (see Figure 6.9). Once again, we use the `using` declaration to locally shorten the external name to `XCE`. A real `XCE` object is provided in the class constructor, as shown on line [40]. Its second, default parameter constitutes the default currency for the application. On line [42], the virtual destructor is defined to allow for inheritance from the `CC_GUI` class.

The following code in `CC_GUI` contains declarations of interesting member functions, which will play a role in the actions of our GUI interface. We will introduce them briefly here, and their definitions are provided in Listing 6.9. First is the `theButtonCallback` *static function*, declared on line [61]. A static member function in a class is defined for the class and not for its objects (Section 4.5). In other words, there is one such function instance regardless of the number of object instances of this class. Hence, it is defined for a class and not for a particular object. This means it can be passed (via a function pointer) to interfaces that expect a bare function pointer. However, static members in a class should be used with the utmost care since they break class safety if used in a multitask environment (thread safety). So, why do we define such a function in the `CC_GUI` class? Because this function needs to be provided as a parameter to one of the objects of the FLTK interface as *a callback function*. It is a function that is called by a component if an action occurs, such as a button click in our case. Fortunately, this is the only role of `theButtonCallback`: once called, it passes control to the `Action_On_Button` function declared on line [78]. Unlike `theButtonCallback`, this function is declared virtual, and it is executed on behalf of the current object (Section 4.11).

Lines [96, 112] declare helper functions. These constitute interfaces between the FLTK legacy code and our classes. Finally, on line [131], a third virtual function `Create_GUI` is declared. This is the primary function whose role is to join all of the necessary actions to display a running user interface on the computer's screen.

Listing 6.8 Definition of the `CC_GUI` class (in *CurrencyCalc_GUI*, *CurCalc_GUI.h*).

```
1    #include <vector>
2    #include <string>
3
4    #include "XML_CurrencyExchanger.h"
5    #include "CurrencyCalcPlayGround.h"
6
7    // Forward declarations
8    class Fl_Choice;
9    class Fl_Float_Input;
10   class Fl_Value_Output;
11   class Fl_Window;
12   class Fl_Widget;
13
14   namespace OL_CE = CurrExchanger::OnLine_CurrExchanger;
15
16
17   // CC - Currency Calculator
18   class CC_GUI
19   {
20       private:
21
22           // Pointers to the FLTK widgets
23           Fl_Choice *                    fChoiceWidget {};
24           Fl_Float_Input *               fEditWidget {};
```

(Coninued)

Listing 6.8 (continued)

```
25          Fl_Value_Output *        fStaticEditWidget {};
26          Fl_Window *              fMainWindow {};
27
28      private:
29
30          // An interface to our currency calculator component
31          using XCE = OL_CE::XML_CurrencyExchanger;
32
33          XCE &    fXML_CurrencyExchanger;
34
35          // Initial code of the reference currency
36          std::wstring    fFromCurrencyCode;
37
38      public:
39
40          CC_GUI( XCE & xce, const std::wstring & fromCurrency = L"PLN" );
41
42          virtual ~CC_GUI();
43
44      private:
45
46          ////////////////////////////////////////////////////////
47          // CALLBACK FUNCTION - do NOT modify !!!
48          ////////////////////////////////////////////////////////
49          //
50          // INPUT:
51          //      widgetPtr - a pointer to the button widget
52          //      obj - a pointer "this" to CC_GUI object
53          //
54          // OUTPUT:
55          //      none
56          //
57          // REMARKS:
58          //      A static function to be put as the FLTK button callback
59          //      Delegates an action to the Action_On_Button().
60          //
61          static void theButtonCallback( Fl_Widget * widgetPtr, void * obj );
62
63      protected:
64
65          ////////////////////////////////////////////////////////
66          // Local function to process button requests
67          ////////////////////////////////////////////////////////
68          //
69          // INPUT:
70          //      none
71          //
72          // OUTPUT:
73          //      true if ok
74          //
75          // REMARKS:
76          //
77          //
78          virtual bool Action_On_Button( void );
79
80      private:
81
82          ////////////////////////////////////////////////////////
83          // Converter of a three-letter code to one word with bytes
84          // set with code characters.
85          ////////////////////////////////////////////////////////
86          //
```

```
87          // INPUT:
88          //       wstr - a wide-string object with 3 letters code
89          //
90          // OUTPUT:
91          //       the code in one word
92          //
93          // REMARKS:
94          //
95          //
96          unsigned long    CurrencyKey_2_Code( const std::wstring & wstr );
97
98          //////////////////////////////////////////////////////////////
99          // Converts one-word currency code to the wide string code
100         //////////////////////////////////////////////////////////////
101         //
102         // INPUT:
103         //       code - a word with letters in each byte, starting
104         //            from the LSB
105         //
106         // OUTPUT:
107         //       wstring with the letters from the input word
108         //
109         // REMARKS:
110         //
111         //
112         std::wstring     Code_2_CurrencyKey( const unsigned long & code );
113
114      public:
115
116         //////////////////////////////////////////////////////////////
117         // This function creates the Graphical User Interface
118         // and runs the application.
119         //////////////////////////////////////////////////////////////
120         //
121         // INPUT:
122         //       none
123         //
124         // OUTPUT:
125         //       FLTK status code
126         //
127         // REMARKS:
128         //       This function does not exit, only upon
129         //       exit from the application
130         //
131         virtual int Create_GUI( void );
132
133   };       // end of CC_GUI
```

6.2.8.2 Definitions of Members of the `CC_GUI` Class and the Callback Mechanism

Listing 6.9 starts a series of definitions of the member functions of the `CC_GUI` class. In this case, we have a long list of FLTK header files, which we omitted here; in the *CurCalc_GUI.cpp* file, these appear instead of line [1]. Since we plan to use some of the SL containers, lines [4–6] provide useful `using` declarations. This is almost always a much better approach than simply opening everything for everybody by writing `using namespace std` (see our comment in Section 3.14.6). Then, on line [9], the *CurCalc_GUI.h* header is included. It contains the definition introduced in Listing 6.8. On line [10], the *StringConverters.h* header is included. It contains possible conversions between the `std::string` and `std::wstring` objects (Josuttis 2012). These are necessary to adapt FLTK (which operates with `std::string`) for our `XML_CurrencyExchanger` component, which utilizes `std::wstring` and allows for internationalization.

Listing 6.9 Implementation of the CC_GUI class (in *CurrencyCalc_GUI, CurCalc_GUI.cpp*).

```
1    // #include group here (FLTK & SL)
2
3    // using declarations
4    using std::string;
5    using std::wstring;
6    using std::vector;
7
8
9    #include "CurCalc_GUI.h"
10   #include "StringConverters.h"
11
12   // Class parametric constructor
13   CC_GUI::CC_GUI( XCE & xce, const wstring & fromCurrency /*= L"PLN"*/ )
14      : fXML_CurrencyExchanger( xce ),
15        fFromCurrencyCode( fromCurrency )
16   {
17   }
18
19   // Destructor does nothing - in case of derivation it is defined virtual
20   CC_GUI::~CC_GUI()
21   {
22   }
```

Lines [13–15] define the class constructor, and line [20] is reserved for the class virtual destructor, for the reasons we have discussed.

Let's take a closer look at the theButtonCallback static function whose definition starts on line [24]. As already mentioned, this is a function that will be registered to the FLTK framework to be called in response to the event of a button click by the user. It accepts two parameters: widgetPtr, which will point at the widget object from FLTK; and obj, which conveys whatever parameter we pass when registering theButtonCallback to the FLTK callback mechanism. And here is a trick: for the future obj, we will pass a pointer this to the CC_GUI object. This way, *a double dispatch* mechanism will be achieved, as illustrated in Figure 6.10.

Such a communication mechanism based on passing a function through its pointer may be encountered in older legacy code such as FLTK. Other platforms rely on similar ideas of signals and/or message passing, but embedded in the object-oriented framework (Appendix A.4).

Programmatically, to perform the previously described action, the passed obj pointer needs to be cast to the CC_GUI pointer type. This is achieved on line [27] with the reinterpret_cast operator, described in Table 3.15 (*GROUP 2*). Then, the call to the virtual Action_On_Button occurs on line [30].

```
23   // CALLBACK FUNCTION - do NOT modify !!!
24   void CC_GUI::theButtonCallback( Fl_Widget * widgetPtr, void * obj )
25   {
26       // Convert the input pointer to our class object
27       CC_GUI * theObj = reinterpret_cast< CC_GUI * >( obj );
28
29       // Call button handler function
30       theObj -> Action_On_Button();
31   }
```

The Action_On_Button function, defined on line [35], performs the action associated with currency exchange computations. Since an exception can happen here, the code is encompassed

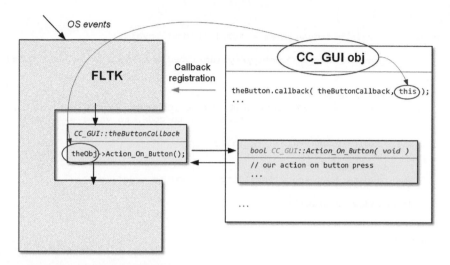

Figure 6.10 Explanation of the callback mechanism in the FLTK framework. A callback function theButtonCallback is registered that also provides a pointer to its CC_GUI object. The OS notifies FLTK about a mouse click, which FLTK translates into a button click; FLTK launches the registered theButtonCallback function, providing a pointer to the FLTK button widget and previously provided pointer to the CC_GUI object. This object is used to call the virtual function Action_On_Button, which finally performs our defined action on a button click.

within the try-catch statement (Section 3.13.2.5), starting on line [37]. On line [42], the value to be converted is read as a raw C string. Hence, it needs to be converted, first to std::string and then to double with the stod function, as on line [45]. The next piece of information for the currency exchange is the code of the destination currency. This is retrieved on line [49] by reading information stored along with the menu items of the fChoiceWidget. The Code_2_CurrencyKey function performs the correct conversion from a numerical code into std::wstring, which is necessary to call the interface of our *CurrencyExchanger* component.

With two input values in the from_val and to_code local variables, on line [53] the main conversion function Convert is called from the fXML_CurrencyExchanger object. If it is successful, the results are written to the corresponding widgets on lines [56, 59], after which the main window is redrawn on line [61] to display the results.

If an error occurs somewhere in the computations, it is caught thanks to the catch statement on line [67], and the whole function returns false on line [69].

```
32    ////////////////////////////////////////////////////////////
33    // Local function to process button requests
34    ////////////////////////////////////////////////////////////
35    bool CC_GUI::Action_On_Button( void )
36    {
37        try
38        {
39
40            ////////////////////////////////////
41            // Get the value from the edit widget
42            const char * editWidget_Text = fEditWidget->value();// first get its text
43
44
45            double from_val = stod( string( editWidget_Text ) );
```

```
46
47          const Fl_Menu_Item * menu_item = fChoiceWidget->mvalue();
48
49          wstring to_code = Code_2_CurrencyKey((unsigned long)menu_item->user_data());
50
51
52          // We are ready to convert
53          if( double to_val {}; fXML_CurrencyExchanger.Convert( fFromCurrencyCode,
54                                        from_val, to_code, to_val ) == true )
55          {
56              fStaticEditWidget->value( to_val );
57
58              // Update text
59              fStaticEditWidget->copy_label( to_string( to_code ).c_str() );
60
61              fMainWindow->redraw();
62          }
63
64          return true;
65
66      }
67      catch( ... )
68      {
69          return false;
70      }
71
72  }
```

CurrencyKey_2_Code on line [83] and Code_2_CurrencyKey on line [99] are examples of helper interfacing functions that convert information between the formats specific to the FLTK and *CurrencyExchange* components. Such *interfacing functions* or *interfacing objects*, called *adapters*, are frequently encountered in real programming due to various platforms and data formats. Here, for instance, on line [85], std::wstring is converted to std::string. Such a conversion is not always possible since std::wstring can contain more information than std::string. But in this case, a compromise is to use only Latin letters, which can usually be converted. Then, the code letters in plain ASCII format are encoded on line [86] into one unsigned long value stored in the menu items of the FLTK menu widget.

Code_2_CurrencyKey performs the opposite action: on lines [102–105], consecutive bytes from the unsigned long value are converted to consecutive code letters of the arr array. These are converted on line [106] to std::string and finally to std::wstring using the to_wstring function.

```
73  /////////////////////////////////////////////////////////////
74  // Converter of a three-letter code to one word with bytes
75  // set with code characters.
76  /////////////////////////////////////////////////////////////
77  //
78  // INPUT:
79  //      wstr - a wide-string object with 3 letters code
80  //
81  // OUTPUT:
82  //      the code in one word
83  unsigned long   CC_GUI::CurrencyKey_2_Code( const wstring & wstr )
84  {
85      string str( to_string( wstr ) );    // wstring ==> string
86      return str[ 0 ] << 16 | str[ 1 ] << 8 | str[ 2 ];
87  }
88
89  /////////////////////////////////////////////////////////////
```

```
90     // Converts one word currency code to the wide string code
91     /////////////////////////////////////////////////////////////
92     //
93     // INPUT:
94     //      code - a word with letters in each byte, starting
95     //          from the LSB
96     //
97     // OUTPUT:
98     //      wstring with the letters from the input word
99     wstring CC_GUI::Code_2_CurrencyKey( const unsigned long & code )
100    {
101        const int kArrSize { 3 };
102        char arr[ kArrSize ] = { 0 };
103        arr[ 2 ] = code & 0xFF;
104        arr[ 1 ] = code >> 8 & 0xFF;
105        arr[ 0 ] = code >> 16 & 0xFF;
106        return to_wstring( string( arr, arr + kArrSize ) );
107    }
```

The main role of the `Create_GUI` function, which begins on line [111], is to create and position various widgets and associate data with them. To simplify things, the positions and dimensions of the widgets are hardcoded in this function. We start with the dimensions of the main window, as set on lines [115, 116]. But in more advanced programs, it is a good idea to store such data in a different place, called *application resources*, which can be read and processed separately if necessary. As a result, the code is not cluttered with data, and the data values can be changed without affecting the code. However, the price is additional code to maintain such flexibility.

The main window object `main_win` of the `Fl_Windows` class is created on line [118]. On line [120], it is assigned to the pointer `fMainWindow`. As a result, the function `Action_On_Button` can redraw the window. This works fine, but we have to be sure the object that is pointed to, such as `main_win`, exists (i.e. is not destroyed) at least as long as the reference to it, such as `fMainWindow`, is in use. This is OK here since as long as the GUI is in action, control does not go out of the `Create_GUI` function. But in larger systems, and especially in parallel programming, maintaining proper object lifetimes is an important and complicated task.

Beginning on line [125], we encounter constants that define the spacing and dimensions of widgets, such as `theEdit` of type `Fl_Float_Input`, created and initialized on lines [136, 137]. This widget is responsible for entering and displaying the value of a currency to be exchanged. On line [139], a pointer is assigned to it to facilitate further access.

```
108    /////////////////////////////////////////////////////////////
109    // This function creates the Graphical User Interface
110    /////////////////////////////////////////////////////////////
111    int CC_GUI::Create_GUI( void )
112    {
113        /////////////////////////////////////////////////////////
114        // Create the main window
115        const int kMainWin_w = 400;
116        const int kMainWin_h = 250;
117        const string kMainWin_Caption( "CurrencyCalc (Polish National Bank)" );
118        Fl_Window    main_win( kMainWin_w, kMainWin_h, kMainWin_Caption.c_str() );
119
120        fMainWindow = & main_win;                // connect through the global variable
121
122
123        /////////////////////////////////////////////////////////
```

```
124     // Some const
125     const int kWidgetSeparator_h = 75;

126     const int kWidgetSeparator_v = 25;
127
128     /////////////////////////////////////////////
129     // Add edit widget
130     const int kEdit_x = 100;
131     const int kEdit_y = 50;
132     const int kEdit_w = 100;
133     const int kEdit_h = 30;
134
135     const string kEdit_Caption( "From "+ string(to_string( fFromCurrencyCode )) );
136     Fl_Float_Input theEdit(kEdit_x,kEdit_y,kEdit_w,kEdit_h, kEdit_Caption.c_str() );
137     theEdit.value( "0" );                  // initial value
138
139     fEditWidget = & theEdit;               // connect through the global variable
140
```

A little more work is necessary to create and properly initialize the combo widget, whose position is defined starting at line [143]. Once again, it is relative to the position of the theEdit widget. As a result, if we change the position of the previous widgets, the others will be adjusted automatically.

The task we face now is how to set up a combo widget in FLTK, represented by the Fl_Choice class, with the currency names stored in the *CurrencyCalc* component. If we succeed, then a user who clicks on the combo will see the names of the currencies they can choose from for exchange. We can access our XML_CurrencyExchanger object using the fXML_CurrencyExchanger reference. With this at hand, on line [148], the XCE::CurrencyMap object is accessed and referenced with the curMap object, which should not be empty.

At this point, two vectors are created: on line [152], menuItemVec to store FLTK's Fl_Menu_Item objects; and on line [155], menuItemTexts to store the std::string objects with the currency names. The problem is that the Fl_Menu_Item object stores only a C-style pointer to the text, whereas the text itself has to be stored somewhere else. Again, we face the problem of synchronizing object lifetimes. In other words, we have to ensure that a pointer stored by a menu item always points at a valid object. Another problem is that menu items expect ASCII text, whereas our *CurrencyExchanged* object holds Unicode characters (i.e. std::wstring). Hence, on lines [157–159], we copy the currency names from curMap to the menuItemTexts vector, at the same time transforming std::wstring objects to std::string. Since menuItemTexts is empty at first, we have to use the back_inserter function on line [157]. On the other hand, text conversion is done with the lambda function (Section 3.14.6) defined on lines [158, 159].

Then, on lines [162–165], the Fl_Menu_Item objects are created, feeding their constructors with the pointer to the previously prepared currency name and currency code returned on line [165] by the CurrencyKey_2_Code function. Note that on line [162], to access the key and currency simultaneously, we use structured binding (Section 3.17). However, only key is used in the loop.

Finally, menuItemVec has to be delimited with *a sentinel object* to indicate its end. Such sentinels are a common technique to indicate the end of a series of objects. The simplest examples are the C-like strings ending with the value 0 to indicate an end-of-string (EOS), as discussed in Appendix A.2.2. Here, on line [169], a sentinel object (the one with all its members set to 0) is pushed back.

Starting at line [172], the theChoiceWidget object of type Fl_Choice is created and initialized with the carefully created menuItemVec object.

```
141    //////////////////////////////////////////////
142    // Add combo widget
143    const int kChoiceWidget_x = kEdit_x + kEdit_w + kWidgetSeparator_h;
144    const int kChoiceWidget_y = kEdit_y;
145    const int kChoiceWidget_w = kEdit_w;
146    const int kChoiceWidget_h = kEdit_h;
147
148    const XCE::CurrencyMap & curMap = fXML_CurrencyExchanger.GetCurrencyMap();
149
150    assert( curMap.size() > 0 );
151
152    vector< Fl_Menu_Item > menuItemVec;
153
154    // A collection of FLTK menu items text
155    std::vector< std::string >   menuItemTexts;
156
157    std::transform( curMap.begin(), curMap.end(), back_inserter( menuItemTexts ),
158                    [] ( const auto & cur ) {
159                        return to_string( cur.second.GetCurrName() ); } );
160
161    int cntr { 0 };
162    for( const auto & [ key, currency ] : fXML_CurrencyExchanger.GetCurrencyMap() )
163    {
164       menuItemVec.push_back( { menuItemTexts[ cntr ++ ].c_str(), 0, 0,
165                reinterpret_cast< void * >( CurrencyKey_2_Code( key ) ) } );
166    }
167
168    // Put a sentinel to the menu list
169    menuItemVec.push_back( { 0 } );
170
171
172    const string kChoiceWidget_Caption( "To " );
173    Fl_Choice theChoiceWidget( kChoiceWidget_x, kChoiceWidget_y, kChoiceWidget_w,
174                               kChoiceWidget_h, kChoiceWidget_Caption.c_str() );
175    theChoiceWidget.menu( & menuItemVec[ 0 ] );
176
177    fChoiceWidget = & theChoiceWidget;  // Connect through the member variable
```

In the last part of the `Create_GUI` function, starting on line [180], the `theStaticEdit` object is created. Then, lines [195–202] create `theButton`, of `Fl_Return_Button` type. To set up the callback mechanisms on a button click, on line [205], `theButton` is connected to the `theButtonCallback` and `this` objects (Figure 6.10).

```
178    //////////////////////////////////////////////
179    // Add const edit widget
180    const int kStaticEdit_x = kEdit_x;
181    const int kStaticEdit_y = kEdit_y + kEdit_h + kWidgetSeparator_v;
182    const int kStaticEdit_w = kEdit_w;
183    const int kStaticEdit_h = kEdit_h;
184
185    const string kStaticEdit_Caption( "" );
186    Fl_Value_Output    theStaticEdit( kStaticEdit_x, kStaticEdit_y, kStaticEdit_w,
187                                      kStaticEdit_h, kStaticEdit_Caption.c_str() );
188    int staticValue = 0;
189    theStaticEdit.value( staticValue );
190
191    fStaticEditWidget = & theStaticEdit; // Connect through the member variable
192
```

```
193    /////////////////////////////////////////////
194    // Add button
195    const int kButtonEdit_x = kStaticEdit_x;
196    const int kButtonEdit_y = kStaticEdit_y + kStaticEdit_h + kWidgetSeparator_v;
197    const int kButtonEdit_w = kStaticEdit_w;
198    const int kButtonEdit_h = kStaticEdit_h;
199
200    const string kButtonCaption( "ReCalc" );
201
202    Fl_Return_Button theButton( kButtonEdit_x, kButtonEdit_y, kButtonEdit_w,
203                                kButtonEdit_h, kButtonCaption.c_str() );
204
205    theButton.callback( theButtonCallback, this ); // Connect the callback function
206
207    /////////////////////////////////////////////
208    // Finalize adding new widgets
209    main_win.end();
210    main_win.show();
211
212    /////////////////////////////////////////////
213    // When all the windows are closed it returns zero
214    return Fl::run();
215
216  }
```

All the widgets have been set up, so we are almost done. Lines [209, 210, 214] let the FLTK framework render them. After their execution, the window appears.

6.2.8.3 Launching the GUI-Based Application

The last thing to do is to launch our application in the `main` function, as shown in the Listing 6.10.

Listing 6.10 Launching the FLTK-based application for the currency exchange (in *CurrencyCalc_GUI, main.cpp*).

```
1    #include <FL/FL_ask.H>
2    #include <filesystem>
3
4    #include "CurCalc_GUI.h"
5    #include "CloseWindow.h"
6
7
8    int main()
9    {
10       CloseConsoleWindow();          // Get rid of the console window
11
12       namespace fs = std::filesystem;
13       // Get full path to the initialization file
14       wstring iniPath( fs::current_path()
15                               / fs::path( CurrExchanger::initDefaultFileName ) );
16
17       // Create the currency exchanger object
18       auto curExchObj = OL_CE::CreateCurExchanger( OL_CE::nbp_addr, iniPath );
19       if( ! curExchObj )
20           return fl_alert( "Cannot load currency info - exiting ..." ), -1;   // Exit
21
22       // Create a GUI object with the provided currency exchanger object
23       CC_GUI   gCC_GUI( * curExchObj );
24
25       // Run application
26       return gCC_GUI.Create_GUI();
27  }
```

Lines [1–5] have the necessary `#includes`. The definition of the `main` function starts on line [8]. `CloseConsoleWindow` is the first function, called on line [10]; its role is to hide the black terminal window. (Its code can be found in the source file.) Then, line [12] creates an alias `fs` to the filesystem namespace. This is used on lines [14, 15] to create a path to the initialization file, which is expected in the same directory as the executed application, conveyed by the `current_path` function.

On line [18], the `curExchObj` object of the `XML_CurrExch_Optional` type is returned. If the operation was successful, it contains a valid `XML_CurrencyExchanger` object. But if for some reason the `curExchObj` optional object is empty, such as if there is no initialization file or no Internet connection, as verified on line [19], the application exits with a short message issued by the `fl_alert` on line [20]. Note that to shorten the code, the `return` statement yields the error code `-1`, which is provided as the rightmost value by the comma `(,)` operator (see *GROUP 16*, Table 3.15).

Finally, on line [23], the `CC_GUI` object is created and linked with the `XML_CurrencyExchanger` object by dereferencing `curExchObj`. The GUI is launched on line [26]; the results are shown in Figure 6.11. The last call returns if the application is closed by a user.

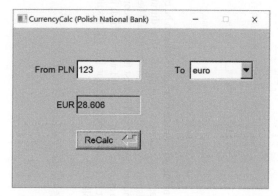

Figure 6.11 Main window of the *CurrencyCalc* application rendered by the FLTK interface.

In this section, we learned about the following:

- Creating simple GUI applications with the FLTK library
- Using the callback mechanism based on a simple function pointer registration
- Managing object lifetime and object inter-dependencies
- Writing interface functions to legacy code

6.3 System Clocks and Time Measurements

Time measurement is one of the most intrinsic features of every microprocessor system. Precise timing is necessary for all digital circuits, as well as for task scheduling by an OS. We also saw current time measurement in the `DisplayCurrentTime` function (Section 3.18.5). But the facilities available to access and measure time depend on the platform (i.e. the OS), as well as on the programming language and its libraries. C++ offers several time-related objects, mostly in the `std::chrono` namespace. The most frequently used members and their properties are listed in Table 6.4. More detailed information can be found in the literature (Stroustrup 2013) or on the Web (Cppreference.com 2019a).

Table 6.4 Basic time operations from the std::chrono namespace (in the headers *<ctime>* and *<chrono>*).

Object	Description	Examples

`std::chrono::system_clock`	A wall clock time from the system-wide realtime clock. It may not be monotonic (time can be adjusted at any moment).	The following shows a function to return a string with the current date and time:
		
		``
		1 // Returns a string with current date & time
		2 string GetCurrentTime(void)
		3 {
		4 using timer = std::chrono::system_clock; // Short name for a timer
		5
		6 std::time_t time_point = timer::to_time_t(timer::now());
		7
		8 return std::ctime(& time_point); // Converts to string
		9 }
		``

`std::chrono::steady_clock`	A monotonic clock (not adjustable). The time points of this clock cannot decrease as physical time progresses. Hence, this clock is suitable for measuring intervals.	On line [4], various types of clock can be chosen, as shown at left. The choice of a clock is application-driven: for a precise time duration, use high_resolution_clock. For a time display, system_clock can be used. The functions now and to_time_t are members of a chosen clock class. The first function records a current time point. The second function converts it to an older object std::time_t, which is easier to convert to a string via construction of the std::ctime object on line [8]. The result of calling GetCurrentTime can look like the following:
`std::chrono::high_resolution_clock`	The clock with the shortest tick period available on a platform.[a]	`Wed Jan 2 23:45:46 2019`

Clock members:

Member	Description
`timer::now`	Returns the current time point
`timer::to_time_t`	Converts a system clock time point to std::time_t
`std::time_t`	An arithmetic type to hold time as a number of seconds since 00:00, Jan 1 1970 UTC.
`std::ctime`	Used to convert time expressed in epochs to calendar local time.

`std::chrono::duration`	A class to represent time intervals.	The function `fun_perform_timer` launches a function supplied as its parameter and measures its performance time. To pass the function, we use the template class `std::function [1, 4]`. In this version, the mechanism is set to process functions taking an `int` parameter and not returning a value. Hence, `void( int )` is set as a template parameter of `std::function` (Section 3.14.9). But C++ is flexible enough to convey a function with any set of parameters, as we will show.

```cpp
1   using fun_void_int = std::function< void( int ) >;
2
3   // Launches fun( fun_param ) and measures its time
4   void fun_perform_timer( fun_void_int fun, int fun_param )
5   {
6       using timer = std::chrono::high_resolution_clock;   // == steady_clock
7
8       // -------------
9       auto timer_start = timer::now();                    // Catch start of time
10
11      fun( fun_param );                                   // run function here ...
12
13      auto timer_end = timer::now();                      // Catch the end of time
14      // -------------
15
16      std::chrono::duration< double > comp_period = timer_end - timer_start;
17
18      cout << "Computation time = " << comp_period.count() << " [s]" << endl;
19
20      cout << "Computation time = " << std::chrono::duration_cast
21          < std::chrono::seconds >( comp_period ).count() << " [is]"   << endl;
22
23      cout << "Computation time = " << std::chrono::duration_cast
        < std::chrono::microseconds >( comp_period ).count()
            << " [us]" << endl;
    }
```

(Continued)

Table 6.4 (continued)

Object	Description	Examples

std::chrono::duration_cast	Converts a time duration to other units.	On line [6], high_resolution_clock is selected. The start time point is caught on line [9], the test function is called on line [11], and then the end time is caught on line [13]. A time duration object is created on line [16]. This is displayed on lines [18, 20, 22] in different units. The previous time-measuring function is verified in the following context:
		
		`24    void arithm_fun( int p ) // A test function`
		`25    {`
		`26       for( auto a : range( p ) )`
		`27          cout << a * a << " ";`
		`28    }`
		`29`
		`30    void fun_perform_timer_test( void )`
		`31    {`
		`32       fun_perform_timer( arithm_fun, 23 ); // Call a measure with p = 23`
		`33    }`
		
		After calling fun_perform_timer_test on a test computer, the last three lines of the output look like this:
		
		`Computation time = 0.00313335 [s]`
		`Computation time = 0 [is]`
		`Computation time = 3133 [us]`

[a] In Visual Studio 2019 on Windows 10, this is the same as std::chrono::steady_clock.

6.4   (✎) **Time Measurement for Function Execution**

Measuring the time required for function execution looks simple – we need to mark start and end times and compute their difference. We will show how to write a wrapper function that encompasses these operations for any function we wish to measure. However, precisely measuring the time consumed by the execution of a few lines of code or a function is not as easy as it might look at first glance. First of all, a function does not run by itself; other OS processes are running in the background, to operate the mouse and connect to the Internet, for example. The background conditions may change from run to run, so in practice, we measure the overall time taken to execute our function and whatever runs with it.

In this section, we extend the `fun_perform_timer` function presented in Table 6.4. The main issue with this function is that it can measure the execution time of any function as long as the function takes an `int` as a parameter and returns `void`. But we'd like to measure the execution time of *any* function – a function that can take and return whatever arguments it wants. C++ comes with mechanisms that allow for passing an arbitrary number of arguments of arbitrary types.

In this section, we will learn about:

- Variadic arguments (bonds)
- Forwarding universal references with `std::forward< decltype( ) >`

As we know, since C++17, a namespace can be created inside another namespace, such as in Listing 6.11, lines [1, 4]. In this nested namespace, a constant `kIterations` is defined on line [6] that will control the number of function calls during its measurement of execution times. The definition of the `measureFuncAvTiming` lambda function for execution time measurement starts on line [22]. The `kIteration` constant is passed to the `iter` in the caption. Then two interesting arguments are passed:

- `func` – A forward (universal) reference conveying a function object to be executed `iter` number of times to measure performance time
- `func_params` – A *variadic list* of parameters that will be passed to the `func`. The variadic list of parameters to a function or template lets us pass *any* number of parameters

A compile-time invariant is checked on line [24]. It ensures that the number of iterations is larger than zero. However, as we already know, unlike the familiar `assert` fuse, which is checked at runtime, `static_assert` is verified during compilation. So, if the condition of `static_assert` evaluates to `false`, an error will be reported, and compilation will stop.

On line [28], the current timestamp is caught by the `time_start` object by calling the `timer::now` function. This and other time-related functions are summarized in Section 6.3.

The function undergoing the performance test is launched `iter` number of times, as orchestrated by the range `for` loop on line [31]. Its range is provided by the auxiliary `range` class, which will be presented in Section 6.5.

On lines [32, 34], `func` is executed with `func_params` as its arguments. However, many variants of `func` and `func_params` are possible; therefore, we use `std::forward` with a deduced type of `func`, obtained by a call to `decltype< func >`. A similar construction is used on line [34] to pass the variadic parameters. This is perfect forwarding, as explained in Section 4.5.1.

Listing 6.11 Definition of the `measureFuncAvTiming` function for measuring the execution time of the provided function (in *CppBookCode, Time.cpp*).

```
1   namespace CppBook
2   {
3       // Nested namespace
4       namespace LTimer
5       {
6           const int kIterations = 10;
7
8           ///////////////////////////////////////////////////////////////
9           // Lambda to measure the execution time of a function taking
10          // any set of parameters.
11          ///////////////////////////////////////////////////////////////
12          //
13          // INPUT:
14          //       func - a function to be called as: func( func_params )
15          // OUTPUT:
16          //       time in milliseconds per single execution of func
17          //
18          // REMARKS:
19          //       func will be called kIterations times and the
20          //       execution time will be averaged
21          //
22          auto measureFuncAvTiming =   [ iter = kIterations ]
                                         ( auto && func, auto && ... func_params )
23          {
24              static_assert( kIterations > 0 );      // check at compile time
25
26              using timer = typename std::chrono::high_resolution_clock;
27
28              auto time_start = timer::now();
29
30                  // Run an algorithm a number of iterations
31                  for( auto i : range( iter ) )
32                      std::forward< decltype( func ) >( func )
33                      (
34                          std::forward< decltype( func_params ) >( func_params ) ...
35                      );
36
37                  // Compute an average execution time of func in milliseconds
38              return   std::chrono::duration_cast<   std::chrono::milliseconds >
39                      ( timer::now() - time_start ).count()
40                      /iter;
41          };
42
43      }
44
45  }
```

Briefly, remember that any function `func` can be passed with any number of arguments of any type. What we want is to pass each lvalue-ref argument as an lvalue-ref, and each rvalue-ref as an rvalue-ref. Perfect forwarding does exactly this (Meyers 2014). Otherwise, the rvalue parameters could be passed through lvalue-refs, what we want to avoid.

By taking the difference between the end and start timestamps, the `measureFuncAvTiming` function returns the duration in milliseconds of an average call to `func`. A value in milliseconds or other time measurement unit can be obtained by calling the `std::chrono::duration_cast` operator (Section 6.3).

What remains is to write a simple function like the following

```
46  void MathFun_RandTest( int iters, double eps, double & result )
47  {
48      // init Mersenne twister
49      std::mt19937 mtRandomEngine( (random_device())() );
50      std::bernoulli_distribution bern( 0.7 );     // 0 or 1 with p=0.7
51
52      result = 0.0;
53      for( int i = 0; i < iters; ++ i )
54          result += bern( mtRandomEngine );
55
56      result /= static_cast< double >( iters ) + eps;
57  }
```

and, with the following code, measure its average execution time per single call:

```
58  auto funTimer { CppBook::LTimer::measureFuncAvTiming };
59
60  double result {};
61
62  auto run_time = funTimer( MathFun_RandTest, 1234567, 1e-5, result );
63
64  cout << "MathFun_RandTes last result: " << result << endl;
65  cout << "MathFun_RandTes run-time: " << run_time << " [ms]" << endl;
```

On line [62], the function `funTimer`, which is the same as the `CppBook::LTimer::meas` `ureFuncAvTiming` lambda function but with a shorter name, launches `MathFun_RandTest` with its parameters several times. `MathFun_RandTest` simply computes an average of the 1 234 567 random numbers drawn from the Bernoulli distribution. For this purpose, the Mersenne random engine is initialized on line [49] with the value returned by the functional operator called on behalf of the `random_device` temporary object (see Section 3.17.3). Finally, the last average value (should be close to p, right?) and the average single execution timing are printed on the screen, as follows:

```
MathFun last result: 0.699677
MathFun run-time: 177 [ms]
```

As we can appreciate, the returned value 0.699677 is close to the 0.7 set on line [50].

6.5 Range Class

C++ 11 introduced a very useful new form of the `for` loop, the *range* `for`, as discussed in Section 3.13.2.2. In conjunction with the `auto` keyword (Section 3.7), it greatly facilitates writing loops, especially when accessing elements of the containers, such as `std::vector` or and `std::list`. It is now very easy to traverse each element from a given set of values, such as

```
for( auto c : { 1, 2, 3 } )
   cout << c;
```

But things get slightly more cumbersome if we wish to traverse a set of values generated by a more complicated formula. For example, starting from 0.0, we wish to generate all consecutive values not exceeding 100.0 and spread by 2.56. With the "standard" `for` loop, this is as simple as writing the following lines of code:

```
for( double f = 0.0; f < 100.0; f += 2.56 )
   cout << f << endl;
```

However, it would be much more convenient if we could harness the new form of the `for` loop and still be able to generate all types of series, like the previous one. For this purpose, we want an iterator with the following syntax

```
range( from, to, step )
```

where `from` stands for a starting value, `to` is the end value (exclusive), and `step` is a value that increases for each step in the iteration. In addition, shortcuts can be introduced; for example, to step by 1, we can use

```
range( from, to )
```

or

```
range( to )
```

to generate all values in the set [0, to) with a step of 1. Interestingly, SL does not provide such a helper (in some frameworks it is called a *linspace*). We can use only `std::iota` to fill an SL container with consecutive values incremented by 1 each time. To remedy this, the `range` class was developed. Before we go to its definition, let's see what it can do by examining the examples in Listing 6.12.

Listing 6.12 Using the `range` class in examples (in *CppBookCode, range_test.cpp*).

```
1   #include "range.h"
2
3
4   void RangeTest( void )
5   {
6      ofstream ostr( "RangeTest.txt" );
7      if( ostr.is_open() == false )
8         return;
9
10     // 1:
11     ostr << "1st test:" << endl;
12
13     vector< float > v = range( 256.0f );
14     copy( v.begin(), v.end(), ostream_iterator< float >( ostr, ", " ) );
15
```

On line [1], we include the range class via its header file. On lines [6–11], a file is created; and if that happens successfully, some text is put into it. Then, a `vector` of `float`s is created and initialized with the consecutive values 0, ..., 255 (inclusive). This is done by assigning to the vector the object `range( 256.0f )`. This works since `range` implements a conversion operator to `std::vector`, as we will discuss. Finally, on line [14], the entire vector is copied, i.e. streamed out to the created file represented by the `ostr` object. In this case, the output looks as follows ([. . .] inserted here to save space):

```
1st test:
0, 1, 2, 3, 4, 5, 6, 7, 8, 9, 10, 11, 12, 13, 14, 15, 16, 17, 18, 19, 20,
21, 22, 23, 24, 25, 26, 27, 28, 29, 30, 31, 32, 33, 34, 35, 36, 37, 38, 39,
40, 41, 42, 43, 44, 45, 46, 47, 48, [...]
240, 241, 242, 243, 244, 245, 246, 247, 248, 249, 250, 251, 252, 253, 254,
255,
```

Let's move to the second example, shown on lines [17–21]:

```
16    // 2:
17    ostr << endl << "2nd test:" << endl;
18
19    vector< size_t > v_size_t( range<>( 0, 100, 13 ) );
20    for( auto a : v_size_t )
21        ostr << a << ", ";
22
```

The main difference is the range generated by calling `range<>( 0, 100, 13 )`. In this case, the values 0, 13, 26, ..., 91 are copied to the `v_size_t` vector. A slight difference is using the `range<>` type instead of the pure `range`. Adding the empty type `<>` allows us to use `range` with its default type for iterations: `size_t`. The output for the second example is as follows:

```
2nd test:
0, 13, 26, 39, 52, 65, 78, 91,
```

In the next example, we use the simple `range` object assigned to the `vvv` object with the `auto` type. In the consecutive `for` loop, another `auto` variable `a` iterates through all values of `vvv`:

```
23    // 3:
24    ostr << endl << "3rd test:" << endl;
25
26    auto vvv = range( 123 );          // 0..122 inclusive, with step 1
27    for( auto a : vvv )
28        ostr << a << ", ";
29
```

```
3rd test:
0, 1, 2, 3, 4, 5, 6, 7, 8, 9, 10, 11, 12, 13, 14, 15, 16, 17, 18, 19, 20,
21, 22, 23, 24, 25, 26, 27, 28, 29, 30, 31, 32, 33, 34, 35, 36, 37, 38, 39,
40, 41, 42, 43, 44, 45, 46, 47, 48, [...]
95, 96, 97, 98, 99, 100, 101, 102, 103, 104, 105, 106, 107, 108, 109, 110,
111, 112, 113, 114, 115, 116, 117, 118, 119, 120, 121, 122,
```

The example shows the operation of the `range` in two loops, iterating through the `float` and `int` values. The first loop traverses the values from 0 up to but not including 256.0, with a step of 16.5. The inner loop goes from the integer −2 up to +16 with a step of 3. In other words, at each step, the value of `step` is added to the current value of the internal state of the `range` iterator:

```
30    // 4:
31    ostr << endl << "4th test:" << endl;
32
33    // Can be used in the nested loops as well
34    for( auto i : range( 0.0, 256.0, 16.5 ) ) // Must be the same type, 0.0 not 0
35    {
```

```
36        for( auto j : range( -2, 16, 3 ) )
37        {
38            ostr << j << ", ";
39        }
40        ostr << endl << i << endl;
41    }
42
43 }
```

The shortened output of the fourth example is as follows:

```
4th test:
-2, 1, 4, 7, 10, 13,
0
-2, 1, 4, 7, 10, 13,
16.5
[...]
-2, 1, 4, 7, 10, 13,
231
-2, 1, 4, 7, 10, 13,
247.5
```

Let's now examine the internals of the range class, shown in Listing 6.13. It is a template class, where a template parameter T defines the type of an iterator. Thus, if we wish to traverse integer values, we can substitute int for T; for floating-point values, T can be float or double, as shown in the previous examples. But the default value is size_t, which denotes a type of nonnegative integer values with a range that can represent the size of any object in bytes (Stroustrup 2013).

Listing 6.13 Definition of the range class (in *CppBookCode, range.h*).

```
1  template < typename T = size_t >
2  class range
3  {
4        const T kFrom, kEnd, kStep;
5
6      public:
7
8        ///////////////////////////////////////////////////////////
9        // Constructor
10       ///////////////////////////////////////////////////////////
11       //
12       // INPUT:
13       //        from - Starting number of the sequence.
14       //        end - Generate numbers up to, but not including this number.
15       //        step - Diff between each number in the sequence (must not be 0).
16       //
17       trange( const T from, const T end, const T step = 1 )
18           : kFrom( from ), kEnd( end ), kStep( step )
19       {
20           assert( kStep != 0 );
21           if( kStep == 0 )
22               throw std::out_of_range( "step param must not be 0" );
23       }
24
25       // Default from==0, step==1
26       range( const T end )
27           : kFrom( 0 ), kEnd( end ), kStep( 1 )
```

```
28        {
29            assert ( kEnd > 0 );
30        }
31
32    private:
33
34        class range_iter
35        {
36            T fVal{};
37            const T kStep{};
38        public:
39            range_iter( const T v, const T step ) : fVal( v ), kStep( step ) {}
40            operator T () const              { return fVal; }
41            operator const T & ()            { return fVal; }
42            const T operator * () const         { return fVal; }
43            const range_iter & operator ++ ()    { fVal += kStep; return * this; }
44
45
46            bool operator == ( const range_iter & ri ) const
47            {
48                return ! operator != ( ri );
49            }
50
51            bool operator != ( const range_iter & ri ) const
52            {
53                // This is a tricky part - when working with iterators
54                // it checks only once for != which must be a hit to stop;
55                // However, simple != does not work if increasing
56                // kStart by N times kSteps skips over kEnd. Therefore this condition:
57                return kStep > 0 ? fVal < ri.fVal : fVal > ri.fVal;
58            }
59        };
60    public:
61        const range_iter begin()   { return range_iter( kFrom, kStep ); }
62        const range_iter end()     { return range_iter( kEnd,  kStep ); }
63
64    public:
65
66        // Conversion to any vector< T >
67        operator std::vector< T > ( void )
68        {
69            auto p = [this]( auto v ){ for( T i {kFrom}; i<kEnd; i+=kStep ) v.push_
                        back(i); return v; };
70            auto n = [this]( auto v ){ for( T i {kFrom}; i>kEnd; i+=kStep ) v.push_
                        back(i); return v; };
71
72            return kStep > 0 ? p( std::vector< T >() ) : n( std::vector< T >() );
                // use RVO here
73        }
74    };
```

range contains three private data members, defined on line [4]. They represent the constant start, end, and step values for the range. Then, on lines [8–30], two constructors are defined; due to the default 1 for the step parameter, we can create the three types of range objects, as already described. Note that for proper operation of the range class, the step parameter cannot be 0; otherwise, the iterations will be infinite. This, in addition to notes in the class comments, is checked in the build version of the software using the assert command. If it happens at runtime, a std::out_of_range exception is thrown.

The important part of the `range` class is its nested private class `range_iter`. It resembles the proxy pattern defined for the `TLongNumberFor` class in Section 4.15.5.1. But in this case, `range_iter` provides a suitable interface required for the iterators. When constructed on line [39], it accepts two values, which are then copied to its `fVal` and `kSteps` member data. `fVal` stores the current state (a "position") of an iterator. `kSteps`, being constant, is used when an iterator is progressing to the next position. `range_iter` overloads a number of operators. The first two, defined on lines [40, 41], are simple conversions to `T` and its reference, which is a common type for the `range` and `range_iter` classes. The overloaded dereferencing operator, shown on line [42], lets us read values. On the other hand, the increment operator on line [43] lets us advance the iterator. The most intriguing is the comparison operator defined on lines [51–58]. Its operation is divided into two directions: negative and positive values of the `kStep` member. In either case, `true` is returned if and only if our `fVal` state is before than `fVal` in the object we compare to (e.g. the end iterator), in accordance with the direction of iterations. Also note that for iteration with floating-point values, we cannot use the simple equation condition.

`range_iter` objects are returned by two members of the `range` class: the `begin` (line [61]) and `end` (line [62]) functions, which are the standard way of expressing the beginning and end of any of the SL collections. `begin` sets the internal state of the iterator to the `kFrom` value, whereas `end` sets its state to the `kEnd` value of the range class.

Here we will make a small digression on *iterators*. These are ubiquitous programming components whose primary role is to traverse collections of data, whatever it may be. Basically, there are two types of iterators: *internal* and *external*. We have already seen and used SL iterators that let us traverse vectors, strings, and maps, for instance. These are external iterators whose primary benefit is that they can be nested over a collection. On the other hand, the `range_iter` inner class is an example of an internal iterator. Its role here is as expected – it serves as a return (proxy) value to the interface composed of the `begin` and `end` members, which lets us use the `range` class, for instance, in the range `for` loop (Section 3.13.2.2).

The last overloaded operator is a conversion to `vector< T >`, defined in `range` on lines [67–73]. With the help of the two lambda functions it lets us convert the `range` class implicitly to `std::vector` with consecutive values as generated by the iteration process. Hence, `range` can also be used to initialize vectors with iterated values, as shown in the previous examples.

6.5.1 Functional Programming and the Ranges Library

C++ has is a more profound concept of a range, which differs from what we presented in the previous section. We talk in this section about *ranges*, i.e. the relatively new programming method aimed mostly at improving chained operations on collections using *pipes*. We have seen many SL operations in which the common interface is a pair of iterators indicating the beginning and end of the elements to be processed, i.e. the range: for instance, `std::find`, `std::copy`, and `std::sort`, presented in Table 3.6. So, what is wrong with passing the range as two separate values? The main obstacle is encountered when one function tries to pass another a range that is the result of an operation. In many contexts, it would be beneficial to have one structure containing all the information instead of two separate iterators passed as the result of one function as an input to the other function without creating local objects to store the intermediate results. For example, the following code

```
vector< int >   vec( 10 );

// Put some values to vec ...

// Sort the values in vec
sort( vec.begin(),vec.end() );
```

in the `range` framework could be simplified as follows:

```
vector< int >   vec( 10 );

// Put some values to vec ...

// Sort the values in vec
sort( vec );
```

Such a compact structure is also less error-prone: for example, it disallows erroneously passing iterators to different collections. Such functionality has been developed in the form of libraries. One of them is *range-v3*, developed by Eric Niebler (2019), which was recently accepted to become part of the new standard C++20. Together with the C++ concepts, it will allow us to write clearer, more compact code. Some exercises with these new techniques are included in the "Questions and Exercises" section of this chapter.

More information on functional programming, ranges, and other inspiring new programming methods in C++ can be found in the book by Ivan Čukić (2019).

6.6 Example Project – Parsing Expressions

In Section 3.19, we discussed C++ operators and expressions. We have used them extensively as building blocks of larger language constructs. But how does the compiler, which is itself a program, recognize whether a+b*c is a valid expression and, if so, how it should be interpreted? Certainly, compilers constitute the art of software design; but in this section, we will look at how to write a simple interpreter that can tell if an expression is correct and another interpreter that can evaluate the value of an expression. For this purpose, we will examine methods of formal language description called *formal grammars*. Then, we will see how to parse an expression in order to tell if it does or does not comply with the grammar rules. We will also learn how to build special data structures that represent expressions in the form of parsing (syntax) trees. Finally, we will learn how to traverse such a tree with a visitor pattern to draw a tree structure or to evaluate the value of an expression. The discussion will allow us to practice previously learned and new programming techniques that involve object-oriented features of modern C++. Summarizing, in this section, we will learn:

- What a formal grammar is, and how to describe arithmetic expressions
- How to get rid of left recursion in a grammar to facilitate its implementation with the *interpreter* design pattern
- What a parsing tree is and how it can be implemented with the *composite* design pattern
- How to extend the interpreter to build a parsing tree that reflects the structure of an expression
- How to traverse a tree with the *visitor* pattern to evaluate an expression (double-dispatch technique)

- How to build a stack data structure to store smart pointers
- Non-owning access to objects with pointers and owning access through the smart pointers
- Reverse Polish notation (RPN) to facilitate expression evaluation
- The prototype pattern to clone compound objects
- Runtime type identification (RTTI) in action with `dynamic_cast`

This plan includes many design patterns, of which the composite and visitor can be especially useful in applications not necessarily related to computer language analyzers. Let's start with a short introduction to the methods of defining grammatical rules that govern computer language constructs.

6.6.1 Defining Language Expressions with Formal Grammar Rules

The C++ operators were presented in Section 3.19. We observed that in addition to the function of an operator, what is important is its precedence as well as its associativity. These are arbitrarily defined by the standard to be unambiguous and to obey the rules indicated in Table 3.15. However, how can these and other language rules be described formally? For this purpose, formal grammars have been devised. These are necessary to obtain a common language definition that us to implement compilers that operate as expected by the users. The subjects of formal grammars and compiler design constitute the core of computer science; they are also very advanced topics treated in many papers and books (Aho et al. 2006). They are outside the scope of this book, but implementing a simple interpreter that copes with basic expressions will demonstrate many useful programming techniques.

A grammar is a collection of grammar productions described using terminal and nonterminal symbols.[3] The following productions

```
E -> E + T | E - T | T          expression
T -> T * F | T / F | F          term
F -> D | ( E )                  factor
D -> 0 | 1 | 2 | ... | 9        digit
```

let us formally describe any expression containing single digits and four binary operators, such as the following

```
3 + ( 4 / 5 - 6 )
```

as well as to tell whether an expression like this one fulfills the rules:

```
3 + ( 4 / ) 5 - 6
```

If so, then we say that the expression is *compliant* with the syntax. Otherwise, we have a syntax error. In the previous grammar productions, red symbols denote *terminal symbols*, i.e. those that are directly typed on a terminal (hence their name). Nonterminal symbols are denoted with black capital letters. They correspond to the formal, or abstract, concepts that form the grammar.

---

3 To describe the syntax of computer languages, the Backus–Naur Form (BNF) has been used for years. It is a metalanguage devised for the definition of the syntax of ALGOL 60. BNF rules are composed of terminal symbols, nonterminal symbols, and meta-symbols such as the alternative |.

Finally, the | symbol denotes a logical alternative between the productions. Hence, D -> 0 | 1 means either 0 or 1 fulfills the D production, and so on.

These grammar rules reflect operator precedence and associativity. The process of fitting grammar rules to an expression is called *parsing*. An example of parsing one of the previous expressions with the previous grammar rules is shown in Figure 6.12.

Parsing is preceded by a *lexical analysis* that splits an expression into meaningful language categories such as numbers and operators called *tokens*. There are special programs, such as *lex* and *flex*, that do the job. But the good news is that for most simple grammars, any regular expression engine, such as the C++ *regex* library discussed in Section 6.2.1, can be used if provided with proper pattern definitions.

We are ready to implement a program that performs the lexical analysis and parsing in accordance with the previous grammar rules. In the first attempt, we may consider implementing nonterminal symbols as functions. On the other hand, the terminal symbols can be directly matched from

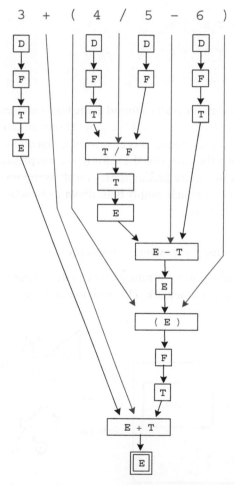

Figure 6.12 Parsing the expression 3+(4/5-6). An expression is syntax-compliant if the entire expression can be completely derived from the grammar rules. Otherwise there is a syntax error. The grammar reflects operator precedence and associativity. Parsing is preceded by lexical analysis, which splits an expression into meaningful language categories such as numbers and operators.

a string representing the input expression. Hence, the first rule from the expression group could be implemented as follows:

```cpp
bool E( void )
{
    if( E() && Match( '+' ) && T() )
      return true;
    else
      // ...

    // ...
}
```

Everything would be fine except that the previous function E would break almost immediately due to infinite recursive call to itself in the third line. This is an inherent problem arising from the structure of our simple grammar. The way around it is to transform the rules in order to eliminate the left recursion. The new version of the grammar, with no left recursion, looks as follows:

```
E   -> T E'
E'  -> + T E' | - T E' | e
T   -> F T'
T'  -> * F T' | / F T' | e
F   -> ( E ) | D
D   -> 0 | 1 | 2 | ... | 9
```

Grammar transformation techniques can be found in the books on formal grammars, such as the classical *Compilers: Principles, Techniques, and Tools* by Aho et al. (2006) and *Modern Compiler Design* by Grune et al. (2012). Nevertheless, it is easy to experimentally verify that the two sets of rules are equivalent: that is, that they describe the same types of expressions. However, eliminating the left recursion introduced two more productions, as well as the mystery e symbol. The latter stands for the epsilon production, which simply boils down to no action, as we will observe soon when analyzing the implementation.

6.6.2 Design of the Expression-Processing Framework

Equipped with the short introduction to grammars, we can draw a complete picture of the components building up our interpreter framework. This is shown in Figure 6.13.

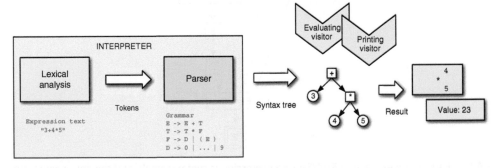

Figure 6.13 Steps of expression interpretation and post-processing. An expression is lexically analyzed and put through the parser, which, based on the grammar rules, checks the syntax and builds the syntax tree. The tree can then be traversed by visitors such as the printing and evaluating visitors. In effect, we can obtain a view of the tree on the screen, or simply its value.

As mentioned earlier, the interpreter consists of the lexical analyzer and parser. Thanks to our simple grammar, these will be joined together under the roof of a simple *interpreter* design pattern. We will implement two of them: the base class will be responsible for checking the syntax of an expression, and the other class will do the same but building the syntax, or parsing, tree during the grammar checking. A syntax tree is a separate data structure that will be implemented using the *composite* design pattern. The structure of a syntax tree exactly reflects the hierarchy and associativity of all the subexpressions. Hence, a syntax tree can be used to analyze the expression further, evaluate its value, simplify the expression, print its structure, or even generate assembly code for its implementation. To achieve these tasks, we will refer to another software component – the *visitor* design pattern. Together with the composite, these two implement *double dispatching*.[4] That is, there can be many different visitors that know how to traverse and what to do in different nodes of a tree. On the other hand, the nodes are aware of the visitor(s) and allow their operation. Such cooperation is very useful not only for syntax trees but for many programming tasks. Imagine, for instance, programming a set of tasks to be performed on a selected subtree of the filesystem, such as searching for a file with a given context, accumulating the total size of all files in the subtree, etc. These can also be implemented using the composite-visitor duet.

Note that remembering examples of design patterns can help with spotting their potential application in many other software components. This, in turn, greatly facilitates their implementation since design patterns provide ready solutions to, or at least approximations of, many common programming problems encountered in various contexts.

6.6.3 The First Expression Interpreter

The first component shown in Figure 6.13 is implemented in the TSimpleExpression Interpreter class, shown in Listing 6.14. Its main actions consist of realizing the productions from the modified grammar with no left recursion, as presented in the previous section. The productions are implemented as the virtual member functions of the TSimpleExpression Interpreter class, whose definition starts on line [3]. But the class has interesting features that we will discuss as well.

On lines [8, 9], the two private data members are defined. The first, fExpressionString, simply stores the input expression. The other, fCurrPos, contains the index of a character in fExpressionString, which is currently matched. Note that the type of fCurrPos is set to be compatible with the size_type expected by the std::string object.

On line [18], the default constructor is defined, whereas on line [19], we see the declaration of the virtual destructor to allow for class inheritance. Again, the = default is used to instruct the compiler to put its default implementation, which introduces the virtual table in this case.

As we know, the default implementations can also be ordered by the compiler for the copy constructor, as well as for the assignment operator. This is done by typing = default on lines [21] and [23].

---

4 A double-dispatching technique but with a callback mechanisms was presented in Section 6.2.8.2.

Listing 6.14 Definition of the `TSimpleExpressionInterpreter` class (in *Parser, SimpleEx pressionInterpreter.h*).

```
1    // Implements the simple expression grammar
2    // free of the left recursion.
3    class TSimpleExpressionInterpreter
4    {
5
6        private:
7
8            std::string           fExpressionString;
9            std::string::size_type fCurrPos {};     // indicates currently examined
10                                                    // position in the expression string
11       public:
12
13           std::string::size_type GetCurPos( void ) const { return fCurrPos; }
14
15       public:
16
17
18           TSimpleExpressionInterpreter( void ) : fCurrPos( 0 ) {}
19           virtual ~TSimpleExpressionInterpreter() = default;
20
21           TSimpleExpressionInterpreter( const TSimpleExpressionInterpreter & )
22                                                                = default;
23           TSimpleExpressionInterpreter & operator = (
24                     const TSimpleExpressionInterpreter & )        = default;
25
```

Also, the moving versions of the copy constructor and an assignment operator can be defaulted, as follows.

```
26           TSimpleExpressionInterpreter(
27                   TSimpleExpressionInterpreter && )  noexcept  = default;
28
29           TSimpleExpressionInterpreter & operator = (
30                   TSimpleExpressionInterpreter && )  noexcept  = default;
```

These instruct the compiler to automatically apply move semantics on all data members, if possible. To do so, the `noexcept` keyword has to be inserted to indicate that the moving operations do not throw any exceptions.

The class `TSimpleExpressionInterpreter` contains the overloaded `operator ()` function, defined on line [47]. Hence, `TSimpleExpressionInterpreter` is a functional object (Section 6.1). Its main action takes place on line [52] and consists of calling the `Expr_Fun` member function. Soon we will see that this is the function corresponding to the expression produced by the grammar. If it returns `true`, then the second condition is checked to verify if the entire input expression has been processed. The fulfillment of the two means the expression has passed the grammar rules. Otherwise, a syntax error occurred, and `false` is returned.

```
31       public:
32
33           /////////////////////////////////////////////////////////////
34           // Functional operator to match an expression to fulfill
35           // the grammar.
36           /////////////////////////////////////////////////////////////
```

```
37        //
38        // INPUT:
39        //              in_str - a string with input expression
40        //
41        // OUTPUT:      true if expression fulfills the grammar, false otherwise
42        //
43        // REMARKS:
44        //              If false returned, then fCurrPos points
45        //              at the last properly matched position.
46        //
47        virtual bool operator () ( const std::string & in_str )
48        {
49            fExpressionString = in_str;
50            fCurrPos = 0;
51
52            return Expr_Fun() && fCurrPos == fExpressionString.size();
53        }
```

Before we analyze the grammar production functions, let's take a look at the Match function, defined on line [70]. This is probably the simplest possible lexical analyzer, which compares a parameter c with a character at the current position in the fExpressionString, as indicated by the fCurrPos member. If these two are the same, then Match returns true, as shown on line [78]. However, before that, fCurrPos is advanced to the next position in the input string. In all other cases, Match returns false.

```
54        protected:
55
56            //////////////////////////////////////////////////////////
57            // This is the simplest lexical analyzer.
58            // It checks if a character matches 1:1 a character
59            // in the fExpressionString at position fCurrPos.
60            //////////////////////////////////////////////////////////
61            //
62            // INPUT:
63            //     c - the character to match in fExpressionString at position fCurrPos
64            //
65            // OUTPUT:  true if c matched, false otherwise
66            //
67            // REMARKS:
68            //     If a match, then fCurrPos is advanced to the next character.
69            //
70            virtual bool Match( char c )
71            {
72                if( fCurrPos >= fExpressionString.size() )
73                    return false;    // the pointer out of scope, exiting ...
74
75                if( fExpressionString[ fCurrPos ] == c )
76                {
77                    ++ fCurrPos;       // advance the pointer to the next position
78                    return true;
79                }
80                else
81                {
82                    return false;      // no match
83                }
84            }
```

Now we encounter a number of virtual member functions that directly implement the grammar rules with no left recursion. The previously mentioned main production is implemented by

Expr_Fun, defined on line [89]. On line [91], it simply calls Term_Fun and Expr_Prime_Fun, exactly as defined in the E -> T E' production. A true value, meaning a syntactically correct expression, is returned only if the two components have been fulfilled.

On the other hand, the Expr_Prime_Fun function, defined on line [96], is responsible for checking the second grammar production: E' -> + T E' | - T E' | e. Since there are alternative rules, separated by the | operator, each branch is implemented as a separate branch of the if-else statements on lines [98, 104]. Considering only the first one, + T E', if + is matched on line [98], then the Term_Fun and Expr_Prime_Fun functions are called in order, as defined in the production. Note that there is also a recursive call to the Expr_Prime_Fun function. But this time we avoid an infinite calling loop, which was the main obstacle when trying to implement the original version of the grammar rules. If the two previous functions return true, then that production is fulfilled, and true is returned to the caller. The final empty production, denoted by e, is implemented on line [110] simply by returning true. The other productions are implemented exactly in the same manner, directly following the grammar rules.

```
85          protected:
86
87
88              // E -> T E'
89              virtual bool Expr_Fun( void )
90              {
91                  return Term_Fun() && Expr_Prime_Fun();
92              }
93
94
95              // E' -> + T E' | - T E' | e
96              virtual bool Expr_Prime_Fun( void )
97              {
98                  if( Match( '+' ) )
99                  {
100                     return Term_Fun() && Expr_Prime_Fun();        // production: + T E'
101                 }
102                 else
103                 {
104                     if( Match( '-' ) )
105                     {
106                         return Term_Fun() && Expr_Prime_Fun(); // production: - T E'
107                     }
108                 }
109
110                 return true;                                      // production: e
111             }
112
113
114
115             // T -> F T'
116             virtual bool Term_Fun( void )
117             {
118                 return Factor_Fun() && Term_Prime_Fun();
119             }
120
121
122             // T' -> * F T' | / F T' | e
123             virtual bool Term_Prime_Fun( void )
124             {
125                 if( Match( '*' ) )
126                 {
127                     return Factor_Fun() && Term_Prime_Fun();   // production: * F T'
128                 }
```

```
129          else
130          {
131              if( Match( '/' ) )
132              {
133                  return Factor_Fun() && Term_Prime_Fun(); // production: / F T'
134              }
135          }
136
137          return true;                                      // production: e
138      }
139
140
141      // F -> D | ( E )
142      virtual bool Factor_Fun( void )
143      {
144          if( Digit_Fun() )
145          {
146              return true; // ok we have matched D
147          }
148          else
149          {
150              if( Match( '(' ) && Expr_Fun() && Match( ')' ) )
151              {
152                  return true;      // ok, this subexpression matches production ( E )
153              }
154          }
155
156          return false;
157      }
158
159
160      // D -> 0 | 1 | 2 | ... | 9
161      virtual bool Digit_Fun( void )
162      {
163          if( Match( '0' ) ) return true;
164          if( Match( '1' ) ) return true;
165          if( Match( '2' ) ) return true;
166          if( Match( '3' ) ) return true;
167          if( Match( '4' ) ) return true;
168          if( Match( '5' ) ) return true;
169          if( Match( '6' ) ) return true;
170          if( Match( '7' ) ) return true;
171          if( Match( '8' ) ) return true;
172          if( Match( '9' ) ) return true;
173
174          return false;
175      }
176
177
178  };
```

Although the grammar allows any expression, the lexical analyzer has been simplified for clarity of discussion. Therefore, the first module to be extended is the lexical analyzer – this task is left as an exercise (number 15 in the "Questions and Exercises" section).

6.6.4 Building the Syntax Tree with the Composite Design Pattern

Passing an expression through the `TSimpleExpressionInterpreter` interpreter returns a binary answer indicating whether the expression does or does not fulfill the grammar rules. However, even more useful would be to generate a data structure whose inherent structure reflects the formation of the input expression. Such a structure is called a *syntax tree*, and examples are presented in Figure 6.14.

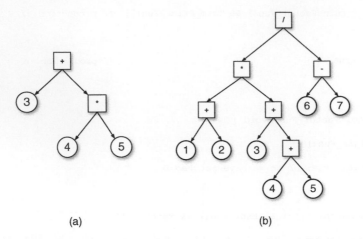

(a)   (b)

Figure 6.14 Syntax trees after parsing the expressions (a) 3+4*5 and (b)(1+2)*(3+(4+5))/(6-7). Each tree reflects the rules of operator precedence and associativity with no parentheses.

In the expression shown in Figure 6.14b, note the construction of the (3+(4+5)) subexpression. Since the + operator is left-associative, without the parentheses 3+4 is executed first, and then the result is added to 5. However, in our case we have this order set differently, as reflected by the tree stucture. The entire factor (3+(4+5)) is then taken to the left side to be multiplied by (1+2), due to the left associativity of the * operator.

Before we find an algorithm for building syntax trees from expressions, let's think of the building blocks for their construction. We have two different categories of nodes: leaf nodes storing numeric values (for simplicity, we assume only digits); and binary nodes, which have two links to the left and right subtrees.

6.6.4.1 The Composite Design Pattern to Define the Nodes of a Tree

Figure 6.15 presents a UML class diagram with the hierarchy of node classes that will be used to build our syntax trees.

This class relation is known as the *composite* design pattern (Gamma et al. 1994). We discussed the composition relation in Section 4.9. Obviously there are common points between the two concepts, but the main difference is that the simple composition relation does not assume any "familial" relation between classes, whereas in the composite design pattern the most characteristic feature is that the composition happens between classes from the same hierarchy. Concretely, BinOperator is derived from the TNode class; hence it is TNode-like. On the other hand, it also contains two TNode class exemplars, fLeftChild and fRightChild. These, in turn, can point at *any* possible object from the TNode hierarchy, whether a ValueLeafNode or even another BinOperator – OK, maybe not directly BinOperator, since it is a pure virtual class but one of its derived classes, such as PlusOperator. Such constructions are common in computer science. An example is the filesystem discussed in Section 6.2.7. In this case, a node can be either a file or a directory (a folder). A directory contains other nodes: files and/or directories, and so on. Another example is a command framework where simple commands coexist with macro commands. Macros, being commands by themselves, consist of a series of prerecorded commands to be executed, and so on.

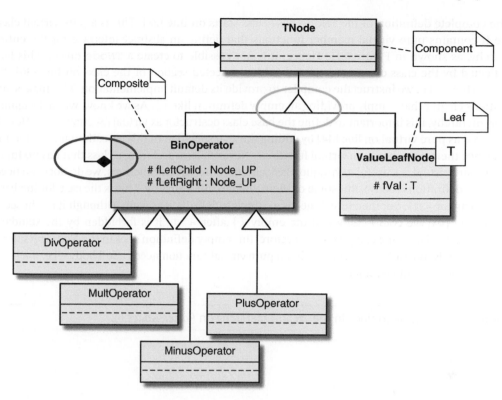

Figure 6.15 UML class diagram of the composite design pattern containing building blocks for the parsing tree. The composite structure arises if the two relations can be observed in a hierarchy. The first is inheritance, outlined with a green circle. The second is the composition between objects in the same hierarchy, outlined by a red circle. The composite structure is common and can be used to express relations between objects in a file-directory tree or between simple and macro commands in a command framework, for instance.

6.6.4.2 Implementation of the TNode Hierarchy and Cooperation with Visitors

Before we dive into the code, we will explain a special relation between all the nodes and the visitor design pattern that will be used to traverse the tree. The two are interrelated: nodes call visitors, and visitors call functions from the nodes. Thus the two groups know about each other. But we cannot simply add their header files to each other – one has to be first. To overcome this problem, something needs to be defined first. In C++, this can be solved by properly arranging the header files and by using only prior declarations of the interrelated classes, with their full definitions provided elsewhere. In the *Nodes.h* header shown in Listing 6.15, we see such declarations at the beginning on lines [9, 13]. These are the definitions of TVisitor and TNode. The first will be used later. But why do we need a declaration of TNode if the definition follows in a few lines? This is necessary to define two important and different pointer types. The first, defined on line [17], is Node_UP, which is an alias to the smart pointer std::unique_ptr that defines the *owning* relation. That is, the Node_UP type will be used to hold pointers to TNode-like objects, which they are responsible for deleting at the proper time, as discussed in Section 5.3. On the other hand, on line [20], a simple NodePtr *non-owning* pointer to TNode is defined. This type is used whenever access to a TNode object is required to perform an action, access its data, and so on, but not to delete it.

The complete definition of the TNode base class starts on line [28]. This is a pure virtual class since it contains pure virtual member functions that define an abstract interface for the entire hierarchy, as shown in Figure 6.15. Hence, it is not possible to create a TNode object. This fact is reflected by the class constructor placed in the protected section of the class on line [36]. By using = default, we instruct the compiler to provide its default implementation. This makes our intentions clearer than simply providing an empty definition like { }. As we know, when designing a class hierarchy, it is important to define the base class destructor as virtual (Section 4.11). Here it is declared as pure virtual on line [44] by adding the = 0 specifier. In this case, though, it is redundant, since there are other pure virtual functions. Nevertheless, declaring a class that has no functions as pure virtual is a useful technique. Basically, for pure virtual functions, we do not even need to provide definitions (body). But some of them will be called anyway. This is the case for the base class destructor ~TNode; therefore, it needs a complete definition as well. Although it might seem that on line [44] we could easily add the empty { } after = 0, it is forbidden by the standard (though accepted by some compilers). Therefore, this empty definition goes in the *Node.cpp* source file. Fortunately, the linker reports whether a pure virtual function needs a full body – i.e. if a body is required but cannot be found.

Listing 6.15 Class definitions in the TNode hierarchy (in *Parser, Nodes.h*).

```
1    #pragma once
2
3
4    #include <memory>
5    #include <cassert>
6
7
8    // Forward class declarations
9    class TVisitor;
10
11
12   // A forward declaration of the base class for the node hierarchy.
13   class TNode;
14
15   // Owning relation - we can declare the std::unique_ptr
16   // with only declared class TNode. Its definition follows.
17   using Node_UP = std::unique_ptr< TNode >;
18
19   // Non-owning relation
20   using NodePtr = TNode *;
21
22
23
24
25   // This is an interface class representing a node
26   // in the tree - it serves only
27   // to be derived from, its objects cannot be created.
28   class TNode
29   {
30
31   protected:
32
33       // Making the constructor protected is also
34       // a way to indicate a class as a base since
35       // only derived classes can be instantiated.
```

```
36          TNode ( void ) = default;
37
38
39     public:
40
41          // To indicate the class is an abstract interface
42          // its destructor is a pure virtual function
43          // what is indicated by adding = 0 to the declaration.
44          virtual ~TNode() = 0;
45
46     public:
47
48          // Pure virtual functions can have implementation
49          // but it is not absolutely required.
50          // Derived types must provide their own implementation if they
51          // are instantiated.
52          // Accept allows operation of a visitor.
53          virtual void Accept ( TVisitor & v ) const = 0;
54
55     public:
56
57          // Re-create yourself - No implementation
58          // for Clone in the base class.
59          virtual Node_UP Clone ( void ) const = 0;
60
61     };
```

In the TNode class and its hierarchy are two distinctive pure virtual functions whose roles we need to explain, as follows:

- The Accept pure virtual function, declared on line [53], provides *a common interface* for the broad group of *visitors*. These are objects that will let us traverse a tree by visiting each of its nodes in a certain order. Accept is called, providing one of the visitor objects as its parameter. This, in turn, is passed alongside the tree to perform its job, whatever it is. The good news is that due to dynamic polymorphism, one Accept per TNode class is enough to accept the entire hierarchy of various visitors, even those that will be devised in the future. We will return to this issue when discussing the visitor hierarchy

- The purpose of the second pure virtual function Clone, declared on line [59], is to define a mechanism for creating a *complete duplicate* of any object from the TNode hierarchy based on a simple pointer to its *prototype*. Such behavior can be achieved by providing Clone in each class derived from the TNode. Due to its behavior, this mechanism is called a *prototype design pattern* (Gamma et al. 1994)

We will see these two in all classes derived from TNode.

6.6.4.3 Implementation of the `ValueLeafNode` Class

Now let's visit another member of the TNode hierarchy. This is the template ValueLeafNode class, whose definition starts in Listing 6.16, lines [64, 65]. It is responsible for storing the value fVal of type V, as shown on line [70]. Objects of this class represent leaves, such as those shown in Figure 6.14. Being a template class makes it easy to define leaves that store non-numeric values. This can be an abstract name of a variable whose value is stored in a look-up table, for instance.

Listing 6.16 Class Definitions in the `TNode` hierarchy – `ValueLeafNode` (in *Parser, Nodes.h*).

```cpp
62  // A leaf (an object) with a value such as
63  // a number, a string, etc.
64  template < typename V >
65  class ValueLeafNode : public TNode
66  {
67
68  private:
69
70      V    fVal {};    // a held value
71
72  public:
73
74      ValueLeafNode( void ) : fVal() {}
75      explicit ValueLeafNode( const V & val ) : fVal( val ) {}
76
77      virtual ~ValueLeafNode() = default;
78
79      ValueLeafNode( const ValueLeafNode & ) = default;
80      ValueLeafNode( ValueLeafNode && ) noexcept = default;
81      ValueLeafNode & operator = ( const ValueLeafNode & ) = default;
82      ValueLeafNode & operator = ( ValueLeafNode && ) noexcept = default;
83
84  public:
85
86
87      V GetValue( void ) const { return fVal; }
88
89      // Accept a visitor
90      void Accept( TVisitor & v ) const override;
91
92  public:
93
94      // Re-create yourself
95      Node_UP Clone( void ) const override;
96
97  };
98
99
100 // A leaf with a floating-point value
101 using NumberLeafNode = ValueLeafNode< double >;
```

On lines [74–82], we see a series of definitions for the constructors and assignment operators of the `ValueLeafNode` class. Since we do not know what type will be used for `V` in the future, the move constructor and assignment operator are also added with the default implementation. This means the compiler will try to use move operations for the `fVal` object, if the `V` class has move operations and they are not throwing exceptions. For this purpose, our implementations of the move semantics are declared `noexcept`. `ValueLeafNode` is not a pure virtual class, so in the source *Visitors.cpp* file are full implementations of the `Accept` and `Clone` virtual functions declared on lines [90] and [95].

Finally, the `NumberLeafNode` alias is defined as the `ValueLeafNode` class instantiated with the `double` type. We can extend this idea when implementing the tree with leaves holding other types.

6.6.4.4 Implementation of the `BinOperator` Class

The `BinOperator` class defined in Listing 6.17, line [103], constitutes a base class for all the binary operators such as `PlusOperator`. The most characteristic part of `BinOperator` is that it owns two branches representing subexpressions of the syntax tree. These are held in the owning pointers `fLeftChild` and `fRightChild`, defined on lines [108, 109]. As alluded to previously, owning the two subexpressions, each the `TNode` type, makes the entire class setup a composite design pattern. But such ownership makes its copy operations much more difficult, as we will discuss shortly. Fortunately, due to the automation of the smart pointers, we do not need to worry about object disposal. The parametric constructor defined on line [114] takes two smart pointers, which are then adopted by moving their held objects to the `fLeftChild` and `fRightChild` members. Moving the objects between the `unique_ptr`s is a standard technique, as discussed in Section 5.3.

However, having the two objects representing subexpressions makes the copying operations nontrivial. This problem was discussed in Section 4.6.3. If we are to copy such an object, how do we copy objects held by the `fLeftChild` and `fRightChild` members? Probably the best way is to make a complete image, which doing so involves creating a series of objects. We will return to this problem when discussing the `Clone` member. To disallow a shallow copy, the copy and move constructors, as well as the assignment operators, are declared = `delete`, as shown on lines [124–128]. Such a declaration in a member function disallows its usage.

Listing 6.17 Class definitions in the `TNode` hierarchy – `BinOperator` (in *Parser, Nodes.h*).

```
102    // A class to represent any binary operator
103    class BinOperator : public TNode
104    {
105
106    private:
107
108        Node_UP      fLeftChild;     // Owning pointer to the left subtree
109        Node_UP      fRightChild;    // Owning pointer to the right subtree
110
111    public:
112
113        BinOperator( void ) = default;
114        BinOperator( Node_UP left, Node_UP right )
115            : fLeftChild( std::move( left ) ), fRightChild( std::move( right ) )
116        {}
117
118        virtual ~BinOperator () = default;
119
120    protected:
121
122        // Disallow simple (shallows) copying.
123        // To copy use Clone()
124        BinOperator( const BinOperator & )  = delete;
125        BinOperator( const BinOperator && ) = delete;
126
127        BinOperator & operator = ( const BinOperator & )  = delete;
128        BinOperator & operator = ( const BinOperator && ) = delete;
129
130    public:
131
132        NodePtr      GetLeftChild( void ) const
133                     { assert( fLeftChild != nullptr ); return fLeftChild.get(); }
134        NodePtr      GetRightChild( void ) const
135                     { assert( fRightChild != nullptr ); return fRightChild.get(); }
```

(Coninued)

Listing 6.17 (continued)

```
136
137         // Passing up for ownership
138         void        AdoptLeftChild( Node_UP up )      { fLeftChild = std::move( up ); }
139         void        AdoptRightChild( Node_UP up )     { fRightChild = std::move( up ); }
140
141   public:
142
143         void Accept( TVisitor & v ) const override = 0;
144
145   public:
146
147         // Re-create yourself - this is a derived class but
148         // again Clone is pure virtual and we don't have
149         // its implementation.
150         Node_UP Clone( void ) const override = 0;
151
152   };
```

Lines [138, 139] define the AdoptLeftChild and AdoptRightChild functions. The role of each is similar to the ubiquitous class *setters*, with an important difference: they *take over* the objects provided by the smart pointers passed as their arguments. To reflect this fact, the names of these functions start with the Adopt prefix. On the other hand, names of functions giving up their held objects usually start with the Orphan prefix. Although not required, such naming conventions systematically increase code readability.

On the other hand, GetLeftChild and GetRightChild, defined on lines [132–134], are simple constant getters that return the "ordinary" non-owning pointer NodePtr.

Finally, notice that similar to the base class TNode, BinOperator defines two pure virtual functions: Accept on line [143] and Clone on line [150]. Interestingly, we do not need to provide their definitions since they will be ensured by the derived classes.

6.6.4.5 Implementation of the PlusOperator Class

All classes representing binary operations are derived from BinOperator, as shown in Figure 6.15. As an example, PlusOperator is shown in Listing 6.18; its definition starts on line [154]. Lines [160, 161] define its parametric constructor. All it has to do is call its base class, passing the provided arguments left and right.

Because PlusOperator is a "real" class, it also needs to provide full definitions of the Accept [170] and Clone [175] virtual functions.

Listing 6.18 Class definitions in the TNode hierarchy – PlusOperator (in *Parser, Nodes.h*).

```
153   // A concrete binary operator
154   class PlusOperator : public BinOperator
155   {
156
157   public:
158
159         PlusOperator( void ) = default;
160         PlusOperator( Node_UP left, Node_UP right )
161             : BinOperator( std::move( left ), std::move( right ) )   // init base class
162             {}
163
164         virtual ~PlusOperator() = default;
165
```

```
166        // Object copying disallowed by the base class
167
168    public:
169
170        void Accept( TVisitor & v ) const override;
171
172    public:
173
174        // Re-create yourself
175        Node_UP Clone( void ) const override;
176
177    };
```

The implementation of the `Accept` member is very simple and the same for all objects of the `TNode` hierarchy. It is shown in Listing 6.19 for `PlusOperator`.

Listing 6.19 Implementation of the `Accept` member function for `PlusOperator` (in *Parser, Nodes.cpp*). The implementation is identical for all other nodes in the `TNode` hierarchy.

```
1    void PlusOperator::Accept( TVisitor & v ) const
2    {
3        v.Visit( * this );
4    }
```

`Accept` reverts the call to a given visitor object, providing a pointer `this` to this node object as its parameter. Such call reverting is enough for visitor v since, based on the type of `this`, an appropriate overloaded `Visit` function will be invoked due to polymorphism. This is the double-dispatching mechanism; we will return to it when describing visitor objects in Section 6.6.7. See also the class diagram in Figure 6.17.

On the other hand, the role and implementation of the `Clone` member function are covered in the next section.

6.6.4.6 Deep Copying Node Objects – The Prototyping Mechanism

Whereas copying objects containing data – such as `NumberLeafNode` – is not a problem, and we can even leave code generation for this action to the compiler by specifying = `default`, there is an inherent problem with copying objects containing pointers to other objects, such as `PlusOperator`. Simply copying pointers is usually undesirable since we end up with two different objects with references to the same data (Section 4.6.3). Therefore, all binary operations implemented with classes derived from `BinOperator` are disallowed any copying and moving operations by defining their copy and move members as = `delete`. So, in the following code snippet, only the first line compiles:

```
1    PlusOperator    p1, p2;        // ok
2    PlusOperator    p3( p2 );      // Compiling error - no copy constructible
3    p1 = p2;                       // Compiling error - no copy by assignment
```

Imagine that we need to duplicate a tree, composed of a number of nodes of different types, having only a pointer to that tree's root node. Such a task might be needed to launch two independent tree annotators, for instance. How do we traverse such a tree, and create a copy of each node and each child node? Even worse, if we have a pointer to a child, we store only a pointer to the base class TNode, so how can we know which node exactly to re-create? This can be done using a special visitor that knows everything about the node hierarchy. But there is a much simpler and more general solution to this ubiquitous problem: the prototype pattern, in the form of special virtual Clone members implemented in each class of the TNode hierarchy. The best way to understand its operation is to analyze the simple code in Listing 6.20.

Each Clone member,[5] such as the NumberLeafNode::Clone whose definition starts on line [1], dynamically creates its clone object, as on line [3], providing itself as a creation pattern in the form of the * this argument to the copy constructor. Then a smart pointer to this newly created object is returned, so we do not need to worry about the lifetime of that object. That's it. The only thing to observe is that Node_UP was defined to store a pointer to the base class TNode. Again, this is an instructive example of C++ polymorphism and the Liskov rule, which states that any derived object can be substituted in place of the base. However, when we take such a pointer, whatever it is, and call its *virtual* Clone member (being virtual is a key point here), the Clone will know precisely what object it needs to create – this is the mechanism behind the prototype pattern.

Listing 6.20 Definitions of Clone functions from various classes of the TNode hierarchy (in Parser, *Nodes.cpp*).

```
1    Node_UP NumberLeafNode::Clone( void ) const
2    {
3        return std::make_unique< NumberLeafNode >( * this );
4    }
```

A slightly more advanced action is performed by Clone members in the classes representing binary operators, such as PlusOperator::Clone, whose the definition starts on line [5]. It needs to create another PlusOperator by calling std::make_unique on line [7], which invokes the PlusOperator parametric constructor. But its two parameters also need to be new subtrees, since we re-create the entire tree and all of its nodes are brand new. Again, we are lucky to have the Clone operation defined for every node – to re-create a subtree, we simply take the child node by calling GetLeftChild and GetRightChild on line [8], and calling their Clone members.

```
5    Node_UP PlusOperator::Clone( void ) const
6    {
7        return   std::make_unique< PlusOperator >(
8                 GetLeftChild()->Clone(), GetRightChild()->Clone() );
9    }
```

This way, the whole cloning operation will recursively pass down the tree, and the new PlusOperator node will be created with two branches with new subtrees.

6.6.5 Interpreter to Build a Syntax Tree

We already defined a simple interpreter, TSimpleExpressionInterpreter, that follows the grammar rules of simple expressions and can tell whether an expression can be derived from these rules (Listing 6.14). We have also defined building blocks in the form of syntax tree nodes, as

---

5 Since Clone produces and abandons an object, it should be named something like Orphan_. However, in the C++ community, it is common to call it Clone or clone, so we also follow this nomenclature.

shown in Figure 6.15. Now we will join the two, so that when parsing the expression and matching a grammar production after a grammar production, the interpreter can also generate the syntax tree that reflects the internal structure of the expression, as shown in Figure 6.14. Thanks to the object-oriented features of C++, we can achieve this task by deriving a new interpreter class from the base class `TSimpleExpressionInterpreter` and tweaking some of the functions.

The new `ExpressionTreeBuilderInterpreter` class is publicly derived from `TSimple ExpressionInterpreter`, as shown in Listing 6.21, line [19]. Hence, in addition to a number of important `#includes`, we need to include the header with the base class, as on line [13].

Listing 6.21 Definition of the `ExpressionTreeBuilderInterpreter` class (in *Parser, ExpressionTreeBuilderInterpreter.h*).

```
1    #include <string>
2    #include <iostream>
3    #include <memory>
4    #include <algorithm>
5
6
7    #include "Nodes.h"
8    #include "Visitors.h"
9    #include "TheStack.h"
10   #include "range.h"
11
12
13   #include "SimpleExpressionInterpreter.h"
14
15
16
17
18   // The interpreter that builds the parsing tree
19   class ExpressionTreeBuilderInterpreter : public TSimpleExpressionInterpreter
20   {
21     public:
22
23
24         ExpressionTreeBuilderInterpreter( void )        = default;
25         virtual ~ExpressionTreeBuilderInterpreter()     = default;
26
27
28         // No shallow copy allowed due to fRoot and other members
29         ExpressionTreeBuilderInterpreter(
30                 const ExpressionTreeBuilderInterpreter & )        = delete;
31         ExpressionTreeBuilderInterpreter(
32                 const ExpressionTreeBuilderInterpreter && )       = delete;
33
34         ExpressionTreeBuilderInterpreter & operator = (
35                 const ExpressionTreeBuilderInterpreter & )        = delete;
36         ExpressionTreeBuilderInterpreter & operator = (
37                 const ExpressionTreeBuilderInterpreter && )       = delete;
38
39     public:
40
41         //////////////////////////////////////////////////////////
42         // Functional operator to match an expression to fulfill
43         // the grammar.
44         //////////////////////////////////////////////////////////
45         //
```

(Coninued)

Listing 6.21 (continued)

```
46      // INPUT:    in_str - a string with input expression
47      //
48      // OUTPUT:  true if expression fulfills the grammar, false otherwise
49      //
50      // REMARKS:
51      //      If false returned, then fCurrPos points
52      //      at the last properly matched position.
53      //
54      virtual bool operator () ( const std::string & in_str )
55      {
56          if( BaseClass::operator()( in_str ) )   // Call the base parser
57              return fNodeStack.Pop( fRoot );      // Take the node off from the stack
58
59          return false;
60      }
61
62  protected:
63
64      using BaseClass = TSimpleExpressionInterpreter;
65
66      using NodeStack = CppBook::UP_Stack_1000< TNode >;  // Useful stack alias
67
68  private:
69
70      NodeStack fNodeStack;       // The stack to store temporary branches of the tree
71
72      Node_UP         fRoot;   // The root node of the parsing tree
73
74  public:
75
76      NodePtr         GetRoot( void ) { return fRoot.get(); }
```

The constructor and virtual destructor on lines [24, 25] are declared as defaults. Since the class will store a `unique_ptr` to the resulting syntax tree, copying and moving are forbidden by defining the appropriate members as deleted on lines [29–36].

Instantiations of the `ExpressionTreeBuilderInterpreter` class are functional objects due to the presence of the overloaded functional `operator ()`, whose definition starts on line [54]. Its action on line [56] is to call the base functional operator and, if successful, copy an object from the top of `fNodeStack` to the `fRoot` member, as done on line [57]. These are defined on lines [70, 72], preceded by the type aliases on lines [64, 66]. The role and implementation of the node stack will be explained in the next section.

As mentioned earlier, in the derived interpreter class, we will reuse some member functions representing the grammar productions. More specifically, we can reuse those that call only other nonterminal actions, whereas those that involve terminal symbols need to be modified slightly.

Let's start with `Digit_Fun`, whose role is to try to match each of the digits from 0 up to 9. In the base class, such matching was enough; and if it was successful, `true` was returned. In the derived overridden version of `Digit_Fun`, whose definition starts on line [78], the first matching task is identical to that in the base class. However, after a successful match on line [80] and before returning `true` on line [83], a new `NumberLeafNode` is created on line [82], which stores the numerical value corresponding to the matched digit symbol. Moreover, the entire node object is pushed onto the node stack `fNodeStack`, where it waits for further processing.

```
77        // D -> 0 | 1 | 2 | ... | 9
78        virtual bool Digit_Fun( void )
79        {
80           if( Match( '0' ) )
81           {
82              fNodeStack.Push( std::make_unique< NumberLeafNode >( 0.0 ) );
83              return true;
84           }
85
```

These actions are repeated for each digit from 0–9, so we skip the implementations here.

```
86           if( Match( '9' ) )
87           {
88              fNodeStack.Push( std::make_unique< NumberLeafNode >( 9.0 ) );
89              return true;
90           }
91
92           return false;
93        }
```

Let's now examine the following `Expr_Prime_Fun` function – whose definition starts on line [97] – and its first production, `E' -> + T E'`. After matching the + symbol on line [99], the term branch is evaluated by calling `Term_Fun` on line [101]. So far, we are performing the same action as in the base class. But after matching + and returning from `Term_Fun`, it is possible to join the nodes that were previously created and saved on the stack nodes into a subtree bound by the `PlusOperator` node. This is done by calling the auxiliary `CreateSubTree` function on line [103] with a new, and still not connected, `PlusOperator` as its argument . The `CreateSubTree` function will be explained shortly. Then `Expr_Prime_Fun` is recursively called on line [104] to verify the `E' -> + T E'` rule.

Nearly identical calling schemes are performed for all the other operators. In each case, `CreateSubTree` is called, with only one difference – the type of the created node object, which reflects the operator just matched by the `Match` function.

```
94     protected:
95
96        // E' -> + T E' | - T E' | e
97        virtual bool Expr_Prime_Fun( void )
98        {
99           if( Match( '+' ) == true )
100          {
101             if( Term_Fun() )            // production: + T E'
102             {
103                CreateSubTree( std::make_unique< PlusOperator >() );
104                return Expr_Prime_Fun();
105             }
106             else
107             {
108                return false;
109             }
110          }
111          else
112          {
113             if( Match( '-' ) == true )
114             {
```

```
115                   if( Term_Fun() )              // production: - T E'
116                   {
117                       CreateSubTree( std::make_unique< MinusOperator >() );
118                       return Expr_Prime_Fun();
119                   }
120                   else
121                   {
122                       return false;
123                   }
124               }
125           }
126
127           return true;               // production: e
128       }
129
130
131       // T' -> * F T' | / F T' | e
132       virtual bool Term_Prime_Fun( void )
133       {
134           if( Match( '*' ) == true )
135           {
136               if( Factor_Fun() )              // production: * F T
137               {
138                   CreateSubTree( std::make_unique< MultOperator >() );
139                   return Term_Prime_Fun();
140               }
141               else
142               {
143                   return false;
144               }
145           }
146           else
147           {
148               if( Match( '/' ) == true )
149               {
150                   if( Factor_Fun() )                   // production: / F T'
151                   {
152                       CreateSubTree( std::make_unique< DivOperator >() );
153                       return Term_Prime_Fun();
154                   }
155                   else
156                   {
157                       return false;
158                   }
159               }
160           }
161
162           return true;                      // production: e
163       }
```

Figure 6.16 illustrates the operation of the CreateSubTree function when processing the 3+4*5 expression. The NumberLeafNode objects with values 3, 4, and 5 are directly pushed onto the stack in the order of their arrival from the parser (Section 4.8.4). However, when a new binary operator node is created, its two child subexpressions are popped off the top of fNodeStack. These are then connected to that operator as its left and right subtrees. Finally, the operator itself is pushed back on top of the stack, and the operations proceed until the entire expression has been parsed or a syntax error has been encountered.

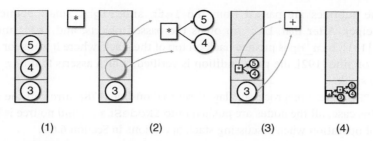

(1)   (2)   (3)   (4)

Figure 6.16 Stack operations of the `CreateSubTree` function when processing the expression 3+4*5. When a new binary operator node is created, its two child subexpressions are popped off the top of the stack. These are then connected to that operator as its left and right subtrees, and finally the operator is pushed back on top of the stack. On the other hand, the `NumberLeafNode` objects are directly pushed onto the stack in the order of their parsing.

Implementation of `CreateSubTree`, whose definition starts on line [176], simply follows the previously described algorithm. Its parameter `bin_op` is a newly created binary operator with empty left and right subexpressions. First the precondition is checked to assert that the stack has at least two nodes that can be processed. Its two topmost nodes need to be removed from the stack, as done on lines [185, 186]: these constitute the right and left subexpressions. In this order, they are connected to the passed `bin_op` by calling its `AdoptLeftChild` and `AdoptRightChild` members on lines [188, 189].

```
164  protected:
165
166      ///////////////////////////////////////////////////////////////
167      // Builds a branch of the parsing tree
168      ///////////////////////////////////////////////////////////////
169      //
170      // INPUT:   bin_op - smart pointer with the input binary operator
171      //
172      // OUTPUT:  node
173      //
174      // REMARKS: bin_op held object is overtaken and pushed onto the stack
175      //
176      void CreateSubTree( std::unique_ptr< BinOperator > bin_op )
177      {
178  #define BUILD_THE_TREE 1
179  #if BUILD_THE_TREE == 1
180
181          assert( fNodeStack.GetStackSize() >= 2 );
182
183          Node_UP left, right;
184
185          fNodeStack.Pop( right );     // Pop the right subexpression
186          fNodeStack.Pop( left );      // Pop the left subexpression
187
188          bin_op->AdoptLeftChild( std::move( left ) );    // Connect left
189          bin_op->AdoptRightChild( std::move( right ) );  // Connect right
190  #endif
191          fNodeStack.Push( std::move( bin_op ) ); // Push onto the stack
192          assert( bin_op.get() == nullptr );      // The input bin_op is orphaned
193      }
194
195  };
```

Note that the subtrees are passed from the `left` and `right` smart pointers using the `std::move` helper. After that, `bin_op` owns the passed objects, and `left` and `right` are empty. On line [191], `bin_op` is pushed back on top of the stack, where it waits for another such action. Finally, on line [192], the postcondition is verified, which asserts that `bin_op` has been passed onto the stack.

The `BUILD_THE_TREE` preprocessor flag, if set to 0 on line [178], turns off the code on lines [179–190]. In this case, all the nodes are pushed onto `fNodeStack`, and no tree is built. We will use this mode of operation when discussing stack operations in Section 6.6.9.

6.6.6   Stack for Smart Pointers

In this section, we will specifically focus on the following issues:

- Template specializations with a specialized stack class to store `std::unique_ptr`
- Proper use of ownership and move semantics
- Dependent and independent names in template definitions

We discussed the template `TStackFor` class in Section 4.8.4. Its main purpose is to provide a stack interface (LIFO functionality) with an internal vector for data support. But `TStackFor`, in its general form as shown in Listing 4.17, assumes that objects pushed onto or popped from the stack are copied. However, when manipulating objects with strong owning semantics, such as the `Node_UP` or any other object held by `std::unique_ptr`, such a strategy cannot work since the objects need to be moved instead. Hence, we need a slightly more specialized version of `TStackFor`. As we pointed out in Section 4.8.2, C++ is ready for such challenges with the *template specialization* mechanism, which allows us to write a special version of a template class for a special occasion: that is, for a specific instantiating type. Such a version of `TStackFor`, specialized to cope with `std::unique_ptr` objects, is presented in Listing 6.22. The class definition starts on lines [2, 3] with `TStackFor< std::unique_ptr< T >, MaxElems >`, which tells the compiler that this a is specialized version if it happens to instantiate a `TStackFor` for any type `T` being held within `std::unique_ptr`. We can freely specify type `T`, as long as it can be held by `std::unique_ptr`, as well as the second numeric parameter `MaxElems`, which stands for the maximum allowable size of the stack.

Lines [7, 9, 12] contain a series of type aliases. These provide shortcuts for the types used in this specialization. In the third case, an additional `typename` was necessary. Such a helper is needed to assure the compiler that the construction refers to a type, and not to a variable in a namespace, for instance. Let's briefly describe what is going on. In C++ templates, there are two types of names:

- *Dependent name* – A name that in some way depends on a template parameter
- *Non-dependent name* – A name that does not depend on a template parameter

The problem is with the first group, i.e. dependent names, since being dependent on a particular type of template parameter means they can represent totally different language categories. For example, the template dependent name `T::my_type` can denote a type, whereas `T::my_static_data` can denote a name of a static object. However, in the two-phase name-lookup process, the C++ compiler needs to figure out precisely what group a particular name belongs to. In the first pass, before a template is provided, the compiler selects non-dependent names. It looks for dependent names when an instantiation happens with a particular type. Hence we can use the `typename` keyword in front of a name that is dependent on a template parameter to tell the compiler that this is the name of a type. If `typename` is not placed in front of a dependent name, the compiler treats it as a non-type name and sifts it out in the first pass. There are many additional rules involved in template parameter matching, particularly concerning the dependent and non-dependent types (*https://stackoverflow.com/q/610245*; Stroustrup 2013; Cppreference.com 2019b; Vandevoorde et al. 2017).

Listing 6.22 Definition of a specialized version of `TStack` specialized for smart pointers (in the *TStack.h*).

```
1    // Stack specialization to operate with std::unique_ptr
2    template < typename T, auto MaxElems >
3    class TStackFor< std::unique_ptr< T >, MaxElems >
4    {
5        public:
6
7            using value_type = std::unique_ptr< T >;
8
9            using DataContainer = std::vector< value_type >;
10
11           // Here we need an additional typename
12           using size_type = typename DataContainer::size_type;
13
14       private:
15
16           DataContainer      fData;
17
18       public:
19
20           DataContainer &   GetDataContainer( void ) { return fData; }
21
22           auto GetStackSize( void ) const { return fData.size(); }
23
24       public:
25
26
```

Returning to the rest of the code, on line [16], the main underlying data container is defined. Recall that this is a `std::vector` storing `std::unique_ptr` data. Hence, `TStackFor` can be seen as a kind of adapter that superimposes a special stack-like interface over a flat vector structure. As expected, there are two member functions. The definition of the `Push` operation starts on line [42]. Note that its parameter `new_elem` is passed by value. Because this is a `unique_ptr`, its held object is taken over and – after checking on line [44] to be sure there is enough space – placed on top of the stack. For this purpose, `emplace_back` is used on line [47], rather than the simple `push_back`. The former has the advantage of directly using the move operation and hence avoiding unnecessary object copying. Note that after `Push` returns, the passed `new_elem` smart pointer is empty (Section 5.3.1.1).

```
27   /////////////////////////////////////////////////////////////
28   // This function puts an element onto the stack
29   /////////////////////////////////////////////////////////////
```

```
30          //
31          //
32          //          INPUT:   new_elem - a smart pointer to the object to
33          //                   be moved onto the stack.
34          //
35          //
36          //
37          //          OUTPUT: true - if operation successful,
38          //                  false - failure, due to insufficient
39          //                  space on the stack (e.g. too many
40          //                  elements)
41          //
42          bool Push( value_type new_elem )
43          {
44              if( GetStackSize() == MaxElems )
45                return false;
46
47              fData.emplace_back( std::move( new_elem ) );
48              // new_elem is empty now
49
50              return true;
51          }
```

The Pop function is defined on line [66]. In our realization, it is perfectly OK to call Pop from the empty stack. Such conditions are checked on line [68], and if the stack is empty, then false is returned. Otherwise, an object is first read out on line [71] from the last element in the underlying vector using the fData.pop_back method. The returned object is a unique_ptr holding an object of type T. Therefore, in the same line, it is first released and reset to the ret_elem. Then, on line [72], an empty now smart pointer is removed from the underlying fData vector (pop_back only reads the last element, leaving it untouched).

```
52              ////////////////////////////////////////////////////////////
53              // This function takes and removes an element from the stack
54              ////////////////////////////////////////////////////////////
55              //
56              //
57              //   INPUT:      new_elem - a reference to the object which
58              //               will be copied with a topmost element
59              //               from the stack. Then the topmost element
60              //               is removed from the stack.
61              //
62              //
63              //   OUTPUT:     true - if operation successful,
64              //               false - failure, due to empty stack
65              //
66              bool Pop( value_type & ret_elem )
67              {
68                  if( GetStackSize() == 0 )
69                      return false;
70
71                  ret_elem.reset( fData.back().release() );    // re-connect pointers
72                  fData.pop_back();    // get rid of the last (empty) element
73
74                  return true;
75              }
76
77      };
```

Finally, on lines [78, 79], a useful template alias is created that defines a group of stacks to hold `std::unique_ptr`s of any type `T` with the maximum number of elements set to 1000.

```
78   template < typename T >
79   using UP_Stack_1000 = TStackFor< std::unique_ptr< T >, 1000 >;
```

Such an alias with partial specialization is possible only with the `using` directive, since the older `typedef` can be used only to specify complete types. Therefore, in new code, the former is a preferred.

Let's also mention that SL offers the `std::stack` class. But our needs regarding the interface are slightly different than that provided in `std::stack`, so we used the previous short implementation.

6.6.7 Traversing Trees with the Visitor Design Pattern

Having now created syntax trees, we can perform actions on them. For example, we can traverse a tree and compute its value. We can also try to simplify an expression by detecting common factors, or we can generate code that will perform whatever semantics are expressed by a tree. Such actions can be coded directly into the classes defining the tree. However, if we had many different actions, this would clutter the code. In such cases, we can use the visitor design pattern.

As shown in Figure 6.13, a tree is composed of N different nodes and there are V different visitors. Each visitor has to traverse the tree, accessing each of its nodes in a certain order. Hence we must implement a rectangular structure of $N \times V$ different actions. The problem now is figuring out which function to call. This is known as the *double-dispatching problem*. As we will see, the correct design of the two hierarchies underpinned with the polymorphic mechanism helps us keep order and easily add new visitors and nodes to this mechanism if necessary. The UML class diagram in Figure 6.17 shows the two class hierarchies and their interaction realized by the `TNode::Accept` and `TVisitor::Visit` complementary functions. As we will see, they solve the double-dispatching puzzle.

Before we go to the code analysis, we will explain a slight problem related to file organization: because the definition of `TNode` depends on `TVisitor` and the definition of `TVisitor` depends on `TNode`, there is a cross-dependency between these two. In C++, this can be resolved using the forward declarations of classes and by properly organizing the header and source files. In our projects, these are organized as shown in Figure 6.18.

Let's consider the organization of the *Nodes.h* and *Nodes.cpp* files. *Nodes.h* can contain only the forward declaration of `TVisitor`, which lets us use references and pointers to `TVisitor`. But this is not sufficient for the compiler to call a member function or access member data from `TVisitor`. Hence the definitions in *Nodes.h* of `TNode` and its related classes can use only references and/or pointers to `TVisitor` – nothing more. Because of this, all actions requiring full access to the definition of `TVisitor` need to be postponed to the *Nodes.cpp* source file. A similar situation with respect to the definition of `TNode` happens in the *Visitors.h* and *Visitors.cpp* files. In other words, *Nodes.h* does not include *Visitors.h*, and *Visitors.h* does not include *Nodes.h*. However, both source files, i.e. *Nodes.cpp* and *Visitors.cpp,* can freely include both headers, *Hodes.h* and *Visitors.h*.

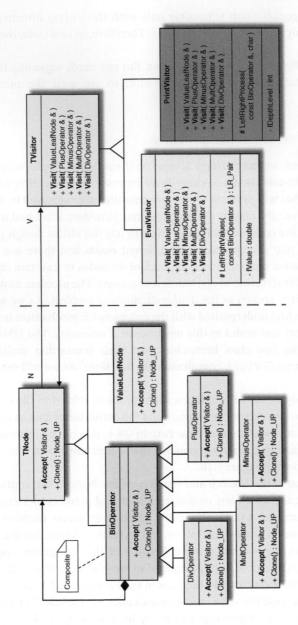

Figure 6.17 UML class diagram of the TNode and TVisitor class hierarchies and relations between them. The TNode composite is a structural pattern. Objects of the TNode hierarchy can be used to build binary trees representing expressions. TVisitor is a behavioral pattern. Concrete visitors are responsible for traversing a tree and performing particular actions. Each TNode is equipped with the Accept member function, which can accept any representative of the TVisitor hierarchy. Complementarily, any TVisitor has a series of Visit member functions, which are overloaded for each concrete node. These build the double-dispatching calling relation.

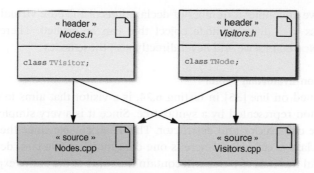

Figure 6.18 UML artifact diagram showing relations of the header and source files with nodes and visitors. A double-dispatch relation requires strict separation of definitions from implementations since both groups of definitions depend on each other. Hence, header files contain only forward declarations of other classes. Sources include both headers.

There are many resemblances between the two class hierarchies. The base class `TVisitor` is defined starting from line [16] in Listing 6.23. Exactly as for the `TNode` classes, the definition of `TVisitor` is preceded on lines [4–12] by a number of forward declarations of the classes whose names need to be known in this context.

On lines [21, 22] are default definitions of the constructor and virtual destructor, which are necessary in the case of class hierarchies. For clarity, we omit other default constructors here.

Listing 6.23 Definition of the visitor class hierarchy (in *Parser, Visitors.h*).

```
1    #include <tuple>
2
3
4    class TNode;
5
6    using NumberLeafNode = ValueLeafNode< double >;
7
8    class BinOperator;
9    class PlusOperator;
10   class MinusOperator;
11   class MultOperator;
12   class DivOperator;
13
14
15   // Abstract base class for all visitors
16   class TVisitor
17   {
18
19   public:
20
21               TVisitor ()     = default;
22       virtual ~TVisitor ()     = default;
23
24   public:
25
26       // Pure virtual function to visit the constructible nodes
27       virtual void Visit( NumberLeafNode & n ) = 0;
28       virtual void Visit( PlusOperator & n ) = 0;
29       virtual void Visit( MinusOperator & n ) = 0;
30       virtual void Visit( MultOperator & n ) = 0;
31       virtual void Visit( DivOperator & n ) = 0;
32
33   };
```

On lines [27–31], we encounter a number of declarations of the pure virtual Visit functions, each reflecting access to a different node object that can be created. There is no Visit for BinOperator or TNode since we will never directly visit those nodes.

6.6.7.1 The Expression-Evaluating Visitor

EvalVisitor, defined on line [35] in Listing 6.24, is a visitor that aims to evaluate the value of the entire expression represented by a syntax tree. Since it is a very simple class, we omitted the definitions of the constructor and destructor. This is acceptable since the virtual destructor defined in the base class is sufficient. There is one data member fValue, defined on line [39], which upon successful traversal of a tree will contain the value of the entire expression.

Lines [66–70] declare the entire series of overridden Visit functions. They strictly follow the corresponding definition from the base class, which is underpinned with the override keyword. Also note that at the same time, these Visits are overloaded for each potential node.

Listing 6.24 Definition of the visitor class hierarchy, cont. (in *Parser*, *Visitors.h*).

```
34    // Expression-evaluating visitor
35    class EvalVisitor : public TVisitor
36    {
37    private:
38
39        double    fValue {};
40
41        const double kDivThresh { 1e-12 };
42
43    public:
44
45        double GetValue( void ) const { return fValue; }
46
47
48    protected:
49
50        using LR_Pair = std::tuple< double, double >;
51
52        /////////////////////////////////////////////////////////////
53        // Auxiliary function to process the left and right nodes.
54        /////////////////////////////////////////////////////////////
55        //
56        // INPUT:    n - a reference to a binary node
57        //
58        // OUTPUT:   a pair of values of the left and right node
59        //
60        EvalVisitor::LR_Pair LeftRightValues( BinOperator & n );
61
62
63    public:
64
65        // Set of overloaded functions for each node in the parsing tree
66        void Visit( NumberLeafNode & n ) override;
67        void Visit( PlusOperator & n ) override;
68        void Visit( MinusOperator & n ) override;
69        void Visit( MultOperator & n ) override;
70        void Visit( DivOperator & n ) override;      // can throw
71
72    };
```

Listing 6.25 contains an implementation of the most representative members of `EvalVisitor`: the `Visit` methods. The definition of the first `Visit` for the `NumberLeafNode` object starts on line [76]. In this case, the only action is to copy the value from the `NumberLeafNode` object to the visitor's inner data member `fValue`, on line [78].

On the other hand, an overloaded version of `Visit`, this time for `PlusOperator`, is defined on line [81]. For this and other binary operators, first the `LeftRightValues` member function is called on line [83]. It returns a tuple with two values that correspond to the values of the left subtree and right subtree. All that remains is to add these values on line [84] and assign them to `fValue`, which always reflects the last value of the subexpression.

Listing 6.25 Implementation of the selected `Visit` members in the `EvalVisitor` class (in *Parser, Visitors.cpp*).

```
73   #include "Nodes.h"
74   #include "Visitors.h"
75
76   void EvalVisitor::Visit( NumberLeafNode & n )
77   {
78       fValue = n.GetValue();
79   }
80
81   void EvalVisitor::Visit( PlusOperator & n )
82   {
83       auto [ l, r ] = LeftRightValues( n );
84       fValue = l + r;      // current value is the sum of left and right
85   }
```

A slightly different implementation can be observed in the `Visit` for `DivOperator`, defined on line [86]. In this case, evaluating division can throw an exception on division by zero, as encoded on lines [90, 91]. In practice, we should react not only on zero but also on division by a value that is too small (Section 3.16). In `EvalVisitor`, this it is controlled by the `kDivThresh` constant member.

```
86   void EvalVisitor::Visit( DivOperator & n )
87   {
88       auto [ l, r ] = LeftRightValues( n );
89
90       if( std::fabs( r ) < kDivThresh )
91           throw std::overflow_error( "Div by 0" );
92
93       fValue = l / r;      // current value is the div of left and right
94   }
```

Finally, let's analyze the `LeftRightValues` function defined on line [103]. As alluded to previously, it is called by each of the binary operators to assess the values of its left and right subtrees. This is accomplished by a call on line [105] to evaluate the left subtree, after which on line [106] the current content of `fValue` is stored in the local variable `left_val`.

```
95    ///////////////////////////////////////////////////////
96    // Auxiliary function to process left and right nodes.
97    ///////////////////////////////////////////////////////
98    //
99    // INPUT:      n - a reference to a binary node
100   //
101   // OUTPUT:     a pair of values of the left and right node
102   //
```

```
103  EvalVisitor::LR_Pair EvalVisitor::LeftRightValues( BinOperator & n )
104  {
105      n.GetLeftChild()->Accept( * this ); // Left first - order matters (left assoc.)
106      auto left_val { fValue };          // Store the left value
107
108      n.GetRightChild()->Accept( * this );
109      auto right_val { fValue };         // Store the right value
110
111      return std::make_tuple( left_val, right_val );
112  }
```

A similar action is repeated on line [108, 109] for the right subtree. Then the values of these two subtrees are returned on line [111] as a tuple.

There are many possible scenarios for implementing the interaction between TNode::Accept and TVisitor::Visit. But in this project we decided that as much as possible, actions would be implemented in the group of visitor objects, relieving the nodes of that burden. This adds to the code's clarity and makes it painless to add new visitors.

6.6.7.2 The Expression-Printing Visitor

The second visitor, PrintVisitor, is defined starting on line [114]. Its role is to print a syntax tree in a terminal window. Each level of the tree should be properly indented to reflect the tree's structure. Like other visitors, on lines [138–142], this one declares the entire suite of overridden and overloaded Visit members for each different type of node. All of them call the auxiliary LeftRightProcess function declared on line [133].

```
113  // A visitor to print structure of the tree
114  class PrintVisitor : public TVisitor
115  {
116  private:
117
118      int     fDepthLevel {};       // current indentation value
119
120      const int fDL_Step { 3 };  // indentation step
121
122  protected:
123
124      /////////////////////////////////////////////////////////////
125      // Auxiliary function to print a bin operator.
126      /////////////////////////////////////////////////////////////
127      //
128      // INPUT:   n - a reference to a binary node
129      //          op - operator symbol character
130      //
131      // OUTPUT:   none
132      //
133      void LeftRightProcess( BinOperator & n, char op );
134
135  public:
136
137      // Set of overloaded functions for each node in the parsing tree
138      void Visit( NumberLeafNode & n ) override;
139      void Visit( PlusOperator & n ) override;
140      void Visit( MinusOperator & n ) override;
141      void Visit( MultOperator & n ) override;
142      void Visit( DivOperator & n ) override;
143
144  };
```

Listing 6.26 shows the two representative functions of `PrintVisitor`. The first `Visit` for the `NumberLeafNode` objects, on lines [3, 4], simply prints its value after properly indenting the output as controlled by the `fDepthLevel` data member. The version of `Visit` for the `PlusOperator` objects, shown on line [7], calls the `LeftRightProcess` function on line [9] with the `'+'` character as its second parameter. Exactly the same action, but with a different second argument, is performed in the case of the remaining binary operators.

Listing 6.26 Implementation of selected members of `PrintVisitor` (in the *Visitors.cpp*).

```
1   void PrintVisitor::Visit( NumberLeafNode & n )
2   {
3       std::cout << std::string( fDepthLevel, ' ' ) << ' ';
4       std::cout << std::string( fDL_Step - 1, '-' ) << n.GetValue() << std::endl;
5   }
6
7   void PrintVisitor::Visit( PlusOperator & n )
8   {
9       LeftRightProcess( n, '+' );
10  }
```

When traversing a tree, the `LeftRightProcess` function, whose definition starts on line [12], is called repeatedly from different nodes on different levels of the tree. Each level is expressed by different indentation value. Therefore, at each call to `LeftRightProcess`, the indentation value is advanced by a constant value, as on line [16]. But before this happens, on line [14], the current indentation value is preserved. It is restored on line [27] at the end of this function. As a result, the deeper levels' indentation is greater by the `fDL_Step` value.

```
11  // Here we have an infix operation: left-this-right
12  void PrintVisitor::LeftRightProcess( BinOperator & n, char op )
13  {
14      auto prev_dl = fDepthLevel;  // get current indentation level
15
16      fDepthLevel += fDL_Step;     // increase indentation
17
18      n.GetRightChild()->Accept( * this );
19
20      std::string sepa( fDepthLevel, ' ' );
21      std::cout << sepa << '|' << std::endl;
22      std::cout << sepa << op << std::endl;
23      std::cout << sepa << '|' << std::endl;
24
25      n.GetLeftChild()->Accept( * this );
26
27      fDepthLevel = prev_dl;       // restore previous indent level
28  }
```

On line [18], the `Accept` from the right node is invoked. On line [20–23], the symbol of the current operation is called with a number of formatting characters. Finally, on line [25], the `Accept` on the left child is called, and the last indentation value is restored.

6.6.8 Testing the Interpreters

In this project, we have designed and implemented classes that together form the simple expression interpreter framework shown in Figure 6.13. Basically, we have two modes of operation, each related to the functionality of the two interpreters: `TSimpleExpressionInterpreter`, which verifies the syntax of an expression; and `ExpressionTreeBuilderInterpreter`, which, when parsing, builds the syntax tree that reflects the structure of the processed expression. In this section, we present two test functions to verify the performance of these two objects.

In `SimpleExpression_Test`, shown in Listing 6.27, the definition starts on line [14] and the `theInterpreter` object of the `TSimpleExpressionInterpreter` class is created on line [17]. It is then used in the loop on lines [28, 29] to test a number of expressions contained in the vector of strings, as defined and initialized on lines [19–25].

Listing 6.27 Definition of the parser test function `SimpleExpression_Test` (in *Parser, ExpressionParser_Test.cpp*).

```
1    #include <iostream>
2    #include <string>
3    #include <vector>
4
5
6    #include "ExpressionTreeBuilderInterpreter.h"
7
8
9    using std::cout, std::endl;
10   using std::string;
11   using std::vector;
12
13
14   void SimpleExpression_Test( void )
15   {
16
17       TSimpleExpressionInterpreter      theInterpreter;
18
19       const vector< std::string > expr_vec  {
20                                        "2+3*(7+3)",
21                                        "2+3+4+5+6+",
22                                        "(((5)))",
23                                        "((2+3)*(4+5)+7)/9",
24                                        "2++3*(7+3)"
25                                      };
26
27       // Check syntax of each expression string
28       for( const auto & expr : expr_vec )
29           cout << expr << " is " << ( theInterpreter( expr ) ? "OK\n" : "not OK\n" );
30
31   }
```

The only answer we can get from this interpreter is whether an expression does or does not comply with the grammar, as shown in the following output message:

```
2+3*(7+3) is OK
2+3+4+5+6+ is not OK
(((5))) is OK
((2+3)*(4+5)+7)/9 is OK
2++3*(7+3) is not OK
```

The `SyntaxTree_Test` function in Listing 6.28, line [1], operates with the `Expression TreeBuilderInterpreter` class from Listing 6.21. The `exprParser` object of this class is created on line [4]. The expression to be processed is defined on line [6].

Line [8] invokes `operator ()` with `good_expr` as its argument. This does the parsing, as described in Section 6.6.5. If `false` is returned, then a syntax error was encountered. In this case, on lines [10, 11], the correct message is output, indicating a possible place where the interpreter got stuck, and the procedure ends.

On the other hand, if the expression is parsed with success, then on line [18], `theRoot` pointer is attached to the root of the syntax tree. We do not know what the type of this node is, but this does not stop us from calling the `Accept` virtual function on line [23] with the `PrintVisitor` object as its parameter. This is polymorphism again. As a result, the structure of the syntax tree is printed in the terminal window, as we will show.

Listing 6.28 Definition of the parser test function `SyntaxTree_Test` (in *Parser, ExpressionParser_Test.cpp*).

```
 1  void SyntaxTree_Test( void )
 2  {
 3
 4      ExpressionTreeBuilderInterpreter    exprParser;
 5
 6      string good_expr( "((1+2)*((3+(4+5))/(6-7)))" );
 7
 8      if( exprParser( good_expr ) == false )
 9      {
10          cout << "Syntax error!\n" << good_expr << "\n";
11          cout << std::string( exprParser.GetCurPos(), ' ' ) << '^' << "\nExiting\n";
12          return;
13      }
14
15      // Here we can do something with the tree e.g. launch a visitor
16
17      // Take a pointer to the root of the tree
18      NodePtr      theRoot { exprParser.GetRoot() };
19      assert( theRoot );
20
21
22      // Print structure of the parsing tree
23      theRoot->Accept( PrintVisitor() ); // Pass a temporary object as an argument
24
25
26      // Let's make a clone of the tree - e.g. to use it in a separate thread
27      Node_UP  theSecondTree { theRoot->Clone() };
28
29
30      // Evaluate the expression
31      EvalVisitor evalVisitor;
32      try
33      {
34          theSecondTree->Accept( evalVisitor );    // Can throw on zero division
35          std::cout << "Val = " << evalVisitor.GetValue() << endl;
36      }
37      catch( std::exception & e )
38      {
39          std::cerr << e.what() << endl;
40      }
41
42  }
```

Although the currently processed tree could be used again, on line [27] its exact copy is created by calling the `Clone` method on the node pointed to by `theRoot` pointer. This is used by `evalVisitor`, created on line [31], to compute and print the value of the entire expression, as coded on line [34, 35]. But since the division can throw an exception, the whole structure is enclosed with the `try-catch` statement starting on line [32].

After executing the previous `SyntaxTree_Test`, the following output is obtained from `PrintVisitor`:

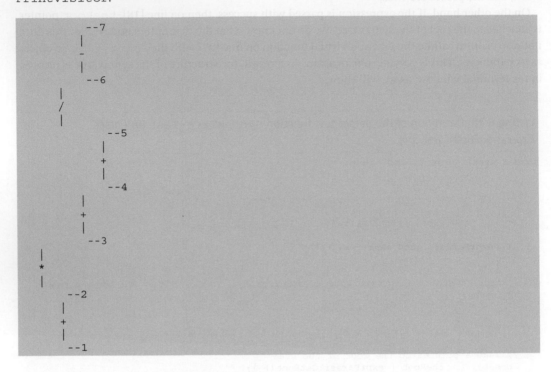

After that, `EvalVisitor` outputs

```
Val = -36
```

In the next section, we will see how the value of an expression can be computed without a syntax tree using a direct operation on the stack with nodes.

Finally, it is worth noticing that the elements of formal grammars, parsing trees, and expression evaluations that we have discussed constitute the salt of the earth in compiler design. Despite their advanced theoretical background, areas such as embedded systems, production automation, and robotics can use these techniques to implement a simple language – a command-like system – a to program or control a device. If the grammar for our command language is simple, after the left-recursion elimination, we can try to implement it, as shown in this section. All of the parsers presented in `TSimpleExpressionInterpreter`, as well as its derived `ExpressionTreeBuilderInterpreter`, belong to the group of top-down LR parsers. These can be used for many simple grammars and also for more complex grammars used for expressions. A characteristic feature of the parsers presented here is that the grammar rules are hardcoded. That is, to change or modify a grammar, we need to change the code and recompile the solution. Usually this is not a problem, but some solutions let us feed a grammar to the parser as an input. In such cases, and also for more complicated grammars, libraries such as *Flex* for lexical analysis and *Bison* for parser construction are recommended (successors of *Lex* and *Yacc*). *Bison* relies on the bottom-up RR parsers and lets us process a broader group of grammars. An interesting C++ implementation of the recursive-descent parser is the Boost Spirit library (*www.boost.org/doc/libs/1_67_0/libs/spirit/doc/html/spirit/introduction.html*): a template-based code that lets us parse a grammar expressed in the BNF notation directly in C++.

When learning C++, skimming *Compilers: Principles, Techniques, and Tools* by Aho et al. (2006) and the slightly more up-to-date *Modern Compiler Design* by Grune et al. (2012) is highly recommended. They provide a much broader view not only of computer language definitions, compilation, code generation, memory management, assembly, and linking, but also of C++ itself. Particular programming techniques used in compilers are frequently encountered in other programming assignments.

6.6.9 Representing Expressions on a Stack in Reverse Polish Notation

We saw the structure of an interpreter that, when parsing an expression, builds the syntax (parsing) tree, which is then traversed by `EvalVisitor` to finally provide the value of an expression. This seems like a lot of constructions. Indeed, if evaluating the value is the ultimate goal, then a much simpler solution can be found. A possible method is to first convert the infix expression into *reverse Polish notation* (RPN), which lets us represent the expression on a stack without using parentheses and then compute the value of that expression. This problem attracted much attention in the early years of computer science. For example, in 1961, Edsger Dijkstra published a report describing his shunting yard algorithm (*https://en.wikipedia.org/wiki/Shunting-yard_algorithm*), which does the job. It may be a surprise, but we followed almost the same idea, as we will soon show. However, before that, let's briefly explain what RPN is.

6.6.9.1 Reverse Polish Notation

RPN (*https://en.wikipedia.org/wiki/Reverse_Polish_notation*) is a way of writing mathematical expressions, fulfilling the precedence and associativity rules of operators with using parentheses. The name comes from the idea of prefix notation proposed by the Polish logician Jan Łukasiewicz in 1924 to facilitate understanding of mathematical expressions. But in computer science, its reversed form, as proposed in 1954 by Arthur Burks and his colleagues, has found many applications. The idea behind RPN is simple. The following example expression in common infix notation

```
3 + 4 * 5
```

can be equivalently written in RPN as follows:

```
3 4 5 * +
```

That is, in RPN, the operators *follow* their operands in a series. The previous formula can be evaluated by reading from left to right. When an operator is encountered, its two preceding operands need to be taken, and the place of this triple in the series is filled with their result. The algorithm continues until only one value is left in the series – this is the value of the entire expression. In our example, working from the left, we find multiplication * first. This and its two predecessors 4 and 5 are taken, and their result 20 is written back. Continuing to the right, the plus operator + is encountered. Again, its two predecessor operands are taken, this time 3 and 20, and the final result 23 is written back. If the expression was

```
(3 + 4) * 5
```

then its RPN version would be

```
5 3 4 + *
```

which evaluates to 35. Interestingly enough, RPN was found by many engineers to be a faster form of evaluating expressions. This was reflected in the famous series of engineering calculators by Hewlett-Packard, such as the HP35.

Based on this description, notice that the most natural way to process infix expressions into their RPN equivalent form, after which they can be easily evaluated, is the stack data structure discussed in Section 4.8.4. Let's trace the evaluation of the last RPN expression using the stack, as shown next.

6.6.9.2 Algorithm for Evaluating an RPN Expression

In the previous section, we outlined the algorithm for evaluating values of RPN expressions. Its steps require an auxiliary stack to hold temporary values, as shown in Figure 6.19. The expression is read from left to right. The operands, such as 5, 3, and 4 in the previous example, are pushed onto the stack. When an operator is encountered, the two topmost values are popped off the stack, such as 4 and 3; and their value – 7, in this case – is pushed onto the stack. This continues until the end of the RPN expression is encountered and only one value is left on the stack. This is the result of the expression: 35 in our example.

The `ComputeValueFrom` function, whose definition starts on line [8] in Listing 6.29, implements this idea. But before we delve into the code, let's summarize the novel C++ techniques that will be used on the way:

- Basics of RTTI for investigating the types of objects when executing code
- Using `typeid`
- Using `dynamic_cast` with references and pointers
- Explicitly calling base member functions

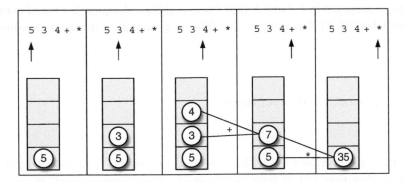

Figure 6.19 Evaluating the RPN expression 5 3 4 + *, The expression is read from left to right. There are two categories of symbols: operands (values) and operators. The operands are pushed onto the stack. When an operator is encountered, then the two topmost values are popped from the top of the stack and used together to compute the value, which is then pushed back onto the stack. The steps continue until the end of the RPN expression is encountered and there is only one final value on top of the stack.

Our input to the ComputeValueFrom function is a vector of nodes, defined by NodeVec on line [1]. This corresponds to the input RPN expression, 5 3 4 + * in Figure 6.19, but the elements are node objects from the TNode hierarchy (Section 6.6.4). The returned value will be represented by the LeafValType whose alias is defined on line [4].

If there are any nodes in the input node_vec, the auxiliary stack auxStack holding LeafValType objects is created on line [21]. Then the nodes from node_vec are processed from left to right in the range loop that starts on line [25], as shown in Figure 6.19. But the problem is as follows: although all elements of node_vec are smart pointers to the TNode base class, the actual pointers are to different objects from the TNode hierarchy. For example, with our simple expression, we will have three LeafValTypes followed by one PlusOperator and one MultOperator. We need to process them differently, as described in the previous RPN processing algorithm, but we have only TNode pointers. So, we have to figure out how, at runtime, to differentiate one TNode pointer to LeafValType from the other TNode pointer to PlusOperator, for instance. In C++, the RTTI mechanism comes to the rescue, as we mentioned in Section 3.19.1 when we discussed *GROUP 2* of the C++ operators. The two RTTI constructions are the typeid and dynamic_cast operators. typeid allows us to check the type of an object referred to with a pointer or a reference, even if that pointer or reference is to the base class from which the class of an object of interest was derived. On the other hand, at runtime, dynamic_cast will try to do a checked conversion of a pointer or a reference to the requestedtype. If the converted types are up, down, or sideways along the inheritance hierarchy, then the conversion will succeed. Otherwise, if dynamic_cast< *a_pointer* > is attempted, a nullptr will be returned. In the case of dynamic_cast< *a_reference* >, a std::bad_cast exception is thrown. We will use these features in our code. First, to distinguish the LeafValType objects, line [29] verifies the typeid of an object held by node, using the typeid of NumberLeafNode. If they agree, then the value of the object is pushed onto the auxStack. Concretely, on line [32] node is cast to the pointer to the NumberLeafNode object, from which the value is read and pushed onto the stack. But how is this done? Because node is a std::unique_ptr, it is not compatible with the NumberLeafNode class. However, it has an overloaded cast operator built in to a pointer of the held class. As a result, std::unique_ptr can be used in all code requiring a pointer or reference to the held object. Hence, GetValue can be called through the node cast to the NumberLeafNode object.

Listing 6.29 Function to compute the value of an expression directly from its RPN representation stored in the stack (in *Parser, NodeStackConverters.cpp*).

```
1   using NodeVec = ExpressionTreeBuilderInterpreter::NodeStack::DataContainer;
2
3
4   using LeafValType = double;
5
6
7   // Computes value of the stack
8   LeafValType ComputeValueFrom( const NodeVec & node_vec )
9   {
10      auto retVal { 0.0 };
11
12      const auto kNumOfElems = node_vec.size();
13      if( kNumOfElems == 0 )
```

(Coninued)

Listing 6.29 (continued)

```
14        return retVal;            // Empty node_vec, return zero & exit
15
16        // The algorithm is as follows:
17        // - The node stack is traversed:
18        // - if a leaf is encountered, then push its value on auxStack
19        // - if a bin operator is encountered, take two topmost values,
20        //   perform the operation, and push back the result on auxStack
21        CppBook::TStackFor< LeafValType, 1000 >    auxStack;
22
23
24        // Traverse all nodes, starting at index 0
25        for( const auto & node : node_vec )
26        {
27            assert( node );
28
29            if( typeid( * node ) == typeid( NumberLeafNode ) )
30            {
31                // A NumberLeafNode
32                auxStack.Push( dynamic_cast< NumberLeafNode * >( node )->GetValue() );
33            }
34            else
35            {
36                // A binary operator - but we don't know yet which one
37
38                assert( auxStack.GetStackSize() >= 2 );
39
40                LeafValType leftNumVal {}, rightNumVal {};
41
42                auxStack.Pop( rightNumVal );    // Get top values
43                auxStack.Pop( leftNumVal );
44
45                // Check what type of operation is in the node
46                if( dynamic_cast< PlusOperator * >( node ) )
47                    auxStack.Push( leftNumVal + rightNumVal );
48                else
49                    if( dynamic_cast< MinusOperator * >( node ) )
50                        auxStack.Push( leftNumVal - rightNumVal );
51                    else
52                        if( dynamic_cast< MultOperator * >( node ) )
53                            auxStack.Push( leftNumVal * rightNumVal );
54                        else
55                            if( dynamic_cast< DivOperator * >( node ) )
56                                if( std::fabs( rightNumVal ) > 1e-32 )
57                                    auxStack.Push( leftNumVal / rightNumVal );
58                                else
59                                    throw std::overflow_error( "Div by 0" );
60                            else
61                                assert( false ); // Must not happen - check in debug
62            }
63
64
65        }
66
67        // Take over the last node from the stack or return empty.
68        assert( auxStack.GetStackSize() == 1 );
69        auxStack.Pop( retVal );
70
71        return retVal;
72    }
```

If a node is not the `NumberLeafNode` type, it is probably one of the four binary operators. So, the only thing left to do is to figure out which one we currently hold in the `node` smart pointer. This is done on lines [46–61] by a chain of `if-else` statements. In each condition, a `dynamic_cast` to a pointer to one of the four operator classes is attempted; if the types agree, then the cast succeeds. In this case, the corresponding operation is performed on the two operands previously popped off the stack on lines [42, 43], and the result is pushed onto `auxStack`. For instance, on line [47], a summation takes place because `PlusOperator` was identified. In this construction, we use the fact that `dynamic_cast` returns `nullptr` if the types do not agree. In such a situation, an attempt to cast to a reference would throw an exception, which we try to avoid when resolving "normal" conditional constructions. `typeid` could also be used instead of `dynamic_cast`.

This construction is used for all operators except `DivOperator`. It is additionally preceded by checking for division by zero, in which case `std::overflow_error` is thrown,[6] as shown on line [59].

Finally, the algorithm stops with only one value left on the stack. This is the final result, which is taken off the stack on line [69] and returned on line [71].

Notice that RTTI was not necessary in the `ExpressionTreeBuilderInterpreter` class or the visitor mechanism. By correctly designing our polymorphic operations, we can avoid using RTTI. There is nothing wrong with it, but the need to check object types in polymorphic code can make us think twice about whether our design could be better. However, sometimes there is no better way. In our example, we decided to keep the `TNode` hierarchy as free as possible from operations related to evaluation and other actions that are left to the visitors. Hence, e.g. the `PlusOperator` on line [47] will not add the two operands for us: it simply represents the plus operation.

The `RPN_Value_Test` function on line [5] glues together parsing the expression and evaluating the expression value, which is done directly from the stack structure by the `ComputeValueFrom` function. But since we are reusing the same `ExpressionTreeBuilderInterpreter` class, we need to change the code slightly to push all the tokens onto the stack and stop building the syntax tree. For this purpose, in the code shown in Listing 6.21, the `BUILD_THE_TREE` preprocessor flag on line [178] should be set to 0. This simply excludes a few lines from the action, and only the last `Push` onto the `fNodeStack` is executed. To verify the proper compilation setting, a simple checkpoint is inserted on lines [7–9]. However, what is more interesting is understanding that by pushing the `TNode` objects onto `fNodeStack`, we obtain the RPN structure of the expression, exactly as shown in the example in Figure 6.19. In other words, our interpreter, fueled by the grammar rules, does infix-to-postfix conversion!

Listing 6.30 Test functions (in *Parser, ExpressionParser_Test.cpp*).

```
1   // Computes the value from the node stack.
2   // This works when compiling with
3   // BUILD_THE_TREE set to 0
4   // (in ExpressionTreeBuilderInterpreter.h)
5   void RPN_Value_Test( void )
6   {
7   #if BUILD_THE_TREE == 1
8       assert( false );          // A fuse to ensure we compiled with the proper parameter
9   #endif
```

(Continued)

---

6 In STL, there is no predefined `div_by_zero` exception, so we can either use `std::overflow_error` or `std::underflow_error` or create a custom exception class.

Listing 6.30 (continued)

```
10
11       ExpressionTreeBuilderInterpreter    exprParser;
12
13       string good_expr( "(1+2)*(3+(4+5))/(6-7)" );        // Expression string
14
15       // Let's call only the base class operator ()
16       if( exprParser.BaseClass::operator()( good_expr ) )
17       {
18          try
19          {
20              std::cout << "Val = " << ComputeValueFrom(
21                          exprParser.GetNodeStack().GetDataContainer() ) << endl;
22          }
23          catch( std::exception & e )
24          {
25              std::cerr << e.what() << endl;
26          }
27       }
28       else
29       {
30          cout << "Syntax error!\n" << good_expr << "\n";
31          cout << std::string( exprParser.GetCurPos(), ' ' ) << '^' << endl;
32       }
33
34    }
```

To make our `exprParser` – defined on line [11] as an object of the `Expression TreeBuilderInterpreter` class – perform parsing without any final postprocessing of the syntax tree, line [16] invokes `operator()` from the *base class*. To accomplish this, we have to put the name of the base class before the name `exprParser` of the object and the name of the member function. In our case, the name of the base class is `TSimpleExpressionInterpreter`, for which an alias `BaseClass` was created on line [64] in Listing 6.21. But we need to provide a qualified name (see Figure 6.2) for the member function, which in our case is `operator ()`. Hence, analogous to the member call scheme in Figure 3.8, a general scheme for calling members of the base class(es) is as shown in Figure 6.20.

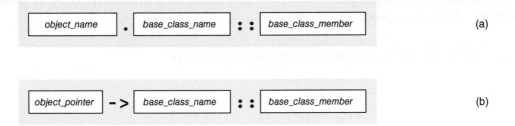

Figure 6.20 Syntax of the base class member call from an object or a reference to the object (a) and by the pointer to an object (b).

Alternatively, line [16] can be written as follows:

```
16        if( ( & exprParser )->BaseClass::operator()( good_expr ) )
```

Then, on lines [20, 21], `ComputeValueFrom` from Listing 6.29 is called with the input vector reflecting the RPN structure of the input expression. Since an exception can be thrown, the call is enclosed by the `try-catch` statement on line [18–23] (Section 3.13.2.5).

Summarizing, in this section, we have learned about the following:

- Basics of formal grammars, lexical analysis, and expression parsing
- Building class hierarchies with interfaces expressed with pure virtual functions
- Expression parsing with the interpreter design pattern
- Implementing syntax trees with the composite design pattern
- Object access with non-owning pointers and owning access with smart pointers
- Stack specialization to store `std::unique_ptr` objects
- Traversing tree structures with the visitor design pattern
- The cloning technique and prototype design pattern to create objects dynamically
- Converting infix expressions into RPN and stack operations
- RTTI with the `typeid` and `dynamic_cast` operators

6.7 Summary

Things to Remember

- Objects can be used to model actions – for this purpose, we designate functional objects that implement the overloaded functional `operator ()`
- The *regex* library provides functionality to match text patterns expressed with regular expressions
- XML can be used for a structured representation of data and its relations
- For better modularity, software components can be organized into static and dynamic libraries
- The handle-body design pattern should be used to separate abstraction (interface) from implementation in order to allow the two to vary independently
- The *filesystem* library provides functions and classes for file and directory operations
- The *chrono* library provides functions and classes for time and date operations
- Formal grammars are used to define computer languages
- The role of the interpreter design pattern is to represent grammar rules and parse language constructions
- The composite design pattern can be used to build self-recursive, tree-like structures, such as syntax trees, file-directory structures, menu and macro menu representations, etc
- The visitor design pattern is used to traverse a collection of objects, such as a tree, to provide double-dispatch access (usually called the `Accept` and `Visit` members)
- The prototype design pattern implements dynamic object construction based on provided prototype objects (usually with the `Clone` method)
- The type of an object can be verified at runtime with the RTTI mechanisms represented by the `typeid` and `dynamic_cast` operators

Questions and Exercises

1. Refactor the system shown in Figure 6.1 to handle menu item actions. Using the composite design pattern, as shown in Figure 6.15, implement a macro command. This command is also derived from the `THandler` class from Listing 6.1. But at the same time, it contains other pre-recorded commands.

2. Implement a cyclic buffer with `THandler` objects (Section 6.1). Use smart pointers.

3. Using the *range-v3* library (*https://github.com/ericniebler/range-v3*), implement the letter histogram component discussed in Section 2.5.

4. Write regular expressions to match the following:

   ■ A date with its fields: the two-digit day number, followed by a dot, then the two-digit month number, a dot, and the four-digit year
   ■ A C++ comment: `// a C++ comment ...`
   ■ A C-like comment: `/* a C comment */`
   ■ A sentence, i.e. text starting with a capital letter and ending with a dot, semicolon, exclamation mark, or question mark

   Then use the following function to test these regular expressions:

```
void regex_test( void )
{
    // input stream
    string str( "jan.koczwara_12@agh.edu.pl" );
    cout << str << endl;

    // R"( )"   for a raw string
    regex pat( R"(([[:alnum:]._]+)@([[:alnum:]._]+)\.([[:alnum:]]+))" );

    // where result(s) what
    if( smatch   match_res; regex_search( str, match_res, pat ) )
        for( auto m : match_res )
            cout << m << endl;
}
```

5. Write unit tests for the currency exchanger project.

6. The exchange project can be arranged in many different ways. For instance, instead of a new `XML_CurrencyExchanger` class, you could write a class to convert an XML file with currency data into a format for the initialization file suitable for the base class. Draw the relations of this approach. What are its benefits and drawbacks? What would happen if you had more different formats for the XML-coded information?

7. Remake the component in the basic version of `CurrencyExchanger` presented in Section 3.18.5 to enclose it in a class instead of the `CurrExchanger` namespace. What are the consequences of the two solutions?

8. In Section 6.2.4, we mentioned the strategy design pattern. It is similar to the handle-body pattern but lets us dynamically change the body object depending on the runtime conditions. Implement a strategy pattern to efficiently sort vectors of different lengths. A suitable sorting algorithm – the one that best fits the current vector length – should be instantiated before the sorting action. Hint: read about sorting algorithm performance with respect to vector length.

9. Based on the example function `RecursivelyTraverseDirectory` presented in Section 6.2.7, write function(s) to traverse a directory and create a sorted list of the files' dimensions.

10. Write a software mechanism to recursively traverse a directory and all of its subdirectories and perform an action supplied in the form of a functional object passed as a parameter (this can be a composite pattern).

11. Refactor the CC_GUI class to keep all the positions and dimensions of the controls in a separate resource file (see Listings 6.8 and 6.9). In the class initialization procedure, open that file, read the data, and properly set up the widgets. Do not forget about controlling data correctness.

12. Design and implement an extended version of the *CurrencyCalc_GUI* project to allow for currency type conversions in both directions, as well as choosing an arbitrary reference currency.

13. Find out how to create a dynamically loaded library in your OS. Remake the static library presented in Section 6.2.6 into a dynamic one, and test its behavior. What are the advantages and disadvantages of both types of libraries?

14. Refactor the SyntaxTree_Test function defined in Listing 6.27 to accept user-supplied expressions.

15. Extend the lexical analysis to allow for white symbols (space, tabs, etc.) and C++ numbers. For this purpose, define and use the *grep* patterns discussed in Section 6.2.1.

16. Derive a new interpreter class that accepts not only numbers but also symbols, so such expressions as a + 3.14 * b are recognizable. Then construct a symbol table containing the associations of symbols with their values and write a visitor to evaluate expressions.

17. Extend the interpreter to accept function calls with various arguments.

18. Design and implement a code-generation visitor for runtime evaluation of any expression. The visitor should generate text, which will be C++ statements. These will form a new program that, after a separate compilation, will provide the final code for evaluating runtime expressions. See "Simple code generation for a stack machine" in (Dick et al. 2012). This idea can be further extended to create your own simple language generator.

19. Implement a simple calculator using the Boost Spirit library (Boost.org 2020).

20. *Reflection* is a technique that lets us inspect a class without having any information about it. Especially when implementing template functions and classes, for example, we might be interested in verifying whether a type for template instantiation contains certain data or the method for a proper call. Such features will be available soon in the C++ standard. But until then, we can try to implement at least some of this functionality. For example, a reflection method can be added to a class, which returns a std.::tuple conveying all of its data (Section 3.17). Such a reflection-aware class can be easily compared, streamed out, etc. This technique is shown in the following code, which presents a partial definition of the TBook class:

```
class TBook
{
    std::string    fAuthor;
    std::string    fTitle;
    int            fPubYear {};
```

```
public:
    // ...

    auto reflection( void ) const
    {
        return std::tie( fAuthor, fTitle, fPubYear );
    }
};
```

a. Augment the `TBook` class with the remaining special functions.

b. Add the overloaded `operator ==` and `operator <`, as well as the streaming operators, taking advantage of the `reflection` method.

c. Extend the `reflection` method to operate in the class hierarchy (make it virtual).

21. When writing generic components using templates it is sometimes important to assure that the supplied types fulfill specific properties. For example, we may allow only signed types or types that can be compared with the `==` and `!=` operators, etc. Such generic expectations of the template arguments can be verified with *the concepts* predicates, the new powerful feature of the C++20 standard.

a. Read and learn about the concepts (e.g. B. Stroustrup: Concepts: The Future of Generic Programming,2017, *https://www.stroustrup.com/good_concepts.pdf*; *https://en.cppreference.com/w/cpp/concepts*). Write your own concept, say `exclusively_unsigned`, to assure that a type comes exclusively from the unsigned types.

b. Refactor the `RevertEndianess` template function from Listing 4.16 to use your `exclusively_unsigned` concept. Verify the compiler messages when a signed type is tried.

c. Design and implement concepts for the `TStackFor` template class used in Section 6.6.6.

22. The `std::optional`, which we used in Section 6.2.5, has two companions:

a. The template `std::variant` that can represent many objects of potentially different types, from which only one is held at a time. Read about the `std::variant` (*https://www.bfilipek.com/2018/06/variant.html*) and refactor the function `GetRoots` from the code from Section 3.16 to return the `std::variant` holding either one or two roots or an error code.

b. The non-template `std::any` which can hold an object of any type which can be further changed in the run-time for example to pass ownership of arbitrary values (*https://www.bfilipek.com/2018/06/any.html*). Consider refactoring the `fVal` member of the `ValueLeafNode` from Listing 6.16 to the `std::any` to stand for any object representing a value such as a `int`, `double` or `std::string`. What are the differences between these two designs?

23. In Section 6.2 we processed the XML file with the *grep* library. However, XML files can be processed with one of many C++ libraries, such as Xerces-C++ (*http://xerces.apache.org/xerces-c/*) or RapidXML (*http://rapidxml.sourceforge.net/*). With the help of one of them write a program to process XML file to extract information on the currency exchange ratios.

24. JSON is another popular format for data storage and representation. There are also some C++ libraries for processing JSON formats, e.g. by Niels Lohmann (*https://github.com/nlohmann/json*) or RapidJSON (*https://github.com/Tencent/rapidjson*). Using one of these header-only libraries write a module to write and read currency information from Section 6.2 to and from the *currency.json* file.

7

Computer Arithmetic

We know that computers store information in bits: that is, in a binary format, 1 or 0. In this chapter, we discuss how this affects computations.

7.1 Integer Value Representation

In Section 2.1, we showed the architecture of a simplified microprocessor system that serves as our computational programming interface. In Section 3.1, we discussed various C++ arithmetic types, which we have used in computations presented in this book. In this section, we present some basic information and discuss integer computer arithmetic. For clarity, let's start with the following definitions:

- The basic unit of information is a *bit*, which conveys a value of either 0 or 1. This gives rise to the binary system with base $B = 2$
- A *byte* is an ordered series of eight bits
- A different *weight value* is associated with each bit position in a byte. For example, the fifth bit, counting from the rightmost 0th position, can be assigned a weight of $2^4 = 16$. There can be different weight assignments, resulting in different arithmetic values
- A byte is the lowest addressable memory unit in a computer system
- A computer *word* is a concatenation of one or an even number of bytes. A word usually corresponds to the bus width of a microprocessor system. For example, in 32-bit systems, words are four bytes long, whereas in 64-bit systems, they are eight bytes long, and so on

Figure 7.1 shows the structure of a byte, including the bit positions, indices i, and weights w_i.

Similar to the value 125, which in a decimal system is interpreted as $1 \cdot 10^2 + 2 \cdot 10^1 + 5 \cdot 10^0$, the value D of a byte shown in Figure 7.1 can be computed as follows

$$D = b_7 \cdot 2^7 + b_6 \cdot 2^6 + \ldots + b_0 \cdot 2^0 \tag{7.1}$$

where b_i are bit values of 1 or 0 in the byte. Given this interpretation, D is always positive and in the range [0...255]. For example, the value of the following byte

0	1	0	1	0	1	1	1

Introduction to Programming with C++ for Engineers, First Edition. Bogusław Cyganek.
© 2021 John Wiley & Sons Ltd. Published 2021 by John Wiley & Sons Ltd.
Companion website: http://home.agh.edu.pl/~cyganek/BookCpp.htm

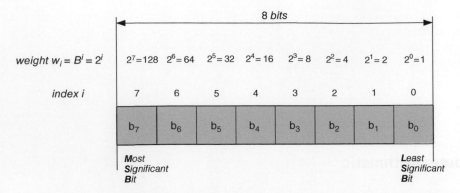

Figure 7.1 A byte is a series of eight bits b_i with the value 1 or 0. The value of a byte is interpreted in accordance with the weights w_i associated with each bit position. If w_i are consecutive integer powers of base $B = 2$, as shown in this image, then we have an integer representation.

using Eq. (7.1) and starting in the rightmost position is as follows:

$$D = 2^0 \cdot 1 + 2^1 \cdot 1 + 2^2 \cdot 1 + 2^3 \cdot 0 + 2^4 \cdot 1 + 2^5 \cdot 0 + 2^6 \cdot 1 + 2^7 \cdot 0 = 1 + 2 + 4 + 16 + 64 = 87$$

In other words, we can write that

$$01010111_2 = 87_{10}$$

where subscripts denote a chosen representation base B for a number. Hence, 2 denotes the *binary* base $B = 2$, and 10 stands for the *decimal* base $B = 10$. Soon, we will also see a representation with $B = 16$, i.e. *a hexadecimal* system, and the less common *octal* system with $B = 8$.

In a general case, the value D can be represented as a sum of N components, as follows:

$$D = \sum_{i=0}^{N-1} b_i w_i \tag{7.2}$$

For integer values, the weights are defined as follows:

$$w_i = B^i \tag{7.3}$$

where B denotes the computation base. Inserting Eq. (7.3) into Eq. (7.2) yields

$$D = \sum_{i=0}^{N-1} b_i B^i \tag{7.4}$$

Naturally, for binary systems, this simplifies to

$$D_{IB} = \sum_{i=0}^{N-1} b_i 2^i \tag{7.5}$$

where the *IB* subscript stands for integer-binary. However, soon we will see that by assigning different weights to the bits, we can also obtain negative and fractional values.

Equation (7.5) denotes a method for converting from a binary representation to a decimal value, i.e. to the equivalent number expressed with $B = 10$. In the next section, we will show how to perform the opposite operation: converting a decimal value to a system with a given base B.

You can play with variants of binary representations and conversions using the *FixBinCalc* application, described in Section 9.5. Also worth mentioning is the binary-coded decimal (BCD) format, which provides a convenient representation of two decimal values encoded in one byte (Section 4.15.1). This format is not as efficient since more "compressed" representations can be devised. But it is common in embedded systems. Also, we used it to pack digits into our `TLongNumberFor` structure in Section 4.15.

7.1.1 Base Conversion Algorithm

To see how to perform a conversion to a given base, let's rewrite Eq. (7.4) as follows

$$D = b_0 B^0 + \sum_{i=1}^{N-1} b_i B^i = b_0 + B \cdot \sum_{i=1}^{N-1} b_i B^{i-1}, \tag{7.6}$$

since whatever B is, the value of $B^0 = 1$. Now, dividing D in Eq. (7.6) by B yields two values, an *integer quotient* and a *remainder,* which, because it always holds that $b_0 < B$, happens to be the last digit b_0 from the binary expansion in Eq. (7.4). That is, we get the following two values:

$$D/B = \left[\sum_{i=1}^{N-1} b_i B^{i-1}, \underline{b_0} \right]. \tag{7.7}$$

Then, repeating this procedure for the quotient $\sum_{i=1}^{N-1} b_i B^{i-1}$, we get the value of b_1, and so on.

This observation leads us to the conversion algorithm. It relies on consecutive divisions of the value by the base B, after which consecutive digits are obtained as remainders of this division, starting in the least-significant digit; the value is substituted for the quotient, and so on, until 0 is obtained.

As an experiment, let's consider the final value we got earlier, 87:

	Q	R
87/10	8	7
8/10	0	8

Reading the column of remainders from the bottom, we get the value 87. Let's try this with the binary base:

	Q	R
87/2	43	1
43/2	21	1
21/2	10	1
10/2	5	0
5/2	2	1
2/2	1	0
1/2	0	1

Again reading the remainder from the bottom, we get the following series: 1010111. In a byte representation, after we insert a leading 0 so we have exactly eight bits, we get the following:

$$87_{10} = 01010111_2$$

The previous algorithm can be used for any other base.

7.1.2 Hexadecimal and Octal Representations

Binary representation is fine, except that binary expansions contain the largest number of digits because they use the smallest integer base, $B = 2$. Hence, larger bases are useful to represent large values. In microprocessor systems and computer science, the most common is the hexadecimal base: $B = 16$. Such a large base works well, but we face the problem of efficient notation for digits greater than 9. For example, how do we write a digit representing 12 and not confuse it with a digit 1 followed by a digit 2? We could use parentheses for this purpose and write (11), (13), or (15). However, it is much handier to use letters for digits greater than 9, in accordance with the following encoding:

Dec	Hex
10	A
11	B
12	C
13	D
14	E
15	F

Let's see it works with our 87_{10} value. With $B = 16$, we get the following digits:

	Q	R
87/16	5	7
5/16	0	5

That is, $87_{10} = 57_{16} = 57_{hex} = 0 \times 57$

Slightly less popular is the octal representation, i.e. $B = 8$. In this case, we get

	Q	R
87/8	10	7
10/8	1	2
1/8	0	1

Hence, $87_{10} = 127_{oct} = 0127$. In C++, we can express the value in all four bases – 2, 8, 10, and 16 – as presented in Table 3.1.

But when converting within a group of systems with bases that are powers of 2, there is an easier way than successive divisions. The following rules apply:

- When converting from a binary stream to hexadecimal, we group bits into four and convert each group of four bits to a hexadecimal digit. In the octal system, the groups contain three bits
- When converting from a hexadecimal value to a binary one, we can convert each digit into its four-bit binary equivalent. The same applies to the octal system, but with three bits

Let's do some experiments, as follows:

87_{dec}	$=_{bin}$	0	1	0	1	0	1	1	1
87_{dec}	$=_{hex}$	5				7			

Similarly, for the octal representation, we get

87_{dec}	$=_{bin}$	0	1	0	1	0	1	1	1
87_{dec}	$=_{oct}$	1		2			7		

However, here is an important question: if we have a decimal value, what is the minimum number of bits to represent it fully? We answered this question in Section 3.1.

7.1.3 Binary Addition

In this section, we consider the problem of adding binary values. Basically, the entire operation is similar to decimal addition, but we need to remember to carry if the result is greater than 1. Let's consider the following example.

100_{dec}	$=_{bin}$	0	1	1	0	0	1	0	0
87_{dec}	$=_{bin}$	0	1	0	1	0	1	1	1
187_{dec}	$=_{bin}$	1	0	1	1	1	0	1	1
Carry		←				←			

Now let's add the same values, but this time represented in the octal and hexadecimal systems:

100_{dec}	$=_{hex}$	6	4
87_{dec}	$=_{hex}$	5	7
187_{dec}	$=_{hex}$	B	B

In this case, we do not have to carry. But in the octal version, we have the following:

100_{dec}	$=_{oct}$	1	4	4
87_{dec}	$=_{oct}$	1	2	7
187_{dec}	$=_{oct}$	2	7	3
Carry			←	

A carry from the most significant digit means the value cannot fit into the current representation. In this case, we either need to extend the sum representation by one digit or store the result and a bit representing the running carry. To detect this situation when doing low-level addition, processors have the carry C bit, as shown in Figure 2.2.

7.1.4 Negative Values and Subtraction

Subtraction also follows common arithmetic rules. However, if the subtracted value (the *subtrahend*) is greater than the value we subtract from (the *minuend*), then we must *borrow*. Let's analyze the following example:

87_{dec}	$=_{bin}$	0	1	0	1	0	1	1	1
100_{dec}	$=_{bin}$	0	1	1	0	0	1	0	0
-13_{dec}	$=_{bin}$	1	1	1	1	0	0	1	1
Borrow				→					
Borrow			→						
Borrow		– – – – –▶							

We encounter three borrows, starting at the fifth bit. However, the last borrow, indicated with a dashed arrow, must be made from an outside bit. This means the result is *negative*. Hence, we need to discuss the representation of negative values in more detail. We will see that subtraction can be performed like addition with a negative value.

Before we start, recall the basic definition of a negative number:

$$a+\left(-a\right)=0. \tag{7.8}$$

Also, it holds that subtraction is equivalent to addition with a negative subtrahend:

$$a-b=a+\left(-b\right). \tag{7.9}$$

The previous two formulas are very useful when implementing the subtraction operation.

Indicating a negative value in text or a formula is that simple. The question is how to include the negative sign (–) in a numeric representation. This is binary information: a number either is or is not negative. Thus, we need to incorporate an additional sign bit to convey this information. That is fine, but there are options for its placement and behavior, as listed in Table 7.1.

Table 7.1 Techniques for representing negative values in a binary representation.

Negative	Description	Example
Sign-magnitude (SM)	The MSB is sacrificed to represent the sign: 0 means a positive value and 1 a negative value. The remaining bits convey positive magnitude. A slight problem is that we have a potential double representation of zero.	A positive value 87_{dec} S------M------ 0 1 0 1 0 1 1 1
Ones' complement (C1)	This representation is obtained after complementing all bits: that is, 0 is changed to 1, and 1 to 0.	1 0 1 0 1 0 0 0
Two's complement (C2)	The most popular and useful way of representing negative values. It is obtained from the C1 representation after adding 1. Thanks to this condition, Eq. (7.8) is immediately fulfilled.	1 0 1 0 1 0 0 1

Taking into account the representation of negative values, we need to modify Eq. (7.5) as follows:

$$D_{SM} = (-1)^S \cdot \sum_{i=0}^{N-2} b_i 2^i \tag{7.10}$$

and

$$D_{C2} = -S \cdot 2^N + \sum_{i=0}^{N-1} b_i 2^i = -S \cdot 2^N + D_{IB} \tag{7.11}$$

where $S = b_{N-1}$ denotes the sign bit with bit indexing, as shown in Figure 7.1. For a byte, the first term in Eq. (7.11) can be either 0 for a positive value or -256 for a negative value. The latter gives us a fast way of finding the negative of a positive value D_{IB}: simply subtract it from 2^N.

With the previous rule, we can easily find the bit representation of -87 as $256 - 87 = 169$. We can verify that the value $169_{\text{dec}} = 10101001_{\text{bin}}$ is -87. From this, we can verify that a negative value always has its MSB set to 1.

From the previous explanation, we see that in most cases, the most convenient binary representation of negative values is C2. A value of 0 is represented with all bits set to 0, and the property in Eq. (7.8) is also fulfilled. In Section 7.1, we noticed that the value D computed in accordance with Eq. (7.1) for a byte is in the range $[0...255]$. That was for positive values only, which in C++ are indicated by providing the `unsigned` suffix to an integer type (Section 3.1). However, in the realm of positive and negative values, values in the range $[-128...+127]$ can be stored in a byte. In C++, these are represented without a suffix or, occasionally, use the `signed` keyword (Table 3.1). Another important property of operations using the C2 format is that subtraction can be directly performed as addition with a negative second term: that is, in accordance with Eq. (7.9). Although addition and subtraction are simple with values in C2 format, we will see that some computations such as multiplication are simpler in an SM representation.

Things to Remember

- The digits to represent a value in a base B are obtained as remainders of successive divisions of a quotient by B, starting with the quotient set to that value
- When converting values from a binary representation to one with the base that is a multiple of 2, such as hexadecimal or octal, we can separately convert the consecutive digits into their bit representations
- Subtraction is equivalent to addition with a negative value for the subtrahend
- For signed values, MSB set to 1 means a negative value
- An unsigned byte can represent the values $[0...255]$. In C2, a signed byte can store $[-128...127]$
- To obtain a C2 representation of a positive number a, we can subtract it from the 2^N value, where N denotes the number of bits in a representation (eight for a byte, and so on)

Although the basic properties and examples presented here are for bytes, they can easily be transformed for computer words composed of many bytes.

7.1.5 Arithmetic Control Flags

We have seen that when adding two digits, we may need to carry. This means the result does not fit into the representation, and the value of 1 must be added to the position to the left. This also holds for subtraction, since subtraction is addition with a negative second term. However, in the case of signed arithmetic, when adding two positive values, their magnitudes may cause the MSB of the result to coincidentally indicate a negative value. This happens if a carry bit is passed from MSB − 1 to the MSB bit position. Such a situation is called an *overflow*, and it is usually indicated by setting a special *V* control bit in the microprocessor. The last control bit is a *zero*, denoted as a *Z* bit, which is set whenever all the bits in the result are set to 0. It is used for comparing numbers, since *Z* set to 1 means the values are equal. The control bits are summarized in Table 7.2.

Table 7.2 Explanation of the control bits in arithmetic operations.

Control flag	Description	Example
Zero Z	1 – The operation result is 0 (all bits of the result set to 0). 0 – The result is not 0.	0 0 0 0 0 0 0 1 + 1 1 1 1 1 1 1 1 ZERO → 0 0 0 0 0 0 0 0 carry ①
Carry C	1 – Result is too large to fit into the bit representation (more positions are required). 0 – Result fits into the representation.	0 1 0 0 0 0 0 1 + 1 1 1 0 0 1 1 1 0 0 1 0 1 0 0 0 ① carry
Overflow V	1 – A carry happened between the two most significant bits. For signed arithmetic, this means adding two positive values produced a negative result. 0 – No carry between two most significant bits.	overflow 0 1 0 0 0 0 0 1 + 0 1 1 0 0 1 1 1 1 0 1 0 1 0 0 0

Notice that when adding two *N* bit values, the results will always fit in $N+1$ bits. As already mentioned, if the carry bit is set, it indicates that the result cannot fit into an *N*-bit representation. On the other hand, for multiplication, we may need up to 2*N* bits.

To understand the role of the overflow *V* bit, let's return to the example from Section 7.1.3. This time, let's assume signed arithmetic using C2 encoding. Adding two values gives the following output:

100_{dec}	$=_{bin}$	0	1	1	0	0	1	0	0
87_{dec}	$=_{bin}$	0	1	0	1	0	1	1	1
-69_{dec}	$=_{bin}$	1	0	1	1	1	0	1	1
Carry						←			
Overflow		←							

Since we assume signed arithmetic, 10111011_{bin} indicates -69_{dec}. However, -69_{dec} corresponds to $256 - 69 = 187$ in unsigned arithmetic, which is exactly what we obtained in Section 7.1.3.

The control bits C, V, and Z appear in the microprocessor register and cannot be read directly from the C++ code. Nevertheless, knowing their roles is important to understand computer arithmetic and to ensure proper values for computations.

Let's also notice another phenomenon related to processing N-bit long values. Trying to assign a value greater than 2^N – to it – for example, by copying from a representation longer than N bits – would result in *overflow*. This is a potentially dangerous situation that in real life can lead to disaster. Therefore it should be forbidden; or, in practice, it should at least be detected and handled. But in C++ for integers, such a situation goes undetected. There are two options:

- Unsigned integers simply wrap around. That is, a module 2^N operation is performed. For example, adding 1 to the LSB digit of an unsigned integer with all its bits set to 1 will result in all bits set to 0. Analogously, subtracting 1 from a LSB of an unsigned integer with all 0 bits will produce a value with all 1s
- For signed integers, *the behavior is undefined*. On some computer platforms, an exception may even be generated

In most cases, neither of these options is the best solution, and overflows should be controlled. We saw such an example in Section 4.15 when trying to assign an 11-digit value to an `unsigned int`. We solved this problem by designing a special class to store arbitrarily long numbers (Section 4.15.3). In other cases, value *saturation* at minimum or maximum allowable values is a better option. But such a feature also comes at a cost. For example, after assessing the required precision, a library can be used to ensure arithmetic with the required precision (Section 7.4.7). Finally, the problem of underflow and overflow for floating-point numbers is further examined in Section 7.4.

Things to Remember

- The result of adding two N-bit values always fits in a maximum of $N+1$ bits
- The result of multiplying N-bit values always fits in a maximum of $2N$ bits
- The carry condition means the result does not fit into the bit representation
- The overflow indicates that adding two positive values produces a negative result due to setting the MSB of the result
- The zero condition indicates a result in which all the bits are 0
- Overflow of an unsigned integer makes it wrap around, which is equivalent to the 2^N modulo operation
- Overflow of signed integers is an undefined behavior and must be avoided
- Computations should be checked to be sure they do not generate arithmetic overflows

7.1.6 Representing Fractions

Figure 7.1 showed a byte structure. As indicated, by associating a weight $w_i = 2^i$ with each ith bit position, we can precisely represent integer values in the range $[0...255]$. However, assigning different weights lets us represent a different range of values. For example, if fractional weights are assumed, then fractions can be represented, as shown in Figure 7.2.

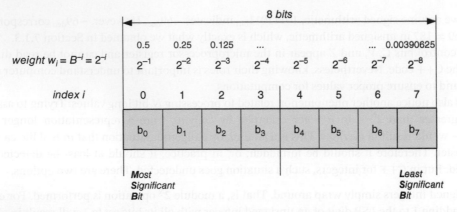

Figure 7.2 Fractional value representation of a byte by assigning weights w_i as consecutive values of 2^{-i}. Unlike integer values, not all decimal fractions can be precisely represented.

More precisely, changing the weight definition w_i in Eq. (7.3) for $B = 2$ as follows

$$w_i = 2^{-(i+1)} \tag{7.12}$$

and inserting into Eq. (7.2) yields

$$D_{FB} = \sum_{i=0}^{N-1} b_i \, 2^{-(i+1)} \tag{7.13}$$

where FB stands for fraction-binary. Comparing Figure 7.1 with Figure 7.2, notice that bit numbering is symmetrical. In this assumption, the MSB for the integer part corresponds to $i = N - 1$, whereas for the fraction, the MSB is placed at $i = 0$. Note also that in both representations, there is *a fixed number* of digits for an integer, as well as fractional parts. Therefore these are *fixed-point* (FX) representations, as opposed to *floating-point* (FP) representations, which will be discussed in Section 7.4.

For example, let's consider the following bit assignment, which served as an example at the beginning of Section 7.1:

0	1	0	1	0	1	1	1

For an integer representation, we used Eq. (7.1). But to compute a fraction, we need to use Eq. (7.13) instead, as follows:

$$D = 2^{-1} \cdot 0 + 2^{-2} \cdot 1 + 2^{-3} \cdot 0 + 2^{-4} \cdot 1 + 2^{-5} \cdot 0 + 2^{-6} \cdot 1 + 2^{-7} \cdot 1 + 2^{-8} \cdot 1 =$$
$$2^{-2} + 2^{-4} + 2^{-6} + 2^{-7} + 2^{-8} = 0.33984375$$

In other words, we can write that $01010111_2 = 0.33984375_{10}$.

We see that the same bit assignments lead to different values. They depend on the weight definitions. Recall that in the integer representation, the MSB value was 1, so all intermediate values could be precisely represented. But in the case of a fraction, the MSB value is $2^{-8} = 0.00390625$, and we can operate in multiples of it. When we divide the value of our example number by the MSB, we get the following:

$$0.33984375 / 0.00390625 = 87$$

Is this a surprise? Not necessarily, if we recall that the integer value of the same bit representation is exactly 87. In other words, a fractional representation means *rescaling* an integer value by the fractional value of the MSB. Formally, a given integer binary value D_{IB} from Eq. (7.5) can be rescaled to a new value as follows

$$\hat{D} = s \cdot D_{IB} + f \tag{7.14}$$

where s denotes scaling and f is an offset value. In our example, we had $D_{IB} = 87$, $s = 2^{-8}$, and $f = 0$. This also means the same C2 encoding can be used to represent a negative fractional value, as discussed in Section 7.1.4.

An important question is how precise the representation in Eq. (7.13) is for real fractions. Notice that the precision P is related to the lowest possible value that can be represented in the LSB:

$$P = B^{-N} = 2^{-N} \tag{7.15}$$

For a byte, $P = 2^{-8} = 0.00390625$. This means all values less than that will be represented as 0 – i.e. they will be disregarded. On the other hand, the maximum representable value is $1.0 - P$, which in our case is 0.99609375. Moreover, operating in multiples of P means not all decimal fractions can be precisely represented in a binary form. We will see that even increasing the number of bits only helps somewhat: doing so limits the representation error but in some cases never leads to a fully precise representation. This is an important observation that explains imprecision in computations due to *rounding error*. We discuss rounding methods in the context of floating-point values in Section 7.4.4.

Let's now devise an algorithm for converting a decimal fraction into the closest binary representation. A value expressed by Eq. (7.13) is less than 1. If it is multiplied by 2, the result is as follows:

$$2 \cdot D_{FB} = \underbrace{b_0}_{0,1} + \underbrace{\sum_{i=1}^{N-1} b_i \, 2^{-i}}_{<1} \tag{7.16}$$

Notice that when a fraction D is multiplied by 2, we get two values: and integer 0 or 1 and a fraction less than 1. The former immediately provides the first bit b_0 from the fractional representation. To find consecutive bits, the second term from Eq. (7.16) is multiplied by 2, and the entire procedure repeats. This continues until one of the following conditions is met: either the fraction is exactly 0, or the maximum number of N bits is reached. However, as we pointed out earlier, for some fractions the bit representation is only an approximation of the real value. Let's verify this procedure, first in the decimal domain with $B = 10$ and a value $D = 0.35$. We get the following series of integers (I) and fractions (F):

	I	F
$0.35 \cdot 10$	3	0.5
$0.5 \cdot 10$	5	0

Reading out the values of I, we immediately obtain 0.35. Let's now change to the binary base: $B = 2$, and the same value $D = 0.35$. For $N = 8$, we get the following:

i		I	F
0	$0.35 \cdot 2$	0	0.7
1	$0.7 \cdot 2$	1	0.4
2	$0.4 \cdot 2$	0	0.8
3	$0.8 \cdot 2$	1	0.6
4	$0.6 \cdot 2$	1	0.2
5	$0.2 \cdot 2$	0	0.4
6	$0.4 \cdot 2$	0	0.8
7	$0.8 \cdot 2$	1	0.6
8	$0.6 \cdot 2$	1	0.2

Knowing the scaling properties from Eq. (7.14), we can obtain the same result as follows:

1. Multiply $0.35 \cdot 2^8 = 89.6$.
2. Take the integer part of the previous result and convert it into a binary representation: $89_{dec} = 01011001_{bin}$.

We see that either way, the value $0.35_{dec} \approx 01011001_{bin}$ is obtained. However, this is only an approximation of 0.35, since the value $0.6 \cdot 2^{-8} = 0.00234375$ was left out. In other words, a rounding error has been generated:

$$\Delta_0 = \left| 0.35_{dec} - 01011001_{bin} \right| = \left| 0.35 - 0.34765625 \right| = 0.00234375$$

Whether this is an acceptable error depends on the application. But we can do better than this. If we consider the eighth bit of the previous series and add it to the seventh, then $0.35_{dec} \approx 01011010_{bin}$, with the following error:

$$\Delta_1 = \left| 0.35_{dec} - 01011010_{bin} \right| = \left| 0.35 - 0.3515625 \right| = 0.0015625.$$

Notice that $\Delta_1 < \Delta_0$. So what we did was choose a different rounding algorithm – rounding to the nearest number instead of rounding toward 0. Here we see how important proper rounding is; this will be discussed further in Section 7.4.4. $\Delta_1 < \frac{1}{2}P = 2^{-9} = 0.001953125$. In an FX representation, the maximum rounding error is fixed to the constant value of $\pm\frac{1}{2}P$, as shown in Figure 7.3.

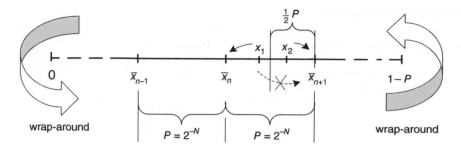

Figure 7.3 The maximum rounding error in the fixed-point representation is limited to $\pm\frac{1}{2}P = 2^{-N-1}$. Real values x_1 and x_2 are represented by the closest fixed-point value. $\bar{x}_n = D_{FB}(n)$ denotes the nth fixed-point value for $0 \leqslant n < 2^N$. Values out of range lead to overflow, which for unsigned numbers results in the value being wrapped around.

Things to Remember

- Unlike integers, the binary representation of some real fractions cannot be precise. The absolute value of the difference is called rounding error
- The maximum rounding error in an FX representation with N fraction bits is $\pm\frac{1}{2}P = 2^{-N-1}$
- To convert a decimal fraction into its binary representation, the fraction is multiplied by 2, and the integer part of the result provides a consecutive representation bit. Then the procedure is repeated for the remaining consecutive fractions until N bits are obtained

7.2 Binary Shift Operations

From daily observations, we know that multiplication and division by 10 are straightforward – we simply shift the decimal point one position to the right or to the left. For example, −12.34, after we shift the decimal point one position to the right, becomes −123.4. Hence, it has been multiplied by 10. On the other hand, when we shift the decimal one position to the left, the new value is −1.234. In this case, the original value has been divided by 10. Thus a right shift by one digit position multiplies the value by the base, whereas a shift to the left divides it by the base. This is true for any base, including binary.

The rules are simple in principle; but as always, there are further details – for example, after the shift, what value should be placed in the vacant position? For example, if we shift bits to the left, then the vacant rightmost bit can be set to 0. However, what will we do with the leftmost bit if the value is signed? If we throw it away, then it can appear that a negative value becomes a positive one or vice versa. Otherwise, can we do a bit rotation – that is, move the leftmost bit into the rightmost position? There are many options, and the possible rules are summarized in Table 7.3.

Shift operations are very efficient ways to manipulate bits. Frequently, integer multiplication or division by 2 and its multiples is faster when implemented using bit-shift operators than with the corresponding arithmetic multiplication or division.

Table 7.3 Shift operations explained.

Shift type	Description and examples	Diagram
Logical shift left	Bits are shifted left by a specified number. The leftmost bit(s) is lost. The rightmost position is filled with a 0 bit.	1 0 1 1 1 0 1 1 = 187 ... 1 / 0 1 1 1 0 1 1 0 = 118 = 374
Logical shift right	Bits are shifted right by a specified number. The rightmost bit(s) is lost. The leftmost position is filled with a 0 bit. ```// Logical shifts unsigned char uy = 187; // == 0b10111011 = -69 uy >>= 1;// == 0b01011101 = 93 uy <<= 1;// == 0b10111010 = 186``` The C++ standard says that the right shift is guaranteed to be logical (0 fill) if the shifted value has an unsigned type or if it has a nonnegative value. Otherwise, the result is implementation-dependent. (See *GROUP 7*, Table 3.15.)	1 0 1 1 1 0 1 1 = 187 ... 0 1 0 1 1 1 0 1 = 93 1
Arithmetic shift left	Like the logical shift left. Note that the sign can be lost.	1 0 1 1 1 0 1 1 = −69 ... 1 / 0 1 1 1 0 1 1 0 = 118 = -138
Arithmetic shift right	The sign bit is copied to preserve the sign. ```// Arithmetic shifts, signed char sx = -69; // == 0b10111011 sx >>= 1;// == 0b11011101 = -35 sx <<= 1;// == 0b10111010 = -70``` (In C++, shifts for the signed values are platform dependent.)	1 0 1 1 1 0 1 1 = −69 ... Repeated 1 to keep the sign 1 1 0 1 1 1 0 1 = −35 1
Rotated shift left	Bits are shifted left, and the leftmost bit is inserted into the rightmost position. Usually available in the microprocessor's machine code. Sometimes additional bits are involved in the chain.	1 0 1 1 1 0 1 1 ... 0 1 1 1 0 1 1 1

Shift type	Description and examples	Diagram
Rotated shift right	Bits are shifted right, and the rightmost bit is inserted into the leftmost position. Usually available in the microprocessor's machine code. Sometimes additional bits are involved in the chain.	

7.3 (✖) Example Project – Software Model for Fixed-Point Representations

We have already seen binary representations for integers and fractions. We considered them separately since they rely on different definitions of the weights in the binary representation. This, in turn, leads to different computational phenomena, such as rounding errors for fractions. Nevertheless, they have many things in common – due to the scaling property, they can be converted each into the other, and they have a fixed position for the decimal point. Also, in many computations, we need to represent values containing both integer *and* fractional parts. In C++, we either have a collection of types to convey signed and unsigned integers, or the floating-point representation to approximate real numbers (Section 7.4). However, the latter consumes at least four or eight bytes for an object, whereas many applications, such as image processing, need shorter representations. Therefore it would be useful to have a data type to represent FX numbers containing integer and fractional parts, and equipped with a set of functions for arithmetic computations. In this section, we will show how to create such a type defining the `FxFor` template class.

7.3.1 Fixed-Point Numbers and Their Arithmetic

Figure 7.4 shows an FX representation that has integer and fractional parts. From Figure 7.4, we can easily determine that

$$N = p + q + 1 \tag{7.17}$$

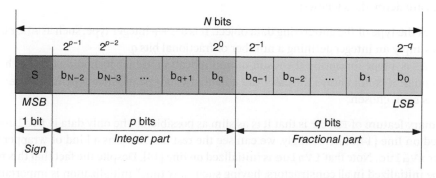

Figure 7.4 Number representation in the fixed-point format containing integer and fractional parts.

Now, properly adjusting Eqs. (7.10) and (7.11), we get the following values:

$$D_{SM} = (-1)^S \cdot \sum_{i=0}^{N-2} b_i \, 2^{i-q} \tag{7.18}$$

and

$$D_{C2} = -S \cdot 2^N + \sum_{i=0}^{N-1} b_i \, 2^{i-q} \tag{7.19}$$

where $S = b_{N-1}$ is the sign bit. For this implementation, we chose SM encoding.

7.3.2 Definition of the *FxFor* Class

As alluded to previously, the purpose of the FxFor template class is to introduce an FX format and basic arithmetic operations. Why do we need it? When dealing with real numbers, an obvious choice is to use the floating-point format, which in C++ is implemented with the two types float and double, which differ in precision. But the two arithmetics have different rounding errors, and in some applications we might be interested in the constant error offered by an FX representation. Using the same byte consumption as double in the fixed domain, we can have a constant error of approximately 2e−10. On the other hand, although float usually consumes only four bytes, when processing big data, such as video streams, reducing the suitable representation to 2 bytes is a viable option: e.g. reducing 16 GB to 8 GB required, etc. Finally, FX arithmetic still has a place in embedded systems, especially those equipped with relatively low-power microprocessors. On the other hand, floating-point allows for a much higher dynamic range for the represented numbers, as we will discuss in Section 7.4.

Before we go to the code, let's outline the new programming techniques we will use:

- Pre- and post-increment operator overloading
- Compile-time computations with constexpr
- Compile-time vs. runtime assertions: static_assert vs. assert

In addition, we will practice writing template member functions (Section 4.8.5), and various bit operations (Section 3.19.1).

The definition of the FxFor template class starts on line [8] in Listing 7.1. Three template parameters are defined, as follows:

- ST defines the type of the underlying data object. It is a C++ integer type, such as short or int
- Prec is simply an integer defining a number of fractional bits q
- ACC_TYPE is a type for storing the result of multiplication. Hence it should be twice the size of ST. Although it is not always the case, the potentially longest possible type unsigned long long has been chosen

The primary feature of FxFor is that it is as slim as possible, so the only data is fValue of type ST, defined on line [14]. Interestingly, we can see the rest of FxFor as a kind of wrapper around the integer fValue. Note that fValue is initialized on line [14]. Despite the fact that this member can also be initialized in all constructors, having such "any time" initialization is important when working with constexpr to satisfy the compiler.

On line [19], a series of simple get/set functions commences. Since we chose the SM representation, the role of `GetInternalValue_in_C2` is to return our internal data in the more common C2 format. The conversion on line [23] operates in accordance with the algorithm described in Table 7.1. The role of the other functions in this group should be clear.

The `constexpr` prefix placed in front of all the functions in this class is interesting. It was first introduced in the example function `RevertEndianness` in Section 4.8.3. `constexpr` is a relatively new programming technique, introduced in C++11 and then modified in subsequent standards. Its purpose is to let a function be compiled and executed during compilation. Hence, it is a kind of pre-execution before the whole translation unit is compiled. The purpose is simple – if we can precompute the value of a function during compilation, rather than at program runtime, we gain performance. The basic rules behind the `constexpr` declared function are as follows:

- If the parameters of the `constexpr` declared function are also `constexpr`, then the function can be compiled and executed, and the result is directly inserted into the final execution code
- Otherwise, the function behaves like any other function: it executes at runtime

But there are other rules that make writing `constexpr` code slightly peculiar. We will see examples of these soon, but summarizing them here helps with understanding the compiler's behavior:

- If a `constexpr` function is compiled on behalf of a `constexpr` object, it is assumed to be a `const` function: that is, it cannot change the state of that object. However, `const` is not automatically added to the function declaration (from C++14), so in "normal" operation it will not be `const` unless `const` is explicitly written by the programmer
- The compiler needs to compile and run the function during the compilation of the whole unit. Therefore, the code needs to be correct. Even if it does compile in a "non-`constexpr`" compilation, compilers tend to be meticulous about some language features, such as uninitialized variables, etc. So, minor code problems that normally generate warnings can stop the compiler from processing `constexpr` functions. The problem is, this usually happens in a stealthy way, and we are not properly informed about the real cause. Hence, debugging `constexpr` code can be problematic sometimes. A practical solution is to make the code run, check all the warnings, and then add `constexpr` if necessary. This hint also applies to debugging template classes
- To verify if something operates as `constexpr`, use `static_assert`. This differs from `assert`, which is executed at runtime
- A difference between a `const` object and a `constexpr` object is that the first is an ordinary object that happened to be declared `const`, so after initialization, its state cannot be changed. The latter, on the other hand, is intended to be compiled and created during compilation, and the result inserted into the final code. This also means such an object implicitly has to be `const`, since once computed before the rest of the code is ready, it cannot be recomputed or changed in any other way
- From a `constexpr` function, only `constexpr` functions can be called
- `constexpr` puts a lot of work put on the compiler, so the compilation time can be significant

Equipped with that knowledge, let's analyze the rest of the code. On lines [30, 36–38], we set some bitmasks. These are frequently used to access a sign bit or the most important bit of the fractional part, for instance. Finally, lines [48–55] define a number of auxiliary functions, which return an absolute value or allow access to the integer and fractional parts. Such operations are possible by proper masking or shifting of bits ("blue" operators in Section 3.19.1).

Listing 7.1 Definition of the template `FxFor` class for representing the FX arithmetic format (in CppBookCode, *FxFor.h*).

```
1   //////////////////////////////////////////////////////////
2   // Class for fixed-point data types.
3   // No saturation, no overflow control.
4   // SupportType - defines an UNSIGNED integer type for the whole number
5   // Prec - defines a number of fractional bits
6   // ACC_TYPE - Accumulator type (for intermediate results)
7   //////////////////////////////////////////////////////////
8   template< typename ST, int Prec, typename ACC_TYPE = unsigned long long >
9   class FxFor
10  {
11  private:
12
13      // Stores the whole number
14      ST    fValue {};
15
16  public:
17
18      // Returns an internal representation in Sign/Magnitude format
19      constexpr ST GetInternalValue( void ) const { return fValue; }
20
21      // Returns an internal representation in C2 format
22      constexpr ST GetInternalValue_in_C2( void ) const
23          { return IsPositive() ? fValue : ( ~fValue | kSignMask ) + 1; }
24
25      constexpr void SetInternalValue( ST new_val ) { fValue = new_val; }
26
27  public:
28
29      // Local const for precision
30      enum: ST      { kPrec = Prec };
31
32  private:
33
34      // Let's define some useful flags
35      enum: ST  {
36              kSignMask   = ST(1) << ( 8 * sizeof( ST ) - 1 ),  // sign bit (integer MSB)
37              kIntegerLSB = ST(1) << kPrec,                     // LSB of the integer part
38              kFractMSB   = kPrec > 0 ? ST(1) << kPrec - ST(1) : 0 // MSB of the fract part
39          };
40
41
42      // A shortcut to this type
43      using FxType = FxFor< ST, Prec, ACC_TYPE >;
44
45  public:
46
47      // Some raw data manipulators
48      constexpr ST DataValueAbs( void ) const
49          { return fValue & ~kSignMask; }  // Return the absolute value (always positive)
50
51      constexpr ST GetMagnitudeOfIntegerPart( void ) const
52          { return DataValueAbs() >> kPrec; }
53
54      constexpr ST GetFractionalPart( void ) const
55          { return fValue & ( kIntegerLSB - 1 ); }
56          // ( kIntegerLSB - 1 ) sets all bits of the fractional part
57
58
```

The code fragment starting on line [59] contains the public construction group. First is the default constructor. Obviously, fValue is set to 0 in the initializer on line [63]. Then, in the constructor body, some preconditions are set in the form of assertions. The first static_assert will be checked during compilation, so all of its arguments must be known at this time. But the second static_assert, which is commented out, does not fulfill this rule since fValue will not be known during compilation. So, this condition cannot be used in the static assertion. On the other hand, the assert on line [67] will not be checked until runtime. Its role is to verify the precondition on a relation between a total number of bits in the supporting type ST and the number of precision bits, both chosen as template parameters by the programmer. This assert is redundant since the previous static_assert, with the same condition, will always be checked before runtime.

The parametric constructor on line [71] accepts one int value to create the FxFor object. So, it serves as a type converter from int to FxFor, as presented in Section 4.15.3.1.

The transformation from integer types is simple – the argument needs to be shifted left by the number of bits in the fractional part, denoted by kPrec. The sign needs to be properly set in the SM format. All this is done on line [74]. We will explain the conversion from double (declared on line [77]) later, since its full definition is located outside the definition of the FxFor class.

```
59   public:
60
61       // ======================================================
62       // Class default constructor
63       constexpr FxFor( void ) : fValue( 0 )
64       {
65           static_assert( sizeof( ST ) * 8 > kPrec );
66           //static_assert( fValue >= 0 );  will not compile since fValue is not known
67           assert( sizeof( ST ) * 8 > kPrec );
68       }
69
70       // Type converting constructors
71       constexpr FxFor( int x )
72       {
73           assert( sizeof( ST ) * 8 > kPrec );
74           fValue = x < 0 ? - x << kPrec | kSignMask : x << kPrec;
75       }
76
77       constexpr FxFor( double x );
78
79
```

The FxFor class copy constructor, whose definition starts on line [80], is a template member function that lets us create one FxFor object from one with different parameters (Section 4.8.5). At the same time, it is also a type-converting constructor that helps transform one FxFor object into another version of FxFor with potentially different template parameters. Note that when analyzing this function, we have to consider not three but all six template parameters: three for this class and (potentially) a different three for the FxFor object passed as the argument f on line [81].

The conversion is not difficult and consists of copying and properly placing the integer and fractional parts of the provided argument, as done on lines [84, 86–87]. Finally, on lines [89–90], the sign is copied as well. But a problem arises if the source object has more bits than the object we copy to. In this case, depending on the value, important data may be lost.

```
80     template< typename D, int P, typename A >
81     constexpr FxFor( const FxFor< D, P, A > & f )           // mixed copy constructor
82     {
83         // First copy the integer part, to not lose the MSB
84         fValue = f.GetMagnitudeOfIntegerPart() << kPrec;
85         // Then copy the most significant part of the fractional part
86         fValue |= f.kPrec > kPrec ? f.GetFractionalPart() >> f.kPrec - kPrec
87                                   : f.GetFractionalPart() << kPrec - f.kPrec;
88         // Finally, set the sign
89         if( f.IsNegative() )
90             MakeNegative();
91     }
92
```

The template member assignment operator, defined on lines [95–96], basically does something similar to the previous copy constructor. The only difference is line [99], which disallows copying of the same objects, called *self-assignment protection*. Although it looks unusual, such a situation can happen, for example, if a container of pointers to the objects is reorganized, sorted, etc. If the self-assignment fuse were omitted, then performing the code on line [102] would erroneously destroy the fractional part, which we would then try to copy on lines [104–105].

```
93     // ====================================================
94
95     template< class D, int P, typename A >
96     constexpr FxType & operator = ( const FxFor< D, P, A > & f )  // mixed assignment
97     {
98         // For different types, it can cause loss of data
99         if( (void*)& f != (void*)this )     // self-assignment protection
100        {
101            // At first copy the integer part not to lose the MSB
102            fValue = f.GetMagnitudeOfIntegerPart() << kPrec;
103            // Then copy the most significant part of the fractional part
104            fValue |= f.kPrec > kPrec ? f.GetFractionalPart() >> f.kPrec - kPrec
105                                      : f.GetFractionalPart() << kPrec - f.kPrec;
106            // Finally, set the sign
107            if( f.IsNegative() )
108                MakeNegative();
109        }
110
111        return * this;
112    }
```

On lines [115–120] are declarations of the type-conversion operators whose role is to perform type conversion but in the opposite direction than the conversion constructor. They can convert an FxFor object into one of the integer types or the FP type, in this case.

```
113    // Conversion operators:
114
115    constexpr operator char()          const;
116    constexpr operator short()         const;
117    constexpr operator int()           const;
118    constexpr operator long()          const;
119
120    constexpr operator double()        const;
121
```

The following code fragments, starting on line [125], contain definitions of some helper functions of the `FxFor` class. These are mostly devoted to checking or changing the sign of the FX number. Their operations are simple and involve bit operations.

```
122      // ======================================================
123      // Helpers:
124
125      constexpr bool IsNegative( void ) const
126          { return ( fValue & kSignMask ) == 0 ? false : true; }
127      constexpr bool IsPositive( void ) const
128          { return ( fValue & kSignMask ) != 0 ? false : true; }    // 0 is also positive
129
130      constexpr void ChangeSign( void ) { fValue ^= kSignMask; }
131
132      constexpr void MakeNegative( void )
133          { assert( fValue != 0 ); fValue |= kSignMask; }        // Turn the sign bit ON
134
135      constexpr void MakePositive( void ) { fValue &= ~kSignMask; }   // Turn sign OFF
136
137      constexpr void MakeAbs( void ) { MakePositive(); }        // Get rid of the sign
138
139      constexpr FxType GetAbs( void ) const
140          { FxType tmp( * this ); tmp.MakeAbs(); return tmp; }   // Return the absolute
141
142
```

Then, on line [146], we declare the series of arithmetic operations. On lines [146–149], these are binary arithmetic operators. However, they rely on the arithmetic update operators declared on lines [151–154]. Line [156] declares the negative operator. It simply changes the sign of the stored value. Then, on lines [160–168], various bit operators are defined. Most of the implementations are very simple and involve few operations. Implementation details for selected arithmetic operators are presented later in this section.

```
143      // ======================================================
144      // Basic library of operations:
145
146      constexpr FxType operator + ( FxType f ) const;
147      constexpr FxType operator - ( FxType f ) const;
148      constexpr FxType operator * ( FxType f ) const;
149      constexpr FxType operator / ( FxType f ) const;
150
151      constexpr FxType & operator += ( FxType f );
152      constexpr FxType & operator -= ( FxType f );
153      constexpr FxType & operator *= ( FxType f );
154      constexpr FxType & operator /= ( FxType f );
155
156      constexpr FxType & operator - ( void );
157
158      // ======================================================
159
160      constexpr FxType operator & ( FxType f ) const;
161      constexpr FxType operator | ( FxType f ) const;
162      constexpr FxType operator ^ ( FxType f ) const;
163
164      constexpr FxType & operator &= ( FxType f );
165      constexpr FxType & operator |= ( FxType f );
166      constexpr FxType & operator ^= ( FxType f );
167
168      constexpr FxType & operator ~ ( void );
169
```

Lines [172–176] declare the pre- and post-increment operators. Note the dummy `int` argument in the latter, i.e. lines [172, 175]. Implementations of some of them follow.

```
170     // =================================================
171
172     constexpr FxType operator ++ ( int );        // postfix
173     constexpr FxType & operator ++ ();           // prefix
174
175     constexpr FxType operator -- ( int );        // postfix
176     constexpr FxType & operator -- ();           // prefix
177
```

Also useful are shift operators, which are overloaded for this class. Their declarations are shown on lines [180–184].

```
178     // =================================================
179
180     constexpr FxType operator << ( int shift ) const;
181     constexpr FxType operator >> ( int shift ) const;
182
183     constexpr FxType & operator <<= ( int shift );
184     constexpr FxType & operator >>= ( int shift );
185
```

Finally, since `FxFor` defines a scalar type, an entire suite of overloaded relation operators is included. These are declared on lines [189–194].

```
186     // =================================================
187     // Comparators:
188
189     constexpr bool operator ==    ( FxType f ) const;
190     constexpr bool operator !=    ( FxType f ) const;
191     constexpr bool operator <     ( FxType f ) const;
192     constexpr bool operator <=    ( FxType f ) const;
193     constexpr bool operator >     ( FxType f ) const;
194     constexpr bool operator >=    ( FxType f ) const;
195
196     };
```

Notice again that all the member functions are declared `constexpr`. As we pointed out earlier, this is not obligatory but helps make the class more robust.

For template classes, implementations of short functions are frequently included in the class definition, whereas longer functions are usually put in the same file but below the class definition (Section 4.8). We follow this methodology with `FxFor`. Some more challenging implementations are discussed in the next section.

7.3.3 Selected Methods of the *FxFor* Class

In this section, we will examine the implementation details of some of the representative member functions. Let's start with the conversion procedure, implemented as the converting constructor on lines [3–4]. It converts from floating-point, represented by the built-in `double` type, to the FX format, represented by our class. Basically, it follows the scaling property described in Section 7.1.6. But at its beginning on lines [6–10], the sign is stored, and the input floating-point value is made positive. Then, on line [13], the standard value cast is applied. It simply cuts off the fractional part using the standard built-in rounding procedure. This way, the integer part is copied on line [16] to the internal representation `fValue`, which is immediately shifted to its proper position on line [17].

Now it is time to obtain and convert the fractional part of the input floating-point value x. A fraction is simply the difference of x and the previously computed integer part, as computed on line [19]. This is scaled on line [21], as guided by Eq. (7.14). This way, the obtained fraction is converted on line [22] to the internal type `ST` and, on line [24], joined with the `fValue` by the simple logical OR operation. Finally, on line [26–27], we take care of the minus sign.

Interestingly enough, if, for example, `minus_sign` was initialized not on line [6] but instead in the following lines, then, although the code would compile under normal conditions, the compiler would abort when working on the `constexpr`.[1] Hence, working with `constexpr` requires additional care.

Listing 7.2 Definition of the type-converting constructor `FxFor( double x )` (in CppBookCode, *FxFor.h*).

```cpp
1   // ====================================================
2   // The type-converting constructor: float to fixed
3   template< typename ST, int Prec, typename ACC_TYPE >
4   constexpr FxFor< ST, Prec, ACC_TYPE >::FxFor( double x ) : fValue( 0 )
5   {
6       bool minus_sign { false };
7       if( x < 0.0 )
8       {
9           minus_sign = true;      // remember the sign,
10          x = -x;                 // then take the absolute value
11      }
12
13      ST int_part = static_cast< ST >( x );   // here we use the standard conversion
14                                  // from the double which cuts off the fraction
15
16      fValue = int_part;
17      fValue <<= kPrec;           // put integer part into its place
18
19      double fract_part = x - int_part;
20
21      double scaled_fraction = fract_part * static_cast< double >( kIntegerLSB );
22      ST fraction = static_cast< ST >( scaled_fraction );
23
24      fValue |= fraction;         // join the two together
25
26      if( minus_sign == true && fValue != 0 )
27          MakeNegative();         // finally consider the sign
28
29  }
```

---

1 Checked with the Microsoft Visual 2019 compiler.

The opposite conversion, shown in Figure 4.22, is implemented as `operator double ()`, as shown on lines [33–34]. Again, on line [37], the scaling Eq. (7.14) is used, but this time in the opposite direction. Hence, on line [38], the fractional part is divided by the value corresponding to the least significant bit of the integer part. In other words, this corresponds to a bit value of the integer 1, which happens to be the value of the `kIntegerLSB` bit in the `fValue` member.

Then, on line [40], the integer part is added to the result; and on line [41], the proper sign is set.

Listing 7.3 Definition of the type-converting `operator double()` (in *CppBookCode, FxFor.h*).

```
30   // We repeat the same code as for the "double" conversion to
31   // avoid implicit conversion from "float" to "double" if a additional
32   // function were used.
33   template< typename ST, int Prec, typename ACC_TYPE >
34   constexpr FxFor< ST, Prec, ACC_TYPE >::operator double() const
35   {
36       // Start from the fraction
37       double retVal = static_cast< double >( GetFractionalPart() )
38                                     / static_cast< double >( kIntegerLSB );
39
40       retVal += GetMagnitudeOfIntegerPart();        // now add the integer part
41       return IsNegative() ? - retVal : retVal;
42   }
```

We will now move on to some characteristic arithmetic operators. First is the prefix increment operator, whose definition starts on lines [44–45]. On line [47], it simply calls the increment operator +=, which we present later. Then, the same object needs to be returned. This is done on line [48], simply by returning * this.

The postfix version of the increment operator starts on lines [53–54]. To distinguish the two, the postfix version is equipped with the dummy formal parameter int. However, its implementation is slightly more complicated, since the "old" version needs to be returned, whereas the object needs to be incremented by 1. Hence, on line [56], a new object is created by calling the copy constructor provided with the * this object. Then, as in the previous function, the object is incremented by calling the += operator with argument 1 on line [57]. Finally, the stored object is returned on line [58]. Knowing the precise operation of the prefix and postfix operators tells us why the postfix operators are much more expensive during computations. This happens mostly because an intermediate object needs to be created and returned. Here it is not a big deal, but imagine doing increments on a matrix.

Listing 7.4 Definition of the prefix and postfix increment operators (in *CppBookCode, FxFor.h*).

```
43   // prefix
44   template< typename ST, int Prec, typename ACC_TYPE >
45   typename constexpr FxFor< ST, Prec, ACC_TYPE >::FxType & FxFor< ST, Prec, ACC_TYPE
     >::operator ++ ()
46   {
47       * this += 1;
48       return * this;
49   }
50
51
52   // postfix
53   template< typename ST, int Prec, typename ACC_TYPE >
```

```
54   typename constexpr FxFor< ST, Prec, ACC_TYPE >::FxType FxFor< ST, Prec, ACC_TYPE
     >::operator ++ ( int )
55   {
56      FxType tmp( * this );    // this unfortunately requires a temporary copy
57      * this += 1;
58      return tmp;
59   }
```

Now it is time for the two most basic arithmetic operations. First is the add and assign operator +=, defined on lines [60–61] (see *GROUP 15*, Table 3.15). Summation is simple, except that the different combinations of the signs need to be properly considered. The signs are read in on lines [65–66]. Then, we select a proper summation algorithm in the double if statements. Let's consider the case where the first argument (i.e. the one represented by this) is negative and the second is positive (i.e. the f object): for example, in the expression −13.5 + 10.0. On line [86], the first object is made positive. If fValue is less than f.fValue, then fValue is subtracted on line [92], and we are finished, since the result will be positive. Otherwise, as in the previous example, the subtraction 13.5 – 10.0 will take place on line [96], resulting in 3.5; its sign will be changed on line [99] to provide the final result, −3.5. But we need to avoid assigning a minus sign to a zero value, as checked on line [98]. This is one of the peculiarities of the SM representation.

Listing 7.5 Definition of the add and assign operator += (in *CppBookCode, FxFor.h*).

```
60   template< typename ST, int Prec, typename ACC_TYPE >
61   typename constexpr FxFor< ST, Prec, ACC_TYPE >::FxType &
62                          FxFor< ST, Prec, ACC_TYPE >::operator += ( FxType f )
63   {
64      // We perform the sign-magnitude arithmetic
65      bool first_is_negative   = IsNegative(),
66      bool second_is_negative  = f.IsNegative();
67
68      if( first_is_negative )
69      {
70         if( second_is_negative )
71         {
72            // Both are negative
73
74            MakeAbs();       // Take the absolute value of the first operand
75            f.MakeAbs();     // Take the absolute value of the second operand
76
77
78            fValue += f.fValue;   // Add the bare magnitudes;
79
80            MakeNegative();        // And negate the result
81         }
82         else
83         {
84            // The first is negative, the second is positive
85
86            MakeAbs();  // simply operate on magnitude (disregarding the sign bit)
87
88            // Here we compare only the magnitudes;
89            // The second is positive, so there is no need to get its abs
90            if( fValue <= f.fValue )    // "soft" to make 0 positive
91            {
92               fValue = f.fValue - fValue;  // and we do NOT change the sign
93            }
94            else
95            {
```

(Continued)

Listing 7.5 (continued)

```
96                  fValue -= f.fValue;
97                  assert( IsPositive() );
98                  if( fValue != 0 )
99                      MakeNegative();        // and negate the result
100             }
101         }
102     }
103     else
104     {
105         if( second_is_negative )
106         {
107             // The first is positive, the second is negative
108
109             f.MakeAbs();  // simply operate on magnitude (disregarding the sign bit)
110
111             // Here we compare only the magnitudes;
112             // The first is positive, so there is no need to get its abs
113             if( fValue >= f.fValue )  // "soft" to make 0 positive
114             {
115                 fValue -= f.fValue;  // and we do NOT change the sign
116             }
117             else
118             {
119                 fValue = f.fValue - fValue;
120                 assert( IsPositive() );
121                 if( fValue != 0 )
122                     MakeNegative();        // and negate the result
123             }
124         }
125         else
126         {
127             // Both are positive
128
129             fValue += f.fValue;
130         }
131     }
132
133     return * this;
134 }
```

The implementation of multiplication in SM is much shorter, as shown in the definition of operator *= beginning on lines [135–137]. Again, the signs of the two operands are read and stored in temporary objects, as shown on lines [140–141]. Then, on line [144], the temporary object theAccumulator is created. Not surprisingly, it is the longest possible bit representation of ACC_TYPE, since its role is to store the result of the multiplication on line [150]. Then theAccumulator needs to be properly scaled by right-shifting the kPrec bits, as done on line [155]. At first, we may think that two such shifts are necessary. But one of them was done previously, since by the arrangement of fValue, the binary point is already kPrec bits to the left. On line [158], the adjusted accumulator is converted and copied to the fValue object. Hence, we have to be sure the result fits with no integer overflow. Finally, the sign is set on lines [161–162], and the current object is returned on line [164].

Listing 7.6 Definition of the multiply and assign `operator *=` (in *CppBookCode, FxFor.h*).

```
135   template< typename ST, int Prec, typename ACC_TYPE >
136   typename constexpr FxFor< ST, Prec, ACC_TYPE >::FxType &
137   FxFor< ST, Prec, ACC_TYPE >::operator *= ( FxType f )
138   {
139       // We perform the sign-magnitude arithmetic
140       bool first_is_negative  = IsNegative();
141       bool second_is_negative = f.IsNegative();
142
143       // First we need an accumulator that is long enough to store the result.
144       ACC_TYPE theAccumulator = DataValueAbs();
145       // we load here an abs value which is then shifted, e.g. if we
146       // load a fixed 1.0 then this value in acc is NOT a unit
147       // but the value shifted to the left by kPrec
148       assert( sizeof( theAccumulator ) >= 2 * sizeof( ST ) );
149
150       theAccumulator *= f.DataValueAbs();    // multiply the POSITIVE magnitudes
151
152       // Now we need to shift the result right by the Prec
153       // to cut off the least-significant kPrec bits (will be lost!).
154       // What is left fits well into the fixed format: int.frac
155       theAccumulator >>= kPrec;
156
157       // Copy the shifted accumulator to the return object
158       fValue = static_cast< ST >( theAccumulator );
159
160       // Finally, set the sign of the result
161       if( ( first_is_negative ^ second_is_negative ) && fValue != 0 )
162           MakeNegative();
163
164       return * this;
165   }
```

`ComputeRoundingError`, whose definition starts on lines [179–180], is a separate function and external to `FxFor`. Its role is to compute the difference between a floating-point value, represented by the argument d, and an FX value, represented by the argument f. This is done by first converting f to the `double` type on line [182] by calling the `static_cast` operator (see *GROUP 2*, Table 3.15). When `static_cast` is encountered, the compiler will look for the available conversion functions and find our `operator double ()`, which does the job. This can be easily verified by placing a breakpoint there during debugging. Finally, the absolute value of the result is returned on line [183]. Curiously, the `std::fabs` function could not be used here since it is not `constexpr`-adapted. Calling only `constexpr` functions from a `constexpr` function is yet another rule for writing `constexpr` code.

Listing 7.7 Definition of the template `ComputeRoundingError` function for computing the difference between floating-point and fixed-point representations (in *CppBookCode, FxFor.h*).

```
166  /////////////////////////////////////////////////////////////
167  // This function returns the difference in representations
168  // between double and FxFor<>
169  /////////////////////////////////////////////////////////////
170  //
171  // INPUT:
172  //      d - an input double value
173  //      f - FxFor<> to be checked
174  //
175  // OUTPUT:
176  //      difference (as a double value) between double
177  //      and fixed representation of this number
178  //
179  template< typename D, int P, typename A >
180  constexpr auto ComputeRoundingError( const double d, const FxFor< D, P, A > f )
181  {
182      auto diff( d - static_cast< double >( f ) );
183      return diff < 0.0 ? - diff: diff;   // std::fabs failed to be constexpr friendly
184  }
```

Finally, on lines [188–191], a number of useful alias names are introduced with the `using` directive. Two special ones for purely fractional types are created on lines [195–196].

Listing 7.8 Definitions of useful alias names for some common types created from the `FxFor` class (in *CppBookCode, FxFor.h*).

```
185  // Here we define the specific data types. Be careful, however,
186  // to check the size of built-in types on your machine!
187
188  using FX_8_8    = FxFor< unsigned short, 8  >;
189  using FX_16_16  = FxFor< unsigned int,   16 >;
190  using FX_24_8   = FxFor< unsigned int,   8 >;
191  using FX_8_24   = FxFor< unsigned int,   24 >;
192
193  // The following types are for normalized numbers
194  // for which their magnitude is less than 1.0.
195  using FX_PURE_FRACT_15 = FxFor< unsigned short, 15 >;
196  using FX_PURE_FRACT_31 = FxFor< unsigned int,  31 >;
```

7.3.4 Applications of *FxFor*

Now that `FxFor` is ready, it is time to check its operation. However, we will start with some useful helpers, shown in Listing 7.9.

Lines [3–4] define a `template constexpr` for a constant value. It takes the value of a constant `pi` assigned to a type given during template instantiation. This way, we can define `gkPi< double >`, `gkPi< float >`, or `gkPi< FX_8_8 >`, as we will see soon.

Listing 7.9 Helper utilities (in *CppBookCode, FixedPtArithm.cpp*).

```
1  // New way of defining constants
2  // with variable templates
3  template< typename T >
4  constexpr T gkPi = T( 3.1415926535897932385 );
```

Lines [6–7] define a custom version of the iostream endl manipulator. This is a helper template function with two template parameters defined with auto. Therefore, their type will be deduced during instantiation based on the types of the passed parameters. The first parameter, REP, defines the number of repetitions of the second parameter, CHAR. The default value of CHAR is set to the end-of-line (EOL) symbol. It simply replaces repeated entries of endl – for instance, endl << endl << endl – with one endl< 3 > in this case. Simply returning a string object with repeated EOLs does the trick. But std::endl is not used, since it always flushes the output stream – which in most cases entails an unnecessary computational burden (Turner 2016). As always, the stream object needs to be returned.

```
5    // A helper multiple end-of-line
6    template < auto REP, auto CHAR = '\n' >
7    std::ostream & endl( std::ostream & o )
8    {
9        // Avoid sending endl - it flushes the stream
10       return o << std::string( REP, CHAR );
11   }
```

Listing 7.10 shows a test function that mostly operates with constexpr. Our first test function, which begins on line [15] and uses the variable template gkPi, creates a floating-point kPi object. The same constant, but for the FX_8_8 FX format, is created on line [20], again using the gkPi template. Then, on line [23], static_assert is called. If it passes, then we can be sure the kPi_8_8 object was created *at compile-time* as the constexpr object. If not, the compiler probably encountered errors; they could even be warnings, as pointed out earlier. Then, lines [26–27] define a floating-point radius and the area of a circle with that radius. These are kept as referential objects, but together they occupy at least 16 bytes. FX 8_8 type objects are more economical. Lines [30–31] again define the radius and area objects, but expressed with the FX_8_8 type. The next static_assert on line [33] will be fulfilled if area_8_8 was properly constructed *at compile-time*.

Listing 7.10 Test function for the FxFor class showing its constexpr properties (in *CppBookCode, FixedPtArithm.cpp*).

```
12   using std::cout, std::endl;
13
14
15   void FxPt_Test_1( void )
16   {
17       constexpr auto & kPi { gkPi< double > };
18
19
20       constexpr FX_8_8  kPi_8_8( gkPi< FX_8_8 > );
21
22       // This checks if kPi_8_8 is created during compilation
23       static_assert( kPi_8_8.GetInternalValue() >= 0 );
24
25       // double
26       constexpr double  radius( 2.0 );
27       constexpr auto area_d ( kPi * radius * radius );
28
29       // FX_8_8
30       constexpr FX_8_8  radius_8_8( radius );
31       constexpr FX_8_8  area_8_8( gkPi< FX_8_8 > * radius_8_8 * radius_8_8 );
32
33       static_assert( area_8_8.GetInternalValue() >= 0 );
34
35
36
```

The static_assert on line [37] is fulfilled if the rounding error is less than a given threshold. An interesting testing benchmark is created here – by reducing the rightmost threshold value on line [37], we can trace the activity of the compiler. At some lower value of the threshold, say 0.00005, the condition is not fulfilled, and the static_assert fires. But this is a vivid sign that the compiler assessed the current state. Information about the object size, values of the computed circle areas, and the error are displayed on lines [40–44].

```
37    static_assert( ComputeRoundingError( area_8_8, area_d ) < 0.005 );
38
39    // area_d and area_8_8 have been already precomputed in compilation
40    cout << "sizeof(double) = "   << sizeof( double );
41    cout << ", area< double > = " << area_d << endl;
42    cout << "sizeof(FX_8_8) = "    << sizeof( FX_8_8 );
43    cout << ", area< FX_8_8 > = " << static_cast< double >( area_8_8 ) << endl;
44    cout << "Diff = " << ComputeRoundingError( area_8_8, area_d ) << endl< 3 >;
```

Having computed the area of a circle, we go a little further and compute the volume of a cylinder on lines [48–60]. Again, we do this in the floating-point and FX domains. The volume is computed using FX_8_8 objects on lines [51–52]. Here, at least two interesting functions are involved. The first is the product of two FX_8_8 objects, from which the second object is locally converted to a temporary object by means of the FX_8_8 constructor. The product is then converted back to double by the static_cast operator, which invokes the double converting operator.

Finally, on line [54], an FX_8_8 object, previously created as constexpr, is copied into a normal runtime object of the larger FX_16_16 type. Here the member template copy constructor from line [80] in Listing 7.1 is called. Then, on line [58], the area is multiplied by the height to obtain the cylinder's volume, and the value is displayed.

```
45    // -------------------------------------------
46    // Compute at runtime
47
48    auto cyl_len { 1000.0 };
49
50    // There will be an overflow
51    cout    << "volume< FX_8_8 > = "
52            << static_cast< double >( area_8_8 * FX_8_8( cyl_len ) ) << endl;
53
54    FX_16_16 area_16_16( area_8_8 );    // init wider from shorter
55
56
57    // Compute a volume of a cylinder
58    area_16_16 *= cyl_len;
59
60    cout << "volume< FX_16_16 > = " << static_cast< double >( area_16_16 ) << endl;
61
62 }
```

Line [63] in Listing 7.11 shows the FxPt_Test_2 test function. Its main purpose is to exemplify the const and constexpr objects, as shown on lines [68–69]. We will again stress the difference: a const object behaves like all other runtime-created objects. Its only restriction is that, once created, it cannot be modified. Note that despite being a const object, the static_assert on line [72] will not compile, since the object is not a constexpr (hence this line is commented out). On the other hand, the constexpr object on line [69] is meant to be created before the whole translation unit is compiled. If this is possible, then the entire process will take place during compilation, and the resulting (also constant) object will be embedded into the resulting code. In this case, the static_assert on line [75] will be fulfilled – first, because it is a constexpr object; and second, because the condition is true.

Listing 7.11 Test function to show differences between the const and constexpr declared objects (in *CppBookCode, FixedPtArithm.cpp*).

```
63   void FxPt_Test_2( void )
64   {
65       // -------------------------------------------
66       // const vs. constexpr
67
68       const FX_8_8      d1 {};    // d1 will be const
69       constexpr FX_8_8 d2 {};    // d2 will be const and computed during compilation
70
71       // Will not compile - is not sufficient, must be constexpr
72       // static_assert( d1.GetInternalValue() >= 0 );
73
74       // This is ok
75       static_assert( d2.GetInternalValue() >= 0 );
76       // Will not compile - d2 is const FX_8_8
77       // d2 *= 2.0;
78   }
```

An attempt on line [77] to modify the d2 object will fail because constexpr on line [69] imposes const properties on the d2 object.

7.4 Floating-Point Representations

Computers are commonly associated with computations. Computer-aided design systems, physical simulations, weather forecasting, cosmic flights, artificial intelligence, etc. – all these and many more are heavily based on mathematical procedures performed by computers. All require numerical value representations in a computer's memory. We discussed integer and FX arithmetic in previous sections. However, if we think of doing computations with values ranging from, for example, -1500.13 up to $+12e+12$, we can see that the formats have a number of important limitations. A mechanism had to be invented for their efficient representation, which would also be compatible with various computer platforms. Such representations have been known at least for half a century in the form of the *floating-point* (FP) format. We have used it many times in the examples presented in this book.

All we needed to do was to choose the `double` or `float` type, and usually we were happy. But let's take a closer look at computations involving these formats. For example, what do we expect the following to display on the screen?

```
1   double first_val       { 0.1 };
2   double scnd_val        { 0.2 };
3
4   double expected_result { 0.3 };
5
6   if( first_val + scnd_val == expected_result )
7       cout << "As expected?" << endl;
8   else
9       cout << "What's going on?" << endl;
```

Is the result a surprise? Probably. But wait a minute: if this does not work as we expected, how can we perform any reliable computations? As we will see, we can, but only if we are aware of what we are doing and what to expect. The problem with the previous code is that there are no 100% precise representations of all or some of the values 0.1, 0.2, and 0.3 in the FP format with a binary base, as we will explain shortly. So, from the beginning, we are working with approximations. Although there are certainly values that can be represented exactly, such as 0.25, from this point on, we should assume that we are always working with *approximate* values. If so, then the natural question is how accurate these approximations are. We will try to answer this question, but let's go back and fix our code. If we rewrite line [6] as follows

```
6   if( std::fabs( ( first_val + scnd_val ) - expected_result ) < 1e-12 )
```

then, instead of the previous

```
What's going on?
```

we get

```
As expected?
```

In the last line, we called the `std::fabs` function to compute the absolute value of the difference between the first sum and `expected_result`, and then we checked whether the result was small enough to consider the two to be sufficiently close together. This "sufficiently close" was arbitrarily set to `1e-12`. This may be the correct value, considering the precision of our computations, but we will also explain how to choose the right value in the following sections.

7.4.1   Number Representation in Floating-Point Format

To analyze the characteristics of computations with floating-point numbers, let's start with the presentation of this format, which is shown in Figure 7.5. The value D of a number is given as follows (Goldberg 1991)

$$D = \left(-1\right)^{S} \cdot M \cdot B^{E} = \left(-1\right)^{S} \cdot \left(d_{o} \cdot d_{1} \ldots d_{p-1}\right) \cdot B^{E} \tag{7.20}$$

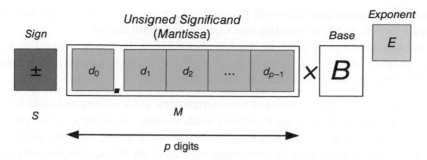

Figure 7.5 Number representation in the floating-point format.

where M denotes an *unsigned significand* (*mantissa* or *fraction*), B is a base, and E denotes the exponent, which is *a negative or positive integer* fulfilling the following condition:

$$E_{\min} \leq E \leq E_{\max} \tag{7.21}$$

The main advantage of using this FP representation, compared with the FX representation discussed in the previous section, is *the larger range of FP numbers*. Hence, the FP representation is used in most numerical computations.

The base B in Eq. (7.20) can be chosen arbitrarily, but it is constant and therefore does not need to be stored in the representation. To explain, we will set a decimal base, i.e. $B = 10$. However, in a computer representation, the base is binary: that is, $B = 2$. The latter has a number of benefits, as we will explain.

For p digits and base B, the value of the significand is given as follows

$$M = d_0 + d_1 \cdot B^{-1} + \cdots + d_{p-1} \cdot B^{-(p-1)} \tag{7.22}$$

where the values of the digits fulfill the condition $0 \leq d_i < B$.

Although a fixed number of digits and exponents is assumed, which boils down to a fixed number of bits for representation, the conveyed value's decimal point can be in various positions – hence, the name *floating-point*. In other words, with FP, we can write 1.23, 12.3, and 123, each with the decimal point in a different position. This is unlike the FX representation discussed in the previous section. The main advantage of FP over the FX representation is the *much greater range* (dynamics) of allowable numbers, assuming the same storage capacity.

We will also add some important facts about the floating-point representation, which will affect our discussion. These also comply with the FP standard:

- In the FP domain, some real values cannot be represented exactly
- Due to roundoff errors, in the FP domain, some algebraic conditions do not always hold. For example, the commutative law may not hold: that is, $(a+b)+c \neq a+(b+c)$ for $a, b, c \in$ FP
- The floating-point representation of numbers is not unique. The preferable way to write the significand is with no leading zeros, to retain the maximum number of significant bits: that is, $d_0 > 0$. This is a *normalized* form[2]

---

2 To increase the range, there is an exception for values with $E = E_{\min}$, called *denormals* (Goldberg 1991).

- Normalization can cause problems with a convenient representation of zero (preferably with all bits set to 0). Hence, a special encoding is necessary, as we will discuss
- Usually, the exponent E, which can be negative, is written in the biased format $E = E_{true} + bias$, in which its value is shifted, so E is always positive (this is the excess method). Such a representation simplifies comparisons of numbers

We have only touched on the specifics of FP computations. Basic understanding of FP computations does not only mean discovering a peculiar math, though – in many systems, proper implementation of FP computations constitutes a serious security matter. For instance, in 1996, a floating-point number representing the horizontal velocity of the Ariane 5 rocket was converted to a 16-bit integer, which caused an overflow followed by an unhandled hardware trap; in the end, the whole launcher exploded (see Figure 7.6).

Figure 7.6 Photo of the Ariane 5 before and after an explosion caused by a floating-point roundoff error. Source: *https://www.youtube.com/watch?v=gp_D8r-2hwk*.

Let's start with some numerical values that show the distribution for various precisions, exponents, and two bases of interest: binary $B = 2$ and decimal $B = 10$. Example distributions for these bases and for positive values are shown in Figures 7.7 and 7.8. The distributions of the floating-point numerals were generated in accordance with Eqs. (7.20)–(7.22). It is evident that even in these simple examples, the possible values do not cover the entire domain and are rather sparse.

Moreover, there is a higher concentration around 0, whereas further from zero, the values are more scarce. Thus, the distributions *are not uniform*. Also, in this simple scheme, there is no good representation for the zero. Nevertheless, the FP standard has special encoding for zero, as we will discuss. All these observations are rather scary – they mean in computations with FP, it is highly unusual to have exact values. We are not living in a perfect world, to this is OK if we can measure how incorrect we are, or even better if we can assess the worst-case scenario. So, let's analyze the potential errors.

As alluded to previously, trying to fit any conceivable real number into an FP representation, taking 32 or 64 bits, inevitably requires choosing the closest FP representation. This process is called *rounding*, and the resulting error is called the *rounding error* (or *roundoff error*).[3] Hence, rounding error is a characteristic feature of FP computations. However, even choosing the closest FP representation is not straightforward, so there are many rounding strategies, as we will discuss. The following situations need to be properly signaled in FP arithmetic:

---

3 See *https://en.wikipedia.org/wiki/Round-off_error*.

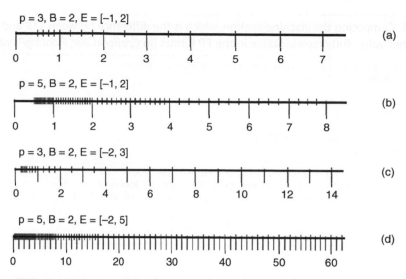

Figure 7.7 Distribution of positive floating-point values for $B = 2$, example precision p, and exponents E. Floating-point values are shown in red. It is easy to see different groups of number "concentrations" corresponding to different exponents E. For example, in plots (a) and (b), four groups are clearly visible, which correspond to $E = -1, 0, 1$, and 2. Spacing within the groups is the same. However, the spacing between the groups increases by a factor of the base B.

Figure 7.8 Distribution of positive floating-point values for $B = 10$, precision $p = 2$, and exponents $E \in [-1, +1]$. Floating-point values are shown in red.

- *Overflow* – The result is too large to be correctly represented
- *Underflow* – The result is too small to be correctly represented
- *Inexact* – The result cannot be represented exactly, so a rounded value is used instead
- *Invalid operation* – E.g. dividing by 0 or computing square root from a negative value

Investigating only the significand in Eq. (7.22), notice that the smallest possible positive value in the last position is simply for $d_{p-1} = 1$, which can be expressed as follows:

$$\varepsilon = 1 \cdot B^{-(p-1)} = B^{1-p}. \tag{7.23}$$

The constant ε, called *a machine epsilon*, is one of the most important values characterizing computations with FP numbers. Since FP numbers are written in a normalized representation, as will be further discussed, ε can be interpreted as the distance between 1 and the closest value greater than 1 (not 0). We will see soon how ε can be used in practical computations with FP values.

For a given FP representation, such as `float` or `double`, the value of the machine epsilon can be easily computed, such as shown in Listing 7.12.

Listing 7.12 Computing the machine epsilon, which is the difference between 1.0f and the next closest higher value, fully representable in the FP format (in *CppBookCode, FloatingPoint.cpp*).

```
1   // Let's find epsilon for single-precision floating-point
2   const float kBase { 2.0f };
3
4   // We will start from this and then this will be successively halved
5   const float kEpsInit { 1.0f };
6
7   // Stores the last computed epsilon
8   float store_eps {};
9
10  // Iterate until adding eps to 1.0f does not change 1.0f
11  for( float eps = kEpsInit; 1.0f + eps != 1.0f; eps /= kBase )
12      store_eps = eps;    // We need to catch the one before the last
13
14  cout << "Machine epsilon = " << store_eps << endl;
15  cout << "Machine epsilon = " << numeric_limits< float >::epsilon() << endl;
```

In the previous code, the machine epsilon is found as the difference between 1.0f and the next closest higher value fully representable in the floating-point format. This requires a few iterations of the loop on lines [11–12]. The variable eps starts with an initial value kEpsInit that is then gradually lowered by dividing by the binary kBase. At some point, the lowest possible nonzero value is reached, which corresponds to the least significant bit of the significand. We need to catch this value since after the next division, it becomes zero and the loop terminates. For this purpose, we use the store_eps variable, which after terminating the loop stores the sought value of the machine epsilon for the float type. On our test computer, the following values are printed:

```
Machine epsilon = 1.19209e-07
Machine epsilon = 1.19209e-07
```

The second result is due to the call on line [15] to the epsilon function from the std::numeric_limits< float > class, which returns the same machine epsilon. This template class delivers useful information about the range and other numerical properties of its provided type, as shown in Table 7.5.

In the next section, we will see how ε can be used to compute the distance between FP numbers.

7.4.2 Distribution of Floating-Point Numbers and the Computational Consequences

Let's analyze the problem of non-uniform distances between FP values. But first, for better insight, let's write the FP values shown in Figure 7.7a. Recall that for the constant $p = 3$ and the binary base $B = 2$, we get $\varepsilon = 0.25$. Also note that due to the four values of the exponent E: $-1, 0, 1,$ and 2, we have four partitions of our FP value D. Within each partition, we have the same spacing δ, as shown in Table 7.4.

On the other hand, we see that ε conveys only the distance between 1 and its nearest higher value. This is concordant with the absolute distance δ between successive FP values only when the exponent $E = 1$. So, in a general case, and based on Eq. (7.20), we conclude that to compute an absolute distance δ, ε needs to be multiplied by the factor B^E:

$$\delta = \varepsilon \cdot B^E \tag{7.24}$$

Table 7.4 FP values from Figure 7.7a for $B = 2$, $p = 3$, $E \in [-1,2]$. There are four groups of FP numbers, each with different separation between the values. The machine epsilon ε is the same and corresponds to the difference between 1 and its nearest higher value, 1.25. The real spacing within each group is given by the product $\delta = \varepsilon \cdot B^E$. But for practical reasons, it is easier to compute $s = \varepsilon \cdot |D|$.

i	0	1	2	3
D	0.5 0.625 0.75 0.875	**1 1.25** 1.5 1.75	2 2.5 3 3.5	4 5 6 7
E	-1	0	1	2
B^E	2^{-1}	2^0	2^1	2^2
$\varepsilon = B^{1-p}$	0.25	**0.25**	0.25	0.25
$\delta = \varepsilon \cdot B^E$	0.125	0.25	0.5	1
$s = \varepsilon \cdot D$	0.125 ... 0.21875	0.25 ... 0.4375	0.5 ... 0.875	1 ... 1.75

In other words, for the absolute distance δ between FP values, we must consider exponents, which in our case is the range $E \in [-1,2]$. An immediate conclusion is that when comparing or subtracting two neighboring FP values, we cannot deal with values less than δ. Our next conclusion is that the spacing between FP numbers becomes larger with the exponent. We observed this effect in Figures 7.7 and 7.8.

The only snag in the previous assessment is that computing δ requires that we know an exponent E of D. Although this can be easily determined (for example, by a bit analysis or with the `frexp` function), a more practical approach is to use the product of ε and the absolute value $|D|$:

$$s = \varepsilon \cdot |D| \tag{7.25}$$

Since, from Eq. (7.20), for normalized FP values it always holds that $|D| \geq B^E$, where E denotes an exponent of D, the following inequality can be easily verified

$$s_{i-1} < \delta_i \leq s_i \tag{7.26}$$

where i denotes the number of a consecutive exponent group (i.e. based on Eq. (7.21), $i \equiv E - E_{\min}$). Substituting Eq. (7.25) into Eq. (7.26), we get

$$\varepsilon \cdot |D_{i-1}| < \delta_i \leq \varepsilon \cdot |D_i| \tag{7.27}$$

Considering that $|D_{i-1}| = |D_i|/B$, and skipping the same index i, we finally get

$$\varepsilon \cdot \frac{|D|}{B} < \delta \leq \varepsilon \cdot |D| \tag{7.28}$$

Feeding Eq. (7.28) with the example values from the experiment shown in Table 7.4, the following inequality is obtained

$$0.125 \cdot |D| < \delta \leq 0.25 \cdot |D|$$

which can be verified by substituting the values of D from Table 7.4.

Of importance is the right side of Eq. (7.28), since for a given value D, the product $\varepsilon \cdot |D|$ gives us a good upper approximation of the minimum FP value than can fit into the FP representation. Now we can use this property to make a more conscious choice for the threshold used when comparing floating-point numbers, as shown in the following code:

```cpp
1   double first_val      { 0.1 };
2   double scnd_val       { 0.2 };
3
4   double expected_result { 0.3 };
5
6   double kThresh { 1e-12 };     // Let's assume an acceptable threshold or set to 0
7
8   double eps = numeric_limits< double >::epsilon();
9
10  double sum = first_val + scnd_val;
11
12  double max_val = std::max( std::fabs( sum ), std::fabs( expected_result ) );
13
14  // Let's modify the threshold to be at least as the second argument
15  kThresh = std::max( kThresh, eps * max_val );
16
17  if( std::fabs( sum - expected_result ) <= kThresh )
18      cout << "As expected?" << endl;
19  else
20      cout << "What's going on?" << endl;
```

We start with a `kThresh` value set on line [6]. Sometimes we know this value from the task we solve, but it might be too low for the FP representation, so on line [15] it is updated to be at least as large as the product of the machine epsilon and the maximum value of the subtracted arguments. In other words, we conclude that two FP values are identical if their difference is not bigger than the scaled machine epsilon.

In numerical analysis, many iterative algorithms follow a similar scheme of subtracting two FP values and checking the result. Usually, the following condition is checked

$$\left| x_{n+1} - x_n \right| \leq \tau \tag{7.29}$$

and if it is fulfilled, the iterations are stopped. In other words, iterations proceed as long as the absolute difference is greater than the assumed threshold. Equation (7.28) gives us a hint how to use the threshold τ, so the previous condition makes sense in the domain of FP numbers. From this point of view and based on Eq. (7.28), the previous equation can be written as follows:

$$\left| x_{n+1} - x_n \right| \leq max\left(\varepsilon \cdot \left| x_n \right|, \varepsilon \cdot \left| x_{n+1} \right| \right). \tag{7.30}$$

In other words, Eq. (7.30) says that x_{n+1} and x_n are approximately equal. On the other hand, the threshold τ is chosen based on experience and the type of mathematical problem, to stop the iterations at a given accuracy. Therefore, in practice, usually the following has to be checked:

$$\left| x_{n+1} - x_n \right| \leq max\left(\tau, \varepsilon \cdot \left| x_n \right|, \varepsilon \cdot \left| x_{n+1} \right| \right). \tag{7.31}$$

As a result, if the difference is less or equal than a predefined threshold or the minimum spacing between the FP values, whichever is greater, the iteration loop has a chance to stop. Based on this, we can sketch a code template for iterative computations that rely on the convergence of the consecutively computed values, as shown in Listing 7.13.

Listing 7.13 A sketch of code for iterative computations until convergence (in *CppBookCode*, *FloatingPoint.cpp*).

```
79
80   double x_n {}, x_n_1 {};
81
82   double eps = numeric_limits< double >::epsilon();
83
84   // An anticipated convergence threshold
85   double thresh { 1e-12 };
86
87   // It is always good to have a fuse if computations do not converge
88   const size_t kMaxIters { 1000 };
89
90   for( size_t n = 0; n < kMaxIters; ++ n )
91   {
92      // do computations, x_n_1 is a new value of x_n
93      // ...
94
95      double loc_thresh = std::max( thresh, eps * std::max( std::fabs( x_n ),
                              std::fabs( x_n_1 ) ) );
96
97      if( std::fabs( x_n_1 - x_n ) <= loc_thresh )
98         break;        // x_n_1 and x_n are approximately equal
99
100     x_n = x_n_1;   // copy for the next iteration
101  }
```

The algorithm involves successive computations of x_n_1 based on the value of x_n computed in the previous step, and so on. Such a scheme repeats in a loop, as on lines [90–101], until the condition in Eq. (7.29) is fulfilled for a certain value of the threshold, which is defined on line [85]. Its value depends on the type of computations, expected convergence properties of the computed functions, etc. Properly choosing the threshold is part of the art of numerical computations, since if it is too large, the result will not be accurate or simply will be wrong. On the other hand, if it is too low, then the iterations can get stuck in an infinite loop. There is also the risk of setting a value that is less than the FP distance for the current values of x_n_1 and x_n. This option is checked on line [95], and loc_thresh is set. The convergence condition is checked on line [97]; if fulfilled, then the loop is immediately terminated due to the break on line [98]. If not, then a common step is to copy the current value x_n_1 to x_n, holding the previous value for the next iteration, as on line [100].

One way or the other, to be sure the loop terminates, it is always a good idea to set an upper limit on the number of iterations. Here, this is done on line [88] by defining kMaxIters, which is then checked in the loop.

In the next section, we will analyze the rounding error when replacing a real value with its nearest FP approximation.

7.4.3 (✘) Real-Value Approximation Error with Floating-Point Representations

To see how to cope with the rounding errors, let's start with an example in the decimal domain, i.e. $B = 10$. Let's assume $p = 3$ digits of precision and that an exact result of some mathematical operation we know is $x = 0.273$. If in our FP system, its closest representation is $\bar{x} = 2.72 \cdot 10^{-1}$, so the difference is $|x - \bar{x}| = 2.73 \cdot 10^{-1} - 2.72 \cdot 10^{-1} = 0.01 \cdot 10^{-1}$. In other words, this is 1 of the *units in the last place* (ULP). If $x = 0.271828$, then the error is only 0.172 of ULP, and so on.

To be more precise, let's define *the absolute difference* between a real value x and its FP approximation $\bar{x}$, as follows:

$$\Delta = |\bar{x} - x| \qquad (7.32)$$

where

$$\bar{x} = D(x) \qquad (7.33)$$

denotes an FP approximation of a real value x in accordance with Eq. (7.20), and with exponent E. The previous is a slight modification of Eq. (7.20), in which we assume that D is a function that converts x to its nearest FP representation.

To be able to compare different values of the exponent E, the *absolute relative difference* is defined as follows:

$$r = \frac{\Delta}{B^E} \qquad (7.34)$$

It conveys information about the difference related to the significand alone and not to the exponent, as we saw in the previous example. In a moment, we will find the range of r. However, note that to determine an error expressed in ULP, we need to divide r by the value expressed by the least significant bit of the significand.

Based on this, to express an error in ULP, we have to relate the distance r to the smallest value of the last position of the significand. That is, r should be divided by the machine epsilon, as follows:

$$R_{ULP} = \frac{r}{B^{1-p}} = \frac{r}{\varepsilon} \qquad (7.35)$$

Let's verify the previous formulas with our two examples with the decimal base ($B = 10$) and precision $p = 3$, for $x_1 = 0.273$ and $x_2 = 0.271828$, and approximated with one value $\bar{x} = 2.72 \cdot 10^{-1}$. For these two cases, we easily obtain the following values:

$$\Delta = |2.73 \cdot 10^{-1} - 2.72 \cdot 10^{-1}| = 0.01 \cdot 10^{-1},$$

$$r = 0.01 \cdot 10^{-1} / 10^{-1} = 0.01, \qquad \varepsilon = 10^{-2},$$

$$R_{ULP} = 0.01 \cdot 10^{3-1} = 1_{[ulp]}$$

In the second case, for $x = 0.271828$, we obtain the following in a similar way:

$$\Delta = |2.71828 \cdot 10^{-1} - 2.72 \cdot 10^{-1}| = 0.00172 \cdot 10^{-1},$$

$$r = 0.00172 \cdot 10^{-1} / 10^{-1} = 0.00172, \qquad \varepsilon = 10^{-2},$$

$$R_{ULP} = 0.00172 \cdot 10^{3-1} = 0.172_{[ulp]}$$

Yet another approach is to compute *the relative error*, which is defined as follows

$$R_R = \frac{|\bar{x} - x|}{|x|} = \frac{\Delta}{|x|} \le r \tag{7.36}$$

where r is given in Eq. (7.34). That is, the relative error R_R is the difference of the real and approximating values, divided by the real value. The inequality in Eq. (7.36) is due to Eq. (7.20), since $d_0 > 0$ and because it holds that $|x| \ge B^E$. In our examples, we get

$$R_R = \frac{0.01 \cdot 10^{-1}}{2.73 \cdot 10^{-1}} \approx 0.00366 \text{ and } R_R = \frac{0.00172 \cdot 10^{-1}}{2.71828 \cdot 10^{-1}} \approx 0.000633,$$

respectively. The values are different because we had different x in these two cases. But R_R stays the same regardless of the exponents. For example, if in the first example we took $x_1 = 2.73 \cdot 10^5$ and $\bar{x} = 2.72 \cdot 10^5$, R_R would still be 0.00366, since the exponents cancel out. That is, we conclude that *the relative rounding error is uniform in the FP domain.*

Figure 7.9 shows that the maximum roundoff error between a real value x and its nearest FP approximation value $\bar{x}_n$ or $\bar{x}_{n+1}$ is up to ½ ULP, whereas the values $\bar{x}_n$ and $\bar{x}_{n+1}$ are separated by 1 ULP.

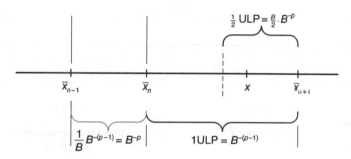

Figure 7.9 Rounding error of approximating a real value x with the closest FP number $\bar{x}_n$ or $\bar{x}_{n+1}$, which differ by 1 ULP. When choosing the nearest FP value, the maximum error is no greater than ½ of ULP.

On the other hand, if we are on the border of the exponent groups – that is, $\bar{x}_{n-1}$ and $\bar{x}_n$, such as between the values 1.75 and 2 in Table 7.4 – then the distance is B less than in the next group, which boils down to B^{-p}. Hence, the maximum error in this case is $½ \cdot B^{-p}$. This way, we come to the following equation:

$$\frac{1}{2} B^{-p} \le r \le \frac{B}{2} B^{-p} \tag{7.37}$$

where r is given in Eq. (7.34). Also note that the two sides of Eq. (7.37) differ by a factor of B. This is called *a wobble*, for which the lower, the better. Thus, we see that the binary base $B = 2$ has yet another advantage of the lowest wobble. Inserting Eq. (7.23) into Eq. (7.37), we get

$$\frac{1}{2} \frac{\varepsilon}{B} \le r \le \frac{1}{2} \varepsilon \tag{7.38}$$

This inequality with values from the example in Table 7.4 reads as follows:

$$0.0625 \leq r \leq 0.125$$

This does not mean r must be greater than 0.0625; it only denotes the upper limits of r.

7.4.4 The IEEE 754 Standard for Floating-Point Arithmetic

As we see from the previous discussion, FP operations require a number of assumptions, such as a choice of a number of bits for the significand and exponent. Moreover, we did not touch on the problem of algorithms for arithmetic operations with FP numbers.

Throughout the years, many FP representations have been proposed. At first, these were suggested by large companies that specialized in computer manufacturing, such as IBM and Cray (Wiki:Floating-point 2020). However, the most commonly encountered FP representation today is provided by the IEEE 754 standard, introduced in 1985 and revised in 2008 (Wiki:IEEE-754 2020). It paved the way for the implementation of FP operations, which we obtain by choosing `float` or `double` in our computations. The bit representation of FP numbers expressed in the IEEE 754 standard is shown in Figure 7.10.

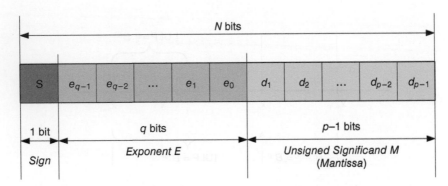

Figure 7.10 Bit representation of floating-point values in the IEEE 754 standard. There are two popular formats: short with a total length of $N = 32$, precision $p = 24$ of the significand, and $q = 8$ bits for the exponent; and long with $N = 64$, $p = 53$, $q = 11$. The most significant bit d_0 of the significand is always 1 and does not need to be stored. This is the hidden bit. This also leaves one free bit which can be used for the sign.

Following are the basic facts about FP representation in the IEEE 754 standard:

- IEEE 754 defines many FP formats, of which the *single-precision* and *double-precision* are probably the most commonly encountered in C/C++ compilers[4]
  - Single-precision format occupies 4 bytes (32 bits) and has $p = 24$ (23 bits stored due to normalization) and $q = 8$ bits. In some C/C++ compilers, this format is represented with `float`

---

4 The standard requires only that `double` is at least as precise as `float`, and that `long double` is at least as precise as double.

- Double-precision format occupies 8 bytes (64 bits) and has $p = 53$ (52 bits stored) and $q = 11$ bits. In some C/C++ compilers, this format is represented with `double`
  - Extended-precision (double-extended) format occupies 10 bytes (80 bits), $p = 65$, $q = 15$. In some C/C++ compilers, this format is represented with `long double`
  - Quadruple-precision format occupies 16 bytes (128 bits) with $p = 113$ bits (supported by some C/C++ compilers with `long double` or special types/flags)
- The most important bit of the significand is not stored, since in a normalized FP representation, it is always 1. This is the *hidden bit* trick (Goldberg 1991). This also explains why using the binary base $B = 2$ is beneficial (also recall that it has the smallest wobble). In addition, this feature explains how the previous bit partitions are organized, also considering the S sign bit
- The standard defines some special values that are especially encoded:
  - Positive infinity ($+\infty$)
  - Negative infinity ($-\infty$)
  - Negative zero (0^-)
  - Positive zero (0^+)
  - Not-a-number (NaN), which is used to represent, for example, the results of forbidden mathematical operations avoiding an exception, such as the square root of a negative value, etc
- The significand and exponent are specially encoded to represent the previous special values (Wiki:IEEE-754 2020). For other encodings, the value 127 in single-precision, or 1023 in double-precision, is added to the exponent
- As shown in Figures 7.7 and 7.8, the "standard" FP formats have a problem with precisely representing 0 and values close to 0. To remedy this, there is a special encoding (all 0s in the exponent bit, and $d_0 = 0$ for the significand) to represent this group of values, which are called *denormals (subnormals)*. But in some systems, using denormals comes with a significant runtime cost[5]
- The IEEE 754 standard defines all necessary mathematical operations on FP values, such as addition, multiplication, and roundings. Rounding is inevitable if the result cannot fit in the FP representation, e.g. due to an insufficient number of bits for precision. There are five rounding modes, as follows:
  - Default round to nearest (ties round to the nearest even digit, i.e. to the value that makes the significand end in an even digit). It can be shown that rounding to nearest leads to the fewest errors (Goldberg 1991)
  - Optional round to nearest (ties round away from 0)
  - Round up (toward $+\infty$)
  - Round down (toward $-\infty$)
  - Round toward 0 (cuts off fractions). This is also the default rounding for the integer types (Section 3.1)
- The IEEE 754 standard allows benign propagation of exceptional conditions, such as overflow or division by zero, in a software-controlled fashion rather than hardware interrupts

---

5 In some systems, to avoid such small values and using denormals, constructions like `x + = 0.05f` are used. This ensures that x is never too close to `0.0f`.

Knowing all this, we can gain further insight into FP representation in accordance with the IEEE 754 standard. For example, considering the bit-allocation scheme shown in Figure 7.10, and Eqs. (7.20)–(7.22), let's interpret the following bit setup:

```
0 10001100 11110000111100000000000
```

The fields in this FP representation can be obtained as follows:

$$S = (-1)^0 = 1$$

$$E = 10001100_b - 127 = 140 - 127 = 13$$

$$M = 1.11110000111100000000000_b = 1 + 2^{-1} + 2^{-2} + 2^{-3} + 2^{-4} + 2^{-9} + 2^{-10} + 2^{-11} + 2^{-12}$$
$$= 1.941162109375$$

Hence, based on Eq. (7.20), the value is

$$D = 1.941162109375 \cdot 2^{13} = 15902.0$$

Note that we had to add a leading 1 to the significand M, since it is not explicitly stored (this is the hidden bit). The previous computations can be performed quite easily, as in the following code snippet:

```
unsigned long df = 0b0'10001100'11110000111100000000000;
float * df_f_ptr = (float *) & df;
cout << "df_float = " << * df_f_ptr << endl;
```

As expected, the output is as follows:

```
df_float = 15902
```

This and other information about the numerical properties of a given type T can be checked by using the data and function members of the numeric_limits< T > class from the *limits* header, as summarized in Table 7.5. The numeric_limits< T > class has a few other members that can be looked up in the *limits* header.

Table 7.5 Common members of `std::numeric_limits` from the SL *limits* library (examples in *CppBookCode, FloatingPoint.cpp*).

SL algorithm function	Description	Examples

`numeric_limits< T >:: epsilon ()`	Returns a machine epsilon value that is the minimum difference between 1.0 and the nearest higher value representable in the FP format.	`#include <limits>`
		
		`cout.setf( ios::boolalpha );   // print plain 'true' or 'false'`
		
		`cout << "numeric_limits< double >::epsilon() = "`
		`    << numeric_limits< double >::epsilon() << endl;`

`numeric_limits< T >:: min ()`	Returns the minimum absolute value for type T.	`cout << "numeric_limits< double >::radix = " << numeric_limits< double >::radix << endl;`
		`cout << "numeric_limits< double >::digits (mantissa) = "`
		`    << numer_c_limits< double >::digits << endl;`

`numeric_limits< T >:: max ()`	Returns the maximum value for type T.	`cout << "numsseric limits< double >::min() = " << numeric_limits< double >::min() << endl;`
		`cout <s< "numeric_limits< double >::max() = " << numeric_limits< double >::max() << endl;`
		
		`cout << "numeric_limits< double >::has_denorm = "`
		`    << numeric_limits< double >::has_denorm << endl;`
		`cout << "numeric_limits< double >::denorm_min() = "`
		`    << numeric_limits< double >::denorm_min() << endl;`
		`cout << "numeric_limits< double >::lowest() = "`
		`    << numeric_limits< double >::lowest() << endl;`

(Continued)

Table 7.5 *(Continued)*

SL algorithm function	Description	Examples
`numeric_limits< T >:: denorm_min()`	Returns the smallest nonzero and denormalized value for type T.	```cout << "numeric_limits< double >::has_infinity = "``` ```<< numeric_limits< double >::has_infinity << endl;```

`numeric_limits< T >:: lowest()`	Returns the most negative finite value for T.	```// round_to_nearest or round_toward_zero```
		```cout << "numeric_limits< double >::round_style = " <<```
		```(numeric_limits< double >::round_style == std::round_to_nearest ?```
		```"round_to_nearest" : "round_toward_zero") << endl;```

`numeric_limits< T >:: radix`	Returns the base of the number system of the FP representation.	```cout << "numeric_limits< double >::round_error() = "```
		```<< numeric_limits< double >::round_error() << endl;```
		
		Output is as follows:
		
		```numeric_limits< double >::epsilon() = 2.22045e-16```
		```numeric_limits< double >::radix = 2```
		```numeric_limits< double >::digits (mantissa) = 53```
		```numeric_limits< double >::min() = 2.22507e-308```
		```numeric_limits< double >::max() = 1.79769e+308```
		```numeric_limits< double >::has_denorm = 1```
		```numeric_limits< double >::denorm_min() = 4.94066e-324```
		```numeric_limits< double >::lowest() = -1.79769e+308```
		```numeric_limits< double >::has_infinity = true```
		```numeric_limits< double >::round_style = round_to_nearest```
		```numeric_limits< double >::round_error() = 0.5```

SL algorithm function	Description	Examples
numeric_limits< T >:: digits	Provides the number of digits in the significand (mantissa).	The following code illustrates the infinity and NaN objects:
| | | ```
double zero { 0.0 };
``` |
| numeric_limits< T >:: has_denorm | Returns true if type T has denormalized values. | ```
double inf { 1.0 / zero };  // let's generate infinity, no exception
const auto kInfinity = numeric_limits< double >::infinity();
``` |
| numeric_limits< T >:: has_infinity | Returns true if type T has a representation for positive infinity. | ```
cout << "infinity = " << inf << endl;
cout << "inf == inf ? " << ( inf == kInfinity ) << endl;
cout << "123.0 + inf == " << 123.0 + inf << endl;
cout << "123.0 / inf == " << 123.0 / inf << endl;

// Let's generate NaN

double nan = sqrt( -0.1 );
cout << "123.0 + nan == " << 123.0 + nan << endl;
``` |
| | | The following output is obtained: |
| | | ```
infinity = inf
inf == inf ? true
123.0 + inf == inf
123.0 / inf == 0
123.0 + nan == -nan (ind)
``` |
| | | Using infinity in computations follows mathematical rules (Korn and Korn 2000). All operations involved with NaN end with NaN; however, no exception is thrown. |

(Continued)

Table 7.5 *(Continued)*

SL algorithm function	Description	Examples
`numeric_limits< T >:: round_style`	Returns a rounding method for type T.	`nextafter` for 0.0 and 1.0 is computed as follows:
`numeric_limits< T >:: round_error()`	Returns the maximum rounding error for type T.	```double val = 0.0;
double next_from_val = nextafter(val, kInfinity);
cout << "nextafter(" << setprecision(20) << val
<< ") = " << next_from_val
<< hexfloat << " (" << next_from_val << ")\n" << defaultfloat;```
`nextafter( val, dir)`	Returns the next representable floating-point number after *val* in direction *dir* (from the *cmath* header).	```val = 1.0;
next_from_val = nextafter(val, kInfinity);
cout << "nextafter(" << setprecision(20) << val
<< ") = " << next_from_val
<< hexfloat << " (" << next_from_val << ")\n"
<< defaultfloat;```
The output is as follows:
`nextafter( 0 ) = 4.9406564584124654418e-324  (0x0.0000000000001000000p-1022)`
`nextafter( 1 ) = 1.0000000000000000222  (0x1.0000000000001000000p+0)`
Note that the next value after 1.0 is 1.0 + machine epsilon found in the previous steps. This is not the same value for 0.0.

7.4.5 The Standard FP Operation Model

It is common practice to define the relation of a mathematical operation with respect to its counterpart in the FP domain. For example, the addition of two real values x and y in the FP domain can be represented as follows:

$$D(x+y)=(x+y)(1+\rho), \text{where} |\rho| \leq \varepsilon \tag{7.39}$$

The + operator can be replaced by other operators, such as −, *, or /. This is called the *standard FP model*.

7.4.6 Computations That Are Conscious of Numerical Errors

So far, we have discussed inevitable errors related to the rounding of real values to their closest representations in the FP domain. However, a second source of errors can be generated during mathematical operations on FP numbers. To understand this, let's consider FP addition, which involves proper *exponent scaling*, followed by *normalization*. For instance, adding two values, i.e. $2.72 \cdot 10^{-1}$ and $1.78 \cdot 10^{-3}$, the latter component's exponent must be scaled to the higher one, as shown in Figure 7.11.

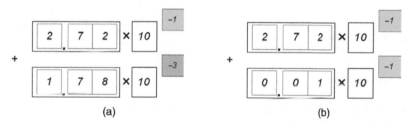

$$+ \qquad \qquad +$$

(a) (b)

Figure 7.11 Adding two FP numbers (a). To perform addition, the values must be scaled to have the same exponent (b). Large differences in the exponents (high dynamics) can lead to the loss of significant digits.

In our example, we get the following:

$$2.72 \cdot 10^{-1} + 1.78 \cdot 10^{-3} => 2.72 \cdot 10^{-1} + 0.01 \cdot 10^{-1} = 2.73 \cdot 10^{-1}$$

We can see that when using only $p=3$ precision digits we lose two digits from the second term due to the shift necessary for the exponent scaling. This can lead to significant errors. The conclusion is that if we have a choice, e.g. when adding a series of FP numbers, we should always order the addition in such a way as to add the values of exponents that are as similar as possible.

Precise descriptions of FP addition, multiplication, and other algorithms can be found in the literature (Knuth 1998). On most modern systems, these are implemented in the microprocessor or a software library. The good news is that adding and subtracting FP numbers is exact if there is no overflow (e.g. due to the *guard digits*). This feature does not hold for multiplication and division, but in this case the relative error does not exceed ½ ULP – assuming there is no overflow.

When performing FP computations, we should be aware of the many peculiarities that can lead to imprecise or even totally incorrect results. The most obvious are the previously mentioned overflow and underflow. However, similarly dangerous is subtracting *numbers that are nearly equal in magnitude*. In such a case, most of the leading digits vanish, and a rounding error may occur that promotes the digit in the last place to a more significant position. For example, when subtracting $2.71828 - 2.71829$, we end up with $1e{-}05$, which reflects only the last digit since all the others are canceled out. But if 2.71828 and 2.71829 were already rounded off, then after subtraction the last digits may be less accurate, since they may already be inaccurate due to the previous rounding. That is, the digits remaining after subtraction convey incorrect information. Even worse, they are promoted to more significant positions of the significand (in our example, 1 in the first position). Errors arising from such situations, called *catastrophic cancelations*, can be very severe. They can arise even in simple computations, such as when finding the roots of a quadratic equation $ax^2 + bx + c = 0$, as discussed in Section 3.16. Its solution is simple, and the roots are given in the analytical form:

$$x_1 = \frac{1}{2a}\left(-b - \sqrt{b^2 - 4ac}\right), \; x_2 = \frac{1}{2a}\left(-b + \sqrt{b^2 - 4ac}\right) \tag{7.40}$$

A problem may arise if $ac \ll b^2$ and $b < 0$. In this case, $\sqrt{b^2 - 4ac} \approx |b|$, and x_1 will suffer from subtracting two almost-identical values. A simple way out, in this case, is to first observe that

$$x_1 x_2 = c \tag{7.41}$$

and to compute x_2 from Eq. (7.40) and then, finally, x_1 from Eq. (7.41). The following code shows this idea:

```
double a {}, b {}, c {};
// Read in a, b, c ...


double x1 {}, x2 {};


double d = b * b - 4.0 * a * c;
if( d > 0.0 )
{
   if( b < 0.0 )
   {
      x1 = (-b+sqrt(d)) / (a + a);// -b becomes positive and we have addition
      x2 = c / x1;
   }
   else
   {
      x1 = ( -b - sqrt( d ) ) / ( a + a ); // adding two negative values
      x2 = c / x1;
   }
}
```

This code needs polishing to become fully operable. However, the main point of this section is to emphasize that rather than naively implementing the formulas shown in a mathematics book, frequently we need to reformulate the problem to avoid errors specific to the floating-point domain.

Many expressions need a closer look in the light of FP computations before implementation. Another example is $x^2 - y^2$, which is almost always better implemented using the familiar equivalent form $(x - y)(x + y)$. Not only do we save one multiplication, but we also avoid catastrophic cancelation errors, which are likely in the first representation (Goldberg 1991).

A terse but practical introduction to the subject of floating-point computations is the paper by Allison (2006). For a more in-depth introduction with mathematical proofs, we recommend the book by Knuth (1998) and the paper by Goldberg (1991). As always, Wikipedia provides an ample source of information on FP computations and the IEEE 754 standard (Wiki:Floating-point 2020; Wiki:IEEE-754 2020).

In the next two sections, we will investigate two classic computational problems that involve FP computations. The first shows how to sum up a series of FP numbers with the best accuracy. In the second example, we will solve the problem of finding a zero crossing for a function, which is ubiquities in optimization. In the example, we will use it to compute an approximate value of the square root of a real number.

7.4.7 Example Project – Evaluating the Summation Algorithms

Summing numerical values is one of the most common numerical operations. If we have a vector of FP values, we can easily sum them with `std::accumulate`, discussed in Section 3.8. But now that we are aware of various subtleties of FP computations, let's analyze how accurate this is. Since we have already dealt with simple summations, in this section we will consider summing the elementwise products of two vectors. This operation, called the *inner product*, is frequently encountered in various domains of science and technology, such as optimization, machine learning, and artificial intelligence. The inner product is defined as follows:

$$P = \mathbf{v} \cdot \mathbf{w} = \sum_{i=0}^{N-1} v[i] \cdot w[i] \tag{7.42}$$

where $v[i]$ and $w[i]$ denote the ith element of the vector $\mathbf{v}$ and $\mathbf{w}$, and N is the number of elements in each. The important aspect of the inner product is that it conveys information about the distance between two vectors. The inner products of normalized vectors (i.e. with modules of 1.0) are -1.0, 0.0, and $+1.0$ for counter-oriented, orthogonal, and concordant ones, as shown in (Figure 7.12).

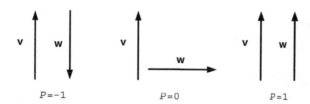

Figure 7.12 The inner products of specific configurations of the vectors **v** and **w**, each of length 1.

A normalized version $\bar{\mathbf{w}}$ of a vector $\mathbf{w}$ is obtained by dividing by its module: that is,

$$\bar{\mathbf{w}} = \frac{\mathbf{w}}{|\mathbf{w}|} \tag{7.43}$$

where |**w**| denotes a vector module defined as follows:

$$|\mathbf{w}| = \sqrt{\mathbf{w} \cdot \mathbf{w}} \tag{7.44}$$

However, as we will soon see, summing values – especially products of values, as in Eq. (7.42) – can be burdened with a significant error if the peculiarities of FP computations are not taken into consideration. To see this, we will investigate the operation of the following summation algorithms:

- The simple multiply-and-add method
- A method that computes the element-wise products, sorts them, and does a summation
- The Kahan summation method, which applies a correction factor on the underflow bits

Each of these algorithms is implemented in a different function. We have gathered all of them, as well as other definitions and test functions, in the `InnerProducts` namespace, which begins on line [8] in Listing 7.14. Some useful aliases are grouped starting on line [11]. Similarly, objects from the standard library are listed starting on line [15].

The function `InnerProduct_StdAlg` starts on line [21]. The only call it makes on line [24] is to `std::inner_product`, which computes the inner product of two vectors v and w, exactly as in Eq. (7.42). For this purpose, the full range of v needs to be provided in its two first arguments. The third is the beginning of w. But the last is an initial start value for the sum in Eq. (7.42). We must be careful to choose its correct type, which agrees with the type of elements in v and w. Otherwise, nasty errors can arise. Alas, we will see that in some cases, `std::inner_product` can be highly inaccurate due to floating-point errors.

Listing 7.14 Evaluating three summation algorithms in the inner product computation (in *CppBookCode*, *InnerProductVerification.cpp*).

```
1   #include <vector>
2   #include <iostream>
3   #include <iomanip>
4   #include <random>
5   #include <numeric>        // for inner product
6
7
8   namespace InnerProducts
9   {
10
11      using DVec = std::vector< double >;
12      using DT = DVec::value_type;
13      using ST = DVec::size_type;
14
15      using std::inner_product;
16      using std::transform;
17      using std::accumulate;
18      using std::sort;
19      using std::cout, std::endl;
20
21      auto InnerProduct_StdAlg( const DVec & v, const DVec & w )
22      {
23          // The last argument is an initial value
24          return inner_product( v.begin(), v.end(), w.begin(), DT() );
25      }
```

The situation can be remedied by summing onto an output sum that has higher precision than the summands. However, such an approach has a number of limitations. First, we need to have a FP representation with higher precision. Using many libraries, such as GMP[6] and *ttmath*,[7] can be cumbersome on some platforms and almost always incurs a runtime penalty.

---

6 GMP is a free library for arbitrary-precision arithmetic (*https://gmplib.org*).
7 A lightweight C++ library for math operations on big integer/floating-point numbers (*www.ttmath.org*).

Based on the analysis of FP summation errors from the previous section, an interesting idea is to first arrange the elements in order of their magnitudes and then add them up. This idea is implemented in the following `InnerProduct_SortAlg` function:

```
26    auto InnerProduct_SortAlg( const DVec & v, const DVec & w )
27    {
28        DVec z;        // Stores element-wise products
29
30        // Elementwise multiplication: c = v .* w
31        transform(   v.begin(), v.end(), w.begin(),
32                back_inserter( z ),
33                [] ( const auto & v_el, const auto & w_el) { return v_el * w_el; } );
34
35        // Sort in ascending order
36        sort( z.begin(), z.end(),
37            [] ( const DT & p, const DT & q ) { return fabs( p ) < fabs( q ); } );
38
39        // The last argument is an initial value
40        return accumulate( z.begin(), z.end(), DT() );
41    }
```

The function needs to precompute the elementwise products of the two input vectors v and w. The result is put into the temporary vector z, defined on line [28]. The products are computed by the `std::transform` function called on lines [31–33]. It takes the full range of the vector v, the beginning of w, and then `std::back_inserter` on line [32] to push the new results directly to z; finally, the lambda function on line [33] multiplies a pair of values passed by reference. Then the products are sorted *in ascending order of magnitude* with `std::sort`, after which, on line [40], they are summed up by `std::accumulate`. These SL algorithms are described in Table 3.6.

The key operation in the previous function is sorting the computed products, as done on line [36] by the `std::sort` function. It might seem that the summation in Eq. (7.42) should not depend on the order of the operands. This is not true in the domain of floating-point computations. By arranging the elements by magnitude, we avoid excessive shifts of the significand that happen when adding FP numbers with highly different exponents (see Figure 7.11). In effect, consecutive sums do not require many shifts of the summands, and the result is usually more accurate compared to summing values with arbitrary magnitudes. The additional cost of this method comes mostly from the sorting performed on line [36]. Last but not least, when calling `std::accumulate` as we do on line [40], always include the initial value of proper types, such as `DT()` in our case, which returns a default zero-initialized value for `DT` (whatever type it is). Writing a simple 0 in this place sometimes leads to malicious errors (hint: a constant 0 is of `int` type).

On the other hand, in the following `InnerProduct_KahanAlg` function, we implement the Kahan summation algorithm. To mitigate the bit loss during addition, it corrects the lower bits at each step of the summation loop, as we will explain.

```
42    // In the Kahan algorithm, each addition is corrected by a correction
43    // factor. In this algorithm, non-associativity of FP is assumed, i.e.:
44    // ( a + b ) + c != a + ( b + c )
45    auto InnerProduct_KahanAlg( const DVec & v, const DVec & w )
46    {
47        DT theSum {};
48
```

```
49      // volatile prevents the compiler from applying any optimization
50      // on the object since it can be changed by someone else, etc.,
51      // in a way that cannot be foreseen by the compiler.
52
53      volatile DT c {};      // a "correction" coefficient
54
55      const ST kElems = std::min( v.size(), w.size() );
56
57      for( ST i = 0; i < kElems; ++ i )
58      {
59          DT y = v[ i ] * w[ i ] - c;   // From y subtracts the correction factor
60
61          DT t = theSum + y;   // Add corrected summand to the running sum theSum
62          // But theSum is big, y is small, so its lower bits will be lost
63
64          c = ( t - theSum ) - y; // Low-order bits of y are lost in the summation.
65          // High-order bits of y are computed in ( t - theSum ). Then, when y is
66          // subtracted from this, the low-order bits of y are recovered (negative).
67          // Algebraically, c should always be 0 (beware of compiler optimization).
68
69          theSum = t;
70      }
71
72      return theSum;
73  }
```

The final sum goes in the theSum variable defined and initialized on line [47]. The correction coefficient c is defined on line [53] as volatile. This tells the compiler not to apply any optimization on c, which could happen since, at first glance, c could be eliminated from this code. Then the summation loop starts on line [57]. It iterates up to the minimum size of either of the input vectors, as controlled by kElems (set on line [55]). On line [59], y is computed as a product of successive elements of the two vectors, which is adjusted by the correction coefficient c. Then, on line [61], t is computed as the sum of theSum and y. Since the running sum held in theSum is usually big, whereas y is comparatively small, when adding the two on line [61], the lower bits of y are lost due to the inevitable right shift of the significand of y (see Figure 7.11). But these bits are "recovered" on line [64]. The higher-order bits of y are computed into the (t - theSum) term. From it, y is subtracted, which leaves only the lower bits of y. This is how we obtain the correction coefficient c, which contains the lower bits of y, as originally proposed by Kahan (1965). On line [69] theSum is copied from t, and the iteration proceeds. The whole trick of recovering the rounding bits y_2 is shown in Figure 7.13.

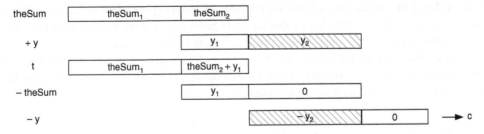

Figure 7.13 Explanation of the recovery of rounding error y_2 in the compensated summation scheme implemented in the InnerProduct_KahanAlg function.

Finally, the following `InnerProducts::InnerProduct_Test` function runs the experiment with two randomly filled vectors. To facilitate the assessment procedure, we use the following relation

$$P = \begin{bmatrix} \mathbf{v}, -\mathbf{v} \end{bmatrix} \cdot \begin{bmatrix} \mathbf{w}, \mathbf{w} \end{bmatrix} = \mathbf{v} \cdot \mathbf{w} - \mathbf{v} \cdot \mathbf{w} = 0 \qquad (7.45)$$

where [**w**,**w**] means concatenation (merging) of the vector **w** with its copy.

The `InnerProduct_Test` function prepares some vectors with random values and tests all the methods we have discussed as so far.

```
74   void InnerProduct_Test( void )
75   {
76       const int kElems = 100000;
77
78       DVec   v( kElems );
79       DVec   w( kElems );
80
81       std::mt19937   rand_gen{ std::random_device{}() };     // Random Mersenne twister
82
83       // ref is a reference wrapper
84       std::generate( v.begin(), v.end(), ref( rand_gen ) );
85       std::generate( w.begin(), w.end(), ref( rand_gen ) );
86
87       // Now let's double our vectors with one negative reflection
88
89       // Lambda has to be mutable to allow change of the variable n
90       v.resize( 2 * kElems );
91       std::generate( v.begin() + kElems, v.end(),
92                          [ n = 0, & v ] () mutable { return - v[ n ++ ]; } );
93       w.resize( 2 * kElems );
94       std::generate( w.begin() + kElems, w.end(),
95                          [ n = 0, & w ] () mutable { return + w[ n ++ ]; } );
96
97       // The inner product should be close to 0.0,
98       // so let's check the two algorithms.
99
100      cout   << "Stand alg error = \t"   << std::setprecision( 8 )
                    << fabs( InnerProduct_StdAlg( v, w ) ) << endl;
101      cout   << "Sort alg error = \t"   << std::setprecision( 8 )
                    << fabs( InnerProduct_SortAlg( v, w ) ) << endl;
102      cout   << "Kahan alg error = \t"   << std::setprecision( 8 )
                    << fabs( InnerProduct_KahanAlg( v, w ) ) << endl;
103  }
104
105  }
```

First, lines [78–79] define two vectors v and w, each containing `kElems` elements. These are then initialized on lines [84–85] with random generator object `rand_gen`, created on line [81]. This is the random Mersenne twister, initialized with the `random_device` object, which we have used a few times before (Section 3.17.3). What is probably new here is the `ref` wrapper, used to pass `rand_gen` by reference to `std::generate` on line [84–85]. But to perform the operation in Eq. (7.45), we need to extend the two vectors. For this purpose, `v.resize` is called on line [90], which doubles the number of elements in v. This way, newly added elements will be initialized with the negative values of the previously inserted random values. This is achieved on line [91] by calling `std::generate` equipped with the lambda function. It returns consecutive negative elements of the vector v, starting at index n = 0, provided in its caption. In order to be able to modify n in its run, the lambda is declared `mutable`. Similarly, on lines [93–94], the vector w is extended. This time, though, its existing values are copied without negation. Finally, the three functions computing the inner product are launched on lines [100–102]. The output of the previous code is as follows:

```
Stand alg error =        7.3001728e+09
Sort alg error  =        12681216
Kahan alg error =        0
```

As we see, in some cases, errors can be catastrophic. Based on this analysis, we can surmise that more often than not, the Kahan algorithm provides more accurate sums than `std::accumulate`, and both have almost identical computation times. Moreover, the Kahan algorithm's computational complexity (execution time) is much less than that of the sorting algorithms.

We will now review what have we learned about in this section:

- There is a method for comparing vectors based on their inner product
- Summing FP values can result in large errors. For better accuracy, the Kahan algorithm is recommended
- The `std::ref` reference wrapper can be used to pass objects by reference
- Only a lambda function declared `mutable` can change values passed in its caption (Section 3.14.6)

7.4.8 Example Project – The Newton Method of Finding the Roots of a Function

Many tasks require finding the *roots* of a function: the arguments for which a function equals zero, as shown in Figure 7.14. For example, in optimization problems, finding the roots of the derivative of a function lets us find local extreme values of that function. We will use this feature to derive an algorithm for computing the roots of a function.

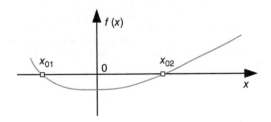

Figure 7.14 Plot of a function having two roots: i.e. it crosses the abscissa at two points x_{01} and x_{02}.

More formally, for a function $f(x)$, we are looking for values x that fulfill the following condition:

$$f(x) = 0 \tag{7.46}$$

Recall how we compute the derivative of a function, as discussed in Section 3.14.8. Based on Eq. (3.4), we came to the approximation formula we repeat here:

$$f'(x) \approx \frac{f(x+\delta) - f(x)}{\delta}$$

This gives us a hint about how our computations can proceed. We start with a certain value of x and, based on the characteristics of the function f around point x, try to find a change δ to x that brings us closer to 0, and so on. Putting this idea into the formula yields

$$f'(x) = \frac{0 - f(x)}{\delta} \tag{7.47}$$

From Eq. (7.47), we easily obtain the formula for the step:

$$\delta = -\frac{f(x)}{f'(x)} \tag{7.48}$$

Equation (7.48) gives us a direct recipe for finding the root of a function $f(x)$. This is the *Newton root-finding method*, summarized in Algorithm 7.1.

Algorithm 7.1 Root-finding algorithm based on Newton's iteration.

Input:	A real-valued function f; start value x_0
Output:	A value x for which $f(x) = 0$
1	$x = x_0$
2	**while** *not-convergent*
3	Compute δ from Eq. (7.48)
4	$x = x + \delta$
5	**return** x

Algorithm 7.1 is only an outline for the real implementation; we need to resolve a number of questions. For example, how do we check the convergence? However, we analyzed a similar problem in Section 7.4.2, so we can use the solution presented there in Listing 7.13. We also discussed function representations and computing function derivatives in Section 3.14.9. So, collecting all of these together under the umbrella of the `NewtonZero` namespace, we come up with the code in Listing 7.15 for computing the roots of a group of real-valued functions.

Listing 7.15 Computing a function's zero-crossing with the Newton approximation method (in *NewtonZero.cpp*).

```
1   #include <iostream>
2   #include <string>
3   #include <functional>
4   #include <algorithm>
```

(Coninued)

Listing 7.15 (continued)

```
5    #include <limits>
6    #include <tuple>
7
8    namespace NewtonZero
9    {
10       using FP = double;
11       using Real_Fun = std::function< FP( FP ) >;
12
```

Once again, to implement a software component composed of a number of `using` declarations and functions, we will use the encompassing namespace rather than a class. In our example, the namespace `NewtonZero` starts line [8]. At first, it is convenient to introduce some type aliases with the `using` directive. On line [10], the FP alias is defined to represent floating-point values throughout the namespace. Such a grouping allows for flexible changes if, for instance, we wished to verify operations with `float`. Line [11] introduces the alias to represent real-valued functions, as discussed in Section 3.14.9. In that section, we also discussed the `deriv` function; for convenience, it is repeated here, starting on line [14].

```
13       // Derivative is also a 1D real function
14       auto deriv( const Real_Fun & fun, const FP x0, const FP eps = 1e-5 )
15       {
16          // Let's use the definition of a derivative
17          return ( fun( x0 + eps ) - fun( x0 ) ) / eps;
18       }
```

The function `FindZero` on line [34] iteratively computes a root of its supplied function `fun`. The computations follow Algorithm 7.1 and the scheme outlined in Listing 7.13. Hence, on line [38], the machine epsilon value is read, which is then used to set the threshold as discussed in Section 7.4.2. The iterating loop starts on line [46]. At each step, on line [51], a function derivative is computed at point x_n by calling `deriv`. But since we will divide by this value, line [54] checks whether it is sufficiently large. Otherwise, the loop is terminated. Here we simply use the epsilon in the role of the minimal threshold of the divisor (see question no. 26 in Q&E).

```
19       ////////////////////////////////////////////////////////////
20       // Finds zero crossing of the supplied function
21       ////////////////////////////////////////////////////////////
22       //
23       // INPUT:  fun - a function object
24       //      start_x - estimated starting point
25       //      thresh - a convergence threshold
26       // OUTPUT:
27       //      a tuple containing a pair of values:
28       //      - the found zero position
29       //      - true if computations converged
30       //
31       // REMARKS:
32       //      Only if true is returned can the result be valid
33       //
34       auto **FindZero**( const Real_Fun & fun, const FP start_x, const FP thresh = 1e-10 )
35       {
36          FP x_n { start_x };
37
```

```
38        const FP cps = std::numeric_limits< FP >::epsilon();
39
40        // Only if true can the computations be correct
41        bool reach_converg { false };
42
43        // It is always good to have a fuse in case computations do not converge
44        const size_t kMaxIters { 1000 };
45
46        for( size_t n = 0; n < kMaxIters; ++ n )
47        {
48           // Set the threshold
49           const FP loc_thresh = std::max( thresh, eps * std::fabs( x_n ) );
50
51           FP df_x = deriv( fun, x_n );
52
53           // Check if we can safely divide
54           if( std::fabs( df_x ) <= eps )
55              break;
56
57           // This is the Newton step
58           FP delta = - fun( x_n ) / df_x;
59
60           // Check for convergence
61           if( std::fabs( delta ) <= loc_thresh )
62           {
63              reach_converg = true;    // Result can be OK
64              break;
65           }
66
67           x_n += delta;    // Update the argument by delta and iterate
68        }
69
70        // Return the result - valid only if reach_converg == true
71        return std::make_tuple( x_n, reach_converg );
72     }
73
74
75  }
```

The parameter delta is computed on line [58], exactly as stated in Eq. (7.48). The convergence condition is checked on line [61]. For this purpose, delta is directly checked, since it is the difference between consecutive values of the variable x_n (compare this with line [97] in Listing 7.13). If the computations converged, i.e. the module of delta is less than the local threshold computed on line [49], then the loop terminates. This is also the only case when the parameter reach_converg is set to true. It is used to distinguish loop termination resulting from other reasons, in which case we cannot provide a valid result. However, if there is no convergence at this step, x_n is updated on line [67] exactly as in step 4 of Algorithm 7.1. On line [71], FindZero returns a pair: the last value of x_n and the flag reach_converg. The former constitutes a valid result only if the latter is set to true. This pair is represented by the std::tuple object, created by the std::make_tuple helper function. This is an efficient method for a function to return many values at once, as discussed in Section 3.17.1. Otherwise, if reach_converg is false, then the loop terminates by exceeding the number of allowable iterations set in kMaxIters. This also means a lack of convergence.

The operation of the `FindZero` function is verified to solve the equation $x^2 + x - 6 = 0$, starting at point -1.5, as set on line [6] of the function `NewtonZero_Test` in the following code. Although the first parameter is an object defined with `std::function`, a lambda function (Section 3.14.6) can also be provided, as shown on line [6].

```
1   namespace NewtonZero
2   {
3
4     void NewtonZero_Test( void )
5     {
6       auto [ val,flag ] = FindZero( [] ( double x ) { return x*x+x-6.0; }, -1.5 );
7
8       std::cout<<"Zero at "<<( flag ? std::to_string(val) : "none" ) << std::endl;
9     }
10  }
```

On line [8], `std::to_string` is called, which converts `val` to `std::string`. This is required in this context, since the `? :` operator expects the same types on both sides of its colon `:`.

It is easy to verify that this square equation has two solutions $x_1 = -3.0$ and $x_2 = 2.0$. Which one is reached depends on the starting point provided as the second parameter to `FindZero`. Hence, the analytical solution has its own advantages, as shown in Section 3.16. But the advantage of the numerical approach, as presented in the `FindZero` function, is that it can work with any provided function. Nevertheless, it requires an initial starting value and threshold, and it operates in an iterative fashion.

7.4.8.1 Function to Compute Square Roots Based on Newton's Iteration

As alluded to previously, finding the roots of a function has many applications, such as optimization problems. Another interesting application is computing functions for which there is no simple implementation. In computations, another function is used, for which we have an easy algorithm. To demonstrate this method, we will compute the square root for a given real value. To see how we can use Newton's method to compute a square root, let's start with the function we wish to compute:

$$f(x) = \sqrt{x} \tag{7.49}$$

It can be written as follows:

$$y = \sqrt{x}$$

Naturally, we assume we do not know how to directly compute $\sqrt{x}$. However, if we square both sides of the previous equation, we get the following

$$y^2 = x$$

which after rearranging yields

$$y^2 - x = 0$$

What this means is that if y happened to be $\sqrt{x}$, the previous equation would be fulfilled. So, let's rename the variables as follows:

$$x^2 - a = 0 \tag{7.50}$$

Now a denotes the constant input argument for which we wish to determine the value of $\sqrt{a}$, while x is a running variable. Equation (7.50) has exactly the form of the zero-finding problem defined in Eq. (7.46). Hence, we can use the previous Newton algorithm to solve Eq. (7.50). The found value of a root will be a good approximation of what we are looking for: $\sqrt{a}$. The previous idea is realized in the code shown in Listing 7.16.

Listing 7.16 Computing the `sqrt` function for real, nonnegative arguments based on the Newton root-finding method (in *CppBookCode, NewtonZero.cpp*).

```
11   namespace NewtonZero
12   {
13
14       // Compute the square root of the arg
15       auto SquareRootApproxNewton( const FP arg )
16       {
17           // This is a reverse function of the square root
18           auto sq_root = [ arg = arg ] ( double x ) { return x * x - arg; };
19
20           return FindZero( sq_root, 1.0 );
21       }
22
```

On line [11], the NewtonZero namespace is opened again. Then, the function SquareRootApproxNewton, defined on line [15], computes the approximate value of the square root of its argument arg. To do this, we only need the definition of the function, as in Eq. (7.50). Again, this is implemented on line [18] using the lambda function. Then, on line [20], the result of FindZero is returned (discussed in the previous section).

```
23       void SquareRoot_Test( void )
24       {
25           std::cout << "Enter positive value to compute the square root ";
26
27           double arg {};
28
29           if ( ! ( std::cin >> arg ) || arg < 0.0 ) return;
30
31           auto [ val, flag ] = SquareRootApproxNewton( arg );
32
33           if( flag )
34               std::cout << "sqrt( " << arg << " )= " << val << std::endl;
35           else
36               std::cout << "Cannot compute the square root" << std::endl;
37
38       }
39
40   }   // End of NewtonZero
```

The `SquareRoot_Test` function, defined on line [23], checks the computations by interacting with the user. Only nonnegative values are allowed for input, as checked on line [29]. On line [31], the structured binding is used to simultaneously receive `val` and `flag`, returned by `SquareRootApproxNewton`.

Finding roots and approximating functions are great numerical analysis problems. Usually, more sophisticated methods such as Taylor series expansion are used. For more on this fascinating domain, we recommend the book by Press et al. (2007). We have only scratched the surface here, but the point is to make more conscious implementations involving FP numbers.

In this section, we learned about the following:

- The Newton algorithm for finding a function's zero-crossing (finding roots)
- Computing a function derivative
- Representing functions with `std::function`
- Checking the convergence of a numerical algorithm that accounts for the specifics of floating-point numbers
- Passing many values from a function using `std::tuple` and `std::make_tuple`
- Applying the Newton zero-finding algorithm to compute the square root function

7.5   Summary

Things to Remember

- Real numbers can be approximated either with fixed-point (FX) or floating-point (FP) representations
- In C++, only built-in integer types use FX representations. FX with fractions can be implemented as a class
- The spacing of FX numbers is uniform
- The spacing of FP values is not uniform – it is larger for numbers with larger exponents
- FP allows for a greater dynamic range of values than FX
- Rounding errors are inevitable when representing real numbers in FX and FP formats
- Computations with FX and FP numbers can result in overflow, underflow, or roundoff errors
- Subtracting close values can lead to severe cancelation errors
- IEEE 754 defines standards for FP representation. The most common are the single-precision (`float`) and double-precision (`double`) formats
- The machine epsilon ε conveys the value represented by the lowest bit of the significand. This is the difference between 1.0 and the next closest higher value representable in the FP format. The product of $\varepsilon \cdot D$ provides a spacing assessment around an FP number D
- In C++, FP values are rounded to the nearest, whereas integer values are rounded toward 0 (cutting off the fraction)
- The `std::numeric_limits< T >` class conveys information about the numerical properties of a type `T`, such as minimum and maximum values, etc

Questions and Exercises

1. Convert the value 87_{10}, analyzed in Section 7.1, to the equivalent representations with the following bases: $B = 3, B = 5, B = 11$.

2. Repeat the subtraction operation from Section 7.1.4, but use Eq. (7.9).

3. Using Eqs. (7.10) and (7.11), derive the formulas and algorithms for summation and multiplication of two values in these representations.

4. Using bit operations, implement the left and right round shifts described in Table 7.3.

5. Using one of the FxFor types defined in Listing 7.8, compute the roots of a second-order polynomial. Analyze the allowable range and maximum error. Devise a method for computing the square root in the fixed-point format.

6. Using FxFor types, in the student grade project in Chapter 3, eliminate the floating-point type double; see Listing 3.3.

7. Refactor the code in Listing 3.4, line [81], to represent matrices with FxFor data. Verify the matrix multiplication in Listing 3.23. What can you change on line [35] to increase computation accuracy and the allowable range?

8. Extend the class FxFor presented in Section 7.3.2 to contain flags signaling overflow situations in operations.

9. In the class FxFor, replace the standard wrap-around rounding with the value-saturation mechanism. That is, when trying to extend the value beyond the storage data capacity, sustain the maximum allowable value.

10. Explain the benefits and pitfalls of the floating-point number representation.

11. What are FP rounding errors?

12. What are overflow and underflow when computing with FP numbers?

13. What is the machine epsilon, and how can it be used in computations with FP numbers?

14. Write a program to generate floating-point values, as shown in Figures 7.7 and 7.8.

15. Using a plot drawing library such as *gnuplot* (*www.gnuplot.info*), draw diagrams with floating-point values.

16. Check std::numeric_limits< T > for float, double, and long double in your system. Check it for int and long.

17. Using the Newton method from Section 7.4.8, write code to compute a local extremum and both roots of the square equation. Compare with the solution given by Eqs. (7.40) and (7.41).

18. The second parameter of the procedure FindZero in Listing 7.16 is the iteration start value, which was arbitrarily set to 1.0. However, the closer it is to a real, but unknown, value of the square root, the faster convergence can be expected. For an estimate of this start value, write a function for finding the square root with the bisection method (see Algorithm 2.3).

19. Modify the code shown in Listing 7.16 to compute $\sqrt[3]{x}$.

20. Let's assume a series of N pairs (x_i, y_i) is given. Develop and implement an algorithm for computing coefficients a, b, and c of the square polynomial of the form $ax_i^2 + bx_i + c \approx y_i$ that fits best the series of pairs.

21. In the function `InnerProduct_SortAlg`, we used `std::sort` to arrange the summands in order. Can you explain why this helps? What should the sort order be? What is the time complexity of this solution?

22. Rewrite the matrix multiplication procedure in Listing 3.23 using the Kahan algorithm for summation.

23. The broad group of definite integrals

$$\int_a^b f(x)dx \tag{7.51}$$

of integrable functions f can be approximated by the following summation:

$$S_N = \sum_{i=1}^N f(c_i)\Delta x_i, \text{ where } c_i \in \langle x_i, x_{i+1} \rangle, \Delta x_i = x_{i+1} - x_i \text{ and } x_1 = a, x_N = b. \tag{7.52}$$

Assuming division of the integration interval $\langle a, b \rangle$ into a number N of equal partitions, the previous summation can be further simplified as follows:

$$\Delta x_i = \Delta x = \frac{x_N - x_1}{N} = \frac{b - a}{N} \text{ and } x_i = i \cdot \Delta x \tag{7.53}$$

The point c_i can be chosen as the middle point between the points x_i and x_{i+1}, as follows:

$$c_i = \frac{x_{i+1} + x_i}{2} = \frac{(i+1) \cdot \Delta x + i \cdot \Delta x}{2} = \Delta x \left(i + \frac{1}{2} \right) \tag{7.54}$$

Insert Eqs. (7.53)–(7.54) into Eq. (7.52), and implement a method for numerically computing the definite integrals for any function. Represent functions programmatically, as discussed in Section 3.14.9.

24. Read, analyze, and implement the trapezoidal method for approximating definite integrals (*https://en.wikipedia.org/wiki/Trapezoidal_rule*). Compare this and the method developed in the previous step.

25. Using the integration procedure devised to compute Eq. (7.52), evaluate the constant π based on the following relation:

$$\pi = \int_0^1 \frac{4}{1 + x^2} dx \tag{7.55}$$

Measure the execution time and accuracy of this approximation as a function of N.

26. Derive the values of the normalized positive minimum $kMin$ and maximum $kMax$ in the IEEE 754 format (Section 7.4.4). Then show that $kMin \cdot kMax = 4 - 2^{-(p-2)}$, where p is the number of bits in the significand. Based on this relation derive the limiting conditions on the minimum and maximum values for the dividend a and the divisor b to assure valid divisions $c = a/b$ in the floating-point domain.

27. Refactor the `FxFor` class (Listing 7.1) by adding definition of the C++20 spaceship operator `<=>`.

8

Basics of Parallel Programming

Today, almost all computer systems, including embedded and mobile systems, are equipped with multicore microprocessors – not to mention graphics programming units (GPUs), which are equipped with thousands of cores. However, all the programs we have written and analyzed until now perform sequentially. That is, although we have multiple functions and calls between them, a microprocessor sequentially processes only instruction at a time. This docs not seem like the most efficient way to use the available hardware resources. Before we go into detail, let's summarize the main topics we will learn about in this chapter:

- Basic concepts of parallel computations
- What concurrent multitasking and threads are
- The risk of using shared objects, and how to protect their access
- How to make standard algorithms like `std::transform`, `std::sort`, and `std::transform_reduce` operate in a parallel mode
- Programming asynchronous tasks with `std::future`
- Basic construction of the OpenMP library – e.g. how to launch and synchronize multiple tasks, and how to make `for` operate in parallel to significantly speed up matrix multiplication

8.1 Basic Concepts of Parallel Computations

Since an example is better than a hundred words, let's start by analyzing the behavior of a simple function `Task_0` run simultaneously on two threads (later, we will show what a thread is and how to make code run on multiple threads). Let's also assume that `Task_0` accesses a global variable x. The situation is outlined in Figure 8.1.

After launching the two threads, each running the same `Task_0`, the output may look like the following

```
0, 10
5, 10
```

Introduction to Programming with C++ for Engineers, First Edition. Bogusław Cyganek.
© 2021 John Wiley & Sons Ltd. Published 2021 by John Wiley & Sons Ltd.
Companion website: http://home.agh.edu.pl/~cyganek/BookCpp.htm

```
1   // ------------------------------------
2   // An example of hazards due to unprotected
3   // shared object
4
5   int x;      // A global shared variable
6
```

Task_0 executed by thread no. 0 **Task_0 executed by thread no. 1**

```
1   void Task_0( void )
2   {
3       auto loc { x }; // Local object
4
5       // Non-protected shared (!)
6       x += 5;
7
8       cout << loc << "," << x << "\n";
9   }
```

```
1   void Task_0( void )
2   {
3       auto loc { x }; // Local object
4
5       // Non-protected shared (!)
6       x += 5;
7
8       cout << loc << "," << x << "\n";
9   }
```

Figure 8.1 An example of parallel execution of two tasks that access the same global object x. Since each instruction for each task can be executed at any time and simultaneously, the results of such free access are unpredictable and usually wrong. The way out of this problem is to make all lines that access common shared objects protected, to allow only one thread to execute at a time. Code that needs this type of protection is called a *critical section*, and the protection can be provided using synchronization objects such as a semaphore or a mutex.

or it may look totally different. On five threads, the output may look like this:

```
0, 15
20, 25
5, 25
10, 25
15, 25
```

More often than not, the results are incorrect and different from run to run. Such a situation is called a *race condition* or a *hazard*. In such a case, we would be lucky to diagnose the incorrect output, since this issue can turn on the red light indicating that something is wrong and needs to be fixed. However, in many cases, errors are stealthy and appear randomly, which makes debugging and verifying parallel code much more difficult.

We have to realize that each instance of Task_0 runs *concurrently*. This intersperses the execution of Task_0's sequential instructions with the execution of analogous instructions, but in different instances (threads). So, for example, an instance run by thread 0 finishes executing line [3], after which thread 5 is faster and manages to execute lines [3–6] of its code. This changes the common object x. If thread 0 now gets its portion of time and executes line [6], the values of x and loc will be far from what is expected and usually random. Also, the expression on line [8], whose intention was to display the two values, is not atomic. That is, its execution can be partitioned between different threads that happen to execute this code at more or less the same time, which leads to haywire output.

There is nothing wrong with Task_0 itself. If run sequentially – for example, in a for loop – it produces correct results that can be easily verified. This simple experiment should alert us that entering the realm of parallel programming can be like entering quicksand. Of course, this is the case only if we are not careful. Knowledge and conscious software design are the best protection measures.

The broad domain of parallel programming is gaining in importance and popularity. Providing more than an introduction is outside the scope of this book, but we can recommend many resources (Pas et al. 2017; Fan 2015; Schmidt and Gonzalez-Dominguez 2017). The intention of this section is to show that with a few new techniques and carefully analyzed cases, writing simple parallel components in C++ is not that difficult. The gain is worth the effort – as we will see, one additional line of code or a single parameter in a function can instantly make our code perform a few times faster than its sequential counterpart. This is in the spirit of C++, which also means better performance.

Before we show these techniques, we will briefly explain the most important concepts related to the domain of parallel programming:

- *Task, multitasking* – A procedure, function, etc. to be executed. Multitasking usually refers to the concurrent realization of multiple tasks
- *Thread, multithreading* – A thread is a separate path of code execution. It can be seen as the code and computer resources necessary to perform a task. Multithreading means the ability to run multiple threads concurrently. Threads can be executed by a single core or multiple cores of a processor. A single core can also run one or more threads by means of the OS's thread-preemption mechanism: a thread can be preempted at any moment and put into the queue of waiting threads; it can be then resumed by the OS as the result of an event, a specific condition, elapsed time, etc
- *Thread pool* – A group of pre-created threads that wait to be assigned to tasks for a concurrent execution. Maintaining a pre-created pool of threads increases performance by avoiding time-costly creations and deallocations of threads, but at a cost of increased resource usage. Once created, the pool of threads is usually maintained until the last parallel region is executed in the program
- *Team of threads* – A group of threads for *work sharing* inside a parallel region. One of the threads is appointed the master and the others are worker threads, as shown in Figure 8.2. The process of spawning multiple threads is sometimes called a *fork*. When threads meet at a common point, this is called a *join* (i.e. they are synchronized)

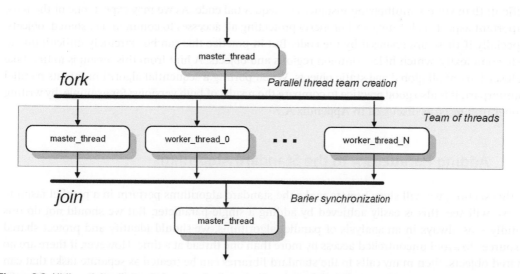

Figure 8.2 UML activity diagram showing the launch of a team of threads.

- *Concurrency* – The simultaneous execution of multiple tasks/threads
- *Shared objects (resources)* – Resources (objects) that can be accessed concurrently by many threads. If a resource can be changed by any of the threads, then special protection techniques should be used to allow access by only one thread at a time, to prevent hazardous results
- *Private objects (resources)* – Resources (objects) that are entirely local to a task/thread and to which other threads do not have access (e.g. via a pointer, etc.); Private objects do not need to be protected for exclusive access since each thread has its own copies
- *Critical section* – Part of the code in a task/thread that accesses a shared object and should be protected to ensure exclusive access of only one thread at a time
- *Mutual exclusion* – A mechanism that allows only one thread to execute uninterrupted its critical section. This is achieved by applying an available thread synchronization object
- *Deadlock* – An error situation in which threads wait for each other to unlock common resources and cannot proceed
- *Atomic instruction* – An instruction that can be completed by a thread without interruption by other threads. Atomic instructions are used to perform safe access to shared resources
- *Synchronization* – The process of waiting for all threads to complete. Such a common point of completion is a *barrier*. Sometimes *synchronization* refers to the mechanism of providing exclusive access to resources. System mechanisms such as semaphores, locks, mutexes, signals, etc. are synchronization objects
- *Thread safety* – A safety policy for an object or class when operating in a multithreading environment. A class is said to be thread-safe if, when an object of that class is created that is local to that thread, it is safe to call any method from that object (this is not the case if e.g. a class contains data members declared `static` or that refer to global objects, etc.). An object is thread-safe if it can be safely accessed by many threads with no additional protection mechanism; this means, if necessary, synchronization mechanisms have been implemented in that object

As we saw in this section and the simple example, writing correct parallel code is much more difficult than simply multiplying instances of sequential code. As we may expect, one of the most important aspects is locating and properly protecting all accesses to common, i.e. shared, objects, especially if these are changed by the code. But in practice this can be extremely difficult due to code complexity, which hides common regions and objects. A hint from this lesson is to first take a closer look at all global and static objects. When porting a sequential algorithm into its parallel counterpart, it is also good practice to compare the results of both versions: for example, by writing proper unit tests, as discussed in Appendix A.7.

8.2 Adding Parallelism to the Standard Algorithms

In this section, we will show how to make the standard algorithms perform in a parallel fashion. As we will see, this is easily achieved by adding a single parameter. But we should not do this blindly – as always in an analysis of parallel algorithms, we should identify and protect shared resources to avoid uncontrolled access by more than one thread at a time. However, if there are no shared objects, then many calls to the standard libraries can be treated as separate tasks that can run in parallel. As we will see, adding `std::execution::par` as the first parameter will make this happen.

In the following sections, we will build parallel systems based on splitting an initial array of data into a number of chunks that will then be independently processed by separate threads, as shown in Figure 8.3. This methodology is called *data parallelism* and usually gives good results when processing massive data, such as mathematical arrays, image and video files, etc. We will rely on programming techniques that make this process as simple and error-free as possible.

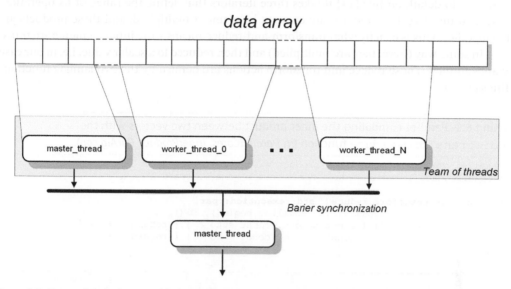

Figure 8.3 Team of threads operating in parallel on an array of data. Each thread takes its assigned chunk of data. Processing is performed independently in an asynchronous fashion. After all the threads finish processing the entire data array, their common results can be gathered and processed further.

Listing 7.14 shows the `InnerProducts` namespace. It contains three serial algorithms for computing the inner product between vectors (Section 7.4.7). Let's recall their characteristic features:

- `InnerProduct_StdAlg` – Calls `std::inner_product` and returns its result
- `InnerProduct_SortAlg` – Creates a vector of individual products between the corresponding elements of the two vectors. These products are then sorted and finally added together. Thanks to sorting, we achieve much more accurate results as compared with the `InnerProduct_StdAlg` algorithm. However, sorting significantly increases computation time
- `InnerProduct_KahanAlg` – A version of the accurate Kahan summation algorithm of the products of the corresponding elements of the two vectors

In this section, we will present new versions of the first two functions: they will perform the same action but in a parallel fashion, potentially taking advantage of available multicore processor(s). A parallel version of the third function is presented in the next section.

The first two parallel functions are as follows:

- `InnerProduct_TransformReduce_Par` – Based on the `std::transform_reduce` algorithm, which, unlike `std::inner_product`, allows for parallel operation. Briefly, *transform-reduce* is a classical scheme of parallel processing in which a problem is split into a number of smaller problems (transformation) that are then solved, after which the partial results are gathered together (reduction)
- `InnerProduct_SortAlg_Par` – A version of the serial `InnerProduct_SortAlg` that calls the parallel implementation of the standard sorting algorithm `std::sort`

The definition of the `InnerProduct_TransformReduce_Par` function begins on line [11] in Listing 8.1. There is only one expression on line [13], although we have split it into multiple lines for better readability. What is important is the new `std::transform_reduce` function with the first parameter `std::execution::par`. In our example, it performs the same action as `std::inner_product`; but, unlike `std::inner_product`, it is able to operate in parallel. Going into detail, on line [14] it takes three iterators that define the range of its operation. That is, two input vectors v and w are element by element multiplied, and these products are added together. This is exactly what transform-and-reduce means – the input elements are transformed in some way (here, they are multiplied) and then reduced to a scalar value, i.e. in our case they are summed. These reduce and transform actions are defined by the two lambda functions on lines [15, 16].

Listing 8.1 Parallel computing the inner product between two vectors with the `std::transform_reduce` function (in *ParallelCores, InnerProduct_ParAlg.cpp*).

```
10    // Parallel version of the inner product with transform-reduce
11    auto InnerProduct_TransformReduce_Par( const DVec & v, const DVec & w )
12    {
13        return std::transform_reduce(  std::execution::par,
14                        v.begin(), v.end(), w.begin(), DT(),
15                        [] ( const auto a, const auto b ) { return a + b; },
16                        [] ( const auto a, const auto b ) { return a * b; }
17            );
18    }
```

`InnerProduct_SortAlg_Par`, defined on line [20], is a parallel version of the serial `InnerProduct_SortAlg` defined in Listing 7.14. Let's compare the two versions. The first difference appears on line [22], as well as in the following `std::transform`. When entering the domain of parallel algorithms, `back_inserter` is the last thing we wish to use. Although it worked fine in the serial implementation, in the parallel world we cannot let many threads back-insert into vector z. But the way around this is simple: we only need to reserve enough space in z, as on line [22]. Thanks to this simple modification, `std::transform` can operate in parallel and independently with any chunk of data. More specifically, the main difference between the serial and parallel versions is on line [27]. The serial approach uses `back_inserter`. In this version, however, we simply provide an iterator to the beginning of z, since it has already been allocated enough space to accommodate all of the results. We don't need to protect z for the exclusive access since each of its elements is accessed only by one thread, whichever it is. Then, on line [31], the parallel version of `std::sort` is invoked. The difference between calling the serial and parallel versions is the presence of the first argument `std::execution::par`.

Finally, the sorted elements need to be summed. In the serial version, we did this with the familiar `std::accumulate`; but it has no parallel version. Instead, we use `std::reduce`, again called with the first parameter set to `std::execution::par`, as shown on line [35].

```
19        // Parallel version of the inner product with sorting
20        auto InnerProduct_SortAlg_Par( const DVec & v, const DVec & w )
21        {
22            DVec z( v.size() );     // Stores element-wise products
23
24            // PARALLEL elementwise multiplication: c = v .* w
25            std::transform(       std::execution::par,
26                    v.begin(), v.end(), w.begin(),
```

```
27                  z.begin(),
28                  [] ( const auto & v_el, const auto & w_el) { return v_el * w_el; } );
29
30          // PARALLEL sort in ascending order
31          std::sort( std::execution::par, z.begin(), z.end(),
32              [] ( const DT & p, const DT & q ) { return fabs( p ) < fabs( q ); } );
33
34          // PARALLEL summation
35          return std::reduce( std::execution::par, z.begin(), z.end() );
36      }
```

The only reason we go to all this trouble with converting algorithms to their parallel counter-parts is performance. Obviously, the performance time of the serial and parallel versions is the best indicator of success. But in practice, we may be surprised, at least in some of the cases. In the next section, we will show how to perform such measurements and explain what they mean.

We have only scratched the surface of parallel execution of the standard algorithms. The best way to learn more is to read the previously cited resources and visit websites such as *www.bfilipek.com/2018/11/parallel-alg-perf.html* and *https://en.cppreference.com/w/cpp/algorithm/execution_policy_tag_t*.

8.3 Launching Asynchronous Tasks

Still in the domain of the *task* of efficiently computing the inner product between two vectors, Listing 8.2 shows the `InnerProduct_KahanAlg_Par` function. This is a parallel version of `InnerProduct_KahanAlg` from Chapter 7. But in this case, rather than simply adding the parallel command `std::execution::par` to the standard algorithms, we will go into the realm of C++ multitasking. As we pointed out earlier, task parallelism can be achieved by launching a team of threads that concurrently process the tasks. In this section, we will exploit this possibility.

The definition of `InnerProduct_KahanAlg_Par` begins on line [5]. First, lines [8–14] define the initial control objects. Since `InnerProduct_KahanAlg_Par` performs in parallel, each task is attached to its specific chunk of data, with `k_num_of_chunks` denoting the number of chunks. In practice, data does not split equally, so usually there is some data left. This is held by `k_remainder`. Each chunk of data is then summed independently. Therefore, each result goes to the `par_sum` container defined on line [16]. Also, a summing function is called independently for each chunk of data. Such tasks are easily defined with lambda functions (Section 3.14.6). In our case, this is `fun_inter`, shown on lines [18–19].

The most characteristic part begins on line [21] with the definition of a `std::vector` storing `std::future< double >` objects. This allows us to define tasks that, after being properly created, can be asynchronously executed. In the loop on lines [25–28], the objects returned by the call to `std::async` with the parameters `std::launch::async`, `fun_inter`, and its local parameters are pushed into the `my_thread_pool` container. But the tasks are only collected – they are not invoked yet. A similar thing happens on lines [31–34] if there is a remainder.

Line [24] is also interesting: its purpose is to define a variable `i` with the same type as the `k_num_of_chunks` object. So, how do we determine the type of an object given the name of or a reference to that object? Line [24] explains how. First we need to call the `decltype` operator, which returns the type of `k_num_of_chunks`, which is then stripped of any decorators such as a reference, a const, etc. using `std::decay`. Finally, we specify what we are interested in: `std::decay<>::type`.

Let's now return to parallel operations. We have prepared our tasks, which are now deposited in the my_thread_pool container. This way, tasks that are created are invoked in the loop on lines [37–38]. More specifically, the call to future<>::get on line [38] launches whatever resources are necessary to execute our tasks. Thanks to our design, these operate independently; hence we were able to use async.

Finally, all the tasks finish their jobs – i.e. are synchronized – before the Kahan_Sum function is called on line [40]. Obviously, its role is to sum up all the partial sums returned by the tasks to the par_sum repository on line [38].

Listing 8.2 Parallel version of the serial inner product InnerProduct_KahanAlg from Listing 7.14 (in *ParallelCores*, *InnerProduct_ParAlg.cpp*).

```
1    // This is a simple data parallelizing the Kahan algorithm.
2    // The input vectors are divided into chunks that are
3    // then processed in parallel but by the serial Kahan algorithm.
4    // The partial sums are then summed up again with the Kahan algorithm.
5    auto InnerProduct_KahanAlg_Par(    const DVec & v, const DVec & w,
6                                       const ST kChunkSize = 10000 )
7    {
8        const auto kMinSize { std::min( v.size(), w.size() ) };
9
10       const auto k_num_of_chunks { ( kMinSize / kChunkSize ) };
11       const auto k_remainder { kMinSize % kChunkSize };
12
13       const double * v_data_begin = & v[ 0 ];
14       const double * w_data_begin = & w[ 0 ];
15
16       vector< double >  par_sum( k_num_of_chunks +( k_remainder>0 ? 1 : 0 ), 0.0 );
17
18       auto fun_inter = [] ( const double * a, const double * b, int s )
19                          { return InnerProduct_KahanAlg( a, b, s ); };
20
21       vector< future< double > >   my_thread_pool;
22
23       // Process all equal-size chunks of data
24       std::decay< decltype( k_num_of_chunks ) >::type i {};
25       for( i = 0; i < k_num_of_chunks; ++ i )
26          my_thread_pool.push_back( async( std::launch::async, fun_inter,
27                  v_data_begin + i * kChunkSize, w_data_begin + i * kChunkSize
28                  , kChunkSize ) );
29
30       // Process the remainder, if present
31       if( k_remainder > 0 )
32          my_thread_pool.push_back( async( std::launch::async, fun_inter,
33                  v_data_begin + i * kChunkSize, w_data_begin + i * kChunkSize,
34                  k_remainder ) );
35
36       assert( par_sum.size() == my_thread_pool.size() );
37       for( i = 0; i < my_thread_pool.size(); ++ i )
38          par_sum[ i ] = my_thread_pool[ i ].get(); // get blocks until async is done
39
40       return Kahan_Sum( par_sum );
41    }
```

The lambda function fun_inter, on line [18], is based on a serial version of InnerProduct_KahanAlg, outlined on line [42]. This is an overloaded version of InnerProduct_KahanAlg but with simple pointers defining the beginning of the two data vectors. As a result, the function easily operates with chunks of data that have been allocated in memory.

```
42   auto InnerProduct_KahanAlg( const double*v, const double*w, const size_t kElems )
43   {
44     // ...
45
46   }
```

Next is the most interesting moment – verifying whether all these parallel methods were worth the effort. We ran the serial and parallel versions on a single machine and compared their execution times; the results obtained on our test system[1] are shown in Table 8.1.

Table 8.1 Execution times for computing inner products between vectors with 20 000 000 elements each. Three groups of algorithms were tested: simple accumulation, sorting and accumulation, and using the Kahan algorithm. In each case, the timings of the sequential and parallel implementations were compared.

Algorithm	InnerProd vs. TransRed	Sort_Ser vs. Sort_Par	Kahan_Ser vs. Kahan_Par
Serial [s]	29	2173	129
Parallel [s]	12	475	11
Speed increase	**2.4**	**4.6**	**11.7**

The most impressive speed increase can be observed for the pair of Kahan-based algorithms. The parallel version outperforms its serial counterpart by more than an order of magnitude! Also, for the algorithms that employ prior element sorting, the speed increases more than four times. This shows that parallel programming is worth the effort. However, in more complex algorithms, an in-depth analysis should be performed in order to spot parts of the code that consume the most processor time. This analysis should be based on measurements and not on guessing. The profiler delivers reliable data to start with, as described in Appendix A.6.3.

8.4 Parallelization with the OpenMP Library

Running parallel versions of some of the algorithms from the SL is simple. But since operations are limited to specific tasks, this mechanism only solves some of the problems involved in implementing parallel systems. We can also design our own threads or run tasks using the ample C++ parallel library (Stroustrup 2013). Doing so has the immediate advantage of building an upper-level interface for the lower-level OS multithreading mechanisms. A correctly designed parallel implementation of the C++ parallel library will work on most modern systems; however, this level of programming requires substantial knowledge, experience, and effort to obtain good results.

The OpenMP library project, which brings us to a slightly higher level of parallel systems programming began in the 1990s. It is aimed at two languages: Fortran and C/C++. It has strong

---

1 Tests performed on a computer with a six-core processor: Intel Xeon E-2186 M @ 2.90GHz.

support from the steering committee, and at the time of writing, version 5.0 has been released (*www.openmp.org*). The most important features of OpenMP are:

- Higher-level programming focusing on tasks that automatically create a team of threads and support synchronization mechanisms
- Operation in a hybrid hardware environment (parallel code can be run on both CPU and GPU)
- Seamless integration with existing C++ code using the preprocessor `#pragma` (Appendix A.1). OpenMP code is added in the form of OpenMP directives with clauses. There are also some OpenMP-specific functions

An in-depth presentation of the most important features of OpenMP could consume a book by itself. In this section, we show only a few basic examples. However, they are very characteristic of the common uses of OpenMP, so we can try other parallel algorithms based on them. There are many good sources of information about OpenMP, including the OpenMP web page (OpenMP 2020). A very accessible introduction is *Guide into OpenMP* by Joel Yliluoma (*https://bisqwit.iki.fi/ story/howto/openmp*). Also, we recommend the recent books by Pas et al. (2017) and Schmidt and Gonzalez-Dominguez (2017). Let's start with a simple example that will demonstrate the basic features of OpenMP.

8.4.1 Launching a Team of Threads and Providing Exclusive Access Protection

The first thing to do when using OpenMP is to add `#include <omp.h>` in the source file, as shown on line [4] in Listing 8.3. The definition of the `OpenMP_Test` function starts on line [8]. Line [13] creates the `outStream` object. This is a string stream to which all output produced by our parallel branches of code will be sent. But we can easily spot that this is a classic example of a shared object. Hence, access to it must be protected to avoid hazards, as will be shown. On line [16], the OpenMP function `omp_get_num_threads` is called. It simply returns the number of threads in the team currently executing the parallel region from which it is called. There is also a counterpart `omp_set_num_threads` function, which lets us set a number of desired threads.

Line [23] contains the first characteristic `#pragma` construction with an OpenMP directive: `omp parallel` says to create and launch a team of threads and to process the following block of code (lines [24–42]) concurrently in each of these threads. `shared( outStream )` explicitly marks the `outStream` object as being shared. However, this does not protect it yet from an uncontrolled access by the threads.

The variable `thisThreadNo` created on line [27] is an example of a private object. That is, each thread contains a local copy. In each, `thisThreadNo` is initialized with the current thread number obtained from a call to the OpenMP function `omp_get_thread_num`. So, if there are 12 threads, the numbers are 0–11. Another local object `kNumOfThreads` on line [30] receives the total number of threads executing the parallel region by calling the previously described `omp_get_num_threads` function (these names can be confusing).

Now we wish to print information about the number of the thread that executes this portion of code, as well as the total number of threads involved. The operation is as simple as using the familiar `std::cout` or `outStream` in our case. However, recall that `outStream` is a shared object and needs to be treated specially: only one thread can perform operations on it at a time, while the others wait. To accomplish such mutual exclusion, on line [36] and again using `#pragma`, we create the `omp critical ( critical_0 )` construction. It tells OpenMP to add a synchronization barrier. As can be easily verified, if `critical` was omitted, the output would be rather messy.[2] Then we can be sure that the operation on lines [38–39] is performed entirely by a single thread until it finishes.

---

2 This can also happen by mistakenly omitting the keyword `omp`.

Line [42] ends the parallel block, and we are back in the sequentially executed part of the code. So, with no additional commands, on lines [49–50] we can print out the number of threads executing on behalf of this block. Likewise, line [53] prints all the information from the outStream object, which was stored there by the threads. Also note that in OpenMP, all thread implementations and manipulations are performed behind the scenes. Therefore it is a very convenient library.

Listing 8.3 Basic OpenMP techniques (in *ParallelCores, EMUtility_ParAlg.cpp*).

```cpp
#include <iostream>
#include <iomanip>
#include <sstream>
#include <omp.h>     // Header for OpenMP



void OpenMP_Test( void )
{
  // This is a shared object - the same for all threads.
  // A problem might happen if many threads want to
  // write it SIMULTANEOUSLY.
  std::ostringstream outStream;

  // We start with serial code executed by one thread line-after-line
  outStream << "Beginning with " << omp_get_num_threads() << " thread(s).\n";
  outStream << "Let's enter the omp parallel ...\n";


  // -----------------------
  // --- This is PARALLEL ---
  // Let's see the TEAM of threads in action
  #pragma omp parallel shared( outStream )
  {
      // This is a local variable;, each thread has
      // its own copy of it.
      auto thisThreadNo = omp_get_thread_num();

      // This is also a local object.
      const auto kNumOfThreads = omp_get_num_threads();

      // Let's use 'critical' to allow execution of
      // only one thread at a time - otherwise there
      // will be a mess on the screen.
      // Do NOT forget the 'omp' keyword here
      #pragma omp critical ( critical_0 )
      {
        outStream  << "I'm thread no. "
                   << thisThreadNo << " / " << kNumOfThreads << "\n";
      }

  }
  // Here is the SYNCHRONIZATION BARRIER - after that, all threads have finished
  // only the master executes
  // --- End of PARALLEL ---
  // -----------------------

  // One (master) thread again, no synchronization necessary.
  outStream     << "After crossing the parallel BARRIER we run "
                << omp_get_num_threads() << " thread(s).\n";

  // Let's see what we gathered
  std::cout << outStream.str() << std::endl;

}
```

The output of this code can be as follows:

```
Beginning with 1 thread(s).
Let's enter the omp parallel ...
I'm thread no. 0 / 12
I'm thread no. 1 / 12
I'm thread no. 3 / 12
I'm thread no. 11 / 12
I'm thread no. 4 / 12
I'm thread no. 5 / 12
I'm thread no. 6 / 12
I'm thread no. 7 / 12
I'm thread no. 8 / 12
I'm thread no. 9 / 12
I'm thread no. 10 / 12
I'm thread no. 2 / 12
After crossing the parallel BARRIER we run 1 thread(s).
```

Notice that a total of 12 threads are created in the team and that the critical section is accessed in a random order. But before and after the parallel region, only one thread is active.

An example of an explicit call to the `omp_set_num_threads` is shown on line [58]. If this is omitted, the number of threads in the team will be set to a default value (usually this is the number of cores in the microprocessor).

```
56    // Before the parallel section can set a number
57    // of threads in a thread-team (do not confuse with cores)
58    omp_set_num_threads( 36 );
```

Also notice that including the *omp.h* header is not sufficient to use OpenMP in our projects. We also need to explicitly turn on the OpenMP compiler option. For example, in Microsoft Visual C++, we open the project's property pages and under C/C++, Language, set Open MP Support to Yes (*/openmp*). In the *gcc* and *clang* compilers, we set the `-fopenmp` flag in the command line.

8.4.2 Loop Parallelization and Reduction Operations

The next example shows what is probably the most common operation with OpenMP: parallelizing the `for` loop. The function `Compute_Pi` shown on line [3] in Listing 8.4 computes the value of the constant π in a parallel way. This is done in accordance with the method outlined by Eq. (7.52), which computes the integral in Eq. (7.55).

In Listing 8.4, we can see two objects. The first, defined on line [5], is a constant dx. The second, on line [8], is a simple variable sum of type `double`. Both are shared, but only sum will be changed, since tithis is the total sum of all of the elements that are added in the loop. Therefore, it needs to be synchronized. But since this operation is very common, OpenMP has a special `reduction` clause that allows for easy, safe updates of the shared variable.

Let's now analyze line [11]. Its first part, `omp parallel for`, is an OpenMP directive that joins the action of creating a team of threads with concurrent execution of the loop (in OpenMP, only `for` can be parallelized this way). That is, dividing the data into chunks and distributing computations to threads, as illustrated in Figure 8.3, are entirely up to OpenMP. If the `#pragma` line is removed, we are left with a perfectly functional sequential version of the code. As mentioned previously, the shared variable `sum` is used to collect the sum of the series computed by all the threads. Therefore, after each thread finishes its job, the partial result needs to be added to `sum`. All of these actions are performed safely by providing the `reduction( + : sum )` clause at the end of line [11].

The `for` loop on lines [12–18] is processed in parts by a team of threads. Note that the iterator `i` on line [12] is a local object and does not need to be treated in any special way. The same is true for `c_i` on line [14]. Also, the update of `sum` on line [17] does not require special protection since OpenMP knows its purpose as a result of the previous `reduction` clause and inserts a proper protection mechanism for us. Finally, the result is computed by the master thread on line [21], after the parallel section.

Listing 8.4 Parallel series summation in OpenMP. An example of a `for` loop with a reduction clause (in *ParallelCores, EMUtility_ParAlg.cpp*).

```
1    // Computes pi with arctan(1) series summation.
2    // N - the number of terms in the series.
3    double Compute_Pi( int N )
4    {
5        const double dx = 1.0 / static_cast< double >( N );
6
7        // This is a SHARED variable
8        double sum {};
9
10       // -------------------------------------
11       #pragma omp parallel for reduction( + : sum )
12       for( auto i = 0; i < N; ++ i )
13       {
14           auto c_i = dx * ( static_cast< double >( i ) + 0.5 );    // A local variable
15
16           // sum is shared, but unique access is guaranteed by the reduction
17           sum += 1.0 / ( 1.0 + c_i * c_i );
18       }
19       // -------------------------------------
20
21       return 4.0 * dx * sum;
22   }
```

The only thing left is to launch `Compute_Pi` with various numbers *N* of elements in the series, as well as to measure the execution time. The `OpenMP_Pi_Test` function, defined on line [23], performs these actions.

First, line [26] creates a list of *N* values to test. Then, on line [28], a sequential loop starts, which on line [32] launches `Compute_Pi`, each time with a different value of N. To measure the execution time, the OpenMP `omp_get_wtime` function is called two times to capture the start and finish timestamps.

```
23   void OpenMP_Pi_Test( void )
24   {
25
26       auto N_list = { 100, 1000, 10000, 100000000 };
27
28       for( const auto N : N_list )
29       {
30           // Returns the number of seconds since the OS startup.
31           auto start_time = omp_get_wtime();                  // Get time start point
32           auto pi = Compute_Pi( N );                          // Do computations
33           auto exec_time = omp_get_wtime() - start_time;      // End time
34
```

```
35        std::cout  << "pi(" << N << ")=" << std::setprecision( 12 )
36                   << pi << " in " << exec_time << std::endl;
37    }
38
39 }
```

The results, printed on lines [35–36], were as follows on our test system:

```
pi(100)=3.14160098692 in 0.0273515000008
pi(1000)=3.14159273692 in 7.90000194684e-06
pi(10000)=3.14159265442 in 5.99999912083e-05
pi(100000000)=3.14159265359 in 0.0788575999904
```

On the other hand, running the code with the #pragma commented out – that is, in a sequential fashion – gave the following output.

```
pi(100)=3.14160098692 in 6.00004568696e-07
pi(1000)=3.14159273692 in 4.60000592284e-06
pi(10000)=3.14159265442 in 4.51999949291e-05
pi(100000000)=3.14159265359 in 0.506925399997
```

The computed values of π are identical for the same N. Naturally, this is good news. But even if we have coded correctly to avoid hazards with unprotected shared variables, there can be differences in numerical values. Why does this happen? Because operations on floating-point values are burdened by phenomena such as rounding errors. In effect, this means addition is not associative in general, as discussed in Section 7.4. Hence, the differences in the order of summation between the sequential and parallel implementations can result in slightly different values.

Interesting conclusions can also be drawn from collating the execution times for corresponding values of N, as shown in Table 8.2. Notice that in all the cases except the last, the sequential version of the code is faster than the parallel version. This may be surprising at first glance. But the explanation is apparent as soon as we recall that creating and calling threads consumes time and memory. Thus it is not efficient to launch threads for tasks with a small amount of data. This also explains why, for significant values of N, the parallel implementation is over six times faster. OpenMP has a special if clause that turns on the parallel mechanism only after a given condition is met. Hence, if line [11] is changed to the following

```
11   #pragma omp parallel for reduction( + : sum )  if( N > 100000000 )
```

the previous code will execute as desired.

Table 8.2 Timings for sequential and parallel versions of the series summation algorithm with respect to the number N of summed elements.

N	100	1000	10 000	100 000 000
Serial [s]	6e-07	4.6e-06	4.52e-05	0.51
Parallel [s]	0.027	7.9e-06	6–05	0.079
Speed increase	2.2e-5	0.58	0.75	**6.5**

8.4.3 Massive Data Parallelization

Our final example shows a parallel implementation of multiplying `EMatrix` objects. The `EMatrix` class was defined in Listing 4.7.

The definition of `operator *` begins on line [2] in Listing 8.5. The code follows the `MultMatrix` function presented in Listing 3.23; the only change is the addition of lines [15–18]. They contain the OpenMP directive with clauses to make the outermost `for` operate in a parallel fashion. We will explain their meaning and then test the performance of this function.

Listing 8.5 Parallel version of `operator *` for `EMatrix` objects (in *ParallelCores*, *EMUtility_ParAlg.cpp*).

```cpp
1   // It can be used as follows: c = a * b;
2   EMatrix    operator * ( const EMatrix & a, const EMatrix & b )
3   {
4       const auto a_cols = a.GetCols();
5       const auto a_rows = a.GetRows();
6
7       const auto b_cols = b.GetCols();
8       const auto b_rows = b.GetRows();
9
10      assert( a_cols == b_rows );            // Dimensions must be the same
11
12      EMatrix  c( a_rows, b_cols, 0.0 );  // Output matrix has these dimensions
13
14      // Split the outermost for loop and run each chunk in a separate thread
15      #pragma omp parallel for \
16              shared( a, b, c, a_rows, b_cols, a_cols ) \
17              default( none ) \
18              schedule( static )
19      // Only the outermost loop will be made parallel
20      for( Dim ar = 0; ar < a_rows; ++ ar )           // Traverse rows of a
21        for( Dim bc = 0; bc < b_cols; ++ bc )         // Traverse cols of b
22          for( Dim ac = 0; ac < a_cols; ++ ac )       // Traverse cols of a == rows of b
23            c[ ar ][ bc ] += a[ ar ][ ac ] * b[ ac ][ bc ];
24
25      return c;
26  }
```

Actually, lines [15–18] are only visible as split into multiple lines: because of the line *ending* with the backslash symbol \, its following (but invisible) newline character is simply ignored by the preprocessor. In this context, \ operates as *a line continuation character*, effectively reducing lines [15–18] to one line, which is necessary to be correctly interpreted as an OpenMP directive. We emphasize that to be a line continuation, \ *must be the last* character in a line. We have already seen \ in another context, i.e. in *two-character escape sequences*, such as \n, \t, and \\. Hence, \ means two different things depending on the context.

The first `omp parallel for` on line [15], seen earlier in `Compute_Pi`, instructs OpenMP to prepare a team of threads that will run portions of `for` concurrently. The division of work is performed by the OpenMP library, but we will be able to give it some clues.

The second line `shared()` on line [16] declares all of the arguments to be shared objects. We know that these need to be treated in a special way to avoid hazards. However, since they are only read here, we do not need to include any synchronization objects like the `critical`, etc.

`default( none )` on line [17] tells the compiler to list all of the objects used in the parallel section. Although all objects by default are treated as shared, their proper classification as shared or private is very important to avoid race conditions.

Finally, in line [18], `schedule( static )` defines the required work-assignment scheme for the threads. This line does not end with a slash, since it closes the entire `omp parallel for` directive. In the `static` scheme, each thread obtains roughly the same amount of work, which is optimal for a balanced workload. There are also other schemes, such as `dynamic` (OpenMP 2020).

The OpenMP directive with clauses pertains only to the first `for` loop on line [20]. The other two, i.e. on lines [21, 22], are local to each thread. Moreover, in each thread, these `for` loops operate sequentially, although *nested threads* are also possible in OpenMP.

Finally, note that all the other objects, such as `ar`, `bc`, and `ac`, are local: each thread will create its own copies of these objects. Therefore, they need not be protected from access by other threads. But as always, we need to be sure they are properly initialized.

If threads need to make a local copy of an object that is defined before `#pragma omp`, the object should be declared with the `private` clause. But this way, objects declared private are not initialized by default. To ensure proper initialization, we must either place the initialization (assignment) in the code or use the `firstprivate` clause.

The `OpenMP_MultMatrix_Test` function, defined on line [27], serves to prepare random matrix objects and run matrix multiplication to measure its performance time. Again, time measurement is accomplished with the `omp_get_time` function.

```
27   void OpenMP_MultMatrix_Test( void )
28   {
29      const auto kCols { 1024 }, kRows { 1024 };
30      EMatrix   a( kCols, kRows ), b( kRows, kCols );
31
32      RandInit( a );
33      RandInit( b );
34
35      auto start_time = omp_get_wtime();                  // Get time start point
36
37      EMatrix   c( a * b );
38
39      auto exec_time = omp_get_wtime() - start_time;    // End time measurement
40
41
42      std::cout << "Middle elem val: " << c[ kCols / 2 ][ kCols / 2 ] << std::endl;
43      std::cout << "Computation time: " << exec_time << std::endl;
44   }
```

The results measured on our test machine are shown in Figure 8.4. Because only one line has the OpenMP directive (and with no other changes to the code), execution was six times faster.

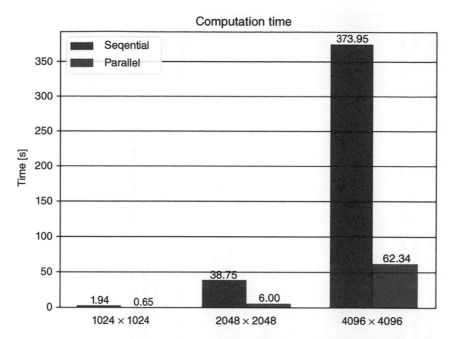

Figure 8.4 Comparing the performance times for multiplying matrices of different sizes in a sequential implementation (blue) and a parallel implementation with OpenMP (red). For large matrices, speed increases by more than six times.

But again, we have only scratched the surface. There have been great achievements in the acceleration of computations. CPU/GPU hybrid systems are especially remarkable and led to the foundation of deep learning and AI. Returning to the problem of matrix multiplication, `EMatrix` is not an optimal representation. Also, more advanced multiplication algorithms are available to take advantage of cache memory (Section 2.1). For example, faster execution speed can be achieved by first transposing the second of the multiplied matrices and then using the multiplication algorithms with the second matrix transposed. As a result, if matrix elements are arranged by rows in memory, cache accesses are more optimal. Table 8.3 summarizes the most common OpenMP constructs, clauses, and functions.

Table 8.3 Common OpenMP constructs, clauses, and functions with examples.

OpenMP directive	Description	Examples
`#pragma omp parallel for [clause[[,]clause]...]`	Fork `for` loop iterations to parallel threads.	In this example, a minimum value and its index are found in a vector. `omp parallel` starts a team of thread; `firstprivate` declares `loc_val` and `loc_offset` to be private for each thread and, at first, initialized exactly as in their definitions; and `shared` declares the objects to be co-used by all threads. `omp for nowait` says to execute the following `for` loop in parallel and not wait for other sub-loops, but to immediately proceed to `omp critical`. This is a guard for the critical section and can be entered by only one thread at a time.
| | | ```cpp
std::tuple< int, int > FindMin( const std::vector< int > & v )
{
    const auto data_num = v.size();
    if( data_num == 0 )
        return std::make_tuple( -1, -1 );

    const auto * src_data_ptr = & v[ 0 ];

    auto sh_val = * src_data_ptr;
    auto sh_offset { 0 };

    // Take an upper limit to find the lowest value
    auto loc_val { std::numeric_limits< int >::max() };
    auto loc_offset { -1 };

    // Use firstprivate to convey the initial values of loc_val and loc_offset.
    // Shared objects are listed in the shared
    #pragma omp parallel default( none ) \
        firstprivate( loc_val, loc_offset ) \
        shared( sh_val, sh_offset, src_data_ptr, data_num )
``` |
`#pragma omp parallel`	Starts independent units of work.	
`#pragma omp single`	Ensures that exactly a single thread executes a block of code.	
`#pragma omp critical`	Construction for mutual exclusion: at any instant only one thread can perform the block encompassed by `critical`.	
`#pragma omp parallel sections`	Creates a team of threads, and starts independent sections. Sections execute in parallel to each other.	
`#pragma omp section`	Starts independent units of work in a section.	
`private( list )`	Declares a variable as private. Each thread contains its own uninitialized copy (for initialization, use `firstprivate`).	
`firstprivate( list )`	Initializes a private variable with the value of the variable with the same name before entering the thread.	
`lastprivate( list )`	Makes the last value of a private variable available after termination of a thread.	
```

```cpp
{
    // Each thread will take its payload and determine
    // its lowest local pixel (reduction for min)
    #pragma omp for nowait
    for( auto i = 0; i < data_num; ++ i )
    {
        auto e = em { src_data_ptr[ i ] };
        if( elem < loc_val )
        {
            loc_val = elem;
            loc_offset = i;
        }
    } // no barrier here due to the nowait clause

    // Enter a critical section here
    #pragma omp critical
    if( loc_val < sh_val )
    {
        sh_val = loc_val;        // Save lowest value in this thread
        sh_offset = loc_offset;  // and its position
    }

    } // a barrier here

    return std::make_tuple( sh_val, sh_offset );
}
```

reduction (*operator* : *list*)	Orders parallel execution of the associative and commutative operations (such as +, *, etc.) with the aggregation of partial results at the thread barrier.
ordered	Forces a sequential order of execution within a parallel loop.
schedule (*kind* [, *chunk size*])	Controls the distribution of loop iterations over the threads. The scheduling modes are *static*, *dynamic*, and *guided*.
shared (*list*)	Declares objects that will be shared among the threads. Each object can be freely accessed by each of the threads at any moment. Hence, objects that are written to have to be protected, e.g. with omp critical.
nowait	Threads don't wait for synchronization at the barrier at the end of the parallel loop construction.
default (*none* | *shared*)	Tells how the compiler should treat local variables. If *none*, then each variable needs to be explicitly declared as shared or private. If *shared*, then all variables are treated as shared.

(Continued)

Table 8.3 (continued)

OpenMP directive	Description	Examples
num_threads (*N*)	Sets the number of threads to be used in a parallel block.	MSE computes the mean squared error from the vectors u and v: $MSE = \sum_{i=0}^{N-1} \left(u[i] - v[i] \right)^2$.
omp_get_num_ threads()	An OpenMP function that returns the number of threads in the current team.	omp parallel for is used to start parallel execution of a team of threads, reduction (+ : sum) introduces a shared variable sum to be safely updated by the threads (so no synchronization is necessary), schedule (static) imposes an even burden on the threads, and if launches parallel execution only if $N > 10000$.
| **omp_set_num_ threads**( *N* ) | Sets the number of threads to *N*. | ```
// Computes the mean squared error (MSE) between two real vectors
double MSE( const std::vector< double > & u, const std::vector< double > & v )
{
    const auto data_num = std::min( u.size(), v.size() );
``` |
| **omp_get_thread_ num**() | Returns a thread number (its ID) within the parallel region. | ```
    if( data_num == 0 )      // Simple error checking
        return -1.0;

    const auto * u_data = & u[ 0 ];
    const auto * v_data = & v[ 0 ];
``` |
| **omp_get_nested**() | Check whether nested parallelism is enabled. | ```
    auto sum { 0.0 };        // Shared due to the reduction clause
``` |
| **omp_set_nested** ( 0/1 ) | Enables or disables nested parallelism | ```
    #pragma omp parallel for default( none ) \
            shared( u_data, v_data, data_num ) \
            reduction( + : sum ) \
            schedule( static ) \
            if( data_num > 10000 )

    for( auto i = 0; i < data_num; ++ i )
    {
        auto diff = u_data[ i ] - v_data[ i ];
        sum += diff * diff;
    }   // Here we have a common barrier

    return sum / static_cast< double >( data_num );
}
``` |

| `omp_get_wtime ()` | Returns an absolute wall clock time in seconds. | In this example, a parallel pipeline is organized in sections. Threads in each section operate in parallel. |

```
void ParSections( void )
{
    const auto N { 100000 };
    // ... init data

    omp_set_nested( 1 ); // Allow for nested parallelism
    // Sections allow for a pipeline organization.
    // Create a team of threads.
    // If sufficient threads, the sections execute simultaneously.
    #pragma omp parallel sections
    {
        // Executes simultaneously with the next secton
        #pragma omp section
        {
            // If sufficient threads, there will be nested parallelism
            #pragma omp parallel shared( N ) num_threads( 2 )
            for( auto i = 0; i < N; ++i )
            {
                // ... compute something
            }
        }
```

(Continued)

Table 8.3 (continued)

OpenMP directive	Description	Examples
		``
// Executes simultaneously with the previous secton
#pragma omp section
{

    #pragma omp parallel shared(N) num_threads(4)
    for(auto i = 0; i < N; ++i)
    {
        // ... compute something
    }

}

}
```
The `omp_set_nested` function allows nested parallelism. The `num_threads` function sets a number of threads to be allocated for the closest parallel section. If a sufficient number of threads are available, then the `for` loop within `section` will execute the nested threads. |
```

8.5   Summary

Things to Remember

- Before refactoring code from a sequential version to a parallel version, measure its performance with the profiler to identify the most time consuming fragments. Do not guess
- Identify shared objects in the code. Those that are changed even by a single thread must be protected to ensure mutual exclusion
- Many of the C++ standard algorithms have parallel implementations, which we can use by providing the `std::execution::par` parameter
- C++ comes equipped with the standard parallel library
- OpenMP offers a safe, fast way to make C++ programs operate in parallel

Questions and Exercises

1. Refactor the matrix addition code shown in Listing 4.10 to allow for parallel operation. Hint: follow the code in Listing 8.5.

2. As shown in Listing 8.5, matrix multiplication requires three loops. In theory, they can be organized in 3! = 6 permutations. Extend the code from Listing 8.5, and measure the performance of different loop structures.

3. Consider the following matrix identity

$$\mathbf{C} = \mathbf{A} \cdot \mathbf{B} = \mathbf{A} \cdot \left(\mathbf{B}^T\right)^T$$

where $\mathbf{B}^T$ means transposition of matrix $\mathbf{B}$. What would be a computational benefit of implementing matrix multiplication in the following two steps?

a. Matrix transposition $\mathbf{B} \rightarrow \mathbf{B}^T$
b. Multiplication of a matrix with the transposed-matrix: $\mathbf{AB}^T$

Implement matrix multiplication in accordance with these two steps, and measure its performance. Compare with the code in Listing 8.5. Hint: analyze the operation of the microprocessor cache memory (Section 2.1).

4. Implement a parallel version of the definite integration for any integrable function. Consult exercise 23 in Section 7.6. Measure its performance.

5. Write test functions for the code snippets shown in Table 8.3, and measure their performance.

6. Data variance provides a measure of how values from a data sample differ from their mean (data deviation measure). One of the methods to compute the variance is based on the following relations:

$$V\left(\mathbf{x}\right) = \frac{1}{N-1} \sum_{i=1}^{N} \left(x_i - m_x\right)^2$$

where

$$m_x = \frac{1}{N} \sum_{i=1}^{N} x_i$$

denotes the mean value of a vector **x**, and *N* stands for the number of elements in the vector.

    a. Implement a serial version of this two-pass algorithm.[3]

    b. Write a test function that will (i) create a vector with randomly generated values from a given distribution and (ii) compute their variance.

    c. Implement a parallel version of the two-pass algorithm. Compare the return values and execution times of the serial and parallel versions.

    d. Apply the compensated summation algorithms discussed in Section 7.4.7. Compare the results.

7. C++20 comes with an interesting feature – *coroutines*. These are functions that can suspend execution and store the current state, to be resumed later with the state restored. This allows for a number of interesting mechanisms such as *asynchronous* tasks, non-blocking I/O handling, value generators, etc. A function becomes a coroutine if it contains any of the following constructions: `co_await`, `co_yield`, or `co_return`. For example, the following `next_int_gen` coroutine returns the consecutive integer value on each call:

```
1   generator< int > next_int_gen( int val = 0 )
2   {
3       for(;;)
4           co_yield val ++;
5   }
```

`co_yield` suspends execution of the `next_int_gen` function, stores the state of `val` object in the `generator< int >`, and returns the current value of `val` through the `generator< int >` object.

    a. Read more about coroutines (*https://en.cppreference.com/w/cpp/language/coroutines*), and write a test function to experiment with `next_int_gen`.

    b. Try to implement a new version of the `range` class from Section 6.5, using coroutines.

8. Implement a parallel version of the MSE defined in Table 8.3 using the `std::transform_reduce`. Compare performance of your implementation with the OpenMP based version.

9. Using the `std::transform_reduce` and the `std::filesystem::recursive_directory_iterator` implement a serial code to recursively traverse a given directory and to sum up sizes of all regular files (see Section 6.2.7). Then design a parallel solution. However, since the above iterator cannot be directly used in a parallel version of the `transform_reduce`, implement a producer-consumer scheme.

---

3 More variance algorithms can be found at *https://en.wikipedia.org/wiki/Algorithms_for_calculating_variance*.

Appendix

This appendix contains sections with various topics related to software development in C++. For instance, the preprocessor, common to the C and C++ languages, is a separate tool for reformatting source code before compilation. We have encountered its directives from the very beginning and treated them as auxiliary to the main programming tasks. However, in the following section on preprocessor directives, all these can be found grouped together in the form of a reference. After that, we provide a short introduction to C. Although programming in C++ does not require learning C, in many cases some basic knowledge of C helps with understanding C++ constructions such as passing parameters to the `main` function. After all, C++ grew up from C. We will also include descriptions of the graphical user interface (GUI) platforms available for C++ programming and the C++ programming toolchain, as well as some information about software testing.

A.1   Preprocessor Directives

The preprocessor is a text-formatting tool that is run just before compilation. Its role is to include files into the translation unit, expand defined names and macros, selectively add/remove parts of the code, remove comments, etc. After the preprocessor runs, the source code can still be meaningful to the programmer, but usually it is not easily readable (in most compilers, such a preprocessed version can be generated upon request). The preprocessor's operations are governed by a relatively small number of preprocessor directives and preprocessing rules shown in Table A.1.

Although preprocessing rules have been nearly the same for years, there are some subtle differences between preprocessing C and C++ code. The most common directives, which are also frequently used in C/C++ code, are `#include`, conditional code inclusion with `#if` – `#endif`, and the include guard `#pragma once` to avoid the problem of multiple inclusion of a header file. These are also used in examples presented in this book. But in modern code, preprocessor directives should be used rarely, since more advanced and safer constructions such as constant objects, `assert`, `cassert`, `constexpr`, etc. are available. Also, modern C++20 introduces *modules*,[1] which in new projects suppress the use of classic headers.

---

1 See "Overview of modules in C++," *https://docs.microsoft.com/en-us/cpp/cpp/modules-cpp?view=vs-2019*.

Introduction to Programming with C++ for Engineers, First Edition. Bogusław Cyganek.
© 2021 John Wiley & Sons Ltd. Published 2021 by John Wiley & Sons Ltd.
Companion website: http://home.agh.edu.pl/~cyganek/BookCpp.htm

Table A.1 Preprocessor directives.

Directive	Description	Examples
| `#include < fname >` | Loads a (header) file *fname* to the translation unit (the same outcome as open-copy-paste). | ```
// Common SL (system) header files
#include <string>
#include <vector>
#include <algorithm>
#include <iostream>
#include <iterator>
#include <array>
#include <random>
#include <fstream>
#include <tuple>
#include <utility>
#include <algorithm>
#include <chrono>
``` |
| `#include " fname "` | The version with `<>` should be used for system headers, since the compiler looks for it in system directories. | ```
// User's headers
#include "range.h"
#include "CurrencyCalc.h"
``` |
| | The second version with `" "` searches first in the user's directory. Hence this version should be used for headers created by a user. | To define a special version of code, we can use

```
#define CODE_VERSION  2

#if CODE_VERSION == 2
          // Code for ver. 2
#endif
``` |

#define *name*
#define *name val*
#define macro(arg)
	Used to define a *name* or a *macro*. These are then expanded and used by other directives of the preprocessor.
	
	A frequently used application is to create an include guard for a header, to define a code version or to define macros that expand before compilation.
	
	Although macros look like functions, they are not, and they obscure the code. Therefore they should not be used unless necessary. Instead, in C++, we can use const values or constexpr (Section 3.13.2.2, *GROUP 4*, Table 3.15).
		We define a macro MAX with two parameters x and y:
		
		`#define MAX(x,y) ((x)>(y)?(x):(y))`
		
		For example:
		
		`cout << MAX( "Fox", "Dog" ) << endl;`
		
		is expanded to
		
		`cout << (("Fox")>("Dog")?("Fox"):` `("Dog")) << endl;`
		
		and then compiled. Do not forget the parentheses in the macro. There can be only one definition of a variable, constant, function, etc. in the program. But header files are included many times, and their inclusions can be chained. Thus, to ensure that a header is included only once, we can use the following preprocessor pattern, called *an include guard*:
		
		`// This is TransDir.h header`
		
		`#ifndef TransDir_h`
		`#define TransDir_h`
		
		`// These definitions are included`
		`// only once`
		
		`#endif // TransDir_h`
		
		First it checks if the *TransDir_h* name has been already defined. If not, it is defined, and the rest of the file is included. Otherwise, nothing between `#ifndef` and `#endif` is included. The other option is to use `#pragma once`.

(Continued)

Table A.1 (continued)

Directive	Description	Examples

(1)
 	
`#ifdef` *name*
 	
(2)
 	
`#if` *condition*
`#else`
`#endif`
	Conditional compilation. There are two versions. In (1), the code is compiled if *name* has been defined with the `#define` directive.
	
	In (2), the code between `#if` ... `#else` is compiled if *condition* is not 0 (true). Otherwise, the code between `#else` ... `#endif` is used.
	`#else` is optional.
		To compile code only on a selected OS
		
		`#if _WIN32`
		
		`    #include <urlmon.h>`
		`    #pragma comment(lib, "urlmon.lib")`
		
		`#else    // A version for other OSs`
		
		`#endif`
		
		The following trick is used to exclude a fragment of code from the build:
		
		`#if 0`
		
		`    // Whatever is here will not be compiled`
		`    ++ x;`
		
		`#endif`
		
		We can restore it quite easily by commenting out the lines containing `#if` and `#endif`.

`#pragma`	Compiler-specific option.	`// A one-time include guard`
		`#pragma once`
		`// Create a parallel for loop with OpenMP`
		`#pragma omp parallel for`

`#undef`	Un-defines a macro or name introduced by a previous `#define`.	Let's change our previous MAX macro and make it "soft."
		
		`#undef MAX`
		`#define MAX(x,y)  ((x)>=(y)?(x):(y))`

`#error`
`#warning`
	`#error` stops compilation.
	`#warning` issues a platform-dependent diagnostic message (sometimes used with `#pragma`).
		`#if !defined(__cplusplus )`
		`#error This code needs the C++ compiler`
		`#endif`

#	Used with the #define macro. It makes the first argument after # be returned as a string in quotation marks.
##	Concatenates a token before and after the operator ##.
__FILE__ __LINE__ __TIME__ __DATE__ __cplusplus	Special predefined preprocessor values ("magic constants"): 1. Current file name (string literal) 2. Current line (numeric) 3. Current time (string) 4. Current date (string) 5. Defined if a C++ compiler is used

The following fragment defines the REQUIRE macro, which checks whether expr is true when executing in the DEBUGGING version of the code. For other versions, it reduces to a semicolon ; denoting an empty expression.

```
#if      DEBUGGING

void REQUIRE_Fun( int expr,
                  const char * expr_name,
                  const char * file_name,
                  const char * line_num );

#define _QUOTE(x) #x
#define QUOTE(x) _QUOTE(x)

// Put REQUIRE to test expressions
#define REQUIRE(expr)                  \
    { REQUIRE_Fun( expr, #expr,        \
      __FILE__, QUOTE(__LINE__) ) ;  }

#else  // DEBUGGING

#define REQUIRE(expr)   ;

#endif // DEBUGGING
```

The DEBUGGING version should define the REQUIRE_Fun function elsewhere. Its role is to display a message to the user or to a log file on a given platform. expr is an expression provided to REQUIRE, whereas #expr is that expression expressed as a string, i.e. within quotation marks " ".

QUOTE(__LINE__) after the first pass of the preprocessor evolves into _QUOTE(num), which after the second pass is converted into num expressed as a string, i.e. something like "num".

In modern C++, we use assert and cassert for this diagnostic purpose.

A.2 Short Introduction to C

C is still frequently used in embedded systems, calls to OS API functions, hardware programming, and some older libraries that are still in operation, such as numerical computations, communication, image format converters, etc. This section is aimed at readers who already know at least the basics of C++ and wish to extend their knowledge of programming techniques characteristic to the C language. Knowing the basics of C also helps with understanding the foundations of C++.

The history of C began in 1972–1973 when Dennis Ritchie from Bell Labs created its first version to facilitate writing utility programs in the Unix OS. Soon, even the Unix kernel was implemented in C. This was a real breakthrough since previous OSs were written in assembly languages, which made their code almost not portable when newer processors appeared on the market. In 1978, *The C Programming Language* by Dennis Ritchie and Brian Kernighan was published, beginning the era of C. Its second edition in 1988 became an ANSII standard for C (Kernighan and Ritchie 1988). Since then, the language has gained in popularity and undergone many revisions. An important revision, C11, was released in 2011. C, along with Simula 67, inspired Bjarne Stroustrup when he was designing C++ (Stroustrup 2007).

Since C++ inherited many features of the C language, and because people have been using C for almost 50 years, it is good to know some of its constructions, functions, and features, especially if we foresee one of the following use cases:

- *Calling OS services* – Since most OSs are written in C, calling their services – for example, when launching new threads, communicating with device drivers, opening files, etc. – at the interface level requires C
- *Parallel processing* – Although C++ has had thread and synchronization libraries since C++11, it is common practice to use some C constructs when developing parallel code. Many parallel programming platforms such as OpenCL, CUDA, and OpenMP allow for some form of C++ code, but there are still many C-like constructions: pointer manipulations, memory copying, etc
- *Embedded systems programming* – Due to the small code footprint, many small microprocessor systems are still based on C code. Also, writing device drivers and interrupt services frequently requires C constructions rather than C++ with the Standard Library
- *Hardware programming in the domain of field programmable gate arrays (FPGAs)* –Although the native languages to program FPGA are VHDL and Verilog, there have been attempts to make hardware programming easier by inventing variants of C. For example Vivado, Synflow, and OpenCL allow us to program vast functionality for the FPGA but in a more efficient way than at the gate level
- *Legacy code* – There are hundreds of libraries and billions of code lines, probably including some in your user's products. For many companies, fast compilation and much easier C code portability are important benefits in systems that have been maintained for years
- *Understanding code in books* – For instance, we referred to such code frequently, such as (Bryant and O'Hallaron 2015; Fan 2015; Press et al. 2007; Grune et al. 2012)

It is no surprise that C is one of the most widely used programming languages. It is also interesting to note that most C++ compilers can compile C code with no problem.

The basic C constructions can be grouped as follows:

- Arrays
- Structures
- Pointers
- Functions

In the following sections, we focus upon flavors specific to C, assuming its C99 version.

A.2.1 Built-in Arrays

The most basic built-in data structure is *an array*. It has a linear organization and access type in the computer's operational memory. An array contains elements of the same type, and the number of elements is known at compile-time.[2] All of these elements are located one after another in a continuous memory space (see Figure 3.2). Let's start with an example and define an array named `tab`, which will contain four elements of `int` type. This can be done as follows:

```
1   enum Dim { kTabSize = 4 };     /* Works in C and C++ */
2   int tab[ kTabSize ] = { 0 };   /* Init all elems to 0 */
```

As mentioned earlier, when defining an array, the number of elements must be known. On line [1], the enumerated type `Dim` with one constant `kTabSize` is defined. This works fine in C, as well as in C++. But in C++, to use a fixed-size array, a better option is to use the `std::array` class (Section 3.10).

A fixed-size array with four elements of type `int` is defined on line [2]. Although not obligatory, in most cases, it is best to initialize the elements of an array immediately. This is done on line [2] by providing the initialization list `{ 0 }`. General schemes for defining fixed-size arrays, without and with initialization, are presented in Figure A.1.

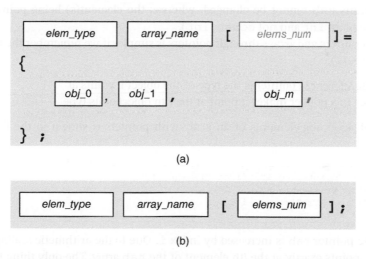

(a)

(b)

Figure A.1 Syntax of built-in arrays. (a) Definition of an array of exactly *elems_num* of *elem_type* and with initialization from the supplied initialization list. If *elems_num* is omitted, then the compiler assumes its number exactly as in the initialization list. If *elems_num* is provided but there are not sufficient values listed in the initializer, then the remaining objects are set to their default values (zero initialization). (b) Array definition with no initialization.

We strive for object initialization at creation time – see the *resource acquisition is initialization* (RAII) principle in C++ (Section 5.2.1.1). The array definition shown in Figure A.1a follows this scheme. If `elems_num` is omitted, then the compiler will set the number and values of elements

---

2 In C99, it is possible to define variable-length arrays (VLAs), whose size can be given by a variable. However, they incur some code overhead and should be avoided.

exactly as in the initializer list. For initialization, both variables and constant objects can be used. Otherwise, if elems_num is provided but there are not enough values in the initializer list, the remaining values are set to default values; for built-in types, this means setting them to 0. On the other hand, if there are more initialization values than stated in elems_num, a compilation error is issued. However, the language is flexible enough to allow us to skip initialization, as shown in Figure A.1b. This option can be used for large arrays when runtime optimization is a primary issue. In such cases, the array values should be set in subsequent lines of code before they are used.

Elements of an array can be accessed with the subscript operator [*i*], as shown on lines [4–5] of the following code snippet. In this case, remember that:

■ The allowable index *i* is in the range from 0 to $N-1$, where N is the number of elements in the array. In our example, the number of elements has already been defined as kTabSize

```
3    /* Set new values to tab */
4    for( int i = 0; i < kTabSize; ++ i )
5        tab[ i ] = i;
```

Another important aspect of fixed-size arrays is that the name of an array is

■ A *constant pointer to the first element* of the array

Hence, tab in our example is of type int * const, and it points at the element located at index 0. This means tab cannot be changed, whereas the element(s) being pointed to can be changed (this is a plain int and not const int).

Manipulating pointers and arrays through pointers is simpler if we remember the following two facts (see Section 3.12):

■ The type of a dereferenced pointer is the type of the object it points at
■ Adding *n* values to a pointer makes it point at the *n*th object of its type

An example of accessing elements of an array with pointers is shown in the following code snippet:

```
6    /* arr is a const pointer to its first element, */
7    /* so we can also write this */
8    for( int i = 0; i < kTabSize; ++ i )
9        * ( tab + i ) = i;
```

On line [9], the pointer tab is increased by index i. Due to the arithmetic scaling of pointers, (tab + i) points exactly at the *i*th element of the tab array. The only thing left to do is to dereference that pointer and assign a value to it. Note that adding to a pointer *scales* in such a way that the next element of the array, not a next byte, is accessed.

In the third version, elements of the array are accessed with the pointer tab_ptr, initially set to point at the first object in the tab array. But this time tab_ptr is updated to point at the elements of the array one by one.

```
1    /* Array access via the pointer */
2    int * tab_ptr = tab;        /* tab is constant, tab_ptr is variable */
3    for( int i = 0; i < kTabSize; ++ i )
4        * tab_ptr ++ = i;
```

The previous operations are illustrated in Figure A.2.

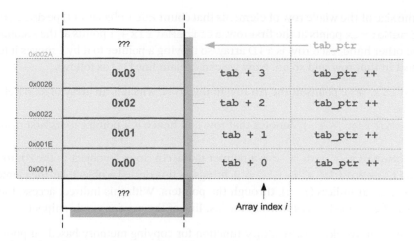

Figure A.2 Accessing elements of an array by adding an offset to the base pointer `tab` and incrementing a pointer `tab_ptr`. Example memory addresses are shown assuming four-byte allocations for `int` objects.

A.2.1.1. Multidimensional Fixed-Size Arrays

A built-in array can contain other built-in array(s) as its elements. This way, we can create multidimensional arrays, as in the following example:

```
1    /* Multidimensional arrays */
2    enum Dims { kRows = 2, kCols = 2 };
3
4    /* kRows is external, kCols internal index */
5    double affineMatrix[ kRows ][ kCols ] = { 0.0 }; /* initialize all elements to 0.0 */
```

Its elements can be accessed using subscripts, as in the following example:

```
6    /* Set all off-diagonal elements to -1 */
7    for( int r = 0; r < kRows; ++ r )
8      for( int c = 0; c < kCols; ++ c )
9        if( r != c )
10           affineMatrix[ r ][ c ] = -1.0;
```

Multidimensional structures can also be accessed with pointers. The following example performs the same action, with only one difference between lines [10] and [15]:

```
11   /* The same with pointers */
12   for( int r = 0; r < kRows; ++ r )
13     for( int c = 0; c < kCols; ++ c )
14       if( r != c )
15         * ( * ( affineMatrix + r ) + c ) = -1.0;
```

To identify the key steps in this expression, let's first identify the type of `affineMatrix`. This is a pointer to the first element, which happens to be a single row: a 1D array of type `double [ kCol]`. Hence, `affineMatrix` follows pointer scaling, which in a single increment advances its value by the size of the whole row of elements that count kCol objects of type double. In other words, affineMatrix points at the first row, affineMatrix + 1 points at the second row, and so on. On the other hand, each row is a 1D array, so moving a pointer to it by 1 moves it to the next double object in that row, and so on. Now we can explain line [15] as follows:

- affineMatrix + r points at the *r*th row in the array, which is an array of kCol elements of type double
- * (affineMatrix + r) denotes that row and hence is a pointer to its first double type object
- * (affineMatrix + r) + c is a pointer to the *c*th double object in the *r*th row
- * (* (affineMatrix + r) + c) brings us this double object, i.e. the element of the affineMatrix at indices (r, c), through the pointers. With this indirect access, the value of the object can be set to -1.0, as shown in the last line of the previous code snippet

Table 3.15 lists the BackwardMemCopy function for copying memory based on pointer operations. Also, the MiniMatrix class exemplifies the use of pointer-based access to matrix elements.

A.2.2 Passing Arrays to Functions – The Main Function

The main function is the first function called on behalf of our program. However, main is not the first code executed after launching the program, since there are some housekeeping tasks to do, such as static and global variable initialization, etc. There should be only one main function in the program, and it should be defined as either one of the two following versions:

1. With no input parameters:

```
int main()
{
    /* body of main */
}
```

2. With call arguments:

```
int main( int argc, char ** argv )
{
    /* body of main */
}
```

The meaning of the second version is explained in in Figure A.3, which shows a call in the terminal window of the example *CPro.exe* with two parameters *2019* and *bin*. The system passes control to the main function with the two parameters. The parameter argc conveys the number of elements in the array of C-style strings, pointed to by the second parameter argv. Thus, argv represents a table with elements that are C-style strings (i.e. tables of char ending with the 0 sentinel). The first string of this table holds the full path of the called application. The next string contains consecutive parameters passed in the command line, and so on. Numerical values need to be converted from the C style strings.

Thus, having received argc in main, we should use only argv[0] to argv[argc-1], although argv[argc] is also guaranteed to be 0 (i.e. nullptr).

The two arguments of main show a C-like way to pass an array to a function: as a pointer to its first element and the total number of elements in the array. Since the array stores C-like text of char * type, the pointer to its first element has the type char **.

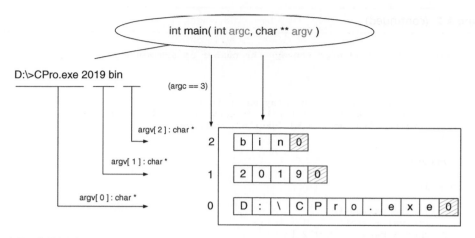

Figure A.3 Calling `CPro.exe 2019 bin` in the command terminal window. The system passes control to the `CPro` main `function` with `argc` and `argv` set as shown. The parameter `argc` conveys the number of elements in the array of C-style strings pointed to by the second parameter, `argv`. The first of these strings contains a full path of the called application. The subsequent strings contain consecutive parameters passed in the command line. Numerical values need to be converted from strings.

Listing A.1 contains a complete C implementation of *CPro.exe*. The program first reads a decimal value and conversion base from the command line and then outputs a converted value in the requested base. The two standard C headers containing declarations of frequently used mathematical and input/output functions are included on lines [1–2]. Line [7] contains the declaration of the `ToBinConvert` function, which is called in `main` to convert a decimal value into its binary representation. Its complete definition is placed after `main`. To write a comment in C, we use the `/* */` symbols. C++ inherited this style and introduced `//` type single line comments.

Listing A.1 C program for converting decimal values. Parameters are passed as arguments to the `main` function (in *CPro, main.c*).

```
1    #include <stdlib.h>
2    #include <stdio.h>
3
4
5
6    /* Function declaration. */
7    void ToBinConvert( int val );
8
9
10
11   /* The CProg converts a decimal value into an
12   equivalent in one of the bases: oct, bin, hex.
13   Param no. 1 is a decimal integer value.
14   An optional param no. 2 is the output base "oct", "bin", "hex"
15   If not provided, then the same value is displayed. */
16
17   /* C program starts with the main function */
18   int main( int argc, char ** argv )
19   {
20       printf ( "Value converter. Calling format:\nCPro.exe dec_val [bin,oct,hex]\n" );
```

(Coninued)

Listing A.1 (continued)

```
21
22        switch( argc )        /* argc conveys the number of arguments */
23        {
24           case 2:
25
26              {  /* Only one param - display as it is */
27                 int val = atoi( argv[ 1 ] ); /* Converts ASCII to int */
28                 printf ( "%d [dec] = %d [dec]\n", val, val );
29              }
30
31              break;
32
33           case 3:
34
35              {  /* Two params */
36                 int val = atoi( argv[ 1 ] );
37                 char * base = argv[ 2 ];
38
39                 /* For the base, we need to check only its first letter */
40                 switch( base[ 0 ] )
41                 {
42                    case 'h': /* check lowercase */
43                    case 'H': /* and uppercase at the same time */
44
45                       /* printf will do the conversion for us */
46                       printf ( "%d [dec] = 0x%x [hex]\n", val, val );
47                       break;
48
49                    case 'O':
50                    case 'O':
51
52                       /* printf will do the conversion for us */
53                       printf ( "%d [dec] = 0%o [oct]\n", val, val );
54
55                       break;
56
57                    case 'b':
58                    case 'B':
59
60                       /* Here we need to do the conversion ourselves */
61                       printf ( "%d [dec] = ", val );
62                       ToBinConvert( val );
63                       printf ( " [bin]\n" );
64
65                       break;
66
67                    default:
68
69                       printf ( "Wrong name param. Should be one of: [bin,oct,hex]\n" );
70                       break;
71
72                 }
73
74              }
75
76              break;
77
78           default:
79
80              printf ( "Call with 1 or 2 params.\nCPro dec_val [hex,oct,bin]\n" );
81              break;
82
83        }
```

```
84
85      return 0;              /* Return value 0 indicates SUCCESS. */
86    }
87
```

The definition of the main function, with its argc and argv parameters, starts on line [18]. On line [20], the printf function is used to display the first message informing us of the calling format for *CPro.exe*. Then, based on the number of passed arguments, control is passed by the switch statement (Section 3.13.2.1) on line [22] either to line [24], if there is only one parameter, or to line [33], if there are two parameters. If there is some other number of parameters, action goes to the default section on line [78], and the program terminates with a short message. Let's briefly analyze what happens if there are two parameters (i.e. the value of argc is 3, as explained in Figure A.3). On line [36], the first parameter is read into argv[1] as a C-like string. This is passed as an argument to the atoi function, which converts the C-like ASCII string into a number. Hence, "123" becomes 123, etc.

On line [37], the second call parameter, which hopefully holds the name of the conversion base, is accessed and assigned to the pointer base. Then we need to check whether the text pointed to by base is *bin*, *oct*, *hex*, or something else, since the user could have made a mistake when typing. To compare strings in C, we can use the strcmp or strncmp function (Section A.2.6). But we made this a little simpler here. Since the three text values start differently, we only check the first letters. We also do this with capital letters: for example, *bin* and *BIN* will mean the same thing. This check is done in the second switch starting on line [40].

Depending on the detected base, control is passed to line [42] for hexadecimal, to line [49] for octal, or to line [57] for binary conversion. Of these, the first two conversions can be done quite easily using the printf function on line [46] or [53], respectively, providing it with a proper formatting string: %x for *hex* or %o for *oct*. Hence, we see that printf accepts a variable number of parameters, of which the first is a formatting string. The formatting string defines the format of the output for each of the consecutive variables by including %[*con_str*], where *con_str* denotes a control string. But there is no easy conversion to binary format, so on line [62], our converting ToBinConvert function is called, as we will explain.

On line [85], we leave main and explicitly return 0 in this case. If return 0 is omitted in main, it is automatically generated by the compiler. But it is better to return a value from a function since it has been explicitly declared. Forgetting return in a function other than main, even if the code compiles on some platforms, can lead to undefined behavior. Further, the returned code value can be read out by other applications to see the result of the operation.

How do we determine the binary representation of a decimal value that is already in memory? It is simple – we need to read its bits one after another, starting from the most significant bit, and print them on the screen. This can be done many ways, but we do not know exactly how long the bitstream is, so it is simplest to start processing from the rightmost bit. But in this case, before printing, we need to reverse the bit order. To do so, a recursive function fits well. ToBinConvert performs these actions in barely three lines of code:

```
88    /* Recursively print bits in reverse order thanks to recursion. */
89    void ToBinConvert( int val )
90    {
91      if( val > 1 )
92        ToBinConvert( val >> 1 );      /* Recursive call */
93
94      printf ( "%d", val & 0x01 );     /* Print the last bit */
95    }
```

On line [91], the input integer `val` is checked to see if it is greater than 1. If so, `ToBinConvert` is called recursively on line [92], but its argument is divided by 2. To avoid costly divisions, a much faster right shift operator `>>`, shifting by one place, is applied (*GROUP 7*, Table 3.15). But when recursion ends due to `val` being equal to 1, all the recursive calls return, launching `printf` on line [94]. This, in turn, outputs "0" or "1" depending on the last bit of `val` from its call time.

When we call this simple example, the following appears in the terminal window:

```
D:\BC++\Projects\CPro\build_win\Debug>CPro 2019 bin
Value converter. Calling format:
CPro.exe dec_val [bin,oct,hex]
2019 [dec] = 11111100011 [bin]
Press any key to continue . . .
```

A.2.3 C Structures

The main difference when using C, as opposed to C++, is that functions are totally separate from structures, which contain only publicly accessible data. The second difference is that there is no automatic mechanism for initializing that data in structures: i.e. there are no constructors, since there are no functions inside the C structures. Finally, in C, structures cannot inherit since there is no inheritance mechanism. On the other hand, C structures can contain other C structures, so a composite relation can exist.

To understand the differences, let's analyze the following example. It implements a representation of the quadratic equation and a few associated functions for its initialization and basic computations.

Listing A.2 Definitions of the `QE` structure to hold coefficients of a quadratic equation in the C language (in *CPro, struct_test.c*).

```
1    /* Simple struct to store coeffs of the quadratic equation */
2    struct QE
3    {
4       float a, b, c;
5    };
6
7    /* struct QE is a tag, and we need to introduce the type QE */
8    /* The name of a struct is a tag, rather than the type. */
9    typedef       struct QE        QE;
```

A structure `QE` is defined on lines [2–5]. It contains three variables a, b, and c. However, unless this is a static or global object, there is *no way to impose an automatic initialization of data* members when an instance of `QE` is created. Also, there is no mechanism for disposing or deallocating memory when `QE` is destroyed. In addition, it is not possible to define a function inside a `struct`, although function pointers are accepted. Moreover, `struct QE` in C is only *a tag*. To introduce a full type `QE`, the `typedef` construction is needed, as shown on line [9].

Finally, there is no way to inherit from a `struct`, although `struct`s can be nested. Compared with C++, these are the fundamental differences that greatly affect the way software is designed, as discussed in Section A.4.

A.2.4 C Functions and Input/Output

As mentioned earlier, a structure QE that is created will not be initialized automatically. Uninitialized data is a major problem and can lead to vicious runtime errors. Therefore, we need to explicitly initialize each QE just after its point of creation (see Listing A.3). For this purpose, we write two functions: Init_0, defined on lines [2–7], which does a default initialization to zero values; and Init, on lines [10–15], which lets us pass an initial value. Note that for both functions, the first parameter is a pointer to the QE object that needs to be initialized. Since there are no references in C, indirect object passing is possible only via pointers. In all cases, we need to make sure the passed pointer is pointing at a valid object before it is used.

Listing A.3   Initializing QE and computing the roots of the quadratic equation (in *CPro, struct_test.c*).

```
1    /* Initialize QE to 0 */
2    void Init_0( QE * qe )
3    {
4        qe->a = 0.0;
5        qe->b = 0.0;
6        qe->c = 0.0;
7    }
8
9    /* Initialize QE to values */
10   void Init( QE * qe, float a, float b, float c )
11   {
12       qe->a = a;
13       qe->b = b;
14       qe->c = c;
15   }
```

Lines [17–20] define the ComputeDelta function is defined. It takes a pointer to a QE object and returns a delta parameter, characteristic of the quadratic equation.

```
16   /* Computes a discriminant of the quadratic equation */
17   float ComputeDelta( QE * qe )
18   {
19       return qe->b * qe->b - 4.0 * qe->a * qe->c;
20   }
```

A test function showing QE and the previous functions in action is defined on lines [22–49].

```
21   /* Function to test the behavior of QE */
22   void Test_QE( void )
23   {
24       /* These objects are not initialized */
25       QE    eq_1;
26       QE    eq_2;
27
28       /* Initialize eq_1 to 0 */
29       Init_0( & eq_1 );
30       Init_0( & eq_2 );
31
```

```
32
33      float a = 0.0, b = 0.0, c = 0.0;
34
35      /* Read 3 params from the keyboard. scanf accepts pointers, so & is used */
36      scanf( "%lf%lf%lf", & a, & b, & c );
37
38      /* Directly set data members of eq_2 */
39      eq_2.a = a;
40      eq_2.b = b;
41      eq_2.c = c;
42
43      /* Compute a discriminant */
44      float delta = ComputeDelta( & eq_2 );
45
46      /* Print delta on the screen */
47      printf ( "delta=%lf\n", delta );
48
49  }
```

Compared to C++, the main problem with this code is that the objects created on lines [25–26] are *not* initialized at first. Initialization has to be performed separately, later in the code, and we have to remember to add it in the right place. In our example, initialization is performed on lines [29–30] by two calls to Init_0.

Note the use of the address & operator, as well as two functions: scanf to input and printf to output data. Both have a formatting string that is the first parameter to each of them. This string, defined simply in C style as a char* constant, defines the format expected for the input or output data. For example, %f means data entered in the floating-point format. Rules for coding format strings can be found in the references (Kernighan and Ritchie 1988) or on the Internet, if necessary. Moreover, note that scanf expects pointers for its data parameters, whereas printf operates directly on data objects.

A.2.5 Unions

We should be aware by now that data in low-level memory always looks the same: a series of bytes. But its meaning depends on the type or, more verbosely, an abstraction superimposed on that data. In some situations – usually, to save space – it is useful to superimpose a few abstractions on the same memory location. These are *unions*.

The C code fragment C_UnionTest in Listing A.4 shows a union LFValue to store either fLongVal or fDoubleVal, but not both at the same time.

Listing A.4 Example of a union in C to store two objects of different types in one memory location (in *CPro, union_test.c*).

```
1   void C_UnionTest( void )
2   {
3       union LFValue
4       {
5           long        fLongVal;
6           double      fDoubleVal;
7       } LF_Obj = { 0 }; /* create LF_obj and init to 0 */
8
9       /* With a union we gain size */
```

```
10       printf ( "s_long = %d, s_float = %d, s_LFValue = %d\n",
11               sizeof( long ), sizeof( double ), sizeof( union LFValue ) );
12
13       /* From LF_Obj we can use only one field at a time */
14       LF_Obj.fLongVal = 120; /* now we use LF_Obj as long */
15
16       /* Print the bytes */
17       int i = 0;
18       printf ( "\nBytes of LF_Obj.fLongVal = 120\n" );
19       for( i = 0; i < sizeof( union LFValue ); ++ i )
20         printf ( "%x\t", * ( (unsigned char*)& LF_Obj + i ) );
21
22       LF_Obj.fDoubleVal = 120.0; /* now we use LF_Obj as a float */
23
24       printf ( "\nBytes of LF_Obj.fDoubleVal = 120.0\n" );
25       for( i = 0; i < sizeof( union LFValue ); ++ i )
26         printf ( "%x\t", * ( (unsigned char*)& LF_Obj + i ) );
27
28       /* However, type punning through a union is not recommended */
29       /* printf (    "\nfLongVal = %ld, fDoubleVal = %lf\n",
30               LF_Obj.fLongVal, LF_Obj.fDoubleVal ); */
31     }
```

When we run the previous code, the following is printed:

```
s_long = 4, s_float = 8, s_LFValue = 8


Bytes of LF_Obj.fLongVal = 120
78        0        0        0          0         0        0        0
Bytes of LF_Obj.fDoubleVal = 120.0
0         0        0        0          0         0        5c       40
```

We see that the size of the `LFValue` union is the size of its largest member, which is eight bytes in this case due to the size of `fDoubleVal`. If we used `struct` instead, then its size would be at least the sum of the sizes of its elements. Since every element of a union is stored at the same memory location, we can use only one member at a time, as shown on lines [14, 22]. But accessing the two fields for typecasting, as shown on line [29], although encountered in some libraries, is not recommended since it depends heavily on the low-level number representation on the specific platform.

As already mentioned, unions were used to save on memory, which is still an important issue in embedded systems. However, in modern C++, unions are deprecated. If we need to store multiple objects, only one of which is active at a time, then we can use `std::variant` instead.

A.2.6 Memory and String Operations

Computer memory is organized as a linear collection of bytes, as discussed in Section 2.1. A series of consecutive bytes of a fixed length is called a *memory block*, a *buffer*, a *byte array*, or a *table*. Of these, strings – i.e. arrays of `chars` – are a special group.[3]

---

3 In C++, these are best represented with `std::string` (Section 3.6). But there is a `std::string::c_str` member function that returns a pointer to C-like string buffer, ending with the 0 sentinel.

When working with C strings, we must remember the following:

- Strings are special memory blocks that contain only printable ASCII characters, each occupying a single byte, represented as the char type.[4] Strings *always* contain a 0 value sentinel to indicate the end of the text, as shown in Figure A.4. An empty string contains 0 at its first position
- The memory buffer storing a string must be large enough to store all characters with the sentinel, and to accommodate all bytes if a new string is copied or concatenated to the buffer

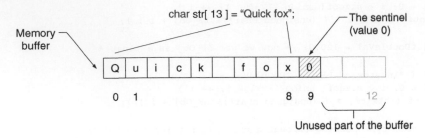

Figure A.4 C-type string definition and representation in memory. To indicate the last character in a string, a sentinel value of 0 is inserted.

As an example, let's count the number of letters in a simple text array:

```
1    char text[] = { "The quick brown fox" };
2
3    int cnt = 0;
4
5    // Measure the length of the text
6    while( * ( text + cnt ) != 0 )
7       ++ cnt;
8
9    printf ( "\"%s\" contains %d letters\n", text, cnt );
```

On line [1], an array of text is defined and initialized with a sentence. Due to the zero sentinel, to find the length of a string, all we need to do is count all letters whose encoding is different than 0. This is done in the loop on lines [6–7], which iterates as long as there are nonzero elements. At each iteration, a consecutive letter is accessed using the * (text + cnt) expression. Then, if code of that letter is not zero, i.e. it is not a string sentinel, the counter cnt is advanced, and the cycle repeats.

Memory buffers, and strings in particular, can be defined and accessed as discussed in Section A.5. The main difference is dynamic memory allocation and deallocation on the heap. In C, these two operations are performed with the malloc and free functions. Two important things about them are as follows. First, each malloc should be followed by its corresponding free, which releases memory. Otherwise, memory leaks are generated. Second, malloc does not initialize memory – it simply reserves a certain region in the computer's memory space.

Tables A.2 and A.3 summarize common functions for string and memory buffer operations in C. Although memory buffer operations compile, they should be avoided in C++ programs. Instead, std::string and associated SL functions should be used, as presented in Section 3.6. Semantically identical memory operations are provided in the SL; these can be accessed with the std prefix, such as std::memmove. They are defined in the *cstring* header.

---

4 To accommodate international symbols in C, 16-bit wide characters are defined as wchar_t (in *wchar.t*). However, in this section we discuss only one-byte strings.

Table A.2 Common C string functions (in `<string.h>`). The C++ SL contains their counterparts – the same names with the `std::` prefix (in `<cstring>`).

Object	Description	Examples
| `strlen` | Returns the length of a C string pointed to by `s` (the sentinel 0 is not counted).<br><br>`int strlen( const char * s );` | A few operations on C strings:<br><br>```
 1    char s1[] = "Quick fox";
 2    char s2[] = "fox";
 3
 4    /* Output length of both strings */
 5    printf ( "len(s1)=%d, len(s1)=%d\n",
 6              strlen( s1 ), strlen( s2 ) );
 7
 8    /* Check if strings are the same */
 9    printf( "cmp(s1,s2)=%d\n", strcmp( s1, s2 ) );
10
11    char s3[ 64 ] = "\0";       /* Large buffer, empty string */
12    strcpy( s3, s1 );           /* Copy s1 to s3 */
13    printf ( "cmp(s1,s3)=%d\n", strcmp( s1, s3 ) );
14
15    strcat( s3, " jumped" );    /* Join two strings */
16    printf ( "s3=%s\n", s3 );
17
18    /* Find if s2 is part of s1 */
19    printf ( "s2 is a part of s1: %s\n",
20              strstr( s1, s2 ) != NULL ? "yes" : "no" );
``` |
| `strcmp`
`strncmp` | Compares two strings. The first character that does not match is compared to see if it has a lower or greater value. Returns:

`<0` if s1<s2
`0`   if s1==s2
`>0` if s1>s2

`int strcmp( const char * s1, const char * s2 );`

The second version compares up to *n* characters. | |
| `strcpy` | Copies `s2` into the buffer pointed to by `s1`. Returns a pointer to `s1`.

`char * strcpy( const char * s1, const char * s2 );` | |

(Continued)
```

Table A.2 (continued)

Object	Description	Examples
| `strcat` `strncat` | Appends `s2` with the sentinel to the buffer pointed to by `s1`. Sentinel 0 in `s1` is overwritten. Returns a pointer to `s1`. <br><br> `char * strcat( const char * s1, const char * s2 );` <br><br> The second version appends the first *n* characters. | An example of reading a line of characters from a file. In C, `fopen` opens a file: <br><br> ```
1  #define line_len 256    /* The way to make constant val */
2  char line_buf[ line_len ] = { 0 };/* Buffer set to 0 */
3
4  FILE * fp_in = fopen( "Fox.txt", "r" ); /* Open a file */
5
6  if( fp_in )
7  {   /* Read a line to the buffer */
8      if( fgets( line_buf, line_len, fp_in ) )
9      {
10         /* Do something ... */
11     }
12
13     fclose( fp_in ); /* After finishing close the file. */
14 }
``` |
| `strstr` | Returns a pointer to the first occurrence of `s2` in `s1` if it exists. Otherwise returns `NULL`, which is the C definition of a 0-valued pointer.

 `char * strstr( const char * s1, const char * s2 )` | |
```

Table A.3 Common C memory functions (in `<string.h>`). The C++ SL contains their counterparts – the same names with the `std::` prefix (in `<cstring>`).

Function	Description	Examples
memset	Fills a block of memory pointed to by dst with num bytes of a value val (interpreted as a byte). Returns dst. `void * memset( void * dst, int val, size_t num );`	The following example allocates, sets, and copies a memory buffer:
memcpy	Copies num bytes from a memory block at src to the memory block at dst. The blocks should not overlap. `void * memcpy( void * dst, const void * src, size_t num );`	
memmove	Copies num bytes from a memory block at src to the memory block at dst. The blocks can overlap. Returns dst. `void * memmove( void* dst, const void* src, size_t num );`	

```
1    int buf_size = 256; /* Size of heap alloc can be set in runtime. */
2
3    unsigned char * buf = malloc( buf_size ); /* Allocate on the heap */
4    if( buf == NULL )
5        return; /* Error, cannot allocate memory. Exiting.*/
6
7    memset( buf, 0x00, buf_size );      /* Fill buf with 0 */
8
9    char * text = "quick brown fox.";
10
11   /* Get text length + sentinel 0 */
12   int text_total_len = strlen( text ) + 1;
13
14   memcpy( buf, text, text_total_len );       /* Copy text to buf */
15
16   char * prefix = "The ";
17
18   /* Move to make room at the beginning of text */
19   memmove( buf + strlen( prefix ), buf, text_total_len );
20
21   memcpy( buf, prefix, strlen( prefix ) ); /* Copy prefix but not 0 */
22
23   print= ( "%s\n", buf );
24
25   free( buf ); /* Do NOT FORGET to release memory. */
```

(Continued)

Table A.3 (continued)

Function	Description	Examples
memcmp	Compares num bytes at locations pointed to by p1 and p2. Returns 0 if the two blocks are the same, or non-zero otherwise. `int memcmp( const void* p1, const void * p2, size_t num );`	To allocate a memory region on the heap, malloc is called on line [3]. Its size can be dynamic, i.e. conveyed in a variable, such as buf_size. If successful, as checked on line [4], a pointer to the region is returned. The buffer is then zeroed by calling memset on line [7]. On line [14], text ending with zero is copied to that buffer. To make room for a few more characters at the beginning, memmove is called on line [19]. New text is then copied on line [21]. But to join the strings, 0 is omitted. Finally, memory is deallocated by calling free on line [25]. If it is not, a memory leak will occur. When run, the following appears on the terminal: `The quick brown fox.`
memchr	Searches a block of memory of num bytes pointed by ptr. If val (interpreted as a byte) is found, then its location is returned, or NULL otherwise. `void * memchr( const void * ptr, int val, size_t num );`	

A.2.7 Binding C and C++ Code

Although in many cases C code can be compiled with a C++ compiler, joining these code components needs a little more attention. First, not all C constructions are correct in a C++ compiler. Second, the format for function encoding is different in the two languages (for complete representation of a function name together with types of its parameters, C++ does name mangling). Because of this, we have to tell the linker which functions require the C-style linkage.

Practically, if we want to bind C code to C++ code, then it is good to place the C parts in separate header(s) and source(s) files (ending with *.c*). Then the C code can be included into the C++ using the following construction:

```
extern "C"
{
  #include "C_header.h"
}
```

This will ensure proper linkage of C functions to the C++ domain. The construction `extern "C"` can also be used in the other direction – in C++, to declare a function that is linked as a C function (*https://isocpp.org/wiki/faq/mixing-c-and-cpp*).

A.3   Linking and Binary Organization of C/C++ Objects

In Section 3.15.5, we discussed a scheme for building a program from many smaller code objects, each from a separate translation unit. To better understand this process, it is interesting to know how the objects are structured and placed in the computer's memory. This knowledge is also important when creating software for custom electronics, such as embedded systems, etc.

When building software components, which frequently contain many classes and dozens of functions, their functionality is important: i.e. what other components can do with them. Such information regarding the source code is found in the *application programming interface* (API) specification. For example, in the next section, we will present libraries for building nice-looking applications with colorful graphical user interfaces. To characterize them, we will only provide a short overview of their APIs. However, no less important is the internal structure of a software component *after* it is built, i.e. its organization at the binary level. It is determined by the type of the processor instruction set, its endianness, data alignment, target platform – such as 64-bit ARM Linux or 32-bit x86 Windows – function-calling convention – how arguments and return values are passed and retrieved, via the stack or with the help of some registers – as well as the binary format of object files, libraries, and executables used, and so on. A specification that precisely describes all of these aspects is called an *application binary interface* (ABI).[5] ABI-compatible systems allow object binding, such as C and C++, as discussed in the previous section, or running programs without extra compilations and builds. Some of these issues are discussed further in this section.

As alluded to previously, the C++ executable or library is usually built in stages. Each successive compilation of a translation unit produces a relocatable object file containing the machine code, global variables, and the symbol table holding the names of global variables and functions. Different relocatable object files are then joined into the executable object file. Figure A.5 shows the structures of the relocatable and executable object files in the *Executable and Linkable Format* (ELF),

---

5 More information on ABIs can be found e.g. at *https://en.wikipedia.org/wiki/Application_binary_interface* and in Herb Sutter, "Defining a Portable C++ ABI," *www.open-std.org/jtc1/sc22/wg21/docs/papers/2014/n4028.pdf*.

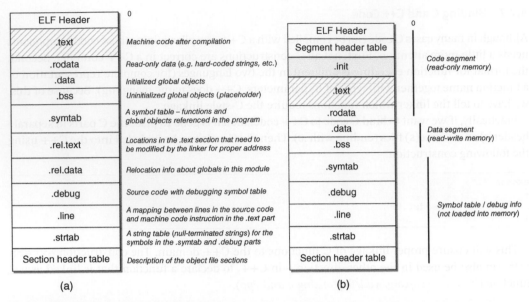

Figure A.5 (a) Relocatable object file and (b) executable object file in the Executable and Linkable Format (ELF) specific to the Linux OS. After compiling a translation unit, the relocatable object file is generated. In contains sections for different purposes. Various objects need to be linked into an executable object file. As a result, the code stored in the *.text* sections and global variables *.data* are relocated and copied. Debug information in the *.debug* and *.line* sections is available only if compiled with the debug flag set (for the *gcc* compiler *–g* option).

which is specific to the Linux OS (Wiki:Portable_Executable 2020). Windows uses the *Portable Executable* (PE) format, and macOS uses the Mach-O format (Wiki:Comparision_Executable 2019).

Machine code generated by the compiler (or an assembler) goes to the ELF *.text* section. The *.data* section contains initialized global objects, whereas *.bss* is a placeholder. A symbol table in *.symtab*, alongside *.rel.text* and *.rel.data,* is used by the linker when resolving and relocating symbol code and data into the executable object file's destination memory. Finally, *.debug* and *.line* are used to synchronize source lines with the positions in the generated code for debugging. These are present only if the code is compiled with the debugging option on. A precise description of the format and the linking process can be found in Bryant and O'Hallaron (2015).

When code is generated by the compiler, it is not known where the code and data will ultimately be placed in memory. Similarly, the locations of functions and data from other translations are not known. Hence, parts of the code and data, called *object files*, and object files previously created in the form of libraries, need to be joined into one library or executable. This task is performed by a program called a *linker* (Section 2.2). More specifically, the two main tasks of linkers are:

- *Symbol resolution* – Uniquely binding each global symbol, and checking for undefined and doubly defined symbols (in which case an error message is generated)
- *Relocation* – Changing code and data into destination memory locations

There are two types of linkers:

- *Static linkers* – Used to build a complete stand-alone executable
- *Dynamic linkers* – Called in the runtime to complete the linking process by loading the shared (dynamic) libraries and binding the symbols

Position-independent code lets us load code into any memory space for execution.

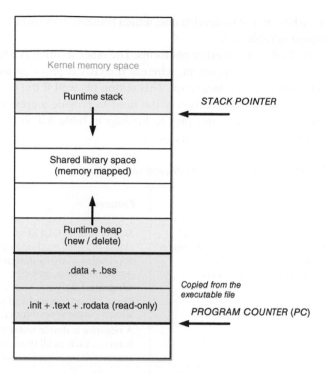

Figure A.6 Runtime memory image of an executable in the Linux OS.

When a program is invoked, special OS code called a *loader* is responsible for loading an image of the program into memory. The memory image is created, as shown in Figure A.6.

The code from *.text* and the global data in *.rodata* are copied from the executable object file. Additionally, the *.init* section is added, which contains the initialization code that is run to set up the environment before calling the user's `main` function.

The data memory space is divided into the user's stack, which usually runs toward lower memory addresses; the runtime heap, growing up the memory address space; and the shared library memory space for *memory-mapped files* (Kerrisk 2010).

The kernel memory space belongs to the OS memory image and is not directly available to the user's code. In systems that have *virtual memory,* the loading process involves mapping virtual memory pages, and the actual page loading is deferred until the relevant code or data address is referenced in the runtime (Bryant and O'Hallaron 2015; Fan 2015).

A.4 Graphical User and Web Interfaces for C++ Projects

Designing a good, versatile, multiplatform, multilanguage GUI library is not an easy task. It may not be possible, considering all the variability and depending on the user's requirements. Hence, the C++ standard does not come with an easy solution in this respect (nor do other languages).

But many attempts have been made to develop one, which resulted in more or less lucky solutions. These are briefly outlined in Table A.4.

In addition, we can easily find a few other platforms. The other solution is a hybrid: the computational part is written as a C++ component, whereas the GUI is provided using a networking platform such as Microsoft's .NET or JavaScript. This option fits well if the GUI is provided by a web browser. But a downside of this solution is the need to provide a cross-language/platform interface – see the description of the Emscripten technology in Table A.4. For more C++ libraries visit e.g. *https://en.cppreference.com/w/cpp/links/libs*.

Table A.4 Common C++-compatible GUI, multimedia, and web libraries.

Library	Characteristics	Features
Qt	One of the most advanced C++ GUI libraries. Comes in two versions: under a commercial license, and as open source (with some limitations). *www.qt.io*	A fully fledged GUI library written based on object-oriented methodology. An interesting application of many design patterns, such as signals and slots, as well as observers. GUI widgets send signals with event information. These can be received and processed by other widgets using special functions called *slots*. A negative is that in order to access all the features, such as all the design tools, a commercial version is required.
FLTK	The Fast Light Tool Kit (FLTK, pron. "fulltick") is a cross-platform C++ GUI toolkit for Linux, Microsoft Windows, and Apple macOS. FLTK comes with complete free source code under the terms of the GNU Library General Public License (LGPL). *www.fltk.org*	Large, relatively easy to build and use C++ library with dozens of graphical widgets for easy GUI programming. Supports 2D and 3D graphics with OpenGL and its built-in OpenGL Utility Toolkit (GLUT) emulator. In Section 6.2.8, we discuss a GUI project based on FLTK for our currency calculator.
wxWidgets	An advanced, free, open source C++ GUI library for Windows, macOS, and Linux. *http://wxwidgets.org/*	Has language bindings to Python, Ruby, etc. For easy design of wxWidgets dialogs and forms, we can use the associated wxDev-C++ designer platform (i.e. a wizard) by Colin Laplace et al. (*http://wxdsgn.sourceforge.net*).
MFC	Microsoft Foundation Classes *https://docs.microsoft.com/en-us/cpp/ mfc/mfc-desktop-applications*	Well-established, revamped GUI library that wraps the Windows API. Comes with Microsoft Visual C++ and runs only on Windows. Good, easy-to-use source wizard that, together with the visual control resource editor, allow for fast prototyping. Substantially supports three types of applications: dialog-based, single-window, and multiple-window formats with dozens of options. See the *FixBinCalc* project mentioned in Section A.5.

Library	Characteristics	Features
gtkmm	Offers a C++ interface for the GUI library GTK+. Free software distributed under the GNU LGPL. *www.gtkmm.org*	Fully object-oriented. Uses C++ class inheritance to derive custom widgets, type-safe signal handlers, SL containers, locals UTF8, namespaces, etc. Cross-platform on Linux (*gcc*), FreeBSD (*gcc*), NetBSD (*gcc*), Solaris (*gcc*, Forte), Win32 (*gcc*, MSVC++), and macOS (*gcc*).
SFML	Simple and Fast Multimedia Library (SFML), mostly for developing games and multimedia applications. Follows the zlib/png license. *www.sfml-dev.org*	Composed of five modules: system, window, graphics, audio, and network. Multiplatform (Linux, Windows, macOS, Android, and iOS). However, it has no easily available widgets such as buttons, edit boxes, combos, etc., which make it difficult to use in some types of GUIs. Bindings for C, .NET, Python, and a few more languages are available.[a]
SDL	Simple DirectMedia Layer, a multimedia, multiplatform library providing easy access to audio, keyboard, mouse, joystick, and graphics hardware. SDL 2.0 is distributed under the zlib license. This license allows you to use SDL freely in any software. *www.libsdl.org*	Good for writing games, emulators, etc. Written in C using the OpenGL and Direct3D libraries. SDL works with C++ on Windows, macOS, Linux, iOS, and Android. There are bindings e.g. to Python.
ImGui	Immediate Mode Graphical User interface for C++ with minimal dependencies. Available under a free and permissive license. *https://github.com/ocornut/imgui*	An impressive, unorthodox graphical library for C++, aimed at content-creation tools, visualization, debug tools, etc. Good choice for integration with game engines, real-time 3D applications, fullscreen applications, embedded and console platforms, etc. For example, it can cooperate with the SDL multimedia library.
Emscripten	Framework for automatic translation of C/C++ code to let it run on the Web at high speed and without additional plug-ins. The C/C++ code is compiled into *asm.js* and WebAssembly using LLVM technology (*http://llvm.org/*). *https://emscripten.org*	An example of bridging the gap between the C/C++ runtime environment and web technologies. Emscripten translates C/C++ code into JavaScript that can be run on the Web, providing the necessary runtime support. That JavaScript code can be executed by *node.js* or from HTML in a browser. On the Emscripten website are examples of successfully ported games that need to render graphics, play sounds, and load and process files, as well as application frameworks like Qt.

[a] A *binding* is a library that allows language A to call functions/procedures written in language B.

A.5 Converting Bin, Oct, Dec, and Hex Values with FixBinCalc

FixBinCalc is an MFC application project we can use to easily convert between six numerical formats: floating-point, fixed-point, decimal, octal, binary, and hexadecimal. It was written by the author when working on FPGA programming to investigate binary values on different microprocessor buses, such as 32-bit or 64-bit. However, it can also be used to measure the difference between binary fixed-point and floating-point representations, as discussed in Section 7.3.4 (Figure A.7).

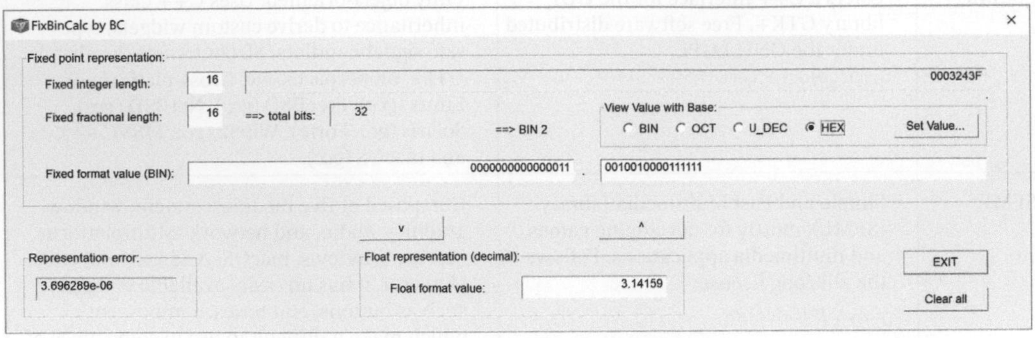

Figure A.7 *FixBinCalc* application for converting numbers between various formats (in *FixBinCalc*).

Finally, although MFC is not a portable platform, it can be useful for fast application prototyping in Windows since it is still supplied as part of the Microsoft Visual Studio environment. MFC has also undergone thorough refurbishing over the last decade. Although this is fine for legacy code, i.e. applications written years ago, the problem with MFC is code maintenance. For new C++ applications that require a GUI, newer technologies are better options, such as modern GUI libraries or the web-based interfaces cited in Table A.4.

A.6   Programming Toolchain

Building software involves many tools. We have discussed the roles of the compiler, linker, and debugger. In addition, to write software, we used an editor. Frequently, all of these come under the umbrella of an integrated development environment (IDE), such as Eclipse or Microsoft's Visual Studio. In this section, we will provide some basic information about three other tools that make our lives easier: *CMake,* which is a project-generating tool; *Git* and *GitHub,* which are source control and maintenance platforms; and the profiler, which lets us measure the performance of our developed software.

A.6.1   Project-Generating Tool (*CMake*)

CMake is a project-generating tool. But why do we need this tool if C++ is defined with no special assumptions about the OS or the specific compiler? The simple answer is that in reality, we all have different computers, different OSs, and, naturally, different software-building tools. Diversity is beautiful, but if we wish to create a universal, multiplatform project, we can end up with a real headache. Even if we minimize our requirements to one particular OS, we immediately face the problem of different compilers and hundreds of different associated settings. For example, it is quite common to have two or three of the latest versions of Microsoft Visual Studio installed, or various versions of *gcc* or *clang* in the jungle of Linux distributions. So, how do we cope with such diversity? One way is to create a project for each IDE/toolchain manually. But we are humans, and we have computers to do this "housekeeping" job for us. And here, project generators such as the *CMake* can help. Briefly, *CMake* is equipped with its own programming language, which lets us express a general idea of what a C/C++ project should look like, and then lets us generate a project on a particular platform (OS + a compiler with an environment). Then this project can be compiled, the built software can be executed, and so on. Let's summarize the main benefits of using *CMake* to define our C++ projects:

- *CMake* lets us define generic rules for a project, which are then realized in order to create a project for a given platform
- *CMake* lets us define relations between projects, such as a library vs. an application that uses this library

CMake is a separate software system with its own syntax and hundreds of definitions and options. The obvious question is, why is this so difficult? Not only do we have to learn all these peculiarities of C++, but then, to be able to build C++ in real environments, we need to become an expert in *CMake*! Fortunately, the news is not that bad. First of all, if we stick to one platform, we can live happily without *CMake*, at least for a while. Second, although at first glance *CMake* might seem to be complicated, we can apply the 20/80 rule that says we can get the vast majority of the benefits while using fewer than 20% of its features.

To use *CMake,* we need to do at least two things:

- Install the latest version of *CMake*[6]
- Prepare a *CMakeLists.txt* file containing instructions for *CMake*

After launching the function `RecursivelyTraverseDirectory`, presented in Table 6.3, the following project directory tree is drawn for the *EmptyPro* project:

```
[+]builtd_linux
[+]build_mac
[+]build_win
|--CMakeLists.txt
[+]include
   |--empty.h
|--ReadMe.txt
[+]src
   |--empty.cpp
   |--main.cpp
```

The *EmptyPro* project is a kind of template project undertaken in this book. You can start using *CMake* by trying it on *EmptyPro*. Then, you can modify *EmptyPro* to fit your needs by adding new files to the *src* and *include* directories, and by changing the project name. To accomplish the latter, you need to change the name of a directory, but also you need to change the project name in the *CMakeLists.txt* file, as we will describe.

We will not go into many details about writing *CMakeLists.txt* files for various projects. However, for many simple projects, the example version shown in Listing 8.1 can be used with only a few modifications.

---

6 A downloadable version can be obtained free from *https://cmake.org/*. In the case of Windows OSs, we recommend installing *CMake* after installing Visual Studio. Remember to allow the *CMake* installer to adjust the system *PATH* for all users.

Listing A.5 An example *CMake* script for generating simple application projects for different OSs (in *EmptyPro*, *CMakeLists.txt*).

```
1   cmake_minimum_required( VERSION 3.6.2 )
2
3   # For a new project it is sufficient to change only its name in the following line
4   set( PROJECT_NAME EmptyPro )
5
6   project( ${PROJECT_NAME} )
7
8   set( CMAKE_BUILD_TYPE Debug )
9   #set( CMAKE_BUILD_TYPE Release )
10
11  if( WIN32 )
12     set( CMAKE_CXX_FLAGS "/DWIN32 /D_WINDOWS /W3 /GR /EHsc /std:c++17 /D_UNICODE /
       DUNICODE" )
13     set( CMAKE_CXX_FLAGS_DEBUG "/MDd /Zi /Ob0 /Od /RTC1 /std:c++17 /D_UNICODE /
       DUNICODE" )
14     message( "Win settings chosen..." )
15  elseif( ${CMAKE_SYSTEM_NAME} STREQUAL "Darwin" )
16     set( CMAKE_CXX_FLAGS "-std=c++17 -Wall" )
17     set( CMAKE_CXX_FLAGS_DEBUG "-g -std=c++17 -Wall" )
18     message( "Mac settings chosen..." )
19  elseif( UNIX )
20     set( CMAKE_CXX_FLAGS "-std=c++17 -Wall" )
21     set( CMAKE_CXX_FLAGS_DEBUG "-g -std=c++17 -Wall" )
22     message( "Linux settings chosen..." )
23  endif()
24
25
26  # Inform CMake where the header files are
27  include_directories( include )
28
29
30  # Automatically add all *.cpp and *.h files to the project
31  file ( GLOB SOURCES "./src/*.cpp"        "./include/*.h" )
32  add_executable( ${PROJECT_NAME} ${SOURCES} )
33
34  # Set the default project
35  set_property( DIRECTORY ${CMAKE_CURRENT_SOURCE_DIR} PROPERTY VS_STARTUP_PROJECT
       ${PROJECT_NAME} )
36
37  message( "CMAKE_BUILD_TYPE is ${CMAKE_BUILD_TYPE}" )
```

Line [1] is a clause for a minimal version of *CMake*. The project name is defined on line [4]. For simple projects, and assuming the same directory structure, this is the only one line you will need to modify by entering the name of your project. We will do this in a moment for the *EasyMatrix* project. Lines [8–9] choose a *Debug* or *Release* project version. Notice that in *CMake*, # is used to enter a comment: this can be used to temporarily comment out a line that may be useful later. Lines [11–23] contain command-line options for various compiler calls. This is the most technical part of our script, which requires knowledge of a particular compiler setup. But once set, these can be used with no further interference. A deeper explanation can be found in the *CMake* documentation.

Line [27] instructs the *CMake* project generator to look for header files in the *include* directory. Similarly, lines [31–32] make *CMake* pull in all source files, i.e. files with the *cpp* extension, from the *src* subdirectory. As a result, our script is highly automatic. An alternative is to explicitly write the names of all our sources, which also has some benefits. Finally, line [35] is specific to Microsoft Visual Studio. Since in addition to our project, projects named *ALL_BUILD* and *ZERO_CHECK* are generated,[7] this makes our project the default. Finally, on line [37], a message is printed if everything went OK.

Now we are ready to generate the first project with *CMake*. All you need to do is to go to the *build_xxx* directory,[8] where *xxx* stands for your OS type, open a terminal window, and type

```
cmake ..
```

which will launch *CMake* with the one-higher directory provided as its input. If it succeeds, then a series of commands from *CMakeLists.txt* is executed, resulting in a series of messages, as shown in Figure A.8.

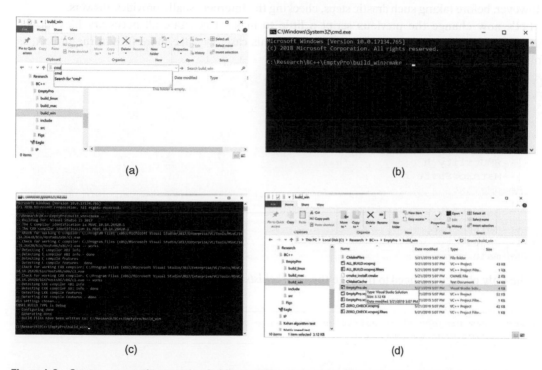

(a)   (b)

(c)   (d)

Figure A.8 Steps to generating a project in Microsoft Visual C++ with *CMake* and the `CMakeLists.txt` script. (a) Type *cmd* in the File Explorer to open the terminal window in the current folder. (b) Type *cmake ..* in the terminal to launch *CMake* with one upper folder as its parameter, i.e. the level of `CMakeLists.txt`. (c) When executing, *CMake* generates messages. (d) If successful, the project files are generated. In case of errors or any changes to `CMakeLists.txt`, this folder should be emptied and the project-generating process repeated.

---

7 These are used to ensure the integrity of the projects. For further explanation, see the *CMake* documentation.
8 Hints: In Linux, to open the terminal, press Ctrl + Alt + T. In Windows File Explorer, go to the directory *build_win* and type *cmake ..* in the file address pane. This will open the command window in this directory (folder) and launch the *CMake* executable with the upper-level directory *build_win* as its parameter.

In our example, the entire suite of project files is generated. From these, *EmptyPro.sln* should be opened in Visual C++, and the *Rebuild Solution* command should be launched. If everything is OK, then the project should be built successfully.[9] In Linux,[10] after generating the project with *CMake*, the build process is activated by launching *make*. An example for the *Grades* project, discussed in Section 3.2, looks like this:

```
boxy@PARSEC:~/Projects/Grades/build_linux$ make
```

Unfortunately, in life, things are not always that easy. If an error happens, then we need to find the first place where it occurred. Then we need to understand the error message. Sometimes this chore is easier if we copy the message to a more convenient editor, where we can split it into more meaningful parts. If they tell us what is wrong, then we can try to figure out how to fix the problem. If errors occur when running the *CMake* script, remember to delete all previously generated files in the *build_xxx* directory. Sometimes an update or a new installation of a compiler suite or *CMake* is necessary. However, before taking such drastic steps, checking the Internet usually provides answers.

Let's now change the previous script a little to make it generate all necessary files for the *EasyMatrix* projects presented in Section 3.5. In this case, we have more files in the project, as follows:

```
[+]build_linux
[+]build_mac
[+]build_win
|--CMakeLists.txt
[+]include
    |--EMatrix.h
    |--EMUtility.h
    |--MarsXorShift.h
|--ReadMe.txt
[+]src
    |--EMatrix.cpp
    |--EMTest.cpp
    |--EMUtility.cpp
    |--main.cpp
```

The only change we need to make to the *CMakeLists.txt* file is on line [4], as follows:

```
3    # For a new project it is sufficient to change only its name in the following line
4    set( PROJECT_NAME EasyMatrix )
```

That is, all we need to do is to provide the proper name of the project. The suite of *CurrencyCalc* projects contains the *CMakeLists.txt* files to generate the library and to generate an application linked to that library (Section 6.2).

---

9 Since Visual Studio 2019, it is also possible to open the *CMake* script directly from the menu: *File > Open > CMake*.
10 If Windows is the main OS, then installing Ubuntu on Windows provides easy access to Linux.

A.6.2 Source Version Control and Repositories

Even simple projects tend to grow rapidly in terms of the number of classes, functions, files, and versions. Things can become really serious if a project is conducted for years by a varying team, and in a dynamically changing environment. There are many discussions and books on the subject, but no one has a single good recipe for success. But again, there are some recommendations that can make the process a little more ordered and manageable. In this section, we discuss:

- Simultaneous work of a team of developers on a single project
- Source backups and repositories
- Project and source versioning

To facilitate these tasks, many platforms have been created and used over the years. But recently, two systems have gained significant popularity:

- *Git* – A version control tool to manage changes and maintain the history of the source code
- *GitHub* – A hosting service built on *Git* repositories. It lets us share repositories, access other users' repositories, back up sources, and collaborate as teams

Figure A.9 shows an action diagram when working with *GitHub*. The best way to learn how to use *GitHub* is to first go through one of the tutorials available on its web page (*https://github.com*) and then to try to create and maintain your own test project. Needless to say, all the projects presented in this book are also available through this repo.

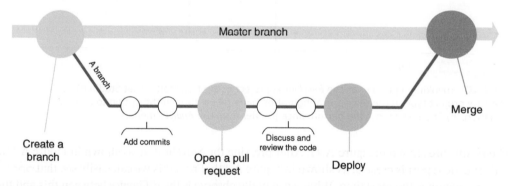

Figure A.9 Flowchart of *GitHub* operations. There is one master branch with a deployable version of the project. A branch creates a new path in a project and lets us work on different features. Each file, after being edited, changed, or deleted, is committed, so the changes and their history are saved in the repo. Pull requests start a discussion about the commits. Before merging to the master, it is possible to deploy from a branch for final testing in production. After testing and verification, the code is merged into the master branch.

Initially it is not necessary to have *Git* on the local computer, since most operations can be performed via access to the *GitHub* website. But after this first stage, it is good to install *Git* and/or to use an IDE that has built-in source-control facilities.

A.6.3 Profiler

A profiler is an application that provides information about the CPU and memory consumption of various parts of our software in operation. Usually, it is launched when the application is in a stable release version and we wish to monitor computer resource use in order to perform further optimizations and code accelerations. In order to make such changes, we must first diagnosis which parts of the code consume most of the resources. In this very short introduction, we will see the role of the profiler embedded in the Microsoft Visual Studio IDE in improving our *EasyMatrix* project, which was presented in Section 3.15.

In order to run a profiler, the following features should be set:

1. In the solution configuration pane, set the *Release* version of the project.
2. In the project settings, choose to generate debug information, as shown in Figure A.10a (yes, this is useful for *Release* versions as well). As a result, we can see the names of functions rather than bare memory addresses.
3. Launch the profiler, as shown in Figure A.10b.
4. Analyze the results.

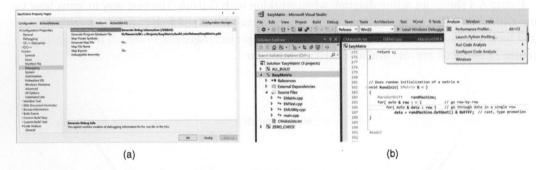

(a)   (b)

Figure A.10 Invoking a profiler for the *EasyMatrix* project in the Microsoft Visual Studio IDE. After setting the *Release* project type in the solution configuration pane, (a) we turn on the option to generate debug information. (b) Then we launch the performance profiler from the *Analyze* menu.

The results are shown in Figure A.11. After pressing the *Start* button, as shown in Figure A.11a, the diagnostic report is created, as shown in Figure A.11b. From this we can easily see that `operator` `*` consumes the most time. What we actually observe is the *difference* between this and the next reported function. In more complicated projects, finding the real hotspots may not be this easy, but looking for large timing differences can provide a hint. In our case, it is not a big surprise that `operator` `*` consumes most of the time, since it performs all the computations. Nevertheless, this analysis leads us to this function for potential improvements. One possibility is developing parallel algorithms, as discussed in Section 8.3.3.

Because we enabled the generation of debug information, double-clicking `operator` `*` in Figure A.11b takes us to the source code, shown in Figure A.11c. The function call chain is also shown.

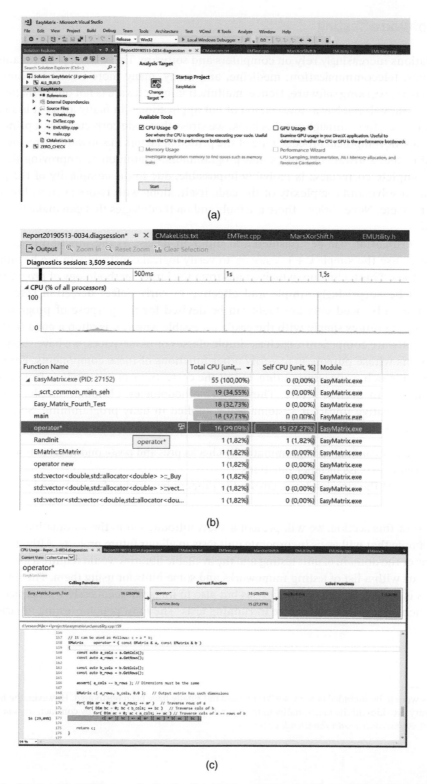

Figure A.11 Panes with profiling results for the *EasyMatrix* project in the Microsoft Visual Studio IDE. (a) Initial profiling window. (b) Timing results after profiling. (c) Calling chain and source code of the most .

A.7   Software Testing

Our civilizations increasingly rely on computers and software. These days, power plants, transport, avionics, telecommunication, medicine, and many, many more industries cannot exist without properly working software. Hence, malfunctioning software is not only a matter of frustrated users who will not buy a new version of our application – in many areas, it is a matter of life or death. Therefore, throughout this book, we stress that code correctness is a primary issue in the software development process. One of the principal factors in software correctness is having well-educated, software designers and programmers, continuously improving their skills. However, complete correctness is probably impossible, due to the complexity of the problems we're trying to solve and complexity of the code itself, along with issues such as limited time, human factors, etc. Nevertheless, there are tools and methodologies that can make the situation less difficult.

Software verification can be considered at different levels. At the function level, we have shown how to use the simple C++ `assert` to verify logical constraints in the beginning and end of functions. This technique, which comes from the larger methodology of *programming by contract*, can be surprisingly simple and effective in early defect detection (Meyer 1997). Although more advanced software tools can be devised for the purpose of programming by contract, keeping things simple with the easily accessible `assert` is often a good trade-off. At the level of software components, such as simple classes or namespaces, we have shown how to write functions whose purpose is to verify other functions of these components. For instance, we use this approach, called *unit testing*, to test the correctness of conversions from decimal to Roman numbers in Section 3.17.2. These two methodologies, although simple, can have a tremendously positive impact if systematically applied in daily programming. Summarizing, they are as follows:

- *Programming by contract* – Programmatically checks pre- and post-conditions to functions, and class invariants in class member functions[11]
- *Unit testing* – At the simplest level, ensure the proper operation of functions and class member functions

In the rest of this section, we will present a short introduction to the automation of unit tests with an example that will let us incorporate unit tests in all our future projects. Although detailed descriptions of the domain of unit testing and the available libraries would require a longer discussion, let's start with a list of testing frameworks and some hints for using them. The role of these frameworks is to facilitate writing unit tests but also to integrate seamlessly with projects and to allow as much automation as possible in running tests. The most popular testing libraries are as follows:

---

11 Contracts were to be included in the C++20 standard but finally have been postponed. However, the *Boost. Contract* library provides all the functionality to incorporate programming paradigms by contract: *www.boost.org/ doc/libs/1_70_0/libs/contract/doc/html/index.html*.

- *Google Test* – Large, multiplatform testing framework (Linux, Windows, or Mac), verified in many projects (*https://github.com/google/googletest/blob/master/googletest/docs/primer.md*). Easily integrates with Visual Studio C++ and is used in our example presented in this section
- *Boost.Test* – A testing framework from the Boost libraries
- *CTest* – Another test library

Our experimental platform will test the *RomanApp* project, which contains all the sources to convert decimal numbers to Roman numerals, as presented in Section 3.17. Here, we list only the most important steps and dependencies; refer to the web links for the most up-to-date information (*https://docs.microsoft.com/en-us/visualstudio/test/writing-unit-tests-for-c-cpp*). The overall procedure to add a test using Google Test is as follows:

1. Be sure you have *Google Test* installed in the Visual Studio framework (run Visual Installer if necessary).
2. Prepare the solution for the project to be tested. In our case, it is named *RomanApp*.
3. Add a new project, choose its name – say, *RomanApp_GTest* – and choose Google Test as its template, as shown in Figure A.12. (If Google Test is not visible, then check its installation again).
4. Add unit tests to *RomanApp_GTest*, as we will show in the following code example.
5. Make sure that when building *RomanApp_GTest,* the compiler and linker can access the *RomanApp* source and compiled modules. In other words, *RomanApp* serves as a "library" for *RomanApp_GTest*. This requires adjusting the project settings, as shown in Figure A.13 (see *https://docs.microsoft.com/visualstudio/test/unit-testing-existing-cpp-applications-with-test-explorer?view=vs-2015#objectRef*).
6. After the solution is built successfully, open the *Test Explorer* pane and click *Run All*. This launches all of the written tests, after which we can check the report to verify which tests passed and which did not.

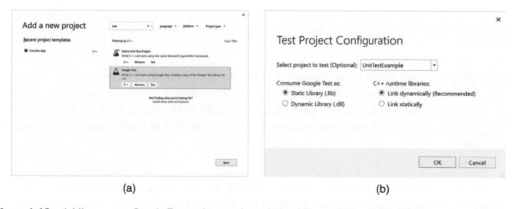

      (a)   (b)

Figure A.12 Adding a new *Google Test* project to the existing Microsoft Visual Studio *RomanApp* solution. (a) Add a New Project wizard. (b) Project configuration window for the *Google Test* framework

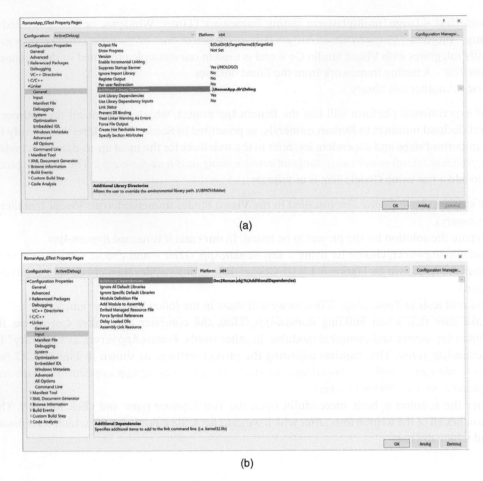

(a)

(b)

Figure A.13 Linker pane settings for `RomanApp_GTest`. (a) Adding the `Dec2Roman.obj` object file to the Additional Dependencies. (b) Setting Additional Library Directories to the path where `Dec2Roman.obj` can be found.

The testing software needs to be properly layered. In our example, the `Decimal_2_Roman_Chain_UnitTest` test function belongs to the main *RomanApp* project. On the other hand, the *Google Test*–based *RomanApp_GTest* only plugs functions to be tested, such as `Decimal_2_Roman_Chain_UnitTest` from our example, into the framework of testing macros, as shown in Listing A.6.

Listing A.6 *Google Test* macros in a source file from the *RomanApp_GTest* project to verify conversions from .decimal to Roman numbers by calling the `Decimal_2_Roman_Chain_UnitTest` function from the *RomanApp* project (in the *test.cpp*).

```
1   #include "pch.h"
2
3   #include "..//..//include//Dec2Roman.h"
4
5   TEST(TestCaseName, TestName) {
6     EXPECT_EQ(1, 1);
7     EXPECT_TRUE(true);
```

```
 8     }
 9
10
11     TEST( DecRoman_TestSuite, ChainTest )
12     {
13         bool result = Decimal_2_Roman_Chain_UnitTest();
14
15         // Nonfatal assertion
16         EXPECT_EQ( result, true ) << "All decimals 1..3999 should pass and vice versa";
17
18         // Fatal assertion
19         ASSERT_EQ( result, true ) << "All decimals 1..3999 should pass and vice versa";
20     }
```

The previous *test.cpp* source file is generated automatically by the project wizard when creating *RomanApp_GTest,* as shown in Figure A.12. It contains some predefined *Google Test* constructions. On line [1], the precompiled header is included through the *pch.h* file. This is a feature specific to the Microsoft Visual Studio platform, which for compatibility reasons we avoided in other projects presented in this book. Using the precompiled header can be switched off in the settings pane opened for the source file. Then, line [3] includes the *Dec2Roman.h* header, which lets us call the Decimal_2_Roman_Chain_UnitTest test function from the main *RomanApp* project. Therefore the name of the header is preceded by the relative path.

The TEST macro, which calls the EXPECT_EQ and EXPECT_TRUE macros on lines [5–7], was automatically added by the wizard to show very basic features of the *Google Test* platform. However, in the same fashion on line [11], we add our own test. First, on line [13], the Decimal_2_Roman_Chain_UnitTest test function is called, and the result of its operation is saved in the result flag. This is then checked by two assertions: the non-fatal EXPECT_EQ on line [16] and the fatal ASSERT_EQ on line [19]. This is all we need to run the test by pressing the green button in the Test Explorer pane, as shown in Figure A.14.

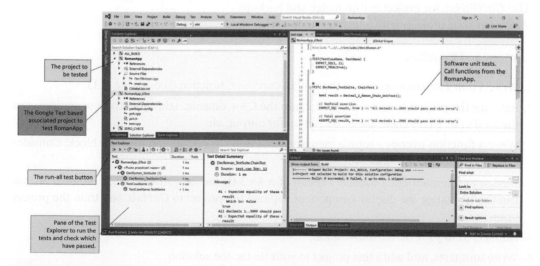

Figure A.14 Visual Studio with two projects: *RomanApp* and its *RomanApp_GTest* testing project, based on the Google Test library. Software unit tests are written using macros defined with Google Test. They call a unit test written to test the specific behavior of *RomanApp*. As shown in the Test Explorer pane, the first test from *test.cpp* passed, while the second one failed.

After we launch the tests, the Test Explorer pane contains the results. As shown in Figure A.14, the first test from line [5] of *test.cpp* obviously passed and is displayed in green. But the second test, which we inserted, failed and is visible in red. Naturally, the reason for this is simple – we have not yet implemented the `ConvertRoman_2_DecimalNumber` function.

Finally, note that in addition to unit testing, there are also the following testing levels (*https://en.wikipedia.org/wiki/Software_testing*):

- *Integration testing* – Verifies the compatibility of the interfaces between software components
- *System testing* – Tests a complete system in order to verify its requirements

We have only scratched the surface of software testing, and there are many different approaches to this broad subject that are definitely worth further investigation. A real step forward in software testing engineering is *extreme programming* with *test-driven development* (TDD) (Fowler 1999). In this approach, writing software starts with tests. Then, after successful refactoring, we are left with the tests and the software that make these tests pass.

Interestingly, there are organized national championships for software testing, and the entire domain is gaining importance. The advent of artificial intelligence will probably change the field of software development and testing even more. Recommended reading in this area is the recent book *Concise Guide to Software Testing* (O'Regan 2019).

A.8 Summary

Things to Remember

- Learn C in order to better understand C++
- Do not mix C code into C++ projects
- Use *CMake* to generate projects that are adjusted to your system and programming framework
- Do not guess: use a profiler to diagnose bottlenecks in your software performance
- Use *Git/GitHub* for project maintenance and backups
- Augment your projects with a testing framework

Questions and Exercises

1. Write a non-recursive version of the `ToBinConvert` function (see Listing A.1).

2. Refactor the project from Section A.2.2 into the C++ domain. Hint: for string operations, use the `std::string` class; use `std::cout` for output, etc.

3. Write a function to copy a source memory block into the destination memory block. Consider cases when memory blocks overlap.

4. Design and implement a console version of a 3×3 tic-tac-toe game. Make it modular so you can easily change the display component. Upload the project to *GitHub*, and train the project branches.

5. Add a GUI to your tic-tac-toe solution.

6. Write unit tests, and add a test project to your tic-tac-toe solution.

7. Run profiling for the inner product functions presented in Section 7.4.7.

8. Read about and play with an experimental version of modules for C++20 in Visual Studio (*https://docs.microsoft.com/en-us/cpp/cpp/modules-cpp?view=vs-2019*). Then refactor one of the simple projects, such as the EMatrix from Section 4.7, to use C++20 modules rather than classic headers.

9. Design and implement an application to show a floating-point value and its corresponding bit settings in various formats of the IEEE 754 standard (see Section 7.4. and Table A.4).

10. Augment the simple text based game from Q&E in Section 2 with the graphics and user's interface.

11. Design and implement a simple house security application that detects if someone is hanging around a house. Hint: Install the OpenCV library for the AI and computer vision operations; write a component to segment a video signal coming from a camera into the static background and the foreground moving objects, then try to develop the rules to distinguish people silhouettes from animals or cars.

12. Design and implement a photo presenter application that given a directory with photos displays them on the screen. Hint: try the SFML or the ImGui libraries (Table A.4). In the next step add smooth image dissolving option and the music.

13. Design and implement an application to convert a pdf document into a simple presentation format. For example, only section titles, as well as figures, tables and their captions are copied from the input document into the output presentation. Hint: use e.g. the PoDoFo library to open and manipulate the pdf files (*http://podofo.sourceforge.net/about.html*). For more C++ libraries visit *https://en.cppreference.com/w/cpp/links/libs*.

Bibliography

Aho, A., Lam, M., Sethi, R., and Ullman, J. (2006). *Compilers: Principles, Techniques, and Tools.* Addison-Wesley.

Alexander, C. (1977). *A Pattern Language: Towns, Buildings, Construction.* Oxford University Press.

Allison, C. (2006). Where did all my decimals go? *Journal of Computing Sciences in Colleges* 21 (3): 47–59.

Augustin. (2017). C++ unit testing in Visual Studio. C++ Team Blog. *https://blogs.msdn.microsoft. com/vcblog/2017/04/19/cpp-testing-in-visual-studio.*

Filipek, B. R. (2018). *C++17 in Detail.* Independently published *https://www.bfilipek.com/2018/08/ cpp17indetail.html.*

Boccara, J. (2016). Strong types for strong interfaces. Fluent {C++}. *https://www.fluentcpp. com/2016/12/08/strong-types-for-strong-interfaces.*

Boccara, J. (2018). Getting the benefits of strong typing in C++ at a fraction of the cost. Fluent {C++}. *https://www.fluentcpp.com/2018/04/06/strong-types-by-struct.*

Boost.org (2020). Boost C++ libraries. *https://www.boost.org.*

Bryant, R. and O'Hallaron, D. (2015). *Computer Systems. A Programmer's Perspective.* Prentice Hall.

Catch Org (2019). Catch2. *https://github.com/catchorg/Catch2.*

Cohn, J. (2019). *Scrum Fundamentals: A Beginner's Guide to Mastery of the Scrum Project Management Methodology.* Independently published.

Coplien, J. (1995). Curiously recurring template patterns. *C++ Report* 7 (2): 24–27.

Cormen, T.H., Leiserson, C.E., Rivest, R.L.i., and Stein, C. (2009). *Introduction to Algorithms.* MIT Press.

Cover, T.M.i. and Thomas, J.A. (2006). *Elements of Information Theory.* Wiley-Interscience.

Cplusplus.com (2020). *http://cplusplus.com.*

Cppreference.com (2018). Filesystem library. *https://en.cppreference.com/w/cpp/experimental/fs.*

Cppreference.com (2019a). Date and time utilities. *https://en.cppreference.com/w/cpp/chrono.*

Cppreference.com (2019b). Template argument deduction. *https://en.cppreference.com/w/cpp/ language/template_argument_deduction*

Cppreference.com (2020a). Template parameters arguments. *https://en.cppreference.com/w/cpp/ language/template_parameters.*

Cppreference.com (2020b). *http://cppreference.com.*

Cppreference.com (2020c). Operator overloading. *https://en.cppreference.com/w/cpp/language/ operators.*

Čukić, I. (2019). *Functional Programming in C++.* Manning Publications Co.

Introduction to Programming with C++ for Engineers, First Edition. Bogusław Cyganek.
© 2021 John Wiley & Sons Ltd. Published 2021 by John Wiley & Sons Ltd.
Companion website: http://home.agh.edu.pl/~cyganek/BookCpp.htm

Cyganek, B. (2013). *Object Detection and Recognition in Digital Images: Theory and Practice*. New-York: Wiley.

Cyganek, B. (2020). CppBook web page. *http://home.agh.edu.pl/~cyganek/BookCpp.htm*.

Dalheimer, M.K. and Welsh, M. (2006). *Running Linux: A Distribution-Neutral Guide for Servers and Desktops*, 5e. O'Reilly Media.

Dick, G., van Reeuwijk, K., Bal, H.E. et al. (2012). *Modern Compiler Design*. Springer.

Dick, J., Hull, E., and Jackson, K. (2017). *Requirements Engineering*. Springer.

Douglass, B. (2006). *Real Time UML*. Boston: Addison Wesley.

Fan, X. (2015). *Real-Time Embedded Systems. Design Principles and Engineering Practices*. Kidlington: Newnes-Elsevier.

FLTK Team (2019). Fast Light Toolkit (FLTK). *www.fltk.org*.

Fowler, M. (1999). *Refactoring: Improve the Design of Existing Code*. Boston: Addison Wesley.

Gamma, E., Helm, R., Johnson, R., and Vlissides, J. (1994). *Design Patterns: Elements of Reusable Object-Oriented Software*. New-York: Addison-Wesley Professional.

Goldberg, D. (1991). What every computer scientist should know about floating-point arithmetic. *ACM Computing Surveys* 23 (1): 5–48.

Google (2019). Googletest Google testing and mocking framework. *https://github.com/google/googletest*.

Grune, D., van Reeuwijk, K., Bal, H.E. et al. (2012). *Modern Compiler Design*. Heidelberg: Springer.

Hinde, D. (2018). *PRINCE2 Study Guide: 2017 Update*. Sybex.

Josuttis, N.M. (2012). *The C++ Standard Library: A Tutorial and Reference*. New-York: Addison-Wesley Professional.

Kahan, W. (1965). Further remarks on reducing truncation errors. *Communications of the ACM* 8 (1): 40.

Kernighan, B. and Ritchie, D. (1988). *C Programming Language*, 2e. Chicago: Prentice Hall.

Kerrisk, M. (2010). *The Linux Programming Interface: A Linux and UNIX System Programming Handbook*. The Starch Press.

Knuth, D. (1998). *The Art of Computer Programming. Seminumerical Algorithms*, 3e, vol. 2. New York: Addison-Wesley.

Korn, G. and Korn, T. (2000). *Mathematical Handbook for Scientists and Engineers: Definitions, Theorems, and Formulas for Reference and Review*, 2e. Dover: Dover Publications.

Liskov, B. (1988). Data abstraction and hierarchy. OOPSLA '87. *https://doi.org/10.1145/62138.62141*.

Martin, R.C. (2009). Getting a SOLID start. Clean Coder. *https://sites.google.com/site/unclebobconsultingllc/getting-a-solid-start*

Matloff, N. and Salzman, J. (2008). *The Art of Debugging with GDB, DDD and Eclipse*. No Starch Press.

McConnell, S. (2004). *Code Complete (Developer Best Practices)*, 2e. New-York: Microsoft Press.

Meyer, B. (1997). *Object-Oriented Software Construction*, 2e. New-York: Prentice Hall.

Meyers, S. (2014). *Effective Modern C++: 42 Specific Ways to Improve Your Use of C++11 and C++14*. Chicago: O'Reilly Media.

Niebler, E. (2019). *Range-v3*. *https://ericniebler.github.io/range-v3*.

OpenMP (2020). *www.openmp.org*.

O'Regan, G. (2019). *Concise Guide to Software Testing*. Springer.

Pas, R.v., Stotzer, E., and Terboven, C. (2017). *Using OpenMP – The Next Step*. The MIT Press.

Patterson, D. and Hennessy, J. (2018). *Computer Organization and Design. The Hardware/Software Interface*. Morgan Kaufman.

Press, W., Teukolsky, S., Vetterling, W., and Flannery, B. (2007). *Numerical Recipes: The Art of Scientific Computing*, 3e. Cambridge: Cambridge University Press.

Rozental, G. and Enficiaud, R. (2019). Boost.Test. *https://www.boost.org/doc/libs/1_72_0/libs/test/doc/html/index.html*.

Schmidt, B.i. and Gonzalez-Dominguez, J. (2017). *Parallel Programming: Concepts and Practice*. Morgan Kaufman.

Sommerville, I. (2016). *Software Engineering*. Addison-Wesley.

Soulami, T. (2012). *Inside Windows Debugging. Practical Debugging and Tracing Strategies*. Microsoft Press.

Stack Overflow (2020). *http://stackoverflow.com*.

Standard C++ Foundation (2019). Get started! *https://isocpp.org/get-started*

Stroustrup, B. (2007). Evolving a language in and for the real world: C++ 1991-2006. *http://www.stroustrup.com/hopl-almost-final.pdf*.

Stroustrup, B. (2012). A tour of C++. Standard C++ Foundation. *https://isocpp.org/tour*.

Stroustrup, B. (2013). *The C++ Programming Language*, 4e. New-York: Addison-Wesley Professional.

Stroustrup, B. (2014). *Programming: Principles and Practice Using C++*, 2e. New-York: Addison-Wesley Professional.

Stroustrup, B. and Sutter, H. (2019). C++ core guidelines. *https://isocpp.github.io/CppCoreGuidelines/CppCoreGuidelines*.

Taligent, I. (1994). *Taligent's Guide to Designing Programs: Well-Mannered Object-Oriented Design in C++*. New-York: Taligent Press.

Thomas, D. and Hunt, A. (2019). *The Pragmatic Programmer: Your Journey to Mastery, 20th Anniversary Edition*, 2e. Addison-Wesley Professional.

Turner, J. (2016). C++ Weekly - Ep 7: Stop using std::endl. *https://articles.emptycrate.com/2016/04/18/stop_using_std_endl.html*.

Unicode Consortium (2020). Unicode. *http://unicode.org*.

Vandevoorde, D., Josuttis, N., and Gregor, D. (2017). *C++ Templates: The Complete Guide*, 2e. New-York: Addison-Wesley Professional.

Wiki:Comparision_Executable (2019). Comparison of executable file formats. *https://en.wikipedia.org/wiki/Comparison_of_executable_file_formats*.

Wiki:Floating-point (2020). Floating-point arithmetic. *https://en.wikipedia.org/wiki/Floating-point_arithmetic*.

Wiki:Huffman_coding (2020). Huffman coding. *https://en.wikipedia.org/wiki/Huffman_coding*.

Wiki:IEEE-754 (2020). IEEE 754. *https://en.wikipedia.org/wiki/IEEE_754*.

Wiki:Portable_Executable (2020). Portable executable. *https://en.wikipedia.org/wiki/Portable_Executable*.

Wiki:Proxy_pattern (2020). Proxy pattern. *https://en.wikipedia.org/wiki/Proxy_pattern*.

Wiki:Roman_numerals (2020). Roman numerals. *https://en.wikipedia.org/wiki/Roman_numerals*.

Wirth, N. (1976). *Algorithms + Data Structures = Programs*. Prentice-Hall.

Yehia, W. (2012). *C++0x, scoped enums*. IBM Developer. *https://www.ibm.com/developerworks/rational/library/scoped-enums/index.html*

Yliluoma, J. (2016). Guide into OpenMP: Easy multithreading programming for C++. *https://bisqwit.iki.fi/story/howto/openmp*.

Index

Introduction to Programming with C++ for Engineers, First Edition. Bogusław Cyganek.
© 2021 John Wiley & Sons Ltd. Published 2021 by John Wiley & Sons Ltd.
Companion website: http://home.agh.edu.pl/~cyganek/BookCpp.htm

Printed and bound by CPI Group (UK) Ltd, Croydon, CR0 4YY

27/10/2024

14580303-0005